CONTENTS

The
New Historicism
R E A D E R

EDITED BY *H. Aram Veeser*

ROUTLEDGE

NEW YORK • LONDON

Published in 1994 by

Routledge
29 West 35 Street
New York, NY 10001

Published in Great Britain by

Routledge
11 New Fetter Lane
London EC4P 4EE

Library of Congress Cataloging-in-Publication Data

The New historicism reader / [edited by] Harold Veeser.
     p.   cm.
   Includes bibliographical references.
   ISBN 0-415-90781-0 (hard). — ISBN 0-415-90782-9 (pbk.)
   1. Criticism.   2. Historicism.   I. Veeser, H. Aram
PN81.N432   1993
801.95—dc20
                                          93-25135
                                            CIP

British Library Cataloguing in publication data is available.

ACKNOWLEDGMENTS

This book surveys the New Historicist diaspora. *"Je resous de m'informer du pourquoi,"* Baudelaire wrote, having seen *Tannhäuser* in 1860, *"et de transformer ma volupté en conaissance"*: "I set out to discover the why of it, and to transform my pleasure into knowledge." I was lucky enough to have many friends who helped me to explore the furthest reaches of New Historicist scholarship.

Discussions began at my own outpost, the very supportive Wichita State University, a place that my colleague Roger Berger's theory reading group—Servanne Woodward, David Ericson, Deborah Gordon, William Woods, Nancy West—made richly cosmopolitan. My colleagues, especially Peter T. Zoller, Mary Sherman, Christopher Brooks, Maureen Hoag, Lawrence M. Davis, and Sarah Daugherty, who critiqued my introduction, and the graduate students—in particular, Sharon Kelley, Corbet Hays, Susan Bradley, and Karen Boren—who provided research assistance and intellectual stimulation, all helped to make this inner station a productive and happy workplace. Steve Heller at Kansas State University provided a keenly helpful reading, and my friend and former colleague James Lee Burke was again a fine spiritual-business advisor.

A wonderful year as George and Delores D. Eccles Fellow at the Humanities Center at the University of Utah gave me ample contact with that rich diasporan enclave, peopled with scholars including Howard Horwitz, Gillian Brown, Anand Yang, Susan Miller; Humanities Center directors Patricia Hanna and Lowell Durham; then-Dean Norman Council; and Humanities Center fellows Marianne Barnett, Kathryn Stockton, and Salam Noor.

At somewhat longer distances, Steven Mailloux, Gerald Graff, Ellen Messer-Davidow, Dominick LaCapra, Jon Klancher, Brook Thomas, and Sean Wilentz saw me over the steppes of historiography and the history of our disciplines. Comrades Paul Smith, Amitava Kumar, Bruce Robbins, Tom Moylan, Fred Pfeil, Moira Ferguson, Michael Ryan, Tim Brennan, Judith Newton, Dipesh Chakrabarty, and Gayatri Spivak introduced me to explosive developments in postcolonial scholarship. David Simpson and Stephen D. Moore went the full distance, the first pulling me towards materialist critique while Moore pressed me towards his own Joycean-Lacanian cataract. One could not, as a friend of the poet Byron told him, live under a cataract all the time. My deep thanks to Gerald Graff for pulling me back, when necessary, to a plainer style.

Edward Said and Stanley Fish have had an indirect yet forceful impact on this volume though Fish would reject my claims for the power of critical consciousness, and Said would abjure my "capitalist poetics."

I have known William P. Germano for two decades and each year my admiration grows. He sent out the feelers for this book, while his able associates at Routledge, Seth Denbo and Eric Zinner—both masters of the monitory fax—brought the cargo home. Terence Hawkes and Janice Price have given encouragement and helped to waft the book across the seas. Michael Esposito greeted delays and changes with his ineffable panache, and put the quality of the book before all other considerations.

The essays included here are classics that have appeared before: "The Role of the King," *The Illusion of Power: Political Theater in the English Renaissance* (Berkeley, California): 59–87; "The Improvisation of Power," *Renaissance Self-Fashioning: From More to Shakespeare* (Chicago: University of Chicago Press, 1980); " 'Eliza, Queene of Shepheardes,' and the Pastoral of Power," *ELR* 10 (1980): 153–182; "Shakespeare's Ear," *Representations* 28 (Fall 1989): 6–13; "George Eliot and *Daniel Deronda*: The Prostitute and the Jewish Question," *Essays from the English Institute* (Johns Hopkins University Press, 1984); "New Americanists: Revisionist Interventions into the Canon," *Boundary 2* 17 (1990); "The Construction of Privacy in and around *The Bostonians*," *American Literature* (Winter 1992); "Romance and Real Estate," *The Gold Standard and the Logic of Naturalism* (Berkeley: University of California Press, 1987), 87–112; "Sentimental Power: *Uncle Tom's Cabin* and the Politics of Literary History," *Sensational Designs: The Cultural Work of American Fiction* (New York: Oxford University Press, 1985), 122–146; " 'Make My Day!': Spectacle as Amnesia in Imperial Politics," *Representations* 29 (Winter 1990): 99–123; "The Logic of the Transvestite: *The Roaring Girl* (1608)," *Staging the Renaissance,* eds. David Kasten and Peter Stallybrass (Routledge), 221–234; "*Adam Bede* and *Henry Esmond*: Homosocial Desire and the Historicity of the Female," *Between Men* (New York: Columbia University Press, 1986), 134–160; "*Mismār Goha*: The Arab Challenge to Cultural Dependency," *South Atlantic Quarterly* 87 (Winter 1988), 109–130; "History is Like Mother," *1981* (Routledge), 206–239; and "Postcoloniality and the Artifice of History: Who Speaks for 'Indian' Pasts?" *Representations* 37 (Winter 1992), 1–26. I wish to thank the editors and publishers who granted me permission to reprint these essays.

My guilty heart goes out to Lawrence Davis, my department chair, Maureen Hoag, my co-director of composition, and Janice Cryer, secretary *extraordinaire,* who lived through this book's genesis and put up with my occasional furtive absences. David Barsamian, Shanti Murua, Isabel Calleja, Judith Siminoe, Zeyad Essa, and Barbara Strunk put up with longer silences, and that archetypal long-distance trader, Henry S. Kazan, taught me all I needed to know about capitalism. Elise Veeser was stalwart, and my brother Cyrus was heroic, lending editorial expertise even as he set sail for his own outpost as Fulbright scholar to the Dominican Republic.

THE NEW HISTORICISM

H. ARAM VEESER

Only a mad desire could motivate the doomed effort to marshal together the best of the New Historicism (NH*). To group and define these wildly individual efforts would demand an even crazier yearning. When I attempted something like this in 1989, I was intrepid, many thought, because NHs were always proclaiming themselves to be unrelated to each other. In the very book that I was introducing, the four bona fide NHs were in denial about indulging in a movement of any sort. Joel Fineman, one of the four, spoke of the NH's "programmatic refusal to specify a methodological program for itself—its characteristic air of reporting, haplessly, the discoveries it happened serendipitously to stumble upon in the course of undirected, idle rambles through the historical archives . . ." (52). Louis Montrose thought NH equally unprogrammatic, saying NHs are "actually quite heterogeneous in their critical practices," and Catherine Gallagher added that the "phenomenon" was one of "indeterminacy." As for the most recognizable NH, Stephen Greenblatt declared that NH was "no doctrine at all" and made other disavowals that provoked one reviewer to say, "the general himself is . . . swearing that he is no theoretician, that his invention of the term NH was virtually accidental." But if it was not a movement in the sense of having a strong common practice, still less was it strictly lined up behind a brigadier. Simon During notes more recently that "books and articles of a bewildering variety have been called NH," and Alan Liu says that their only unifying thread is their agreement that they have no unifying thread. Faced with their collective identity crisis, I confessed that "the NH is a phrase without an adequate referent." Reviewers quoted that phrase more than any other, except perhaps for another exactly opposite passage, the passage in which I reassured readers with the five key assumptions that do reappear and bind together the NHs.

*NH signifies *New Historicism*, NHs signifies *New Historicists*, and *NHt* signifies *New Historicist* throughout this introduction.

1

THE FIVE FUNDAMENTAL ASSUMPTIONS

In the absence of a doctrine, manifesto, and strong common practice, the only sure recourse is to the NH texts themselves. My own five-point definition grew from a close reading of these documents, but even then I was tentative. Any such list would reduce NH's wondrous complexity, and unfortunately reviewers have liked my five points for just that reason. Yet the first four points have held up pretty well, and the fifth has vastly thickened and defined its sinew. NH really does assume: 1) that every expressive act is embedded in a network of material practices; 2) that every act of unmasking, critique, and opposition uses the tools it condemns and risks falling prey to the practice it exposes; 3) that literary and non-literary "texts" circulate inseparably; 4) that no discourse, imaginative or archival, gives access to unchanging truths or expresses unalterable human nature; and 5) that a critical method and a language adequate to describe culture under capitalism participate in the economy they describe.[1] All the articles in this book consistently embrace these five tenets, except for the five essays grouped as "Some Fractures and the Future of NH," whose authors contend that some truths do not change—that white heterosexual males consistently enjoyed privileges, for example, while women, gays, and subcontinental Indians consistently paid the price.

Assumption 5 (that it's high time for criticism to catch up with capitalism) raises all the urgent questions that have always swirled around NH. Is it liberal or Leftist? Literary or historical? Feminist or neuter? Reformist or radical? Canon-making or canon-smashing? Stabilizing or capsizing? Most NH would object that these binary differences between entities (between liberal and radical, for example) arise only by repressing differences within entities (the houses of liberalism, radicalism, and feminism all have many mansions). Yet readers have a right to know: does NH get us somewhere new or does it reinforce the literary, disciplinary, social, sex-gender, international status quo?

Nothing better captures NH's potential conservatism than does the wax-museum stolidity implied by M. A. Abrams's 1992 edition of the *Glossary of Literary Terms*. Abrams isolates four characteristics:

1. The idea that ideology positions readers as subjects—black middle-class postcolonial lesbian, working-class second-generation Italian-American heterosexual marxist—called a virtual halt to the practice of speaking as if for a common humanity.

2. Second, Foucault's Knowledge/Power fusion gave intellectuals the confidence that their knowledge had power, but the powersource—housed in oppressive institutions—clamped down on their subversive desires to promote cultural change.

3. A third idea, dialogism, also acknowledged that conflict defined social inter-

action. But the project, embraced by liberal critics who sought to apply Bakhtin, was insistently to demonstrate that unifying, stable institutions and structures usually managed to contain and neutralize disruptive energies. The novel, like the state, actually seemed to enjoy its own internal hemorrhaging.

4. Fourth, as an alternative to Marxist polemical writing and upsettingly deconstructive or feminist ecriture, a writing practice called thick description rapidly gained New Historicist backing. Thick description—used by anthropologists to distinguish a wink from a blink, and by cultural historians to study what people thought they were doing when they conducted charivaris and cat massacres—gave New Historicists a hermeneutic for unraveling social texts without discussing class struggle, emergent groups, or macroeconomic change.

Apolitically tame and quietistic, all four tendencies—subject-positioning, Power/Knowledge, internal dialogism, and thick description—suggest that NH is bent on neutralizing solidarity, subversion, disruption, and struggle.

But if NH seems committed to what David Simpson has called the strong containment thesis, in practice it has radically disrupted business as usual in the study of literature. It especially upsets narrow, prescriptive, authoritarian critics who insist that art must attack the dominant social, political, and economic order. Barbara Harman suggests that a reversal of ordinary assumptions is at stake when she remarks that "the strength of Greenblatt's analysis is a function of its ability to demonstrate the self's deep implication in its founding culture, even where we have always assumed that we were witnessing an opposition" (63). As D. A. Miller succinctly puts the most broadly shared and defiant NH axiom, "even if it were true that literature exercises a destabilizing function in our culture, the current consensus that it does so does not."[2] To say that the most radical-oppositional critics are really the most conforming-conservative critics may seem to be an insight worthy of Orwell's *1984*. Yet at the same time it liberates NHs from certain preconceptions and allows them to study centuries-worth of literature within capitalism on precisely its own terms. The essays below confront the market's bizarrely distorting effects (anorexia, homophobia, agoraphobia) and their spectacular impact on representation (naturalism, photography, film, trompe l'oeil). NH studies of nineteenth- and twentieth-century texts indicate an important shift within the NHs' "poetics of culture," which now is committed to showing that capitalism and market relations metabolize all of art as well as life.

NHs have entertained from the first the heresy of a good capitalism. Greenblatt was again out in front: "Society's dominant currencies, money and prestige, are invariably involved," he writes ("Poetics of Culture" in Veeser, 12), and the revealingly entitled *Shakespearean Negotiations* radically proposes that all aesthetic representation anticipates or embodies market relations.[3] And yet for Greenblatt the "circulation of social energy" meant something like rhetorical *energia* or force. *Economy* and its metaphors mean something very much more specifically capitalist for later NHs. Michaels, Gallagher, Thomas, Pease, Tompkins, and Rogin, in their pieces printed below, disagree about the inherent subversiveness of art. But they all agree that contemporary life at its best embodies mobility and impersonality. Two legal maxims sum up the modern and postmodern conditions. One is the great legal jurist Blackstone's comment, reprinted as Michaels's epigraph, that "property best answers the purposes of civil life, especially in commercial countries, when its transfer and circulation are totally free and unrestrained."[4] The second comes from another historian of the English law, Sir Henry Maine, and is quoted in Brook Thomas's essay: the "movement of progressive societies has ... been a movement *from status to contract.*" All these later NHs agree that capitalism requires hollow, empty personalities that resemble money itself—a medium totally free, unconstrained by silly principles that would inhibit their entering any contract or compromise. Hovering in its own borderland between text and material context, between aggression and embarrassment, between literature and non-literature, between lucky "finds" and universal verities, NH has gravitated in its studies to the go-betweens, middlemen, long-distance traders, translators, and cross-cultural brokers—Rushdie's Chamcha, Shakespeare's Iago, the conquistador Cortez's Aztec "wife," La Malincha—those mobile figures who oscillate much after the fashion of market prices and NHs themselves.[5]

CONVERTING DETAILS INTO KNOWLEDGE: THE CLASSIC MOVES

One might in fact say that all the features I have enumerated flesh out one fundamental oscillation between two sorts of contingency. Contingency means "that which may or may not happen," which is chancy, aleatory, uncertain. But it fundamentally means, as Marlon Ross has pointed out, to touch together, "a happening dependent upon another happening," a causal connection. For just one example, the anecdote—that signature NH move—is accidentally contingent and therefore shows that writing history is an arbitrary, illogical business. But it also expresses conditional contingency, the making of explanatory connections, and so it reveals that everything is logically connected to everything else. This unresolved tension between arbitrary and conditional contingency makes the NH volatile and inexhaustible.[6]

But critics of the NH have tended to perceive its allegiance to one contigency or the other, never to both. Thus arises the charge that NH eschews totalities, teleologies, and grand narratives, turning instead to details, local knowledge, and what Frank Lentricchia calls "the gritty, ground-level texture" of life. Each *unique* detail, episode, or essay comes to *re*present, *dup*licate, *stand in for* much more than its insignificant self. This logical difficulty has emboldened NH's detractors, who have long charged that NH poses "a context, text, and in between a relation of pure suggestiveness" (Liu 743). Simpson indicts NH for its "Geertzian paradigm of semiotic saturation . . . wherein all facets of a culture are imbued with functional-expressive meaning, so that any interaction of text and context (or any other text) is by definition charged with exemplary significance" (14). Even the NH critic's own airplane rides and minor traumas take on disproportionate importance. Are these indictments justified? A closer look at one representative essay will yield some answers.

An NH essay speeds the reader through a series of gestalt shifts that leave the brain spinning in its pan. Yet the soul can travel no faster than a trotting camel, according to the Arab proverb, and in fact a typical essay resolves into five discrete, measured operations. "Marlowe and the Will to Absolute Play," the chapter in Greenblatt's *Renaissance Self-Fashioning* that just precedes the chapter reprinted in this volume, moves through five moments—anecdote, outrage, resistance, containment, and the critic's autobiography—all in a tight twenty-five pages.

The opening acts "less as explanatory illustration than as disturbance, that which requires explanation" (Greenblatt, *Learning to Curse*, 5). The chapter begins laconically: "On 26 June 1586 a small fleet, financed by the Earl of Cumberland, set out from Gravesend for the South Seas." With the fleet under way and the twice-terminal name *Gravesend* safely behind, Greenblatt turns over the microphone to an actual, historical merchant-adventurer, John Sarracoll, who picks up the tale. The English fleet set in at Sierra Leone, merchants and crew admiring a beautiful "town of the Negroes . . . of about two hundred houses, and walled about with stakes so thick, that a rat could hardly get in or out. . . ." A postscript drops this final news: "our men at their departure set the town on fire" and burned it to ashes.

No easy answers unlock the conundrum of an awed admirer who burns down the object of admiration. Greenblatt registers puzzlement and outrage. Having found this shocking passage where no old historicist would look, Greenblatt reads it as no old historicist could. He tries to imagine what Sarracoll thought, why he wrote what he did. Does an "aesthetic element" in the Englishmen's admiration for the town "conflict with or somehow fuel the destructiveness?" And if Sarracoll feels no uneasiness at all, "why does he suddenly shift and write not *we* but *our men*? . . . when he recalls the invasion, why does he think of rats?" Although Sarracoll's *rats* and his change of *we* to *our men* would attract few historians' interest, Greenblatt pries at these hairline verbal fractures to get an inside look at something also beneath most historians' notice—a single *human subject*. Greenblatt concludes that only a very empty person could write such a document, that absence of feeling is an ethical vacancy, as is now inescapably evident in "the moral blankness that rests like thick snow on Sarracoll's sentences" (194). Sarracoll's bland moral vacancy, so like that of Arfie in *Catch-22* and Pyle in Graham Greene's *The Quiet American*, seems endemic to imperialism. But so is its negation, resistance and rebellion. Greenblatt now introduces just such a nay-sayer, Christopher Marlowe, who rebels against every secular and divine orthodoxy, including heterosexuality. Marlowe's "life suggests the very opposite of that 'peculiar equilibrium'" and "rushes to embrace the tragic with a strange eagerness." In Marlowe's dramas the moral rhythms that usually soothe English conscience, rhythms such as pride-goes-before-a-fall, fail to materialize. Human personality is radically reduced to "a senseless lump of clay/That will with every water wash to dirt." Most of all, Marlowe insists on the "essential meaninglessness of theatrical space, the vacancy that is the dark side of its power to imitate any place." Marlowe gets in the face of authority and stands outside society.

But in that sense Marlowe represents precisely the version of the artist—iconoclast, foe of hypocrisy, intransigent outsider—that D. A. Miller calls the liberal-consensual version, a version whose universality Jane Tompkins and other critics here call into question. Greenblatt anticipates these later challenges when, midway through the essay, he performs the strong containment move: authority flicks the would-be-satanic Marlowe aside. In Marlowe's supposedly destabilizing drama, attacks on social norms—Tamburlaine's excessive violence, Barabas's amorality, Edward's homosexuality, Faustus's skepticism—are "exposed as unwitting tributes to that social construction of identity against which they struggle." By embracing what society deems evil, "they have unwittingly accepted [society's] crucial structural elements." At such moments—archetypal, inevitable moments for an NH steeped in Foucault's microphysics of disciplinary society—leftist, feminist, oppositional, liberationist critics have traditionally walked out: Who wants to hear that the good fight is doomed to fail? Yet "the crucial issue is not man's power to disobey," he writes, "but the characteristic modes of desire and fear produced by a given society, and the rebellious heroes never depart from those modes" (209). By turning Marlowe from a socially destabilizing writer into a socially reinforcing one, Greenblatt makes him a true rebel, one whose "unwitting tributes to society" undermine the liberal consensus that great art is oppositional.

The unavoidable, final move is autobiographical. Greenblatt feels compelled to ask if the NH can itself avoid exhausted modes of desire and fear. In a last, deeply characteristic NHt gesture, Greenblatt summarizes Marlowe's heroes in terms that could describe the NHs themselves:

> Rather they take courage from the absurdity of their enterprise, a . . . supremely eloquent, playful courage . . . a penchant for the outlandish and absurd, delight in role-playing, entire absorption in the game at hand and consequent indifference to what lies outside the boundaries of the game . . . (220)

Having reinstated biographical criticism, Greenblatt now restores autobiography. We learn, alarmingly, that Greenblatt silently watched a man—who winked at him!—steal a tourist's camera in Naples. With equal alarm, we now see that the absorbing game of criticism supersedes outrage, that the delights of playing the game offset political impotence, that the more important matters lying outside the game leave a critic indifferent. This penchant for playful, aggressive forgetfulness sounds like Nietzschean amorality or postmodern play at its worst. (What if Greenblatt had silently watched a rape in Naples?) Yet the five critics who appear at the end of this volume (see "Fractures and the Future") find they can use NH strategies and still commit their work to liberatory politics. They can because NH occupies (as we have just seen) the shifting ground between history (Sarracol) and literature (Marlowe), between true rebellion and unwitting tribute, between analysis of the literary text and scrutiny of the critic's troubled self. Strong containment versus art-as-opposition, accidental discovery (of Sarracol's log) versus fateful contiguity (the log makes Marlowe blindingly transparent), and now playful amoral theatrical outsider versus the NHt critic engaged in (as Gallagher avows) "an attempt to de-moralize our relationship to literature, to interrupt the moral narrative of literature's benign disruptions with which we soothe ourselves" (Veeser, 46). With this fifth, allusive autobiographical moment, the NHt essay completes a full cycle.[7]

RESISTING THE NEW HISTORICISM

Opposed to the moralizing of literature, NH has met its own share of opposition. True, hard-core, traditional scholars praise the NH's "gorgeous vitality" (Litvak) and popular magazines—shell-shocked by twenty years of deconstructive jargon—hug plain-speaking NH like a long-lost twin.[8] Some first-wave objections to NH have been answered or set aside. The charge made often in the early eighties that NH had failed to theorize itself seems laughably wrong now that meta-critical essays build up like Chinese lacquer around every NHt twist and angle.[9]

But other long-standing objections have been harder to shake off. The charge of quietism, based on NH's alleged strong-containment position and its demonstrations that all subversive moves were doomed to be contained by and perverted to serve the uses of Power, remains (as the Pease essay here suggests) very much alive.[10] Judith Newton's charge that the NH recycles—without much attribution—long-established feminist arguments and strategies, and Marguerite Waller's contention that Greenblatt remains wedged in patriarchal assumptions, both deserve further discussion. In the present collection, Jane Gallop reads the coded language of women's critical anthologies in order to trace the complex internal branchings of feminism after 1981. Gallop's foray into historical scholarship represents a new departure for her. Her success in this mode reminds the reader that NH has been equally a women's tradition, its major figures including Natalie Zemon Davis, Joan W. Scott, Leah Marcus, Catherine Gallagher, Wai-

Chee Dimock, Myra Jehlen, Nancy Armstrong, Cathy N. Davidson, Carol Clover, Susan Stewart, Gillian Brown, and Sharon Cameron.

The charge laid by Walter Cohen in 1982—that "arbitrary connectedness" vitiates NH conclusions—has echoed down the years. Historians remain deeply troubled by what they perceive to be methodological anarchy. Where, they might ask, does my unalphabetized list of feminist NHs in the preceding paragraph find its organizing principle? To read a historian's review of Greenblatt, Gallagher, or even Thomas, who follows most closely the historians' own genealogical and "coverage" protocols—is to glimpse the chasm that divides the literature faculty from their historian colleagues.

Francois Furet complained, for example, that his colleagues devoted to the study of *mentalites,* the historically important operations of feelings, love, conscience, instinct, had resulted in an "unending pursuit of new topics" no better grounded or motivated than changing fashions in trousers or cars. Lynn Hunt preemptively criticizes social historians for moving "from one group to another (workers, women, children, ethnic groups, the old, the young) without developing much sense of cohesion or interaction between topics." Cultural history as practiced by NHs might also fall into the trap of defining itself topically and thus "degenerate into an endless search for new cultural practices to describe, whether carnivals, cat massacres, or impotence trials."[11]

And yet historians have themselves fielded an NH team. Walter Laqueur, Natalie Zemon Davis, Lynn Hunt, Anson Rabinbach, Sean Wilentz, a brilliant group of New West historians (Richard White, Peggy Pascoe, Patricia Limerick) and many other familiar names—Robert Darnton, Roger Chartier, Carlo Ginzburg, Emmanuel Le Roy Ladurie—often sound notes in an NH key. Sean Wilentz has usefully summarized three assumptions that unite the New Cultural Historians:

1. All polities "are ordered and governed by 'master fictions' as well as by . . . force." Certain fictions—the Nazi Aryan cult, divine right of kings, charisma in Negara—may appear as sheer fantasy today, whereas others—the myths of justice, equality, and popular sovereignty, "partake of a mixture of fact, myth, and wishful thinking." (4)

2. Not just public verbal forms (speeches, sermons, parliamentary debates) but rather all kinds of signs and rhetoric—public and private, verbal and nonverbal—are open for interpretation. "Personal diary jottings about recalcitrant slaves, disobedient children, and mired cattle can tell us things about political relations in colonial Virginia not to be found in the most impassioned pamphlet on natural law."(5)

3. Thick description will enable historians to sort out the levels of rhetorical meaning—to understand when a blink is a wink, to discern "the subtle dynamics of agreement and disagreement." (5)

All these points would be congenial to the NHs represented in this volume.

But resistances to the NH continue to multiply. Some critics have demanded an investigation, for example, of the NH misappropriation of lexical funds. Words that once had fairly stable referents, such as imperialism, colonialism, and logic, today float free. Neologistic phrases like new historicism, linguistic colonialism, imperialist poetics, academic imperialism, and logics of disintegration make up a goodly part of any younger professor's table talk. These terms evoke no small display of pique on the part of Marxists, who have haggled for decades over the precise meanings of these words. Genuine Marxists are scarce, but post-colonialist critics also deplore the loose misuse of the left-lexicon: "imperialism" and "colonialism," "exploitation" and "appropriation." Tim Brennan writing in a recent issue of *Race & Class* denounces what he calls the merely *metaphorical* mis-uses of perfectly clear and precise terms, terms that Brennan feels have been slyly taken over and turned into mere tropes. He makes the same point that George Orwell made in his famous essay equating the degeneration of English with the rise of fascism. To speak, for example, of the *imperial designs* harbored by English departments toward history and anthropology departments, is to drain the sap right out of the term *imperialism*. Without the red juice of Marxist struggle-philosophy, *imperialism* loses all the polemical force that it might have had as a theoretical weapon against actual global imperialism. But NH could return the very plausible counterclaim that global, territorial imperialism is busily replicated across a much wider social field, including the domestic and private space of the home. Elaborating, Simon During notes the "sixties' enlargement on what could be named 'political' and engaged politically." The NHs' expanding of the word *economy* may well be faithful to this sixties enlargement of *politics*. Wai-Chi Dimock has no loyalty, for example, to Marxist economics.[12] In keeping with NH's emphasis on the personal, she examines Ralph Waldo Emerson's emotional economy upon the occasion of his son's early death. Emerson suffers anguish because he cannot feel regret, or at least not enough regret. Dimock writes: "He feels some pain when his son dies, sure enough; but that pain turns out to be no more than what he would have felt had he lost a large sum of money" (85). Dimock pursues an NHt strategy as she unearths the great man's outre calculations and shows how his language with its market logic enables him to assess an emotional bankruptcy of which that logic is itself the cause. After a discussion of *economy* such as Dimock's, one must agree with Brennan. This is not what Adam Smith and Ricardo meant at all.

NH: FASHIONABLE PRESENT, DODGY PASTS

Those critics who resist NH commitments to local knowledge, accidental contingency, and foregrounding of the personal really object to a much older tradition of American criticism and philosophical pragmatism. Where after all did NH get its moves? The NH is old-fashioned, as Brook Thomas persuasively argues. NH can promote its program in *Chaucer Review* and *Modern Philology*, where deconstruction and postcolonialism get marked, "Return to Sender." Perhaps this is so because NH has rejuvenated traditional humanist practices, such as biographical criticism.[13] Historians tend to say NH came from them, and indeed (as David Simpson points out) Roy Harvey Pearce should be credited with the invention of the term *new historicism* in his 1972 book, *Historicism Once More.* Thomas has investigated these claims carefully in a superbly written book that cultural critics called shrewd and well-informed but that historians approached with suspicion. One such reviewer said that Thomas should not have bothered to write the book and simply should have directed us to Morton White's superior 1949 book on the same topic (written when Greenblatt was six years old and Gallagher hadn't yet been born.) Linda Orr explains some of the suspicion and hostility. Tracing historians' two-hundred year effort to deny their own literariness, debts to rhetoric, and need for emotive language, Orr quips that NH is literature's revenge on history.

If we do return to Morton White, we can see what it is that separates NH from even the newest old historicism. White traces the late-nineteenth- and early-twentieth-century American pragmatist tradition, and finds there several useful definitions with which NHs would for the most part agree:

> By 'historicism' I shall mean the attempt to explain facts by reference to earlier facts; by 'cultural organicism' I mean the attempt to find explanations and relevant material in social sciences other than the one which is primarily under investigation.[14]

Organicism and historicism define the NH cosmos, as well but with this difference. Whereas historians traditionally balanced their sociological organicity and their linear historicity, NHs let their organicism eclipse their historicism. Simon During refers to the NHs' "lucid, diachronically torpid, synchronically hectic literary histories" (183). Devotees of sweeping, centuries-spanning narrative (diachrony) find the organicist project (synchrony) obnoxious. David Simpson has argued that no essential section (*coupe d'essence*) or cultural biopsy can accurately take society's measure (one of "the aggressively simple theories derived from Clifford Geertz"). Brook Thomas steps up the attack on Geertzian thick description, which recreates a detailed, integrated setting. Thomas remarks that the "organic model is hard to dispel"—implying it should be dispelled. Marjorie Levinson has delivered the ultimate insult. The wish to reconstruct a milieu in which "to restore to the dead their own living language" is precisely unaltered *old* historicism. With this charge, we come full circle. NH has evaporated.

Yet NH refuses to disappear, in part because it refuses to surrender the power to read from individual lives to macro-social structures, and vice-versa. Organicist? Humanist? Seduced by chimeras of social relevance? Perhaps. Yet NH has won over critics and readers well-schooled in poststructuralism and Marxisms who nonetheless search for connections between social structures, literary texts, and their own gender, sexuality, class position, ethnic background, relations to bosses and parents—in short, to their lives.

Not that NH has supported a self-centered identity politics. NH has also done that rarest of things—it has touched other disciplines and inspired non-academicians. Avid readers of the NH often contend that NHt analysis has given them ways to reconnect their personal lives with large societal shifts. Disappointingly, deconstruction had ignored the shifts, while Marxisms had ignored the personal lives. NH insisted that "the intensely personal moment . . . is intertwined with the great public cris[e]s," and this hook-up lit many people's imaginations.[15] In the late seventies Foucault's now-translated work and his lectures at Berkeley—the home of NH—dragged critics' attention back to the human subject. After Foucault, the human being had to be resituated somewhere between the integral humanist person and the structuralist fabrication. Foucault also complicated the prevailing sixties notion that power was hoarded like shares of preferred stock.[16] Rather, it was passed from Gucci handbag to backpack to hip pocket, the "Hey, boy" at work becoming the "Yes, Boss" at home. NH would also accept the pragmatists' view that "history is not merely a chronicle of the past, but rather a pragmatic weapon for explaining the present and controlling the future." As White and Thomas fully document, history had ceased to be "a tale of regal insanity and political intrigue" (48). NH inherited nineteenth- and twentieth-century North American pragmatism and twisted it to fit Foucault's microphysics of power.

But new historicisms go back even further. Fineman exploits his gift for outrageous statement by calling the early Greek historian Thucydides "the first New Historicist" (51), since Thucydides's anecdotes first disrupted an otherwise seamless narrative of Greek triumphs and virtues. Thomas brilliantly documents the NHs' debt to von Ranke, Burckhardt, and Nietzsche, then to Robinson and the Beards, as well as the more obvious debts to the many poststructuralist and New Left projects. At his most New Historical when traversing from literature to law—and, in his essay here, to legal realists including Oliver Wendell Holmes and Louis Brandeis—Thomas has expanded upon Hayden White's powerful book, *Metahistory,* which shook up historians by pointing out their unconscious reliance on rhetorical figures.

Another little-talked-of debt, this one to the elite Courtauld and Warburg Institutes that did such brilliant Renaissance scholarship in the forties and fifties, complicates the revenge-of-literature motif. Whereas the Warburg group acquired a snobbish erudition ("I have allowed quotations . . . to remain only in the original languages"),[17] NHs are more passionately moved to recover original *ver-*

nacular and demotic "languages"—popular rites, rituals, and body language. NH inversions deserve to be more fully explored in the genealogical manner that Brook Thomas has shrewdly laid out.

The NH gives its would-be genealogists a headache in part because it wants to forget its opponents and its intellectual ancestors, or at least to select the ones it prefers. As Patrick Brantlinger points out, NH has no strong wish to claim its American-pragmatist forebears, who so readily supported U.S. imperialism.[18] Nietzsche is an equally shameful progenitor, as is even Foucault, now that so many have condemned him for hypostasizing Power and denying that anyone could successfully resist it. The NH's convenient amnesia, its energetic forgetting or *aktive Vergesslichkeit*, may clear the road to further action, but it plays Old Harry with any effort to tell the NH story.[19]

A HAPPY HOLLOWNESS

In failing to know its own history, NH pays silent homage to deconstruction, for literary writing as understood by Derrida and de Man always fails on a rather magnificent scale. All writing is a tomb enclosing nothing, but literary writing ostentatiously flubs its efforts to refer to the world, express authorial emotion, communicate in transcendental symbols, or differentiate itself from rhetoric.[20] Having learned the thrilling effects of linguistic failure, NH simply assumed that the same joys attended *personal* failure. "We might say," During concludes, "that individuating escape routes are never incorporated into the social system more effectively than when they reveal the hollowness of the social system's conceptual struts, when the individuals feign, rather than naively endorse, faith." The hollow man or woman plays a crucial role in all New Historicism. Whether La Malincha—Cortez's interpreter, who brings down her own Aztec society—or Iago, professing beliefs that he does not hold, the hollow go-between is absolutely crucial. Whereas hold-over modernists still bewail disillusionment, inauthenticity, the *trahison des clercs,* and alienation, NH considers such laments bloated and pretentious. It treats modernist moralizing the way the Sex Pistols treat England's Queen. Its anthems to emptiness blast with garage-band intensity, causing Terry Eagleton and other plaintiffs to charge that NH fetishizes torture and death. "The flayed, crucified, disemboweled body has become a veritable emblem for this approach," Eagleton complains. "Sub-Nietzschean defeatism" rules the NH roost. But NHs consider Eagleton an old fart. Their initial fang-bearing denials of Marxism have modulated into condescending faint praise—a potentially more dangerous attitude, when one recalls (to pursue the punk analogy) that the explosive Hell and the Pistols subsided into Devo and New Wave. Will NH end not with a bang but a pop?

Perhaps the taming of the NH is still far down the road—even though Simpson has already called it "pop Foucault." Foucault and NH emphasize very different logics of capitalism. Foucault studies the individual dissolved in advancing microstructures of power and represents (in Edward Said's words) "an irresistible colonizing movement that paradoxically fortifies the prestige of both the individual scholar and the system that contains him."[21] NH emphasizes by contrast the self-disrupting logics of capitalism. The Latin *contingere* means, antithetically, "closely linked" and "thrown together by chance," or connected and disconnected—a logical scandal that NH's "arbitrary connnectedness" repeats. Another scandal is the contradictory valuation and debasement of the human individual, an oscillating effect captured in contributor Catherine Gallagher's remarks about Dickens's *Our Mutual Friend:*

> Eugene and Lizzie are equally garbage and treasure to each other; indeed, they are treasure because they are garbage . . . (62)

Uncannily alive to paradoxes that inhabit the money form—debasing and empty (garbage), it lays the foundation for modern citizenship, rights, and love (treasures)—Gallagher yet refuses to moralize and preach. Rather she graphs with stunning precision and evident pleasure the ways capitalism promotes thrusting, tireless human desires and the ways literature alchemizes those desires into art.

WHY THE RENAISSANCE FIRST?

If NH finds its own practices doubled in free-market circulation, capital penetration, and self-referenced simulacra that refer—like pornography—to an untouchable, illusory "reality," then why should this literary-critical tendency have made its first home the primitive, nascent capitalist societies of early modern Europe? Instead of fully developed turbulent free markets and selves liberated from quasi-feudal status hierarchies, the Renaissance fostered a potentially modern culture just emerging within "a jumble of traditional rules and offices designed to govern older, very different theatrical practices and a set of ordinances drawn up hastily in response to particular and local pressures" ("Circulation of Social Energy" 16). Why did NH first gain purchase in Renaissance studies? Many critics resort, in explanation, to Renaissance exceptionalism, calling the Renaissance the origin of subjectivity and individualism. This thesis goes back to Burckhardt in the nineteenth century, but it retains persuasive force.[22] Jean Howard has remarked, for example, that "these scholars construe the [Renaissance] period in terms reflecting their own . . . exhilaration and fearfulness of living in a gap in history" (17). Marlon Ross posits the same sort of homology when he argues that "we might say about Greenblatt's relation to his historical materials what he has said of the Europeans who destroyed Indian culture. 'In tearing down what both appealed to them and sickened them, they strengthened their power to resist their dangerous longings' (*Renaissance Self-Fashioning* 183)" (505). The Renaissance is the delivery room in which NHs witnessed their own birth.

The first four selections printed here testify to the unimaginable excitement that men and women of the Renaissance must have felt as the rigid constraints of medieval institutions and physical hardships began to fall away.[23] Those pleasures are abundantly clear in Stephen Orgel's *The Illusion of Power* but so are the perils: the individual's surging sensations of power may befuddle and destroy him. Orgel demonstrates that the absolute power of a monarch—exercised daily in edicts and executions—may be less solid than a court masque or cardboard stageset. Charles I finds out too late that he is chiefly a theatrical king whose real power base has crumbled away.

Greenblatt shows that the rigid structures of English and Venetian society may yield to a cunning agent who exploits those structures. Othello almost achieves admission to the tony men's club—upper Venetian society—and his failures allow us to glimpse early modern subjectivity in the making. Fineman finds the glimmerings of a later Freudian subjectivity in Shakespeare's sonnets, and so his piece too brings to the reading of early texts a tingling sensation of self-discovery and recognition. The "Why's" of NH's Renaissance genesis have been widely debated, but one canny explanation comes from David Simpson. Unlike his own field, Romanticism, the Renaissance was not yet theory-saturated or equipped to defend against the reductive NHt reading of Marxism. It needed refreshing new critical approaches to refurbish its thoroughly canonical texts. NH reads these classics in terms of extra-"literary" analogues, and instead of creating a new canon reaffirms the old one. Now Shakespeare connects with everything![24]

FIVE ASSUMPTIONS AS ILLUSTRATED IN THIS VOLUME

I. EMBEDDEDNESS

These early-modern men's and women's tormented or ecstatic writhings can profitably return us to the five basic tendencies that I outlined in 1989 and summarized briefly above. Consider the first-named assumption, that every expressive act is embedded in a network of material practices. The Renaissance period makes this embeddedness particularly clear. It was then, according to Jonathan Dollimore, that state power and cultural forms "most visibly merge." Pastoral, the masque, and the institution of patronage offer a rudely explicit lesson on the inseparability of culture and power. So completely had literature merged with social and economic practices that, according to Dollimore, "Jane Tompkins has argued that the Renaissance inherited from the classical period a virtually complete disregard of literature's meaning and a correspondingly almost exclusive emphasis on its effect. What mattered, ultimately, was action, not signification, behavior, not discourse." Tompkins's point, the same point that she makes in the selection below, is that literature does social work. Similarly, Greenblatt observes in his article that literary production and rhetorical education were completely bound up together in this period. "In *The Tudor Play of Mind*, Joel Altman has recently demonstrated the central importance for English Renaissance culture of the *argumentum in utramque partem*, the cultivation of the scholar's power to speak equally persuasively for diametrically opposed positions. The practice permeated intellectual life in the sixteenth century and was, Altman convincingly argues, one of the formative influences on the early drama." Orgel's piece demonstrates not just the emptiness of the king's illusions but also that the very epitome of empty, false shows—a court masque—could serve as a medium of nation-shaking contest and debate. A lavish masque that the lawyers produced at the king's command presented a powerful argument on the lawyers' own behalf. It concludes pointedly refuting Charles's claim to have an absolute prerogative, or ultimate authority, in all affairs of state:

> The world shall give prerogative to neither
> We cannot flourish but together.

Today a reader must step into history in order to understand how odd an exchange this really was. Here were two parties representing interests that had locked in a deadly contest that led to the Ship Money Case in 1641 and literally cost Charles and the hereditary aristocracy their head in 1649. That this momentous and nation-shattering conflict should work itself out through the highly allegorical, displaced medium of the court masque suggests some of the uses of hollowness. Deeply embedded in material conflicts, the masque fully illustrates the first NHt assumption—that material and aesthetic practices incite each other. They cannot flourish but together.

II. FALLING PREY TO THEIR OWN CRITIQUE

Orgel's vivid recreation of the political contests enacted through court masques also illustrates a second principal NHt assumption, namely, that every act of unmasking, critique, and opposition uses the tools it condemns and risks falling prey to the practice it exposes.[25] This was indeed the fate that overcame the lawyers who mounted "The Triumph of Peace" for King Charles I. The lawyers wanted to tell Charles that he had lost touch with reality. But they told him in a masque, the ultimate out-of-touch fantasy form. Their scoldings and veiled threats, instead of the intended subversive thrusts, turned into harmless compliments and delighted Charles so mightily that he ordered the performance repeated. Medium in this case nullified message.

NH's oft-noticed ambivalence and embarrassment, its occasional angst-laden confessions, may be the consequence of assumption two. Louis Montrose remarks that "integral to this new project of historical criticism is a realization and ac-knowledgement that the critic's own text is as fully implicated . . . as is the doc-ument under study." Doomed ceaselessly to perceive their own guilty investment in the systems they publicly deplore, they have further cause to see themselves mirrored in a Renaissance that prized and cultivated self-exposing, self-assem-bling confession, whether in church, on the rack, at the Globe, or through the sonnet.[26] NHs' own confessions have rarely gained them absolution. Frank Len-tricchia contends that their self-undermining confessions link them to the main-line tradition of aesthetic humanism and "our colleagues in literary study, who take not a little pleasure from describing themselves as powerless" (in Veeser, 241), while Stanley Fish attributes these "uneasy," "nervous," self-blaming ges-tures to either "large ambitions that have been frustrated" or the "familiar aca-demic" conviction that "we must be doing something wrong because people are listening to us and offering us high salaries" (315). Others who deplore NH self-unmaskings land somewhere between Lentricchia, who urges critics to believe in their revolutionary power, and Fish, who counsels the critics to "sit back and enjoy the fruits of their professional success" (315). The Rogin article below turns the screw yet tighter. Noting that adults increasingly see films that appear to have been made for children, he observes that they keep their self-respect by "admiring the skills by which they have been infantilized" (Robin Wood, quoted by Rogin). "This self-aware quality," remarks Rogin, "should be read not as maturity but as escape from troubling depths" (119). NH could be said to stage the same escape—as could Rogin himself.

III. LITERATURE AND NON-LITERATURE: SAME DIFFERENCE

Greenblatt, Orgel, and Fineman also disclose the ways in which—and this is the third point on which NHs broadly agree—literary and non-literary texts cir-culate inseparably. History and literature have been endlessly juxtaposed before now, but never in quite so insouciant a fashion. When critics obeyed the histo-rians' reigning protocols, they pressed the life from their work, During observes. NH is the first critical movement to ignore the historians' conservative complaints.

In Greenblatt's "Improvisation of Power," a chapter from Peter Martyr's *De orbe novo*, a travelogue of Spanish conquistadors in the New World, is the best gloss on Shakespeare's tragedy of a Moorish soldier in Venice and Malta. For Orgel, the "most complete expression of the royal will" was to be found neither in the king's weak army nor his erratically obeyed edicts but rather in his lavishly funded court theatricals that provided Charles with his own self-scripted illusions of power. Fineman shows that literary and non-literary texts can interpenetrate over a great historical divide. The Symbolic motif of writing overwhelms, in

Shakespeare's *Sonnets,* the Imaginary motif of visual, Petrarchan compliment. In this "capture" of the Imaginary-visible-narcissistic-and-mirroring mode by the Symbolic-written-intersubjective mode, Shakespeare prefigures Jacques Lacan. By connecting two symbol-doctors across a four-and-a-half-century gap, Fineman completes the circuit joining psychoanalysis and poetry. A sixteenth-century imaginative text by Shakespeare and a twentieth-century scientific text by Lacan occupy exactly the same epistemological plane.

The world irresistibly contaminates the literary text. Montrose draws on the pioneering work of Daniel Javitch, *Poetry and Courtliness in Renaissance England* (Princeton: Princeton University Press, 1978) to show how beautiful language and ugly politics collude. He illustrates in the selection here how certain powerful magnates and peers mounted their own theatrical receptions for the queen in order to smooth over the conflicts that had arisen between her and them. One of the most powerful, Gyles Brydges, Lord Chandos, had resisted the Crown's dictates, used his private army to terrorize his own vassals and peasants, and in short acted as a law unto himself. His pastoral festivities in honor of the queen's visit epitomize the ironies and hypocrisies of courtly behavior. Observing that the local magnate's appointee, a lord high constable who had overtaxed and even murdered some of the local country people, appeared before Elizabeth in the costume of a sheep, Montrose notes the "remarkable sublimation" of local conditions and events in "a grimly comic miming of satire's wolf-in-sheeps'-clothing motif." Montrose reveals the Renaissance origins of what we tend to consider—following George Orwell—a peculiarly modern tendency to aestheticize real-life horror. The high constable's nasty/funny charade joins other instances of the political-literary macabre, the sick jokes at the scaffold in Orwell's "A Hanging," the human ears spilled from a jar in Carolyn Forche's "The Colonel," or—a superb recent example critiqued by Bruce Robbins—the body-dump outings in Joan Didion's *Salvador.* In all these instances literary critics ably expose entrenched, thuggish power attempting to amuse itself. An era when the Tudors had not yet consolidated their monopoly of violence allows NHs to catch, in their natural habitat, the dangerously free subjectivities liberated by early-modern capitalism that have used the arts to found one fascism, junta, and political dystopia after another.

IV. NO TEXT ACCESSES UNCHANGING TRUTHS

But in asking why the NH arose particularly within Renaissance scholarship, one must question all the claims made on behalf of what we might call Renaissance exceptionalism. All these claims about the extraordinary nature of the sixteenth century—that it is the time when state and culture most visibly merge, that the seventeenth century inherited the classical disregard for literature's meaning and looked instead only to its persuasive effect, that (as Peter Burke has suggested) the sense of anachronism—that things can be out of date—originates with the Renaissance, that the psychoanalytic subject had its origins in the Shakespearean subject—all these claims require circumspect review.[27] Could one not say that every age is an exception?

Greenblatt has said that NHs study the Renaissance "by analogy to ourselves," a remark that one could take to mean that subjectivity never changes. And indeed Lentricchia condemns the apparent anti-historicism embodied in what he sees as NH's defeatist argument that "the Renaissance is *our* culture because it is the origin of our disciplinary society" (Veeser, 239). But it is more accurate to say that the Renaissance epitomizes the moment of historical fracture: "European humanists were right to perceive a significant cultural rift between their era and the one that preceded it," especially given the "emergence of social structures previously unknown to the stage of world history." [28] Feminism—another such historical break—has placed the older break in question. Joan Kelly-Gadol's question, "Did women have a Renaissance?" (Parker xxx), aptly captures the NHt willingness to overturn period pieties. One group's Renaissance may be another's ice age. Some women remain skeptical about NH. Is it a renascence in scholarship for them? Judith Lowder Newton flatly replies, No. "Non-feminist 'new historicism,' " she writes, "has been widely criticized for its tendency to insist upon the totalizing power of hegemonic ideologies, ideologies implicitly informed by elite male values and often presented as typical of the way culture itself is constructed as a whole" (Veeser, 166). NHs' emphases on Power necessarily confine it to the study of powerful men, in other words. Marguerite Waller has also argued that "Greenblatt's text [*Renaissance Self-Fashioning*] is unselfconsciously sexist" (3). By whole-heartedly entering the imaginative world of Sir Thomas Wyatt's self-fashioning lyrics, the critic "does not undo the act of usurpation and colonization being perpetrated either on Wyatt's text or on the reader who does not identify with the thrills and disillusionments of the male traffic in women" (5). Other feminists have registered similarly disturbing objections to the NH enterprise.[29] At the same time, Greenblattian investigations of pathological masculinity can give feminists new forms of ammunition. A crystalline example comes as so often from Elizabeth Fox-Genovese. Fox-Genovese writes that Locke's misogyny "inadvertently furnished future feminists with a language of rights and rationality."[30] Oppositional acts are revealed as gestures—fun to make, but empty. They are—as J. L. Austin said of literary speech-acts—in a peculiar way hollow or void.[31]

The awakening to this unhappy fact has come about in just the last twenty years. Nancy Hartsock, Judith Newton, and other vigorous fighters have cried "Foul," and denounced as conspiracy the recent moves to question narratives of opposition just when long-oppressed groups of women, gays, people of color, and workers have finally begun to tell their own stories.

But NH lets us see that it was not for Renaissance men only that individualistic feeling suddenly gathers to a head. Gallagher's article on Margaret of Cavendish and Marjorie Garber's chapter below on *The Roaring Girl,* based on the real-life Mary Frith, show that explosively released subjectivities could thrive in female bodies, too. Women in a patriarchy headed by a dangerous, crafty queen were uniquely well situated to test the limits of freedom, constraint, desire, and repression. Mary Frith, a.k.a. Moll Cutpurse, can star in a Renaissance play that is "about the circulation of parts, about women with penises and testicles and men who lack them" in part because the real Moll could dress as a man throughout a career that moved from pickpocketing to prostitution to bawdry and—long after she saw herself represented in *The Roaring Girl*—finally to tavern keeping. Mobility, exchange, appetite, identity shifts, traffickers, go-betweens, fixers, markets, money, bodies—Renaissance women clarify these exemplary NHt themes.

Orgel, Greenblatt, Montrose, and Fineman memorably pursue, in the classic essays below, the shifting, proud, doomed subjectivities that Renaissance literature helped to make profoundly alterable, rarely stable, and never secure. The backwash reaches into Chaucer's era. But the rolling force of it all tumbles down the years and crashes on the nineteenth century.

V. NEW ECONOMICS DEMAND A NEW POETICS

The fifth NHt assumption—that literature in capitalism requires a capitalist poetics—receives magnificent elaboration in the post-Renaissance studies included here. Progress from status to contract demands that all goods and even personal traits be alienable, marketable, and perpetually up for sale. In a contract, each party, now hollowed-out, requires the other party to complete the whole, and because the whole itself now stands beyond the contracting parties, a third term like the state for Hobbes or the general equivalent for Marx or the phallus for Freud or *la langue* for Saussure must arise. The general equivalent in all cases scoops out the human subject and absorbs the subject's essence.

GARBAGE AND TREASURE

Please note the NH difference. The hollowness of the self that so enraged and demoralized everyone from T. S. Eliot to Bertolt Brecht now inspires respect and study, not recrimination and calls for revolution. NH initiates a truly radical change. It accepts the inevitability of emptiness.

The raucous wake had already begun. Roland Barthes, in "The Death of the Author," denied the very existence of selves (he writes *Barthes on Barthes* not to form his identity but rather to erase it). Lacan's empty subject, Foucault's exuberant "lament" for the disappearing human subject, and Derrida's death of the addressee inscribed in the written mark (in *Limited, Inc.,* for example)—all these helped bear the pall.[32]

To see how this positive response to hollowness works itself out, we may begin with Gallagher's essay on George Eliot's *Daniel Deronda*, which, included below, shows what has happened to money and to Jewish subjectivity in England over three centuries. The terms have all shifted, and Daniel Deronda, the attractive leading man, bears little resemblance to Barabas, a package of nastiness. Deronda is, like Barabas, identified with money. But money itself has changed. An early establishing shot finds Daniel in the classic Laura Mulvey, male-gaze position, observing but unseen, as (in the gambling casino in Leubrunn) Gwendolyn Harleth excitedly wins and loses money. Her excitement strikes Daniel as sordid, and when she pawns a necklace to get more gambling money, he redeems it and returns it to her, along with a stern note.

Gallagher comments that the roulette wheel stands for the free market, part for whole. The wheel respects no ranks or genders, only money, just like the market itself. Deronda, like a traditional father, orders his "daughter" (in Gallagher's words) to "vacate the marketplace and depend on his legacy alone." He tries to restore a paternalist, sex-gender system. To recall Sir Henry Maine's idiom, *Status* would—if Daniel had his way—replace gaming-table *contract*. Deronda wants to escape the market. The market drags him back. Daniel makes the shattering discovery that his mother is an actress, an artist, virtually a prostitute, and a Jew, while Gwendolyn abandons casinos only to be sucked into the equally debasing English marriage market. Now a mere commodity, Gwendolyn is forced to receive the insulting gift of her husband's concubine's jewelry, a gift that makes her own concubinage all too clear. Daniel and Gwendolyn watch themselves slide from the realm of independent self-production to the hell of circulation.

What saves Daniel is Jewish nationalism—Zionism—which negates the market because it is opposed to a "viciously cosmopolitan" Jewishness that would "resolve all national interests into the algebra of loans." Jewish nationalism gives Deronda a fixity of purpose and a geographical destination. Asking herself why Eliot should repudiate the generous cosmopolitan culture in which Eliot herself was immersed, Gallagher discovers the neurotic insecurities grounding a capitalist poetics. "It's the problem more than the solution that's compelling," she says. The fertile problem is how to create "a self-sustaining anxiety."

This new anxiety differs from the "salutary anxiety" that Greenblatt so penetratingly explores. That Renaissance anxiety tends to come from without. The powerful people contrive to make the weaker people anxious. The great Protestant divine Hugh Latimer conceals a royal pardon until a condemned woman accepts a doctrinal point of religion; theatrical suspense tightens the throat and stomach of its happily terrorized audience; the Duke in *Measure for Measure* makes Juliet fear needlessly for her brother's life; and Prospero strikes a paralyzing and ceaseless anxiety into everyone on his island. But the *self-sustaining* anxiety Gallagher sees in *Deronda* comes from within, from Deronda's upsetting discovery that he originates in theatricality, circulation, gambling, brokering, and the market. His self-generating anxiety drives Deronda into action, into a search for stability, a cultural center, a geographical home. Anxiety originates not in Power but in his own rootless subjectivity.

The problem, not the solution, is compelling, because the solution can resolve nothing. Were the novel actually to observe Daniel settling down in Palestine, the restless mobility that defines capitalist poetics would have to cease. Capital cannot stand cessation any more than nature can support a vacuum. A case could be made for the accuracy of NH perceptions. Daniel's Zionism has indeed carried out its program. The Jewish settlement of Palestine failed to end Jewish anxiety and incited the Intifada. "Self-sustaining anxiety" can be humanly admirable only until it tries to dispel itself.

The unstable market that creates subjective anxieties receives analysis in Pease, Michaels, Tompkins, Thomas, and Rogin, as well. Donald Pease observes that some prominent Americanists, such as Quentin Anderson in *The Imperial Self,* have discerned a romance of interpretation that traps readers and critics in intolerably anxious circular logic. Anderson saw in his Columbia students after the 1968 student riots an "extreme passivity designed to 'suffer' the unmastered materials of the external world." "The material so suffered ceases to remain external and turns instead into the fluent and circumambient energies of the creative self." Attracted by this theory of anxieties sublimated in art, Pease approvingly cites Gerald Graff, the superb historian of university literature teaching:

> The symbolic-romance theory, stressing as it did the inability of American narratives to resolve their conflicts within any social form of life, provided expression for disappointments left over from the 30s toward a society that had failed to fulfill its ideal image of itself but evidently could not be righted by social action. (213)

Pease deplores the usual response to this disappointment. Instead of retreating from the disheartening public realm to the reassurances that one can after all dominate a text, external nature, previous interpretations, a former self "in a relentlessly circular economy" (O'Hara calls this the romance of interpretation), Pease demands a renewed public program. Given the Bercovitch hitch, this call gets a bit tricky, since in all likelihood Pease's most strident opposition will only strengthen the power of academic studies as they are traditionally performed in the ivory tower.[33]

Pease therefore makes a signature NHt move by assuming the role of the go-between. He asserts that New Americanists, of whom he is one, "occupy a double relation" as "liaisons between cultural and public realms." In defiance of conventionalists such as Fish and Michaels who say that you can never step outside your culture in order to evaluate it, for you will then have no terms of evaluation left, Pease insists that his group is "at once within the field and external to it." He and his associates—Jonathan Arac, Paul Bové, Daniel O'Hara, Rob Wilson—operate as "representatives of subjects excluded from the field imaginary" of Bercovitch and consensus American studies. This self-assured return to confident declarations of one's own representativity and objectivity would sound like whistling in the dark to the other contributors to this volume.

Pease's essay enters this volume as the lone champion of a more widely shared critique of NH. At least half the contributors to my earlier volume disputed the NHt claim that criticism has no political mandate or valency. That critique continues to thrive in ever more nuanced versions that Pease so lucidly elaborates. These counterarguments have failed to persuade the NH mainstream to alter their course.

They have especially failed to persuade Walter Michaels, known as the Great Satan by cultural materialists like Pease who would still claim that literary criticism can effectively oppose and disrupt an unjust system. Dangerous threats to social stability? Michaels speaking for Berkeley NH replies, "Our studies show the opposite." Going well past the Bercovitch theory about Puritans' approving dissensus, Michaels says that all representational modes push each other towards increasingly corporate styles of being. Daguerrotype and photography, the legal decisions about corporate responsibility, anti-trust battles, monetary debates and gold-bug agitation, bankruptcy legislation all profoundly redefine humanity. We have a new technology of being human: "what seems monstrous now is the discovery that for a man to be a man, he must also be a corporation—a man *is* a corporation." Observations such as this one (which is about Frank Norris's great novel, *The Octopus*) pervade Michaels's brilliantly argued work.

Michaels's article printed here discusses the American writer Hawthorne's opposition to the logic of the market, his apparent wish to recover an organic community of hereditary and inalienable property. Michaels asserts that the apparently feudal, reactionary desire for inalienable title—a born gentleman can never be less than that—is by no means anachronistic in the 1850s when Hawthorne wrote *Gables*. Congress had before it a bill providing that slaves "could not be bought or sold by creditors." In addition, radical reformers were urging that homestead land be made inalienable, so as to keep it from the hands of speculators. Hawthorne's novel resists the unregulated capitalist market, much as did these hedges against unrestrained slave and land sales. Holgrave embodies this resistance within the novel. And yet Holgrave has himself circulated through many jobs. He seems to be a pure product of the market economy, a self-made operator and manipulator. His current profession, that of daguerreotypist, even more completely embodies the innovations and degradations that drive the market. Daguerreotypy had commercialized and debased image making, replacing oil portraiture forever. The market that Hawthorne sets out to escape reasserts itself at the center of his novel.

Thus, while Holgrave represents profoundly anti-market forces in the novel, stands for hereditary title (he recovers land he has never seen but that somehow *belongs* to him), and practices daguerreotypy, an art that gives him access to deep truths about people, he is himself the pure product of republican fluctuation. The stronghold of clear title stands on the quicksand of free-for-all corporate capitalism. Michaels's reading strongly suggests that characters may represent stability one minute and fluctuation the next, or more alarmingly, both at once. As in capitalism itself, every representation is always up for grabs.

STATUS TO CONTRACT

Brook Thomas brilliantly tracks hollow personality to yet other legal and aesthetic norms that frame it. In an essay on privacy in Henry James's *The Bostonians*, Thomas focuses on a handshake. Noting that with this handshake the heroine Verena agrees to keep silent about an illicit meeting, and comparing the handshake to another physical sign, the kiss, Thomas extracts a lesson about movement from status to contract as the basis for social relationships. Contending that status is more primitive than contract, Thomas remarks that her "privacy is constructed by maintaining a space . . . an emptiness at her core that makes her dependent upon relations" ("Privacy"). Every good novel, too, sets up a contract with its reader that makes it "dependent on relations." This is clearly a further step both toward understanding capitalist personality and inventing a capitalist poetics. "Verena's remarkable capacity to establish relationships with people results not from a fullness, but an emptiness," Thomas observes. Her eventual husband, Basil, attributes "to Miss Tarrant a singular hollowness of character" (*Bostonians*). A private personality means, for Henry James, creating a space *between*, "a space that establishes connections while simultaneously helping to define the parties involved." Personality and privacy depend on contracts and thus owe "much to the ideal of the period's market exchanges," says Thomas. An oppositional, left-leaning critic himself, Thomas would like to make the Jeremiah move and transcend his culture. Yet every bit as much as Michaels and Gallagher, he doubts that he can execute that move. Drawn back into the vortex of lack and desire, Thomas succumbs to the logic of the go-between.

In her powerful argument in support of the literary value of women's sentimental fiction, Jane Tompkins shows perhaps most forcefully of all the contributors that time and place shape each succeeding version of human subjectivity. Thus the multitudinous nineteenth-century Americans who read *Uncle Tom's Cabin* and wept at the doll-like little Eva were not "unaccountably moved to tears by matters that are intrinsically silly and trivial." Instead they were caught up in a monumental effort "to reorganize culture from women's point of view." In Harriet Beecher Stowe's understanding, "it is the *modern* view that is naive." It is silly to believe that political change can save humankind. Politics is the *problem*, not the *solution*. Only action through the private, domestic, women's sphere can relieve that problem. Thus, "Stowe relocates the center of power in American life, placing it not in the government, nor in the courts of law, nor in the factories, nor in the marketplace, but in the kitchen." Tompkins demonstrates effectively that within a few decades, great literature was marked down to the status of laughable pap. The reasons were social and economic, and American criticism, "which had been evangelical and religious . . . evolved during the 1870s and '80s into a concern for the material conditions of social life." In consequence, novels once thought "superb" now were seen to be "full of idealized characters, authorial didacticism, overt religiosity," to be "morally false and artistically naive." Besides illustrating most effectively that no texts offer access to unchanging truths, Tompkins performs the added NH service of leaving us nowhere solid to stand. Instead of trumpeting the moral probity of women writers who stood for justice and—because they had no male prerogatives to run off and become boat captains—made their stand in the home, Tompkins also lets us see how pernicious this latter ideal could be. In a remarkable passage, she cites Catherine Beecher, Stowe's elder sister. Beecher's famed *Treatise on Domestic Economy* (1841; rev. as *The American Woman's Home* [1866]) expresses the hope that this cheering example of power centered in the home would

> soon spread, and ere long colonies from these prosperous and Christian communities would go forth to shine as "lights of the world" in all the now darkened nations. Thus the "Christian family" would become the grand ministry . . . in training our whole race.

The imperial designs expressed here render the inspiring feminist message somewhat hollow.

Equally hollow to post-colonial ears will be the Bush-Reagan years' political culture as analyzed here by political scientist Michael Rogin. Rogin finds that anxiety comes home to roost in the state itself. Arguing that "a multinational-dominated internationalized economy that resists state control sets the stage for a defensive nationalism," Rogin sees the state as an actor (quite literally so, in Reagan's case) who lacks power either to control the economy or to mobilize the populace but can still conduct covert military action (Bush was CIA director). *Daniel Deronda* confronts the same situation—eroding national power in an increasingly cosmopolitan world—and finds a projected solution in Jewish nationalism. For Reagan-Bush and (perhaps) beyond, the answer is a weird new NHt trope, the covert spectacle—backstairs Watergate and front-page Grenada, backchannel Iran-Contra and prime-time smart-bombing. Such tactics developed gradually. "The full-fledged absorption of American foreign policy by symbolic gesture," concludes Rogin, "awaited the Reagan presidency."

Rogin's stunning analyses remind the reader of this volume how much more there is to learn from critics than from talk shows. In other essays, Rogin has demonstrated how the one group—Jewish black-face performers, for example— obtains freedom and psychic mobility at the price of another group's fixity— that is, the stereotyping of African-Americans. And with his discussions of psychic mobility and the theatrical triumphs achieved by impotent rulers, he returns us full circle to Greenblatt's nauseatingly mobile Iago and Orgel's paper tiger Charles I.

FUTURES AND FRACTURES

The final section of the book deserves its own introduction. For in Garber, Chakrabarty, Gallop, and Harlow, we find non-NHs appropriating NHt methods selectively. They do so in part because their own work has changed—Gallop and Garber moving from purer psychoanalytic viewpoints to projects contaminated by historical circumstance, Sedgwick historicizing her seemingly ahistorical paradigm—a model in which pandemic homosociality ensures the degradation of women—and the often relentlessly historicizing Harlow and Chakrabarty adapting the synchronic, organicist tactics of NH. These are fractures of NH—selective grabs that ignore what cannot be used. Chakrabarty and Harlow cold-shoulder NH's skeptical unwillingness to confirm particular versions of history. Gallop expands the permissible range of NHt evidence—what seems a chance typo or an inadvertently omitted footnote proves, for Gallop, the key to pervasive editorial repressions and political suppressions. Garber too exceeds NH's roomy limits. Analyzing wordplay in *The Roaring Girl,* she suddenly begins to pun and goof on her sister critics' texts and even their names. The changing of costumes, roles, and genders slips from the cordoned-off-for-safety Jacobean city comedy and runs wild in the normally sedate milieu of the critic. The autobiographical move, long an NHt tactic, gravitates to the center of analysis. Gallop's article here proceeds from her having "always enjoyed being a bad girl" of criticism; Sedgwick writes poems, was spoiled and spanked, eats too much; Chakrabarty wears bell bottoms; Garber wears men's clothes. When did we know so much about critics' lives?

The two most unexpected inclusions in this volume are Harlow and Chakrabarty. Chakrabarty observes that in an India very apt to take on British models of subjectivity, very few autobiographies have been written. Those that have appeared include almost no intimate details. Chakrabarty asks the piercing questions:

> How do we read this text, this self-making of an Indian male who was second to no one in his ardor for the public life of the citizen, yet who seldom, if ever, reproduced in writing the other side of the modern citizen, the interiorized private self unceasingly reaching out for an audience?

> Public without private? Yet another instance of the "incompleteness" of bourgeois transformation in India? (10)

Or, he asks later, just another case of the "lazy native"? The NH has at least provoked the questions.

After a bout of deconstruction (she translated Derrida's text, *Spurs*, for the American edition), Barbara Harlow turned her back on theory and went to the American University in Cairo. Now a committed postcolonial scholar, she writes here in an unexpectedly NHt vein, even beginning in classic NHt fashion with an anecdote. In the Arab world, she tells us, a story goes around, the story of "Goha's Nail."

> Goha offered his house for sale, but attached one condition: that he retain ownership of just one of the nails in the house. This condition did not dissuade the prospective purchaser at the time, but he was surprised somewhat later when Goha appeared at the door, asking to check on his nail.

The story proceeds, with Goha returning with a blanket during a severe storm in order to guard his nail from any elemental threat. Finally he moves back into the house. Initially the story was a wry look at the British agreement to evacuate Egypt only on the condition that they keep their base in the Suez Canal. Now it represents any Western attempt to maintain an active presence in the Arab Middle East.

This favorite NHt device—salutary anxiety, covert spectacle, Goha nail—operates like the rhetorical figure *chiasmus*, or crossing. It demonstrates the textuality of history and the historicity of texts. The key idea is that the former owner need only retain title to a single nail in order to control and reoccupy the whole building. This key trope unlocks many examples as the Harlow article unfolds. The Egyptian president Sadat's policy of *infitah*, or economic "open door," lends itself beautifully to Harlow's anecdote-analogy, for the West and Israel go immediately into the house and claim their Egyptian nail. (One could add that the ill-fated policy ended with Sadat dead as a doornail.) The article printed here may itself be read as a double crossing, the unwanted return of High Theory to reclaim the errant deconstructor-turned-postcolonial critic. Readers of Harlow's other work, such as *Resistance Literature*, will be pleased to find that she has at last chosen to construct a resilient, airy, symmetrical verbal structure, but the hell of it is, she uses the NH—another Goha nail.

WHAT WILL THEY BE UP TO NEXT?

NHt practices seem infinitely extendable. Its intensive "thick descriptive" readings of a wink and a tear. Its analysis of contrasts between a handshake and a kiss in *The Bostonians*. Its insistently childlike questions: what gender are vampires, why has Prospero no wife, why was England's the only all-transvestite theater? Its annoying habit of pointing out disturbing continuities: Sappho's links to German nationalism; family pets, petting, and teenage pregnancy; fear of the free market (agoraphobia) and fear of food (anorexia); the sexist eighteenth-century female thermometer to measure women's sexual excitability as a spur to the first-wave women's liberation movement. Its perverse distensions of the realm of the aesthetic: murdering peasants as an art form; bodies, death, and pauper funerals; rock'n'roll and the art of soldiering in Indochina; spectacle and amnesia in American politics; the human ear in Shakespeare's sonnets and the servant's hand in the "master's bedroom." These new subjectivities, continuities, economies, and poetics mark out only a fraction of the the the terrain NH has begun to explore.

The young and the restless (as Fish calls NHt critics) have dropped their pebbles into even the most placid waters—the medieval period. That field "has from the beginning served the postmedieval Western historical consciousness as one of the primary sites of otherness by which it has constituted itself," contends Lee Patterson (2), who has led NHt medievalist inquiry. Younger medievalists have greeted the NH as a way to uproot an entrenched positivist methodology. Medievalists may now study NH takes on their discipline: "Peasant Consciousness, Chaucer's Miller, and the Structure of the *Canterbury Tales*," "Narrative and Power in Hoccleve's *Regiment of Princes*," "A Chaucerian Critique of the Petrarchan Academy," "Authorial Signature and Social Identity in Late Fourteenth-Century England," or "Narrative and Capital in Late Medieval Scotland."[34] These essays juxtapose with exacting historical analysis the raciest developments in literary theory and so avoid what Caroline Walker Bynum has called "presentism," the fallacy of insisting on the modernity of medieval texts. NH's arrival has changed the face of medieval studies, and it has refigured the relationship between that period and others. It has helped critics to perceive changes in the "threats" that women posed to men's work. The Bible and medieval texts represented Delilah as sexually dangerous, whereas Milton presents her as dangerously domestic. The great Puritan limns in Delilah the allure of that prevalent and Protestant sphere reserved for women: in *Samson Agonistes*, she represents the realm of private domesticity and the economy of the wife.[35]

The nineteenth-century European economic takeoff and the border-smashing imperialism that extended European control over eighty-five percent of the earth's surface by 1913 have proven remarkably conducive to NHs who finesse disciplinary borders and ransack the historical archives. The last few years have seen, for example, Steven Mailloux's fascinating development of a *rhetorical hermeneutics* capable of linking through metaphors of food and nutrition the controversies embroiling texts such as *Peck's Bad Boy* and Eugene Sandow's physical-fitness manuals. They have seen in Gillian Brown's "The Empire of Agoraphobia" that food took on additional symbolic weight, this time representing the loved-and-hated border between women and the world. Brown shows that nineteenth-century American women felt increasingly trapped by rigid separate-spheres culture: relegated to the private domestic sphere, their public sphere contact reduced to *shopping*, many women succumbed to immobility, invalidism, or mummifying fears of open spaces (agoraphobia). Other women defiantly resisted the world's every intrusion, even the benign, vital infusions of food (anorexia). Brown's striking anecdotes (drawn from medical literature) lead into a brilliant new reading of *Bartleby the Scrivener* as anorexic agoraphobe. And these years have seen Marjorie Levinson's fine reading of the sexual rhetorics used by Byron and other aristocrats to attack the social upstart John Keats—an attack on "verbal priapism" that arguably still shapes Euro-American views of poetry today.

The list of splendid NH readings could be extended almost without end. Is NH history? Is it literature? Is it garbage? Is it treasure? It may be too early to answer such questions. One suspects that the Caroline lawyers were right: they cannot flourish but together. The contributors to this volume can in any case speak eloquently to all the issues that NH has raised. Insofar as NH has its canonical past and its promising future, both are well represented in this book.

NOTES

1. Vincent Leitch "subscribes to the charter of new historicism outlined by Veeser" but also warns, helpfully, that NH is not, as some theorists believe, a movement limited to those at the University of California-Berkeley associated with the journal *Representations;* it was "manifested first during the late 1970s in the writings of Greenblatt, Lentricchia, Said, and others." *Cultural Criticism, Literary Theory, Poststructuralism* (New York: Columbia University Press, 1992), 164. Leitch is referring to *The New Historicism*, ed. H. Aram Veeser (New York and London: Routledge, 1989), cited hereafter as Veeser.

2. D. A. Miller, *The Novel and the Police* (Berkeley: University of California Press; quoted in Catherine Gallagher, in Veeser, 45.

3. See "The Circulation of Social Energy," *Shakespearean Negotiations* (Berkeley: University of California Press, 1988), in which Greenblatt most carefully details market economy and its relationship to literary work. He feelingly recaptures the literature lover's desire to "bind and fix" fleeting pleasure and elusive values in a "stable and permanent source," that is to say, the literary work, which then offers "an escape from shared contingency." Greenblatt dismisses this desire in a powerful, one-sentence paragraph: "This project, endlessly repeated, repeatedly fails for one reason: there is no escape from contingency" (3). Literary works share in the general ephemerality of things. As Jane Tompkins writes in her essay here, "*The Scarlet Letter* is a great novel in 1850, in 1876, in 1904, in 1942, and in 1966, but each time it is great for different reasons." Greenblatt carries forward this market-based aesthetic philosophy in *Marvelous Possessions,* especially in the final chapter, "The

Go-Between," about the brokers/traders/traitors who sold out their own peoples and civilizations but also catalyzed new hybrids and in large part authored modern subjectivities.

4. Blackstone, "Of Title by Alienation," *Commentaries on the Laws of England* (Philadelphia: Lippincott, Grambo, & Co., 1855); in Michaels, 85. For the Critical Legal Studies left-deconstructive version, see Duncan Kennedy, "The Structure of Blackstone's Commentaries," *Buffalo Law Review* 28 (Spring 1979): 205–382.

5. David Simpson objects that "this celebration of contingency can . . . be thought of as 'subversive' only as long as it is nested within the postmodernist ethic of occasionality as in some sense libidinally liberating" (*Subject to History,* 13). He acutely notes that NHs acknowledge their placement within a "distinctly overarching" capitalism (13). He, Liu, McGann, Marjorie Levinson, and Jon Klancher have all written dazzlingly "critical materialist" essays. See Klancher, Levinson, "Back to the Future," and Simpson, "Introduction," *Subject to History: Ideology, Class, Gender* (Ithaca: Cornell University Press, 1991).

6. See Marlon B. Ross, "Contingent Predilections: The Newest Historicisms and the Question of Method," *The Centennial Review* 34 (Fall 1990), especially 490–493.

7. Liu shrewdly analyzes the autobiographical impulse. Saying that NH is "in effect a profoundly narcissistic method," he contends that, "disbelieving in a regulated method of reaching the historical other from the domain of the text, it at last studies itself in the anxious pose of reaching for the other" ("The New Historicism," 746). For examples of autobiographical moves see the epilogue to *Renaissance Self-Fashioning,* Montrose's finale in "The Elizabethan Subject and the Spenserian Text," and the last paragraph of Leonard Tennenhouse, "Strategies of State and Political Plays." Liu provides these references.

8. Adam Begley, author of the *Times Magazine* article ("The Tempest around Stephen Greenblatt" [28 March 1993]: 32–38) emphasizes NH's fast-moving prose, a feature easily caricatured by Camille Paglia as "Joan Didion crossed with *National Geographic* . . . The anecdotal, microchip manner of NH is yuppie grazing, cuisine minceur in a quiche-and-fern bistro."

9. See, for example, the interventions by Greenblatt, Montrose, Gallagher, Tennenhouse, Fineman, During, Horwitz, Litvak, Levinson, Liu, Mailloux, Klancher, Rosenberg, Pecora, Thomas, Fish, White, and Leinwand. The briefest summary would result in doubling the length of this introduction. So rich is this secondary literature that a volume of meta-critical NH essays will doubtless appear soon.

10. For a parallel account of what Simpson calls NH's *strong containment* thesis, see David Carroll, "Institutional Authority and Literary Power," in *Taking Chances: Derrida, Psychology, and Literature,* ed. Joseph Smith and William Kerrigan (Baltimore: Johns Hopkins University Press, 1984).

11. Lynn Hunt, "Introduction: History, Culture, and Text," *The New Cultural History*, ed. Lynn Hunt (Berkeley: University of California Press, 1989): 1–22.

12. Dimock cites Jacques Derrida, *Positions*, trans. Alan Bass (Chicago: University of Chicago Press, 1981) 60–67; and "From Restricted to General Economy: A Hegelianism without Reserve," in *Writing and Difference,* trans. Alan Bass (Chicago: University of Chicago Press, 1978), 251–77. See also "Economimesis," *Diacritics.*

13. "New historicists tend to keep alive much of the legacy and practice of traditional humanism, which some of its critics demonstrate (see Veeser)," remarks Leitch (164).

14. Morton G. White, *Social Thought in America: The Revolt Against Formalism* (New York: Viking, 1949), 12. NH has also been judged and seen itself as a "revolt against formalism." Fineman writes, "The term 'New Historicism' initially carried with it a somewhat polemical air, for the literary criticisms and critical histories that pronounced themselves New Historicist . . . presented themselves as overdue corrections of, or as morally and politically motivated reactions against, the formalism—more precisely and more pejoratively, the 'mere formalism' (which . . . was thought to be apolitical, sexist, hermetic, elitist, etc.)—that . . . had come to be associated with everything from the kind of close, immanent textual readings said to be endemic to the New Criticism, to the scientistic, agentless, essentialist, cross-cultural typologizations said to be characteristic of what was called Structuralist, to the kinds of deconstructive, but still mandarin and still strictly textual, and therefore still formalist, and therefore still objectionable, formulations—mere formulations—identified with either the phenomenologically or the rhetorically conceived versions of what came to be called Post-Structuralism" (in Veeser, 51).

15. Greenblatt, *Renaissance Self-Fashioning,* 119.

16. Adam Begley extends this lively metaphor in his *New York Times Magazine* article (36).

17. Stephen Orgel, introduction, *The Renaissance Imagination: Essays and Lectures by D. J. Gordon,* collected and ed. Stephen Orgel (Berkeley: University of California Press, 1975), x.

18. Patrick Brantlinger, review of Brook Thomas, "The New Historicism and Other Old-Fashioned Topics," in *American Historical Review* (December 1992): 1484. Thomas affirms that Dewey, James, and Peirce founded a progressive, liberal tradition that has broken down in "Watergate, Vietnam, and the Reagan era" (95).

19. Nietzsche speaks of *aktive Vergesslichkeit* as the only way to throw off the paralyzing obsessions with *past* events and the indispensable precondition for future achievement. On this "malady of history," see *The Uses and Abuses of History for Life,* trans. Adrian Collins (New York: Macmillan, 1957), 5–73.

20. Simon During provides these phrases. See During, "New Historicism," *Text*

and Performance Quarterly 11 (July 1991), 180. "Literature is marked not by its completion and immanent value but by the wiles, the turns and tropes in which it feigns fullness." Analogous is Greenblatt's division between the public and private, "the (finally doomed) individual drive to find and express a 'true' self, a self not given on another's terms, breed feignings, secrecy, rumors of defalcations from official truths, and so on, that Greenblatt applies a de Manian to a Foucauldian programme."

21. *Culture and Imperialism* (New York: Knopf, 1993), 278.

22. Burckhardt, writing in 1860, considered the Italian Renaissance in particular, but his nostalgia for the towering individualism of Renaissance merchant-princes extended to all cities that experienced the first heroic phases of capitalism. See the discussion of Burckhardt, "titanic individualism," and contemporary Renaissance scholarship in David Quint, "Introduction," *Literary Theory, Renaissance Texts* (Baltimore: Johns Hopkins University Press, 1986)1–20. Two indispensable texts for the study of emerging individualism are C. B McPherson, *The Political Theory of Possessive Individualism: Hobbes to Locke* (London: Oxford University Press, 1962) and Carole Pateman, *The Sexual Contract* (Stanford: Stanford University Press, 1988).

23. Lawrence M. Davis points out that this traditional view of the medieval period is not fair—cf. the joy of life and learning in Dublin and in Muslim culture in Spain (personal correspondence).

24. David Simpson, private correspondence.

25. A colleague, Stephen D. Moore, has pointed out that my language of unmasking has explicit debts to deconstruction. (And in fact Gayatri Spivak's discussions of Derrida and postcolonialism inspired my wording.) Moore's extraordinary work is best represented by his *Literary Criticsm and the Gospels: The Theoretical Challenge* (New Haven: Yale University Press, 1989) and *Mark and Luke in Poststructuralist Perspectives: Jesus Begins to Write* (New Haven and London: Yale University Press, 1992). For provocative NHt readings of the Midrash, see Daniel Boyarin, especially "The Case of the Married Monk," *Representations* 36 (Fall 1991), 87–113.

26. Alan Liu has brilliantly suggested the many ways in which NHs find themselves implicated in their own texts. "The New Historicism, I conclude, is our latest post-May 1970, post-May 1968, post 1917, . . . post 1789 (and so forth) imagination of an active role for intellect in the renascence of society" (752). This yearning imagination accounts both for the attractiveness of the Renaissance proper to NHs seeking their own renascence as politically powerful figures who guide society—Miltons and Machiavellis, perhaps. I would argue that they have actually settled for the more imaginably parallel *imago* of the long distance trader, that sub-group of adventurous, gambling Levantines who ranged across Asia and Africa finessing borders, brokering deals, and sending new products into Europe.

27. See Peter Burke, *The Renaissance Sense of the Past* (New York: St. Martin's Press, 1969), 138–41 and Dipesh Chakrabarty, "The Death of History? His-

torical Consciousness and the Culture of Late Capitalism," *Public Culture* 4 (Spring 1992): 47–66.

28. Patricia Parker, *Shakespeare and the Question of Theory* (New York and London: Methuen, 1985), xvii. Among the new socioeconomic factors were the arrival of capitalism, families' change from units of production to units of consumption, the rise of pauperism and the loss of traditional means of coping with it (such as manorial alms-giving), changes in the sex-gender system (Gayle Rubin's term) that undermined simpler mimetic theories of artistic representation.

29. See Carroll Smith-Rosenberg, "The New Woman and the New History," *Feminist Studies* 3 (Fall 1975): 185–98; Ellen Pollak, "Feminism and the New Historicism: A Tale of Difference or the Same Old Story?" in *The Eighteenth Century: Theory and Interpretation.*

30. Elizabeth Fox-Genovese, "Property and Patriarchy in Classical Bourgeois Thought," *Radical History Review* 4 (Spring/Summer 1977): 52; quoted in Anson Rabinbach, "Rationalism and Utopia as Languages of Nature: A Note," *International Labor and Working Class History* 31 (Spring 1977): 33.

31. *How to Do Things with Words* (Cambridge, Mass.: Harvard, 1962), 22: "a performative utterance will, for example, be *in a peculiar way* hollow or void if said by an actor on the stage, or if introduced in a poem, or spoken in a soliloquy. . . . Language in such circumstances is . . . parasitic upon its normal use. . . ."

32. Stephen D. Moore pointed out these references to me. For a thorough analysis of the death of the subject, see Paul Smith, *Discerning the Subject* (Minneapolis: University of Minnesota Press, 1988.)

33. By "Bercovitch hitch" I mean Sacvan Bercovitch's influential thesis that American culture and its polity is never harmed or disrupted by opposition and dissent. It is strengthened by them. The Puritan founders, inveterate dissenters, wanted their followers to dissent, too—so long as fundamental power relationships remained undisturbed. See Sacvan Bercovitch's brilliant attempt at autobiographical criticism, "Reflections of an Americanist," *The Journal of American History* (December 1991): 972–87, as well as his *The American Jeremiad* (Madison: University of Wisconsin Press, 1978).

34. All these tags appear as subtitles of articles in Lee Patterson, ed., *Literary Practice and Social Change in Britain, 1380–1530* (Berkeley: University of California Press, 1990).

35. See John Guillory, "Dalila's House: Samson Agonistes and the Sexual Division of Labor," in *Rewriting the Renaissance: The Discourse of Sexual Differences in Early Modern Europe,* ed. Mary Nyquist and Margaret W. Ferguson (London: Methuen, 1988): 148–76.

THE BEGINNINGS

1

THE ROLE OF KING

STEPHEN ORGEL

Hostile critics saw in the royal histrionics only frivolity or hypocrisy, and even sympathetic observers regularly referred to masques as "vanities." This, indeed, is Prospero's term for his own masque, "some vanity of mine art."[1] The description is exact and the charge irrefutable: these works are totally self-regarding. They are designed to be so. "All representations," wrote Ben Jonson, "especially those of this nature in court, public spectacles, either have been or ought to be the mirrors of man's life."[2] But mirrors, like so many Renaissance symbols, may be viewed in various and contradictory ways, and their moral implications lie in the eye of the beholder. They are emblems of worldliness and pride, frail glasses "which are as easy broke as they make forms."[3] They are also the way to self-knowledge. English didacticism in 1559 could do no better than provide a mirror for magistrates; and Hamlet's player holding the mirror up to nature is not encouraging her self-esteem. For the Jacobean translator of Ovid, the myth of Narcissus embodied the full ambiguity of the power of reflection. The youth's mother, reports George Sandys, *enquiring whether he should live untill he were old,* Tiresias *replied:* If he know not himselfe. *As strange as obscure; and seeming contradictory to that Oracle of* Apollo: To know a mans selfe is the chiefest knowledge. *The lacke hereof hath ruined many: but having it must needs ruine our beautifull* Narcissus: *who only is in love with his owne perfections.*"[4] This is a paradigm for the Stuart court and the mirror of its theater.

Roles in plays, to Puritan observers, were impostures and lies. The very act of imitation, in drama as in art, usurped a divine prerogative, and theatrical productions were therefore often seen to be at the heart of the court's degeneracy and impiety. But from another point of view the parts we choose to play are not impersonations but ideals. They are what we wish to be, and they reveal not so much the way we want others to see us as the way we want to see ourselves.

Here are some ways in which the Stuart court wanted to see itself.

THE MASQUE OF QUEENS

In 1609 Ben Jonson and Inigo Jones created a heroic masque for Queen Anne and her ladies. *The Masque of Queens* provided a martial context for womanly virtue—whereas King James, we will recall, was an ardent and programmatic pacifist. The production opened on a coven of witches and an ugly hell; infernal dances and charms provided an elaborate and extended antimasque. Suddenly the hall was filled with a blast of loud music, "with which not only the hags themselves but the hell into which they ran quite vanished, and the whole face of the scene altered, scarce suffering the memory of such a thing. But in the place of it appeared a glorious and magnificent building figuring the House of Fame, in the top of which were discovered the twelve masquers sitting upon a throne triumphal erected in form of a pyramid and circled with all store of light."

Eleven of the masquers had the roles of warrior queens from history. In Jones's costume designs, the Amazonian qualities are expressed through a variety of details: an elegant bodice adapted from armor, a plumed helmet, masculine half-sleeves, bases, and instead of dancing pumps, light boots. For the twelfth queen, Anne of Denmark, Jonson invented the figure of Bel-Anna, Queen of the Ocean. Only the design for her headdress has survived. Jones has crowned her with an armillary sphere, a celestial globe. Just such a model as this had demonstrated to Ficino the power of human knowledge and the essential divinity of the mind.

Jones's drawing of the House of Fame is the earliest surviving design for stage machinery in England. The drawing shows the front of a hexagonal building; it has double doors within a huge central arch, above which sit the twelve masquers on their pyramidal throne. The figures on the roof are probably musicians; the two deities in the clouds on either side of the cornice are identified by Jonson as "eminent figures of Honor and Virtue." The façade is adorned with statues. Those on the lower tier represent "the most excellent poets, as Homer, Virgil, Lucan, etc., as being the substantial supporters of Fame," while those on the upper are "Achilles, Aeneas, Caesar, and those great heroes which these poets had celebrated." The conception, Jonson says, derives from Chaucer.

The architecture of the building is a characteristic amalgam of styles. It has certain Palladian elements—the central arch, the pilasters, the windows of the lower story—but the basic motif of the upper tier is the gothic trefoil. In the same way, the statuary on the façade pays homage to classical heroes, but the house itself is a realization of the work of the greatest English medieval poet. The union of classic and romantic, heroic and chivalric, was a continual ideal of James's reign, and Jones's setting is an architectural assertion of the success of the synthesis. But Jonson also makes it clear that in the House of Fame, heroism is a secondary virtue: the heroes are glorified not by their deeds alone, but by the enduring and transforming power of poetry. Every hero has his poet, and the building is inspired by Chaucer. The whole vision presents the Jacobean court with its own best image.

Heroism is the royal consort; but the highest virtue is that of the pacific king, not a warrior, but a classical scholar and poet.

This was the setting for the entry of the masquers. The pyramidal throne suddenly turned around, and in its place the winged figure of Fame appeared. The great gates then opened, and the ladies were borne forth into the hall in three triumphant chariots, drawn respectively by "far-sighted eagles, to note Fame's sharp eye," griffins, "that design / Swiftness and strength," and, for the queen's carriage, lions, "that imply / The top of graces, state and majesty."

OBERON

Like his mother, Henry Prince of Wales was an ardent masquer, and like his father, an antiquarian and patron of the arts. For the two seasons following *The Masque of Queens,* 1610 and 1611, he commissioned from Jonson and Jones two entertainments designed to restore to life the world of ancient British chivalry. For the first, *Prince Henry's Barriers,* he chose a role from the Arthurian romances, Meliadus, lover of The Lady of the Lake. In Jonson's fiction, the young prince is summoned by Merlin and King Arthur to revitalize English knighthood—the production centered about feats of arms in which Henry distinguished himself. A contemporary spectator records that "the Prince performed this challenge with wondrous skill and courage, to the great joy and admiration of all the beholders, the Prince not being full sixteene yeeres of age."[5]

But the martial side of the prince's nature apparently disturbed King James, who vetoed a similar project for the next year. In honor of Henry's creation as Prince of Wales, Jonson and Jones devised instead the masque of *Oberon, The Fairy Prince.* Spenserian romance joins with classical myth to create a Britain that unites the traditions of chivalry with classical order. Silenus and his satyrs celebrate the accession of Oberon, heir of King Arthur—Greek and British mythology are, for Jonson, part of a single tradition. Indeed, in a gloss Jonson even suggests that the English word "fairy" is cognate with the Greek *fèras,* a late form of *théras,* satyrs. The synthesis is again apparent in Jones's costume for the young prince. King James's heir is a medieval knight and Roman emperor combined; he also wears recognizable elements of contemporary dress. The Roman skirt, for example, has been transformed into Jacobean trunk hose. Oberon is not an impersonation, but a version of the true prince.

The palace Jones designed for Oberon is another synthesis, an anthology of architectural styles. A rusticated basement seems to grow out of the rocks. The parterre has a Palladian balustrade. A splendid pedimented archway fills the central façade, supported by grotesque Italian terms, and accented by Doric pilasters and Serlian windows. Crenellated English medieval turrets are topped with tiny baroque minarets; two pure Elizabethan chimneys frame an elegant dome in the style of Bramante.

Jones's inspiration here is not merely eclectic. Rather this design makes a programmatic visual statement about the national culture and the sources of its heroism. England becomes great through the imposition of classical order upon British nature; the rough native strength of the castle is remade according to the best models, civilized by the arts of design, by learning and taste. In the same way the Prince of Faery, the new Prince of Wales, comes out of the woods, tames the rough satyrs, and descends to salute his father, the real King James, in the Palladian architecture of the Whitehall Banqueting House.

Such productions reveal a great deal about the age's sense of itself and its intense hopes for this young man. The king, for all his pacific policies (which in any case were not especially popular) was awkward and largely without charm. Henry's untimely death in 1612 robbed England not only of a patron for her poets and artists, but of a romantic hero as well.

NEPTUNE'S TRIUMPH FOR THE RETURN OF ALBION

In 1623 Prince Charles, the Duke of Buckingham, the prince's private secretary Sir Francis Cottington, and an odd assortment of others including the court dwarf Archibald Armstrong, went to Spain to negotiate the prince's marriage with the Infanta Maria, sister of Philip IV. The Spanish match was a favorite project of King James; it represented a major European alliance, and seemed to promise an eventual reconciliation with the Catholic faith and the powers that adhered to it. But it also involved large concessions to the Catholic cause in England, and was therefore understandably unpopular with the British public. The prince and his negotiators were eager for an agreement, and undertook to meet all conditions; but the Spanish court rightly felt that Charles's promises regarding the necessary changes in the English laws of religious conformity were unrealistic, and after almost a year of discussions the plan was abandoned. The prince's party sourly returned home in October 1624, to find their failure greeted with popular rejoicing. To the king, however, the whole episode must have seemed a galling fiasco, and the court provided no celebrations of its own.

Three months later Jonson and Jones prepared a long-delayed welcome home. *Neptune's Triumph for the Return of Albion* does more than put the best face on a bad situation. It provides a context within which the fiasco may be seen as a victory. Jonson's fiction begins, like so many of his later masques, as fact: it opens in the Banqueting House itself. The stage presents nothing but two pillars dedicated to Neptune; the masque has not yet begun. A poet enters, ostensibly to distribute playbills; the court cook appears, and requests an account of the forthcoming entertainment. The poet expounds his allegory:

The mighty Neptune, mighty in his styles,
And large command of waters and of isles,
Not as the lord and sovereign of the seas,
But chief in the art of riding, late did please
To send his Albion forth . . .
Through Celtiberia; and to assist his course,
Gave him his powerful Manager of Horse,
With divine Proteus, father of disguise,
To wait upon them with his counsels wise
In all extremes. His great commands being done,
And he desirous to review his son,
He doth dispatch a floating isle from hence
Unto the Hesperian shores to waft him thence.

In this allegory, King James is Neptune, Prince Charles Albion; Buckingham is visible under his title of Master of the King's Horse in the first of Albion's associates; and Cottington, who had served as a secret agent, is Proteus. The journey is "through Celtiberia" because their route took them first to Paris, but the reason for the expedition is carefully glossed over. The floating island is then described. The royal party will make its appearance enthroned beneath a mystical Tree of Harmony, the banyan, first planted in India by the sun himself. The tree becomes a symbol of the harmonious strength of the court; every one of its branches sends out roots, and becomes a new trunk supporting the whole.

The cook demands more entertainment, the comedy of an antimasque. The poet replies that his work is high art, addressed only to the intellect. But the cook then articulates Jonson's own concept of theater at court: these presentations speak to the whole man, and must satisfy all his senses; they are given in the Banqueting House because they are not merely poems but banquets, ravishing sights and sounds, sweet smells; they feed all parts of the observer's sensibility. And the cook himself then produces the comic dancers, in the form of meats and vegetables from his own gigantic cooking pot.

Now the poet's masque begins. The heavens open, revealing Apollo and Mercury (patrons respectively of the poetry of the masque and the prose of the antimasque), accompanied by the muses and the goddess Harmony. To their music the floating island appears, and moves forward bearing the masquers. Jones's island is covered with an arbor, as the text requires; but it is an arbor of palms, not a banyan tree. In part, this doubtless reflects merely the architect's ignorance of Asian botany; however the choice of palms can hardly have been accidental. The all-powerful Neptune's island bears emblems of peace; the returning prince appears beneath the branches that heralded Christ's entry into Jerusalem.

The association of James's pacifism with the peace of God, and of his capital with the holy city, formed an important part of Jacobean official imagery from the very beginning of the reign, and as a way of justifying unpopular policies, particularly in ecclesiastical matters, it became increasingly insistent. James was regularly represented as Solomon (for example, he is so depicted by Rubens on the Banqueting House ceiling), and the Anglican church under the Stuart monarchy was held to preserve the pristine purity of Christ and the Apostles. The line of argument ran this way: England was converted by Joseph of Arimathea, long before Constantine and the conversion of Rome. The decay of Christianity began with the advent of Augustine and his popish monks, but the abolition of the English monasteries had allowed the ancient faith to flower again. All of this is implied in Jones's emblematic palms.

But the masque makes a more overt set of claims for the monarchy as well. James is explicitly represented, after all, not as Solomon but as Neptune. With the descent of the masquers the island disappears, and Jones's scene opens to reveal a marine palace. James's Palladian Banqueting House is now translated into the deep perspective of a maritime fantasy. Behind the allegorization of the king as Neptune lies a long tradition. In the same way, Sir Walter Ralegh had sung the Ocean's love to Cynthia, the moon, ruler of the sea; and Jonson and Jones in 1609 had presented Queen Anne not as the sovereign of the realm but as Bel-Anna, Queen of the Ocean. There is, of course, a simple military reality behind this: the strength of an island kingdom depends heavily on its navy. But there are mythographic realities as well that tell us a good deal more about the way the Stuart court saw itself. Neptune appears in the masque "Not as the lord and sovereign of the seas"—he is that in any case—"But chief in the art of riding."

The connection between these two aspects of the royal persona would not have seemed obscure to a Jacobean audience who knew that King James's favorite sport was riding. But Jonson's allusion goes deeper, to a myth in which Neptune was the creator and tamer of the embodiment of the ocean's energy, the horse. From Plato onward, horsemanship had served as a symbol for the imposition of reason upon the wildness of nature or the violence of the passions. This is why the implications of the term *chivalry* are so much more complex than its derivation—from *chevalerie*, horsemanship—would suggest. To bring the destructive energies of nature under control, both within and without, was the end of Renaissance education and science. Every gentleman was thus properly a type of Neptune; and on a larger scale, the myth provided a pattern for the relation between king and commonwealth.

That the pattern was unrealistic goes without saying. The only mind operating in Jonson's allegory is the monarch's. Albion's return is a triumph because it is executed at Neptune's command; the whole action is presented as a serene extension of the royal will. This is a political myth, an accurate record of the way James viewed his government in his last years. His son's autocracy is only a step beyond. But the danger of political myths lies in their tendency to exclude political realities: the mirror of the king's mind allows him to know only himself. By 1624 the commonwealth, unlike the sea or the horse, had developed a very strong mind of its own. And indeed, in this penultimate year of his reign, political realities denied the king even his theatrical triumph. The French and Spanish ambassadors could not be invited to attend together, and each threatened the most dire diplomatic reprisals if the other were given priority. Within two days of the performance, James was forced to cancel the masque.

THE TRIUMPH OF PEACE AND *COELUM BRITANNICUM*

The development of Charles I's autocracy is one of the most extraordinary chapters in British legal history. In 1629, outraged by what he took to be continual inroads on the crown's authority, frustrated by inadequate revenues and the failure of numerous proposals for new taxes, the king dissolved Parliament and determined to rule without it. He managed to do so for the next eleven years. The 1630s saw the most complete consolidation of royal power in British history; by 1635 the king claimed the rights of direct taxation, the granting of monopolies in all industries, the control of all ecclesiastical offices including those in private households, the enforcement of absolute religious conformity—even the manufacture of soap was declared to be a royal prerogative. No area of the nation's life was too insignificant for Charles to want to regulate it: for example, by royal edict alehouses were forbidden to sell tobacco, and London inns to serve game. (The latter measure was conceived as a way of making town life so unpleasant for country gentlemen that they would be persuaded to return home to manage their estates.)

There were many challenges to the legality of the royal prerogatives. In every case, the basic question was whether laws could be made by royal fiat, without the assent of Parliament. Gradually over the decade, usually by the barest possible majority, the courts came to support the king. By 1638, when the Star Chamber handed down its decision in the famous ship-money case[6] that *rex* was *lex*, that king was law, the British monarchy was *statutorily* the most powerful in Europe. The political realities were, of course, quite different. Only *authority* can derive from statute. A government's power depends on its ability to enforce its authority. The crown might impose taxes, but people increasingly refused to pay them; and if they could not be persuaded to do so by noble rhetoric and high ideals, the king's only recourse was an army that had to be paid out of uncollected taxes. Such realities produced in Charles only patient bafflement at the stubborn unregeneracy of so ungrateful a populace; he ruled according to a political theory that had the quality of a hermetic allegory. In a very profound way the stage at Whitehall was his truest kingdom, the masque the most accurate expression of his mind.

The legal profession was on the whole uncomfortable about royal prerogatives, and unsympathetic to the crucial principle of Divine Right, which made the king responsible only to God. In 1634 the Inns of Court took the remarkable step of retaining Inigo Jones and James Shirley in an attempt to speak to the king in his own language. The lawyers presented a masque at Whitehall that was, for all its courtly splendor, diplomatically but unequivocally critical of the royal policies, and undertook, through the power of poetry and the marvels of spectacle, to persuade the royal spectator to return to the rule of law.

The impulse to produce *The Triumph of Peace* came, oddly enough, from a royal command. William Prynne, author of *Histrio-Mastix*, with its treasonable attack on court theatricals, had been indicted, and his trial was about to begin. The prisoner was a barrister of Lincoln's Inn, and had dedicated the offending volume to his fellow lawyers. Charles demanded that the legal fraternities definitively repudiate their colleague and publicly declare their loyalty to the crown. What gesture of loyalty could be more appropriate than the presentation of a lawyers' masque at court?

The Inns lavishly complied. Shirley composed his text in consultation with a committee of barristers; the subject of *The Triumph of Peace* was the relationship between the king and the law. The setting Jones provided for the masque's opening was an Italian piazza. In fact, Shirley had given the architect a choice; the text calls for a scene "representing the Forum or Piazza of Peace." Jones chose not a classical Roman forum, but the center of the life of an Italian Renaissance city-state, the architectural embodiment of republican principles. In contrast, two years earlier, when Jones created a similar setting for the king's masque *Albion's Triumph,* the architecture had been a clear expression of imperial ideals.

The Roman analogy is carefully avoided in *The Triumph of Peace.* Extravagantly and with unparallelled splendor the legal profession asserted to the crown their joint responsibilities:

> The world shall give prerogative to neither;
> We cannot flourish but together.

Not surprisingly, considering the nature of the medium, the message failed to get across. The masque was a huge success; the royal solipsist saw in it nothing but adulation, and was graciously pleased to order it repeated.[7]

Two weeks later the king presented his own view of his place in the commonwealth. Thomas Carew's and Inigo Jones's *Coelum Britannicum* was the greatest theatrical expression of the Caroline autocracy. Carew's allegory is about the radical reformation of society, the purifying of the mind and passions, the power of language and apparitions to exorcise the rebellious spirit; it even undertakes to create a new body of poetic symbolism, as if to redeem through its imagery the imperfect nature that art imitates. The masque conceives the royal will as central to an unprecedented degree. In its fable, Jove has taken the Caroline court as a model for his own, and has banished licentiousness and ignoble passion from the heavens. The opening scene is a ruined city, the decadent civilization that is to be revitalized and ennobled. Its shutters part, and the gigantic figure of Atlas fills the stage. For the Renaissance, Atlas was the exemplar of cosmic wisdom. Jones's heroic figure, crowned and bearing the heavens on his shoulders, is the link between earth and heaven, an allegory of the monarch described in *Basilikon Doron*. The great globe opens, revealing the constellations, those glorifications of ancient lust and violence, the mythology of an outworn past. Each in its turn is deposed and extinguished, until heaven at last stands empty, ready to receive a chaste and heroic iconography.

The reformation then begins. Atlas and the sphere vanish and a mountainous landscape appears. From beneath the stage come ancient Britons, the kingdom's history restored to life. (They are the figures shown seated on the rocks.) Above, wild nature is framed by the palms of the royal peace. This setting is to open, revealing first a garden and a princely villa, and then an elegant pastoral perspective with Windsor Castle in the distance, while the heavens will part to show beneficent deities smiling on Charles's reign.

The grandiloquence of the masque's conception lay as much in its engineering as in its poetry. Carew's text gives a vivid sense of the spectator's experience:

. . . there began to rise out of the earth the top of a hill, which by little and little grew to be a huge mountain that covered all the scene; the underpart of this was wild and craggy, and above somewhat more pleasant and flourishing; about the middle part of this mountain were seated the three kingdoms of England, Scotland and Ireland, all richly attired in regal habits appropriated to the several nations, with crowns on their heads, and each of them bearing the ancient arms of the kingdoms they represented. At a distance above these sat a young man in a white embroidered robe, upon his fair hair an olive garland, with wings at his shoulders, and holding in his hand a cornucopia filled with corn and fruits, representing the genius of these kingdoms. . . .

At this the underpart of the rock opens, and out of a cave are seen to come the masquers, richly attired like ancient heroes; the colours yellow embroidered with silver, their antique helms curiously wrought, and great plumes on the top; before them a troop of young lords and noblemen's sons bearing torches of virgin wax; these were apparelled after the old British fashion in white coats embroidered with silver, girt, and full gathered, cut square-collared, and round caps on their heads, with a white feather wreathen about them; first these dance with their lights in their hands, after which the masquers descend into the room and dance their entry.

The dance being past, there appears in the further part of the heaven coming down a pleasant cloud, bright and transparent, which coming softly downwards before the upper part of the mountain, embraceth the genius, but so as through it all his body is seen; and then rising again with a gentle motion bears up the genius of the three kingdoms, and being past the airy region, pierceth the heavens, and is no more seen. At that instant the rock with the three kingdoms on it sinks and is hidden in the earth. This strange spectacle gave great cause of admiration, but especially how so huge a machine, and of that great height, could come from under the stage, which was but six foot high.

The full force of Caroline idealism, the determination to purify, reorder, reform, reconceive a whole culture, is here fully realized in apparitions and marvelous machinery. The most complete expression of the royal will in the age lay not in the promulgation of edicts, erratically obeyed, nor in military power, inadequately furnished, but in Inigo Jones's ability to do the impossible.

EPILOGUE

Or rather, to seem to do so: the truth of the royal productions was the truth of appearances. Power was asserted only through analogies, faith affirmed only through symbols. That such forms of expression should now seem to us at best obscure, at worst insincere, says much for the success of the Puritan revolution. History has vindicated William Prynne; however extravagant its rhetoric, the Puritan invective against royal theatricals reveals, ironically, an accurate sense of their most powerful effects. Viewed from outside the Banqueting House, the masque could be seen to provide the monarchy chiefly with an impenetrable insulation against the attitudes of the governed. Year after year designer and poet re-created an ideal commonwealth, all its forces under rational control, its people uniquely happy and endlessly grateful.

It is a mistake to think that there was deception in this vision, or cynicism in the king's satisfaction with it—history is not so simple. The vision was a perfectly accurate projection of the way Charles saw his realm. His idealism was politically naive, no doubt, but it was not hypocritical, and more important, he was not alone in it. It was consistently supported by the judiciary, and in 1638 the highest court in the land decreed, in the ship-money decision, that prerogative rule was indeed the rule of law. Much of Caroline legal and political history has the quality of a court masque. The darkest moral we are justified in drawing from subsequent events is that if kings will be philosophers, they had better not be Platonists. After a decade of ideals, a disenfranchised Parliament at last declared its authority by virtue of the realities of its power, and the absolute rule of the Stuart monarchy was revealed as a royal charade, a theatrical illusion. Andrew Marvell testifies to the histrionic power of the final act:

> . . . thence the *Royal Actor* born
> The *Tragick Scaffold* might adorn;

> While round the armed Bands
> Did clap their bloody hands;
> *He* nothing common did or mean
> Upon that memorable Scene:
> But with his keener Eye
> The Axes edge did try:
> Nor call'd the *Gods* with vulgar spight
> To vindicate his helpless Right,
> But bow'd his comely Head
> Down, as upon a Bed.[8]

The player king produced, even in Cromwell's loyal retainer, the full Aristotelian measure of admiration, pity, and dread.

NOTES

1. *The Tempest* 4.1.41.
2. *Love's Triumph through Callipolis,* lines 1–3.
3. *Measure for Measure* 2.4.123–26.
4. *Ovid's Metamorphoses Englished* (Oxford, 1632), p. 103.
5. Stephen Orgel and Roy Strong, *Inigo Jones* (Berkeley, 1973), 1:159.
6. The king had revived an Elizabethan tax on coastal towns for the support of the navy. In 1633 the tax was extended to inland districts, and met with considerable resistance, the opponents arguing that the imposition of ship-money constituted taxation by royal fiat. The test case was Rex v. Hampden, 1637; the decision was overturned by Parliament in 1641.
7. For a detailed discussion of the masque's complex political context, and a full analysis of the allegory, see *Inigo Jones* 1:63–66.
8. "An Horatian Ode upon Cromwell's Return from Ireland," lines 53–64.

2

The Improvisation of Power

Stephen Greenblatt

Spenser and Marlowe are, from the perspective of this study, mighty opposites, poised in antagonism as radical as that of More and Tyndale in the 1530s. If Spenser sees human identity as conferred by loving service to legitimate authority, to the yoked power of God and the state, Marlowe sees identity established at those moments in which order—political, theological, sexual—is violated. If repetition for Spenser is an aspect of the patient labor of civility, for Marlowe it is the means of constituting oneself in an anonymous void. If Spenser's heroes strive for balance and control, Marlowe's strive to shatter the restraints upon their desires. If in Spenser there is fear of the excess that threatens to engulf order and seems to leave an ineradicable taint on temperance itself, in Marlowe there is fear of the order that threatens to extinguish excess and seems to have always already turned rebellion into a tribute to authority. If Spenser writes for an aristocratic and upper-middle-class audience in a self-consciously archaizing manner, thereby participating in the decorative revival of feudal trappings that characterized Elizabethan courtly ritual,[1] Marlowe writes for the new public theater in a blank verse that must have seemed, after the jog-trot fourteeners of the preceding decades, like reality itself. If Spenser holds up his "other world" to the gaze of power and says, "Behold! This rich beauty is your own face," Marlowe presents *his* and says, "Behold! This tragi-comic, magnificent deformity is how you appear in my rich art." If Spencer's art constantly questions its own status in order to protect power from such questioning, Marlowe undermines power in order to raise his art to the status of a self-regarding, self-justifying absolute.

There is not, of course, anything in Spenser or Marlowe comparable to the violent polemical exchange between More and Tyndale, but there is at least one resonant moment of conjunction that will serve to exemplify the opposition I have just sketched here. In book 1, canto 7 of *The Faerie Queene*, dismayed by the news that Redcrosse has been overthrown by the giant Orgoglio, Una providentially encounters Prince Arthur, the embodiment of Magnificence—the virtue, according to the letter to Raleigh, that "is the perfection of all the rest, and containeth in it them all." This is Arthur's first appearance in the poem, and there follows an elaborate description of his gorgeous armor, a description that includes the following stanza on his helmet's crest:

> Vpon the top of all his loftie crest,
> A bunch of haires discolourd diuersly,
> With sprincled pearle, and gold full richly drest,
> Did shake, and seem'd to daunce for iollity,
> Like to an Almond tree ymounted hye
> On top of greene *Selinis* all alone,
> With blossomes braue bedecked daintily;
> Whose tender locks do tremble euery one
> At euery little breath, that vnder heauen is blowne.
>
> *(1.7.32)*

As early as the late eighteenth century, a reader records his surprise to find this passage almost verbatim in part 2 of *Tamburlaine*.[2] It occurs in the scene in which Tamburlaine is drawn on stage in his chariot by the captive kings, "with bits in their mouths," the stage direction tells us, "reins in his left hand, in his right hand a whip, with which he scourgeth them." Exulting in his triumphant power, Tamburlaine baits his captives, hands over the weeping royal concubines to satisfy the lust of his common soldiers, and—his own erotic satisfaction—imagines his future conquests:

> Through the streets with troops of conquered kings,
> I'll ride in golden armor like the Sun,
> And in my helm a triple plume shall spring,
> Spangled with Diamonds dancing in the air,
> To note me Emperor of the three-fold world,
> Like to an almond tree ymounted high,
> Upon the lofty and celestial mount,
> Of ever green *Selinus* quaintly decked
> With blooms more white than *Hericina's* brows,
> Whose tender blossoms tremble every one,
> At every little breath that thorough heaven is blown.
>
> *(4.3.4094–4113)*

What is sung by Spenser in praise of Arthur is sung by Tamburlaine in praise of himself; the chivalric accoutrement, an emblem of Arthur's magnanimous knighthood, is here part of Tamburlaine's paean to his own power lust. Lines that for Spenser belong to the supreme figure of civility, the chief upholder of the Order of Maidenhead, the worshipful servant of Gloriana, for Marlowe belong to the fantasy life of the Scythian Scourge of God. Marlowe's scene is self-consciously emblematic, as if it were a theatrical improvisation in the Spenserean manner, but now with the hero's place taken by a character who, in his sadistic excess, most closely resembles Orgoglio.[3] And even as we are struck by the radical difference, we are haunted by the vertiginous possibility of an underlying sameness. What if Arthur and Tamburlaine are not separate and opposed? What if they are two faces of the same thing, embodiments of the identical power? Tamburlaine's is the face Arthur shows to his enemies or, alternatively, Arthur's is the face Tamburlaine shows to his followers. To the Irish kern, Spenser's Prince of Magnanimity looks like the Scourge of God; to the English courtier, Marlowe's grotesque conquerer looks like the Faerie Queene.

How shall we characterize the power that possesses both faces and can pass from one to the other? In a famous passage in *The Prince*, Machiavelli writes that a prince must know well how to use both the beast and the man, and hence the ancients depicted Achilles and other heroes as educated by Chiron the centaur. This discussion is an early instance of the celebration of psychic mobility that has continued to characterize discussions of Western consciousness to the present time. Thus in his influential study of modernization in the Middle East, *The Passing of Traditional Society*, the sociologist Daniel Lerner defines the West as a "mobile society," a society characterized not only by certain enlightened and rational public practices but also by the inculcation in its people of a *"mobile sensibility* so adaptive to change that rearrangement of the self-system is its distinctive mode."[4] While traditional society, Professor Lerner argues, functions on the basis of a "highly constrictive personality" (51), one that resists change and is incapable of grasping the situation of another, the mobile personality of Western society "is distinguished by a high capacity for identification with new aspects of his environment," for he "comes equipped with the mechanisms needed to incorporate new demands upon himself that arise outside of his habitual experience"(49). Those mechanisms Professor Lerner subsumes under the single term *empathy*, which he defines as "the capacity to see oneself in the other fellow's situation" (50). In the West, this capacity was fostered first by the physical mobility initiated by the Age of Exploration, then confirmed and broadened by the mass media. "These," he writes, "have peopled the daily world of their audience with sustained, even intimate, experience of the lives of others. 'Ma Perkins,' 'The Goldbergs,' 'I Love Lucy'—all these bring us friends we never met, but whose joys and sorrows we intensely 'share' " (53). And the international diffusion of the mass media means a concomitant diffusion of psychic mobility and hence of modernization: "In our time, indeed, the spread of empathy around the world is accelerating" (52).

To test the rate of this acceleration, Professor Lerner devised a set of questions that he and his assistants put to a cross-section of the inhabitants of the Middle East, to porters and cobblers, as well as grocers and physicians. The questions began, "If you were made editor of a newspaper, what kind of a paper would you run?" and I confess myself in complete sympathy with that class of respondents who, like one shepherd interviewed in a village near Ankara, gasped "My God! How can you say such a thing? . . . A poor villager . . . master of the whole world" (24). Professor Lerner invariably interprets such answers as indicative of a constrictive personality incapable of empathy, but in fact the Turkish shepherd, with his Tamburlainian language, reintroduces the great missing term in the analysis of modernization, and that term is *power*. For my own part, I would like in this chapter to delineate the Renaissance origins of the "mobile sensibility" and, having done so, to shift the ground from "I Love Lucy" to *Othello* in order to demonstrate that what Professor Lerner calls "empathy," Shakespeare calls "Iago."

To help us return from the contemporary Middle East to the early seventeenth century, let us dwell for a moment on Professor Lerner's own concept of Renaissance origins: "Take the factor of physical mobility," he writes, "which initiated Western takeoff in an age when the earth was underpopulated in terms of the world man-land ratio. Land was to be had, more or less, for the finding. The great explorers took over vast real estate by planting a flag; these were slowly filled with new populations over generations" (65). It didn't exactly happen this way. Land does not become "real estate" quite so easily, and the underpopulation was not found but created by those great explorers. Demographers of Mesoamerica now estimate, for example, that the population of Hispaniola in 1492 was 7–8 million, perhaps as high as 11 million. Reduction to that attractive man-land ratio was startlingly sudden: by 1501, enslavement, disruption of agriculture, and, above all, European disease had reduced the population to some 700,000; by 1512, to 28,000.[5] The unimaginable massiveness of the death rate did not, of course, go unnoticed; European observers took it as a sign of God's determination to cast down the idolaters and open the New World to Christianity.

With the passage from the sociologist's bland world of ceremonial flag-planting in an empty landscape to violent displacement and insidious death, we have already moved toward Shakespeare's tragedy, and we move still closer if we glance at an incident recounted in 1525 by Peter Martyr in the Seventh Decade of *De orbe novo*. Faced with a serious labor shortage in the gold mines as a result of the decimation of the native population, the Spanish in Hispaniola began to raid neighboring islands. Two ships reached an outlying island in the Lucayas (now called the Bahamas) where they were received with awe and trust. The Spanish learned through their interpreters that the natives believed that after death their souls were first purged of their sins in icy northern mountains, then borne to a paradisal island in the south, whose beneficent, lame prince offered them innumerable pleasures: "the souls enjoy eternal delights, among the dancings and songs of young maidens, and among the embracements of their children, and whatsoever they loved heretofore; they babble also there, that such as grow old, wax young again, so that all are of like years full of joy and mirth."[6] When the Spanish understood these imaginations, writes Martyr, they proceeded to persuade the natives "that they came from those places, where they should see their parents, and children, and all their kindred and friends that were dead: and should enjoy all kind of delights, together with the embracements and fruition of beloved things" (625). Thus deceived, the entire population of the island passed "singing and rejoicing," Martyr says, onto the ships and were taken to the gold mines of Hispaniola. The Spanish, however, reaped less profit than they had anticipated; when they grasped what had happened to them, the Lucayans, like certain German Jewish communities during the Crusades, undertook mass suicide: "becoming desperate, they either slew themselves, or choosing to famish, gave up their faint spirits, being persuaded by no reason, or violence, to take food" (625).

Martyr, it appears, feels ambivalent about the story. He is certain that God disapproves of such treachery, since many of those who perpetrated the fraud subsequently died violent deaths; on the other hand, he opposes those who would free enslaved natives, since bitter experience has shown that even those Indians who have apparently been converted to Christianity will, given the slightest opportunity, revert to "their ancient and native vices" and turn savagely against those who had instructed them "with fatherly charity" (627). But, for our purposes, Martyr's ambivalence is less important than the power of his story to evoke a crucial Renaissance mode of behavior that links Lerner's "empathy" and Shakespeare's Iago: I shall call that mode *improvisation*, by which I mean the ability both to capitalize on the unforeseen and to transform given materials into one's own scenario. The spur-of-the-moment quality of improvisation is not as critical here as the opportunistic grasp of that which seems fixed and established. Indeed, as Castiglione and others in the Renaissance well understood, the impromptu character of an improvisation is itself often a calculated mask, the product of careful preparation.[7] Conversely, all plots, literary and behavioral, inevitably have their origin in a moment prior to formal coherence, a moment of experimental, aleatory impulse in which the available, received materials are curved toward a novel shape. We cannot locate a point of pure premeditation or pure randomness. What is essential is the Europeans' ability again and again to insinuate themselves into the preexisting political, religious, even psychic structures of the natives and to turn those structures to their advantage. The process is as familiar to us by now as the most tawdry business fraud, so familiar that we assume a virtually universal diffusion of the necessary improvisational talent, but that assumption is almost certainly misleading. There are periods and cultures in which the ability to insert oneself into the consciousness of another is of relatively slight importance, the object of limited concern; others in which it is a major preoccupation, the object of cultivation and fear. Professor Lerner is right to insist that this ability is a characteristically (though not exclusively) Western mode, present to varying degrees in the classical and medieval world and greatly strengthened from the Renaissance onward; he misleads only in insisting further that it is an act of imaginative generosity, a sympathetic appreciation of the situation of the other fellow. For when he speaks confidently of the "spread of empathy around the world," we must understand that he is speaking of the exercise of Western power, power that is creative as well as destructive, but that is scarcely ever wholly disinterested and benign.

To return to the Lucayan story, we may ask ourselves what conditions exist in Renaissance culture that make such an improvisation possible. It depends first upon the ability and willingness to play a role, to transform oneself, if only for a brief period and with mental reservations, into another. This necessitates the acceptance of disguise, the ability to effect a divorce, in Ascham's phrase, between the tongue and the heart. Such role-playing in turn depends upon the transformation of another's reality into a manipulable fiction. The Spanish had to perceive the Indians' religious beliefs as illusions, "imaginations" as Martyr's English translator calls them. Lucayan society, Martyr observes, is based upon a principle of reverent obedience fostered by a set of religious fables that "are delivered by word of mouth and tradition from the Elders to the younger, for a most sacred and true history, insomuch as he who but seemed to think otherwise, should be thrust out of the society of men" (623). The Lucayan king performs the supreme sacral functions and partakes fully in the veneration accorded to the idols, so that if he were to command one of his subjects to cast himself down from a precipice, the subject would immediately comply. The king uses this absolute power to ensure the just distribution, to families according to need, of the tribe's food, all of which is stored communally in royal granaries: "They had the golden age, *mine* and *thine*, the seeds of discord, were far removed from them" (618). Martyr then perceives the social function of Lucayan religious concepts, the native apparatus for their transmission and reproduction, and the punitive apparatus for the enforcement of belief. In short, he grasps Lucayan religion as an ideology, and it is this perception that licenses the transformation of "sacred and true history" into "crafty and subtle imaginations" (625) that may be exploited.

If improvisation is made possible by the subversive perception of another's truth as an ideological construct, that construct must at the same time be grasped in terms that bear a certain structural resemblance to one's own set of beliefs. An ideology that is perceived as entirely alien would permit no point of histrionic entry: it could be destroyed but not performed. Thus the Lucayan religion, in Martyr's account, is an anamorphic representation of Catholicism: there are "images" carried forth with solemn pomp on "the holy day of adoration"; worshipers kneel reverently before these images, sing "hymns," and make offerings, "which at night the nobles divide among them, as our priests do the cakes or wafers which women offer" (622); there are "holy relics" about which the chief priest, standing in his "pulpit," preaches; and, as we have seen, there is absolution for sin, purgatory, and eternal delight in paradise. The European account of the native religion must have borne some likeness to what the Lucayans actually believed; why else would they have danced, singing and rejoicing, onto the Spanish ships? But it is equally important that the religion is conceived as analogous to Catholicism, close enough to permit improvisation, yet sufficiently distanced to protect European beliefs from the violence of fictionalization. The Spanish were not compelled to perceive their own religion as a manipulable human construct; on the contrary, the compulsion of their own creed was presumably strengthened by their contemptuous exploitation of an analogous symbolic structure.

This absence of reciprocity is an aspect of the total economy of the mode of improvisation that I have sketched here. For what we may see in the Lucayan story is an early manifestation of an exercise of power that was subsequently to become vastly important and remains a potent force in our lives: the ownership of another's labor conceived as involving no supposedly "natural" reciprocal obligation (as in feudalism) but rather functioning by concealing the very fact of ownership from the exploited who believe that they are acting freely and in their own interest. Of course, once the ships reached Hispaniola, this concealed ownership gave way to direct enslavement; the Spanish were not capable of continuing the improvisation into the very mines. And it is this failure to sustain the illusion that led to the ultimate failure of the enterprise, for, of course, the Spanish did not want dead Indians but live mine workers. It would take other, subtler minds, in the Renaissance and beyond, to perfect the means to sustain indefinitely an indirect enslavement.

I have called improvisation a central Renaissance mode of behavior, but the example on which I have focused is located on a geographical margin and might only seem to bear out Immanuel Wallerstein's theory that Western Europe in the sixteenth century increasingly established its ownership of the labor and resources of those located in areas defined as peripheral.[8] But I would argue that the phenomenon I have described is found in a wide variety of forms closer to home. It may be glimpsed, to suggest two significant instances, in the relation of Tudor power to Catholic symbolism and the characteristic form of rhetorical education.

The Anglican Church and the monarch who was its Supreme Head did not, as radical Protestants demanded, eradicate Catholic ritual but rather improvised within it in an attempt to assume its power. Thus, for example, in the Accession Day celebration of 1590, we are told that the queen, sitting in the Tilt gallery, "did suddenly hear a music so sweet and so secret, as every one thereat greatly marvelled. And hearkening to that excellent melody, the earth as it were opening, there appears a Pavillion, made of white Taffeta, being in proportion like unto the sacred Temple of the Virgins Vestal. This Temple seemed to consist upon pillars of porphyry, arched like unto a Church, within it were many lamps burning. Also, on the one side an Altar covered with cloth of gold; and thereupon two wax candles burning in rich candlesticks; upon the Altar also were laid certain Princely presents, which after by three Virgins were presented unto her Majesty."[9] This secular epiphany permits us to identify two of the characteristic operations of improvisation: displacement and absorption. By displacement I mean the process whereby a prior symbolic structure is compelled to coexist with other centers of attention that do not necessarily conflict with the original structure but are not swept up in its gravitational pull; indeed, as here, the sacred may find itself serving as an adornment, a backdrop, an occasion for a quite secular phenomenon. By absorption I mean the process whereby a symbolic structure is taken into the ego so completely that it ceases to exist as an external phenomenon; in the Accession Day ceremony, instead of the secular prince humbling herself before the sacred, the sacred seems only to enhance the ruler's identity, to express her power.[10]

Both displacement and absorption are possible here because the religious symbolism was already charged with the celebration of power. What we are witnessing is a shift in the institution that controls and profits from the interpretation of such symbolism, a shift mediated in this instance by the classical scholarship of Renaissance humanism. The invocation of the Temple of the Vestal Virgins is the sign of that transformation of belief into ideology that we have already examined; the Roman mythology, deftly keyed to England's Virgin Queen, helps to fictionalize Catholic ritual sufficiently for it to be displaced and absorbed.

This enzymatic function of humanism leads directly to our second instance of domestic improvisation, for the cornerstone of the humanist project was a rhetorical education. In *The Tudor Play of Mind*, Joel Altman has recently demonstrated the central importance for English Renaissance culture of the *argumentum in utramque partem*, the cultivation of the scholar's power to speak equally persuasively for diametrically opposed positions. The practice permeated intellectual life in the early sixteenth century and was, Altman convincingly argues, one of the formative influences on the early drama.[11] It is in the spirit of such rhetorical mobility that Erasmus praises More, as we have seen, for his ability "to play the man of all hours with all men" and that Roper recalls the young More's dazzling improvisations in Cardinal Morton's Christmas plays.

The hagiographical bias of Roper's and most subsequent writing on More has concealed the extent to which this improvisational gift is closely allied to a control of power in the law courts and the royal service: the mystification of manipulation as disinterested empathy begins as early as the sixteenth century. As a corrective, we need only recall More's controversial works, such as *The Confutation of Tyndale's Answer*, whose recurrent method is through improvisation to transform the heretic's faith into a fiction, then absorb it into a new symbolic structure that will ridicule or consume it. Thus Tyndale had written: "Sin we through fragility never so oft, yet as soon as we repent and come into the right way again, and unto the testament which God hath made in Christ's blood: our sins vanish away as smoke in the wind, and as darkness at the coming of light, or as thou cast a little blood or milk into the main sea." More responds by maliciously improvising on Tyndale's text: "Neither purgatory need to be feared when we go hence, nor penance need to be done while we be here, but sin and be sorry and sit and make merry, and then sin again and then repent a little and run to the ale and wash away the sin, think once on God's promise and then do what we list. For hoping sure in that, kill we ten men on a day, we cast but a little blood into the main sea." Having thus made a part of his own, More continues by labeling Tyndale's argument about penance as "but a piece of his poetry"—an explicit instance of that fictionalization we have witnessed elsewhere—and concludes, "Go me to Martin Luther . . . . While that friar lieth with his nun and woteth well he doth nought [i.e., knows he does evil], and saith still he doth well: let Tyndale tell me what repenting is that. He repenteth every morning, and to bed again every night; thinketh on God's promise first, and then go sin again upon trust of God's testament, and then he calleth it casting of a little milk into the main sea."[12]

Improvisation here obviously does not intend to deceive its original object but to work upon a third party, the reader, who might be wavering between the reformers and the Catholic Church. If the heretic speaks of sin redeemed by God's testament as milk, More returns that milk to sin, then surpasses the simple reversal by transforming it to semen, while he turns the sea that imaged for Tyndale the boundlessness of divine forgiveness into the sexual insatiability of Luther's nun.

These perversions of the reformer's text are greatly facilitated by the fact that the text was already immersed in an intensely charged set of metaphorical transformations—that is, More seizes upon the brilliant instability of Tyndale's prose with its own nervous passage from Christ's blood to sin conceived progressively as smoke, darkness, blood, and finally milk. More's artful improvisation makes it seem that murder and lust lay just beneath the surface of the original discourse, as a kind of dark subtext, and he is able to do so more plausibly because both violence and sexual anxiety are in fact powerful underlying forces in Tyndale's prose as in More's. That is, once again, there is a haunting structural homology between the improviser and his other.

I would hope that by now *Othello* seems virtually to force itself upon us as the supreme symbolic expression of the cultural mode I have been describing, for violence, sexual anxiety, and improvisation are the materials out of which the drama is constructed. To be sure, there are many other explorations of these materials in Shakespeare—one thinks of Richard III wooing Anne[13] or, in comedy, of Rosalind playfully taking advantage of the disguise that exile has forced upon her—but none so intense and radical. In Iago's first soliloquy, Shakespeare goes out of his way to emphasize the improvised nature of the villain's plot:

> Cassio's a proper man, let me see now,
> To get this place, and to make up my will,
> A double knavery . . . how, how? . . . let me see,
> After some time, to abuse Othello's ear,
> That he is too familiar with his wife:
> He has a person and a smooth dispose,

> To be suspected, fram'd to make women false:
> The Moor a free and open nature too,
> That thinks men honest that but seems to be so:
> And will as tenderly be led by the nose . . .
> As asses are.
> I ha't, it is engender'd; Hell and night
> Must bring this monstrous birth to the world's light.
> *(1.3.390–402)*[14]

We will try shortly to cast some light on why Iago conceives of his activity here as sexual; for the moment, we need only to observe all of the marks of the impromptu and provisional, extending to the ambiguity of the third-person pronoun: "to abuse Othello's ear / That he is too familiar with his wife." This ambiguity is felicitous; indeed, though scarcely visible at this point, it is the dark essence of Iago's whole enterprise which is, as we shall see, to play upon Othello's buried perception of his own sexual relations with Desdemona as adulterous.[15]

What I have called the marks of the impromptu extend to Iago's other speeches and actions through the course of the whole play. In act 2, he declares of his conspiracy, " 'tis here, but yet confus'd: / Knavery's plain face is never seen, till us'd," and this half-willed confusion continues through the agile, hectic maneuvers of the last act until the moment of exposure and silence. To all but Roderigo, of course, Iago presents himself as incapable of improvisation, except in the limited and seemingly benign form of banter and jig.[16] And even here, he is careful, when Desdemona asks him to improvise her praise, to declare himself unfit for the task:

> I am about it, but indeed my invention
> Comes from my pate as birdlime does from frieze,
> It plucks out brain and all: but my Muse labours,
> And thus she is deliver'd.
> *(2.1.125–28)*

Lurking in the homely denial of ability is the image of his invention as birdlime, and hence a covert celebration of his power to ensnare others. Like Jonson's Mosca, Iago is fully aware of himself as an improviser and revels in his ability to manipulate his victims, to lead them by the nose like asses, to possess their labor without their ever being capable of grasping the relation in which they are enmeshed. Such is the relation Iago establishes with virtually every character in the play, from Othello and Desdemona to such minor figures as Montano and Bianca. For the Spanish colonialists, improvisation could only bring the Lucayans into open enslavement; for Iago, it is the key to a mastery whose emblem is the "duteous and knee-crooking knave" who dotes "on his own obsequious bondage" (1.1.45–46), a mastery invisible to the servant, a mastery, that is, whose character is essentially ideological. Iago's attitude toward Othello is nonetheless colonial:

though he finds himself in a subordinate position, the ensign regards his black general as "an erring barbarian" whose "free and open nature" is a fertile field for exploitation. However galling it may be to him, Iago's subordination is a kind of protection, for it conceals his power and enables him to play upon the ambivalence of Othello's relation to Christian society: the Moor at once represents the institution and the alien, the conqueror and the infidel. Iago can conceal his malicious intentions toward "the thick-lips" behind the mask of dutiful service and hence prolong his improvisation as the Spaniards could not. To be sure, the play suggests, Iago must ultimately destroy the beings he exploits and hence undermine the profitable economy of his own relations, but that destruction may be long deferred, deferred in fact for precisely the length of the play.[17]

If Iago then holds over others a possession that must constantly efface the signs of its own power, how can it be established, let alone maintained? We will find a clue, I think, in what we have been calling the process of fictionalization that transforms a fixed symbolic structure into a flexible construct ripe for improvisational entry. This process is at work in Shakespeare's play, where we may more accurately identify it as *submission to narrative self-fashioning*. When in Cyprus Othello and Desdemona have been ecstatically reunited, Iago astonishes Roderigo by informing him that Desdemona is in love with Cassio. He has no evidence, of course—indeed we have earlier seen him "engender" the whole plot entirely out of his fantasy—but he proceeds to lay before his gull all of the circumstances that make this adultery plausible: "mark me, with what violence she first lov'd the Moor, but for bragging, and telling her fantastical lies; and she will love him still for prating?" (2.1.221–23). Desdemona cannot long take pleasure in her outlandish match: "When the blood is made dull with the act of sport, there should be again to inflame it, and give satiety a fresh appetite, loveliness in favor, sympathy in years, manners and beauties" (2.1.225–29). The elegant Cassio is the obvious choice: "Didst thou not see her paddle with the palm of his hand?" Iago asks. To Roderigo's objection that this was "but courtesy," Iago replies, "Lechery, by this hand: an index and prologue to the history of lust and foul thoughts" (2.1.251–55). The metaphor makes explicit what Iago has been doing all along: constructing a narrative into which he inscribes ("by this hand") those around him. He does not need a profound or even reasonably accurate understanding of his victims; he would rather deal in probable impossibilities than improbable possibilities. And it is eminently probable that a young, beautiful Venetian gentlewoman would tire of her old, outlandish husband and turn instead to the handsome, young lieutenant: it is, after all, one of the master plots of comedy.

What Iago as inventor of comic narrative needs is a sharp eye for the surfaces of social existence, a sense, as Bergson says, of the mechanical encrusted upon the living, a reductive grasp of human possibilities. These he has in extraordinarily full measure.[18] "The wine she drinks is made of grapes," he says in response to Roderigo's idealization of Desdemona, and so reduced, she can be assimilated to

Iago's grasp of the usual run of humanity. Similarly, in a spirit of ironic connois-seurship, he observes Cassio's courtly gestures, "If such tricks as these strip you out of your lieutenantry, it had been better you had not kiss'd your three fingers so oft, which now again you are most apt to play the sir in: good, well kiss'd, an excellent courtesy" (2.1.171–75). He is watching a comedy of manners. Above all, Iago is sensitive to habitual and self-limiting forms of discourse, to Cassio's reaction when he has had a drink or when someone mentions Bianca, to Othello's rhetorical extremism, to Desdemona's persistence and tone when she pleads for a friend; and, of course, he is demonically sensitive to the way individuals interpret discourse, to the signals they ignore and those to which they respond.

We should add that Iago includes himself in this ceaseless narrative invention; indeed, as we have seen from the start, a successful improvisational career depends upon role-playing, which is in turn allied to the capacity, as Professor Lerner defines empathy, "to see oneself in the other fellow's situation." This capacity requires above all a sense that one is not forever fixed in a single, divinely sanc-tioned identity, a sense Iago expresses to Roderigo in a parodically sententious theory of self-fashioning: "our bodies are gardens, to the which our wills are gardeners, so that if we will plant nettles, or sow lettuce, set hyssop, and weed up thyme; supply it with one gender of herbs, or distract it with many; either to have it sterile with idleness, or manur'd with industry, why, the power, and corrigible authority of this, lies in our wills" (1.3.320–26). Confident in his shaping power, Iago has the role-player's ability to imagine his nonexistence so that he can exist for a moment in another and as another. In the opening scene he gives voice to this hypothetical self-cancellation in a line of eerie simplicity: "Were I the Moor, I would not be Iago" (1.1.57). The simplicity is far more apparent than real. Is the "I" in both halves of the line the same? Does it designate a hard, impacted self-interest prior to social identity, or are there two distinct, even opposing selves? Were I the Moor, I would not be Iago, because the "I" always loves itself and the creature I know as Iago hates the Moor he serves or, alternatively, because as the Moor I would be other than I am now, free of the tormenting appetite and revulsion that characterize the servant's relation to his master and that constitute my identity as Iago. I would be radically the same / I would be radically different; the rapacious ego underlies all institutional structures / the rapacious ego is con-stituted by institutional structures.[19]

What is most disturbing in Iago's comically banal and fathomless expression—as for that matter, in Professor Lerner's definition of empathy—is that the imag-ined self-loss conceals its opposite: a ruthless displacement and absorption of the other. Empathy, as the German *Einfühlung* suggests, may be a feeling of oneself into an object, but that object may have to be drained of its own substance before it will serve as an appropriate vessel. Certainly in *Othello*, where all relations are embedded in power and sexuality, there is no realm where the subject and object can merge in the unproblematic accord affirmed by the theorists of empathy.[20]

As Iago himself proclaims, his momentary identification with the Moor is a strategic aspect of his malevolent hypocrisy:

> In following him, I follow but myself.
> Heaven is my judge, not I for love and duty,
> But seeming so, for my peculiar end.
> *(1.1.58–60)*

Exactly what that "peculiar end" is remains opaque. Even the general term "self-interest" is suspect: Iago begins his speech in a declaration of self-interest— "I follow him to serve my turn upon him"—and ends in a declaration of self-division: "I am not what I am."[21] We tend, to be sure, to hear the latter as "I am not what I seem," hence as a simple confirmation of his public deception. But "I am not what I am" goes beyond social feigning: not only does Iago mask himself in society as the honest ancient, but in private he tries out a bewildering succession of brief narratives that critics have attempted, with notorious results, to translate into motives. These inner narratives—shared, that is, only with the audience— continually promise to disclose what lies behind the public deception, to illuminate what Iago calls "the native act and figure" of his heart, and continually fail to do so; or rather, they reveal that his heart is precisely a series of acts and figures, each referring to something else, something just out of our grasp. "I am not what I am" suggests that this elusiveness is permanent, that even self-interest, whose transcendental guarantee is the divine "I am what I am," is a mask.[22] Iago's constant recourse to narrative then is both the affirmation of absolute self-interest and the affirmation of absolute vacancy; the oscillation between the two incompatible positions suggests in Iago the principle of narrativity itself, cut off from original motive and final disclosure. The only termination possible in his case is not revelation but silence.

The question remains why anyone would submit, even unconsciously, to Iago's narrative fashioning. Why would anyone submit to another's narrative at all? For an answer we may recall the pressures on all the figures we have considered in this study and return to our observation that there is a structural resemblance between even a hostile improvisation and its object. In *Othello* the characters have always already experienced submission to narrativity. This is clearest and most important in the case of Othello himself. When Brabantio brings before the Signiory the charge that his daughter has been seduced by witchcraft, Othello promises to deliver "a round unvarnish'd tale . . . / Of my whole course of love" (1.3.90–91), and at the heart of this tale is the telling of tales:

> Her father lov'd me, oft invited me,
> Still question'd me the story of my life,
> From year to year; the battles, sieges, fortunes,

> That I have pass'd:
> I ran it through, even from my boyish days,
> To the very moment that he bade me tell it.
>
> *(1.3.128–33)*

The telling of the story of one's life—the conception of one's life as a story[23]—is a response to public inquiry: to the demands of the Senate, sitting in judgment or, at the least, to the presence of an inquiring community. When, as recorded in the fourteenth-century documents Emmanuel Le Roy Ladurie has brilliantly studied, the peasants of the Languedoc village of Montaillou are examined by the Inquisition, they respond with a narrative performance: "About 14 years ago, in Lent, towards vespers, I took two sides of salted pork to the house of Guillaume Benet of Montaillou, to have them smoked. There I found Guillemette Benet warming herself by the fire, together with another woman; I put the salted meat in the kitchen and left."[24] And when the Carthaginian queen calls upon her guest to "tell us all things from the first beginning, Grecian guile, your people's trials, and then your journeyings," Aeneas responds, as he must, with a narrative of the destiny decreed by the gods.[25] So too Othello before the Senate or earlier in Brabantio's house responds to questioning with what he calls his "travel's history" or, in the Folio reading, as if noting the genre, his "traveler's history." This history, it should be noted, is not only of events in distant lands and among strange peoples: "I ran it through," Othello declares, from childhood, "To the very moment that he bade me tell it." We are on the brink of a Borges-like narrative that is forever constituting itself out of the materials of the present instant, a narrative in which the storyteller is constantly swallowed up by the story. That is, Othello is pressing up against the condition of all discursive representations of identity. He comes dangerously close to recognizing his status as a text, and it is precisely this recognition that the play as a whole will reveal to be insupportable. But, at this point, Othello is still convinced that the text is his own, and he imagines only that he is recounting a lover's performance.

In the 45th sonnet of Sidney's *Astrophil and Stella*, Astrophil complains that while Stella is indifferent to the sufferings she has caused him, she weeps piteous tears at a fable of some unknown lovers. He concludes,

> Then think my dear, that you in me do read
> Of Lovers' ruin some sad Tragedy:
> I am not I, pity the tale of me.

In *Othello* it is Iago who echoes that last line—"I am not what I am," the motto of the improviser, the manipulator of signs that bear no resemblance to what they profess to signify—but it is Othello himself who is fully implicated in the situation of the Sidney sonnet: that one can win pity for oneself only by becoming a tale of oneself, and hence by ceasing to be oneself. Of course, Othello thinks that he has triumphed through his narrative self-fashioning:

> she thank'd me,
> And bade me, if I had a friend that lov'd her,
> I should but teach him how to tell my story,
> And that would woo her. Upon this hint I spake:
> She lov'd me for the dangers I had pass'd
> And I lov'd her that she did pity them.
>
> *(1.3.163–68)*

But Iago knows that an identity that has been fashioned as a story can be unfashioned, refashioned, inscribed anew in a different narrative: it is the fate of stories to be consumed or, as we say more politely, interpreted. And even Othello, in his moment of triumph, has a dim intimation of this fate: a half-dozen lines after he has recalled "the Cannibals, that each other eat," he remarks complacently, but with an unmistakable undertone of anxiety, that Desdemona would come "and with a greedy ear / Devour up my discourse" (1.3.149–50).

Paradoxically, in this image of rapacious appetite Othello is recording Desdemona's *submission* to his story, what she calls the consecration of her soul and fortunes "to his honors, and his valiant parts" (1.3.253). What he has both experienced and narrated, she can only embrace as narration:

> my story being done,
> She gave me for my pains a world of sighs;
> She swore i' faith 'twas strange, 'twas passing strange;
> 'Twas pitiful, 'twas wondrous pitiful;
> She wish'd she had not heard it, yet she wish'd
> That heaven had made her such a man.
>
> *(1.3.158–63)*[26]

It is, of course, characteristic of early modern culture that male submission to narrative is conceived as active, entailing the fashioning of one's own story (albeit within the prevailing conventions), and female submission as passive, entailing the entrance into marriage in which, to recall Tyndale's definition, the "weak vessel" is put "under the obedience of her husband, to rule her lusts and wanton appetites." As we have seen, Tyndale explains that Sara, "before she was married, was Abraham's sister, and equal with him; but, as soon as she was married, was in subjection, and became without comparison inferior; for so is the nature of wedlock, by the ordinance of God."[27] At least for the world of Renaissance patriarchs, this account is fanciful in its glimpse of an original equality; most women must have entered marriage, like Desdemona, directly from paternal domination.

"I do perceive here a divided duty," she tells her father before the Venetian Senate; "you are lord of all my duty,"

> but here's my husband:
> And so much duty as my mother show'd
> To you, preferring you before her father,
> So much I challenge, that I may profess,
> Due to the Moor my lord.
>
> *(1.3.185–89)*[28]

She does not question the woman's obligation to obey, invoking instead only the traditional right to transfer her duty. Yet though Desdemona proclaims throughout the play her submission to her husband—"Commend me to my kind lord," she gasps in her dying words—that submission does not accord wholly with the male dream of female passivity. She was, Brabantio tells us,

> A maiden never bold of spirit,
> So still and quiet, that her motion
> Blush'd at her self,
>
> *(1.3.94–96)*

yet even this self-abnegation in its very extremity unsettles what we may assume was her father's expectation:

> So opposite to marriage, that she shunn'd
> The wealthy curled darlings of our nation.
>
> *(1.2.67–68)*

And, of course, her marriage choice is, for Brabantio, an act of astonishing disobedience, explicable only as the somnambulistic behavior of one bewitched or drugged. He views her elopement not as a transfer of obedience but as theft or treason or a reckless escape from what he calls his "guardage." Both he and Iago remind Othello that her marriage suggests not submission but deception:

> She did deceive her father, marrying you;
> And when she seem'd to shake and fear your looks,
> She lov'd them most.
>
> *(3.3.210–11)*[29]

As the sly reference to Othello's "looks" suggests, the scandal of Desdemona's marriage consists not only in her failure to receive her father's prior consent but in her husband's blackness. That blackness—the sign of all that the society finds frightening and dangerous—is the indelible witness to Othello's permanent status as an outsider, no matter how highly the state may value his services or how sincerely he has embraced its values.[30] The safe passage of the female from father to husband is irreparably disrupted, marked as an escape: "O heaven," Brabantio cries, "how got she out?" (1.1.169).

Desdemona's relation to her lord Othello should, of course, lay to rest any doubts about her proper submission, but it is not only Brabantio's opposition and Othello's blackness that raise such doubts, even in the midst of her intensest declarations of love. There is rather a quality in that love itself that unsettles the orthodox schema of hierarchial obedience and makes Othello perceive her submission to his discourse as a devouring of it. We may perceive this quality most clearly in the exquisite moment of the lovers' reunion on Cyprus:

> OTHELLO   It gives me wonder great as my content
> To see you here before me: O my soul's joy,
> If after every tempest come such calmness,
> May the winds blow, till they have waken'd death,
> And let the labouring bark climb hills of seas,
> Olympus-high, and duck again as low
> As hell's from heaven. If it were now to die,
> 'Twere now to be most happy, for I fear
> My soul hath her content so absolute,
> That not another comfort, like to this
> Succeeds in unknown fate.
> DESDEMONA   The heavens forbid
> But that our loves and comforts should increase,
> even as our days do grow.
> OTHELLO   Amen to that, sweet powers!
> I cannot speak enough of this content,
> It stops me here, it is too much of joy.
>
> *(2.1.183–97)*[31]

Christian orthodoxy in both Catholic and Protestant Europe could envision a fervent mutual love between husband and wife, the love expressed most profoundly by Saint Paul in words that are cited and commented upon in virtually every discussion of marriage:

> So men are bound to love their own wives as their own bodies. He that loveth his own wife, loveth himself. For never did any man hate his own flesh, but nourisheth and cherisheth it, even as the Lord doth the congregation: for we are members of his body, of his flesh and of his bones. For this cause shall a man leave father and mother, and shall be joined unto his wife, and they two shall be one flesh. This mystery is great, but I speak of Christ and of the congregation.[32]

Building upon this passage and upon its source in *Genesis*, commentators could write, like the Reformer Thomas Becon, that marriage is a "high, holy, and blessed order of life, ordained not of man, but of God, yea and that not in this sinful world, but in paradise that most joyful garden of pleasure." But like the Pauline text itself, all such discussions of married love begin and end by affirming the larger order of authority and submission within which marriage takes its rightful place. The family, as William Gouge puts it, "is a little Church, and a little Commonwealth . . . whereby trial may be made of such as are fit for any place of authority, or of subjection in Church or Commonwealth."[33]

In Othello's ecstatic words, the proper sentiments of a Christian husband sit alongside something else: a violent oscillation between heaven and hell, a momentary possession of the soul's absolute content, an archaic sense of monumental scale, a dark fear—equally archaic, perhaps—of "unknown fate." Nothing *conflicts* openly with Christian orthodoxy, but the erotic intensity that informs almost every word is experienced in tension with it. This tension is less a manifestation of some atavistic "blackness" specific to Othello than a manifestation of the colonial power of Christian doctrine over sexuality, a power visible at this point precisely in its inherent limitation.[34] That is, we glimpse in this brief moment the *boundary* of the orthodox, the strain of its control, the potential disruption of its hegemony by passion. This scene, let us stress, does not depict rebellion or even complaint—Desdemona invokes "the heavens" and Othello answers, "Amen to that, sweet powers!" Yet the plural here eludes, if only slightly, a serene affirmation of orthodoxy: the powers in their heavens do not refer unmistakably to the Christian God, but rather are the nameless transcendent forces that protect and enhance erotic love. To perceive the difference, we might recall that if Augustine argues, against the gnostics, that God had intended Adam and Eve to procreate in paradise, he insists at the same time that our first parents would have experienced sexual intercourse without the excitement of the flesh. How then could Adam have had an erection? Just as there are persons, Augustine writes, "who can move their ears, either one at a time, or both together" and others who have "such command of their bowels, that they can break wind continuously at pleasure, so as to produce the effect of singing," so, before the Fall, Adam would have had fully rational, willed control of the organ of generation and thus would have needed no erotic arousal. "Without the seductive stimulus of passion, with calmness of mind and with no corrupting of the integrity of the body, the husband would lie upon the bosom of his wife," and in this placid union, the semen could reach the womb "with the integrity of the female genital organ being preserved, just as now, with that same integrity being safe, the menstrual flow of blood can be emitted from the womb of a virgin."[35] Augustine grants that even Adam and Eve, who alone could have done so, failed to experience this "passionless generation," since they were expelled from paradise before they had a chance to try it. Nevertheless, the ideal of Edenic placidity, untried but intended by God for mankind, remains as a reproach to all fallen sexuality, an exposure of its inherent violence.[36]

The rich and disturbing pathos of the lovers' passionate reunion in *Othello* derives then not only from our awareness that Othello's premonition is tragically accurate, but from a rent, a moving ambivalence, in his experience of the ecstatic moment itself. The "calmness" of which he speaks may express gratified desire, but, as the repeated invocation of death suggests, it may equally express the longing for a final *release* from desire, from the dangerous violence, the sense of extremes, the laborious climbing and falling out of control that is experienced in the tempest. To be sure, Othello *welcomes* this tempest, with its charge of erotic feeling, but he does so for the sake of the ultimate consummation that the experience can call into being: "If after every tempest come such calmness . . . ." That which men most fear to look upon in the storm—death—is for Othello that which makes the storm endurable. If the death he invokes may figure not the release from desire but its fulfillment—for *death* is a common Renaissance term for orgasm—this fulfillment is characteristically poised between an anxious sense of self-dissolution and a craving for decisive closure. If Othello's words suggest an ecstatic acceptance of sexuality, an absolute content, they suggest simultaneously that for him sexuality is a menacing voyage to reach a longed-for heaven; it is one of the dangers to be passed. Othello embraces the erotic as a supreme form of romantic narrative, a tale of risk and violence issuing forth at last in a happy and final tranquillity.

Desdemona's response is in an entirely different key:

> The heavens forbid
> But that our loves and comforts should increase,
> Even as our days do grow.

This is spoken to allay Othello's fear, but may it not instead augment it? For if Othello characteristically responds to his experience by shaping it as a story, Desdemona's reply denies the possibility of such narrative control and offers instead a vision of unabating increase. Othello says "Amen" to this vision, but it arouses in him a feeling at once of overflowing and inadequacy:

> I cannot speak enough of this content,
> It stops me here, it is too much of joy.

Desdemona has once again devoured up his discourse, and she has done so precisely in bringing him comfort and content.[37] Rather than simply confirming male authority, her submission eroticizes everything to which it responds, from the "disastrous chances" and "moving accidents" Othello relates, to his simplest demands,[38] to his very mistreatment of her:

> my love doth so approve him,
> That even his stubbornness, his checks and frowns,—
> Prithee unpin me,—have grace and favour in them.
> *(4.3.19–21)*[39]

The other women in the play, Bianca and Emilia, both have moments of disobedience to the men who possess and abuse them—in the case of Emilia, it is a heroic disobedience for which she pays with her life.[40] Desdemona performs no such acts of defiance, but her erotic submission, conjoined with Iago's murderous cunning, far more effectively, if unintentionally, subverts her husband's carefully fashioned identity.

We will examine more fully the tragic process of this subversion, but it is important to grasp first that Othello's loss of himself—a loss depicted discursively in his incoherent ravings—arises not only from the fatal conjunction of Desdemona's love and Iago's hate, but from the nature of that identity, from what we have called his submission to narrative self-fashioning. We may invoke in this connection Lacan's observation that the source of the subject's frustration in psychoanalysis is ultimately neither the silence nor the reply of the analyst:

Is it not rather a matter of frustration inherent in the very discourse of the subject? Does the subject not become engaged in an ever-growing dispossession of that being of his, concerning which—by dint of sincere portraits which leave its idea no less incoherent, of rectifications which do not succeed in freeing its essence, of stays and defenses which do not prevent his statue from tottering, of narcissistic embraces which become like a puff of air in animating it—he ends up by recognizing that this being has never been anything more than his construct in the Imaginary and that this construct disappoints all of his certitudes? For in this labor which he undertakes to reconstruct this construct *for another*, he finds again the fundamental alienation which made him construct it *like another one*, and which has always destined it to be stripped from him *by another*.[41]

Shakespeare's military hero, it may be objected, is particularly far removed from this introspective project, a project that would seem, in any case, to have little bearing upon any Renaissance text. Yet I think it is no accident that nearly every phrase of Lacan's critique of psychoanalysis seems a brilliant reading of *Othello*, for I would propose that there is a deep resemblance between the construction of the self in analysis—at least as Lacan conceives it—and Othello's self-fashioning. The resemblance is grounded in the dependence of even the innermost self upon a language that is always necessarily given from without and upon representation before an audience. I do not know if such are the conditions of human identity, apart from its expression in psychoanalysis, but they are unmistakably the conditions of theatrical identity, where existence is conferred upon a character by the playwright's language and the actor's performance. And in *Othello* these governing circumstances of the medium itself are reproduced and intensified in the hero's situation: his identity depends upon a constant performance, as we have seen, of his "story," a loss of his own origins, an embrace and perpetual reiteration of the norms of another culture. It is this dependence that gives Othello, the warrior and alien, a relation to Christian values that is the existential equivalent of a religious vocation; he cannot allow himself the moderately flexible adherence that most ordinary men have toward their own formal beliefs. Christianity is the alienating yet constitutive force in Othello's identity, and if we seek a discursive mode in the play that is the social equivalent of the experience Lacan depicts, we will find it in *confession*. Othello himself invokes before the Venetian Senate the absolute integrity of confession, conceived, it appears, not as the formal auricular rite of penitence but as a generalized self-scrutiny in God's presence:

> as faithful as to heaven
> I do confess the vices of my blood,
> So justly to your grave ears I'll present
> How I did thrive in this fair lady's love,
> And she in mine.
> *(1.3.123–36)*[42]

The buried identification here between the vices of the blood and mutual thriving in love is fully exhumed by the close of the play when confession has become a virtually obsessional theme.[43] Theological and juridical confession are fused in Othello's mind when, determined first to exact a deathbed confession, he comes to take Desdemona's life:

> If you bethink yourself of any crime,
> Unreconcil'd as yet to heaven and grace,
> Solicit for it straight . . . .
> Therefore confess thee freely of thy sin,
> For to deny each article with oath
> Cannot remove, nor choke the strong conceit,
> That I do groan withal: thou art to die.
> *(5.2.26–28, 54–57)*

The sin that Othello wishes Desdemona to confess is adultery, and her refusal to do so frustrates the achievement of what in theology was called "a good, complete confession."[44] He feels the outrage of the thwarted system that needs to imagine itself merciful, sacramental, when it disciplines:

> thou dost stone thy heart,
> And makest me call what I intend to do
> A murder, which I thought a sacrifice.
> *(5.2.64–66)*

We are at last in a position to locate the precise nature of the symbolic structure into which Iago inserts himself in his brilliant improvisation: this structure is the centuries-old Christian doctrine of sexuality, policed socially and psychically, as we have already seen, by confession. To Iago, the Renaissance skeptic, this system has a somewhat archaic ring, as if it were an earlier stage of development which his own modern sensibility had cast off.[45] Like the Lucayan religion to the conquistadors, the orthodox doctrine that governs Othello's sexual attitudes—his simultaneous idealization and mistrust of women—seems to Iago sufficiently close to be recognizable, sufficiently distant to be manipulable. We watch him manipulate it directly at the beginning of act 4, when he leads Othello through a brutally comic parody of the late medieval confessional manuals with their casuistical attempts to define the precise moment at which venial temptation passes over into mortal sin:

IAGO	To kiss in private?
OTHELLO	An unauthoriz'd kiss.
IAGO	Or to be naked with her friend abed,
	An hour, or more, not meaning any harm?
OTHELLO	Naked abed, Iago, and not mean harm?
	It is hypocrisy against the devil:
	They that mean virtuously, and yet do so,
	The devil their virtue tempts, and they tempt heaven.
IAGO	So they do nothing, 'tis a venial slip.

(4.1.2–9)

Iago in effect assumes an extreme version of the laxist position in such manuals in order to impel Othello toward the rigorist version that viewed adultery as one of the most horrible of mortal sins, more detestable, in the words of the *Eruditorium penitentiale*, "than homicide or plunder," and hence formerly deemed punishable, as several authorities remind us, by death.[46] Early Protestantism did not soften this position. Indeed, in the mid-sixteenth century, Tyndale's erstwhile collaborator, George Joye, called for a return to the Old Testament penalty for adulterers. "God's law," he writes, "is to punish adultery with death for the tranquility and commonwealth of His church." This is not an excessive or vindictive course; on the contrary, "to take away and to cut off putrified and corrupt members from the whole body, lest they poison and destroy the body, is the law of love."[47] When Christian magistrates leave adultery unpunished, they invite more betrayals and risk the ruin of the realm, for as Protestants in particular repeatedly observe, the family is an essential component of an interlocking social and theological network. Hence adultery is a sin with the gravest of repercussions; in the words of the great Cambridge Puritan William Perkins, it "destroyeth the Seminary of the Church, which is *a godly seed* in the family, and it breaketh the covenant between the parties and God; it robs another of the precious ornament of chastity, which is a gift of the Holy Ghost; it dishonors their bodies and maketh them temples of the devil; and the Adulterer maketh his family a Stews."[48] It is in the bitter spirit of these convictions that Othello enacts the grotesque comedy of treating his wife as a strumpet and the tragedy of executing her in the name of justice, lest she betray more men.

But we still must ask how Iago manages to persuade Othello that Desdemona has committed adultery, for all of the cheap tricks Iago plays seem somehow inadequate to produce the unshakable conviction of his wife's defilement that seizes Othello's soul and drives him mad. After all, as Iago taunts Othello, he cannot achieve the point of vantage of God whom the Venetian women let "see the pranks / They dare not show their husbands" (3.3.206–7):

> Would you, the supervisor, grossly gape on,
> Behold her topp'd?
>
> *(3.3.401–2)*

How then, without "ocular proof" and in the face of both love and common sense, is Othello so thoroughly persuaded? To answer this, we must recall the syntactic ambiguity we noted earlier—"to abuse Othello's ear, / That he is too familiar with his wife"—and turn to a still darker aspect of orthodox Christian doctrine, an aspect central both to the confessional system and to Protestant self-scrutiny. *Omnis amator feruentior est adulter*, goes the Stoic epigram, and Saint Jerome does not hesitate to draw the inevitable inference: "An adulterer is he who is too ardent a lover of his wife."[49] Jerome quotes Seneca: "All love of another's wife is shameful; so too, too much love of your own. A wise man ought to love his wife with judgment, not affection. Let him control his impulses and not be borne headlong into copulation. Nothing is fouler than to love a wife like an adultress . . . . Let them show themselves to their wives not as lovers, but as husbands."[50] The words echo through more than a thousand years of Christian writing on marriage, and, in the decisive form given them by Augustine and his commentators, remain essentially unchallenged by the leading Continental Reformers of the sixteenth and early seventeenth century, by Tudor ecclesiastical authorities, and even by Elizabethan and Jacobean Puritans who sharply opposed so many conservative Anglican doctrines. There is, to be sure, in all shades of Protestantism an attack on the Catholic doctrine of celibacy and a celebration of married love, a celebration that includes acknowledgment of the legitimate role of sexual pleasure. But for Reformer as for Catholic, this acknowledgment is hedged about with warnings and restrictions. The "man who shows no modesty or comeliness in conjugal intercourse," writes Calvin, "is committing adultery with his wife," and the *King's Book*, attributed to Henry VIII, informs its readers that in lawful matrimony a man may break the Seventh Commandment "and live unchaste with his own wife, if he do unmeasurably or inordinately serve his or her fleshly appetite or lust."[51]

In the Augustinian conception, as elaborated by Raymond of Peñaforte, William of Rennes, and others, there are four motives for conjugal intercourse: to conceive offspring; to render the marital debt to one's partner so that he or she might avoid incontinency; to avoid fornication oneself; and to satisfy desire. The first two motives are without sin and excuse intercourse; the third is a venial sin; the fourth—to satisfy desire—is mortal. Among the many causes that underlie this institutional hostility to desire is the tenacious existence, in various forms, of the belief that pleasure constitutes a legitimate release from dogma and constraint. Thus when asked by the Inquisition about her happy past liaison with the heretical priest of Montaillou, the young Grazide Lizier replies with naive frankness, "in those days it pleased me, and it pleased the priest, that he should know me carnally, and be known by me; and so I did not think I was sinning, and neither did he."[52] "With Pierre Clergue," she explains, "I liked it. And so it could not displease God. It was not a sin" (157). For the peasant girl, apparently, pleasure was the guarantee of innocence: "But now, with him, it does not please me any more. And so now, if he knew me carnally, I should think it a sin" (151). A comparable attitude, derived not from peasant culture but from the troubadours, evidently lies behind the more sophisticated courtship of Romeo: "Thus from my lips, by thine my sin is purged."[53]

It should not surprise us that churchmen, Catholic and Protestant alike, would seek to crush such dangerous notions, nor that they would extend their surveillance and discipline to married couples and warn that excessive pleasure in the marriage bed is at least a potential violation of the Seventh Commandment. "Nothing is more vile," says Raymond's influential *summa*, "than to love your wife in adulterous fashion."[54] The conjugal act may be without sin, writes the rigorist Nicolaus of Ausimo, but only if "in the performance of this act there is no enjoyment of pleasure."[55] Few *summas* and no marriage manuals take so extreme a position, but virtually all are in agreement that the active *pursuit* of pleasure in sexuality is damnable, for as Jacobus Ungarelli writes in the sixteenth century, those who undertake intercourse for pleasure "exclude God from their minds, act as brute beasts, lack reason, and if they begin marriage for this reason, are given over to the power of the devil."[56]

Confessors then must determine if the married penitent has a legitimate excuse for intercourse and if the act has been performed with due regard for "matrimonial chastity," while Protestants who have rejected auricular confession must similarly scrutinize their own behavior for signs that their pleasure has been too "spacious."[57] "Lust is more spacious than love," writes Alexander Niccoles in the early seventeenth century; it "hath no mean, no bound . . . more deep, more dangerous than the Sea, and less restrained, for the Sea hath bounds, but it [lust] hath none."[58] Such unbounded love is a kind of idolatry, an encroachment upon a Christian's debt of loving obedience to God, and it ultimately destroys the marital relationship as well. Immoderate love, another Puritan divine warns, "will either be blown down by some storm or tempest of displeasure, or fall of itself, or else degenerate into jealousy, the most devouring and fretting canker that can harbor in a married person's breast."[59]

These anxieties, rich in implication for *Othello*, are frequently tempered in Protestant writings by a recognition of the joyful ardor of young married couples, but there remains a constant fear of excess, and, as Ambrose observed centuries earlier, even the most plausible excuse for sexual passion is shameful in the old: "Youths generally assert the desire for generation. How much more shameful for the old to do what is shameful for the young to confess."[60] Othello himself seems eager to ward off this shame; he denies before the Senate that he seeks

> To please the palate of my appetite,
> Nor to comply with heat, the young affects
> In me defunct . . . .
> (1.3.262–64)[61]

But Desdemona makes no such disclaimer; indeed her declaration of passion is frankly, though by no means exclusively, sexual:

> That I did love the Moor, to live with him,
> My downright violence, and scorn of fortunes,
> May trumpet to the world: my heart's subdued
> Even to the utmost pleasure of my lord.
> (1.3.248–51)[62]

This moment of erotic intensity, this frank acceptance of pleasure and submission to her spouse's pleasure, is, I would argue, as much as Iago's slander the cause of Desdemona's death, for it awakens the deep current of sexual anxiety in Othello, anxiety that with Iago's help expresses itself in quite orthodox fashion as the perception of adultery.[63] Othello unleashes upon Cassio—"Michael Cassio, / That came a-wooing with you" (3.3.71–72)—the fear of pollution, defilement, brutish violence that is bound up with his own experience of sexual pleasure, while he must destroy Desdemona both for her excessive experience of pleasure and for awakening such sensations in himself. Like Guyon in the Bower of Bliss, Othello transforms his complicity in erotic excess and his fear of engulfment into a "purifying," saving violence:

> Like to the Pontic sea,
> Whose icy current and compulsive course
> Ne'er feels retiring ebb, but keeps due on
> To the Propontic and the Hellespont,
> Even so my bloody thoughts, with violent pace,
> Shall ne'er look back, ne'er ebb to humble love,
> Till that a capable and wide revenge
> Swallow them up.
>
> *(3.3.460–67)*

His insupportable sexual experience has been, as it were, displaced and absorbed by the act of revenge which can swallow up not only the guilty lovers but—as the syntax suggests—his own "bloody thoughts."

Such is the achievement of Iago's improvisation on the religious sexual doctrine in which Othello believes; true to that doctrine, pleasure itself becomes for Othello pollution, a defilement of his property in Desdemona and in himself.[64] It is at the level of this dark, sexual revulsion that Iago has access to Othello, access assured, as we should expect, by the fact that beneath his cynical modernity and professed self-love Iago reproduces in himself the same psychic structure. He is as intensely preoccupied with adultery, while his anxiety about his own sexuality may be gauged from the fact that he conceives his very invention, as the images of engendering suggest, as a kind of demonic semen that will bring forth monsters.[65] Indeed Iago's discourse—his assaults on women, on the irrationality of eros, on the brutishness of the sexual act—reiterates virtually to the letter the orthodox terms of Ungarelli's attack on those who seek pleasure in intercourse.

The improvisational process we have been discussing depends for its success upon the concealment of its symbolic center, but as the end approaches this center becomes increasingly visible. When, approaching the marriage bed on which Desdemona has spread the wedding sheets, Othello rages, "Thy bed, lust stain'd, shall with lust's blood be spotted" (5.1.36), he comes close to revealing his tormenting identification of marital sexuality—limited perhaps to the night he took Desdemona's virginity—and adultery.[66] The orthodox element of this identification is directly observed—

> this sorrow's heavenly,
> It strikes when it does love—
> *(5.2.21–22)*

and on her marriage bed/deathbed Desdemona seems at last to pluck out the heart of the mystery:

OTHELLO   Think on thy sins.
DESDEMONA   They are loves I bear to you.

OTHELLO	And for that thou diest.
DESDEMONA	That death's unnatural, that kills for loving.

(5.2.39–42)

The play reveals at this point not the unfathomable darkness of human motives but their terrible transparency, and the horror of the revelation is its utter inability to deflect violence. Othello's identity is entirely caught up in the narrative structure that drives him to turn Desdemona into a being incapable of pleasure, a piece of "monumental alabaster," so that he will at last be able to love her without the taint of adultery:

> Be thus, when thou art dead, and I will kill thee,
> And love thee after.

(5.2.18–19)

It is as if Othello had found in a necrophilic fantasy the secret solution to the intolerable demands of the rigorist sexual ethic, and the revelation that Cassio has not slept with Desdemona leads only to a doubling of this solution, for the adulterous sexual pleasure that Othello had projected upon his lieutenant now rebounds upon himself.[67] Even with the exposure of Iago's treachery, then, there is for Othello no escape—rather a still deeper submission to narrative, a reaffirmation of the self as story, but now split suicidally between the defender of the faith and the circumcised enemy who must be destroyed. Lodovico's bizarrely punning response to Othello's final speech—"O bloody period!"—insists precisely upon the fact that it was a speech, that this life fashioned as a text is ended as a text.

To an envious contemporary like Robert Greene, Shakespeare seems a kind of green-room Iago, appropriating for himself the labors of others. In *Othello* Shakespeare seems to acknowledge, represent, and explore his affinity to the malicious improviser, but, of course, his relation to the theater and to his culture is far more complex than such an affinity could suggest. There are characters in his works who can improvise without tragic results, characters who can embrace a mobility of desire—one of whose emblems is the male actor playing a female character dressed up as a male—that neither Iago, nor Othello, nor Desdemona can endure. Destructive violence is not Shakespeare's only version of these materials, and even in *Othello*, Iago is not the playwright's only representation of himself. Still, at the least we must grant Robert Greene that it would have seemed fatal to be imitated by Shakespeare. He possessed a limitless talent for entering into the consciousness of another, perceiving its deepest structures as a manipulable fiction, reinscribing it into his own narrative form.[68] If in the late plays, he experiments with controlled disruptions of narrative, moments of eddying and ecstasy, these invariably give way to reaffirmations of self-fashioning through story.

Montaigne, who shares many of Shakespeare's most radical perceptions, invents in effect a brilliant mode of *non-narrative* self-fashioning: "I cannot keep my subject still. It goes along befuddled and staggering, with a natural drunkenness. I take it in this condition, just as it is at the moment I give my attention to it."[69] Shakespeare by contrast remains throughout his career the supreme purveyor of "empathy," the fashioner of narrative selves, the master improviser. Where Montaigne withdrew to his study, Shakespeare became the presiding genius of a popular, urban art form with the capacity to foster psychic mobility in the service of Elizabethan power; he became the principal maker of what we may see as the prototype of the mass media Professor Lerner so admires.

Finally, we may ask, is this service to power a function of the theater itself or of Shakespeare's relation to his medium? The answer, predictably, is both. The theater is widely perceived in the period as the concrete manifestation of the histrionic quality of life, and, more specifically, of power—the power of the prince who stands as an actor upon a stage before the eyes of the nation, the power of God who enacts His will in the Theater of the World. The stage justifies itself against recurrent charges of immorality by invoking this normative function: it is the expression of those rules that govern a properly ordered society and displays visibly the punishment, in laughter and violence, that is meted out upon those who violate the rules. Most playwrights pay at least professional homage to these values; they honor the institutions that enable them to earn their keep and give voice to the ideology that holds together both their "mystery" and the society at large.

In Marlowe, as we have seen, we encounter a playwright at odds with this ideology. If the theater normally reflects and flatters the royal sense of itself as national performance, Marlowe struggles to expose the underlying motives of any performance of power. If the theater normally affirms God's providence, Marlowe explores the tragic needs and interests that are served by all such affirmations. If the Elizabethan stage functions as one of the public uses of spectacle to impose normative ethical patterns on the urban masses, Marlowe enacts a relentless challenge to those patterns and undermines employment of rhetoric and violence in their service.

Shakespeare approaches his culture not, like Marlowe, as rebel and blasphemer, but rather as dutiful servant, content to improvise a part of his own within its orthodoxy. And if after centuries, that improvisation has been revealed to us as embodying an almost boundless challenge to the culture's every tenet, a devastation of every source, the author of *Othello* would have understood that such a revelation scarcely matters. After all, the heart of a successful improvisation lies in concealment, not exposure; and besides, as we have seen, even a hostile improvisation reproduces the relations of power that it hopes to displace and absorb.

This is not to dismiss the power of hatred or the significance of distinctions—it matters a great deal whether Othello or Iago, the Lucayans or the Spaniards prevail—only to suggest the boundaries that define the possibility of any improvisational contact, even contact characterized by hidden malice.

I would not want to argue, in any event, that Shakespeare's relation to his culture is defined by hidden malice. Such a case can no doubt be made for many of the plays—stranger things have been said—but it will sound forced and unconvincing, just as the case for Shakespeare as an unwavering, unquestioning apologist for Tudor ideology sounds forced and unconvincing. The solution here is not, I suggest, that the truth lies somewhere in between. Rather the truth itself is radically unstable and yet constantly stabilized, as unstable as those male authorities that affirm themselves only to be undermined by subversive women and then to be reconstituted in a different guise. If any reductive generalization about Shakespeare's relation to his culture seems dubious, it is because his plays offer no single timeless affirmation or denial of legitimate authority and no central, unwavering authorial presence. Shakespeare's language and themes are caught up, like the medium itself, in unsettling repetitions, committed to the shifting voices and audiences, with their shifting aesthetic assumptions and historical imperatives, that govern a living theater.

Criticism can legitimately show—as I hope my discussion of *Othello* does—that Shakespeare relentlessly *explores* the relations of power in a given culture. That more than exploration is involved is much harder to demonstrate convincingly. If there are intimations in Shakespeare of a release from the complex narrative orders in which everyone is inscribed, these intimations do not arise from bristling resistance or strident denunciation—the mood of a Jaques or Timon. They arise paradoxically from a peculiarly intense *submission* whose downright violence undermines everything it was meant to shore up, the submission depicted not in Othello or Iago but in Desdemona. As both the play and its culture suggest, the arousal of intense, purposeless pleasure is only superficially a confirmation of existing values, established selves.[70] In Shakespeare's narrative art, liberation from the massive power structures that determine social and psychic reality is glimpsed in an *excessive* aesthetic delight, an erotic embrace of those very structures—the embrace of a Desdemona whose love is more deeply unsettling than even an Iago's empathy.

EPILOGUE

A few years ago, at the start of a plane flight from Baltimore to Boston, I settled down next to a middle-aged man who was staring pensively out of the window. There was no assigned seating, and I had chosen this neighbor as the least likely to disturb me, since I wanted to finish rereading Geertz's *Interpretation of Cultures,* which I was due to teach on my return to Berkeley the following week. But no sooner had I fastened my seat belt and turned my mind to Balinese cockfighting than the man suddenly began to speak to me. He was traveling to Boston, he said, to visit his grown son who was in the hospital. A disease had, among other consequences, impaired the son's speech, so that he could only mouth words soundlessly; still more seriously, as a result of the illness, he had lost his will to live. The father was going, he told me, to try to restore that will, but he was troubled by the thought that he would be incapable of understanding the son's attempts at speech. He had therefore a favor to ask me: would I mime a few sentences so that he could practice reading my lips? Would I say, soundlessly, "I want to die. I want to die"?

Taken aback, I began to form the words, with the man staring intently at my mouth: "I want to . . ." But I was incapable of finishing the sentence. "Couldn't I say, 'I want to live'?" Or better still (since the seat belt sign had by this time flashed off), he might go into the bathroom, I suggested lamely, and practice on himself in front of a mirror. "It's not the same," the man replied in a shaky voice, then turned back to the window. "I'm sorry," I said, and we sat in silence for the rest of the flight.

I could not do what the man had asked in part because I was afraid that he was, quite simply, a maniac and that once I had expressed the will to die, he would draw a hidden knife and stab me to death or, alternatively, activate some device secreted on board the plane that would blow us all to pieces (it's not for nothing that I have been living in California for the past ten years).

But if paranoia tinged my whole response, there were reasons for my resistance more complex than the fear of physical attack. I felt superstitiously that if I mimed the man's terrible sentence, it would have the force, as it were, of a legal sentence, that the words would stick like a burr upon me. And beyond superstition, I was aware, in a manner more forceful than anything my academic research had brought home to me, of the extent to which my identity and the words I utter coincide, the extent to which I want to form my own sentences or to choose for myself those moments in which I will recite someone else's. To be asked, even by an isolated, needy individual to perform lines that were not my own, that violated my sense of my own desires, was intolerable.

When I first conceived this book several years ago, I intended to explore the ways in which major English writers of the sixteenth century created their own performances, to analyze the choices they made in representing themselves and in fashioning characters, to understand the role of human autonomy in the construction of identity. It seemed to me the very hallmark of the Renaissance that middle-class and aristocratic males began to feel that they possessed such shaping power over their lives, and I saw this power and the freedom it implied as an important element in my own sense of myself. But as my work progressed, I perceived that fashioning oneself and being fashioned by cultural institutions—

family, religion, state—were inseparably intertwined. In all my texts and documents, there were, so far as I could tell, no moments of pure, unfettered subjectivity; indeed, the human subject itself began to seem remarkably unfree, the ideological product of the relations of power in a particular society. Whenever I focused sharply upon a moment of apparently autonomous self-fashioning, I found not an epiphany of identity freely chosen but a cultural artifact. If there remained traces of free choice, the choice was among possibilities whose range was strictly delineated by the social and ideological system in force.

The book I have written reflects these perceptions, but I trust that it also reflects, though in a manner more tentative, more ironic than I had originally intended, my initial impulse. For all of the sixteenth-century Englishmen I have written about here do in fact cling to the human subject and to self-fashioning, even in suggesting the absorption or corruption or loss of the self. How could they do otherwise? What was—or, for that matter, what is—the alternative? For the Renaissance figures we have considered understand that in our culture to abandon self-fashioning is to abandon the craving for freedom, and to let go of one's stubborn hold upon selfhood, even selfhood conceived as a fiction, is to die. As for myself, I have related this brief story of my encounter with the distraught father on the plane because I want to bear witness at the close to my overwhelming need to sustain the illusion that I am the principal maker of my own identity.

NOTES

1. On the feudal revival, see Arthur B. Ferguson, *The Indian Summer of English Chivalry* (Durham, N.C.: Duke University Press, 1960), Frances A. Yates, "Elizabethan Chivalry: The Romance of the Accession Day Tilts," in *Astraea: The Imperial Theme in the Sixteenth Century* (London: Routledge, 1975), pp. 88–111, and Roy Strong, *The Cult of Elizabeth: Elizabethan Portraiture and Pageantry* (London: Thames and Hudson, 1977).

2. John Steevens, cited in *The Works of Edmund Spenser: A Variorum Edition*, ed. Edwin Greenlaw et al. (Baltimore: Johns Hopkins University Press, 1932–57), 1:252.

3. It is not certain who borrowed from whom, though I think the dominant view, that Marlowe borrowed from Spenser, is quite likely. For the parallels between Spenser and Marlowe, see also Charles Crawford, "Edmund Spenser, 'Locrine,' and 'Selimus,' " *Notes and Queries* (9th ser.) 7 (1901), pp. 62–63, 101–3, 142–44, 203–5, 261–63, 324–25, 384–86.

4. Daniel Lerner, *The Passing of Traditional Society: Modernizing the Middle East* (New York: Free Press, 1958; rev. ed. 1964), p. 49.

5. The figures are from Sherburne Cook and Woodrow W. Borah, *Essays in Population History: Mexico and the Caribbean* (Berkeley: University of California Press, 1971), pp. 376–411.

6. Peter Martyr (Pietro Martire d'Anghiera), *De Orbe Novo*, trans. M. Lok, p. 623. The Seventh Decade was finished in the middle of 1525. On Peter Martyr, see Henry R. Wagner, "Peter Martyr and His Works," *Proceedings of the American Antiquarian Society* 56 (1946), pp. 238–88. There is a rather pallid modern translation of *De Orbe Novo* by Francis A. MacNutt (New York: Putnam's, 1912).

7. It is the essence of *sprezzatura* to create the impression of a spontaneous improvisation by means of careful rehearsals. Similarly, the early English drama often strove for this effect; see, for example, *Fulgens and Lucres* where the seemingly incidental conversation of "A" and "B" is fully scripted.

8. Immanuel Wallerstein, *The Modern World-System: Capitalist Agriculture and the Origins of the European World-Economy in the Sixteenth Century* (New York: Academic Press, 1974).

9. Roy Strong, *The Cult of Elizabeth: Elizabethan Portraiture and Pageantry*, p. 153.

10. As an example of the operation of displacement in the visual arts, one may consider Breughel's *Christ Bearing the Cross*, where the mourning figures from Van der Weyden's great *Descent from the Cross* are pushed out to the margin of the canvas and the swirling, festive crowd all but obscures Christ. Similarly, for absorption we may invoke Dürer's self-portrait of 1500, where the rigidly frontalized, verticalized, hieratic figure has taken into itself the Christ Pantocrator.

11. Joel B. Altman, *The Tudor Play of Mind: Rhetorical Inquiry and the Development of Elizabethan Drama* (Berkeley: University of California Press, 1978). See also Jackson I. Cope, *The Theater and the Dream: From Metaphor to Form in Renaissance Drama* (Baltimore: The Johns Hopkins University Press, 1973), esp. chaps. 4–6. Cope argues brilliantly for the central importance of improvisation in the drama of the Renaissance, but for him improvisation is in the service finally of "a real coherence" of "the eternal order" of the myths of renewal (p. 210). One passes, by means of an apparent randomness, a chaotic flux, to a buried but all-powerful form. Improvisation is the mask of providence, and Cope concludes his study with a discussion of *The Tempest* as a "mythic play" of natural resurrection and Christian doctrine. I would argue that the final effect of improvisation in Shakespeare is the reverse: we always begin with a notion of the inescapability of form, a sense that there are no surprises, that narrative triumphs over the apparent disruptions, that even the disruptions serve narrative by confirming the presence of the artist as a version of the presence of God. And through improvisation we pass, only partially and tentatively, to a sense that in the very acts of homage to the great formal structures, there open up small but constant glimpses of the limitations of those structures, of their insecurities, of the possibility of their collapse.

12. *Confutation*, 8:1, pp. 90–92. My attention was drawn to this passage by Professor Louis L. Martz who discussed it in a lecture at the Folger conference

"Thomas More: The Man and His Age." On More's "art of improvisation" see Martz, "The Tower Works," in *St. Thomas More: Action and Contemplation*, pp. 63-65.

13. Richard III virtually declares himself an improviser: "I clothe my naked villainy / With odd old ends stol'n forth of holy writ" (1.3.335–36). He gives a fine demonstration of his agility when he turns Margaret's curse back on herself. Behind this trick perhaps is the fact that there were in the popular culture of the Renaissance formulaic curses and satrical jigs into which any names could be fitted; see Charles Read Baskervill, *The Elizabethan Jig and Related Song Drama* (Chicago: University of Chicago Press, 1929), pp. 66-67.

14. All citations of *Othello* are to the Arden edition, ed. M. R. Ridley (Cambridge, Mass.: Harvard University Press, 1958). Iago's description of Cassio, "a finder out of occasions" (2.1.240–41), is a far more apt description of himself as an improviser.

15. This interpretation is argued powerfully in an unpublished essay, "On the Language of Sexual Pathology in *Othello*," by Edward Snow of George Mason University. A similar case is made by Arthur Kirsch in a sensitive psychoanalytic study, "The Polarization of Erotic Love in *Othello*" (*Modern Language Review* 73 [1978], pp. 721–40). Kirsch suggests that what becomes insupportable for Othello is "the fulsomeness of his own sexual instincts and, as his verbal and physical decomposition suggests, his jealous rage against Cassio is ultimately a rage against himself which reaches back to the elemental and destructive triadic fantasies which at one stage in childhood govern the mind of every human being" (p. 737).

16. Iago's performance here, which Desdemona unnervingly characterizes as "lame and impotent," is one of the ways in which he is linked to the playwright or at least to the Vice-like "presenter" of a play; see Bernard Spivack, *Shakespeare and the Allegory of Evil: The History of a Metaphor in Relation to His Major Villains* (New York: Columbia University Press, 1958).

17. One might argue that Shakespeare, like Marx, sees the exploiter as doomed by the fact that he must reduce his victim to nothingness, but where Marx derives a revolutionary optimism from this process, Shakespeare derives the tragic mood of the play's end.

18. For Iago's "corrosive habit of abstraction," see Maynard Mack, "The Jacobean Shakespeare: Some Observations on the Construction of the Tragedies," in *Stratford-upon-Avon Studies: Jacobean Theatre* 1 (1960), p. 18. For Iago as a "portrait of the artist," see Stanley Edgar Hyman, *Iago: Some Approaches to the Illusion of His Motivation* (New York: Atheneum, 1970), pp. 61–100.

19. The vertigo intensifies if we add the sly preceding line: "It is as sure as you are Roderigo, / Were I the Moor, I would not be Iago." One imagines that Roderigo would unconsiously touch himself at this point to make sure that he *is* Roderigo.

Iago is a master of the vertiginous confounding of self and other, being and seeming:

> Men should be what they seem,
> Or those that be not, would they might seem none.
>
> *(III, iii, 130–31)*

> He's that he is; I may not breathe my censure,
> What he might be, if, as he might, he is not,
> I would to heaven he were!
>
> *(IV, i, 267–69)*

20. See, for example, Theodor Lipps:

> The specific characteristic of esthetic pleasure has now been defined. It consists in this: that it is the enjoyment of an object, which however, so far as it is the object of *enjoyment*, is not an object, but myself. Or, it is the enjoyment of the ego, which however, so far as it is esthetically enjoyed, is not myself but objective.
>
> Now, all this is included in the concept empathy. It constitutes the very meaning of this concept. Empathy is the fact here established, that the object is myself and by the very same token this self of mine is the object. Empathy is the fact that the antithesis between myself and the object disappears, or rather does not yet exist. ("Empathy, Inner Imitation, and Sense-Feelings," in *A Modern Book of Esthetics*, ed. Melvin Rader [New York: Holt, Rinehart and Winston, 1960], p. 376.)

To establish this "fact," Lipps must posit a wholly esthetic dimension and what he calls an "ideal," as opposed to a "practical" self. In *Othello* there is no realm of the purely esthetic, no space defined by the intersection of negative capability and the willing suspension of disbelief, and no separation of an "ideal" from a "practical" self.

21. To complicate matters further, both declarations occur in a cunning performance for his dupe Roderigo; that is, Iago is saying what he presumes Roderigo wants to believe.

22. Thus Iago invokes heaven as the judge of his self-interested hypocrisy, for *self* and *interest* as stable entities both rely ultimately upon an absolute Being.

23. Elsewhere too, Othello speaks as if aware of himself as a character: "Were it my cue to fight," he tells the incensed Brabantio and his own followers, "I should have known it, / Without a prompter" (1.2.83–84). His acceptance of the commission to fight the Turks is likewise couched in an inflated diction that suggests he is responding to a cue:

> The tyrant custom, most grave senators,
> Hath made the flinty and steel couch of war
> My thrice-driven bed of down: I do agnize
> A natural and prompt alacrity

> I find in hardness, and would undertake
> This present wars against the Ottomites.
> (1.3.229–34)

24. Emmanuel Le Roy Ladurie, *Montaillou: The Promised Land of Error*, trans. Barbara Bray (New York: Braziller, 1978), pp. 8–9. In a review essay, Natalie Zemon Davis calls attention to the narrative structure of the testimony, a structure she attributes not to the pressure of the Inquisition but to the form of village culture: "Some of these details were probably remembered over the decades—good memories are part of oral culture—but most form a reconstructed past: from a general memory of an event, a narrative is created that tells with verisimilitude how the events could have unfolded. The past is a story" ("Les Conteurs de Montaillou," *Annales: Economies, Sociétés, Civilisations* 34 [1979], p. 70).

    On narrativity as a mode, see Louis Marin, *Utopiques: jeux d'espaces* (Paris: Minuit, 1973); Svetlana Alpers, "Describe or Narrate? A Problem in Realistic Representation," *New Literary History* 7 (1976–77), pp. 15–41; Leo Bersani, "The Other Freud," *Humanities in Society* 1 (1978), pp. 35–49.

25. *The Aeneid of Virgil*, trans. Allen Mandelbaum (New York: Bantam Books, 1972), bk. 1, lines 1049–51.

26. I very reluctantly accept the Quarto's *sighs* for the Folio's *kisses*; the latter need not, as editors sometimes claim, suggest an improbable immodesty but rather may express Othello's perception of Desdemona's nature, hence what her love has given him. Moreover, the frank eroticism of *kisses* is in keeping with Desdemona's own speeches; it is Othello who emphasizes a pity that she voices nowhere in the play itself. On the other hand, *sighs* admits a simpler reading and by no means excludes the erotic.

    There is another interpretive problem in this speech that should be noted: the last two lines are usually taken as a continuation of Desdemona's actual response, as recalled by Othello. But they may equally be his interpretation of her feelings, in which case they may say far more about Othello than about Desdemona. A competent actor could suggest either possibility. There is a further ambiguity in the *her* of "made her such a man": I hear *her* as accusative, but the dative cannot be ruled out.

27. *The Obedience of a Christian Man*, in William Tyndale, *Doctrinal Treatises and Introductions to Different Portions of The Holy Scriptures*, ed. Henry Walter (Cambridge: Parker Society, 1848), p. 171.

28. Both the Folio and the Second Quarto read "You are the Lord of duty," but the paradox of an absolute duty that must nevertheless be divided is suggestive.

29. Iago is improvising on two earlier remarks of Brabantio:

> and she, in spite of nature,
> Of years, of country, credit, everything,
> To fall in love with what she fear'd to look on?

(1.3.96–98)

and

> Look to her, Moor, have a quick eye to see:
> She has deceiv'd her father, may do thee.
> *(1.3.292–93)*

In a society deeply troubled by clandestine marriage, the circumstances of Desdemona's union already brand her as faithless, even at the moment Othello stakes his life upon her faith, while, quite apart from these circumstances, it would seem for the male psyche depicted in the play that the very act of leaving her father borders obscurely on sexual betrayal.

30. See George K. Hunter, "Othello and Colour Prejudice," *Proceedings of the British Academy 1967* 53 (1968), pp. 139–63; Leslie A. Fielder, *The Stranger in Shakespeare* (New York: Stein & Day, 1972), chap. 3.

   A measure of the complex significance of Othello's blackness may be taken from a glance at the competing interpretive possibilities of Desdemona's "I saw Othello's visage in his mind" (1.3.252):

   > "Do not be surprised that I have married an older black man who looks to you grotesque and terrifying. I have married not a face, a complexion, but a mind: a resolute, Christian mind."

   > "I saw Othello's valuation of himself, his internal image, the picture he has in his mind of his own face. I saw how much he had at stake in his narrative sense of himself, how much his whole existence depended upon this sense, and I was deeply drawn to this 'visage.' "

   > "I saw Othello's visage—his blackness, his otherness—in his mind as well as his complexion: there is a unity in his being. I am subdued to precisely this quality in him."

31. Ridley, in the Arden edition, adheres to the Quarto's "calmness" at line 185. Most editors prefer the Folio's "calms."

32. Ephesians 5.28–32, as cited in the marriage liturgy (*The Book of Common Prayer 1559*, ed. John Booty [Charlottesville: University of Virginia Press, 1976], p. 297). The passage is quoted by Arthur Kirsch, "The Polarization of Erotic Love in *Othello*," p. 721, who draws conclusions closely parallel to some of my own, though he differs in emphases and methodology.

33. Becon and Gouge are cited in William and Malleville Haller, "The Puritan Art of Love," *Huntington Library Quarterly* 5 (1941–42), pp. 44–45, 46.

34. From its inception, Christianity competed fiercely with other sexual conceptions and practices. For a detailed and moving study of one episode in this struggle, see Le Roy Ladurie's *Montaillou*. Michel Foucault has attempted the beginnings of a modern history of the subject in *La volonté de savoir* (Paris: Gallimard, 1976).

35. *The City of God*, trans. Marcus Dods (New York: Modern Library, 1950), bk. 14, chap. 24, pp. 473–75.

36. For the inherent violence of sexuality, see Lucretius, *The Nature of the Universe*, trans. Ronald Latham (Baltimore: Penguin, 1951): "Lovers' passion is storm-tossed, even in the moment of fruition, by waves of delusion and incertitude. They cannot make up their mind what to enjoy first with eye or hand. They clasp the object of their longing so tightly that the embrace is painful. They kiss so fiercely that teeth are driven into lips. All this because their pleasure is not pure, but they are goaded by an underlying impulse to hurt the thing, whatever it may be, that gives rise to these budding shoots of madness" (pp. 163–64).

37. Richard Onorato has called my attention to the way Iago, who is watching this scene, subsequently uses the word *content*. "nothing can, nor shall content my soul," he tells himself, "Till I am even with him, wife, for wife" (2.1.293–94). Later, when under his influence Othello has bade "farewell content" (3.3.354), Iago proffers the consoling words, "Pray be content" (3.3.457).

38. When Othello asks Desdemona to leave him a little to himself, she replies, "Shall I deny you? no, farewell, my lord" (3.3.87).

39. "Prithee unpin me" requires that the actress, as she speaks these words, call attention to Desdemona's erotic submission to Othello's violence.

40. As Gabrielle Jackson pointed out to me, Emilia feels that she must explain her refusal to observe her husband's commands to be silent and go home:

> Good gentlemen, let me have leave to speak,
> 'Tis proper I obey him but not now:
> Perchance, Iago, I will ne'er go home.
> *(5.2.196–98)*

The moment is felt as a liberating gesture and redeems her earlier, compliant theft of the handkerchief, but it is both too late and fatal. The play does not hold out the wife's disobedience as a way of averting tragedy.

41. Jacques Lacan, *The Language of the Self: The Function of Language in Psychoanalysis*, trans. Anthony Wilden (Baltimore: The John Hopkins University Press, 1968), p.11.

42. In effect, Othello invokes larger and larger spheres of self-fashioning: Othello to Desdemona, Othello to Desdemona and Brabantio, Othello to the Senate, Othello to heaven. We might add that the narrative element in formal auricular confession may have been heightened by the fact that confessors were instructed not to interrupt the penitent but to let him begin with a full and circumstantial account.

43. The word *confession* and its variants (*confess'd, confessions*) is repeated eighteen times in the course of the play, more often than in any other play in the canon.

44. See Thomas N. Tentler, *Sin and Confession on the Eve of the Reformation* (Princeton: Princeton University Press, 1977), and chapter 2 of Greenblatt, *Renaissance Self-Fashioning*.

45. This is a frequent response in the literature of colonialism; we have encountered it in Spenser's *View of the Present State of Ireland*, where he sees the Irish as living in certain respects as the English did before the civilizing influence of the Norman Conquest.

46. Tentler, p. 229. The *Eruditorium penitentiale* points out that in cases of necessity it is possible to kill or steal justifiably, "but no one may fornicate knowingly without committing a mortal sin." Tentler observes, "This kind of thinking is an exaggeration even of medieval puritanism. Yet it is also true that the climate of religious opinion allowed and perhaps even encouraged such exaggerations."

   Cf. Francis Dillingham, *Christian Oeconomy or Household Government* (London: John Tapp, 1609): "Julius Caesar made a law that if the husband or the wife found either in adultery, it should be lawful for the husband to kill the wife or the wife the husband. Death then by the light of nature is fit punishment for adulterers and adulteresses" (p. 13).

47. George Joye, *A Contrarye (to a certayne manis) Consultacion: That Adulterers ought to be punyshed wyth deathe. Wyth the solucions of his argumentes for the contrarye* (London: n.p., 1559?), pp. G4ᵛ, A4ᵛ. "The sacred integrity therefore of this Christ's holy church, the inviolable honor of holy matrimony ordained of God, the preservation of the private and public peace, all honesty, godly zeal to virtue, to the salavation of our souls and to God's glory should constrain every Christian heart to counsel, to exhort and to excite all Christian magistrates to cut off this contagious canker of adultery from among us, lest in further creeping, . . . it daily corrupteth the whole body of this noble realm so that it else be at last so incurable that . . . neither the vice nor yet the just remedy will be suffered" (A6ᵛ).

   The death penalty for adulterers was briefly adopted by the Puritan Parliament in the seventeenth century; see Keith Thomas, "The Puritans and Adultery: the Act of 1650 Reconsidered," in *Puritans and Revolutionaries: Essays in Seventeenth-Century History*, ed. Donald Pennington and Keith Thomas (Oxford: At the Clarendon Press, 1978), pp. 257–82.

48. William Perkins, *A Godly and Learned Exposition of Christs Sermon in the Mount* (Cambridge: Thomas Pierson, 1608), p. 111. See Robert V. Schnucker, "La position puritaine à l'égard de l'adultère," *Annales: Economies, Sociétés, Civilisations* 27 (1972), pp. 1379–88.

49. Quoted, with a mass of supporting material, in John T. Noonan, Jr., *Contraception: A History of Its Treatment by the Catholic Theologians and Canonists* (Cambridge, Mass.: Harvard University Press, 1966), p. 80. The Stoic marital doctrine, Noonan observes, "joined the Stoic distrust of pleasure and the Stoic insistence on purpose" (p. 47); early Christians embraced the doctrine and hardened its formulation in combatting the gnostic sects.

50. Noonan, p. 47.

51. John Calvin, *Institutes of the Christian Religion*, bk. 2, chap. 8, section 44, quoted in Lawrence Stone, *The Family, Sex and Marriage in England 1500–*

1800 (New York: Harper & Row, 1977), p. 499; *The King's Book, or a Necessary Doctrine and Erudition for Any Christian Man* (1543), ed. T. A. Lacey (London: Society for Promoting Christian Knowledge, 1932), pp. 111–12. See likewise John Rogers, *The Glasse of Godly Loue* (1569), ed. Frederick J. Furnivall, New Shakespeare Society, ser. 6, no. 2 (London: N Trübner, 1876), p. 185:

> Also there ought to be a temperance between man and wife, for God hath ordained marriage for a remedy or medicine, to assuage the heart of the burning flesh, and for procreation, and not beastly for to fulfill the whole lusts of the devilish mind and wicked flesh; for, though ye have a promise that the act in marriage is not sin . . . yet if ye take excess, or use it beastly, vilely, or inordinately, your mistemperance makes that ill which is good (being rightly used), and that which is clean, ye defile through your abusing of it.

In the seventeenth century, William Perkins informs his readers that the "holy manner" in marital intercourse involves moderation, "for even in wedlock, excess in lusts is not better than plain adultery before God." "This is the judgment of the ancient Church," notes Perkins, citing Ambrose and Augustine, "that Intemperance, that is, immoderate desire even between man and wife, is fornication" (*Christian Oeconomie*, trans. Thomas Pickering [London: Felix Kyngstone, 1609], pp. 113–14).

52. Le Roy Ladurie, *Montaillou*, p. 151. In fact the priest, who was, in Le Roy Ladurie's words, "an energetic lover and incorrigible Don Juan" (p. 154), held a somewhat different position. "One woman's just like another," he told Grazide's mother, "The sin is the same, whether she is married or not. Which is as much as to say that there is no sin about it at all" (p. 157). Le Roy Ladurie interprets his views on love as follows: "Starting from the Cathar proposition that 'any sexual act, even between married persons, is wrong,' he applied it to suit himself. Because everything was forbidden, one act was no worse than another" (pp. 158–59).

53. 1.5.107. Le Roy Ladurie quotes from the *Brévaire d'amour*. "A lady who sleeps with a true lover is purified of all sins . . . the joy of love makes the act innocent, for it proceeds from a pure heart" (p. 159).

   See Friar Laurence's warnings to Romeo about excessive love:

> These violent delights have violent ends
> And in their triumph die, like fire and powder,
> Which, as they kiss, consume . . . .
> Therefore love moderately: long love doth so.
> *(2.6.9–14)*

54. Tentler, p. 174.

55. Tentler, p. 181: "hoc est in executione ipsius actus nulla voluptatis delectatione teneatur."

56. Tentler, p. 183. According to the *King's Book*, over those who have violated

married chastity, "the Devil hath power, as the angel Raphael said unto Thobit, They that marry in such wise that they exclude God out of their hearts, and give themselves unto their own carnal lusts, as it were an horse or a mule, which have no reason; upon such persons the Devil hath power" (p. 112).

For a humanist's version of these notions, see the following aphorisms from Juan Luis Vives's *Introductio ad Sapientam:*

> The pleasure of the body is, like the body itself, vile and brutal.
> Sensual delectation bores the soul and benumbs the intellect.
> Sensual delectation is like robbery, it vilifies the soul. This the reason why even the most corrupted man seeks secrecy and abhors witnesses.
> Sensual pleasure is fleeting and momentaneous, totally beyond any control and always mixed with frustration.
> Nothing debilitates more the vigor of the intellect than sexual pleasure.
> (Carlos G. Noreña, *Juan Luis Vives* [The Hague: Martinus Nijhoff, 1970], p. 211)

For an attenuated modern version, see the first televised speech delivered from the Sistine Chapel on 27 August 1978 by Pope John Paul I; the pope prayed that families "may be defended from the destructive attitude of sheer pleasure-seeking, which snuffs out life" (*S.F. Chronicle*, 28 August 1978, p. 1).

57. In the early seventeenth century, Samual Hieron counsels married couples to recite the following prayer before going to bed: "Allay in us all sensual and brutish love, purifying and sanctifying our affections one towards another, that we may in nothing dishonor this honorable state, nor pollute the bed of marriage . . . but may use this thine ordinance in the holy sort, that carnal lusts may be slaked and subdued, nor increased or inflamed thereby" (*A Helpe Unto Devotion*, 3d ed. [London: H.L., 1611], p. 411).

58. *A Discourse of Marriage and Wiving* (London, 1620), quoted in Ronald Mushat Frye, "The Teachings of Classical Puritanism on Conjugal Love," *Studies in the Renaissance* 2 (1955), pp. 156–57.

59. William Whately, *A Bride-bush* (London, 1619), quoted in Frye, p. 156.

60. Noonan, p. 79.

61. A major textual crux, and I have taken the liberty, for the sake of clarity and brevity, to depart from Ridley's reading which is as follows:

> the young affects
> In my defunct, and proper satisfaction.

As Ridley says, "after all the discussion, Othello's meaning is moderately clear. He is too mature to be subjugated by physical desire"; but he goes on to read *proper* as "justifiable," where I would read it as "my own." Ridley's *moderately* should be emphasized.

62. Yet another crux: the Quarto reads "very quality" instead of "utmost pleasure." I find the latter more powerful and persuasive, particularly in the context of Desdemona's further mention (1.255) of "The rites for which I love him."

    Iago twice echoes Desdemona's declaration: "It was a violent commencement in her, and thou shalt see an answerable sequestration" (1.3.342–43) and again "Mark me with what violence she first loved the Moor" (2.1.221).

63. Desdemona is, in effect, a kind of mirror reversal of Cordelia: where the latter is doomed in the first act of the play by her refusal to declare her love, the former is doomed precisely for such a declaration.

    Professor Spivack, along with most critics of the play, sees Iago as the enemy of the religious bond in marriage (pp. 49–50); I would argue that it is precisely the nature of this bond, as defined by rigorists, that torments Othello.

64. On "property" see Kenneth Burke, A Grammar of Motives (Berkeley: University of California Press, 1969): "Iago may be considered 'consubstantial' with Othello in that he represents the principles of jealousy implicit in Othello's delight in Desdemona as a private spiritual possession. Iago, to arouse Othello, must talk a language that Othello knows as well as he, a language implicit in the nature of Othello's love as the idealization of his private property in Desdemona. This language is the dialectical opposite of Othello's; but it so thoroughly shares a common ground with Othello's language that its insinuations are never for one moment irrelevant to Othello's thinking. Iago must be cautious in leading Othello to believe them as true: but Othello never for a moment doubts them as values" (p. 414). As so often happens, I discovered that Burke's brilliant sketch had anticipated the shape of much of my argument. Burke has an essay on the ritual structure of the play in Hudson Review 4 (1951), pp. 165–203.

65. I have read two powerful unpublished essays that analyze the male sexual anxieties in the play at a level prior to or beneath the social and doctrinal one discussed here: Edward Snow, "On the Language of Sexual Pathology in Othello" and C. L. Barber, " 'I'll pour this pestilence into his ear'; Othello as a Development from Hamlet."

66. In act 4, Othello had first thought of poisoning Desdemona and then was persuaded by Iago to "strangle her in her bed, even the bed she hath contaminated" (4.1.203–4). The blood he fantasizes about later may be simply an expression of violence (as he had earlier declared, "I will chop her into messes" [4.1.196]), but it is tempting to see it as a projection of the blood that marked her loss of virginity and hence, in his disturbed formulation, as "lust's blood." For a sensitive exploration of the anxiety over virginity, staining, and impotence in Othello, see Stanley Cavell, "Epistemology and Tragedy: A Reading of Othello," Daedalus 108 (1979), pp. 27–43.

67. Like Oedipus, Othello cannot escape the fact that it is he who has committed the crime and must be punished.

    We should, in all fairness, call attention to the fact that Othello in the end views his wife as "chaste," but the language in which he does so reinforces the orthodox condemnation of pleasure:

> cold, cold my girl,
> Even like thy chastity.
> *(5.2.276–77)*

Indeed the identification of the coldness of death with marital chastity seems to me a *confirmation* of the necrophilic fantasy.

68. Shakespeare's talent for entering into the consciousness of others and giving supreme expression to incompatible perspectives has been a major preoccupation of criticism since Coleridge and Keats. For a recent exploration, see Norman Rabkin's concept of "complementarity": *Shakespeare and the Common Understanding* (New York: Free Press, 1967).

   In *The Anxiety of Influence* (New York: Oxford University Press, 1973), Harold Bloom remarks, "Shakespeare is the largest instance in the language of a phenomenon that stands outside the concern of this book: the absolute absorption of the percursor" (p. 11).

69. "Of Repentance," in *The Complete Essays of Montaigne*, trans. Donald M. Frame (Stanford: Stanford University Press, 1958), pp. 610–11. It is hardly irrelevant for our purposes that Montaigne describes this method in an essay in which he rejects the confessional system.

70. On pleasure and the threat to established order, see Georges Bataille, *Death and Sensuality: A Study of Eroticism and the Taboo* (New York: Walker & Co., 1962), and Mikhail Bakhtin, *Rabelais and His World*, trans. Helene Iswolsky (Cambridge, Mass.: MIT Press, 1968).

   See also Herbert Marcuse, *Eros and Civilization* (New York: Random House, 1955); Michel Foucault, *Discipline and Punish: The Birth of the Prison*, trans. Alan Sheridan (New York: Pantheon, 1977); Leo Bersani, *A Future for Asyanax: Character and Desire in Literature* (Boston: Little, Brown and Company, 1976).

   In *Unredeemed Rhetoric: Thomas Nashe and the Scandal of Authorship* (Baltimore: Johns Hopkins University Press, 1982), Jonathan Crewe of Berkeley investigates comparable issues in the work of Thomas Nashe.

3

"ELIZA, QUEENE OF SHEPHEARDES," AND THE PASTORAL OF POWER

LOUIS ADRIAN MONTROSE

Pastoral power might seem an oxymoronic notion, for pastoral literature is ostensibly a discourse of the powerless in dispraise of power. In his study of Elizabethan poetic kinds, Hallet Smith characterizes "the central meaning" of Elizabethan pastorals as "the rejection of the aspiring mind. The shepherd demonstrates that true content is to be found in this renunciation."[1] Smith's perspective on pastoral equates "theme" with "meaning"; my perspective distinguishes "form" from "function." The repertoire of pastoral forms includes images and metaphors; conventions of person, place, and diction; and distinctive generic features and their combinations. This repertoire was exploited and elaborated by Elizabethan poets and politicians, by sycophants and ideologues, by the Queen herself. My argument is that the symbolic mediation of social relationships was a central function of Elizabethan pastoral forms; and that social relationships are, intrinsically, relationships of power.[2]

The Arte of English Poesie, a guide to the practice of courtship and courtly poetry that was dedicated to Queen Elizabeth, claims that modern poets have devised pastoral poetry, "not of purpose to counterfait or represent the rustical manner of loves and communication: but under the vaile of homely persons, and in rude speeches to insinuate and glaunce at greater matters and such as perchance had not bene safe to have been disclosed in any other sort."[3] Puttenham suggestively describes a verbal complex that is literally pastoral in form, pervasively amorous in content, and intrinsically political in purpose. Puttenham calls allegory both "the figure of false semblant" and "the Courtier": "the Courtly figure *Allegoria*, is ... when we speake one thing, and thinke another, and that our wordes and our meanings meete not" (p. 186). In his peroration, Puttenham tells the Queen—"if it please your Majestie"—that her courtier should "dissemble his conceits as well as his countenances, so as he never speake as he thinkes, or think as he speaks, and that in any matter of importance his words and his meaning very seldome meete"; and that "our courtly Poet" should "dissemble not only his coun-

88

tenances & conceits, but also all his ordinary actions of behaviour, or the most part of them, whereby the better to winne his purposes & good advantages" (pp. 299–300). In Puttenham's own courtly discourse, the courtly poet and the courtier finally merge. Within this context of socio-literary analogies and ironies, Puttenham's own version of pastoral exemplifies his version of allegory. The otiose love-talk of the shepherd masks the busy negotiation of the courtier; the shepherd is a courtly poet prosecuting his courtship in pastoral forms.

In pastoral forms, Queen Elizabeth and her subjects could pursue their mutual courtship subtly and gracefully; they could perform a wide range of symbolic operations upon the network of social relationships at whose center was the sovereign. Queen Elizabeth is the cynosure of my essay as she was of Elizabethan pastoralism. But if the poet's task was to celebrate, the critic's task is to understand the uses of celebration. My purpose is to explore the range of motives in pastorals whose subject, audience, or performer was the Queen, and to situate this Elizabethan flowering of royal pastoral forms within the historical process of which it was a part.[4]

I PRINCESS AND MILKMAID

If Elizabeth's most memorable pastoral persona is to be a resplendent queen of shepherds, her quaintest is to be a humble milkmaid. In those anxious years under the rule of her Catholic half-sister Mary, Elizabeth seems already to have created for herself a rustic, "mere English" version of pastoral; it complements that which was to be created for her by her poets. Holinshed reports an incident that took place while Princess Elizabeth was under house-arrest at Woodstock (1554–1555):

> Thus this woorthie ladie oppressed with continuall sorrow, could not be permitted to have recourse to anie friends she had; but still in the hands of hir enimies was left desolate, and utterlie destitute of all that might refresh a dolfull hart, fraught full of terror and thraldome. Whereupon no marvell, if she hearing upon a time out of hir garden at Woodstocke, a certeine milkmaid singing pleasantlie, wished hir selfe to be a milkemaid as she was, saieng that hir case was better, and life more merier than was hirs in that state as she was.[5]

The episode is perhaps apocryphal but nevertheless attractive and instructive. The rejection of aspiration and the celebration of *otium* expressed here and in so many Elizabethan pastorals exemplifies what Puttenham characterizes as the recreative function of poetry: "the common solace of mankind in all his travails and cares of this transitory life" (p. 24). When they fulfill this function, pastorals and other imaginative forms are (in Kenneth Burke's fine phrase) "equipment for living." They are symbolic instruments for coping with the goddess Fortuna, with the endemic anxieties and frustrations of life in an ambitious and competitive society. Pastorals that celebrate the ideal of content function to articulate—and thereby, perhaps, to assuage—*dis*content. Elizabeth's pastoral impulse juxtaposes her experience of contingency and personal danger in a violent, deceptive world with an idealized lowly life in a world of unalienated labor synchronized with the orderly cycles of nature—the diurnal and seasonal rounds and the productivity of domesticated animals. Leisure and labor, aspiration and content, interact ambiguously in an hierarchical political context. A princess caught in a position of impotence and constraint projects herself into a lowly milkmaid. The subject is not the simple milkmaid but the complex princess-as-milkmaid; through Elizabeth's perspective, the actual powerlessness and compulsory physical labor of the peasant are transformed into a paradoxical experience of power, freedom, and ease. It was only society's elite, like Princess Elizabeth, who were in a position to be tragic actors upon the world-stage of history. The operations of pastoral forms may have provided them with a symbolic means to express and manage the threats and fears of living at or near the apex of the hierarchy, the center of power. But for the great, the material reality of a peasant's life can hardly have been a desirable or even a feasible option.

While a captive princess, Elizabeth might give pastoral form to a sentimental fantasy; as a queen regnant, she used pastoral forms as instruments of policy. In her speech to Parliament in 1576, in another response to the constant urging by the many men around her that she marry, Elizabeth wrote: "If I were a milkmaid with a pail on my arm, whereby my private person might be little set by, I would not forsake that poor state to match with the greatest monarch."[6] Elizabeth's rhetoric builds subtly upon an analogy of sexual and social hierarchies: a milkmaid is both a maiden and a peasant, both sexually and socially inferior to "the greatest monarch," the powerful male whom she would spurn. Elizabeth's hyperbole renders the marginal states of virginity and poverty as sources of power. The rhetorical point of the hypothesis, however, is that she herself is *not* a milkmaid, not a mere private woman but a great monarch in her own right. And if, as a poor and private milkmaid, she might eschew marriage on personal grounds, so much the more must she do so on political grounds: to marry would be to relinquish the anomalous but very real power that she enjoys as a maiden queen in a masculine and patriarchal world. She puts her policy succinctly in a remark to the earl of Leicester: "I will have here but one Mistress, and no Master."[7]

Elizabeth was fond of saying that she was married to her people, and she assured the Commons "that, though after my death you may have many stepdames, yet shall you never have a more natural mother than I mean to be unto you all."[8] As virgin, spouse, and mother, Elizabeth gathered unto herself all the Marian attributes. It was left to her preachers, propagandists, and poets to isolate the remaining female archetype—the whore—in the Catholic Mass, the Papacy, and the Queen of Scots. For purposes of public relations, however, Elizabeth might cast even Mary Stuart as a milkmaid. In the interval between Mary's trial and her execution, Elizabeth worked hard on speeches to Parliament, intended for publication and popular consumption, in which she reluctantly justified her government's proceedings:

> And if, even yet, now the matter is made but too apparent, I thought she truly would repent—as perhaps she would easily appear in outward show to do—and that for her none other would take the matter upon them; or that we were but as two milk-maids, with pails upon our arms; or that there were no more dependency upon us, but mine own life were only in danger, and not the whole estate of your religion and well doings: I protest . . . I would most willingly pardon and remit this offence.[9]

The royal rhetorician consistently invokes the pastoral contrast not as a desired escape from the burdens of *negotium* but as a foil for the exercise of power, not as a rejection of aspiration but as an assertion of authority.

According to William Empson, pastoral's characteristic operation is to put "the complex into the simple"; its characteristic effect is "to imply a beautiful relation between rich and poor" in which "the best parts of both [are] used."[10] His formulations are pertinent to some Elizabethan versions of pastoral. The pastoralization of the Elizabethan body politic puts the complex into the simple and puts public relationships of power into intimate relationships of love—a love that is variously spiritual, maternal, and erotic. It creates beautiful and benevolent relationships between the royal shepherdess and her flock, and between the queen of shepherds and the spiritual and temporal pastors who guard her flock: that is, between the sovereign and the whole people, and between the sovereign and the political nation, the elite through whom she governs her people. The gentleman lawyers of Gray's Inn, a nursery of the political nation, celebrated these relationships in the spectacular court revels of Shrovetide 1595.[11] The central device, Proteus's Adamantine Rock, splits open in the Queen's presence and the liberated masquers dance forth, drawn by the "trew adamant of Hartes" (l. 197), which is both England and England's Queen:

> Under the shadow of this blessed rock
> In Britton land while tempests beat abroade,
> The lordly and the lowly Shepheard both
> In plenteous peace have fedd their happy flockes.
> *(ll. 246–49)*

Characteristic examples of each of these pastoral forms of political relationship are to be found in the work of George Peele, one of the most assiduous and able of Elizabethan mythmakers. In *Descensus Astraea* (1591), a city pageant for the installation of the new Lord Mayor of London, the Queen is identified with the pagan virgin goddess of Justice. This identification was a popular one in the later part of the reign; Peele's innovation is to make his Eliza-Astraea a shepherdess, a "Celestiall sacred Nymph, that tendes her flocke / With watchfull eyes, and keeps this fount in peace."[12] Peele's pageant is part of an annual rite renewing the special relationship between the sovereign and the citizens of London; the pageant symbolizes that relationship as one between a shepherdess and her flock. "Astraea with hir sheephook on the top of the pageant" speaks reassuringly to her sheep and to her audience: "Feed on my flocke among the gladsome greene / Where heavenly Nectar flowes above the banckes" (11. 54–55). Astraea dwelt on earth during the Golden Age; a Golden Age of peace, prosperity, and Protestantism has descended upon England with the advent of "Our faire Astraea, our Pandora faire, / Our Eliza, or Zabeta faire" (11. 40–41). Peele expresses in delicate pastoral form the vital and wary economic relationship between the crown and the companies of London merchants, tradesmen, and artisans; he sublimates the expanding market economy of an age of gold into the maternal plenitude of a Golden Age.

One of Peele's numerous bids for aristocratic patronage was "An Eclogue Gratulatorie entituled to the right honorable, and renowned Shepheard of Albions Arcadia: Robert Earl of Essex and Ewe" (1589). In this Spenserian mixture of encomium and complaint, Peele elaborates the relationship of Essex and his forces to their royal mistress by a rather precious pastoral allegory. Essex "is a great Herdgroome, certes, but no swaine, / Save hers that is the Flowre of Phaebes plaine" (ll. 48–49); "He waits where our great Shepherdesse doth wunne, / . . . his lustie flocke him by" (ll. 56, 58). Peele includes a memorable contribution to the pastoral mythologizing of Sidney as "the great Shepherd good Philisides" (l. 62), and of Essex as Sidney's spiritual and ideological heir:

> With him he serv'd, and watcht and waited fate,
> To keepe the grim Wolfe from Elizaes gate.
> And for their Mistresse thoughten these two swains,
> They moughten never take too mickle paines.
>
> *(ll. 66–69)*

Peele's sentiment notwithstanding, Eliza often found such pains reckless and self-serving.[13] Indeed, she herself might use Peele's pastoral metaphor as an instrument of instruction and chastisement. When Thomas Arundell of Wardour returned from the Continent in 1596 an "Earl of the Holy Empire," the Queen of England expressed her displeasure in a pointed pastoral: "Betweene Princes and their Subjects there is a most straight tye of affections. As chaste women ought not to cast their eye upon any other than their husbands, so neither ought subjects to cast their eyes upon any other Prince, than him whom *God* hath given them. I would not have my sheepe branded with another mans marke; I would not they should follow the whistle of a strange Shepherd."[14] Prince, Husband, and Shepherd are analogized as superior terms in hierarchical opposition to Subject, Wife, and Sheep. The virgin Queen must have relished thoroughly her own paradoxical analogy.

Elizabeth enthusiastically adopted into her discourse the splendid pastoral persona given her by her poets. And her poets managed to find their own encomiastic uses for the rustic pastoral persona recurrently invoked by the Queen. When she entered the estate of the Countess of Derby at Harefield in the summer of 1602, Elizabeth was confronted by a dairymaid named Joan. Joan invited Elizabeth to spend the night in her dairy house and told her she would be better accommodated there than at the great house. Here at last, on what was to be her final progress, the aged queen had her opportunity to experience the life of a milkmaid. Joan went on to tell the visitors quite candidly that the intent of her hospitality was to oblige them to work at the harvest: "to carry them into the fields; and make them earne their entertaynment well and thriftily: and to that end I have heere a *Rake* and *Forke*, to deliver to the best Huswife in all this company."[15] The note in the printed text informs us that at this point the Queen was presented with "2 Juells." The episode has no more intrinsic dramatic or poetic merit than most Elizabethan royal entertainments. But the fascination and the power of such multi-media happenings lie elsewhere, in their facile deployment of the whole range of Elizabethan encomiastic strategies in a melding of life with art. A rake and a pitchfork for the best of huswives are also jewels in the shapes of a rake and a pitchfork for the best of queens. Like the entertainment of which they are a part, the jewels are both tangible and symbolic offerings in a transaction between giver and recipient. The pert dairymaid's allegorical gifts make a striking emblem for Elizabethan pastoral itself: objects and relations in the material world of peasant labor are sublimated into forms of lordly splendor. Like the poet's figuratively ornamented pastorals, the dairymaid's bejewelled rake and pitchfork "counterfait or represent the rustical manner of loves and communication" so as "to insinuate and glaunce at greater matters." It is to the sources and the substance of those matters that I now turn.

II   BODY POLITIC AND *CORPUS CHRISTI*

Michael Drayton rephrases a commonplace of Renaissance poetics when he writes that "pastorals, as they are a Species of Poesie, signifie fained Dialogues, or other speeches in Verse, fathered upon Heardsmen . . . who are ordinarie persons in this kind of Poeme, worthily therefore to be called base, or low . . . . The subject of Pastorals, as the language of it ought to be poor, silly, & of the coursest Woofe in appearance." The interrelated principles of hierarchy, analogy, and decorum produce a literary kind that is base in style, in subject, and in its status within a system of literary forms, within a verbal body politic. In his next sentence, however, Drayton reveals the inherent paradox of this pseudo-simple form: "Neverthelesse, the most High, and most Noble Matters of the World may be shaddowed in them, and for certaine sometimes are." Drayton's qualification alludes to the pastorals of Saint Luke's Gospel and Vergil's fourth eclogue: "The Blessing which came . . . to the testimonial Majestie of the Christian Name, out of *Sibyls* Moniments, cited before *Christ's* Birth, must ever make *Virgil* venerable with me; and in the *Angels* Song to Shepheards at our Saviours Nativitie Pastoral Poesie seemes consecrated."[16] Vergil's fourth eclogue celebrates an unborn child who will make time run back to the Golden Age. Christian exegetes accommodate Vergil's oracular and encomiastic Roman mythmaking by a creative misreading: the eclogue is an inspired nativity hymn, a prophecy of the advent of Christ and the Christian dispensation.

The amorous lyric—invitational, celebratory, or plaintive, Petrarchan, mytho-logical, or rustic—is characteristic of the great Elizabethan pastoral anthology, *Englands Helicon* (1600), and of Elizabethan pastoral poetry in general. But the Christological reading of Vergil's Golden Age eclogue and the pastoral imagery of the nativity and ministry of Christ may occasionally infuse the landscape of Elizabethan pastorals with an aura of religious mystery. *Englands Helicon* contains an example in E.B.'s "Sheepheards Song: A Caroll or Himme for Christmas."[17] Here the paradoxical languages of pastoral and religion merge: "For loe the worlds great Sheepheard now is borne / A blessed Babe, an Infant full of power" (ll. 33–34); "Sprung is the mirthful May, / Which Winter cannot marre" (ll. 39–40). Edmund Bolton, who is presumably the "E.B." of "The Sheepheards Song," also contributed to *Englands Helicon* "A Canzon Pastorall in honour of her Majestie" (p. 17). This lyric fuses pastoral's spiritual and amorous strains into a royal en-comium alluding to the month of the Queen's own nativity: "With us as May September hath a prime" (l. 8). Bolton's pastoral song for a national goddess appropriates the language of the shepherd's Christmas hymn: "Winter though every where / Hath no abiding heere: / . . . The Sunne which lights our world is alwayes one" (ll. 25–26, 28). Implicit in the juxtaposition of these two lyrics is the whole complex of verbal strategies I have called the Elizabethan pastoral of power.

The grounding of pastoral's power in the conjunction of classical and biblical mysteries, so eloquently described by Drayton, is better exemplified in the early fifteenth-century Nativity pageants of the Wakefield Master than in almost any Elizabethan pastorals. In the *Prima Pastorum*, in fact, one of the shepherds quotes and interprets the Vergilian prophecy at the dramatic moment of its fulfillment, at the birth of Christ. The events dramatized in these plays make spiritual love and power immanent in a world that is not allegorically but literally humble and pastoral. This quality fuses the sacred and the profane, the mysterious and the naturalistic, the biblical and the contemporary, in a popular and collective art form which exploits—as Renaissance texts rarely do—the radical social implications of pastoral's Christian context. Most Elizabethan pastorals were produced by poets and scholars under the patronage or influence of court and aristocracy or by gentleman amateurs; the social milieu and informing spirit of the Nativity pageants are alien to Elizabethan pastorals.

The religious mystery of Christ's double nature generates the pastoral paradox that Christ is both the Lamb of God and the Good Shepherd. In relationship to Christ, to a transcendent Lord metaphorized as a Pastor, *all* human creatures belong to a single flock of sheep. But among themselves, within the political domain, human creatures are most rigorously classified and stratified. The "Exhortation, concerning good order and obedience, to rulers and magistrates" (1559) is an authoritative exposition of Tudor ideology: "Everye degre of people, in theyr vocation, callyng, and office hath appointed to them, theyr duety and ordre. Some are in hyghe degree, some in lowe, some kynges and prynces, some inferiors and subjects, priestes, and layemenne, Maysters and Servauntes, Fathers and chyldren, husbandes and wives, riche and poore."[18] To translate into the discourse of pastoral: some are shepherds and some are sheep—some are the shearers and some are the shorn. A tension between temporal hierarchy and spiritual communion was woven into the fabric of traditional Europe's Christian culture; in pastoral forms, this tension might combine with a tension between literal and metaphorical shepherds, between peasants and lords. Such tensions are expressed and contained at the end of the Nativity pageant of the Chester cycle, when the three naturalistically presented shepherds who have witnessed the first Christmas resolve to become preachers of the Gospel; as V. A. Kolve puts it, "these shepherds of sheep have become shepherds of men."[19]

The verse from the Gospel of Luke (1:52) that was used as the Canticle for Vespers—"He hath put down the mighty from their seat, and hath exalted the humble"—was in daily use before the Reformation of the English Church. But, as Kolve writes,

> the text came into special prominence . . . during the Christmas season at the feast of the Innocents, when the custom grew up of electing from the choir a Boy Bishop for the day and allowing the boys to sit in the seats of their elders and superiors and to conduct certain of the divine offices. The truth enshrined in that custom was felt to be a part of the deepest significance of the Incarnation. England took the festival to its heart; it seems to have been more common there than anywhere else in Europe. And thus, this theme of the exaltation of the humble had a particular Nativity reference. Though it originally concerned the Virgin, it came to apply to the Innocents slaughtered by Herod, and directly to Jesus Himself: on Christmas a babe is born in a mean stable who will displace the powerful

> and privileged . . . . We see here wedded the two ideas: the humble over-
> throwing the mighty; the young overthrowing the old. It is a profound part
> of the meaning of the Nativity, and no Corpus Christi cycle neglects it.
> (pp. 156–57)

In the apocalyptic perspective of the cycle plays, the only true king is the King of Kings; even Christian rulers might be contaminated by Herod's image.[20] Elements of the inversion and levelling that were explicit in the divine pastoral of the Nativity texts might subtly infiltrate other pastoral forms. This context had to be expunged or transformed if pastoral metaphors were to function effectively as benign images of the stable and rigorously hierarchical social order which Tudor governments sought to establish and preserve.

The sixteenth-century movement toward the centralization of nation-states under the rule of dynastic monarchs proceeded internally against the power of local magnates and regional loyalties, and internationally against Reformation religious crises, political instability, and armed conflict. Changes in the nature and location of power and authority are inseparable from changes in the stucture and function of the symbolic forms in which power and authority are expressed, controlled, and enhanced. In regard to royal ceremonial, Roy Strong points out that

> the medieval heritage of festival was basically ecclesiastical, celebrating
> the prince in relation to Holy Church, his sacred anointing at his corona-
> tion, his presentation of myrrh, frankincense, and gold at Epiphany or the
> washing of the feet of the poor on Maundy Thursday. These occasions
> were inherited by the great dynasties of Europe in the sixteenth century
> but extended and overlaid by what might be described as a liturgy of State.
> This can be followed in its most extreme form in Protestant countries,
> where the splendours of Catholic liturgical spectacle were banished at the
> Reformation along with the old medieval saints' days. To replace these
> came State-promoted festivals.[21]

The Henrician regime abolished the rite of the Boy Bishop by royal proclamation and enacted statutes forbidding possession of the English Bible to anyone below the status of gentleman. A copy of Thomas Langley's *Abridgement of Polydore Vergil* bears this telling inscription: "I bout this boke when the Testament was obberagatyd [abrogated], that shepeherdys myght not red hit. I prey God amende that blyndnes. Wryt by Robert Wyllyams keppynge shepe upon Seynbury hill 1546."[22] The Catechism in the *The Book of Common Prayer* (1559), which all English children were supposed to know by heart, included a version of the pastoral "rejection of the aspiring mind"; it was a personal acknowledgment of the duty "to submit myself to all my governors, teachers, spiritual Pastors and masters. To order myself lowly and reverently to all my betters."[23] The monumental Statute of Artificers (1563) was notably concerned with the regulation of agrarian laborers and youths. Within the analogical system of thought that sanctioned social hierarchy, pastoral mystifications of relations between the humble and the mighty, the young and the old, were reinforced by examples of benevolent relationships between superiors and inferiors that were literally pastoral (the shepherd and his flock) and spiritually pastoral (Christ and humanity).

Power relationships might be metaphorized as pastoral relationships in various aspects of social life. But the pastoral analogy was a particularly apt ideological instrument for a government trying to subordinate the wills of all subjects to the will of their Queen, a government which had promulgated royal supremacy and popular uniformity in religion. References to the Virgin were excised from the English translation of the liturgy, and the pageants involving the Virgin were excised from the Corpus Christi plays. The process of suppressing the plays was virtually complete by 1580.[24] By that time, a professional city drama and amateur courtly poetry had begun to flourish. They were fostered by the Crown and employed in the creation of a syncretic Elizabethan mythology, iconography, and ritual. The Elizabethan suppression of the cult of the Virgin Mary, of the craft cycles, and of medieval spirituality and much of its related folk culture, inevitably involved the suppression of the popular and vital version of pastoral that was expressed in Nativity pageants.

These suppressions were in fact only a stage in a larger process of appropriation and transformation. A virgin Queen who united church and state, brought relative peace and security to her people, and secured the triumph of the reformed religion attracted to herself the feminine symbolism of the Virgin Mary as well as the pastoral symbolism of Christ's Nativity and the Church's ministry. The custom of celebrating the Queen's accession day began to flourish following the suppression of the northern rebellion and the York Corpus Christi play in 1569, and the promulgation of the Papal Bull excommunicating Elizabeth on Corpus Christi Day 1570. Roy Strong suggests that "Accession Day represented a development of the medieval tradition of combining a feast day of the Church with secular rejoicing. The Reformation had swept away many important Catholic feast days, above all Corpus Christi. . . . The rise of the Queen's Day festivities enabled these energies to be concentrated into a stream designed to glorify the monarchy and its policies."[25] In 1576, the Elizabethan Church made the Queen's accession day one of its very few official holy days; it became known as "The Birthday of the Gospel." And the Queen's own birthday, which happened to fall on the eve of the Virgin's Nativity, also came to be celebrated as a national holiday. It is no wonder that Catholic propagandists attacked the cult of the Queen as an abominable blasphemy, and that Puritans occasionally made so bold as to denounce it as idolatry. These dissenting voices of reaction and revolution frame what was an extraordinary transformation of cultural symbols—a transformation partly spontaneous and popular, partly calculated and official. It seems to have worked to various ends: to the emotional benefit of the populace, the political benefit of the government, and the economic benefit of the artists and craftsmen, performers and patrons, who helped to body it forth.

Yates and Strong have argued persuasively that there must have been a collective *psychological* need for rites and images to replace those obliterated in the Reformation. I would add that rulers and poets also had a vital "professional" need for them. The iconoclastic tendencies of reform threatened both the monarchy and the arts in which it symbolized itself. Eventually, the threat was realized in the Puritan revolution against the ideology of Stuart court culture—a revolution epitomized in Milton's response to the royalist "idolatry" of *Eikon-Basilike* with a tract entitled *Eikonoklastes* (1649). The Elizabethan government had to find ways to channel and delimit iconoclasm and to check the momentum of reform if the symbols through which its power was manifested were to remain untainted and efficacious.[26] This process of containment and decontamination was relatively successful in the short run, in part because "symbolic formations and patterns of action tend to persist longer than power relationships in changing socio-cultural systems" (Cohen, *Two-Dimensional Man*, p. 36). As Cohen explains, the ambiguity, flexibility, and multivocality characteristic of symbolic forms provide a measure of continuity in social change:

> Social life is highly dynamic, continuously changing, and if the symbols associated with these relations change erratically there will be no order, and life will be chaotic and impossible. . . . Symbols are continuously interpreted and reinterpreted. . . . It is this very "conservative" characteristic of theirs that makes symbolic formations so fundamental for the establishment and continuity of social order. One of the contradictions of social change is that it is effected through continuities. (pp. 37–38)

The pastoral images, motifs, and stylistic conventions of Elizabethan culture were grounded not only in literary history but also in contemporary religious and socio-economic experience; they constitute one of the "symbolic formations" contributing to the establishment and continuity of the Elizabethan regime in a period of religious and socio-economic upheaval. Elizabethan culture inherited and imported a richly heterogeneous pastoral tradition: pagan and biblical, satiric and romantic, rustic and courtly, religious and erotic. The makers of Elizabethan culture exploited an affinity between pastoral form and the feminine symbolism that mixed Marian and Petrarchan elements with a Neoplatonic mythography of love. Such a combination of symbolic formations was perfectly suited to the unique character of this ruler: a woman, a virgin, an anointed sovereign, and the governor of a reformed Christian church. Royal pastoral was developed into a remarkably flexible cultural instrument for the mediation of power relations between Queen and subjects.

One of the richest literary realizations of this symbolic complex is also one of the earliest: Colin Clout's "laye of fayre *Elisa*, Queene of shepheardes all," in *The Shepheardes Calender* (1579).[27] By placing his pastoral encomium of Elizabeth in the fourth eclogue, Spenser was challenging comparison with Vergil's "messianic eclogue." Colin, Spenser's pastoral persona, metamorphoses an Ovidian aetiological myth into a Tudor genealogical myth:

> For shee is *Syrinx* daughter without spotte,
> Which *Pan* the shepheards God of her begot:
>   So sprong her grace
>   Of heavenly race,
> No mortall blemishe may her blotte.
>   *(ll. 50–54)*

In the learned commentary pretentiously published with the *Calender*, E. K. glosses Pan both as Christ and as Henry VIII. The genealogy alludes to the immaculate conception of a blessed virgin, cleverly countering Catholic insinuations of Elizabeth's bastardy with an insinuation of her divinity. It also echoes the Anglican apologetics that justified the Queen's claim to be God's heir to the spiritual and temporal sovereignty of England. If we follow out the Ovidian logic of the myth, which E. K. retells concisely in his gloss, we see that Elisa is also the personification of pastoral poetry: the "offspring" of the love chase and the nymph's transformation were the reeds from which Pan created his pipe. Spenser's treatment of the symbolic union of Pan and Syrinx suggests three successive dimensions of meaning: in the simple allegorical correspondence that E. K. gives us, Elisa is Elizabeth Tudor, daughter of Henry and Anne and supreme governor of the English church and state; the Elisa of *Aprill* is also the idealized personification of the body politic, created by the Queen's poets, artisans, preachers, and councillors to focus the collective energies and emotions of her subjects and to harness and direct their diverse and potentially dangerous personal aspirations; finally, Elisa is the re-creation of the various accretions of Elizabethan symbolism into a new and complex image within Spenser's text. The first and second Elisas are subsumed by the third, who is engendered by the poet and his muse.

The genealogical myth is repeated at the center of the encomium. The pastoral poet now includes himself with the frame of the image that he is creating; the overworked and sunburned shepherd is present at a Nativity scene:

> *Pan* may be proud, that ever he begot
>   such a Bellibone,
> And *Syrinx* rejoyse, that ever was her lot
>   to bear such an one.
> Soone as my younglings cryen for the dam,
> To her will I offer a milkwhite Lamb:

>   Shee is my goddesse plaine,
>   And I her shepherds swayne,
>   Albee forswonck and forswatt I am.
>   *(ll. 91–99)*

"This our new Poete" (as E. K. calls him) has seized upon the combination of sources in which "Pastorall Poesie seemes consecrated" and has transformed them into a pastoral consecration of the English, Protestant, and Tudor present. Spenser's *Aprill* brilliantly epitomizes the synthetic achievement of the English literary Renaissance that it inaugurates. It fuses Vergilian imperial pastoral, Gospel nativity pastoral, and Arcadian erotic pastoral; eclogue, hymn, and love song. Elizabeth achieves an ideological fusion of classical *imperium* and Christian reform; Spenser's Elizabethan celebration achieves a poetic fusion of classical and humanist with medieval and native literary traditions.

The shepherd's *gift*—both his *talent* and his *offering*—is the power to create symbolic forms, to create illusions which sanctify political power; his expectation is a reciprocal, material benefit. At the center of the idealizing pastoral form within which the poet has created Elisa, the humble shepherd-courtier worships her. The adoring shepherd offers a milk-white lamb to his goddess; the ambitious young poet offers an encomiastic pastoral to his Queen. The poet who fathers Elisa is Elizabeth's subject and her suppliant. The eclogue thus suggests the dialectic by which poetic power helps to create and sustain the political power to which it is subservient. Spenser's *Aprill* is more than a brilliant and influential example of Elizabethan pastoral celebration. Its very subject is the paradoxical artistic and social process by which Elizabethan pastoral celebration comes into being.

III   COURT AND COUNTRY

The popular and medieval pastoral of the craft cycles was being weeded out at the same time that the elite and Renaissance pastoral of the lyric, romance, and masque was being cultivated. In the stylistic and thematic juxtapositions of *The Shepheardes Calender*'s moral, plaintive, and recreative eclogues, Spenser seems to strive for a synthesis of old and new. But most of the pastoral entertainments devised for presentation to the Queen in court and on progress strive to replace the old with the new. These occasional, celebratory, and ritualistic creations exemplify the dialectic between enduring symbolic forms and the flux of social relations. Although some of the entertainments performed on progress were more explicitly pastoral than others, the very institution of the progress had strong affinities with Elizabethan pastoral forms and thematics. The progress was, after all, a movement from the court and the city to the country, from Westminster and London to aristocratic estates, royal hunting lodges, and provincial towns. Temporarily removing from the physical center of power and trade, population and plague, the Queen on progress was living a pastoral romance. If the progress had the pastoral function of periodically renewing court and monarch by immersion in things healthy and natural, simple and traditional, it was also eminently pastoral in that it insinuated and glanced at matters greater than rustic bride-ales and mythological fantasies. It was a paradoxical fusion of *otium* and *negotium*, holiday and policy.

Elizabeth's summer progresses began with the reign and were an almost annual occasion for two decades. From the end of the 1570s until the beginning of the 1590s, Queen and government were preoccupied by diplomacy and warfare; progresses diminished while drama and masquing flourished in the court. Then, at the beginning of the 1590s, the Queen started travelling again and continued to do so until almost the end of her life. Plans were made but never realized that would have taken her as far as Shrewsbury and York, where the Councils of the Marches and the North administered the remoter regions of her island realm. Over the years, however, she did manage to see and be seen by great numbers of her subjects in the most populous, prosperous, and loyal regions of England. One of her recent biographers suggests that "over a large part of south-east and central England Elizabeth was a known, if not quite a familiar figure; there can have been few people in these areas who did not get a chance to see her."[28] In addition to the orations and debates, pageants and fireworks, dances and dramas that regularly entertained her, there were rituals of greeting and parting and of gift-giving by the local hosts at the boundaries of every shire, town, and estate. The Queen travelled in an entourage sometimes numbering upwards of five hundred. From her itinerant court emanated an aura of splendor and an illusion of authority that far belied the limits of her government's police power, administrative efficiency, and fiscal resources. Thus the progress was more than an instrument of public relations and a refreshing change of scene; it was an extraordinarily elaborate and extended periodic ritual drama, in which the monarch physically and symbolically took possession of her domains.

Elizabethan progresses and pageants and other public spectacles ranging from Garter rites to executions may usefully be thought of as examples of what social anthropologists call "social dramas." These are collective temporal forms, characteristic of all societies,

in which the political and the symbolic orders interpenetrate and affect one another. Each drama tries to effect a transformation in the psyches of the participants, conditioning their attitudes and sentiments, repetitively renewing beliefs, values and norms and thereby creating and recreating the basic categorical imperatives on which the group depends for its existence. At the same time, some or many of the participants may attempt

> to manipulate, modify or change, the symbols of the drama to articulate minor or major changes in the "message." (Cohen, *Two Dimensional Man,* p. 132)

This concept illuminates a basic feature of state spectacles: their various entertainments are framed within a larger social drama; performers, writers and artisans, sponsors, the Queen and her entourage, spectators—*all* are encompassed as participants within the social drama. The entertainments performed during a progress are plays-within-a-play. Of course, the entertainments acknowledge this fusion of art and life quite explicitly and in various ways: the Queen is directly addressed or she is included within the fictions; debates are referred to her wise judgment; conflicts are resolved, savage men are civilized, virgins escape defilement, blind men regain their sight simply by virtue of her magical presence. Elizabeth did not need to be provided with acting parts—she merely played herself. And she did so consummately well, as a dispatch from an attentive Spanish ambassador testifies: "She was received everywhere with great acclamations and signs of joy, as is customary in this country, whereat she was exceedingly pleased and told me so, giving me to understand how beloved she was of her subjects and how highly she esteemed this. . . . She would order her carriage sometimes to be taken where the crowd seemed thickest, and stood up and thanked the people."[29] Of Elizabeth's own performances on progress, Sir John Neale observed half a century ago that "the supreme moments of her genius were these, and if with their masques and verses her progresses belong to the history of the drama, they are no less part of the unwritten story of government propaganda."[30] To this I would add that the progresses and their entertainments did not serve the interests of the Queen and her government exclusively; they also proffered occasions and instruments to those in pursuit of offices and honors, gifts and pensions, influence and power. In other words, the symbols of celebration could be manipulated to serve simultaneously a variety of mutual interests and self-interests. They might influence the attitudes and sentiments of the royal actress herself, as well as those of her audience and her fellow performers.

Re-creating a text in the context of its performance will add substance to the preceding generalizations. My text is that of the scenarios, speeches, and songs intended for performance before the Queen at Sudeley during the progress of 1591.[31] The Sudeley entertainment has received little critical attention; admittedly, its literary merits are relatively slight. Such entertainments, however, have a significance that is genuinely historical *and* literary. They exhibit particularly well the social instrumentality of figurative language, the dialectic between power relations and symbolic forms.

Let us begin at the front door. "At her Majesties entrance into the Castle, an olde Shepheard spake this saying":

Vouchsafe to heare a simple shephard: shephards and simplicity cannot part. Your Highnes is come into Cotshold, an uneven country, but a people that carry their thoughts, levell with their fortunes; low spirites, but true harts; using plaine dealing, once counted a jewell, nowe beggary. These hills afoorde nothing but cottages, and nothing can we present to your Highnes but shephards. The country healthy and harmeles; a fresh aier, where there are noe dampes, and where a black sheepe is a perilous beast; no monsters; we carry our harts at our tongues ends, being as far from dissembling as our sheepe from fiercenesse; and if in anything we shall chance to discover our lewdnes, it will be in over boldnesse, in gazinge at you, who fills our harts with joye, and our eies with wonder. As for the honoreble Lord and Lady of the Castle, what happines they conceive, I would it were possible for themselves to expresse. . . . This lock of wooll, Cotsholdes best fruite, and my poor gifte, I offer to your Highnes: in which nothing is to be esteemed, but the whitenes, virginities colour; nor to be expected but duetye, shephards religion. (p. 477)

A pastoral "rejection of the aspiring mind" and a beautiful relationship between peasantry, aristocracy, and sovereign are expressed in the elegant and fashionable courtly rhetoric of a shepherd too simple to be anything but honest and plain. We are plunged immediately into the paradox—or the duplicity—of the pastoral style. The secular religion of devotion to a mistress that is the theme of so many Elizabethan pastorals appears here in its undisplaced political form, as duty to a social superior.

The old shepherd's vision of life in the Cotswolds idealizes the remnants of a feudal agrarian society. In fact, the English countryside was being profoundly transformed by the centralizing efforts of the Elizabethan regime, great advances in farming and husbandry techniques, demographic growth, and the expansion of a market economy.[32] Sheep were vital to the economy and society of the Cotswolds, and to the complex relations of production and distribution affecting the welfare of the whole nation.[33] Thus it was particularly appropriate that the Queen meet a shepherd in this part of Gloucestershire. The topography of the Cotswolds was ideally suited to the sheep-raising that flourished there, and the physical details of landscape and population are accurately reflected in the shepherd's speech. But the economic significance of animal husbandry, farming, and wool industries disappears into encomiastic iconography: in wool, "nothing is to be esteemed, but whitenes, virginities colour." Here pastoral's metaphorizing process is quite explicitly a process of purification. The shepherd's assertion demonstrates that the creation of figurative pastoral discourse involves a distortion, a selective exclusion, of the material pastoral world. One of the most remarkable features of this appropriation of pastoral forms by Renaissance court culture is its transformation of what in other contexts was a vehicle of agrarian complaint, rustic celebration, and popular religion into a vehicle of social mystification.

On the second day of the Sudeley entertainments, the pastoral style and setting change from rustic and local to learned and mythological. But the scenario continues to develop its royal theme: a celebration of the power of virginity and the virginity of power. The scenario enacts an episode from the first book of Ovid's *Metamorphoses* and then, in effect, metamorphoses it: Daphne, pursued by Apollo, is changed into a tree; Apollo's song concludes that "neither men nor gods, can force affection." "The song ended, the tree rived, and DAPHNE issued out, APOLLO ranne after," himself apparently quite unregenerate. "DAPHNE running to her Majestie uttred this": "I stay, for whether should chastety fly for succour, but to the Queene of chastety." Daphne is retrieved from the effects of Apollo's lust and craft by the power of Elizabeth's presence, "that by vertue, there might be assurance in honor" (pp. 479–80). Cotswold has become Arcadia. Elizabeth is the queen of this pastoral and sylvan domain; she incarnates Diana, to whom Ovid's Daphne is votary. When Ovid's Daphne cries to her father Peneus to help her, she is changed into the laurel. At Sudeley, Daphne's metamorphosis is less an escape than a demonic imprisonment from which she must be liberated. The Queen's virtuous magic derives from a kind of matriarchal virginity; her powers transcend those of the lustful and paternal pagan gods.

Daphne makes an offering to her savior: "these tables, to set downe your prayses, long since, *Sibillas* prophesies, I humbly present to your Majesty, not thinking, that your vertues can be deciphered in so slight a volume, but noted" (p. 480). She alludes to the oracular source of Vergil's "messianic" eclogue and to the sense of strain that arises when "the most high and noble matters of the world" are confined within poor and silly pastoral forms. The logic of combining Vergilian imperial pastoral with Ovidian erotic pastoral lies in the aetiological character of the Daphne myth as it is treated in the *Metamorphoses*. Apollo establishes the laurel as his tree and institutes the triumph:

> Thou shalt adorne the valiant knyghts and royall Emperours:
> When for their noble feates of armes like mightie conquerours,
> Triumphantly with stately pompe up to the Capitoll,
> They shall ascende with solemne traine that doe their deedes extoll.[34]

Such allusions deftly link the Sudeley entertainment to an ingenious political myth that claimed the spiritual and temporal authority of the primitive church and the Empire of Constantine as the inheritance of the Elizabethan regime. Frances Yates interprets this aspect of the Elizabeth cult in terms of an international policy:

> By claiming for the national church that it was a reform executed by the sacred imperial power as represented in the sacred English monarchy, the Elizabeth symbol drew to itself a tradition which also made a total, a

universal claim—the tradition of sacred empire. . . . The arguments for sacred empire—that the world is at its best and most peaceful under one ruler and that then justice is most powerful—are used to buttress her religious rights as an individual monarch. The monarch who is One and sovereign within his own domains has imperial religious rights, and he can achieve the imperial reform independently of the Pope. (*Astraea*, pp. 58–59)

This remarkably allusive entertainment weaves together Ovidian mythology, Vergilian and Sybilline prophecy, and Imperial policy with an iconography of virtuous desire adapted from Petrarch's *Canzoniere* and *Trionfi*. Petrarch wrote of Laura as another Daphne, the inspiration of his laureate verse; Elizabethan courtier-poets worshipped their royal mistress as another Laura.[35] At Sudeley, Daphne is liberated from her Ovidian arboreal form, and the triumph of heroic warfare is modulated into a Triumph of Chastity befitting a virgin empress.

The resonant complex of associations that unfolds during the entertainments of the first and second days at Sudeley is brought to a climax and conclusion on the third day. The festivities were in fact spoiled by bad weather but the intended scenario is preserved. "This it should have beene, one clothed all in sheepe-skins, face & all, spake this by his interpreter":

> May it please your highnes, this is the great Constable and commanda-dore of Cotsholde; he speaks no language, but the Rammish tongue; such sheepishe governours there are, that can say no more to a messenger than he, ([*here the* Constable *utters*] Bea!) this therfore, as signifying his duety to your Majestye, and al our desires, I am commanded to be his interpreter. Our shepheards starre, pointing directly to Cotshold, and in Cotshold, to Sudley, made us expect some wonder, and of the eldest, aske some counsel: it was resolved by the ancientst, that such a one should come, by whome all the shepheards should have their flocks in astonishment: our Constable commaunds this day to be kept holliday, all our shepheards are assembled, and if shepheards pastimes may please, how joyful would they be if it would please you to see them. (p. 481)

Royal compliment is leavened by rustic comedy. The combination of Ovidian metamorphosis and pastoral metaphor is consummated in the presentation of the high constable of Cotswold—a shepherd of shepherds—actually transformed into a sheep.

Although we have returned from Arcadia to the rustic here-and-now of the Cotswolds, the place and time are irradiated by the Queen's coming. "Her Majesty was to be brought amonge the shepheards amonge whome was a King and a Queene to be chosen" (p. 481). The scene would have introduced quite artfully the reversals appropriate to an apocalyptic moment. The pretty trifles performed by the shepherds and shepherdesses include a squabble over mastery between shepherd king and queen. Elizabeth is set apart from the kings of the earth when the shepherdess triumphantly concludes that "the Queene shall and must commaunde, for I have often heard of a King that could not commaunde his subjects, and of a Queene that hath commaunded Kings" (p. 482). When the shepherds consult their almanac regarding "the starr, that directs us hither" (p. 483), their eyes fall on the Queen's birthday, which had passed a few days before: "The seventh of September, happines was borne into the world." The prognostication which follows brings the pageant to its consummation in the here-and-now, in a mutual transformation of life and art: "At foure of the clocke this day, shal appeare the worldes wonder that leades England into every land, and brings all lands into England" (p. 484). The pastoral show has shifted from the metamorphosis of Daphne to the apotheosis of Elizabeth. The shepherds discover that the Queen is already in their midst; "espying her Majesty," they kneel and worship. It is a rare instance of prophecy's immediate fulfillment:

> This is the day, this the houre, this the starre: pardon dread Soveraigne, poor shepheards pastimes, and bolde shepheardes presumtions. We call our selves Kings and Queenes to make mirth; but when we see a King or Queene, we stand amazed. . . . For our boldnes in borrowing their names, and in not seeing your Majesty for our blindnes, we offer these shepheards weedes, which, if your Majestye vouchsafe at any time to weare, it shall bring to our hearts comfort, and happines to our labours. (p. 484)

So concludes the printed text of Her Majesty's entertainment at Sudeley. Poor shepherds playing kings adore their authentic sovereign lady. Celebrating the anniversary of her nativity, they laud the preaching of her gospel and the advent of a national and Protestant *imperium*.

Half a century earlier, the Protestant Princess Elizabeth had been living under constant threat and suspicion, a rural exile from her Catholic half-sister's court. Now she is the governor of state and church, the cynosure of court and country; she is moving through her land on a royal progress, in the procession of a blessed virgin. In entertainments like this, we find a confluence of the varied resources of national, religious, and personal symbolism that goes beyond appropriation of the Marian cult to associate the advent of Elizabeth with the Advent of Christ. The arrival of the Queen in this notable sheep-farming area at a time just after her birthday provides the circumstances for a metamorphosis of the scene that was acted in the pastoral Nativity pageants of the Corpus Christi plays. Thematically unified though loosely episodic in form, the cycle of pageants at Sudeley is given a kind of closure by its final offering. At her entry, the Queen receives a lock of wool; at the conclusion of the festivities, she receives what is presumably some rich garment made from Cotswold wool. During the entertainment's performance, wool is transformed into apparel; rural society is transformed into a pastoral playground; the Queen's visit is transformed into a theophany. The final gift offering to the Queen, from rustics who have played kings, conflates the adoration of the Magi and the adoration of the Shepherds with a felicitous economy typical of the humble form, "poor, silly, & of the coursest Woofe in appearance," in which, "neverthelesse, the most High, and most Noble Matters of the World may bee shaddowed." Vergilian eclogue and evangelical narrative, the two great traditions in which "Pastorall Poesie seemes consecrated," have been skillfully combined. The shepherds' final act of homage and offering combines intimacy and awe; it is a synecdoche for the social drama in pastoral form that the Queen and her hosts have performed. An eminently political occasion has been elevated into a spiritual mystery.

Reflecting on the Elizabethan iconography of empire, Frances Yates writes suggestively that "the lengths to which the cult of Elizabeth went are a measure of the sense of isolation which had at all costs to find a symbol strong enough to provide a feeling of spiritual security in face of the break with the rest of Christendom" (*Astraea*, p. 59). Yates implies that the cult is not only an instrument of foreign policy but also a source of strength, perseverance, and legitimation for the Queen personally and for the nation collectively. I would add that the persistence and elaboration of this cult during the reign undoubtedly served collaterally as an instrument of domestic policy, as another symbolic means by which the crown might procure the loyalty, obedience, and service of both the unenfranchised masses and the political nation. I have suggested that the Sudeley pageantry creates a complex and hyperbolic role for the Queen and a simple, collective, and idealized relationship between the Queen and her subjects. To specify the functions of this entertainment requires speculation about the motives and interests of its sponsor. My speculations proceed on the principles that human motives are complex, that the interest groups in Elizabethan society are heterogeneous, and that a multiplicity of meanings and functions can be articulated in the same symbolic form.

Sudeley Castle had been built during the troubled reign of Henry VI, in a period of great civil discord and dynastic power struggles among the nobility. In order to endure, the Tudor dynasty had to check such baronial disorder. But without its prior existence, Elizabeth's grandfather would probably not have been able to prosecute successfully his own relatively weak claim to the throne. Lawrence Stone stresses that

the greatest triumph of the Tudors was the ultimately successful assertion of a royal monopoly of violence both public and private. . . . The first task of the Tudors was to rid the country of the overmighty subject whose military potential came not far short of the monarchy itself. . . . This was

a task which could only be achieved by a hundred years of patient en-
deavour on a broad front using a wide diversity of weapons. It called for
a social transformation of extreme complexity, involving issues of power,
technology, landholding, economic structure, education, status symbols,
and concepts of honour and loyalty.[36]

It is precisely within this context of social transformation that the apparently
frivolous Sudeley entertainment should be understood. It is a minor but not insignificant event in the Elizabethan social process: it figures and manipulates
relations of domination and subordination in cultural forms. Both the royal visitor
and her baronial host are playing their parts in another of those continuous acts
of reciprocal courtship, display, and conciliation by which Elizabeth and the English peerage managed with relative success to maintain the stability of their caste
and a consensus of interests throughout the reign.

Giles Brydges, Queen Elizabeth's host, was third Lord Chandos and one of
some sixty peers of the realm. The Brydges were a long-established gentle house
that produced notable servants and soldiers for the Tudor dynasty; they had been
raised to the peerage by Mary. According to Stone, the titular peerage "comprised
the most important element in a status group, a power *elite*, a Court, a class of
very rich landlords, an association of the well-born"; the peerage should be viewed
as "the only common factor in a whole series of overlapping ranking variables in
a hierarchical society" (*Crisis of the Aristocracy*, p. 64). Stone cites Lord Chandos
as one of the great landowners who at Court "were less influential and less respected than a mere favourite like Ralegh, and of negligible consequence in comparison with a powerful official like Sackville or Egerton" (p. 63). Giles Brydges
may have lacked influence at Queen Elizabeth's court, but at the local level his
power rivaled hers. "In the late sixteenth century," notes Stone, "Lord Chandos
was known as 'King of the Cotswolds'."

In Gloucestershire in the 1570's, Giles Lord Chandos used armed retain-
ers with guns at the ready to frighten off the under-sheriff, protected servants of his who robbed men on the highway near Sudeley Castle, so that
the inhabitants dared not arrest the thieves nor the victims prosecute their
assailants, rigged juries, and put in a high constable of the shire who used
his office to levy blackmail on the peasantry. When summoned to the
Council of Wales he did not deign to come, retorting loftily that "I had
thought that a nobleman might have found more favor in your Courte,
then thus to be delt with (as I am) lyke a common subjecte." (*Crisis of the
Aristocracy*, pp. 229–30)

Such facts help us imaginatively to return a now-lifeless Elizabethan text to its
living context in the material relations of Elizabethan people.

By his actions and by his words, Lord Chandos exemplifies the exploitative rural elite who were traditional targets of agrarian satire and protest of the kind that could be heard at the opening of the *Secunda Pastorum*. The version of life in the Cotswolds presented to the Queen under this lord's auspices, however, has been metamorphosed into an extravagant but benign pastoral pageant of holiday games, prestations, and celebrations. The welcome, the gifts, and the acts of homage made by the shepherds to the Queen are presented on behalf of "the honoreble Lord and Lady of the Castle" (p. 477); presumably, the Queen's lordly host hopes to ensure a reciprocal flow of the perquisites, honors and offices, and grossly undervalued tax assessments that the aristocracy considered its due. The shepherds' prominence in the entertainments and in exchanges with the Queen is deceptive. The essential trick of this version of pastoral is to appropriate shepherd figures as mediators of a beautiful relationship between peer and monarch in which the best parts of both are used. The scenarios of the Sudeley festivities suggest a remarkable sublimation of the local conditions and events described by Stone: a terrorized and exploited peasantry are presented as happy shepherds and shepherdesses at play; a predatory high constable is replaced by "one clothed all in sheepeskins, face & all," who merely "baa's" meekly, in what seems a grimly comic miming of pastoral satire's "wolf-in-sheep's clothing" motif; a truculent and obstreperous magnate ("the King of the Cotswolds") turns Sudeley into Bethlehem in a show of love and fealty to "a Queene that hath commaunded Kings."

The social functions of the Sudeley entertainment and other such public spectacles are multiple and diverse. Yates suggests a collective psycho-social function for the Eliza cult, benefitting the Queen and the nation in terms of international politics and religious conflict; and I have suggested a supplementary socio-political function, benefitting the monarchy and the Elizabethan regime in terms of the loyalties of the English people. More particularly, in a context in which the commons were actually present as performers or as spectators, pageants like the one at Sudeley might fortify loyalty toward the crown among those whose relationship to the landlords who were their immediate and tangible superiors was one of endemic suspicion or resentment. "In the sixteenth century," writes Christopher Hill, "the threat to the unprivileged came not so much from the central government as from the local feudal lord, against whom the monarchy might be conceived as a protector. This was often found to be an illusion . . . the king's interests were inseparably bound up with those of the landed ruling class. Yet he *had* an interest in preventing the grosser forms of injustice, and in the maintenance of law and order" (*Reformation to Industrial Revolution*, p. 55). Thus the pastoral pageants at Sudeley and others like them might affirm a benign relationship of mutual interest between the Queen and the lowly, between the Queen and the great, and among them all.[37]

This complex and convenient ambiguity was produced by the interaction of *segmentary* power relations with *multivocal* symbolic forms:

> All politics, all struggle for power, is segmentary. This means that enemies
> at one level must be allies at a different level. . . . It is mainly through the
> "mystification" generated by symbolism that these contradictions are re-
> petitively faced and temporarily resolved. . . . The degree of "mystifica-
> tion," and of the potency of the dominant symbols that are employed to
> create it, mounts as the conflict, contradiction, or inequality between peo-
> ple who should identify in communion increases. . . . It is indeed in the
> very essence of the symbolic process to perform a multiplicity of functions
> with economy of symbolic formation. (Cohen, *Two-Dimensional Man*, p.
> 32)

There can be several dimensions to the political dynamic of Elizabethan pastoral
forms such as those of the Sudeley entertainment: they may function to transcend
socio-economic stratification in "a beautiful relation between rich and poor,"
to atone the commons, the gentles, and the Queen of England; they may function
to assert a bond of reciprocal devotion and charity between lowly subjects
and sovereign, perhaps strengthened by the implication of a common interest
opposed to the aristocracy; and they may function to confirm and preserve the
delicate balance of interests between the crown and the political nation, so that
power, wealth, and prestige will continue to be shared exclusively among the
shepherds of men. In the first instance, the whole people is united against a foreign
threat; in the second, the crown and the commons are united against a baronial
threat; in the third, the crown and the social elite are united against a popular
threat. From every angle, the political dynamic was advantageous to Eliza, Queen
of shepherds.

What is most impressive about Elizabethan pastorals of power is how successful
they really are at combining intimacy and benignity with authoritarianism. This
success must be attributed in large part to the fact of the monarch's sex and to
the extraordinary skill with which she and her courtier-poets turned that potential
liability to advantage. Sir John Hayward, who had been imprisoned by the Queen
for his *History of Henry IV*, ungrudgingly admired her mastery of the royal role:
"Now, if ever any persone had eyther the gift or the stile to winne the hearts of
people, it was this Queene . . . in coupling mildnesse with majesty as shee did,
and in stately stouping to the meanest sort."[38] "Coupling mildnesse with majesty"
describes perfectly the paradoxical effect and the particular utility of royal pastoral—of putting the complex into the simple, of placing Eliza among her shepherds and among her sheep. The "symbolic formation" of pastoral provided an
ideal meeting ground for Queen and subjects, a mediation of her greatness and
their lowness; it fostered the illusion that she was approachable and knowable,
lovable and loving, to lords and peasants, courtiers and citizens alike. What was
ostensibly the most modest and humble of poetic kinds lent itself effortlessly to
the most fulsome of royal encomia. The charisma of Queen Elizabeth was not

compromised but rather was enhanced by royal pastoral's awesome intimacy, its sophisticated quaintness. Such pastorals were minor masterpieces of a poetics of power.

IV   EPILOGUE

In the speech which opened his first English Parliament (1603), King James lectured the assembled lords, gentlemen, and citizens on the analogies of power: "I am the Husband, and all the whole Isle is my lawful Wife; I am the Head, and it is my Body; I am the Shepherd, and it is my Flocke."[39] Elizabeth's political predilection was as absolutist as James's but her own pastoral strategies were usually subtler, especially when she was playing to Parliament or the populace. Her performances were graced by a sure sense of public relations that her successors lacked or disdained. But there was more at work than the accidents of royal personality in the fragmentation and polarization of a national, Protestant, and humanist English culture during the Jacobean and Caroline reigns. P. W. Thomas suggests that

> there were it seems two warring cultures. But it is more accurate to talk of a breakdown of the national culture, an erosion through the 1630's of a middle ground that men of moderation and good will had once occupied. . . .
>
> The Civil War was about the whole condition of a society threatened by a failure of the ruling caste both to uphold traditional national aims and values, and to adapt itself to a rapidly changing world.[40]

In the 1630s, in the isolated splendor of the Caroline court, Queen Henrietta Maria sponsored and performed in Neoplatonic pastoral fantasies like *The Shepherd's Paradise* (1630) and *Florimène* (1635); while in *Lycidas* (1638), Milton was giving new force to Spenser's earlier pastoral attacks on a derelict and corrupt church hierarchy: "Blind mouths! that scarce themselves know how to hold / A Sheep-hook" (ll. 119–20).[41]

It was at the Hampton Court Conference (1604), when a Puritan divine mentioned presbytery, that King James remarked angrily, "no Bishop, no King."[42] His quip was to prove an ironic history lesson. When *Poems of Mr. John Milton* was registered for publication by the Puritan polemicist in 1645, he superscribed to *Lycidas* (first printed 1638) a note that it "By occasion foretells the ruin of our corrupted Clergy then in their height"; now Milton could claim membership in a tradition of vatic poets. First among the English poems in his 1645 collection, Milton placed "On the Morning of Christ's Nativity" (written 1629). In the ode's harmonious incorporation of Vergilian Golden Age eclogue and naive Christmas

carol, in Drayton's words "Pastorall Poesie seemes consecrated." And in the political context of the mid-1640s, Milton's first publication of his youthful work
takes on added resonance. For the poem's energy is not focused on ingeniously
paradoxical descriptions of the Incarnation or on homely details of the Nativity,
but on the intense imagining of a revolutionary moment:

> And Kings sat still with awful eye,
> As if they surely knew their sovran Lord was by.
>
> *(ll. 59–60)*

> Th' old Dragon under ground,
> In straiter limits bound,
>   Not half so far casts his usurped sway,
> And wroth to see his Kingdom fail,
> Swinges the scaly Horror of his folded tail.
>
> *(ll. 168–72)*

> In Urns and Altars round,
> A drear and dying sound
>   Affrights the *Flamens* at their service quaint;
> And the chill Marble seems to sweat,
> While each peculiar power forgoes his wonted seat.
>
> *(ll. 192-96)*

For Milton, spiritual revolution is also historical revolution; it demands a revival
and completion of the English Reformation. This implies a transformation of
polity and of culture, a recovery of the authentic sources and forms of pastoral
power.

NOTES

1. *Elizabethan Poetry* (1952; rpt. Ann Arbor, 1968), p. 10.

2. In this essay, I construe "power" and "politics" in broadly social terms. See
   Abner Cohen, *Two-Dimensional Man: An Essay on the Anthropology of
   Power and Symbolism in Complex Societies* (1974; rpt. Berkeley, 1976), p.
   xi: " 'Power' is taken to be an aspect of nearly all social relationships, and
   'politics' to be referring to the processes involved in the distribution, maintenance, exercise and struggle for power. . . . Power does not exist in a 'pure
   form' but is always inherent in social relationships."

3. Ed. Gladys D. Willcock and Alice Walker (Cambridge, Eng., 1936), p. 38.
   (Subsequent page references will be to this edition.) I accept the ascription
   of this work to George Puttenham. In quotations from this and other Elizabethan texts, I have modified obsolete typographical conventions.

4. My own selective and speculative study is indebted to the comprehensive

survey of royal pastorals in Elkin Calhoun Wilson, *England's Eliza* (1939; rpt. London, 1966), pp. 126–66.

5. *Holinshed's Chronicles of England, Scotland, and Ireland,* 6 vols. (1808; rpt. New York, 1965), IV, p. 133.

6. Quoted in J. E. Neale, *Elizabeth I and Her Parliaments 1559–1581* (New York, 1958), p. 366.

7. Sir Robert Naunton, *Fragmenta Regalia* (written circa 1630; printed 1641), ed. Edward Arber (London, 1870), p. 17.

8. Parliament of 1563. Quoted in Neale, *Elizabeth I and Her Parliaments 1559–1581,* p. 109.

9. Quoted in J. E. Neale, *Elizabeth I and Her Parliaments 1584–1601* (New York, 1958), p. 117.

10. *Some Versions of Pastoral* (1936; rpt. New York, 1968), pp. 22 and 11–12.

11. The text is preserved in BL MS Harley 541; I quote from the excerpts printed in Marie Axton, *The Queen's Two Bodies* (London, 1977), pp. 85–87.

12. Lines 20–21. All quotations are from *The Life and Minor Works of George Peele,* ed. David H. Horne (New Haven, 1952). Further line references will be noted parenthetically in the text.

13. See my study of the politics of Sidney's royal entertainments: "Celebration and Insinuation: Sir Philip Sidney and the Motives of Elizabethan Courtship," *Renaissance Drama,* N.S. 8 (1977), 3–35.

14. William Camden, *Annales or, the History of the most Renowned and Victorious Princesse Elizabeth,* trans. R. N., 3rd ed. (London, 1635), p. 469; quoted in Wilson, *England's Eliza,* p. 212. Elzabeth's pastoral metaphor could also be beneficent. For example, she nicknamed Sir Christopher Hatton her "Bellwether" and her "Mutton"; Sir Thomas Heneage wrote to Hatton (July 1581) that the Queen "willed me to send you word, with her commendations, that you should remember she was a Shepherd, and then you might think how dear her Sheep was unto her" (see Eric St. John Brooks, *Sir Christopher Hatton* [London, 1946], pp. 99–100, 302–03).

15. The text is printed from MS in John Nichols, *The Progresses and Public Processions of Queen Elizabeth,* 3 vols. (1823; rpt. New York, 1966), III, 586–95; I quote from p. 588.

16. "To the Reader of His Pastorals" (1619), in *The Works of Michael Drayton,* ed. William Hebel *et al.,* 5 vols. (Oxford, 1961), II, 517.

17. *Englands Helicon,* ed. Hugh Macdonald (1949; rpt. Cambridge, Mass., 1962), pp. 135–36. Further quotations are from this edition.

18. *Elizabethan Backgrounds,* ed. Arthur F. Kinney (Hamden, Conn., 1975), p. 60. This homily was first printed in 1547.

19. *The Play Called Corpus Christi* (Stanford, 1966), p. 154.

20. See Kolve, pp. 104–05 and 143.

21. *Splendour at Court: Renaissance Spectacle and Illusion* (London, 1973), pp. 21–22.

22. Quoted in A. G. Dickens, *The English Reformation* (New York, 1964), p. 191.

23. Rpt. in *Liturgies and Occasional Forms of Prayer Set Forth in the Reign of Queen Elizabeth,* ed. W. K. Clay (1847; rpt. New York, 1968), p. 213.

24. See Harold C. Gardiner, S. J., *Mysteries' End* (New Haven, 1946).

25. *The Cult of Elizabeth: Elizabethan Portraiture and Pageantry* (London, 1977), p. 119. On Accession Day rites, see J. E. Neale, *Essays in Elizabethan History* (London, 1958), pp. 9–20; Frances A. Yates, *Astraea: The Imperial Theme in the Sixteenth Century* (London, 1975), pp. 88–111; and Strong, *The Cult of Elizabeth,* pp. 117–62.

26. On iconoclasm, see John Phillips, *The Reformation of Images: Destruction of Art in England, 1535–1660* (Berkeley, 1973); on the production, distribution, and desecration of the royal image, see Roy C. Strong, *Portraits of Queen Elizabeth I* (Oxford, 1963).

27. The lay was reprinted separately in *Englands Helicon.* References are to the often reprinted one-volume Oxford Standard Authors edition of Spenser's *Poetical Works,* ed. J. C. Smith and E. de Selincourt. In the following discussion, I borrow some phrases from my longer study of the *Calender.* " 'The perfecte paterne of a Poete': The Poetics of Courtship in *The Shepheardes Calender,*" *Texas Studies in Literature and Language,* 21 (Spring 1979), 34–67.

28. Paul Johnson, *Elizabeth I: A Study in Power and Intellect* (London, 1974), p. 226.

29. *Calendar of State Papers, Spanish* (1568–1579), pp. 50–51, quoted in Neville Williams, *Elizabeth, Queen of England* (London, 1967), p. 233.

30. "The Sayings of Queen Elizabeth" (1926), rpt. in *Essays in Elizabethan History,* p. 96.

31. Printed in *Speeches Delivered to Her Majestie this Last Progresse,* etc. (Oxford, 1592; rpt. in *The Complete Works of John Lyly,* ed. R. Warwick Bond, 3 vols. (Oxford, 1902), I. 477–84. Parenthetical citations in my text will be to volume one of this edition. Bond's ascription of the work to Lyly on stylistic grounds has received no substantiation. I have chosen this entertainment for detailed study because it is pastoral, short, and skillful in its rhetorical strategies.

32. *The Agrarian History of England and Wales, Volume IV, 1500–1640,* ed. Joan Thirsk (Cambridge, Eng., 1967), is comprehensive and technical. There are concise surveys in Christopher Hill, *Reformation to Industrial Revolution,* rev. ed., The Pelican Economic History of Britain, Volume 2, 1530–1780 (Harmondsworth, 1969), pp. 61–71; and D. C. Coleman, *The Economy of England 1450–1750* (New York, 1977), pp. 31–47.

33. See Peter J. Bowden, *The Wool Trade in Tudor and Stuart England* (London,

1962), p. xv: "Wool was, without question, the most important raw material in the English economic system. . . . Every class in the community, whether landlord, farmer, merchant, industrial capitalist or artisan, had an interest in wool, and it was the subject of endless economic controversy." On Cotswold ecology, see Thirsk, *Agrarian History*, pp. 64–66.

34. *Ovid's Metamorphoses: The Arthur Golding Translation* (1567), ed. John Frederick Nims (New York, 1965), I, 687–90. Like Golding's translation, the Sudeley pageant is considerably more pastoral in its treatment of the Daphne myth than is Ovid's original. In Spenser's *Aprill*, the Muses bring bay branches to adorn Elisa; E. K. glosses them as "the signe of honor and victory, and therefore of myghty Conquerors worn in theyr triumphes, and eke of famous Poets" (*Poetical Works*, p. 434).

35. See Wilson, *England's Eliza*, pp. 230–72; Yates, *Astraea*, pp. 112–20.

36. *The Crisis of the Aristocracy 1558–1641* (Oxford, 1965), pp. 200–1.

37. Compare Joel Hurstfield, *Freedom, Corruption and Government in Elizabethan England* (London, 1973), p. 46: "To understand the relationship between the Tudor people and their governments, it is essential to take into account that this was minority rule, an uneasy and unstable distribution of power between the Crown and a social elite in both the capital and the shires, and that this governing class, this elite, itself played a double role. It was under pressure to conform and was at the same time the channel of communication for a vast mass of propaganda in defense of the existing order, pumped out through press and pulpit, through preambles to Acts and through proclamations read out in the market-place, through addresses to high court judges in Star Chamber and by high court judges at the assizes, through all the pageantry and symbolism of royal progresses."

38. Hayward, *Annals*, ed. John Bruce (London, 1840), pp. 6–7, quoted in Neale, *Essays in Elizabethan History*, p. 92.

39. *The Political Works of James I*, ed. C. H. McIlwain (1918; rpt. New York, 1963, p. 292.

40. "Two Cultures? Court and Country under Charles I," in *The Origins of the English Civil War*, ed. Conrad Russell (London, 1973), pp. 184 and 193.

41. Texts and parenthetical line numbers follow John Milton, *Complete Poems and Major Prose*, ed. Merritt Y. Hughes (New York, 1957).

42. See David Harris Willson, *King James VI & I* (1956; rpt. New York, 1967), p. 207.

4

SHAKESPEARE'S EAR

JOEL FINEMAN

In my book on Shakespeare's sonnets I argued, on more or less formal, even formalist, grounds that in his sonnets Shakespeare invented what is an altogether novel but subsequently governing model of subjectivity in our literary history—recognizing that the word *literary* in the phrase *literary history* has a particular historical formation, just as the word *history*, in the same phrase, is a function of, an effect of, a particular literary form. This argument about the invention of Shakespearean subjectivity, whether right or wrong, is a strong one because it straightforwardly asserts that, at a specific level of generality, and within the context of a specific, notably self-conscious, literary tradition, there is something exigent, necessary, predetermined about the construction and reception of Shakespeare's lyric subject. Putting the point as bluntly as possible, I argued in my book that in his sonnets Shakespeare comes upon, i.e., he "invents," the *only* ways in which or through which subjectivity, understood as a particular literary phenomenon, can be coherently thought and effectively produced in the literature of the West.

Summarizing, very briefly, the main lines of that argument, I began by saying that Shakespeare writes at the end of a tradition—one quite central to the development of the Renaissance sonnet—that identifies the literary, and therefore literary language, with idealizing, visionary praise, a tradition in which there obtains, at least figuratively speaking, an ideal Cratylitic correspondence, usually figured through motifs of visual or visionary language, between that which is spoken and that which is spoken about. However, because Shakespeare, when he sits to sonnets, registers the conclusion of this tradition of the poetics and poetry of praise—a tradition that reaches back to the invention of the "literary" as an intelligible theoretical category—he, Shakespeare, is obliged, in order to be literary, to recharacterize language as something duplicitously and equivocally verbal rather than as something truthfully and univocally visual. It was my argument that this linguistic revision of a traditional language of vision both enables and

116

constrains Shakespeare to develop novel literary subjects or verbal representation for whom the very speaking of language is what serves and works to cut them off from their ideal and visionary presence to themselves. Citing Shakespeare's sonnet 152, I called this generic Shakespearean subject the subject of a "perjured eye," and I further maintained that the reader of Shakespeare's sonnets, precisely because Shakespeare's sonnets remark themselves as something verbal, not visual, of the tongue and not the eye, will therefore find, though in a paradoxical way, that the language of the sonnets performs, and thereby stands as warrant for, what the sonnets speak about.

According to this argument, a variety of literary features—at the level of theme, motif, and trope—contribute to and follow from what I take to be an historically significant entropic evacuation of the poetics of idealization. Further, according to this argument, these literary features, taken together, in turn determine, in quite specific ways, the psychologistic profile of the literary subject who opens his mouth to speak in the aftermath of praise. For example, guided by the way Shakespeare's sonnets move from the young man subsequence to the dark lady subsequence, and distinguishing between a bliss that is always virtually achieved and, in contrast, a desire that is always, by virtue of its constitution, structurally unsatisfiable, I argued that Shakespeare's sonnets, because they displace ideal vision by corrupt language, thereby confront the traditionally homogeneous speaker of epideictic lyric with an essential, and theretofore unspeakable, heterogeneity, with the result that the speaker of Shakespeare's sonnets, fleshing out this difference, becomes the subject of an altogether unprecedented verbal desire for what is not admired. In the book, putting this point very grandly, I said that Shakespeare's sonnets, because they explicitly put the difference *of* language into words, thereby invent and motivate the poetics of heterosexuality, by which I meant to specify a necessarily misogynist desire, on the part of a necessarily male subject, whom the sonnets call "Will," for the true-false Woman who exists as a peculiar and paradoxical but still necessary "hetero-," or other or difference, to the essential sameness of a familiar and profoundly orthodox "homo-." In this way, paradoxing the orthodox, Shakespeare's sonnets manage to activate at a psychologistic level what are of course, in the literary tradition Shakespeare inherits, conventional, but not characterologically textured, erotic topoi. (One local virtue of such an account, I thought, is that it allows one to speak to the gender determinations of Shakespeare's sonnets—and, beyond the sonnets, to the gender determinations that operate in Shakespeare's other writings—in a way that does not import into the discussion unspoken assumptions about agency and motivation that stand at conceptual odds with—indeed, usually undercut from the start—the ethical and political concerns of reductively psychologistic criticism of Shakespearean characterology.) In passing I will say, parenthetically, that this atavistic and sentimental allegiance to the idea and idealization of the autonomous human and humanist subject, male or female, precisely because it begs the question of the subject, amounts to a characteristic failure of Shakespearean criticism—characteristic and Shakespearean because such criticism, whatever its explicit ideological intentions, not only responds to but also capitulates to the historical hegemony of Shakespearean characterology: this is surely the greatest weakness of much contemporary criticism of Shakespeare.

It will be recognized that the subjectivizing consequences, within the domain of literature, that my argument about Shakespeare's sonnets wants to derive from the disjunctive conjunction of, on the one hand, a general thematics of vision and, on the other, a general thematics of voice, bears striking similarities to Jacques Lacan's account of the constitution of the subject through the capture of what he calls an Imaginary register—which Lacan figures through visionary motifs—by what he calls a Symbolic register—which Lacan figures through motifs of spoken speech. I briefly remarked this affinity in my book, and argued that the similarity derived from the fact that the Lacanian subject in particular, and the psychoanalytic subject in general, were epiphenomenal consequences of the Renaissance invention of the literary subject. Some people have disagreed with this claim, preferring to put things the other way around. In either case, however, whether we see Lacan as Shakespearean or Shakespeare as Lacanian, the argument I developed, depending as it did on exigent determinations arising out of the relation of visionary presence to verbal representation, lays itself open to the kind of criticism Jacques Derrida has directed against what he understands to be Lacan's logocentric, phallogocentric, sexist account of the construction of the linguistic subject. For Derrida, and for poststructuralism in general, there is a more radical difference constitutive of, yet different from and extrinsic to, the structuralist difference of language, a difference—more precisely an activity of *différance*, both difference and deferral—that Derrida figures in terms of writing and textuality, the peculiar phenomenality of which serves to break the totalizing structurations of Lacan's broken subject. Even though the argument of my book restricts itself to a discussion of the domain of literature, it is open to the same kind of critique, for in establishing its large opposition between, on the one hand, the thematics and ontology of literary vision and, on the other, the thematics and ontology of literary voice, the book assimilates the activity of writing to speech, thereby leaving to the side the fact that Shakespeare's sonnets are necessarily written and not necessarily spoken, just as their words on the page are necessarily visualized as typographic letters and not necessarily heard as vocalized words. I acknowledged this possible objection in the introduction to my book, but argued that Derrida's criticisms of Lacan, especially as these are formulated in the name of writing and textuality, are themselves a part, and a systematic part, of the system of the perjured eye, rather than a critique thereof. And that—I quote from the introduction—

Derrida's subsequent attempt to rupture Lacan's rupture, Derrida's putatively postsubjective account of supplemental *différance* seems, from the point of view of Shakespeare's sonnets, nothing but another "increase" that "from fairest creatures we desire" [here referring to the first line of Shakespeare's first sonnet, "From fairest creatures we desire increase"], a subjective indeterminacy already predetermined . . . by the exigencies of literary life [here assuming the wrinkle, literally the "crease," that Shakespeare introduces into the poetics of copious "increase"] . . . . What Derrida calls "writing," the thematics of the deconstructive "trace" Derrida associates with *écriture*, is not beyond Shakespeare's sonnets but is instead anticipated and assimilated by them to the theme of language, with the two of these together being opposed to the theme of vision.[1]

I would still say much the same—in fact, precisely the same—but I am nevertheless now more interested in how it happens this wrinkle or crease of textuality—what Derrida calls *écriture*, what Lacan calls the Real, a Real that can be neither specularized nor represented but the marks of which are the condition and consequence of both specularity and representation—precipitates and is precipitated by the disjunctive coordination of the specular and the spoken. I am interested in this because, having formulated, I believe, in the book on Shakespeare's sonnets—though, again, only at a specific level of generality and, again, I could be wrong—the formal constraints governing the formation of literary subjectivity in our literary tradition, I am now concerned, in the book I am writing on Shakespeare's plays called *Shakespeare's Will*, to understand how and why it happens these formalist constraints are realized at a particular moment, by a particular individual, and with particular consequences. Thus, where the book on Shakespeare's sonnets was concerned with the formal invention of a generic Shakespearean persona, I am now concerned to understand how it happens that a particular and idiosyncratic person, Shakespeare, informs and is informed by that formal persona; and this is an interesting question, I think, because it helps to explain how it happens that a single individual, Shakespeare, the person, speaks to and founds an institution, the Shakespearean. To answer this question, however, it is necessary to understand why in our literary tradition it is necessarily writing, as such, that exists as that which constitutively intermediates between voice and vision.

In the context of this question, i.e., the question of the text and its relation to vision and speech, I turn now to the famous, so-called Rainbow Portrait of Queen Elizabeth (fig. 1), which is the picture I selected for the cover of my book on Shakespeare's sonnets, on the grounds that, to my mind, it illustrates the book's argument. The meaning of this picture, tentatively attributed to Isaac Oliver, has always been somewhat enigmatic, but what interests me in particular about the picture, and is the reason why I chose it for the cover of my book, is the somewhat bizarre design of ornamental, isolated eyes and mouths and ears with which the painting decorates the queen's elaborate dress. This iconography, of eyes and

Figure 1. The "Rainbow" portrait of Queen Elizabeth I, attributed to Isaac Oliver, c. 1600. Reprinted from Joel Fineman, *Shakespeare's Perjured Eye: The Invention of Poetic Subjectivity in the Sonnets*, by permission of the Marquess of Salisbury, Hatfield House.

mouths and ears, derives, one assumes, from Vergil's famous description of Rumor or *Fama* in book 4 of *the Aeneid*—"as many tongues, so many sounding mouths, so many pricked ears"—a conflation transmitted to the Renaissance through such authors as Boethius and Chaucer—though just why a celebratory portrait of the queen should so directly associate her with the negatively charged figure of Rumor—e.g., Spenser's House of Fame—is something of a mystery, though by no means an irresolvable one.[2] The topos is of course known to and favored by Shakespeare, e.g., in *Titus Andronicus*: "Like the house of Fame, / The palace full of tongues, of eyes, and ears" (2.1.126–27); *2 Henry IV*: "Open your ears, for which of you will stop / the vent of hearing when loud Rumor speaks" (Ind.1); or *2 Henry VI*, "Where fame, late ent'ring at his heedful ears, / hath plac'd thy beauty's image" (3.3.62–63). That Shakespeare characteristically concatenates ears-eyes-and-voice is also well known, e.g., Bottom in *A Midsummer Night's Dream*: "The eye of man hath not heard, the ear of man hath not seen" (4.1.211–12); or when Troilus "invert[s] th' attest of eyes and ears" (5.2.122), just as this concatenation is something Shakespeare tends to associate with the specifically rhetorical, e.g., in *The Merry Wives of Windsor*, *"Pistol*: He hears with ears. *Evans*: [. . .] What phrase is this? 'He hears with ears'? Why, it is affectations" (1.1.148–50). Given all this, what is genuinely mysterious and surprising about the Rainbow Portrait, especially if we assume this large picture was originally displayed at court, is the way the painting places an exceptionally pornographic ear over Queen Elizabeth's genitals, in the crease formed where the two folds of her dress fold over on each other, at the wrinkled conclusion of the arc projected by the dildolike rainbow clasped so imperially by the virgin queen. I think of this ear as one version of the "increase" that "from fairest creatures we desire" to which I earlier referred. (In reproduction, the vulvalike quality of the ear is perhaps not so readily apparent, but, enlarged and in florid color, the erotic quality of the image is really quite striking, as is the oddly colorless quality of the rainbow, a kind of dead rainbow.)

For reasons that I think are relatively obvious, I took this picture as a straightforward illustration of two central arguments in my book on Shakespeare's sonnets, first, that the difference between language and vision, i.e., the difference between eyes and mouths, is what precipitates a specific fetishistic erotics, the vulvalike ear, an erotics that is correlative to an equally fetishistic principle of sovereign power that is imaged by the picture's depiction of the queen as a whole. This kind of bifold erotics calls forth this kind of sovereignty, or "Bifold Authority," and vice versa. So too, I took the painting's caption, on the left, in the odd, dimensionless space that writing tends to occupy in pictures, as a summary statement of the way in which certain deconstructive thematics, whatever their intentions, necessarily participate within the system they intend to rebuke, a point I consider important, given a variety of recent, more or less abortive, attempts to deconstruct the Renaissance text. "Non sine sole Iris," as the picture puts it, i.e., "No rainbow without the Sun," is for me a very eloquent and true description of the way the iridescent fragmentation of a photo-logocentric light works, and always has been seen to work, to resecure the ruling order of the sun.

What I want to mention here, or really what I will be obliged simply to assert, is that there are reasons to associate this salacious ear that both covers and discovers the genitals of Queen Elizabeth with a specific and historically determinate Renaissance sense of textuality; and this is a point worth following out, I think, first, because it suggests an identifiable complicity that links, by means of an unspoken necessity, Renaissance textuality, sexuality, and ideology one to each of the two others, in a link or collation the historical stability and specificity of which at least raises the possibility that it is Renaissance textuality, as such, that predicates a particular system of sexuality and ideology. Second, I think this point would be worth following out because, if demonstrated, it would again follow that various contemporary, deconstructive conceptualizations of reading once again recapitulate—or rather, effect a repetition that capitulates to—the movements and motifs of the Renaissance text, and this not simply at the level of topoi but in a more general registration of the phenomenality of the textual.

As I say, I cannot here develop this argument in any detailed, textured way— if it happens anyone wants to see a preliminary version of this argument, he or she can take a look at my essay on "The Rape of Lucrece," "Shakespeare's *Will*: The Temporality of Rape."[3] I can, however, gesture toward that argument by means of two quotations. The first is from a poem on hearing by John Davies, which comes from his *Nosce Teipsum*, i.e., "know thyself," a collection of poems on the immortality of the soul. The poem on "Hearing" follows a corresponding poem on "Sight," one that articulates various Renaissance commonplaces about "the quick power of sight," and it is in contrast to this immediacy of vision that Davies in the succeeding poem identifies the ear as organ of delay:

> These wickets of the Soule area plac't on hie
> Because all sounds doe lightly mount aloft;
> And that they may not pierce too violently,
> They are delaied with turnes and windings oft.
>
> For should the voice directly strike the braine,
> It would astonish and confuse it much;
> Therefore these plaits and folds the sound restraine,
> That it the organ may more gently touch.
>
> As streames, which with their winding banks doe play,
> Stopt by their creeks, run softly through the plaine,
> So in th' Eares' labyrinth the voice doth stray,
> And doth with easie motion touch the braine.
>
> It is the slowest yet the daintiest sense.[4]

As that which slows the logos, leading it astray within its labyrinthine folds and plaits, the Ear for Davies functions as the intermediating maze that saves the brain from a too quick arrival of the sense or voicing of speech, a speech that would otherwise strike the brain like an astonishing flash of light. It is for this reason, taking Davies's poem as index of something larger than itself, that we can understand the Ear, a specifically Renaissance Ear, as instrument of delay and deferral—what Derrida calls the *différance*, both spatial and temporal, that is prior to any difference whatsoever, and what Shakespeare, I have tried to argue, as in my essay on "The Rape of Lucrece," also comprehends in terms of a subjectivizing temporal distention and dilation when he writes his metaphor of "post." I believe this helps to explain why for Shakespeare the ear is so often a figure of momentous suspense, as in *Hamlet*, when the fall of Ilium "takes prisoner Pyrrhus' ear," and I believe also that this Shakespearean ear eventually determines Derrida's account of the reader's, any reader's, relation to a text, any text. Compare, for example, Davies's poem on hearing with this passage from Derrida's essay on Nietzsche, "Otobiographies":

You must pay heed to the fact that the *omphalos* that Nietzsche compels you to envision resembles both an ear and a mouth. It has the invaginated folds and the involuted orificiality of both. Its center preserves itself at the bottom of an invisible, restless cavity that is sensitive to all waves which, whether or not they come from the outside, whether they are emitted or received, are always transmitted by this trajectory of obscure circumvolutions.

The person emitting the discourse you are in the process of teleprinting in this situation does not himself produce it; he barely emits it. He reads it. Just as you are ears that transcribe, the master is a mouth that reads, so that what you transcribe is, in sum, what he deciphers of a text that precedes him.[5]

The metaphoremes, and the erotics that informs them, that appear in Derrida's text do not come from nowhere; quite the contrary, I propose that they come from the Renaissance in general, and from Shakespeare in particular. To show that, however, it would be necessary to show that for Shakespeare it is specifically the ear that is the organ of the text, of the specifically typographic text, and that is something that must, for now, be postponed, though Shakespeare's sonnet 46 would be one place to begin.[6]

NOTES

This essay originally was delivered at a meeting of the Shakespeare Association, 30 April 1988, in Boston.

1. Joel Fineman, *Shakespeare's Perjured Eye* (Berkeley, 1986), 46.

2. Vergil *Aeneid* 4.183: "Tot linguae, tot idem ora sonant, tot subrigit auris" (*subrigit,* from *surgo* or *surrigo,* "rise, raise"). The number is infinite because there are as many mouths as men. There is an obvious Foucauldian reading of the Rainbow Portrait—i.e., of the queen's total surveillance—that implies a surveyed and supervised subject of power.

3. Joel Fineman, "Shakespeare's *Will* : The Temporality of Rape," *Representations* 20 (Fall 1987): 25–76.

4. John Davies, *The Complete Poems*, ed. Alexander B. Grosart, 3 vols. (Blackburn, Eng., 1869), 1:106.

5. Jacques Derrida, "Otobiographies," trans. Avita Ronnell, in *The Ear of the Other* (New York, 1985), 36.

6. Remember the "question" of the text—cf. Dora, Lacan, the moon and the semicolon—i.e., the rhetorical question. People don't want to read nowadays; they substitute thematic reaction for reading. The force of the story is to show that textuality predicates a specific sexuality and ideology, and that if people aren't willing to read, they will be caught up in this fetishistic project.

5

GEORGE ELIOT AND *DANIEL DERONDA:* THE PROSTITUTE AND THE JEWISH QUESTION

CATHERINE GALLAGHER

I would like to reopen a question that seems to have been prematurely closed: What conception of authorship, what ideas about its nature, simultaneously attracted hundreds of English women to that career in the nineteenth century and severely handicapped them in practicing it? Many of you will immediately think that this question, of all questions about women writers, has been amply answered, for you will recall that Sandra Gilbert and Susan Gubar, as well as numerous other feminist critics, point to the historical association of authorship with generative paternity.[1] Women, presumably, were driven to write in order to "create" for themselves, but they found that the male metaphor of literary creativity—the patriarchal metaphor—excluded them from the province of letters, and their books consequently rehearse this sense of exclusion and handicapped (castrated) creativity. Such an analysis concentrates on the historical connections linking author, father, and male God to the exclusion of all other associations that might have occurred to nineteenth-century writers.

Moreover, the critics themselves seem to subscribe to the underlying association of writing with creative generativity. They are merely offended that women were thought unfit for this procreative art. Although these critics sometimes suggest that the male myth of the generative Word was designed to compensate for the fictional nature of all fatherhood, they seldom carry this critique of creativity very far, and remain content to point out that generativity is a "naturally" female characteristic, implying that the natural metaphor of the mother-author was the very thing the patriarchal metaphor was designed to preempt.

I would like to argue that another, very different association also helped structure the conjunction of gender and authorship in the nineteenth century. When women entered the career of authorship, they did not enter an inappropriately male territory, but a degradingly female one. They did not need to find a female metaphor for authorship; they needed to avoid or transform the one that was already there. The historical association—disabling, empowering and central to

124

nineteenth-century consciousness—that I would like to discuss is not the meta-phor of the writer as father, but the metaphor of the author as whore.

This metaphor has an ancient pedigree. Classicists tell us that although few women in the Greek classical period actually wrote, the association of writing with femaleness in general and prostitution in particular spread with the increase in literacy itself. A link between writing and malevolent forms of female power can be found in several fragments; a too-close association with letters was also believed to emasculate a man.[2] Underlying these associations is a notion of written language far removed from the idea of the procreative Word. It has been noted that Aristotle was uncertain about whether writing most resembled the natural generativity of plants and animals or the unnatural generation of money, which, in usury, proliferates through mere circulation but brings nothing qualitatively new into being. At times, Aristotle speaks of poetic making as a method of natural reproduction; at other times, he speaks of the written word as an arbitrary and conventional sign multiplying unnaturally in the mere process of exchange. The former idea of language promotes the metaphor of literary paternity; the latter the metaphor of literary usury[3] and, ultimately, literary prostitution.

The whole sphere to which usury belongs, the sphere of exchange as opposed to that of production, is traditionally associated with women. Women are items of exchange, a form of currency and also a type of commodity. Of course, in normal kinship arrangements, when the exchange is completed and the woman becomes a wife, she enters the realm of "natural" (in the Aristotelian sense) pro-duction. But the prostitute never makes this transition from exchange to produc-tion; she retains her commodity form at all times. Like money, the prostitute, according to ancient accounts, is incapable of natural procreation. For all her sexual activity, indeed because of all of her sexual activity, she fails to bring new substances, children, into the world.[4] Her womb, it seems, is too slippery. And yet she is a source of proliferation. What multiplies through her, though, is not a substance but a sign: money. Prostitution, then, like usury, is a metaphor for one of the ancient models of linguistic production: the unnatural multiplication of interchangeable signs.

From ancient times, then, we have evidence of two radically different ways of thinking about authors, one based on a masculine metaphor, the other on a fem-inine metaphor. Both are associated with forms of multiplication, of proliferation, and yet they cannot be made parallel, for they operate on completely different assumptions about the nature of linguistic procreation. The gender distinction in literary theory is not between male fathers who *can* multiply and female eunuchs who *cannot*, not between male language and female silence, but between the natural production of new things in the world and the "unnatural" reproduction of mere signs. According to the father metaphor, the author generates real things in the world through language; according to the whore metaphor, language pro-liferates itself in a process of exchange through the author.

This essay does not attempt to choose between these metaphors or to develop an abstract truth about authorship. Rather, it describes specific historical associations confronting professional women writers in the nineteenth century, when the metaphor of the author as whore was commonplace. My purpose, then, is to register the peculiar Victorian resonances of the metaphor and to use it as a way both of interpreting the ending of George Eliot's career and of understanding her last novel, *Daniel Deronda*.

As in classical times, prostitution in the nineteenth century is linked to writing through their joint inhabitation of the realm of exchange. It is impossible to specify one universally accepted Victorian idea of the way exchange functions inside the general economy, but we can venture to assert that the processes of exchange, of circulation, are distinguished from those of production by all political economists. The sphere of production, rather than that of circulation, is then identified as the source of value, the source of real wealth. The Marxist critique of political economy, with its distinction between the production and realization of surplus-value, only refines the qualitative difference between these economic realms. These realms, of course, interpenetrate, for the essence of capitalism, as both political economists and their critics agree, is production that depends on the exchange of two underlying commodities: labor (or labor-power) and money. The stated source of value (and of surplus-value), however, remains the productive labor of the worker, that which brings some new things into the world.

Nineteenth-century economic thought, then, systematically accords the processes of exchange an epiphenomenal status even as it conceives of exchange as the ever-present condition of production. The marketplace (as distinct from the workplace) is truly a mechanism of *realization*: value is a shadowy potential until it is realized in exchange, but exchange only realizes the value already created in production. Circulation can never be a source of value. If in usury money seems to multiply through exchange alone, we are told, that is mere illusion, for all increases in wealth depend on someone's labor.

Those who hold this labor theory of value must wish the marketplace to be a simple reflection of values established in the productive sphere. The free market desired by laissez-faire political economists is first and foremost a market in labor, and the price of labor should determine, in the final analysis, the price of other commodities. A market unresponsive to that determination or overly responsive to other determinations is what much nineteenth-century economic theory is designed to do away with. A marketplace not directly bound to production, the value of a commodity wildly incommensurate with the value of the labor embodied in the commodity, is almost universally regarded as a bad thing. And as this economic discourse finds more popular expressions in either the liberal or the socialist traditions, one detects a growing hostility toward groups that seem to represent a realm of exchange divorced from production: for example, traders in general but especially costermongers in works like Mayhew's *London Labour and the London Poor*, prostitutes in the works of Mayhew, Acton, W. R. Greg and others, and Jews in the works of almost everybody.

The latter two representatives, the prostitutes and the almost always Jewish usurer, are ubiquitous in nineteenth-century writing about authorship. Examples abound, from Sainte-Beuve's often-quoted remark that all persons of renown are prostitutes, to Thackeray's ironic defense of Eugène Sue: "He gets half-a-crown a line for this bad stuff, and has, one may say with certainty, a hundred thousand readers every day. Many a man and author has sold himself for far less."[5] The activities of authoring, of procuring illegitimate income, and of alienating one's self through prostitution seem particularly closely associated with one another in the Victorian period. Thackeray identifies two reasons for this historical conjuncture: the development of cheap serial publication (in which authors were often paid by the line) and the growth of a massive popular readership in the 1830s and 1840s. These conditions most directly affected what we now call popular literature, but the decreasing cost of publication, advances in education, and changes in copyright law made it impossible for any professional writer to claim to be independent of the marketplace. The author, moreover, does not go to market as a respectable producer with an alienable commodity, but with *himself or herself* as commodity. The last half of the eighteenth century is the period both when the identity of text and self begins to be strongly asserted and when the legal basis for commodifying texts (as distinct from books) comes into being in copyright law. This combination puts writers in the marketplace in the position of selling themselves, like whores.

If, on the other hand, writers refrain from identifying their true selves with their texts, they get caught in another strand of the web of exchange, for language itself, especially published writing, is then often identified with money as an alien, artificial, and entrapping system of circulation. In Thackeray's *Pendennis* and Trollope's *The Way We Live Now*, for example, literary exchange resembles usury and inflationary retailing. It should be noted, moreover, that the Victorian usurious writer is often female and thus a composite image of usurer and whore. Many nineteenth-century statements about the false, imitative, and merely conventional nature of women's writing, statements that have been used to prove that the woman writer was considered a eunuch, should be reread with these metaphors of exchange in mind. For each indignant outburst against female authors emphasizes these authors' unearned ascendancy in the marketplace. George Eliot's "Silly Novels by Lady Novelists," W. R. Greg's falsely moral women novelists, and Hawthorne's scribbling women are all distinguished from productive laborers. Eliot is most emphatic about this distinction in her essay (1856) in which she argues that " 'In all labour there is profit;' but ladies' silly novels, we imagine, are less the result of labour than of busy idleness."[6]

These women do not, then, inhabit the sphere of literary *production*, but that is only half of their sin. The other half lies in the fact that they are nevertheless prolific. Their novels sell, and what is more, they sell because they merely recirculate a conventional language. The ladies, Eliot tells us, "are remarkably unanimous in their choice of diction";[7] their characters and incidents, she claims, are also identical. All the matter, she emphasizes, is drawn from novels and goes back into the making of more novels. Such women rake off profits without production, without labor.

The links George Eliot made between a certain kind of female literature, inflation, dishonest retailing, and usurious exchange were common, and easily called to mind the woman of pure exchange, the woman as commodity, the prostitute. What is surprising about Eliot, however, is her claim that exchange is the essence of all authorship. Eliot's dominant metaphor for authorship, both in her novels and essays, is not genealogy but commerce. And her commercial language often stresses exchange over production. For example, in her note on "Authorship," written sometime in the 1870s, she not only describes authorship in metaphors of exchange but also defines it as an act of commodity circulation. In this note, she plays down the role of production by baldly stating that writing is not the author's definitive activity. To be an author, she explains, is a social activity, a "bread winning profession," whereas merely "to write prose or verse as a private exercise and satisfaction is not a social activity."[8] "Social" here means, first of all, economic. In this note, as in numerous other notes and essays throughout her career, Eliot identifies the characteristics of her chosen profession, and the first characteristic is its location in the marketplace. The difference between the mere writer and the author is that the author writes for money.

Since mere writing is not a social act, the note on "Authorship" tells us, "nobody is culpable" for it. Writing is innocent; publication is guilty and also perilous. As Eliot presents them in numerous late essays, authors are the creatures of an economy that constantly imperils their identities and their products. In other markets, she claims, production and exchange are harmoniously coordinated; in the literary market, however, they are at odds. That which defines the authors, exchange, always also seeks to undo them, to make them profitable but unproductive. The market will encourage the author to recirculate, "to do over again what has already been done, either by himself or others."[9] This danger is elaborated by Eliot through the usury metaphor in her *Theophrastus Such* essays.[10]

The *Theophrastus Such* essays also construct the threat of the prostituting, "amusing" author who purveys poison, spreads disease, and generates unnatural passions and excessive appetites. In "Debasing the Moral Currency," for example, burlesques of great literature are first likened to an inflated currency and then to an inflamed woman with a combustible liquid: "I confess," writes the essayist, "that sometimes when I see a certain style of young lady, who checks our tender admiration with rouge and henna and all the blazonry of an extravagant expenditure, with slang and bold *brusquerie* intended to signify her emancipated view of things, and with cynical mockery which she mistakes for penetration, I am sorely tempted to hiss out '*Petroleuse*!'"[11] Here the image of *Liberté* as a whore emerges directly out of the liberty of the cultural marketplace.

The inflationary usurer and the infectious or combustible "expensive" woman—these are the assured but dangerous inhabitants of the authorial sphere, the degradingly feminine sphere of exchange. Why did Eliot so insistently place authors in this unsavory company by emphasizing their dependence on circulation? What deep attraction drew Eliot to the commercial definition despite its perils? The answer is twofold. The first and most obvious reply takes us back to a consideration of why, initially, loose women are associated with the marketplace. Money may be a sign of sterility and even of an outcast status, but it is nevertheless an emblem of liberation from patriarchal authority. The woman in the marketplace is presumably free from the patriarch, both in the sense that she needs the permission and approval of no single man and in the sense that finding her determination in the nexus of relationships with clients or the public enables her to escape the identity imposed by a father. By associating herself with the marketplace, Eliot evades any specifically patriarchal authority that her literal and her literary forefathers might try to impose, replacing the mystifications of genealogy with the realities of economics.

The commercial definition of authorship, though, has an even more complex role in Eliot's discourse. Established as a *fact*, it creates the necessity for its own transcendence in the realm of *value*. By defining the author as a writer in the marketplace, Eliot not only minimizes the anxiety attached to one metaphor but also establishes a different metaphoric core of anxiety for her own work. The guilt of illegitimate genealogical appropriation may be occluded, but the guilt of usurious and whorish commercial appropriation then immediately opens up.

This, however, is a profitable opening for Eliot. For out of it emerges the demand for a different economy, a demand constantly stimulated but never quite met by her own texts. By relentlessly exposing the unnaturalness of the commercial literary economy—its severance from "real wants" and independence of standards of quality in the commodity—Eliot promotes the artificial construction of a superseding *moral* economy.

But although the perils of the commercial economy that necessitate the moral economy are elaborately detailed in the late essays and poems, the moral economy itself remains vague. From the note on "Authorship," we learn that the moral economy would ensure "real" productivity, for it would regulate publication on the basis of quality. Good work, moreover, would add a truly new substance to the world, would make "a real contribution."[12] And yet, despite these appeals to originality, Eliot never equates productivity with natural generation. One of the few things the late essays make clear about the moral economy of culture is its sharp separation from nature. The most dangerous belief afoot, Theophrastus Such tells us, is that identified by Sainte-Beuve, the belief "that culture is something innate, that it is the same thing as nature."[13]

The moral economy, then, must break with the commercial literary economy and yet remain an economy, a sphere of exchange. Eliot's last novel, *Daniel Deronda*, allows us to investigate the problematic implications of this double imperative and to see why, within the terms of Eliot's discourse, cosmopolitan culture finally fails to be that sufficiently differentiated sphere.

Daniel Deronda displays the same preoccupations as Eliot's other late works. Usury, prostitution, and art become, in the course of the novel, interchangeable activities. They are made not identical, but fungible with each other by a complex pattern of metaphors, plot reversals, and ironic exchanges too intricate to describe here. Perhaps the most instructive part of this pattern, though, is the figure that Daniel himself makes in it. Daniel, the supposed saint and savior, is the novel's major negotiator of these exchanges and the only character who stands for each activity of exchange in turn.

Daniel Deronda opens on a cosmopolitan world of pure exchange and immediately introduces the major representatives of that sphere: the beautiful but sinister and reckless woman and the Jewish pawnbroker. The gambling casino at Leubrunn, which functions, the epigraph tells us, as the medium rather than the origin of the story, is a society itself mediated by a roulette wheel. When that wheel is in motion, it suspends normal social distinctions and creates an ironic momentary Utopia of equality at the expense of fraternity. The roulette game is a mystified, abstracted, and grotesquely passive war of all against all. The various players, as seen through Daniel's eyes, see only the roulette wheel and do not see one another. The wheel seems to make money appear and disappear, but in reality, the players are only exchanging money, as Daniel later explains to Gwendolen; one's gain is another's loss in this form of nonproductive money-getting. Like all money gained in the realm of pure exchange, roulette winnings are a double sign of credit and debit.

They are, indeed, exactly like the profits the Jewish pawnbroker makes from the exchange of Gwendolen Harleth's necklace in the very next episode; and it is this identity that underlies the irony of Gwendolen's bitter reflection that "these Jew dealers were so unscrupulous in taking advantage of Christians unfortunate at play!"[14] The business of the Jew and the play of the Christian are altogether isomorphic, and their symmetry derives from the doubleness of the sought-after sign: the nine louis given to Gwendolen in exchange for her necklace, like all signs in usurious exchange, represent a double indebtedness. From Gwendolen's point of view, the nine louis represent a loss; she feels she has not been paid enough for the necklace. In her mind, the Jew really owes her something—has something of hers that is worth more than she has been paid; from the usurer's point of view, Gwendolen has merely prepaid a debt to him that she would have incurred for the use of his money.

This vast game of beggar-your-neighbor, in which the debtors can claim to be the creditors, and vice versa, is Gwendolen's natural sphere. At least, as we first see her through Daniel's eyes, she seems particularly appropriate to it because she is herself a double sign. The book opens with the questions: "Was she beautiful or not beautiful? . . . Was the good or the evil genius dominant?" (35). Daniel concludes, "Probably the evil," and then goes on to "save" Gwendolen by increasing the minus side of her account.

In this way, Daniel, through his very disapproval, enters into an exchange with Gwendolen that pairs him with the pawnbroker. Gwendolen herself makes the association when she remembers that Daniel's hotel is in the same street as the pawnbroker's shop; she imagines Daniel scrutinizing and evaluating her as Mr. Wiener scrutinizes and evaluates her jewels. But surely, it might be objected, this pairing of Daniel with the pawnbroker is a pairing of opposites, as Daniel's immediate retrieval and restoration of the necklace make clear. Daniel sends Gwendolen two items along with the redeemed necklace: (1) a supposedly anonymous note saying, "A stranger who has found Miss Harleth's necklace returns it to her with the hope that she will not again risk the loss of it," and (2) a handkerchief from which "a large corner . . . seemed to have been recklessly torn off to get rid of a mark" (49). The whole packet comprises a message that seems to say the opposite of what a pawn ticket, a promissory note, or, indeed, any kind of money generally says. For the signs Daniel sends Gwendolen represent not the promise to pay off a specified person or government, but an acknowledgment that an ostentatiously anonymous person (a stranger, a recklessly torn-off mark, the sign of a flamboyantly discarded identity) has already paid. They resemble, then, an anonymous receipt closing a particular transaction, but their prohibition against exchange also extends beyond the immediate transaction, making them a species of anti-money. They are a specific directive against further exchange: the stranger hopes that Miss Harleth "will not again risk the loss" of the necklace by pawning it. Moreover, since the necklace is made of stones that had belonged to Gwendolen's father, their return, accompanied by Daniel's stern note, could easily be seen as the valorization of genealogy over exchange: the father orders the daughter to vacate the marketplace and remain dependent on his legacy alone.

Superficially, then, Daniel and the pawnbroker are a pair of opposites. And yet if we consider the effect of Daniel's actions on Gwendolen, his exchanges with her only make him a more formidable version of the usurer. Gwendolen quite rightly refuses to see his package as a restoration of her loss; it represents, rather, the further depletion of her self-esteem. She can no longer fancy that the pawnbroker owes her something. By buying back the necklace, at the usurer's higher price, and then returning it to her, Daniel increases her deficit by putting her in debt to him. The signs that he sends Gwendolen—the necklace, the note, and the handkerchief—replace the usurious signs of double indebtedness with tokens of unidirectional, unambiguous debt. In attempting to get rid of her doubleness, Daniel vastly increases Gwendolen's indebtedness and makes it impossible for her to repay him. Since the note is anonymous, she cannot even object to the liberty

Daniel has taken without exposing herself to humiliation. Finally, she can only quit the scene of these encounters with a sense of permanent and demeaning disadvantage. If Daniel redeems anyone in this exchange, he redeems the pawn-broker, whose profits are realized and whose debts are canceled. And that is in summary the plot of the whole novel: a young man who thinks he has a mission to save wayward women turns out to have a mission to save a nation of usurers.

Daniel's warning to Gwendolen, furthermore, only drives her from one arena of exchange to another. Unlike Leubrunn, which gives Gwendolen fantasies of escaping the determinations of her sex, the English marketplace to which she returns is explicitly sexual and contaminated by illicit relationships. Henleigh Grandcourt seeks Gwendolen as a *wife* and not a mistress, but the novel purposely collapses this distinction, reverses the terms by a series of exchanges, and proves that a wife can be a prostitute both in her own eyes and in those of her husband. By knowingly taking the place of, allowing herself to be exchanged for, Grand-court's mistress, Lydia Glasher, Gwendolen becomes a sign of the very thing she is not, the abandoned woman of passion, the mistress, the whore. It is this iden-tification through exchange that repels Gwendolen, and it is this identification to which she must ultimately submit. By being exchanged with the woman of ex-change in her marriage to Grandcourt, she will remain forever a sign of exchange and, in her own mind at least, a sign of the very illicit sexuality she cannot herself enjoy.

Gwendolen is finally transformed into a commodity condemned to perpetual resale to the same consumer, a state maintained by the periodic checks Grandcourt sends her mother. Her new status is traumatically forced on her consciousness by the receipt, on her wedding night, of yet another package, this one from Lydia Glasher. Like Daniel's earlier package, it also contains jewels and a note. In a sense, Lydia's package cancels Daniel's because this time the note emphasizes that the enclosed jewels are not legitimately Gwendolen's. The note reads, "These diamonds, which were once given with ardent love to Lydia Glasher, she passes on to you. You have broken your word to her, that you might possess what was hers . . . The man you have married has a withered heart. His best young love was mine; you could not take that from me when you took the rest. It is dead; but I am the grave in which your chance of happiness is buried as well as mine" (406). The box, now a casket full of diamonds, continues to stand for Lydia Glasher's passionate sexuality, which has been taken from her but cannot therefore be bestowed on Gwendolen. The note insists that Gwendolen receive the box as simply one payment for the alienation of her own sexuality, an alienation that must be perpetually transacted with the same man. In thus paying Gwendolen, Lydia also pays her back, with a vengeance, emphasizing that Gwendolen's very lack of passion, her lack of any but a financial motive for marrying Grandcourt, makes her the real whore and simultaneously denies her the whore's pleasure and freedom.

Unlike Daniel's package, then, Lydia's package tells Gwendolen that there is no way out. She does not have a choice between fatherly authority and alienating exchanges. The father is dead and yet lives on in the very exchanges that seemed before to mark his liberating absence. But if, once again, we look at the way these two packages function in Gwendolen's psychic development, we can see that they are very similar. Lydia's act resembles Daniel's because it, too, establishes a unidirectional, unambiguous debt that can never be repaid. If Daniel's first pairing in the narrative is with the pawnbroker, his second is with Lydia Glasher, the illicitly sexual woman. And this identification sharpens as the novel progresses, for Gwendolen (like almost everyone else in the book) thinks Daniel is the illegitimate son of Sir Hugo Mallinger, whose legal heir (because Sir Hugo has failed to produce a legitimate son) is Henleigh Grandcourt. Gwendolen thus identifies Grandcourt's displacement of Daniel with her own displacement of Lydia and Lydia's children. Both Daniel and Gwendolen think of Daniel as the representative of the illicitly sexual and wronged woman.

Through two kinds of illicit sexual exchange, then, the characters in *Daniel Deronda* themselves become interchangeable, not because they are reduced to uniformity but because, like money, they expand into doubleness. They come to mean what they are not; loss and gain are reversed. Daniel and Gwendolen especially become legible to each other only by an understanding of their mutual illegitimacy. And "illegitimacy" is the word neither can say because it conjures up the secret signified of both, that which is embodied, or rather disembodied, in the elusive creature, Daniel's missing mother. She is the central mystery in the novel, the woman with an "enigmatic veiled face," who fills not just Daniel's imagination, but Gwendolen's too, with "dread" and "shame" (206). They think, and we think, that their own lives refer to hers and that hers refers to dreadful, shameful sexuality. They think, and we think, that this sexuality causes the problems of identity and alienation from which they both suffer, deprives them of a stable ground, and makes them both, in different ways, reluctant signs of things antithetical to them.

It seems an odd twist, then, when the dreadful, shameful veiled core of meaning to which so much in the novel alludes turns out not to be a loose woman, a public or private concubine, but an *artist*, the greatest lyric actress of her time. All through his life, Daniel has thought that he stood as the sign of his mother's sexual sin; in the climax of the novel, however, he finds that his life means something else entirely. Instead of having been abandoned as a sign of shameful sex, Daniel was literally traded for an artistic career; he is, in this sense, the representative of his mother's career because he is the thing that she exchanged for it. Daniel is just like the little boy we briefly glimpse in the opening chapter, who stands with his back to the gaming table as his mother plays: "He alone had his face turned towards the doorway, and fixing on it the blank gaze of a bedizened child stationed as a masquerading advertisement on the platform of an itinerant show, stood close behind a lady deeply engaged at the roulette-table" (36). Daniel and the little boy stand for the play by having been left for it. As the reader's mind later takes in the fact that the metaphorical roulette-table means artistic rather than sexual exchange, the interchangeability of these two activities is reasserted.

"Reasserted," rather than asserted, because, long before Daniel's mother is unveiled, the novel repeatedly emphasizes the close connection between selling oneself as a sexual commodity and selling oneself as an artist. The points of connection in the narrative are too numerous to list completely, but the most obvious and often-remarked instances are the degenerate actor Lapidoth's attempt to pander his daughter Mirah, first as a singer and then as a prostitute, and Gwendolen's proposal to go on the stage just before she sells herself to Grandcourt. The constant association of Gwendolen's affinity for the stage and her desire to remain in the realm of exchange strengthen the same connection on a somewhat more abstract level.

But although these connections are obvious, their implications are not. What is the nature and extent of the identification between prostitution and art in *Daniel Deronda*? With the entrance of the Alcharisi, the novel seems intent on making a universal association between artists and prostitutes, one component of which is the very difference between them. The Alcharisi was as dedicated to artistic traditions as Herr Klesmer, the novel's explicit example of a pure and authentic artist. Hers was the long and arduous apprenticeship that Gwendolen is incapable of. Hers too was the natural power lacking in Mirah. Her training and genius, it would seem, save her from the threat of prostitution that both Gwendolen and Mirah face. Indeed, all three women's stories indicate that art and prostitution are *alternatives* in women's lives, but alternatives with such similar structures that their very alternativeness calls attention to their interchangeability.

The structural similarity between the two careers emphasized in the Alcharisi's story is their joint exclusion of generational reproduction. Like a prostitute, the Alcharisi is a slippery womb out of which Daniel has fallen. Thus Daniel does, in a sense, represent her preference for many men over one: "Men followed me from one country to another. I was living a myriad lives in one. I did not want a child" (688-89). Similarly, she emphasizes that her entry into a cultural marketplace freed her from becoming a mere link in a family line: "[My father] wished I had been a son; he cared for me as a makeshift link . . . . He hated that Jewish women should be thought of by the Christian world as a sort of ware to make public singers and actresses of. As if we were not the more enviable for that! That is a chance of escaping from bondage" (694).

Both the woman artist and the prostitute, then, are established in the sphere of exchange that excludes "natural" generation and substitutes for it an exhilaratingly dangerous love affair with a multitude. The female performer, as a contemporary noted, must "sacrifice maiden modesty or matronly reserve" in order to be "stared at, commented on, clapped or hissed by a crowded and often unmannered audience, who forget the woman in the artist."[15] This immediate and threatening relationship to the cultural consumer, though, is only one of the ways in which the performer acts out the relationship between art and exchange. Another aspect of performance recalls the metaphor of the usurer and further breaks down the distinction not only between kinds of artist but also between the repulsive and admirable elements of their art. It is, indeed, a single trait of the performer that makes her both type and antitype of the artist. The performer, according to an 1875 essay by George Henry Lewes, which seems to state both his and Eliot's opinion on the topic, is a mere medium for other artists. He is only a painted thing, Lewes complains, who simply *represents* the creation of the poet.[16] The word *represent,* emphasized in Lewes's essay, is used repeatedly about Alcharisi: "All feeling," we are told, "immediately became matter of conscious representation" for her; "I cared for the wide world," she tells her son, "and what I could represent in it" (691). Never is she described as an originator of substance. Lewes's essay goes on to argue that actors command too high a price, both in fame and money. Their market values, he insists, are inflated, for they are only "luxuries."[17] The performer, then, is another instance of the usurious artist who dominates Eliot's late work. It is thus little wonder that Jews have only two professions in this book. The Alcharisi reports that her husband, Daniel's father, "wound up his money changing . . . and lived to wait upon me" (696).

But it is this same element of theatrical performance that makes Eliot use it as a synecdoche for what is best in art. The performance requires the submergence of the self in the words and thoughts of another; it requires, then, the development of the kind of self Eliot considered ideal, the "self that self restrains" in the interests of some larger, corporate identity. To forget the woman in the artist, to become the medium of the collective project of culture, Eliot often argues, is to enable the spiritual economy. Every time she invokes the usury metaphor, then, or refers to the inauthentic and parasitic nature of theatrical performance, she raises objections to that very moral economy of art she elsewhere invokes.

In *Daniel Deronda* we can see Eliot struggling with this contradiction and only resolving it finally by separating the moral economy from art. For the novel shows us that artistic exchange, even when separated from monetary exchange, produces effects very like those of financial circulation. In "The Modern Hep! Hep! Hep!," the last of the *Theophrastus Such* essays, Eliot sums up those effects in the word "alienism." Alienism is a spiritual disease that, she tells us, is sometimes euphemistically called "cosmopolitanism." Jews are particularly prone to it because, having no homeland of their own, they are often forced to live in the medium of abstract universalism created by international finance. Although Eliot argues that the Jews have not yet been made "viciously cosmopolitan by holding the world's money-bag," and hence resolving "all national interests" into "the algebra of loans," she fears that such cosmopolitanism would result from any relaxation of their separatism.[18] If Jews are to be virtuous, she insists, they must have at least a spiritual nationality and at best a reconstituted homeland.

Money, however, is not the only breeder of "alienism," a word with striking Arnoldian resonances. In *Culture and Anarchy*, Arnold called his bearers of culture, his "saving remnant," "aliens," and called upon the English to overcome their insularity and embrace the "best that has been thought and said" no matter what its origin.[19] In "The Modern Hep! Hep! Hep!" it is precisely this sort of cultural internationalism that Eliot deplores: "A common humanity is not yet enough to feed the rich blood of various activity which makes a complete man. The time is not come for cosmopolitanism to be highly virtuous . . . It is admirable in a Briton with a good purpose to learn Chinese, but it would not be a proof of fine intellect in him to taste Chinese poetry in the original more than he tastes the poetry of his own tongue."[20]

The character who suffers from this aspect of culture in *Daniel Deronda* is Daniel himself—Daniel, whose first inklings of identity came through books and who is disempowered by a *too* diffuse sympathy, a lack of particularity always associated with the decentering power of wide reading: "His imagination had so wrought itself to the habit of seeing things as they probably appeared to others, that a strong partisanship, unless it were against an immediate oppression, had become an insincerity for him . . . A too reflective and diffusive sympathy was in danger of paralysing in him that indignation against wrong and that selectedness of fellowship which are the conditions of moral force." He seeks an "influence that would justify partiality" (412–13). Ironically, in depriving him of his Jewishness, his mother has turned him into another version of the Jew: the cultured cosmopolitan, the alien.

By embracing Jewish nationalism, then, Daniel saves the Jews and himself from abstract universalism. He will save them, it is hoped, from money, and himself from cosmopolitan culture, by replacing both with the mystic merger of souls described in the Cabbala. Eliot is drawn to the Cabbala for its principle of exchange, but she never confuses this with the exchanges of authorship. "In the doctrine of the Cabbala," Mordecai explains to Daniel, "souls are born again and again in new bodies till they are perfected and purified, and a soul liberated from a worn-out body may join the fellow-soul that needs it . . . . When my long-wandering soul is liberated from this weary body, it will join yours, and its work will be perfected" (599–600). This is the moral economy for which both money-changing and art are exchanged in *Daniel Deronda*. The substitution is effected, once again, through an exchange of jewelry; Daniel's ring, which had been his money-changing father's, had been given to him by his artistic mother, and had provided him entrée into the pawnshop of Ezra Cohen, is taken by the pander Lapidoth as a kind of payment for his children. The alienation of all the negative things Jewishness stands for in the book enables the pure exchange of souls symbolized in Daniel's marriage to both Mirah and Mordecai.

It is true that this union seems to have textuality at its heart, but that textuality rigorously excludes all that Eliot has previously meant by "art." For art, like money in this novel, is international, widely disseminated through modern printing, and bent on the creation of fungible, cosmopolitan selves. The Cabbala, on the other hand, is a set of exclusive, closely guarded and hand-copied esoteric texts, bent on the creation of a cumulative but nevertheless unique Jewish self. Indeed, Mordecai's way of disseminating his culture evinces a desire to dispense even with these texts. His teaching of little Jacob, for example, proceeds by "a sort of outpouring in the ear of the boy" of "a Hebrew poem of his own." Jacob cannot even understand the words, but Mordecai assures himself that "The boy will get them engraved within him . . . it is a way of printing" (532–33). Mordecai may believe that this kind of "printing" will one day influence Jacob, but as Eliot would be the first to point out, this activity has nothing to do with authorship. No one is culpable for it.

What should we make of this repudiation of the realm of exchange deep enough to undermine even the exchanges of a cosmopolitan culture in which Eliot herself was immersed? We should first place it within a general reflux away from internationalism in England. Imperial competition, the loss of London's power as the undisputed center of international finance, and various other difficulties in international relations were building toward a new mood of nostalgic nationalism. In its own very tangential way, through the link of Jewish rather than English nationalism, the novel connects with all this and takes the necessary step beyond Arnoldian internationalism.

Daniel Deronda's achievement, though, certainly does not lie in its expression of renewed nationalistic spirit. It is the problem much more than the solution that we find compelling in this novel, the creation of a self-sustaining anxiety. And intricate investigation of the problem seems to refer to Eliot's particular experiences in the realm of exchange. Here, of course, one can only speculate, but these reflections on her career made at its close, when her anxieties had perhaps begun to subside, might give us new insights into Eliot's fears of authorship. Again, these do not include a fear of writing or any anxiety about handling pens. Rather, they center around the relationship between her public, authorial identity, her pseudonym George Eliot, and her private identity, the ambiguous Marian Evans Lewes. It must be remembered that the impropriety of the latter is what led to the adoption of the former. "George Eliot," as Ruby Redinger has amply demonstrated, was not just an enabling fictional masculine identity but was for many years a serious screen to disguise the author's identity. For it was feared, by Lewes, Eliot, and her publishers, that no one would buy the books of the scandalous Marian Evans.[21] Indeed, Eliot's great anxiety about how much she would make from her books seems entirely determined by the illicitness of her relationship to George Henry Lewes. Eliot alone of all Victorian authors felt as a constant reality the interchangeability, the equivalence of difference, between prostitution and authorship. For as Bracebridge Hemyng pointed out in his 1861 study of prostitution, there were two kinds of prostitutes: women who traded their services for the money of many men, and women who were privately kept, without benefit of marriage, by one man.[22]

This reflection gives a new meaning to that perhaps apocryphal account of what the name "Eliot" stands for: "To L. I owe it."[23] The name might be a veritable I.O.U., a recognition of indebtedness as much as a statement of gratitude, and a promissory note for future exchanges. With Eliot's authorship she purchased her status as something other than a whore. What she denied in her private designation, Marian Evans Lewes, she coyly admits in her public designation: I am not married to this man; I owe him money or I am his concubine. In May of 1880, she married John Cross, and George Eliot, author, and Marian Evans Lewes, scandalous woman, went out of existence in the same instant.

NOTES

1. Sandra M. Gilbert and Susan Gubar, *The Madwoman in the Attic* (New Haven: Yale University Press, 1979).

2. F. D. Harvey, "Literacy in the Athenian Democracy," *Revue des Etudes Grecques* 79 (1966): 621. Also, Susan G. Cole, "Could Greek Women Read and Write?" *Women's Studies* 8 (1981): 137, 155. Both critics cite Menander, frag. 702k:
   Teach a woman letters? A terrible mistake!
   —Like feeding extra venom to a horrifying snake.
   Cole also draws a connection between prostitution and reading and writing (p. 143). Moreover, Charles Segal claims, primarily on the basis of Sophocles' *Trachiniae* and Euripides' *Hippolytus*, that there is a general Greek suspicion of writing that associates it with trickery, concealed love, and female desire. Segal argues that there is a tendency in Greek literature to associate writing with the hidden, dangerous, interior space of female desire, "a duplicitous silent speaking that can subvert the authority of king and father. As a concentrated form of seduction and persuasion, such 'female' writing is doubly a threat to the masculine ideal of straightforward talk and forthright action" ("Greek Tragedy: Writing, Truth, and the Representation of the Self," in *Mnemai: Classical Studies in Memory of Karl K. Hudley,* ed. Harold J. Evjen [Chico, Calif.: Scholars Press, 1984], pp. 56–57).

3. This discussion is based on Marc Shell's *The Economy of Literature* (Baltimore: Johns Hopkins University Press, 1978), pp. 91–102.

4. I am indebted to Professor Thomas Laqueur of the University of California, Berkeley, History Department, who directed me to several ancient texts on the infertility of women whose intercourse is too frequent and too passionate. The infertility of prostitutes is, for example, cited by Lucretius as an instance

of the general rule that excessive sexual activity leaves women barren. See *The Nature of the Universe* (London: Penguin Books, 1970), p. 170.

5. W. M. Thackeray, "Les Mystères de Paris (The Mysteries of Paris), par Eugène Sue. Thieves' Literature of France," repr. in Helga Grubitzsch, *Materialien zur Kritik des Feuilleton-Romans* (Wiesbaden: Akademische Verlagsgesellschaft Athenaion, 1977), p. 247.

6. George Eliot, "Silly Novels by Lady Novelists," *Westminister Review* N.S. 10 (1856): 461.

7. Ibid., p. 448.

8. "Authorship," *Leaves from a Notebook: The Works of George Eliot*, vol. 8 (New York: Nottingham Society, n.d.), pp. 209–10.

9. Ibid., p. 211.

10. See, for example, "The Too-Ready Writer," who, with "too much interest at his back," has not even a perception that can truly be called his. Despite his complete lack of productive capacity, however, the too-ready writer, like the usurer, manages to turn his real indebtedness to the intellectual labor of others to his credit. "You perceive," sneers the essayist, "how proud he is of not being indebted to any writer: even with the dead he is on the creditor's side, for he is doing them the service of letting the world know what they meant better than [they] . . . themselves had any means of doing." *The Impressions of Theophrastus Such: The Works of George Eliot*, vol. 8 (New York: Nottingham Society, n.d.), p. 118.

11. *Theophrastus Such*, p. 189.

12. "Authorship," p. 211.

13. *Theophrastus Such*, pp. 88–89.

14. George Eliot, *Daniel Deronda*, ed. and intro. Barbara Hardy (repr., Baltimore: Penguin Books, 1970), p. 48. All subsequent references to this novel are to this edition and are cited parenthetically in the text by page number.

15. "Women Artists," *Westminster Review* N.S. 14 (1858): 164.

16. George Henry Lewes, *On Actors and the Art of Acting* (Leipzig: B. Tachnitz, 1875), repr. in *Literary Criticism of George Henry Lewes*, ed. Alice Kaminsky (Lincoln: University of Nebraska Press, 1964), p. 112.

17. Ibid.

18. *Theophrastus Such*, p. 157.

19. Matthew Arnold, *Culture and Anarchy*, ed. R. H. Super (Ann Arbor: University of Michigan Press, 1965), pp. 145–46.

20. *Theophrastus Such*, p. 149.

21. Ruby V. Redinger, *George Eliot: The Emergent Self* (New York: Alfred A. Knopf, 1975), pp. 391–400.

22. Bracebridge Hemyng, *Those Who Will Not Work*, companion vol. to Henry

Mayhew's *London Labour and the London Poor* (London: Charles Griffin & Co., 1861), p. 213.

23. It cannot be said that Eliot was conscious of the "I-O-Lewes" nature of the name she chose. In his *Life of George Eliot* (New York: Thomas P. Crowell & Co., 1904), J. W. Cross says only, "I may mention here that my wife told me the reason she fixed on this name was that George was Mr. Lewe's Christian name, and Eliot was a good mouth-filling, easily pronounced word" (p. 219). Blanche Colton Williams offers no attribution when she says in *George Eliot* (New York: Macmillan Co., 1936), " 'George' she borrowed from Lewes. 'To L—I owe it' gave her 'Eliot,' which, however, was explained simply as 'a good mouth-filling word' " (pp. 131–32). But even if we decide that the interpretation of the name is entirely Williams's speculation, we are still left with the novelist's own very revealing explanation, which might have been the inspiration for Blanche Williams's interpretation. For to say that "Eliot" is a "good, mouth-filling word" is to remind us again that her identity as novelist is what saves her from the status of prostitute implied by financial dependence on Lewes.

6

NEW AMERICANISTS: REVISIONIST INTERVENTIONS INTO THE CANON

DONALD E. PEASE

The term "New Americanists" derives from the lengthy review article entitled "Whose American Renaissance?" Frederick Crews contributed to the twenty-fifth-anniversary issue of the *New York Review of Books* (October 27, 1988). Crews uses the term in ways homologous with other neologisms—new historicism, neo-Marxism, poststructuralism—devised to mark shifts in the organizing principles and self-understanding of a field. Crews's "New Americanists" deploy these and other revisionist practices to intervene in the restructuring of American Studies. In keeping with this usage, Crews applies the term to the authors of close to thirty essays in two volumes of collected essays, as well as five recent books by single authors.[1]

After separating his American Renaissance from the New Americanists', Crews presumes to reclaim legal proprietary rights over his field. But instead of exercising the proprietary liberties of *The Liberal Imagination* (1950) and banishing the New Americanists from his American Renaissance, Crews concludes the review with a staggering acknowledgment:

> The truth is that for any works written before the last seventy years or so, the most influential academics get to decide who's in and who's out. And the New Americanists themselves seem destined to become the next establishment in their field. They will be right about the most important books and the most fruitful ways of studying them because as they always know in their leaner days, those who hold the power are right by definition.[2]

Crews cannot recognize New Americanists as members of his field. At the startling conclusion of the review, however, he recognizes the New Americanists as the "next establishment in *their* field" (my emphasis). But without anywhere else in the review having proposed terms supportive of this recognition, his conclusion seems written by someone of another mind about the New Americanists than Frederick Crews. Instead of taking final possession of Crews's *American Renaissance*, that final paragraph seems a contextually dispossessed literary property, but one developed within a text-milieu separable from the one articulated in the remainder of the review.

In articulating these concluding sentences in terms he elsewhere discredits, Crews, at the conclusion of the review, makes clear the ideological crisis New Americanists effect for his field. And my preceding sentences, as they reconstruct "Crews" in terms held self-evident by New Americanists, deconstitute the "Crews" of *The Liberal Imagination*. In bringing Crews's earlier constructions together with this reconstruction, my analysis articulates what might be called a crisis in the field-Imaginary of American Studies.

By the term field-Imaginary I mean to designate a location for the disciplinary unconscious mentioned earlier. Here abides the field's fundamental syntax—its tactic assumptions, convictions, primal words, and the charged relations binding them together. A field specialist depends upon this field-Imaginary for the construction of her primal identity within the field. Once constructed out of this syntax, the primal identity can neither reflect upon its terms nor subject them to critical scrutiny. The syntactic elements of the field-Imaginary subsist instead as self-evident principles.

Throughout my discussion of Crews's review, I have treated *The Liberal Imagination* as the location of Crews's field-Imaginary. A partial list of the titles of master-texts within the field of American Studies will enable me to describe its field-Imaginary as if it represented a primal scene: F. O. Matthiessen's *American Renaissance* (1941); Henry Nash Smith's *Virgin Land* (1950); R. W. B. Lewis's *The American Adam* (1955); Richard Chase's *The American Novel and Its Tradition* (1957); Harry Levin's *The Power of Blackness: Hawthorne, Poe, Melville* (1958); Leslie Fiedler's *Love and Death in the American Novel* (1960); Marcus Bewley's *The Eccentric Design* (1963); Leo Marx's *The Machine in the Garden* (1965); Richard Poirier's *A World Elsewhere* (1966); Quentin Anderson's *The Imperial Self (1971)*; Sacvan Bercovitch's *American Jeremiad* (1973).

While these master-texts in American Studies provide slightly different meta-narratives with which Americanists define their practices, all of these titles presuppose a realm of pure possibility (*Virgin Land, A World Elsewhere*) where a whole self (*American Adam, The Imperial Self*) can internalize the major contradictions at work in American history (*The Machine in the Garden, The Power of Blackness*) in a language and in a set of actions and relations confirmative of the difference between a particular cultural location and the rest of the world (*Love and Death in the American Novel, The Eccentric Design, The American Novel and Its Tradition, American Jeremiad, American Renaissance*).

I described earlier this autonomous place apart from a culture as the construction of *The Liberal Imagination*, but as this list of titles should indicate, *The Liberal*

Imagination works with pre-oedipal wishes, narcissistic drives, and primal words to produce a compelling primal scene. Here the urge for absolute union with cultural goods becomes wholly indistinguishable from identification with instinctual drives. In this realm, intensities take the place of referentials and negations possess no language with which to be distinguished from affirmations.

Like the primal scene within an individual's psyche, the scenario organizing the field-Imaginary of American Studies depends upon the *separation* it enables *from* potentially traumatic material. The binding power of materials from this primal scene becomes visible in Crews's review at those moments when the New Americanists either criticize this separation as an ideological construction or propose a relation between the separated realms. Whenever New Americanists question the separation of the cultural from the public realm, they undermine the (imaginary) relation between Crews's primal identity as a specialist in American Studies and the field's primal scene.

Crews explicitly negotiates the difficulties resulting from this crisis in the field-Imaginary and tacitly present in his review in his discussion of his former colleague Henry Nash Smith's essay in a volume of essays by New Americanists. In this essay Smith, the author of *Virgin Land* (1950), does for that founding text what Crews never does in his review; he reconsiders the text in terms of a New Americanist critique. Whereas Smith did not intend his designation of the nineteenth-century West as "virgin land" to be ideological, Richard Slotkin, in *The Fatal Environment* (1985), finds this designation to be, in both its conception and deployment, an ideological cover-up for Indian removal, frontier violence, government theft, land devastation, class cruelty, racial brutality, and misogyny. In reconsidering, Smith acknowledges some truth to these claims, but then wisely remarks that at the time he was working on *Virgin Land* (1947–50), the critical self-consciousness with which Slotkin scrutinized its ideology was simply not available: "This cluster of concepts, which I would call an American ideology, is constantly present in *Virgin Land* but, so to speak, off stage, only occasionally given explicit recognition."[3] Crews, however, never cites the substance of Smith's remark, nor does he comment on what was crucially at stake for the field of American Studies in Smith's change of mind. In place of such commentary, Crews questions the motives of the editors of *Ideology and Classic American Literature*, who included Smith's posthumous essay as "a kind of trophy." Crews then goes on to concern himself with the "liberal attitude" displayed in Smith's change of mind. Smith, Crews writes, "acceded to Slotkin's implied [sic] critique of his work, confessing that he had been blind to the way such catchwords as 'free land' and 'frontier initiative' had been used to rationalize atrocities."[4]

In this passage, Crews misrecognizes the New Americanists' threat to *his* field in the displaced form of Henry Nash Smith's (posthumously published) response to Richard Slotkin's defacement of *Virgin Land*. In *The Fatal Environment*, Slotkin constructs an alternate primal scene within which New Americanists construct themselves and define their objects. This alternate radically threatens the identity Crews constructed out of *Virgin Land* (and the other founding texts in his field-Imaginary). To restore that identity, Crews, in this passage, uses Smith's placement within an alien text-milieu to conduct a rescue mission for the corpse of one of the founding fathers of the field's primal scene.

By invoking this image of a rescue mission for a founding father's corpse, I intend to reactivate Crews's language deployed in *The Sins of the Fathers* and to propose a location for Crews's concluding review paragraph. Throughout his study of Hawthorne, Crews depends upon a psychoanalytic understanding of the guilt accrued to Hawthorne by his ancestors' misdeeds in New England's witch-haunted glades. Crews, following Levin's *Power of Blackness*, argues that Hawthorne's narratives obsessively return to the primal scene of ancestral guilt to reconstruct the psyche in its terms. In *The Fatal Environment*, Slotkin constructs an alternate primal scene out of what might be called the political unconscious of the *Virgin Land* and of *The Power of Blackness*. Slotkin's book proposes this scene (and his meta-narrative about it) as an alternate context within which Americanists can construct their critical personae, canonical objects, and disciplinary practices.

In *Virgin Land*, Smith idealized the American West as that permanent place in nature where Americans could separate from their pasts and recover the forever inviolable status of a new beginning. Smith wrote *The Virgin Land* in the postwar years when returning veterans needed a place in which to recover from the traumas of a war fought over conflicting ideologies. As a romance-fulfillment of a wished-for America of endlessly renewable possibilities, possibilities which could be readily transported abroad in the Americanization of Western European nations, a *Virgin Land* eliminated ideological considerations about this place as un-American. But writing in the post-Vietnam era, Slotkin rereads *Virgin Land* in terms that recall American imperialism—its generalized domination of nature and native cultures. As an anti-romance of America's origins, Slotkin's *Fatal Environment* finds in Smith's *Virgin Land* a paradigmatic context for the naturalization of racist and sexist stereotypes. As the primal scene of America's endlessly recoverable origin, *Virgin Land*, Slotkin argues, is predicated upon the denial of the difference between "virgin land" and every other place in the culture. After underscoring the violence in this denial, Slotkin associates the originary violence he finds in the denial of difference of America's primal self-image with the violence of America's western settlers directed against native peoples. More significantly, Slotkins's work, *The Fatal Environment*, thereby re-establishes the relationship between the cultural and political spheres Smith's *Virgin Land* denies.

In order to recover the separation of these spheres, Crews performs his characteristic act of denegation. He ignores the political content of Slotkin's ideological critique of *Virgin Land* and attends instead to Smith's placement of that founding text within *The Fatal Environment*. In rescuing the body of Smith's text from that alien context, Crews contrasts the "characteristically magnanimous style" of "the late Henry Nash Smith's classic (and classically liberal [sic]) *Virgin Land*" with the "catch-words" of the "macabre" Slotkin thesis.[5] In other words, he frees Smith's founding text from an alien New Americanist context through the exercise of negative capability—he negates the specificity of Slotkin's thesis, then reduces the terms of Slotkin's critique to "catch-words" like "macabre" obsession. Following his impoverishment of Slotkin's critique, Crews repossesses Smith's revisionist account in *Virgin Land* by reading the work as an example of "magnanimous style." For by identifying with Smith's style, in place of what he considers Slotkin's impoverished politics, Crews effectively separates that style from *The Fatal Environment's* politics and then reconstructs for Smith a fresh start in *Virgin Land.*

By removing Smith from *The Fatal Environment*, where New Americanists construct their field identities, Crews indirectly discloses the rationale for his own misrecognitions: for Crews, New Americanists quite literally exist outside the assumptions consititutive of his field. Their externality to Crews's field and their construction within another indicates both that a crisis in the field-Imaginary (its common sense) is taking place and that this crisis is becoming apparent in the war of paradigms.

NEW AMERICANISTS AND NEW HISTORICISTS FROM THE OUTSIDE/IN

So far Crews's review has proven useful in several ways: in defining a shift in the orientation of the field, in exemplifying the crisis in identity produced by this shift, and in the correlation between these crises and the liberal end of ideology consensus. Stated differently, Crews's discussion of New Americanists indicates the intimate relationship between the paradigms within American Studies and the dominant myths about the nature of the American character. These paradigms do not refer to existing facts, but are constituted out of the field-Imaginary of American Studies whose primal scene they constitute. When a critic, such as Slotkin, offers an alternate Imaginary out of which to constitute the field of American Studies, he threatens the identity of those constituted in the previous field-Imaginary. In reaction to this (imaginary) threat, Crews recovers the America produced out of the cold war consensus.

Throughout his review, Crews differentiates his field's practices from those of the New Americanists' by the difficulty he displays in placing them. That he places them within the academy, yet outside his field, is significant for Crews's having misrecognized the separation (on which he bases his identity) between the cultural and the political. Crews fails to acknowledge New Americanists as members of his field because they insist on literature as an agency within the political world and thereby violate the fundamental presupposition of the liberal imagination. In returning a historical context to American Studies, New Americanists have developed a subfield within American Studies called New Historicism. The New Historicism constructs for New Americanists an ideological agency which returns questions of class, race, and gender from the political unconscious of American Studies. That agency depends for its effectiveness upon the skill in close reading developed by the previous generation of Americanists: their new critical ability to convert even the most incoherent of texts into an apparent unity. Such New Historicists can turn the raw materials of history (chronicles, unofficial memoirs, fashions, economic statistics, anecdotes) into objects of New Americanists' attention by reconstructing these texts' relations with canonical works. Since these constructions address the ways in which New Historicists and professional historians treat historical materials differently, I will, before defending them, restate the most frequent criticisms professional historians have directed against the New Historicists—that they are unable to follow the rules of disinterested inquiry and that they formulate arbitrary connections between text and context.

In relating the otherwise forgettable objects of everyday life to historical meta-narratives, New Historicists turn one of the prerogatives of a close reader into an historical agency. Like the close reader, the American New Historicist constructs relations between otherwise unrelated political, economic, and historical materials and the meta-texts of American Studies. They remake American history by making it seem in need of a field made up of close readings. When official history is written after the manner in which New Americanists read texts, that history no longer remains beholden to the strictures of empiricist or realist or conventionalist historiography—any more than a close reading does. By reading into archival materials the mediations necessary for historic placement, American New Historicists have substantially revised the textuality of American history.

As Paul Bové has persuasively demonstrated, their newly discovered power over history has led some New Historicists to inflated claims about literature's effect on political change.[6] One familiar version of these claims depends upon the homologous relationship between the "textuality" of history and the "historicity" of the text. Now on one level this homology and the claim dependent upon it are simply true. For, even if the New Historicism had not led to changes in the practices of professional historians, or effected any great change in the culture at large, it has, in the practices of the New Americanists, significantly changed the field of American Studies. Having interpellated historical documents and related interpretive constructions into the textuality of American literature, the New Historicist has in fact historicized the literary text. But the culture in which these historical changes have taken place remains the relatively restricted field of American Studies, a field, as Crews's review indicates, particularly volatile at the present time, with a number of divergent practices in the process of emergence. Given its resourcefulness in the production of new relations, the New Historicism pro-

vides New Americanists with a way of affiliating their emergent disciplinary practices with emancipatory social or political movements. But the relationships
American New Historicists establish between those social movements and their
emergent practices are, as I hope to demonstrate, quite complicated.

When New Americanists read the relations between social movements and
their own emergent practices, their readings sometimes turn the structural unit
of signification for a disciplinary practice—displacing the preceding unit with one
significantly different—into a homology for the basic reflex of an emancipatory
social or political praxis—the opposition of a dominated group to an oppressor.
When they articulate their new practices in terms of this homology, but without
nonacademic political associations, New Americanists activate what we might call
the ideology of discipline formation. That is, they identify and symbolically affiliate what is innovative in their disciplinary practices with a social movement's
opposition to an oppressor. This identification is ideological in the sense that it
constitutes for the New Americanists an imaginary scenario about what actually
takes place when someone learns a new discipline. Reconstructed out of the imaginary relations within this scenario, the rigorous methodology, while being
learned, occupies the position of the oppressor, but after the discipline's methods
are thoroughly learned, that same rigorous methodology occupies the position of
the emancipator. The release is as much a part of the structure of disciplinary
instruction as is the oppression. It is only when the ideology about the instruction
takes precedence over its actual content that the scene of disciplinary instruction
turns into a generalized opposition directed against an oppressive power.

Thus far, this account legitimizes New Historicism's claim to cultural power,
but it questions the generalized oppositional context within which some American
New Historicists have described their discipline. This delegitimation partially
corroborates, but also importantly revises, Crews's claim that their ideology should
exclude the New Americanists from academic fields. As Gerald Graff has reminded us,[7] American Studies followed English Studies in assigning academic
status to the demands for equality and justice of disenfranchised social groups.
By redefining them within the terms of their field, previous Americanists fulfilled
these political demands but only in the idealizing terms of the liberal imagination.
This liberalization from *within* the field of American Studies, as Allen Grossman
has pointed out, compensated for the diminution of progressive political programs
outside the academy.

The acceptance of modern letters in the mother tongue as a university
subject runs fairly parallel, as is obvious with the liberalization of the polity
in England and America and particularly with the emancipation of women,
so far as it occurred. Where the university could not ignore a class or
group, it was inclined to offer it a pathway to academic legitimacy that
satisfied claims upon status but excluded from the means to rule.[8]

If American Studies redefined liberty as a freedom from emancipatory demands, the liberal imagination, in its exercise of negative capability, denied those demands any specific political representation. Demands for women's or Blacks' rights became identified instead with all the other public matters from which the liberal psyche should separate itself. But the New Americanists' inclusion among their ranks of representatives from newly enfranchised political groups refuses the reduction of real political gains into the symbolic attitudes struck by the liberal imagination. Insofar as the liberal imagination represents the denial of political questions, the academic field it supervises becomes, for the New Americanists, an appropriate battlefield to fight for the return of these questions to the literary imagination.

As we have seen, the New Historicism enables New Americanists to reconstruct the relation between public and cultural matters previously denied. When a New Historicist makes explicit the relationship between an emancipatory struggle taking place outside the academy and an argument she is conducting within the field, the relationship between instruction in the discipline's practices and participation in emancipatory political movements can no longer be described as imaginary. Such *realized* relations undermine the separation of the public world from the cultural sphere and join, as Jonathan Arac puts it, "the nexus of classroom, discipline and profession to such political areas as those of gender, race and class as well as nation."[9]

FROM THE COLD WAR CONSENSUS TO THE NEW DISSENSUS

In their representations of public questions and political groups previously excluded from their field, New Americanists can be—they are by Crews—described as external to American Studies. When their work continues the struggles taking place outside the academy or realizes the connection between their disciplinary practices and oppositional political movements, New Americanists separate their discipline from the liberal consensus.

In characterizing the difference between the liberal "end of ideology" consensus represented within his field and the New Americanists' oppositional practices, Crews turns to Sacvan Bercovitch, whose notion of "dissensus" politics at once discriminates New from previous Americanists and designates their pluralistic project as unassimilable to any consensus. Since any consensus, in Bercovitch's estimation, reproduces the cold war ideology, only a dissensus view will counter that ideology.

To discriminate among New Americanists and distinguish their oppositional practices from Bercovitch's notion of dissensus, I now turn to that notion. While he never explicitly defines dissensus, Bercovitch uses the term to convey the discontinuity between generations—setting the heterogeneity of his contributors' dissenting opinions about American literature against that generation's liberal consensus. Used to indicate a gathering of diverse views, Bercovitch's term tacitly corroborates the cold war consensus it explicitly opposes. Yet Bercovitch's dissensus restores value only to the principle of dissent. For this dissensus does not emerge out of his contributors' resistance to specific cultural arrangements or presupposition of a prior consensus. It is not a further development of political arguments only partially pursued by the preceding generation of Americanists or of residual forces needing realization. Neither is it an inclusion of contexts or historical facts missing from the prior history, yet crucial for adequate historical understanding. It is not any of these things because such contestatory relations between the new dissensus and the old consensus would do just what Bercovitch insists can (must) never be done, that is, argue for the effectiveness of an oppositional movement. Instead of proposing a description of his Cambridge project in New Americanist literary history as the history of an oppositional consensus in the process of formation, Bercovitch identifies any consensus derivable from his dissensus as the characteristic work of American Ideology. Previous efforts at a literary history (whether by Spiller, in the forties with fifty-five contributors, or by Parrington, in the twenties with one) resulted, Bercovitch claims, in a "consensus about the term 'literary' that involved the legitimation of an entire canon, and a consensus about the term 'history' that was legitimated by a certain concept of America."[10] The consensus about both terms was best expressed, Bercovitch agrees with Crews, by F. O. Matthiessen in his landmark study *American Renaissance*, where he explained that Whitman, Thoreau, Melville, Hawthorne, and Emerson all "felt it was incumbent on their generation to give fulfillment to the potentialities freed by the Revolution, to provide a culture commensurate with America's political opportunity."[11]

In fact, the consensus Matthiessen represented (which, as we have seen, included R. W. B. Lewis, Trilling, Smith, Chase, Marx, Poirier, Fiedler, Anderson, and, in complicated ways, an earlier cultural version of Bercovitch) emphasized *strains* in the American literary impulse that led out of Parrington's notion of history and into alternative worlds organized by romance, style, cultural heroism, and (in the case of Fiedler's *Love and Death in the American Novel*) neurosis. Considered from one perspective, all the practitioners of American New Historicism are in revolt against the ahistoricism of the preceding generation's consensus. Given his ground-breaking study of the monologic effect in both American literature and culture of the revolutionary mythos, however, Bercovitch cannot affiliate himself with the new generations's revolt nor indeed any oppositional model. He believes that the *mythos* of the revolution supported the cultural form he calls the American Jeremiad, which functions at times of organic crises (like the present) as a force for social integration in American society. Bercovitch also believes that any oppositional movement is, of necessity, both structured in this revolutionary mythos and dependent upon that mythos for cultural power. And having, in *The American Jeremiad*, rejected in advance any possible grounds for the conversion of dissent (whether expressed implicitly by literary works or explicitly by political groups) into the bases for actual social change, Bercovitch observes that American radicalism is always represented in ways that reaffirm the culture rather than undermine it. For Bercovitch, the history of American radical movements only reveals the incomparable cooptative power of American ideology rather than the movement's power to effect social change. American ideology refutes and absorbs subversive cultural energies, Bercovitch cogently observes, "harnessing discontent to the social enterprise" by drawing out protest and turning it into a rite of ideological assent.[12]

While Bercovitch proposed this description of American culture quite early in his career—as an expert in Puritan literature—the claim did not command the recognition from the field of American Studies until he used the writings of American Renaissance authors, Melville, Hawthorne, Thoreau, Emerson, and Whitman, as examples of the rhetoric of the American Jeremiad. In keeping with his understanding of the subsumptive power of an explanation borrowing on the revolution for its authority, Bercovitch cannot describe the new dissensus in terms of an opposition to the old consensus, but rather as the result of its breakdown. The old consensus no longer seems to account for the evidence, Bercovitch sensibly explains; hence, the context it once provided now conceals more than it reveals. In American Studies what we have instead of this context, Bercovitch contends, "is a Babel of contending approaches, argued with a ferocity reminiscent of the polemics that erupted in the last great days of Rome."[13] However, insofar as it correlates the work of his twenty-one contributors with the end of an Empire, Bercovitch's New Cambridge History project not only does not eradicate but actively deploys the rhetoric of revolution. More significantly, Bercovitch welcomes the breakdown that the pervasive interpretive confusion resulting from this Babel forebodes.

In related observations about New Historicicm, Stephen Greenblatt has recently argued that mainstream literary history produced a prevailing consensus quite similar to the one Bercovitch claims was at work in the old American literary history. Mainstream literary history, Greenblatt remarks, tends "to be monological, that is, it is concerned with discovering a single political vision, usually identical to that said to be held by the entire literate cultural class."[14] But Greenblatt then describes the old version of literary history in a way significantly different from Bercovitch. This old historicist version is old, Greenblatt claims, because it accepted historical fact as a phenomenon to be observed rather than to be produced by particular social groups in conflict with other social groups—as it is by the New Historicists. Whereas for Bercovitch the elaboration of conflict always works in the service of an American ideology, always able to find unity in diversity, for Greenblatt the New Historicists' multiplication of irreconcilable conflicts produces a context for their mutual contestation. Against Bercovitch's notion of an expressive unity in the old consensus, Greenblatt views literary works themselves as sites of internalized political conflict, "fields of force, places of dissension and shifting interests, occasions for the jostling of orthodoxies and subversive interests."[15]

Following Greenblatt's line of thought, we can begin to consider the limitations in Bercovitch's model of dissensus by noting the context for contentious dialogue he eliminates from consideration. By defining the new dissensus solely in terms of the breakdown of the old, Bercovitch relegates any of its political effectiveness to signs of this breakdown. Without any context within which dissensus Americanists can argue among themselves over the outcomes of the conflicts among dominant and subordinate social groups, among the rhetorics most effective for the reconstruction of American history, or among the shapes emergent historical forces should assume, the new dissensus only continues the old consensus—but under the displaced form of its breakup into unrelated fragments.

To give the new dissensus political effectiveness, Bercovitch should re-evaluate his oppositional model, beginning with his notion of the Jeremiad. For, at the time Bercovitch claims for it greatest cultural power, the pre-Civil War years of American Renaissance, it was, in fact, breaking apart as an adequate consensus formation. During the debates over the conflicted, highly charged, and mutually contestatory issues of expansionism, the national bank, slavery, and secession, the revolutionary mythos was put into service differently by each interest group— thereby losing its power to reconcile their disputes and integrate the factions. Unlike either the old consensus or the present dissensus, the oppositional movements which then formed had great political effectiveness. Their political means of continuing their rhetorical arguments, the Civil War, resulted in a transformation of the nation's polity—slaves were set free and the South underwent radical reconstruction, as did various previously disenfranchised groups in the North. Bercovitch's notion of dissensus, insofar as it is structured by the *separation* of the politics of dissent from the already established consensus, represses the social change an oppositional movement can produce. If, in his commentary on writers from the pre-Civil War era, he at times imposes his notion of the ideology of consensus onto American writers in his overseeing of the Cambridge project, he uses his prior description of the American Jeremiad to subsume and co-opt the differences among his contributors. In pre-designating any coalition of dissenters to be complicit with the integrative function in American ideology, Bercovitch proposes as the basis for his dissensus the breakdown of the ideology. But that breakdown, insofar as it presupposes *The American Jeremiad* as the source of integration, only signifies the historic effect of that work on the Cambridge project. As the *unity* the dissensus Americanists corroborate, *The American Jeremiad* provides their project with a tacit consensus. That tacit consensus in turn continues the work of ideological separation effected by the liberal consensus.

FROM THE COLD WAR DISSENSUS TO A NEW AMERICANIST COUNTER-HEGEMONY

To understand what is politically effective about the cultural conversation in-itiated by the New Americanists and what differentiates that conversation from dissensus, we need to consider the conversation it displaces. As we have seen, that conversation in the cold war epoch explicitly related the construction of the field of American Studies to liberal anticommunist consensus. Lionel Trilling began this cultural conversation when he used his reading of America's canonical writers to enforce that consensus:

> The fact is the American writers of genius have not turned their minds to society. Poe and Melville were quite apart from it; the reality they sought was only tangential to society. Hawthorne was acute when he insisted that he did not write novels but romances—he thus expressed his aware-ness of the lack of social texture in his work.[16]

Richard Chase, in a book published seven years after *The Liberal Imagination*, explicitly relates Trilling's distinction between the romance and the novel to the politics of the cold war consensus. For Chase, the romance, insofar as it represents the difference between negative capability and ideological structures, is represen-tative of America's cultural capital. Chase reproduces this cultural capital by de-ploying the romance as his means of constructing canonical texts. But then Chase advances Trilling's hypothesis another step by asserting that "the abstractness and profundity of romance allow it to formulate moral truths of universal validity."[17] And once he has identified the function of the romance with the cultural entitle-ment to speak universal truths, Chase assigns this power not to the romances themselves but to the liberal imagination capable of claiming this power as its own. The liberal imagination recognizes in the romance

> an assumed freedom from the ordinary novelistic requirements of verisi-militude, development, and continuity; a tendency toward melodrama and idyl; a more or less formal abstractness and, on the other hand, a ten-dency to plunge into the underside of consciousness; a willingness to abandon moral questions or to ignore the spectacle of man in society, or to consider these things only indirectly or abstractly.[18]

In an intervention which significantly changes the terms of this conversation, Russell Reising, in one of the books Crews reviews (*The Unusable Past: Theory and the Study of American Literature*) underscores the relationship between Trill-ing's work and the liberal anti-Stalinism of consensus historians. Their embattled relationship with progressive liberal historians led anti-Stalinists to two funda-mental strategies:

> (1) They replaced the progressive dualistic line up of historical forces with a triadic (sometimes called dialectical) model that postulated some "middle landscape" which synthesized various oppositions and (2) they rejected a materialistic emphasis on economics for an analysis of culture, focusing on human expression in psychology, art and literature. Whereas Progressives wanted to understand what in fact was the reality of history, counter-Progressives stressed the primacy of how people felt about reality and how their myths, images and symbols dramatized these feelings.[19]

Through his analysis of the relationship between Trilling's literary project and the more or less contemporary work of the consensus historians, this New Americanist underscores the ideological work the liberal imagination effected in the political world.

Following Trilling, Chase identifies this ideological work with the genre of the romance, then internalizes this separation as the regulative norm of American Studies. Geraldine Murphy, a New Americanist Crews does not mention in his review, has usefully identified Chase's development of Trilling's consensus with the "vital center" hypothesis of such cold war consensus historians as Arthur Schlesinger. In the cultural contradictions Chase isolated as the chief canonical feature in the American romance, Murphy discerns the construction of an American cultural front united against communism:

> the cultural front of this apocalyptic struggle between East and West pitted a socialist realism controlled by the State for its own propagandistic purposes against a subjective symbolistic, abstract modernism—the kind of art that readily symbolized the independent critical role of the artist in democratic society.[20]

In Murphy's reading of the liberal consensus, this opposition to communism produced a united cultural front in the fifties, but a cultural front that, following the disappearance of Stalinism as a vital opponent, was destined to lose any political effectiveness. Following the heating up of the Vietnam war in the sixties, the cold war itself, as the unquestioned basis for articulating the cultural capital of America, became the object of political opposition. And following the emergence of civil rights, women's rights, and student movements throughout the country, the cold war consensus lost its power to contain opposition.

The selves American citizens constructed out of the emancipatory politics of the sixties desublimated the political energies the liberal imagination had previously held in check. But their previous containment within a separate cultural sphere significantly qualified the effectiveness of these desublimated energies. Having been held in check by an *imaginary separation*, these energies were initially expressive of the power to break through imaginary barriers. The students' demands for political arrangements organized around the fulfillment of libidinal drives resulted in part from the transference into the political sphere of the impulses and drives previously identified as those experienced within the realm of the American romance. When students formulated demands within a political world that Ahab and Ishmael and Natty Bumppo and Emerson and Whitman had previously voiced only within the realm of the literary romance, they voiced their refusal to acknowledge the difference between the cultural and the public realm.

By insisting that the inner aspirations developed through their reading of the American romance should be realized within the public world, these students undermined Trilling's central premise of "Reality in America." In this essay, Trilling definitively separated the realm of the literary romance, where desire for wholeness could be fulfilled, from the realm of politics, where it could not. By breaking down the imaginary barrier separating the romance they had internalized from the external norms of American *Realpolitik*, the students desublimated the powerful energies produced as the ideological work of the liberal imagination, but in a political realm that had become for them indistinguishable from a utopian romance. The sixties, in other words, turned the politics of the forties inside out. Not Stalinism but liberal consensus became the threat to the whole self. And the response to this threat was the appearance, within the public world, of the primal scene of the American Romance. When students demanded from their public world what American characters had demanded in romance, they denied the imaginary separation, predicated by the Liberal Imagination, between the cultural and the political. Consequently, their politics literalized, in the public world, the imaginary of the American Romance.

In partial recognition of the need to restore the barrier separating these realms, Quentin Anderson, in a book published three years after the student riots of 1968, redesignates Trilling's liberal imagination *The Imperial Self*.[21] This change in the name of the self who acts from within the cultural sphere adapts the students' ideological critique of America's foreign policy in the Vietnam era to the characterization of the self constituted within America's foundational literary texts. In conscripting the name that had united various oppositional political groups against American foreign policy to describe the self produced out of the American Romance, Anderson reinstates the barrier separating cultural from political matters. But this time, the divisions appeared within the psyches of students who had previously refused to acknowledge the difference between the public and private realms. However, following the publication of *The Imperial Self*, Anderson's Columbia students, at any rate, would recognize a homology between the selves produced within American romances and within American foreign policy and would understand, as the rationale for this identification, a hypertrophy of narcissistic impulses productive of imperialism:

I believe that the habit scholars have of calling Emerson misty or abstract, calling Whitman a successful charlatan, calling Henry James ambiguous, are but ways of referring to an inchoate perception of the absolutism of the self which is described in this essay. This absolutism involves an extreme passivity, which is complemented by, must be complemented by, the claim of the imperial self to mastery of what has almost overwhelmed it.[22]

In this passage, Anderson does not bring Trilling's and Chase's prior formulations into consideration for explicit revision, nor does he explicitly identify the liberal imagination as a version of the imperial self. Instead, he produces a protocol for relearning Trilling's instruction as the difference between the imperial self within the American Romance and America's imperialist foreign policy. But the imperial self produced out of the absolutist demands for mastery of previously unmastered materials differs crucially from the imperialist policies of a government. The cultural imperial ego is produced out of an extreme passivity designed to "suffer" the unmastered materials of a world external to the creative imagination. Following this act of passive aggression, the material so suffered ceases to remain external and turns instead into the fluent and circumambient energies of the creative self.

Redefined as an unrealizable inner drive to master external matters, the imperial ego, for Anderson, rules the difference between its inner America and the rest of the world. The imperial ego *within* at once depends upon the public policy of U.S. imperialism for its definition, yet negates such a policy as antithetical to its authentic (real cultural) interests. And self-ruled rather than interested in ruling others, Anderson's imperial self overrules the need to materialize any other political interests. It restores the private cultural realm as the appropriate domain of the liberal imagination and condemns any realization of that imagination in the public world as a version of plain old U.S. imperialism.

In the Vietnam era of liberationist politics, Anderson's *Imperial Self* worked as an exemplary version of the American Jeremiad. In his critique of the nation's founding works, Anderson engages the oppositional energies released within the student counterculture, but then subsumes them within the dominant cultural realm that Trilling and Chase had previously cordoned off from politics. In the absence of any American Stalinists or communists or Marxists for liberal consensus critics to oppose, the liberal subjects Americans constructed out of the liberationist movements of the day become the implicit object of Anderson's liberal critique. Instead of proposing exemplary representations within past American literature for these counter-consensus movements, Anderson as a representative of the liberal consensus rediscovers within them the symptoms of absolutist drives, which, when acted upon in the public world, turned counter-imperialism into imperialism.

Published at the outset of the post-Vietnam era (and revised after his move to

Columbia), Sacvan Bercovitch's *American Jeremiad* constructs a totalized cultural domain for Anderson's *Imperial Self* to supervise when he designates all oppositional political forces as figurations of the oppositioned structure at work in a pervasive revolutionary *mythos*. Daniel T. O'Hara cogently describes the collusion between Bercovitch's Jeremiad structure and the cold war consensus as a

> scene of Cold War cultural persuasion . . . the latest in a series of collective mythic acts of national self-definition that go back to the formation of the revolutionary ethos and before that to the Puritans' compact on *The Mayflower* to found a brilliant city on the Hill. The Soviet Union replaces Satan and his snares, the imperial British, and the slave-holding secessionists as the latest cultural Other, the always already potentially present Enemy Within against which the authentic American must strive to create a distinctive identity.[23]

Thus, for Bercovitch every oppositional movement is susceptible to cooptation within what we might call the "surplus opposition" of the cold war consensus. Because he cannot envision any political culture in the United States other than one organized according to the supernumerary binarity of the cold war consensus, Bercovitch, as we have seen, proposes a dissensus politics. But, as his placement within this cultural conversation makes clear, Bercovitch's politics of dissensus only elevate *The American Jeremiad* into the consensus principle of the cold war liberals. And when, in the Cambridge project, it becomes the anthology's principle for the reorganization of American literary history, it continues the cold war consensus by taking opposition to a point of powerless dissensus. Without any arena for articulating different, dissenting voices into an empowering reconstruction of the field of American Studies, these individual, dissenting voices become simulacra of the structuring oppositions that articulated the cold war. Whereas, for Bercovitch, there was no way outside oppositional containment, for many New Americanists at work in his Cambridge History project (and elsewhere), there exists the possibility of countering the hegemony. Frederick Crews's review testifies to the New Americanists' effectiveness in reorganizing the field of American Studies.

NEW AMERICANISTS AND THE COUNTER-HEGEMONY

To understand what's at stake in the New Americanists' counter-hegemony, we need to turn first to Gramsci, who formulates the dynamic "wars of position" in which counter-hegemonic forces can be successfully mobilized against hegemony. A war of position takes place, as Joseph Buttigieg has pointed out, during periods of organic crisis, when the collective will organized according to one interpretation of reality gives way, after years of struggle, to alternative interpretations.[24] Gramsci locates the origin of organic crisis in moments of drastic cultural change which illuminate the incurable contradiction at work within prevailing organizing principles. Gramsci is as interested "to research into how precisely permanent collective wills are formed" out of a "concrete fantasy" as he is to study where "there exists in society the necessary and sufficient conditions for its transformation." To overturn the hegemonic successfully requires that oppositional forces construct their own version of a "concrete fantasy" whose "level of reality and attainability" will elicit identification from previously disadvantaged minority groups and will enable the construction of a prevailing alternate interpretation of reality able to turn the pervasive conflict of interpretations to the use of certain groups.[25]

Throughout this discussion of the New Americanists, I have argued the relationship between their emergence and the change in what Gramsci calls the "concrete fantasy" (what I have described as a crisis in the field-Imaginary) of American Studies. I depend upon this category because it accounts for both the remarkable integration in the meta-narrative thematic of American Studies and for the psychological resistance to any counter-hegemonic critique of the tacit assumptions at work in those narratives. Descriptive of the pre-linguistic identification of the field practitioner with the field's assumptions, principles, and beliefs, the field-Imaginary designates the place in American culture for the overdetermination of "romance." Naming at once the genre within the field, the means of producing and interpreting its canonical objects, the relations between the field's practitioners, the mediation between the field and the culture, and the means of separating culture from politics, the romance overdetermines the field of American Studies.

In *Professing Literature*, Gerald Graff discusses the historic role in the construction of American Studies of symbolic-romance theory in terms compatible with my own:

> The symbolic-romance theory, stressing as it did the inability of American narratives to resolve their conflicts within any social form of life, provided expression for disappointments left over from the thirties toward a society that had failed to fulfill its ideal image of itself but evidently could not be righted by social action.[26]

When transferred onto the field of American romance, these unresolved conflicts become the pure potentialities and infinite capabilities of the whole self. And following Graff, what might be called the field-Symbolic of American Studies, the codification by its practitioners of primal scene materials into disparate interpretations and close readings, produces a thick description for this symbolic romance. When translating field-Imaginary materials into their interpretations,

Americanists have enforced the field's tacit assumptions that their primal identities have internalized. In their secondary elaborations of their disparate critical practices, these Americanists have rationalized their tacit assumptions into the common sense of the field, thereby disseminating signs and codes in terms of what counts as legitimate knowledge. In their readings, then, Americanists like Crews have simply recirculated the assumptions, norms, and beliefs which they have internalized on the primal scene as beyond question. And the central practices of these older Americanists have turned their romance with the primal scene of American Studies into what Daniel T. O'Hara called the romance of interpretation.[27] So, whereas the primal scene of the romance is predicated upon the separation of an internal from an external realm, O'Hara's romance of interpretation translates the power to separate from a public realm into the power to dominate a text, external nature, previous interpretations, a former self, in a relentlessly circular psychic economy.

In denying the separation constitutive of the field, however, New Americanists have changed the field-Imaginary of American Studies. The political unconscious of the primal scene of their New Historicist readings embodies *both* the *repressed relationship between* the literary and the political and the *disenfranchised groups previously unrepresentable in this relationship.* And as conduits for the return of figures and materials repressed through the denial of the relationship of the field to the public world, New Americanists occupy a double relation. For as *liaisons between* cultural and public realms, they are at once within the field yet external to it. Moreover, as representatives of subjects excluded from the field-Imaginary by the previous political unconscious, New Americanists have a responsibility to make these absent subjects representable in their field's past and present.

Predicated upon the linkage between the cultural and the public, the New Americanists' field-Imaginary correlates cultural with political materials in the primal scene. A brief list of New Americanists' titles should indicate this shift. Smith's *Virgin Land* gives way to Annette Kolodny's *Lay of the Land* and Slotkin's *Fatal Environment;* R. W. B. Lewis's *American Adam* becomes Myra Jehlen's *American Incarnation,* Carolyn Porter's *Seeing and Being,* or Henry Louis Gates's *Figures in Black;* Chase's *American Novel and Its Tradition* ends up Russell Reising's *Unusable Past;* Roy Harvey Pearce's *Continuity of American Poetry* translates to Paul Bové's *Destructive Poetics,* while Bercovitch's *American Jeremiad* finishes as Frank Lentricchia's *Criticism and Social Change.* All of these titles restore in their primal scenes the relations between cultural and political materials denied by previous Americanists. These recovered relations enable New Americanists to link repressed sociopolitical contexts *within* literary works to the sociopolitical issues *external* to the academic field. When they achieve critical mass, these linkages can change the hegemonic self-representation of the United States' culture.

NOTES

1. *The American Renaissance Reconsidered: Selected Papers from the English Institute, 1982–1983*, ed. Walter Benn Michaels and Donald E. Pease (Baltimore: Johns Hopkins University Press, 1985); Russell S. Reising, *The Unusable Past: Theory and the Study of American Literature* (New York: Methuen, 1986); *Ideology and Classic American Literature,* ed. Sacvan Bercovitch and Myra Jehlen (Cambridge: Cambridge University Press, 1986); Donald E. Pease, *Visionary Compacts: American Renaissance Writings in Cultural Context* (Madison: University of Wisconsin Press, 1987); Jane Tompkins, *Sensational Designs: The Cultural Work of American Fiction, 1790–1860* (New York: Oxford University Press, 1985); David S. Reynolds, *Beneath the American Renaissance: The Subversive Imagination in the Age of Emerson and Melville* (New York: Alfred A. Knopf, 1988); Philip Fisher, *Hard Facts: Setting and Form in the American Novel* (New York: Oxford University Press, 1985). See Frederick Crews, "Whose American Renaissance?" *New York Review of Books* 35, no. 16 (October 27, 1988): 68–69.

2. Crews, "Whose American Renaissance?" p. 81; Lionel Trilling, *The Liberal Imagination: Essays on Literature and Society* (New York: Viking, 1950).

3. Henry Nash Smith, "Symbol and Idea in Virgin Land," in *Ideology and Classic American Literature*, p. 23.

4. Crews, "Whose American Renaissance?" p. 74.

5. Crews, "Whose American Renaissance?" p. 74.

6. See Paul Bové, *Intellectuals in Power: A Genealogy of Critical Humanism* (New York: Columbia University Press, 1986), particularly "Intellectuals at War: Michel Foucault and the Analytics of Power."

7. See Graff, *Professing Literature*, pp. 209–25.

8. Allen Grossman in "Criticism, Consciousness and the Sources of Life: Some Tasks for English Studies" in *Uses of Literature*, ed. Monroe Engel (Cambridge: Harvard University Press), p. 25.

9. Jonathan Arac, *Critical Genealogies: Historical Situations for Postmodern Literary Studies* (New York: Columbia University Press, 1987), p. 307.

10. Sacvan Bercovitch, "The Problem of Ideology in American Literary History," *Critical Inquiry* 12, no. 1 (Summer 1986):632.

11. Bercovitch, "The Problem of Ideology," p. 633.

12. Bercovitch, "The Problem of Ideology," p. 644.

13. Bercovitch, "The Problem of Ideology," p. 633.

14. Stephen Greenblatt, "Introduction," *Genre* 15, nos. 1–2 (Spring and Summer 1982):5.

15. Greenblatt, "Introduction," p. 6.

16. Trilling, *The Liberal Imagination*, p. 212.

17. Richard Chase, *The American Novel and Its Tradition* (Garden City: Doubleday, 1957), p. xi.

18. Chase, *The American Novel*, p. ix.

19. Russell Reising, *The Unusable Past*, p. 95.

20. Geraldine Murphy, "Romancing the Center: Gold War Politics and Classic American Literature," *Poetics Today* 9, no. 4 (1988):738.

21. Quentin Anderson, *The Imperial Self: An Essay in American Literary and Cultural History* (New York: Random House, 1971), pp. ix–x.

22. Anderson, *The Imperial Self*, p. 14.

23. Daniel T. O'Hara, "Socializing the Sublime in American Renaissance Writers," *SAQ* 88, no. 3 (Summer 1989):701.

24. See Joseph A. Buttigieg, "The Exemplary Worldliness of Antonio Gramsci's Literary Criticism," in *boundary 2* 11, nos. 1–2 (1982–83):21–39.

25. Antonio Gramsci, "The Modern Prince," in *The Modern Prince and Other Writings*, ed. Louis Marks (New York: International Publishers, 1957), pp. 169, 184, 166, 174, and 154.

26. Graff, *Professing Literature*, p. 219.

27. In *The Romance of Interpretation: Visionary Criticism from Pater to de Man* (New York: Columbia University Press, 1985). O'Hara revises the interpretive romance hypothesis—which analyzes the ways in which the literary critic's transferences and counter-transference with literary texts produce an inflationary critical self—in *Lionel Trilling: The Work of Liberation* (Madison: University of Wisconsin Press, 1988), which is simply the best interpretive study of Trilling's entire career available.

7

THE CONSTRUCTION OF PRIVACY IN AND AROUND *THE BOSTONIANS*

BROOK THOMAS

To start: a scene from *The Bostonians.* The transplanted southerner Basil Ransom has returned to Boston from New York on a business trip and decides to look up Verena Tarrant, whom he had met the year before while visiting his cousin Olive Chancellor, a reformer and women's rights advocate. Basil knows that Olive despises him for his conservative views but even so risks stopping by with the hopes of locating Verena. Seeing instead the old abolitionist Miss Birdseye leaving Olive's house, Basil gets from her Verena's Cambridge address and elicits from her a promise not to tell Olive that she had seen him. Believing in the "victory of truth" and that Verena will convert Basil to their cause "privately," Miss Birdseye assents: "She *will* affect you! If that's to be your secret, I will keep it."[1]

Proceeding to Cambridge, Basil finds Verena and goes with her for a long walk. The question arises as to whether Verena will tell Olive of the visit. "How will she know," Basil asks, "unless you tell her?"(*B*, 243). "I tell her everything," responds Verena (*B*, 243), all the while suggesting that she might after all keep the visit secret.

> "Well, if I don't tell Olive, then you must leave me here," said Verena, stopping in the path and putting out a hand of farewell.
>
> "I don't understand. What has that to do with it? Besides I thought you said you *must* tell," Ransom added. In playing with the subject this way, in enjoying her visible hesitation, he was slightly conscious of a man's brutality—of being pushed by an impulse to test her good-nature, which seemed to have no limit. It showed no sign of perturbation as she answered:
>
> "Well, I want to be free—to do as I think best. And, if there is a chance of my keeping it back, there mustn't be anything more—there must not, Mr. Ransom, really."

"Anything more? Why, what are you afraid there will be—if I should simply walk home with you?"

"I must go alone, I must hurry back to mother," she said, for all reply. And she again put out her hand, which he had not taken before.

Of course he took it now, and even held it a moment; he didn't like being dismissed, and was thinking of pretexts to linger. "Miss Birdseye said you would convert me, but you haven't yet," it came into his head to say (*B*, 244–45).

Later we learn that Ransom's visit, "buried in unspoken, in unspeakable, considerations," becomes "the only secret [Verena] had in the world—the only thing that was all her own" (*B*, 288).

Staged around a handshake—the most common gesture standing for the enactment of a contractual agreement—this scene creates a private space between Basil and Verena, giving to her a secret that is her only possession in the world. In this essay I want to examine the construction of privacy in *The Bostonians*, especially the possibility for it under the terms set down by the marriage contract. But I want to do more. Even though frequently we refer to privacy, it is not entirely clear what we refer to when we do. As the author of a legal text on the right of privacy notes, "The word 'privacy' has taken on so many different meanings and connotations in so many different legal and social contexts that it has largely ceased to convey any single coherent concept."[2] Or, as a book co-authored by the lawyer who defended *Ulysses* against charges of obscenity puts it, "The word 'privacy' has different meanings for all of us."[3] The notion of privacy seems to evoke private meanings. Given this confused sense of privacy, there still might be some lessons to be learned from James's fictional construction of the private, even if we no longer accept them as lessons from the Master.

One reason for the legal confusion over privacy is that law in the United States distinguishes between two kinds of privacy. On the one hand, there is the so-called constitutional right of privacy that protects against governmental actions; on the other, there is the common law or tort right to privacy that protects against actions by other private parties. The confusion is heightened by the fact that the Constitution makes no mention of a right of privacy, nor is one mentioned in the common law until the late nineteenth century, when two American lawyers gave it a rationale and a name. Constitutional privacy is in large measure a creation of the Warren Court, especially Justice Douglas, who argued that various amendments of the Bill of Rights contain "penumbras," which, when taken together, create "zones of privacy" into which the government should not intrude.[4] For instance, a Constitutional right of privacy is the basis for the decision in *Roe v. Wade*, which limits the government's power to interfere with a woman's choice to have an abortion. In contrast, the common-law right to privacy grows out of a *Harvard Law Review* essay published in 1890. Its authors, Samuel Warren and Louis Brandeis, like James, attended Harvard. Constructed out of James's milieu and at almost the same time that he was writing, this right to privacy would seem to be the one most pertinent to his works.

Brandeis and Warren graduated first and second in their law school class. Warren came from a wealthy Boston family. Brandeis would become the first Jewish member of the Supreme Court. Brandeis's biographer quotes Roscoe Pound as saying that their article did "nothing less than add a chapter to our law."[5] Its intent was to protect human dignity from the prying of others. They were especially concerned about abuses by the press:

> The press is overstepping in every direction the obvious bounds of propriety and of decency. Gossip is no longer the resource of the idle and of the vicious, but has become a trade, which is pursued with industry as well as effrontery. To satisfy a prurient taste the details of sexual relations are spread broadcast in the columns of the daily papers. To occupy the indolent, column upon column is filled with idle gossip, which can only be procured by intrusion upon the domestic circle. The intensity and complexity of life, attendant upon advancing civilization, have rendered necessary some retreat from the world, and man, under the refining influence of culture, has become more sensitive to publicity, so that solitude and privacy have become more essential to the individual; but modern enterprise and invention have, through invasions upon his privacy, subjected him to mental pain and distress, far greater than could be inflicted by mere bodily injury.[6]

This hostility to the press has sparked imaginative accounts of their article's origin. According to legend, Warren sought Brandeis's help in response to press coverage of his family's social life. In 1883 Warren married Miss Mabel Bayard, daughter of Thomas Francis Bayard, Sr., a senator from Delaware who was nearly nominated for president by the Democrats, although his southern connections raised suspicion about him with some northerners. As secretary of state, Bayard forged a cooperative alliance with Great Britain known as "hands across the Atlantic."[7] It is only appropriate, then, that the famous writer of transatlantic novels, Henry James, knew Bayard's daughter, having met her on a visit to Washington, D.C., in 1882. Impressed by her charm, he wrote to his mother that she and her friends were, "Such as one ought to marry, if one were marrying."[8] James wasn't marrying, but a year later Mabel was. According to one of Brandeis's biographers, the Warrens "set up housekeeping in Boston's exclusive Back Bay section and began to entertain elaborately. *The Saturday Evening Gazette*, which specialized in 'blue blood items,' naturally reported their activities in lurid detail."[9] Reporters, we are told, sneaked into social affairs as waiters. For six years, according to the authors of a book on privacy, Warren and Brandeis considered legal means to halt such intrusions, using that time meticulously to arrange "the words that convey the ideas that constitute [their] argument."[10]

Recently this account of the article's origins has been disputed. Unearthing very few reports of the Warrens' social life, less sympathetic scholars speculate that the actual cause of Warren's outrage was the handling of Senator Bayard in 1889.[11] But whether the image of Samuel Warren knocking a camera out of a disguised reporter's hands is a fabrication or not, it is clear that many of the so-called best men of the time were concerned about the intrusiveness of the press. For instance, Warren and Brandeis cite a *Scribner's* article written the same year by E. L. Godkin, the editor of *The Nation*. Godkin argues that the threat to privacy grows out of the development of new technologies of publicity. Admitting that there is "some substance" to the claim that "the love of gossip is after all human," he adds:

> But as long as gossip was oral, it spread, as regarded any one individual, over a very small area, and was confined to the immediate circle of his acquaintances. It did not reach, or but rarely reached, those who knew nothing of him. It did not make his name, or his walk, or his conversation familiar to strangers. And what is more to the purpose, it spared him the pain or mortification of knowing that he was gossiped about. A man seldom heard of oral gossip about him which simply made him ridiculous, or trespassed on his lawful privacy, but made no positive attack on his reputation. His peace and comfort were, therefore, but slightly affected by it.

In contrast, widely circulated papers reveal someone's imperfections to people miles away. Even worse, they allow him to read "exactly what is said about him." Thus he must suffer "the great pain of feeling that everybody he meets in the street is perfectly familiar with some folly, or misfortune, or indiscretion, or weakness, which he had previously supposed had never got beyond his domestic circle."[12]

The press's power to affront personal dignity intrigued James. In *The Reverberator* (1888), for example, a vulgar American reporter almost halts the marriage of a sophisticated French-American man to an innocent American woman when he publishes information that she confidentially tells him about the private life of her family-to-be. Shocked, the family considers her unworthy of membership in its exclusive circle. Whether or not we can trust a biographer's summary of journalistic accounts of the private life of the Warren family, James's plot indicates that Warren and Brandeis had available vivid, if fictional, evidence of the press's lack of scruples. Their concern was not with libel, which was already covered by the law. Instead, they wanted to guarantee legal protection against the sort of intrusions that James imagines, *whether the information was true or not.*[13] They sought this protection by claiming that, although it had never been articulated, the common law guaranteed a right to privacy or, as they put it, "the right 'to be left alone.' "[14]

The political consequences of such a right to privacy in our own day are not at all clear. Some liberals point to its Mugwump origins to link it to an elitist, bourgeois ideology. For evidence they could point to an 1890 editorial in *The Nation*. Commenting on the Warren and Brandeis article, it deplores violations of privacy but is pessimistic about providing for its protection, because, "In all democratic societies today the public is disposed either to resent attempts at privacy, either of mind or body, or turn them into ridicule."[15] To defend privacy seems, in other words, undemocratic. Shortly thereafter, however, an editorial in *Scribner's Magazine* takes issue with this assumption. "It is important to note," it insists, "that privacy is not by any means an attribute of aristocracy as opposed to democracy." Nonetheless, the *Scribner's* article only fuels the fire of those who find the defense of privacy conservative. It begins, "In the great future battle of the world between the two systems of Socialism and Individualism, one of the vital points of difference is to be *privacy*."[16]

But if late-nineteenth-century capitalists linked the threat to privacy to socialism, today some capitalists decry a right to privacy while some radicals cry out for it. For instance, the radical feminist Andrea Dworkin is incensed with the recent *New York Times* and *NBC News* policy of reporting the names of rape victims: "If a woman's reporting a rape to the police means she will be exposed by the media to the scrutiny of voyeurs and worse, a sexual spectacle with her legs splayed open in the public mind, reporting itself will be tantamount to suicide." Like Warren and Brandeis years earlier, Dworkin considers the truth of the reporting irrelevant. "The media," she says, "use you until they use you up." What the rape victim needs, she argues, sounding very much like our Mugwumps, is "privacy, dignity, lack of fear."[17]

In contrast, we have Judge Richard Posner's pronouncements on privacy. It is hard to fit Posner's complicated thinking under simple labels, but he is certainly not a socialist. He is, however, extremely critical of a tort right to privacy: "Very few people want to be left alone. They want to manipulate the world around them by selective disclosure of facts about themselves. . . . Reputation is what others think of us, and we have no right to control other people's thoughts. Equally we have no right, by controlling the information that is known about us, to manipulate the opinions that other people hold of us. Yet this is the essence of what most students of the subject mean by privacy."[18]

Posner's stand on privacy is consistent with that aspect of his thought that makes him an economic conservative: he is a staunch defender of the freedom of the market. Thus he disagrees with Warren and Brandeis's attempt to provide legal protection for those who want to keep information about themselves, true or not, from circulation in the market. Posner would seem to agree with the reporter in *The Reverberator* that such information belongs to the public. Any consideration of the political effect of a right to privacy should take into account Warren and Brandeis's attempt to resist the logic of the market.

The attempt to have the right to privacy resist the logic of the market forced the two lawyers to distinguish privacy from property rights. The attempt to disassociate a right from rights of property in the United States in the late nineteenth century might at first glance seem a foolish move. After all, labor leaders and political radicals decried the legal privileges granted to the propertied and declared that the major social conflict was one between the interests of workers and the interests of property. But, as legal historians point out, this was not the age of property in the law but the age of contract.[19] The law may have protected vested interests of property; nonetheless, the *value* of property was subordinate to the contract relation. Whereas in the eighteenth century there was a general tendency to assume the intrinsic value of a piece of property, in the highly developed market economy of the late nineteenth century value was determined by contractual exchanges in the marketplace. The consequences of the reign of contract for the attempts to guarantee a right to privacy are best understood if we remember Locke's crucial distinction between life and labor. For Locke labor is alienable from the person and thus becomes a form of property. Life, however, is not alienable. To subordinate the right to privacy to that of property is to make it alienable. But the entire point of a right to privacy is to protect aspects of the personality from circulation in the marketplace. Privacy, therefore, had to be related to an inalienable part of one's personality.

One way of looking at the history of the tort right to privacy is to note how difficult it has been to disassociate it from property.[20] Godkin's argument about reputation is a good example. Reputation, Godkin argues, is one of man's most valuable possessions, as important (or more important) for the comfort and happiness of life as "tangible property." As he quotes Shakespeare:

> Who steals my purse steals trash; 'tis something, nothing;
> 'Twas mine, 'tis his, and has been slave to thousands;
> But he that felches from me my good name
> Robs me of that which not enriches him,
> And makes me poor indeed—[21]

But even though Godkin insists on reputation as being more valuable than money, the courts protected reputation by linking it to tangible property. Because reputation could increase earning power, it, like labor, was a form of property. For instance, one of Albion W. Tourgée's most ingenious attacks on the separate-but-equal law challenged in *Plessy v. Ferguson* was that, in labeling Homer Plessy, who was seven-eighths white, black, the Jim Crow law deprived him of his reputation as a white man, which affected his earning power and consequently violated the Fourteenth Amendment's protection of life, liberty, and property. The Supreme Court did not deny Tourgée's argument that reputation was a form of property; it merely denied the relevancy of his argument to the law in question.

If reputation itself is marketable, how can it be an inalienable part of someone's personality? Indeed, the seeming inability completely to disassociate the right to privacy from property would seem to point to the folly of arguments like Warren and Brandeis's that appeal to the notion of an "inviolate personality" capable of resisting the market. As a generation of literary critics has been trained to believe, the very notion of an inviolate, private self is a construct. Students of late-nineteenth-century United States culture have used this insight to suggest that far from resisting the logic of the market, the notion of an inviolate, private self is a product of it. For instance, Philip Fisher problematizes the opposition between public and private by arguing that in *The Bostonians* the private self does not preexist the public but is created by disappearing from it. The "genius" of James's novel, he asserts, "is not to ask the question of how, out of normal human materials" a performing public self is constructed; "Instead [James] begins with Verena's instinctively public self and asks how, out of this, an intimate and human-scale personality might be won." Verena's "full possession of an individual self," he argues, comes from her final act of disappearing from the public.[22]

Fisher's reading seems to complicate a genteel, Mugwump vision of a private, autonomous self that preexists the realm of publicity. It is worth noting, however, that the Mugwump vision was not quite as essentialist as contemporary critics make it out to be. For Godkin a private self is not an ahistorical self. "Privacy," he maintains, "is a distinctly modern product, one of the luxuries of civilization, which is not only unsought for but unknown in primitive or barbarous societies."[23] Even if we dispute Godkin's Eurocentric views of civilization and barbarism, they demonstrate that for him a private self is not given but is produced by a particular civilization, a civilization that he feels is well worth preserving. Likewise, the purpose of Warren and Brandeis's article was to demonstrate that the common law is a historically adaptable institution that contains within it the principles to provide legal protection against new threats to a particular version of the self. Present commentators almost always overlook the fact that Warren and Brandeis refer to a right *to* privacy, not a right *of* privacy, which is the common phrase today. They shouldn't. The difference is subtle, but a right *to* privacy implies that unless it is guaranteed an inviolate personality will be impossible to maintain, whereas a right *of* privacy implies something that an inviolate personality has as an inalienable possession. A right *to* privacy is more a creation of the law, a right *of* privacy more an appeal to natural rights.

My point is that Warren and Brandeis come closer than some give them credit for to Robert Post's very contemporary argument that the issue at stake concerning privacy "is not whether the law ought to protect personality, but rather how the law ought to conceptualize personality for the purposes of legal protection."[24] The Mugwumps conceptualized personality in a very particular way and felt that it should be protected. What is interesting when we look at James in conjunction with their concept of personality is that he too asserts a notion of personality, but one that problematizes the Mugwump version. In problematizing it he does not, however, reduce it to a pure product of the public sphere or the market. The private self in James *does* respond to new market conditions and new techniques of publicity. But even though those forces help to shape the nature of the self, they do not completely determine its shape.

The problem with Fisher's reading is that it corrects the notion that a private self preexists a public realm by turning the relationship upside down. James's novel works by a "reversal of terms." He underlines a "strategy of self-creation that *inverts* the strategy of publicity and visibility that are the machinery of the celebrity" (my emphasis).[25] The private is formed by disappearing from what must be a preexisting public realm. The legal distinction between the Constitutional and tort rights of privacy points to the flaw in such an inversion. To recall, Constitutional privacy is concerned with violations of privacy by the government; tort privacy with violations by other private parties. If privacy can be violated by private parties, a simple opposition between public and private won't do. Instead, we need to distinguish between different realms of the private.[26] For instance, whereas it seems to make sense to contrast the private self to the "public" realm of the market, in the late nineteenth century the market was very much considered a part of the private realm. After all, a main principle of laissez-faire economics was that the public realm of government should not interfere with private business contracts between free individuals.[27] But even if we grant that the realm of the market was for the most part considered private rather than public, it still makes sense to consider the market *less* private than the domestic sphere into which Verena disappears at the end of *The Bostonians*. It is the almost sacred realm of the domestic circle that Warren and Brandeis and Godkin seem most concerned to protect. They share that concern with Justice Douglas, who in *Griswold v. Connecticut* appealed to the sanctity of the domestic circle to uphold the right of a married couple to use contraceptives. Waxing eloquent, he asks: "Would we allow the police to search the sacred precincts of marital bedrooms for telltale signs of the use of contraceptives? The very idea is repulsive to the notions of privacy surrounding the marriage relationship. We deal with a right of privacy older than the Bill of Rights—older than our political parties, older than our school system. Marriage is a coming together for better or for worse, hopefully enduring, and intimate to the degree of being sacred."[28]

The domestic circle may be considered by many of us the most sacred zone of privacy, but, as Douglas's quotation makes clear, it is not an *asocial* realm. Indeed, at the heart of the domestic circle is a contractual relation, that between husband and wife. The nature of that contract complicates any exploration into the notion of privacy.

The marriage contract, lawyers in the late nineteenth century granted, is a special sort of contract. In an 1867 essay Godkin favorably evoked Sir Henry

Maine, who argued that the "movement of the progressive societies has . . . been a movement *from Status to Contract*."[29] Casting off feudal relations based on status, progressive societies were founded on contractual relations of free and equal individuals. Honoring the "freedom" of contract as no society before it, the United States could claim to be the most progressive of progressive societies. But the marriage contract raises an important problem. Involving two mutually consenting adults, it nonetheless creates a relationship of status, a relationship that the United States Supreme Court called "the foundation of the family and of society."[30] A society supposedly founded on freedom of contract, in fact, had an equally important foundation in a domestic relation of status.

Because the social order depends upon the proper ordering of the private domestic realm, the contract creating that space has a quasi-public nature. Thus, in an age in which the courts considered interference with market transactions an unwarranted violation of the freedom of contract, they asserted their right to regulate the marriage contract. Divorce, for instance, was not simply a matter of two individuals who could freely enter into or out of a contractual relation. As Justice Thomas M. Cooley of Michigan wrote, "There are three parties to every divorce proceeding, the husband, the wife, and the state; the first two parties representing their respective interests as individuals; the state concerned to guard the morals of its citizens, by taking care that neither by collusion nor otherwise, shall divorce be allowed under circumstance as to reduce marriage to a mere temporary arrangement of conscience or passion."[31]

One of the most respected legal minds of his day, Cooley was very reluctant to interfere with business contracts between private citizens. Nonetheless, like most of his generation, he believed in governmental regulation of the marriage contract. Cooley is also the person who provided Warren and Brandeis with their crucial phrase, "the right 'to be left alone'."[32]

As we have seen, Warren and Brandeis link the right to be left alone with the domestic circle, a sanctified private realm supposedly immune to public and private interference. What needs to be emphasized, however, is that the state relinquishes its regulatory power over the domestic circle only after the marriage contract creates the proper status relations. Once the domestic circle is properly ordered, its regulation can be left to husband and wife, who are expected to perform their proper duties, duties established by a clear-cut legal hierarchy.

As some critics of traditional marriage pointed out, the courts' attitude toward marriage was similar to the attitude southern courts had adopted toward slavery. In both cases courts tried to guarantee a proper relation of status but refused to interfere with it once it was established.[33] The end of slavery did not mean the end of the courts' treatment of marriage in the same way. In fact, emancipation fueled fears of miscegenation, which led to powerful reassertions of the government's right to regulate the terms of the marriage contract. For instance, in a decision that declared homes the "nurseries of the States," an Alabama court dissolved an interracial marriage. Who, it wondered, can "estimate the evil of introducing into the most intimate relations, elements so heterogeneous that they must naturally cause discord, shame, disruption of family circles, and estrangements of kindred? While with their interior administration, the State should interfere but little, it is obviously of the highest public concern that it should, by general laws adapted to the state of things around them, guard against disturbances from without."[34]

Because the domestic circle had such an important social role, it was established by a contract much more public in nature than the business contract. This public contract created a sacred sphere that should not be violated by public or private parties. Private as that sphere might seem, however, it was not a sphere in which husband and wife could legally assert "the right to be left alone" against one another. On the contrary, the marriage contract created one legal body out of two. James's works can help us sort out the complications that the marriage contract presented to notions of a private personality. It's time, then, to return to *The Bostonians*.

The relationship established between Verena and Basil in Cambridge is defined by two very different contrasts. One is between their encounter and the location in which it begins to take shape. Their intimacy is first established in Memorial Hall at Harvard, a semipublic space commemorating the private deaths of the "sons of the university" who gave their lives in public service during the Civil War. As James puts it, "They were discussing their affairs, which had nothing to do with the heroic symbols that surrounded them; but their affairs had suddenly grown so serious that there was no want of decency in their lingering there for the purpose" (*B*, 247).

The other contrast is between their relationship and the one that Verena has with Olive. Because Verena ends up promising to marry Basil, most critics assume that the relationship between the two women stands for an alternative to traditional marriage. To a certain extent this is true, but we need to see what alternative it suggests. Many contemporary critics look at Olive's feminism and assume that she opposes the institution of marriage. To be sure, she would "hate it for herself" (*B*, 84). But that hatred has to do with the fact that marriage for her was possible only with a man. Olive is not necessarily opposed to the *institution* of marriage. Indeed, Verena's initial radical disapproval of the marriage-tie "gave [Olive] a vertigo" (*B*, 84). She especially "didn't like the 'atmosphere' of circles in which such institutions were called into question" (*B*, 84). Unlike Verena, she is not an advocate of "free union" (*B*, 84).

Olive's negative response to Verena's radicalism reminds us that only a minority of those supporting women's rights clamored for the abolition of marriage. While decrying existing inequalities, more conservative reformers continued to consider marriage a special form of contract, sanctified by a higher power. More radical reformers also believed in marriage but felt that equality could be ensured only if the marriage contract matched the freedom of business contracts. For instance, free-love advocate, spiritualist, and first female Wall Street broker Victoria Woodhull, whom James used as a model in "The Siege of London," proclaimed that in marriage "There is neither right nor duty beyond the uniting—the contracting—individuals."[35]

When they first meet, Verena's ideas are close to Woodhull's; Olive's are more conservative. Quite traditional in her views, Olive idealizes a relationship that requires renunciation. What distinguishes her from traditional advocates of marriage is that she asks Verena to renounce heterosexual attraction. Verena's temporary acceptance of Olive's terms allows their relationship to develop without what many in their society felt was a natural barrier to a truly egalitarian relationship in marriage. Indeed, the hierarchical status constructed by the marriage contract was justified by "natural" forces of heterosexuality. Freed from such forces, Verena and Olive can strive for Olive's ideal of a special, egalitarian union.[36] Appropriately, the language describing their relationship evokes the ideals of marriage.

As Olive acknowledges, the "union of soul" that she seeks with Verena would take a "double consent" (*B*, 80). Based on mutual consent, their relationship creates a "partnership of their two minds" (*B*, 156). That partnership is not, however, based on radical notions of "free union" (*B*, 84) in which the partners are free to dissolve it at will. Instead, Olive seeks, as in a marriage contract, a promise that "would bind them together for life" (*B*, 110). That she seeks from Verena a promise not to marry would seem to undercut my claim that James uses their relationship to experiment with the possibility of a truly egalitarian "marriage." But her subsequent refusal to accept Verena's spoken promise when it is offered, preferring to "trust" her "without a pledge" (*B*, 137), serves to emphasize the way in which Olive hopes for a union more tightly bound than the existing marriage contract. The marriage contract, after all, depends on legal sanction to enforce its lifelong bond. Olive's idealized bond demands a perpetual renewal based on mutual trust. Coming together in a partnership that compensated for the lack each one possessed, Verena and Olive form an "organic whole" (*B*, 156).

Verena and Olive's relative success in creating one body out of two is in stark contrast to Basil's lone attempt to form a partnership. Having difficulty making ends meet as a southern lawyer in New York City, "he had formed a partnership with a person who seemed likely to repair some of his deficiencies—a young man from Rhode Island, acquainted, according to his own expression, with the inside track" (*B*, 187).[37] Rather than compensate for Basil's deficiencies—one of which was capital—his new partner grabbed what little money the partnership had and took off for Europe.

As successful as Verena and Olive's "partnership" (*B*, 172) seems by contrast, its very appearance of success allows James to suggest an indirect criticism of the institution of marriage that Olive herself is not willing to make. If Verena and Olive's union creates an organic body that compensates for their respective deficiencies, what it lacks, as we have seen, is a space for Verena to call her own. The problem is not simply that Verena's relationship with Olive grants her a public role, whereas her relationship with Basil confines her to a private one. To be sure, Verena and Olive work together to present a voice to the public, whereas Basil will deny Verena that voice. But if the voice is Verena's, it is controlled by Olive. Olive's control is linked to the nature of their domestic life together. Olive, though opposed to marriage for herself, is extremely domestic. On his first visit to her, Basil is most struck by the tasteful arrangement of his cousin's home. Like the proper wife, "Olive Chancellor regulated her conduct on lofty principles" (*B*, 23). "Her house," we are told, "had always been thoroughly well regulated" (*B*, 173). This domestic regulation is one of the most important things that Olive offers to Verena, who comes from a most unregulated family. But even though such regulation heightens her cultural refinement, it leaves her with no space of her own.

This is not to say that at the end of the novel she will find it with Basil. James is highly conscious of how the private sphere of the domestic circle creates a realm in which individual privacy is hard to come by. This, indeed, is part of the message of *The Reverberator*. It is easy to read that work as James's attack on the press's intrusion into the private realm of the domestic circle. But James also directs his satire against the proper French-American family, the "house of Probert," that is held together by a delicate "bond" that makes "each for all and all for each" (*R*, 68–69). Acting as a corporate body, it would forbid son and brother Gaston to marry a lovely but unrefined American who in her innocence betrays family secrets to the press. "Family secrets" is the right phrase, for everyone in the family knows about them. As imagined by James, this family is so close that no secrets are allowed, although a lot of hypocrisy is. For instance, the family seems willing to relent in its judgment of Francie if she would only lie and say that she was forced into confiding to the journalist. But innocent Francie insists on the truth, forcing Gaston to choose between his family and his lover. In a crucial scene, his friend, an American artist, advises him to marry—"To save from destruction the last scrap of your independence" (*R*, 205). Gaston's family, he tells him, is rendering him "incapable of individual life" (*R*, 205). Gaston ends up proving his independence by choosing to marry, but, in a typical Jamesian move, that choice creates the conditions for yet another domestic circle. Similarly, in *The Bostonians* Verena escapes from one domestic relation into another.

In most respects her relationship with Basil promises to be even more confining than her relationship with Olive. In addition to being predicated on her willingness to hold "her tongue" (*B*, 253) and no longer to speak in public, her relation to Basil introduces the force of sexuality into Verena's life, a force that makes it impossible to maintain the delicate balance of equality for which Olive and Verena strive. Indeed, the holding of Verena's tongue and the force of male sexuality are linked early in the book when Olive warns her, "There are gentlemen in plenty who would be glad to stop your mouth by kissing you" (*B*, 136).

The image of Verena's mouth being stopped by a kiss invites direct comparison with the scene between Basil and Verena in Cambridge. If that scene culminates in a handshake, the act most symbolic of contractual relations between equal partners, the kiss is the act most symbolic of sealing the contract between man and wife. The nature of Verena's life in marriage is anticipated by the imagery of the final scene. Wrenching Verena from Olive "by muscular force" (*B*, 448), Ransom thrusts the "hood of Verena's long cloak over her head, to conceal her face and her identity" (*B*, 449).

As Lynn Wardley has pointed out, Verena's marriage with Basil does not, as Fisher would have it, signal the end of her performing self for a private self, since Verena will continue to perform. The difference is that she will now perform with Basil as her private audience.[38] She has not disappeared from the public realm to assert the "full possession of an individual self," because the domestic sphere she is about to enter, while decidedly private, will not allow her the space for a self to exist. Indeed, the marriage contract incorporates her into the body of her husband.

The book's ending does not mean, however, that James offers no space whatsoever for a private self to be constructed. Such a space occurs, even if momentarily, during the handshake between Verena and Basil. Like the kiss about which Olive warns Verena, Verena's handshake with Basil leads to a holding of her tongue. But whereas the kiss would put an end to her addresses to the public so as to reserve them for Basil, the handshake implies that she will keep her meeting with Basil secret from Olive, another private party. Furthermore, she does not submit to her silence but offers it on the condition that Basil leave her a space of her own. If offering her hand seals a moment of intimacy between her and Basil, it also establishes boundaries between them: " 'Well, if I don't tell Olive, then you must leave me here,' said Verena, stopping in the path and putting out a hand of farewell" (*B*, 244). To be sure, at first Basil refuses to enter into the agreement she offers. He even momentarily enjoys playing with her and testing her good nature while being "slightly conscious of a man's brutality" (*B*, 244). But Verena's resistance continues, working to control the "natural" brutality that would force itself upon her: "Well, I want to be free—to do as I think best. And, if there is a chance of my keeping it back, there mustn't be anything more—there must not, Mr. Ransom, really" (*B*, 244).

Of course, Verena's desire to be "free" can be read ironically in light of the book's ending. Far from offering her freedom, this moment can be read as leading to her subsequent submission to Basil's masculine will. Nonetheless, at this moment a delicate balance is achieved when Basil, despite irritation at "being dismissed" (*B*, 245), takes the hand she once again offers. In James's world a space in which a private self can take shape is constructed in such a balanced moment.

The nature of that moment can be appreciated by comparing it to perhaps the most famous moment in American literature sanctifying a private relationship between a man and a woman: the meeting of Hester and Dimmesdale in *The Scarlet Letter*. Whereas Hawthorne's lovers meet in the forest, James's, as we have seen, meet in a semi-public realm. Part of the sanctity of their moment together results from the sanctity of that semi-public space, not their withdrawal into nature. Furthermore, whereas Hester and Dimmesdale share privacy because of their illicit sexual union, Verena and Basil create the possibilities of privacy through the establishment of boundaries. As Olive puts it, trying to wrench Verena's secret from her later in the novel, "Verena Tarrant, what *is* there between you?" (*B*, 370). A private personality for James does not result from protecting a self that preexists social relations. Nor does it result from the union of two selves into one that underlies the so-called sanctity of the domestic sphere. It does not even result from disappearance from the public. Instead, it has to do with the creation of a space *between,* a space that establishes connection while simultaneously helping to define the parties involved as individuals.

What complicates the establishment of this space *between* in James is that it depends upon an empty space *within* the two parties involved. We can see this most obviously with Verena. Verena's remarkable capacity to establish relationships with people results not from a fullness, but an emptiness, "the extraordinary generosity with which she could expose herself, give herself away, turn herself inside out, for the satisfaction of a person who made demands of her" (*B*, 380). Her role as medium is her most obvious manifestation of this "generosity."[39] She seems capable of speaking the voice of whoever is in control of her. Her generosity suggests that James has merely given her the traditional definition of a woman as an empty vessel, waiting to be filled and given identity by her union with a man. For instance, during his first encounter with her Basil comes close to attributing "to Miss Tarrant a singular hollowness of character" (*B*, 61). But the "hollowness" that defines Verena's essence turns out to inhabit other characters as well. It is, after all, deficiencies, not a fullness, that cause Basil, Verena, and Olive to seek out partnerships. Furthermore, if Verena's voice seems capable of being taken possession of by whomever she is around, it is that very voice that seduces Basil, penetrating the core of his being so that he, in turn, wants to take sole possession of it.

Taking possession of another is as much a sin for James as it is for Hawthorne. Unlike Hawthorne, however, he does not imagine an alternative to it to be a full moment of organic unity. In contrast, James's alternative balances the generosity that he associates with Verena against the resistance that she displays in her handshake with Basil. Owing much to the ideal of the period's market exchanges, that balanced vision also points to its limits.

The ideological power of contract as a mode of exchange depends upon an image of balance, an image of two free and equal parties willingly consenting to a transaction from which both can benefit. What needs to be stressed, however, is that in the business contract this image excludes truly *interpersonal* exchanges. This is because, although the exchange ideally leads to financial profit for both involved, it concerns alienable property—not the essence of the people themselves. Accumulated property can be merely added onto an already existing self.

James's image of exchanges is quite different. For James no essential self exists outside of exchanges and yet precisely for that reason all exchanges are interpersonal and thus affect the very nature of the self. This is because, as we have seen, a self cannot achieve definition without a "space *between*" that only interpersonal relations can provide, while, at the same time, interpersonal relations are impossible without an emptiness *within* the self, an emptiness making one vulnerable to penetrations—and dominations—by another. This image of exchange leads to a very different account of how business contracts lead to profit.

Rather than present a world in which a balanced agreement between equal partners can lead to mutual profit—as Basil hoped for in forming his law partnership—James presents a world in which profit results from imbalances, dominations, and submissions. Even in those transactions in which both parties reap a financial gain, for James a personal loss is involved. Indeed, rather than assume that the basis of a contract is a preexisting balance between bargaining partners whose agreement signals a meeting of the wills, James shows that a balance can be achieved only, as Verena temporarily does, through the resistance of one party to the will of another.

This vision puts him at odds with many of the most outspoken critics of the marriage contract of his day—but not because he is an apologist for marriage. I have already pointed out how he uses Olive and Verena's relationship to challenge the image of an organic bond idealized by some reformers. But he also challenges those radicals who demanded that husband and wife be considered free and equal contracting parties, like those entering into a business contract. Like Locke, such reformers felt that someone could enter into exchanges and alienate property (or labor as a form of property) without affecting an essential, inalienable self. James, however, presents a self that is defined by the exchanges into which it enters, just as the marriage contract alters the status of the contracting parties. As a result, rather than use the business contract as a model for reforming the marriage contract, he uses the imbalances that critics noted in the marriage contract to suggest that such imbalances inhabit *all* exchanges; that all exchanges, like the marriage contract, involve imbalanced structures of the status of the person that they in part construct. Nonetheless, within this framework—there was no other available to him—James does present an exchange that achieves a momentary balance as Basil and Verena, in shaking hands, create a space between themselves, a space that both constructs and—so long as it exists—helps to maintain a private self otherwise denied Verena.

The moment of privacy constructed between Verena and Basil in this scene helps us to understand another contract that James tries to negotiate in his works: that between reader and text. I want to turn to the terms of that contract as a way to address two recent charges leveled against James. The first is the complaint by some feminists that he denies Verena any possible autonomy.[40] The second that he is a champion of a discredited notion of artistic autonomy. My responses to these complaints are linked. Yes, James does deny Verena autonomy, but he also explicitly compares her to a work of art. Since few would deny that James regards art very highly, it follows that James's denial of autonomy to Verena should not be seen negatively. It also follows that James does not champion artistic autonomy. What he does champion, I would claim, is artistic "privacy."

Artistic privacy in James can be understood by comparing it to Warren and Brandeis's use of art to establish a right to privacy. In order to distinguish privacy from property, Warren and Brandeis turned to a series of copyright cases that often involved works of art. To be sure, to claim copyright is to transform a work into a form of property available for circulation through *publication*. But Warren and Brandeis were interested in those cases that established the artist's right to withhold publication. That right, they claimed, establishes the precedent for a right to be left alone. They could rely on these cases to establish a right to privacy because of the special position that artistic creation occupies in our culture. On the one hand, it can be alienated and become a form of property. On the other, prior to its act of alienation, it seems to be coextensive with the life of its creator. To attempt to possess it without his permission, they argued, is not so much the theft of a piece of property—its market value may be worthless—as it is a violation of his personal dignity, that is, his privacy. For them a work of art seems to be simultaneously a potential piece of alienable property and an expression of its creator's innermost self.

James complicates this already complicated situation by reminding us that an innermost self is itself the product of relationships with others. Warren and Brandeis may evoke an inviolate personality, but in James's world personality is by definition prone to violation. This Jamesian sense of personality is associated with a notion of art different from that of the two lawyers. Just as an innermost self is the product of relationships, so too a work of art has no life unless it is brought into relation with an audience. On the one hand, that relation makes it vulnerable to possession; on the other, the work has the capacity to possess its audience. Furthermore, as James knows, although the law attempts to maintain a clear-cut distinction between works of fiction and life, allowing authors to proclaim their works fictional as protection against libel suits, works of art with a mimetic component often involve an urge to appropriate life or some aspect of it. Nonetheless, the life of a work of art depends upon the existence of a space between itself and the very life that it would appropriate, for if its act of appropriation were complete it would lose its status as art. Thus for James a work is not, as it is for Warren and Brandeis, coextensive with its creator until he alienates it as a piece of property to the public. Instead, it is defined by a variety of relations, although it cannot be reduced to any one. First, there is the gap between it and its creator; second, between it and readers who would possess it; third, between it and the life that it would possess. Its "privacy" depends upon establishing a "space between" in at least these three directions. Such privacy is not a moment of autonomy in which a work can speak for itself. Instead, it is constructed by maintaining a space that keeps it from being dominated by the very relations that define it, just as a self maintains its privacy by resisting effacement by the exchanges that help to shape it. It depends, in other words, upon a moment like that moment of courtship in *The Bostonians* when Verena, so vulnerable to being possessed by others, maintains the power to possess her would-be possessors.

The most important link between Verena and a work of art is this capacity to be simultaneously vulnerable and seductive. Her seductiveness comes from her charm, which for Mrs. Burrage gives her the appearance of an autonomous work of art whose originality creates its own value: "When a girl is as charming, as original, as Miss Tarrant, it doesn't in the least matter who she is; she makes herself the standard by which you measure her; she makes her own position" (*B*, 307). But, as we have seen, Verena's "originality" derives not from her autonomy but from an emptiness at her core that makes her dependent upon relations. That dependency, in turn, makes her the most fascinating figure in the book. She may not drive the plot, but it is generated by her "generosity." Making her vulnerable to possession by those around her, this generosity also opens her to life. For instance, on the beautiful spring day that Basil visits Verena in New York, Olive leaves them alone and walks along the streets "barely conscious of the loveliness of the day, the perfect weather, all suffused and tinted with spring" (*B*, 303). In contrast, although Verena is at first nervous about her walk with Basil, once she "was fairly launched the spirit of the day took possession of her" (*B*, 324).[41]

The openness that makes Verena vulnerable to possession also accounts for her seductive and original charm. Both her vulnerability and seductiveness are in turn related to her voice. Neither Olive nor Basil is originally attracted to the ideas that she expresses. Olive, as we have seen, is repulsed by her notions of free union; Basil, by almost everything. As he tells Miss Birdseye, "Does a woman consist of nothing but her opinions? I like Miss Tarrant's lovely face better, to begin with" (*B*, 219). Verena's ideas, it seems, are alienable from Verena's body. And more than from her body, from her voice. Completely charmed by her voice as she performs in New York, Basil takes for granted that "the matter of her speech was ridiculous. . . . She was none the less charming for that, and the moonshine she had been plied with was none the less moonshine for her being charming" (*B*,

264). Indeed, it is Verena's voice that proves so seductive. For Basil, Verena's voice, not her opinions, represents her "character." As he tells Mrs. Luna, Olive's sister, "You like me for my opinions, but entertain a different sentiment for my character. I deplore Miss Tarrant's opinions, but her character—well, her character pleases me" (B, 421).

But lest we think that only the ideas of women seem alienable from the voices that stand for their characters, it is important to remember that Verena also separates her attraction to Basil from his opinions. Challenged by Olive about her attraction to a former slave owner, she with "majesty" responds, "I don't loathe him—I only dislike his opinions" (B, 371). Just as Basil is seduced by Verena's voice, so she marvels at "how wonderfully he can talk" (B, 377). The "spell" that each casts on the other, like the spell that works of art cast on their audiences, cannot be explained by mere reference to ideas and argument.

The separability of a work or a character from its ideas seems to return us to a doctrine of individual autonomy, for it implies that there is some mysterious essence to both work and character that cannot be reduced to their ideas. Eliot, for instance, praised James for having a mind so fine that no idea can violate it. But this commonplace reading of James's inviolability is more appropriate to Warren and Brandeis's notion of personality and art than James's. Rather than establishing autonomy, the failure of a character or work of art to be identical with its ideas actually forces it into relations of dependency. Autonomy would occur not when there is a discrepancy between voice and content but when there is an organic merger of the two. Indeed, the failure to merge the two makes Verena's voice vulnerable to appropriation by others who speak through her as a medium. There is, in fact, no better expression of the emptiness at the core of her being than the discrepancy between her voice and the ideas it expresses. That emptiness, however, allows her to be both vulnerable and seductive. So too with a novel, especially because its *medium* is language, which by nature cannot be, as perhaps music can, pure voice.

Constituted by language, a literary work possesses a voice that is not identical to the ideas it expresses, a discrepancy that renders readers' efforts to reduce it to ideas a violation of its "privacy." At the same time, because language would not be language unless it expressed ideas, any reading that attempts completely to separate a work from its ideas is as flawed as the effort to alienate a worker's labor without altering his self. Just as Verena and a work of art are not identical to the ideas they express, so a worker is not identical to his labor. This lack of identity would seem to indicate that ideas, like labor, are alienable from the essential character of a person or a work of art. Verena should be able, in other words, to enter into exchanges of ideas with Olive or Basil that would leave her essential self untouched. But because she is defined by a lack, rather than by a preexisting autonomy, this is impossible. Her self is at least partially involved in any exchange that she enters, just as the worker's self is at least partially involved in any exchange that he makes for his labor. This is most obvious in Verena's pro-spective marriage with Basil. In marriage Verena's character will be altered be-cause the very structure of the relationship established by the marriage contract is not negotiated through a free exchange of ideas but already dominated by ideas held by Basil.

The point is, then, not only that a discrepancy between voice and ideas creates a dependency on relationships, but that people and works are defined by the specific relationships into which they enter. The ways in which Olive and Basil relate to Verena offer two negative models for the contract between reader and text.

Possessed by Verena's voice, both Basil and Olive attempt to possess it. Basil's mode of possession grows out of his recognition of gendered difference, difference defined for him by a hierarchical relationship of status. Having separated the charm of Verena's voice from what it says, Basil does not care so much to influence its content, which he dismisses as moonshine. For him Verena's voice is a purely formal performance. He merely wants to reserve its performances for himself. In contrast, Olive, in striving for an egalitarian union, demands a perfect merger of form and content. That merger, however, demands a loss of difference. As a result, her way of achieving union becomes in one important respect more proprietary than Basil's. If Basil allows Verena her voice and dismisses its content, Olive appropriates it as a medium to express her own ideas. Thus she is like numerous readers who use a work of literature as a vehicle to make public their own point of view. Basil reads Verena's voice performatively; Olive, constitutively. For James a contract between reader and text that will preserve a text's privacy depends upon a resistance to such acts of possession.

Of course, in *The Bostonians* such resistance is not sustained. The balance be-tween a work's power to possess its would-be possessors and their power to possess it may be impossible to maintain. "Balanced" readings of a work (including my attempt at one in this essay) may be impossible. Nonetheless, something is lost if we abandon the effort to respect the spaces that help to constitute aesthetic "privacy." Trying to define what that "something" is forces me to add some final complications to my argument about the differences between James's and Warren and Brandeis's notions of privacy.

That Warren and Brandeis turn to copyright cases involving works of art to separate privacy from property rights is not surprising. As Renaissance New His-toricists have argued, the construction of an institutional space known as the aesthetic paralleled the construction of a legal space making way for the institution of modern forms of private property that assume a subjectivity best described as "possessive individualism."[42] As C. B. Macpherson has shown, this subjectivity was constructed in theories of social contract that implicitly legitimated the rise of a modern market economy. In such a world theorists of the aesthetic claimed that it resisted the power of the market to turn all into a commodity. Warren and Brandeis's use of copyright law to establish an inviolate personality that resists the forces of the market is a specific example of this general argument. Recent critics have challenged the possibility of such resistance. Instead, they argue, any such resistance is produced by the forces it claims to resist. At stake is the very existence of spaces known as the "private" or the "aesthetic."

In part, James confirms the argument against standard notions of both the private and the aesthetic. For him no private personality or aesthetic space exists prior to exchanges. Nonetheless, James continues to hold out for notions of both the private and the aesthetic. Despite their avoidance of essentialism, Jamesian notions of both seem as doomed to failure as Warren and Brandeis's effort to separate privacy from property rights. Indeed, just as the major threat to the two lawyers' right to privacy today is not, as some Mugwumps feared, socialism but a market economy that would turn everything—including personality—into a commodity, so the major threat to a Jamesian notion of the aesthetic is the effort by recent critics to subsume it completely under the category of rhetoric so that a work's value is measured by the amount of persuasion that it accomplishes in the marketplace of ideas. Unable to resist efforts by readers to possess it, a work seems as incapable of maintaining "privacy" as it does of possessing an originating autonomy.

But at this point James poses a challenge to the challengers, for, although he adopts the vocabulary of property relations to describe aesthetic relations, he forces us to see that what it means to possess a work of art is double-edged. On the one hand, someone can hold title to a work and copyright the earning power brought about by its publication; on the other, someone with no legal claim to it can "possess" it through an imaginative act of appropriation. The first is clearly within the realm of legal notions of property. The second, however, is difficult to artic-ulate in legal terms. Indeed, what lawyer would claim that a reader's imaginative possession of a work is a claim to legal ownership over it? This second form of possession does not fit under the law of copyright.

If aesthetic possession cannot be completely separated from legal notions of property, neither can it be simply translated into legal discourse without a loss. It is inseparable because a work cannot be imaginatively possessed without being made available to the public through some form of publication, which brings it into the realm of copyright law. Nonetheless, once we have appropriated James's notion of privacy from his published works, it has no clear-cut place in the present legal system. The United States' legal system works in part by assigning rights, just as Warren and Brandeis assign the right of privacy to particular people. But to whom would it assign a Jamesian right to privacy, which depends upon a space that belongs to no one person although it is a product of human exchanges? Not easily translatable into legal discourse, *The Bostonians'* construction of privacy continues to raise questions today about how our legal system grants title to a right that it has constructed. Its power to raise questions about aspects of the legal system at the time that it was published forces me to question my previous appropriation of Verena to construct an allegory of reading.

If there is a difference between legal and metaphoric possessions of works of art, there is also a difference between possessing works of art and possessing people. The law does not totally cover the metaphoric modes of possessing either; it does, however, offer literal ways of possessing both. The former involves the law of copyright, which was being refined as James was writing. The latter involves the law of slavery that had been abolished a generation before the book is set. Nonetheless, this post-Reconstruction book suggests that other forms of legal possession exist when it has its aging representative of abolitionism grant Ransom access to Verena. Miss Birdseye hopes that Verena will privately reform this conservative southerner who grew up in a society that classified master and slave and husband and wife as parallel parts of the law of domestic relations. Instead, Basil persuades Verena to enter into a contract with him that their society feels constructs a private realm. In that realm Verena's artistry, like a work of art in the copyright cases that Warren and Brandeis cite, will be withheld from the public. Verena, however, is not a work of art (although she is constructed by one). Thus she enters a relationship covered by marriage laws, not copyright. My discussion of the nature of the contract legitimated by those laws should help to explain why the narrator has good reason to fear that Verena's tears at the book's end "were not the last she was destined to shed" in "the union, so far from brilliant, into which she was about to enter" (*B*, 449).

NOTES

1. Henry James, *The Bostonians* (New York: Macmillan and Co., 1886), 221. Future references to this work will be cited parenthetically within the text and designated (*B*). The other work by James cited parenthetically in the essay will be *The Reverberator* from *The Novels and Tales of Henry James*, v. 13, (New York: Scribner's, 1908), cited as (*R*).

2. J. Thomas McCarthy, *The Rights of Publicity and Privacy* (New York: C. Boardman, 1987), 1–3.

3. Morris L. Ernst and Alan U. Schwartz, *Privacy: The Right to Be Let Alone* (New York: Macmillan, 1962), 1.

4. *Griswold v. Connecticut*, 381 U.S. 479 at 484 (1965).

5. Alpheus Mason, *Brandeis: A Free Man's Life* (New York: Viking, 1946), 70.

6. Samuel Warren and Louis Brandeis, "The Right to Privacy," *Harvard Law Review* 4 (1908): 196. The most influential account of the tort law of privacy since Warren and Brandeis is William L. Prosser, "Privacy," *California Law Review* 48 (1960): 383–423.

7. Charles Callan Tansill, *The Foreign Policy of Thomas F. Bayard, 1885–1897* (New York: Fordham Univ. Press, 1940).

8. Henry James, *The Letters of Henry James*, ed. Leon Edel (Cambridge: Harvard Univ. Press, 1974) 1:408.

9. Mason, *Brandeis*, 46.

10. Ernst and Schwartz, *Privacy*, 47.

11. James H. Barron, "Warren and Brandeis, *The Right to Privacy*, 4 Harvard L. Rev. 193 (1890): Demystifying a Landmark Citation," *Suffolk University Law Review* 13 (1979): 875–922; Lewis J. Paper, *Brandeis* (Englewood Cliffs, N.J.: Prentice-Hall, 1983).

12. E. L. Godkin, "The Rights of the Citizen: IV. To His Own Reputation," *Scribner's Magazine* 8 (1890): 66.

13. In France a law was on the books that levied a fine of 500 francs on every publication in a periodical of a fact of private life. Warren and Brandeis cite this law in "The Right to Privacy." Whether James was aware of it or not is unclear from the action of *The Reverberator*. On the one hand, he makes it clear that the French papers planning to reproduce *The Reverberator* article must be more careful about what they print than their American counterpart; on the other, the action that the French-American family contemplates if they overstep their bounds is a "suit for defamation" (*R*, 170).

14. Warren and Brandeis, "The Right to Privacy," 195. They cite Thomas M. Cooley, *Treatise on the Law of Torts*, 2nd ed. Brandeis reuses the phrase thirty-eight years later in his famous dissent in a governmental wiretapping case, indicating that for him at least intrusions by government and private parties violate the same right. The "right to be let alone," he asserts, is "the most comprehensive of rights and the right most valued by civilized men." *Olmstead v. United States*, 277 U.S. 438 at 478 (1928). James frequently describes characters who seek this right. In *The Aspern Papers* the note sent by Miss Bordereau's niece to the narrator expresses her aunt's desire that the narrator's colleague "would let her alone" (*The Novels and Tales of Henry James*, vol. 12 [New York: Scribner's, 1908]). In *The Reverberator* three different people or groups of people are described as wanting to be left alone. The American girl, Miss Francie, "who had not even the merit of knowing how to flirt," only "asked to be let alone" (*R*, 58); the French-American family thinks of itself as "quiet people who only want to be left alone" (*R*, 197); and the son is told by his artist friend that it would be fair play for the family itself to "let [him] alone" (*R*, 203).

15. "The Right to Privacy," *The Nation*, 25 December 1890, 496–97.

16. "The Point of View," *Scribner's Magazine* 9 (1891): 261.

17. Andrea Dworkin, "The Third Rape," *Los Angeles Times*, 28 April 1991, M6.

18. Richard A. Posner, "The Right to Privacy," *Georgia Law Review* 12 (1978): 400, 408. Posner levels another attack against a right of privacy in the intro-

duction to his book on law and literature. See *Law and Literature: A Misunderstood Relation* (Cambridge: Harvard Univ. Press, 1988), 4–5.

19. See Grant Gilmore, *The Death of Contract* (Columbus: Ohio State Univ. Press, 1974); Duncan Kennedy, "The Structure of Blackstone's *Commentaries*," *Buffalo Law Review* 28 (1979): 205–382; and Peter Gabel and Jay M. Feinman, "Contract Law as Ideology," in *The Politics of Law: A Progressive Critique*, ed. David Kairys (New York: Pantheon, 1982), 172–85.

20. Walter Benn Michaels argues that "the explicit attempt to shift privacy away from property nonetheless produced a dramatic extension of property rights, produced, in effect, new property." "The Contracted Heart," *New Literary History* 21 (1990): 526 n. 13.

21. Quoted in Godkin, "Reputation," 59.

22. Philip Fisher, "Appearing and Disappearing in Public: Social Space in Late-Nineteenth-Century Literature and Culture," in *Reconstructing American Literary History*, ed. Sacvan Bercovitch (Cambridge: Harvard Univ. Press, 1986), 180, 178. For an overlapping, but different view, see Ian F. A. Bell, "The Personal, the Private, and the Public in *The Bostonians*," *Texas Studies in Literature and Language* 32 (Summer 1990): 240–56.

23. Godkin, "Reputation," 65.

24. Robert C. Post, "Rereading Warren and Brandeis: Privacy, Property and Appropriation," unpublished ms., 18.

25. Fisher, "Appearing and Disappearing," 180, 179.

26. Fisher makes such an effort, but not in a way that complicates his opposition between the public and the private.

27. A major complication for laissez-faire thinkers was the rise of corporations. For instance, Godkin refers to railroad corporations as "those large quasi-public enterprises." "Reputation," 63.

28. *Griswold v. Connecticut*, at 485–86.

29. Sir Henry Maine, *Ancient Law: Its Connection with the Early History of Society and Its Relation to Modern Ideas* (1861; rpt., New York: Dorset, 1986), 141. Godkin's evocation of him appears in "The Labor Crisis," *North American Review* 105 (1867): 183.

30. *Maynard v. Hill*, 125 U.S. 190 at 211 (1887).

31. *People v. Dawell*, 25 Mich. 247 at 257 (1872).

32. See n. 14 above.

33. Amy Dru Stanley, "Conjugal Bonds and Wage Labor: Rights of Contract in the Age of Emancipation," *Journal of American History* 75 (1988): 477. For problems that the legal similarities between slavery and marriage cause Stowe in *Uncle Tom's Cabin,* see my *Cross-examinations of Law and Literature* (New York: Cambridge Univ. Press, 1987), 113–37.

34. *Green v. State*, 58 Ala. 190 (1877), cited Michael Grossberg, *Governing the*

Hearth: Law and The Family in Nineteenth-Century America (Chapel Hill: Univ. of North Carolina Press, 1985), 138.

35. Quoted in Stanley, "Conjugal Bonds," 474. Woodhull's spiritualism granted her sense of the marriage contract the sanctity of a higher power as well. On feminism and spiritualism, see Ann Braude, *Radical Spirits* (Boston: Beacon, 1989).

36. It seems obvious to us today that Olive and Verena's relationship is based on homosexual rather than heterosexual attraction. I am not, however, convinced that James consciously constructed such an attraction between them. Whether he did or not does not affect my argument, which is merely that he removes from their relationship that force that determined the "natural" positions of status in marriage.

    On feminist ideals of marriage, see William Leach, *True Love and Perfect Union: The Feminist Reform of Sex and Society* (New York: Basic Books, 1980). Leach's discussion of the feminist call for a doctrine of "no secrets" about the mysteries of marriage might seem to imply that the lack of secrets between Olive and Verena is an effort to live up to this ideal. But the "no secrets" doctrine was based on the belief that previously unspoken aspects of marriage (like sex) should be made public so as to demystify marriage and place it on a rational foundation. In contrast, the lack of secrets between Olive and Verena results from the similarity of their union to that of traditional marriage in which ideally husband and wife had no secrets. Try to imagine Olive making public details of her life with Verena.

37. Albion W. Tourgée has a fictional character describe a law partnership as a marriage: "If lawyers are in a partnership they ought to be like husband and wife,—no secrets between them." *With Gauge & Swallow, Attorneys* (Philadelphia: J. B. Lippincott, 1890), 136.

38. Lynne Wardley, "Woman's Voice, Democracy's Body, and *The Bostonians,*" *English Literary History* 56 (Fall 1989): 639–65.

39. On Verena as a spiritualist, see Howard Kerr, *Mediums, and Spirit-Rappers, and Roaring Radicals; Spiritualism in American Literature, 1850–1900* (Urbana: Univ. of Illinois Press, 1972), 190–222; and Susan Wolstenholme, "Possession and Personality: Spiritualism in *The Bostonians,*" *American Literature* 49 (1978): 580–91.

40. See, for instance, Jean Fagan Yellin's remark: "Because James's young heroine Verena is essentially selfless, there is never any possibility that she will achieve autonomy." *Women & Sisters: The Antislavery Feminists in American Culture* (New Haven: Yale Univ. Press, 1989), 164.

41. In consciously evoking Verena's role as a medium, her ability to be taken possession of by spirits, this description calls attention to one of the most important strategies in the book. Alfred Habegger has noted that the book divides in two. The first half is predominantly a satire of the reformist and spiritualist movements; the second, a psychological exploration of the attractions between Verena and Olive and Verena and Basil. In the first half James

satirically discredits the spiritualist vocabulary of magic and the occult associated with Verena. But in the second half he finds himself returning to it as he struggles to describe the seemingly mysterious attractions connecting his major characters. At times his use of it is almost unnoticeable, as when he frequently refers to Verena's "charm." At other times it is quite explicit. Contemplating how rapidly she has been persuaded by Basil's courting toward the end of the book, Verena "felt it must be a magical touch that could bring about such a cataclysm. Why Basil Ransom had been deputed by fate to exercise this spell was more than she could say—poor Verena, who up to so lately had flattered herself that she had a wizard's wand in her own pocket" (*B*, 385). The vocabulary of magic and spiritualism does more than explain the "spells" cast by characters on one another. It becomes the only available vocabulary to explain the seductive attraction of art. The two, in fact, merge in Verena. For Habegger's argument see: "The Disunity of *The Bostonians,*" *Nineteenth-Century Fiction* 24 (1969): 193–209.

42. C. B. Macpherson, *The Political Theory of Possessive Individualism* (New York: Oxford Univ. Press, 1962). For a powerful feminist supplement to Macpherson's argument see Carole Pateman, *The Sexual Contract* (Stanford: Stanford Univ. Press, 1988).

8

ROMANCE AND REAL ESTATE

WALTER BENN MICHAELS

*Experience hath shewn, that property best answers
the purposes of civil life, especially in commercial
countries, when its transfer and circulation are totally
free and unrestrained.*
Blackstone, "Of Title by Alienation,"
Commentaries on the Laws of England

Visiting Salem in 1904, Henry James asked to be shown the "House of the Seven Gables" and was led by his guide to an "object" so "shapeless," so "weak" and "vague," that at first sight he could only murmur, "Dear, dear, are you very sure?" In an instant, however, James and the guide ("a dear little harsh, intelligent, sympathetic American boy") had together "thrown off" their sense that the house "wouldn't do at all" by reminding themselves that there was, in general, no necessary "relation between the accomplished thing for ... art" and "those other quite equivocal things" that may have suggested it, and by noting in particular how Hawthorne's "admirable" novel had so "vividly" forgotten its "origin or reference."[1] Hawthorne would presumably have seen the point of James's response; his own Preface warned readers against trying to "assign an actual locality to the imaginary events" of the narrative, and for the romance as a genre he claimed an essential "latitude" with respect to reference, a latitude not allowed novelists, who aimed at a "very minute fidelity ... [to] experience."[2] The distinction drawn here between the novel and the romance, between a fundamentally mimetic use of language and one that questions the primacy of reference, has, of course, become canonical in American literary criticism, even though (or perhaps just because) its meaning remains so uncertain. Does Hawthrone intend the romance (as some recent critics think) to pose a self-consciously fictional alternative to the social responsibilities of the novel? Or does he intend the romance (as some other even more recent critics think) to provide in its radical fictionality a revolutionary al-

186

ternative to the social conservativism of the novel?[3] The last paragraph of the Preface suggests that neither of these formulations may be correct.

Looking for the Seven Gables in Salem, Hawthorne says, is a mistake because it "exposes the Romance to an inflexible and exceedingly dangerous species of criticism, by bringing [its] fancy pictures into positive contact with the realities of the moment" (3). The implication seems to be that the romance—unlike the novel—is too fragile to stand comparison with reality, but Hawthorne immediately goes on to suggest that the difference between the romance and the novel is perhaps less a matter of their relation to reality than of their relation to real estate. He has constructed *The House of the Seven Gables* "by laying out a street that infringes upon nobody's private rights, and appropriating a lot of land which had no visible owner, and building a house, of materials long in use for constructing castles in the air" (3). The romance, then, is to be imagined as a kind of property, or rather as a relation to property. Where the novel may be said to touch the real by expropriating it and so violating someone's "private rights," the romance asserts a property right that does not threaten and so should not be threatened by the property rights of others. The romance, to put it another way, is the text of clear and unobstructed title.

THE MONEY POWER

Of course, haunted-house stories (like *The House of the Seven Gables*) usually involve some form of anxiety about ownership. Frequently this anxiety concerns actual financial cost. Stephen King, the author of *The Shining*, has put this powerfully in a discussion of the movie *The Amityville Horror*. "What it's about," he says,

> is a young couple who've never owned a house before; Margot Kidder is the first person in her family actually to have owned property. And all these things start to go wrong—and the horrible part is not that they can't get out, but that they're going to *lose the house*. There was some point where things were falling, and the door banging, and rain was coming in, and goop was running down the stairs, and behind me, in the little movie house in Bridgton, this woman, she must have been 60, was in this kind of ecstasy, moaning, "Think of the bills, think of the bills." And that's where the horror of that movie is.[4]

Which is not to say that the financial implications of the haunted house are limited to the actual repair costs of the physical damage done by the ghosts. Think of the plight of the Amityville couple as investors in real estate: having risked everything to get themselves into the spectacularly inflationary market of 1975, they find themselves owning the only house on Long Island whose value is declining—the only one for a few years, anyway, until the rising interest rates, as intangible as ghosts but even more powerful, would begin to produce a spectral effect on housing prices everywhere. It may be worth noting that in 1850 Hawthorne was writing at the start of one of the peak periods in nineteenth-century American land speculation, a period in which, according to the agricultural historian Paul Wallace Gates, "touched by the fever of land speculation, excited people throughout the country borrowed to the extent of their credit for such investments."[5]

But the actual price of real estate may not finally be as crucial to the haunted house as the fact of ownership itself and the questions that necessarily accompany that fact: who has title? what legitimates that title? what guarantees it? Again, contemporary examples abound. Because of certain "impediments" on their house, the Lutzes in Amityville never did get clear title, although they had what their lawyer called "the best that could be fashioned for their mortgage."[6] Another movie, *Poltergeist*, centers on what is in effect a title dispute between a real estate development company and the corpses who inhabit the bulldozed cemetery the developer builds on. But title disputes have also a more intimate connection to Hawthorne and to *The House of the Seven Gables*. The most prominent and respectable witch brought to trial before Hawthorne's ancestor, the "persecuting" magistrate John Hathorne, was an old woman named Rebecca Nurse, whose family were comparative newcomers to Salem and much resented by the old and increasingly impoverished villagers. The Nurses had bought land from James Allen (land he had inherited from the Endicotts) and were paying for it in twenty yearly installments. In 1692, when Rebecca was accused, they had only "six more years to go before the title was theirs," but the villagers still thought of them as *arrivistes* and continued to call their place "the Allen property."[7] Hathorne was fleetingly touched by Rebecca's respectability and by her claim to be "innocent and clear" of the charges against her, but he held her for trial anyway, and in the end she was one of the first witches hanged. *The House of the Seven Gables* remembers the day of Rebecca's hanging in Maule's curse on the Pyncheons, "God will give you blood to drink"—the dying words of Rebecca's fellow victim, Sarah Good. More important, Hawthorne revives the connection between witchcraft and quarrels over property by beginning his narrative with a title dispute. Owner-occupant Matthew Maule, who "with his own toil . . . had hewn out of the primal forest . . . [a] garden-ground and homestead," is dispossessed by the "prominent and powerful" Colonel Pyncheon, "who asserted plausible claims to the proprietorship of this . . . land on the strength of a grant from the legislature" (7). Maule, of course, is executed for witchcraft, with Pyncheon leading the pack of executioners.

In one sense, this reworking of the witch trials is a little misleading; as Hawthorne himself notes, one of the few redeeming qualities of the witch hunters was "the singular indiscrimination with which they persecuted, not merely the poor and aged as in former judicial massacres, but people of all ranks, their own equals, brethren, and wives" (8). But the Pyncheon persecution of the Maules does not follow this model. Indeed, it precisely inverts the pattern described in Boyer and Nissenbaum's extraordinary *Salem Possessed: The Social Origins of Witchcraft*, where the accusers are shown to have been characteristically worse off socially and economically than the accused. Hawthorne does not, however, represent the struggle between Pyncheons and Maules merely as a conflict between the more and less powerful or even in any simple way as a conflict over a piece of land. He presents it instead as a conflict between two different modes of economic activity, and in this he not only anticipates recent historians' findings but begins the complicated process of articulating his own defense of property.

The devil in Massachusetts, according to Boyer and Nissenbaum, was "emergent mercantile capitalism."[8] Hawthorne understood the question in terms more appropriate to someone whose political consciousness had been formed during the years of Jacksonian democracy. Maule embodies a Lockean legitimation of property by labor, whereas the Pyncheons, with their pretensions to nobility, are something like old-world aristocrats—except that the pre-Revolutionary fear of a titled aristocracy had, during the Jackson years, been replaced by the fear of "money aristocracy," and Judge Pyncheon is certainly more capitalist than nobleman. From this standpoint, the difference between Maule and Pyncheon is less a difference between bourgeois and aristocrat than between those whom Jackson called "the agricultural, the mechanical, and the laboring classes" and those whom he called the "money power." And yet, *The House of the Seven Gables* by no means enacts a Jacksonian confrontation between the "people" and those who sought to exercise a "despotic sway" over them. Instead, the fate of property in *House* suggests the appeal of a title based on neither labor nor wealth and hence free from the risk of appropriation.

"In this republican country," Hawthorne writes, "amid the fluctuating waves of our social life, somebody is always at the drowning-point" (38). This "tragedy," he thinks, is felt as "deeply . . . as when an hereditary noble sinks below his order." Or rather, "more deeply; since with us, rank is the grosser substance of wealth and a splendid establishment, and has no spiritual existence after the death of these but dies hopelessly along with them." The central point here, that America is a country where, as a French observer put it, "material property rapidly disappears,"[9] is, perhaps, less important than the implied comparison between the impoverished capitalist and the dispossessed aristocrat. The capitalist who loses everything loses everything, whereas the nobleman, losing everything material, retains his nobility, which has a "spiritual existence." This title cannot be bought or sold; unlike the land you have "hewn out of the forest," it cannot be stolen either. Aristocracy's claim to land is unimpaired by the inability to enforce that claim. Indeed, it is in a certain sense strengthened, or at least purified, since the assertion of what Blackstone calls the "mere right of property," a right that stands independent of any right of possession, is the assertion of a right that is truly inalienable: it cannot be exchanged for anything else, it cannot be taken from you, it cannot even be given away.

Such a claim to property has, from the start, its place in *The House of the Seven Gables*. The Preface's "castles in the air" suggest in their immateriality a parallel between romance and the property rights of impoverished aristocrats. And in the text itself, what Hawthorne calls the Pyncheons' "impalpable claim" to the rich territory of Waldo County in Maine repeats this structure. Although the "actual settlers" of this land "would have laughed at the idea" of the Pyncheons asserting any "right" to it, the effect of their title on the Pyncheons themselves is to cause "the poorest member of the race to feel as if he inherited a kind of nobility" (19). This pretension is treated somewhat nervously in Hawthorne's text as a kind of atavistic joke, but the principle on which it is based—title so perfect that it is immunized from expropriation—was by no means completely anachronistic in the 1850s. For example, antislavery polemicists like Harriet Beecher Stowe and William Goodell admitted the comparative superiority of those slave states and societies where, as Goodell puts it, slaves are treated as "real estate" in the sense that they are "attached to the soil they cultivate, partaking therewith all the re-straints upon voluntary alienation to which the possessor of the *land* is liable, and they cannot be seized or sold by creditors for the satisfaction of the debts of the owner."[10] Of course, it could be argued that this restraint upon alienation should itself be considered a feudal relic, reflecting primarily a nostalgia for the time when land had not yet been transformed into a commodity and, thus, Pyncheons and slaveholders alike could be seen as throwbacks. But, in fact, the notion of inalienable title was central also to one of the most radically progressive social movements of the 1840s and 1850s, the "land for the landless" agitation (opposed by southern slaveholders and northern capitalists both) that culminated in the Homestead Act of 1862.

At the heart of the homestead movement was the conviction that the land should belong to those who worked it and not to the banks and speculators. Attempting to protect themselves from speculation, the most radical reformers urged that homestead land be made inalienable, since obviously land that could not be bought or sold could not be speculated upon either. This attempt failed, but Congress did in fact require that "no land acquired under the provisions of [the Homestead Act] should in any event become liable to the satisfaction of any debt contracted prior to the issuing of the patent."[11] Thus, homestead lands, like slaves in Louisiana, represented at least a partial escape from alienability. And, indeed, the desire for such an escape was so strong that Homestead Act propa-gandists were sometimes willing to sacrifice their Maule-like claim to property through labor for a Pyncheon-like claim to the status of an absentee landlord. In a pamphlet entitled *Vote Yourself a Farm*, the pamphleteer reminds his readers that "if a man have a house and home of his own, though it be a thousand miles off, he is well received in other people's houses; while the homeless wretch is turned away. The *bare right* to a farm, though you should never go near it, would save you from many an insult. Therefore, Vote yourself a farm."[12] In effect, the Pyncheons have voted themselves a farm, or rather, more powerfully, the bare right to one. Hawthorne himself, figuring the romance as uncontested title and inalienable right, has sought in the escape from reference the power of that bare right. His "castles in the air" of the Preface are equally Hepzibah Pyncheon's "castles in the air" (65), her "shadowy claims to princely territory." And her "fantasies" of a "gentility" beyond the reach of "commercial speculations" are his claims to a "street that infringes upon nobody's" rights and to "a lot of land" without any "visible owner." Even the map of Waldo that hangs on Hepzibah's kitchen wall images the security of romance's bare right; "grotesquely illuminated with pictures of Indians and wild beasts, among which was seen a lion" (33), the map's geography is, Hawthorne says, as "fantastically awry" as its natural history. It is itself one of those "fancy-pictures" that perish if "brought into contact" with reality, an antimimetic map, charting a way out of republican fluctuation and novelistic imitation.

For if the romance seeps out of the Preface and into the text as an impalpable claim to impalpable property, the novel, too, embodies an ongoing relation to property, in the form of certain "mistakes" provoked by the lies of mimesis. The novel's commercial world consists of "magnificent shops" with "immense panes of plate glass," with "gorgeous fixtures," with "vast and complete assortments of merchandize," above all, with "noble mirrors . . . doubling all this wealth by a brightly burnished vista of unrealities" (48). We are unable to see through these unrealities just as we are unable to see through those other "big, heavy, solid unrealities such as gold, landed estate . . . and public honors" (229). Hawthorne here conceives of mass production as a form of mimesis and of the factories that make these stores possible as novels producing the realistically unreal. At the same time, the novel is a figure for appropriation and for those men—like the aristocrat-turned-capitalist Judge Pyncheon—who "possess vast ability in grasping, and arranging, and appropriating to themselves" those unrealities. In fact, the mirror of capitalism is itself reproduced in such men whose own "character," "when they aim at the honors of a republic" (130), becomes only an "image. . . . reflected in the mirror of public opinion" (232). Before the Revolution, "the great man of the town was commonly called King" (63); now he must make himself over into a facsimile of the people. They see themselves reflected in him, and he, "resolutely taking his idea of himself from what purports to be his image" (232), sees himself reflected in them. Only "loss of property and reputation," Hawthorne says, can end this riot of mimesis and bring about "true self-knowledge."

Judge Pyncheon, who looking within himself sees only a mirror, never seeks such self-knowledge; and the novel, aiming at a "very minute fidelity" to the "ordinary course of man's experience," never seeks it either—its goal is the department-store doubling of unrealities. Only the romance, with its dedication to "the truth of the human heart," and, in the text itself, only the daguerreotypist Holgrave can represent the "secret character" behind the mirror and restore appropriated property to its rightful owner. It is, of course, extraordinary that Holgrave, who inveighs against all property, should come to represent its legitimation, and it is perhaps even more extraordinary that the photograph, almost universally acclaimed in the 1850s as the perfection of mimesis, should come to represent an artistic enterprise hostile to imitation. To understand these reversals, we need to look a little more closely at the technology of imitation and at the social conditions in which that technology and the romance itself were developed.

Holgrave's career, says Hawthorne, was like "a romance on the plan of Gil Blas," except that Gil Blas, "adapted to American society and manners, would cease to be a romance" (176). Although only twenty-one, Holgrave had been (among other things) a schoolmaster, a salesman, and a dentist. His current occupation of daguerreotypist is, he tells Phoebe, no more "likely to be permanent than any of the preceding ones" (177). According to Hawthorne, such mobility is typical of the "experience of many individuals among us, who think it hardly worth the telling" (176), and certainly too ordinary to be the stuff of romance. Hawthorne exaggerates, of course, but not much. Several recent historians have noted the high degree of geographic mobility in the 1840s and 1850s, mostly among young men who, for economic reasons, frequently changed locations and jobs. This phenomenon, according to Robert Doherty, was particularly noticeable in major commercial centers like Salem, where it was associated also with increased social hierarchism. In rural agricultural areas, young men tended to stay put, and the distribution of property was comparatively even. In towns like Salem, however, "commerce and manufacturing produced great inequalities of wealth,"[13] and over one-third of Salem's population in the fifties consisted of transients. Most of these were propertyless young men whose geographic mobility came from hopes of a corresponding economic mobility. Sometimes these hopes were gratified. Many men, Doherty suggests, "spent a period of youthful wandering and then settled in at about age 30 and began to accumulate property."[14] Many more, however, "failed to gain even minimal material success." Some of these "propertyless . . . men stayed in town," Doherty writes, some "drifted from place to place, but all were apparent casualties of a social system which denied them property."[15]

The development of such an underclass had obvious social significance, and it suggests also ways in which a career like Holgrave's might not only be inappropriate for romance by virtue of its ordinariness but would even constitute a reproach to the commitment to property on which the romance is based. For a real-life Holgrave in Salem in 1851 stood a three-to-one chance of becoming what Doherty calls a "casualty," never accumulating any property and remaining stuck forever at the bottom of an increasingly stratified society. Hawthorne's Holgrave, needless to say, escapes this fate. Like only a few real-life young men, he rises from "penniless youth to great wealth," and one might perhaps interpret this rise as Hawthorne's ideological intervention on behalf of the openness of American society.

Except that, as we have seen, what made Hawthorne most nervous about American society was precisely its openness, its hospitality to fluctuation.[16] In this respect, the actual economic mobility of life in Salem, the fact that some men rose (according to Doherty, about 23 percent) and some men fell (about 13 percent), would be infinitely more disturbing to Hawthorne than the existence of a permanent class of the propertyless. If inalienable rights can be neither lost nor acquired, how then can we explain Holgrave's happy ending, his sudden rise to property? One clue is that he does not actually earn his wealth; he marries it. Which is not to say that Hawthorne is being ironic about his hero's merits—just the opposite. The whole point here is that property that has been earned is just as insecure (and, in the end, illegitimate) as property that has been appropriated by some capitalist trick. Thus, for Hawthorne the accumulation of property must be remade into an accession to property, and the social meaning of Holgrave's career turns out to be that it is not really a career at all. His period of wandering gives him instead the chance to display a stability of character that provides a kind of psychological legitimation for the fact of ownership: "Amid all his personal vicissitudes," Hawthorne writes, Holgrave had "never lost his identity . . . he had never violated the innermost man" (177). Like the romance itself, which, despite its apparent freedom from the responsibilities of the novel, "must rigidly subject itself to laws," (1), Holgrave appears "lawless" but in fact follows a "law of his own" (95). Anchoring property not in work but in character, he defuses both the threat posed by the young transients who failed to acquire property (Hawthorne simply legislates them out of existence) and the threat posed by the transients who did acquire property (since he makes that acquisition a function not of social mobility but of the fixed character of the "innermost man"). Apparently a pure product of the "republican" world of fluctuation, Holgrave turns out instead to embody the unchanging truth of romance.

But if Holgrave's career offers Hawthorne the opportunity to transform the social meaning of the new class of landless transients, Holgrave's art, the daguerreotype, hits even closer to home and requires an even more spectacular inversion. The terms of this inversion are quickly apparent in Holgrave's claim that the daguerreotype, despite its apparent preoccupation with "the merest surface," "actually brings out the secret character with a truth that no painter would ever venture upon" (91). It was, of course, far more usual for writers of the forties and fifties to make just the opposite point. The "unrivalled precision" of the daguerreotype and the paper photograph, painters were warned, "renders exact imitation no longer a miracle of crayon or palette; these must now create as well as reflect . . . bring out the soul of the individual and of the landscape, or their achievements will be neglected in favor of the facsimiles obtainable through sunshine and chemistry."[17] For Hawthorne, however, it is the *daguerreotype* that penetrates to the soul, seeing through republican honors to "the man himself."

The triumph of the daguerreotype in *The House of the Seven Gables* is the portraits—Hawthorne's and Holgrave's—of Judge Pyncheon dead. Early daguerreotype portraits were often marred by a certain blurriness. The very oldest surviving portrait, John Draper's picture of his sister Catherine, taken in 1840, was sent to an English photographer accompanied by apologies for the "indistinctness" that results, Draper wrote, from any movement, even "the inevitable motions of the respiratory muscles." But where "inanimate objects are depicted," Draper went on to remark with satisfaction, "the most rigid sharpness can be obtained."[18] Holgrave's job is thus made easier by the fact that the judge has stopped breathing, but the real point here is that the daguerreotype always sees through to the fixed truth behind the fluctuating movements of the "public character." It is as if the subject of a daguerreotype is in some sense already dead, the truth about him fixed by the portrait—just as the actual "fact of a man's death," Hawthorne writes in connection with Pyncheon's posthumous reputation, "often seems to give people a truer idea of his character" (310). The daguerreotype, always a representation of death, is also death's representative.

As is the romance. In a passage that anticipates by some forty years Henry James's famous remarks on "the coldness, the thinness, the blankness" of Hawthorne's America, the French journalist Michel Chevalier was struck by the absence in America of those elements that in Europe served, as he put it, to "stir" the "nerves." James would miss the sovereign, the court, little Norman churches; the effect of American life on a "French imagination," he thought, "would probably be appalling."[19] But Chevalier was thrilled, not appalled. He did miss what he called the "sensual gratifications": "wine, women, and the display of princely luxury . . . cards and dice." But, Chevalier says, the American has a way of more than making up for the absence of traditional stimulants; seeking "the strong emotions which he requires to make him feel life," the American "has recourse to business. . . . He launches with delight into the ever-moving sea of speculation. One day, the wave raises him to the clouds . . . the next day he disappears between the crests of the billows. . . . If movement and the quick succession of sensations and ideas constitute life, here one lives a hundredfold more than elsewhere."[20]

If the cold blankness of American life figured for James the difficulty of finding something to represent, that blankness was to Chevalier the setting for a business life of "violent sensations," and to Hawthorne the violent movements of business were the violence of mimetic representation itself. The world of the "money power," Andrew Jackson warned in his Farewell Address, is "liable to great and sudden fluctuations" that render "property insecure and the wages of labor unsteady and uncertain."[21] "The soil itself, or at least the houses, partake in the universal instability," Chevalier exclaimed.[22] Hawthorne required the romance to fix this instability, to render property secure. Where representations are unrealities produced by mirrors, the romance represents nothing, not in compensation for the coldness of American life but in opposition to its terrible vitality. Business makes the American "feel life," but that life is a mimetic lie, whereas "death," Hawthorne says, "is so genuine a fact that it excludes falsehood" (310). Celebrating the death—one might better call it the execution—of Judge Pyncheon, the romance joins the witch hunt, the attempt to imagine an escape from capitalism, defending the self against possession, property against appropriation, and choosing death over life.

THE SLAVE POWER

The conjunction of death and secure property has its place in another text of 1851, one intended not as a romance but, in its author's words, as a "representation . . . of real incidents, of actions really performed, of words and expressions really uttered."[23] Riding by his slave quarters late at night, Simon Legree hears the singing of a "musical tenor voice": " 'When I can read my title clear / To mansions in the skies,' " Uncle Tom sings, " 'I'll bid farewell to every fear / And wipe my weeping eyes.' "[24] Tom is preparing for the martyrdom toward which Legree will soon help him, and his sense of heaven as a "home" to which he has clear title is barely metaphoric. Slaves, of course, were forbidden to own property, but Stowe thought of them as, by definition, the victims of theft. Slavery, "appropriating one set of human beings to the use and improvement of another" (2:21), robbed a man of himself, and so freedom involved above all the restitution of property. Only in death did the slave's title to himself become "sure"; only in death did Uncle Tom's cabin actually become his.

It is not, in itself, surprising that freedom in the mid-nineteenth century, the period that C. B. Macpherson has called the "zenith" of "possessive market society,"[25] should be understood as essentially a property relation, but it does provide in *Uncle Tom's Cabin* some unexpected and little-noted points of emphasis. When, for example, George Shelby frees his slaves, he tells them that their lives will go on pretty much as before but with the "advantage" that, in case of his "getting in debt or dying," they cannot be "taken up and sold" (2:309). The implication here is that Shelby himself would never sell them, and in fact, voluntary sales play a comparatively minor role in Stowe's depiction of the evils of slavery. A paragraph from Goodell's *The American Slave Code* helps explain why: "This feature of liability to seizure for the master's debt," Goodell writes,

is, in many cases, more terrific to the slave than that which subjects him to the master's voluntary sale. The slave may be satisfied that his master is not willing to sell him—that it is not for his interest or convenience to do so. He may be conscious that he is, in a manner, necessary to his master or mistress. . . . He may even confide in their Christian benevolence and moral principle, or promise that they would not sell him. . . . But all this affords him no security or ground of assurance that his master's creditor will not seize him . . . against even his master's entreaties. Such occurrences are too common to be unnoticed or out of mind.[26]

According to Goodell, then, the slave, whose condition consists in being subordinated to the absolute power of his master, may in the end be less vexed by the absoluteness of that power than by its ultimate incompleteness. It is as if the greatest danger to the slave is not his master's power but his impotence. Thus, Eliza and little Harry flee the Shelbys because, although the Shelbys were "kind," they also "were owing money" and were being forced to sell Harry—"they couldn't," she says, "help themselves" (1:128). And when Augustine St. Clare dies, his entire household is overwhelmed not so much by grief as by "terror and consternation" at being left "utterly unprotected" (2:144).

What the slaves fear, of course, is being taken from a kind master to a cruel one; this threat, Goodell thinks, makes them constantly insecure, and the mechanics of this insecurity are the plot mechanism that sells Uncle Tom down the river. But in describing the reaction of St. Clare's slaves to his death, Stowe indirectly points toward a logic of slavery that runs deeper than the difference between good and bad masters, deeper even than the master-slave relation itself. As a matter of course, she notes, the slave is "devoid of rights"; the only "acknowledgment" of his "longings and wants" as a "human and immortal creature" that he ever receives comes to him "through the sovereign and irresponsible will of his master; and when that master is stricken down, nothing remains" (2:144). The point here is not that one man in the power of another may be subjected to the most inhumane cruelties; nor is it the more subtle point that the power of even a humane master dehumanizes the slave—for Stowe, the power of the kind master and the cruel master both can be tolerated, since even a Legree, refusing Tom his every want and longing, at least acknowledges those wants by refusing them and thus acknowledges his humanity. Rather, the most terrifying spectacle slavery has to offer is the spectacle of slaves *without masters*. Since the "only possible acknowledgment" of the slave as a "human and immortal creature" is through his master's "will," when in debt or in death the master's will is extinguished, the slave's humanity is extinguished also. The slave without a master stands revealed as nothing more than "a bale of merchandise," inhuman testimony to the absolute transformation of a personal relation into a market relation.

Stowe, like most of her contemporaries, customarily understood slavery as "a relic of a barbarous age."[27] The conflict between the "aristocratic" "Slave Power" and "republican" "free labor" would prove "irrepressible," William Seward proclaimed in a tremendously influential speech,[28] and the supposed "feudalism" of the South was a northern byword. More recently, Eugene Genovese, reviving the irrepressible-conflict interpretation of the Civil War, has described the slave-holding planters as the "closest thing to feudal lords imaginable in a nineteenth-century bourgeois republic"[29] and has argued that the South was a fundamentally precapitalist society. But, as we have begun to see, Stowe was basically more horrified by the bourgeois elements of slavery than by the feudal ones. She and Goodell both were struck by the insecurity of the slave's life, and she, in particular, saw that insecurity as the inevitable fate of property in a free market. The evil of slavery lies, then, not in its reversion to a barbaric paternalism but in its uncanny way of epitomizing the market society to which she herself belongs. Rejecting the claims of southern apologists that slavery provides a social and economic refuge from capitalism, Stowe imagines it instead as a mirror of the social and economic relations coming to the fore in the bourgeois North.

Hence the slave trade, what she calls the "great Southern slave-market," dominates her picture of the South, and, despite their feudal status, the slaves in her writings share the anxious lives of Hawthorne's "republican" northerners—"somebody is always at the drowning-point." The "fluctuations of hope, and fear, and desire" (2:245) they experience appear now as transformations of their market value. Their emotions represent their status as the objects of speculation. "Nothing is more fluctuating than the value of slaves,"[30] remarks a Virginia legislator in *The Key to Uncle Tom's Cabin*. A recent Louisiana law had reduced their value: Texas's imminent admission to the Union as a slave state would increase it. The Virginians speak of their "slave-breeding" as a kind of agriculture and of their female slaves as "brood-mares," but Stowe penetrates more deeply into the nature of the commodity by imagining the product without *any* producer. What everybody knows about the "goblin-like" Topsy, that she just "grow'd," is only part of the answer to a series of questions asked her by Miss Ophelia: " 'Do you know who made you? . . . Tell me where you were born, and who your father and mother were.' " " 'Never was born,' " Topsy replies, " 'never had no father nor mother. . . . I was raised by a speculator' " (2:37). If production in *The House of the Seven Gables* is done with mirrors, production in *Uncle Tom's Cabin* is an equally demonic magic trick, substituting the speculator for the parent and utterly effacing any trace of labor, human or divine.

This replacement of the parent by the speculator assumed an even more lurid countenance when, instead of being separate, the two figures were embodied in the same man, as when a father might sell his daughter. Stowe reproduces a poem by Longfellow called "The Quadroon Girl," in which a planter and slaver bargain in the presence of a beautiful young girl:

> "The soil is barren, the farm is old,"
> The thoughtful planter said;

> Then looked upon the Slaver's gold,
>   And then upon the maid.
>
> His heart within him was at strife
>   With such accursed gains;
> For he knew whose passions gave her life,
>   Whose blood ran in her veins.
>
> But the voice of nature was too weak;
>   He took the glittering gold!
> Then pale as death grew the maiden's cheek,
>   Her hands as icy cold.
>
> The slaver led her from the door,
>   He led her by the hand,
> To be his slave and paramour
>   In a strange and distant land![31]

Writers like George Fitzhugh defended slavery claiming that it replaced the "false, antagonistic and competitive relations" of liberal capitalism with the more natural relations of the family. "Slavery leaves but little of the world without the family,"[32] he wrote in *Cannibals All!*; in a thoroughly paternalist society, all men, black and white, would be related to one another. Writers like Stowe and Longfellow inverted Fitzhugh's defense while preserving its terms. They, too, were concerned to defend the family against the market, but in their view slavery only weakened the "voice of nature." It might be appropriate to think of one's children as property, but to make that property alienable was to annihilate the family by dissolving nature into contract. "For the sake of a common humanity," Stowe wrote, she hoped that Longfellow's poem described "no common event."[33]

Longfellow's poem is somewhat ludicrous, and its effect, perhaps, is to make the danger it imagines seem absurdly remote—in fact, no common event. But the transformations that capitalism works upon parental and erotic relations appear elsewhere in a more penetrating (although in some respects equally lurid) form. Indeed, these transformations, intensified and above all internalized, constitute what I take to be the heart of Hawthorne's concerns in *The House of the Seven Gables*, the chief threat against which the defense of property is mounted. I would therefore like to close by returning to that text and to what might be called its own representation of the quadroon girl.

"If ever there was a lady born" (201), Holgrave tells Phoebe, it was Alice Pyncheon, the daughter of a Pyncheon with aristocratic ambitions who, returning to Salem after a long stay in Europe, fervently hoped to gain "actual possession" of the Waldo territory and, having established himself as a "Lord" or "Earl," to return to England. According to tradition, the only man with access to the deed to Waldo was Matthew Maule, the grandson of the original "wizard," who was rumored still to haunt his old home "against the owner of which he pretended to hold an unsettled claim for ground-rent" (189). Summoned to the house, this young Maule (himself supposed, by the young ladies at least, to have a bewitching eye) demands to see Alice as well as her father. Ushered into his presence, the beautiful girl looks at Maule with unconcealed "admiration," but the "subtile" Maule sees only arrogant indifference in her "artistic approval" of his "comeliness, strength, and energy" (201). Her "admiration" is so open because it is so empty of desire; she looks at him, Maule thinks, as if he were "a brute beast," and he determines to wring from her the "acknowledgment that he was indeed a man." The "business" he has with her father now turns on Alice and on what Hawthorne calls the "contest" between her "unsullied purity" and the "sinister or evil potency . . . striving to pass her barriers" (203).

Alice is prepared to enter this apparently uneven struggle between "man's might" and "woman's might" because, as she tells her father, no "lady, while true to herself, can have ought to fear from whomsoever or in any circumstances" (202). She knows herself possessed of a "power" that makes "her sphere impenetrable, unless betrayed by treachery within" (203). Hence, she allows her father to stand by while Maule, gesturing in the air, puts her into a trance from which Pyncheon, suddenly alarmed, is unable to rouse her. " 'She is mine!' " Maule announces, and when Pyncheon rages against him, Maule asks quietly, " 'Is it my crime, if you have sold your daughter. . . ?' " (206).

Obviously this story repeats in some crucial respects the narrative of "The Quadroon Girl," but in pointing to this similarity I do not mean to claim that the bewitching of Alice Pyncheon is an allegory of the slave trade. Hawthorne seems to have been largely indifferent to the issue of slavery; a few years later, he would urge Charles Summer to "let slavery alone for a little while" and focus instead on the mistreatment of sailors in the merchant marine.[34] I mean instead to see in this story some sense of how deep the notion of inalienability could run and especially of how deeply undetermined it could be by conditions closer to home than the slave trade and less exotic than witchcraft. For Alice Pyncheon fancies herself immune to possession (in effect, to appropriation) simply because she feels no desire. She thinks of herself as a kind of impregnable citadel. Desires, like so many Trojan horses, would make her vulnerable; wanting no one and nothing, she is free from what Hawthorne, in McCarthyesque fashion, calls "treachery from within," and so impervious to aggression from without. That she in fact succumbs to Matthew Maule does not invalidate her analysis—it only shows that the enemy within need not take the form of felt desire. In their dreams, Hawthorne says, the Pyncheons have always been "no better than bond-servants" (26) to the Maules. Thus, Alice's Pyncheon blood makes her as much an alienable commodity as does the quadroon girl's black blood. And although *she* feels no desire, her father does, "an inordinate desire," Hawthorne calls it, "for measuring his land by miles instead of acres" (208). The bewitching of Alice is here imagined as a business transaction; witches, it turns out, are capitalists by night, and having appropriated her spirit as the Pyncheons did his land, Matthew Maule makes Alice live out her life in unconscious mimicry of the original Salem girls: breaking out, wherever she might be, into "wild laughter" or hysterical tears, suddenly dancing a "jig" or "rigadoon," obeying the every command of "her unseen despot" (209).[35]

Despot is a crucial word here; Andrew Jackson described the National Bank as exerting a "despotic sway"[36] over the financial life of the country; Harriet Beecher Stowe called slavery "a system which makes every individual owner an irresponsible despot";[37] Hawthorne calls Maule, the capitalist wizard, an "unseen despot." The force of the term is in all three cases to represent (internal) conflict as (external) oppression. For example, the point of characterizing the Bank as despotic was to associate it with old-world aristocracy and literally to represent it as un-American. Readers of Jackson's veto message cannot help but be struck by his obsessive concern with "foreign stockholders" in the Bank and with the anonymous threat they pose to "our country." By the same token, Stowe, fearing slavery (if I am right) as an emblem of the market economy, nevertheless thought for many years that the slave problem could be solved by repatriation to Africa, as if exorcising the slaves would rid the South of feudalism and the North of capitalism. Hawthorne, too, imagines a Maule become a Holgrave, renouncing "mastery" over Phoebe and leaving her "free" out of "reverence for another's individuality" (212). Indeed, the very idea of the romance asserts the possibility of immunity to appropriation in an Alice Pyncheon-like fantasy of strength through purity.

For what does the notion of inalienability entail if not a property right so impenetrable that nothing on the outside can buy it or take it away from you and so pure that nothing on the inside will conspire to sell it or give it away? That no actual possession of land could meet these criteria we have already seen. What slavery proved to Stowe was that even the possession of one's own body could not be guaranteed against capitalist appropriation. "The slaves often say [she quotes an "acquaintance"] when cut in the hand or foot, 'Plague on the old foot. . . . It is master's, let him take care of it; nigger don't care if he never get well.' "[38] Even the slave's soul, she thought, could not be kept pure when the "nobler traits of mind and heart" had their own "market value": "Is the slave intelligent?—Good! that raises his price two hundred dollars. Is he conscientious and faithful? Good . . . two hundred dollars more. Is he religious? Does that Holy Spirit of God . . . make that despised form His temple?—Let that also be put down in the estimate of his market value, and the gift of the Holy Ghost shall be sold for money."[39] Only death offered an escape from this "dreadful commerce." Legree says to George Shelby, who has made him an offer on Uncle Tom's corpse, "I don't sell dead niggers" (2:282).

In Hawthorne's republican world, however, everything is for sale. If not exactly dead niggers, then at least some version of them, like the Jim Crow gingerbread men Hepzibah Pyncheon sells to her first customer. And if not exactly the Holy

Spirit, then at least the "spirit" of Alice Pyncheon, held for debt by her father's "ghostly creditors," the Maules. In fact, the whole project of the romance, with its bizarrely utopian and apparently anachronistic criteria for legitimate ownership, had already played a significant, if ironic, role in opening the American land market. The irony, of course, is that Hawthorne and others like him were uncompromisingly opposed to speculation in land. Jackson, for example, reacted against his own early career as a land speculator by defending, in Michael Rogin's words, "original title against actual residents whose longstanding possession was contaminated at the core."[40] But if the goal was purity, the effect on the western frontier was chaos; criteria like Jackson's were so rigorous that they left no man's title secure. Hence, the separation of title from possession, the very condition of romance's attempt to defend against speculation, turned out to be the condition that enabled speculators to flourish. Apparently imagining the terms of a text that would escape republican fluctuation, Hawthorne imagined in fact the terms of the technology that made those fluctuations possible.

The problematic at the heart of this reversal becomes even sharper if we turn from commerce in land to commerce in people. Stowe opposed slavery, but she did so, as we have seen, in defense of property. Slaves, she thought, were the victims of theft; their property rights in their own persons had been violated. Attacking southern feudalism, she spoke for free labor and against slave labor. But insofar as her critique of slavery came to be a critique of the "Southern market," it had inevitably to constitute a repudiation of free labor as well. What Stowe most feared was the notion of a market in human attributes, and of course, free labor is just shorthand for a free market in labor. Hence, her conception of freedom was itself a product of the economy epitomized for her in the slave trade—free market, free trade, in Blackstone's words, "free and unconstrained" "circulation" of "property."

Hawthorne valued freedom too; it was essential to the "individuality" he cherished and to the "reverence" for individuality he held highest among the virtues. Matthew Maule leaves Alice Pyncheon's spirit "bowed" down before him; Holgrave demonstrates his own "integrity" by leaving Phoebe hers. But the specter of "treachery within" cannot be so easily laid to rest. For the real question raised by Alice's story is whether "reverence" for "individuality" is not ultimately an oxymoron. How should we read what Hawthorne calls Alice's loss of "self-control"? We may read it as a conflict between two forces—the individual self and the market—opposed in principle to one another.[41] In this instance, the market wins—but it need not, and indeed, when Holgrave liberates Phoebe, it does not. Or we may read it as a conflict in which the individual is set against a market that has already gained a foothold within—the McCarthyesque imagination of conspiracy. Here the enemy is still regarded as fundamentally other but is seen successfully to have infiltrated the sphere of the self—it must be exorcised.

But if we remember that Alice, as a Pyncheon, is already in bondage to the

Maules, and if we remember that this fact of her birth seems to her the guarantee of her "self-control," we may be led to a third reading. Here Alice is ultimately betrayed not only by her father's desire but by the very claim to individual identity that made her imagine herself immune to betrayal—the enemy cannot be repulsed by the self or exorcised from the self, since the enemy of the self is the self. "Property in the bourgeois sense," C. B. Macpherson has written, "is not only a right to enjoy or use; it is a right to dispose of, to exchange, to alienate."[42] Property, to be property, must be alienable. We have seen the fate of Hawthorne's attempt to imagine an inalienable right in land; now we can see the fate of his attempt to imagine an inalienable right in the self. The slave cannot resist her master because the slave is her master. If, from one perspective, this looks like freedom, from another perspective it looks like just another one of what Stowe called "the vicissitudes of property."

NOTES

1. Henry James, *The American Scene* (Bloomington, Ind., 1968), 270–71.

2. Nathaniel Hawthorne, *The House of the Seven Gables*, ed. Seymour L. Gross (New York, 1967), 1. Subsequent page references are cited in parentheses in the text.

3. The texts I have in mind here are Michael Davitt Bell's *The Development of American Romance* (Chicago, 1980) and an article by Brook Thomas, "*The House of the Seven Gables*: Reading the Romance of America," *PMLA* 97 (March 1982): 195–211. Thomas contrasts the "freedom of the romance" to the "conservativism of the novel" (196) and suggests that Hawthorne "chose to write romances . . . because they allowed him to stay true to the American tradition of imagining an alternative to the society he inherited" (195–96). Bell sees a similar tension within the romance itself, in an opposition between the "artifice and insincerity of forms" and the "anarchic energy" of the "strange new truths" (xiv) of American life in the mid-nineteenth century.

   In *House*, this opposition is embodied by the Pyncheons and Holgrave, but not, according to Bell, satisfactorily, since the "revolutionary" "alternative to the empty forms of the past" represented by Holgrave and Phoebe seems too "personal" to form "the basis of a new social system" and too transitory to "avoid recapitulating the historical cycle" that created the "repressive formalism" in the first place (182–83). Thomas reads the end in similar terms but somewhat more optimistically, arguing that Hawthorne "seems to have retained a hope for the future," imagining in Phoebe's marriage to Holgrave "a real possibility for a break with the past" (209).

   But in my reading, the point of the romance is neither to renew the past nor to break with it; it is instead to domesticate the social dislocation of the 1840s and 1850s in a literary form that imagines the past and present as utterly continuous, even identical, and in so doing, attempts to repress the possibility of any change at all. For critics like Bell, *The House of the Seven*

Gables fails in the end because Holgrave's "radicalism" succumbs to "conservatism" (184); democracy succumbs to aristocracy; ultimately, the "dangerous" and "subversive" fictionality of the romance succumbs to the "safe and conservative" referentiality of mimesis (14, 18). But what seemed dangerous and subversive to Hawthorne was not so much the "crisis" of reference intrinsic to the romance (Bell calls it a "crisis of belief" [149] and of "correspondence" [153]) as the violently revolutionary power of mimesis, the representing form of a market society inimical to the social stability, the individualism, and the rights to property that Hawthorne meant the romance to defend. Thus the novel actually ends triumphantly, with a transformation of "business" into inheritance and mimesis into "fairy-tale."

4. *New York Times Magazine,* 11 May 1980, 44.

5. Paul Wallace Gates, "The Role of the Land Speculator in Western Development," in *The Public Lands*, ed. Vernon Carstensen (Madison, 1968), 352. "The peak years of speculative purchasing," Gates goes on to say, "were 1854 to 1858, when a total of 65,000,000 acres of public domain were disposed of to purchasers of holders of land warrants" (360).

6. Jay Anson, *The Amityville Horror* (New York, 1978), 17. The main obstacle appears to have been that the only heir of the deceased former owners was the son who had murdered them, Ronald. Since Ronald, having killed his parents, was legally barred from inheriting their estate, it is unclear exactly from whom the Lutzes were buying the property. For true horror fans, however, Anson is gratifyingly explicit about who actually ended up owning their "dream house" when the demoralized Lutzes fled to California. "Just to be rid of the place, they signed their interest over to the bank that held the mortgage" (260).

7. Marion L. Starkey, *The Devil in Massachusetts* (1949; reprint, New York, 1969), 77.

8. Paul Boyer and Stephen Nissenbaum, *Salem Possessed* (Cambridge, Mass., 1974), 209.

9. Michel Chevalier, *Society, Manners, and Politics in the United States*, ed. John William Ward (Ithaca, N.Y., 1961), 98.

10. William Goodell, *The American Slave Code* (1853; reprint, New York, 1969), 65. The central state in question is Louisiana.

11. George M. Stephenson, *The Political History of the Public Lands* (New York, 1917), 243. For a characteristically helpful discussion of the ideology of homesteading, see Henry Nash Smith, *Virgin Land* (Cambridge, Mass., 1950), 165–210.

12. The quotation is in Stephenson, *Political History of the Public Lands*, 109–10.

13. Robert Doherty, *Society and Power* (Amherst, Mass., 1977), 52–53. "Agriculture," Doherty notes, "produced greater equality, and the only communi-

ties approaching equitable distribution of property were low-level, less developed rural hinterlands" (53).

14. Ibid., 47.

15. Ibid., 49.

16. Hawthorne apparently found the idea of a fixed income as attractive personally as it was socially. James Mellow quotes his sister Ebe: "One odd, but characteristic notion of his was that he should like a competent income that would neither increase nor diminish. I said that it might be well to have it increase, but he replied, 'No, because then it would engross too much of his attention' " (Mellow, *Nathaniel Hawthorne in his Times* [Boston, 1980]), 94.

17. Quoted in Robert Taft, *Photography and the American Scene* (New York, 1938), 133–34.

18. Ibid., p. 30.

19. Henry James, *Hawthorne* (Ithaca, N.Y., 1967), 35.

20. Chevalier, *Society, Manners, and Politics*, 298–99. Writing in August 1835, Chevalier notes, "Great fortunes, and many of them too, have sprung out of the earth since the spring; others will, perhaps, return to it before the fall. The American does not worry about that. Violent sensations are necessary to stir his vigorous nerves."

21. Andrew Jackson, "Farewell Address," in *American Democracy: A Documentary Record*, ed. J. R. Hollingsworth and B. I. Wiley (New York, 1961), 374.

22. Chevalier, *Society, Manners, and Politics*, 299.

23. Harriet Beecher Stowe, *The Key to Uncle Tom's Cabin* (New York, 1969), 1. Written in 1853, this book was an extraordinarily successful attempt to defend the veracity of *Uncle Tom's Cabin* by providing massive documentation for the incidents it narrated and the characters it described.

24. Harriet Beecher Stowe, *Uncle Tom's Cabin* (Columbus, Ohio, 1969), 2:246. All subsequent references to this work are cited in parentheses in the text.

25. C. B. Macpherson, *Possessive Individualism* (New York, 1964), 272.

26. Goodell, *American Slave Code*, 65–66.

27. Stowe, *Key*, 62.

28. William H. Seward, "The Irrepressible Conflict," in Hollingsworth and Wiley, *American Democracy*, 468–69. The "experience of mankind," Seward claimed, had "conclusively established" that two such "radically different political systems" could never coexist. "They never have permanently existed together in one country," he said, "and they never can."

29. Eugene D. Genovese, *The Political Economy of Slavery* (New York, 1967), 31.

30. Stowe, *Key*, 289.

31. Quoted in ibid., 295.

32. George Fitzhugh, *Cannibals All!* in *Ante-Bellum*, ed. Harvey Wish (New York, 1960), 129.

33. Stowe, *Key*, 294.

34. Quoted in Mellow, *Nathaniel Hawthorne,* 435.

35. In this connection, it may be worth remembering not only Hawthorne's lifelong fear and dislike of mesmerism but also Stowe's remark that "negroes are singularly susceptible to all that class of influences which produce catalepsy, mesmeric sleep, and partial clairvoyant phenomena" (*Key*, 46). Mesmerism, as a threat to property, works most easily on those whose title to themselves is least secure, but no one in Hawthorne's world can be entirely safe from the threat of expropriation.

36. Andrew Jackson, "Farewell Address," 374. See also his "Veto of the Bank Bill," in Hollingsworth and Wiley, *American Democracy*, 309–21.

37. Stowe, *Key*, 204.

38. Ibid., 22.

39. Ibid., 280.

40. Michael Paul Rogin, *Fathers and Children: Andrew Jackson and the Subjugation of the American Indian* (New York, 1976), 96. Although he does not explicitly point to the intrinsically self-defeating character of the demand for pure title, Rogin does go on to note that occupancy laws were opposed by "aspiring speculators" as well as by "purists over contractual rights" (97).

41. Such a reading is adopted in effect by Michael T. Gilmore, who argues that Hawthorne, writing *The House of the Seven Gables*, "was unable to suppress his misgivings that in bowing to the marketplace he was compromising his artistic independence and integrity" ("The Artist and the Marketplace in *The House of the Seven Gables*," *ELH* 48 [Spring 1981]: 172–73). Gilmore's valuable essay seems to me typical of much recent work on the artist in the market in that it calls attention to the importance of the market only to draw ever more firmly the line between the values of that market and the values of art. The point I am urging in this essay is the rather different one that for Hawthorne qualities like independence and integrity (artistic or otherwise) do not exist in opposition to the marketplace but are produced by and contained within it.

42. Macpherson, *Possessive Individualism*, 92.

9

SENTIMENTAL POWER: *UNCLE TOM'S CABIN* AND THE POLITICS OF LITERARY HISTORY

JANE TOMPKINS

Once, during a difficult period of my life, I lived in the basement of a house on Forest Street in Hartford, Connecticut, which had belonged to Isabella Beecher Hooker—Harriet Beecher Stowe's half-sister. This woman at one time in her life had believed that the millennium was at hand and that she was destined to be the leader of a new matriarchy.[1] When I lived in that basement, however, I knew nothing of Stowe, or of the Beechers, or of the utopian visions of nineteenth-century American women. I made a reverential visit to the Mark Twain house a few blocks away, took photographs of his study, and completely ignored Stowe's own house—also open to the public—which stood across the lawn. Why should I go? Neither I nor anyone I knew regarded Stowe as a serious writer. At the time, I was giving my first lecture course in the American Renaissance—concentrated exclusively on Hawthorne, Melville, Poe, Emerson, Thoreau, and Whitman—and although *Uncle Tom's Cabin* was written in exactly the same period, and although it is probably the most influential book ever written by an American, I would never have dreamed of including it on my reading list. To begin with, its very popularity would have militated against it; as everybody knew, the classics of American fiction were, with a few exceptions, all succès d'estime.

In 1969, when I lived on Forest Street, the women's movement was just getting under way. It was several years before Chopin's *The Awakening* and Gilman's "The Yellow Wallpaper" would make it onto college reading lists, sandwiched in between Theodore Dreiser and Frank Norris. These women, like some of their male counterparts, had been unpopular in their own time and owed their reputations to the discernment of latter-day critics. Because of their work, it is now respectable to read these writers who, unlike Nathaniel Hawthorne, had to wait several generations for their champions to appear in the literary establishment. But despite the influence of the women's movement, despite the explosion of work in nineteenth-century American social history, and despite the new historicism that is infiltrating literary studies, the women, like Stowe, whose names were household words in the nineteenth century—women such as Susan Warner, Sarah J. Hale, Augusta Evans, Elizabeth Stuart Phelps, her daughter Mary, who took the same name, and Frances Hodgson Burnett—these women remain excluded from the literary canon. And while it has recently become fashionable to study their works as examples of cultural deformation, even critics who have invested their professional careers in that study and who declare themselves feminists still refer to their novels as trash.[2]

My principal target of concern, however, is not feminists who have written on popular women novelists of the nineteenth century, but the male-dominated scholarly tradition that controls both the canon of American literature (from which these novelists are excluded) and the critical perspective that interprets the canon for society. For the tradition of Perry Miller, F. O. Matthiessen, Harry Levin, Richard Chase, R. W. B. Lewis, Yvor Winters, and Henry Nash Smith has prevented even committed feminists from recognizing and asserting the *value* of a powerful and specifically female novelistic tradition. The very grounds on which sentimental fiction has been dismissed by its detractors, grounds which have come to seem universal standards of aesthetic judgment, were established in a struggle to supplant the tradition of evangelical piety and moral commitment these novelists represent. In reaction against their worldview, and perhaps even more against their success, twentieth-century critics have taught generations of students to equate popularity with debasement, emotionality with ineffectiveness, religiosity with fakery, domesticity with triviality, and all of these, implicitly, with womanly inferiority.

In this view, sentimental novels written by women in the nineteenth century were responsible for a series of cultural evils whose effects still plague us: the degeneration of American religion from theological rigor to anti-intellectual consumerism, the rationalization of an unjust economic order, the propagation of the debased images of modern mass culture, and the encouragement of self-indulgence and narcissism in literature's most avid readers—women.[3] To the extent that they protested the evils of society, their protest is seen as duplicitous—the product and expression of the very values they pretended to condemn. Unwittingly or not, so the story goes, they were apologists for an oppressive social order. In contrast to male authors such as Thoreau, Whitman, and Melville, who are celebrated as models of intellectual daring and honesty, these women are generally thought to have traded in false stereotypes, dishing out weak-minded pap to nourish the prejudices of an ill-educated and underemployed female readership. Self-deluded and unable to face the harsh facts of a competitive society, they are portrayed as manipulators of a gullible public who kept their readers imprisoned in a dreamworld of self-justifying clichés. Their fight against the evils of their society was a fixed match from the start.[4]

The thesis I will argue in this chapter is diametrically opposed to these portrayals. It holds that the popular domestic novel of the nineteenth century represents a monumental effort to reorganize culture from the woman's point of view; that this body of work is remarkable for its intellectual complexity, ambition, and resourcefulness; and that, in certain cases, it offers a critique of American society far more devastating than any delivered by better-known critics such as Hawthorne and Melville. Finally, it suggests that the enormous popularity of these novels, which has been cause for suspicion bordering on disgust, is a reason for paying close attention to them. *Uncle Tom's Cabin* was, in almost any terms one can think of, the most important book of the century. It was the first American novel ever to sell over a million copies and its impact is generally thought to have been incalculable. Expressive of and responsible for the values of its time, it also belongs to a genre, the sentimental novel, whose chief characteristic is that it is written by, for, and about women. In this respect, *Uncle Tom's Cabin* is not exceptional but representative. It is the *summa theologica* of nineteenth-century America's religion of domesticity, a brilliant redaction of the culture's favorite story about itself—the story of salvation through motherly love. Out of the ideological materials at their disposal, the sentimental novelists elaborated a myth that gave women the central position of power and authority in the culture; and of these efforts *Uncle Tom's Cabin* is the most dazzling exemplar.

I have used words like "monumental" and "dazzling" to describe Stowe's novel and the tradition of which it is a part because they have for too long been the casualties of a set of critical attitudes that equate intellectual merit with a certain kind of argumentative discourse and certain kinds of subject matter. A long tradition of academic parochialism has enforced this sort of discourse through a series of cultural contrasts: light "feminine" novels vs. tough-minded intellectual treatises; domestic "chattiness" vs. serious thinking; and summarily, the "damned mob of scribbling women" vs. a few giant intellects, unappreciated and misunderstood in their time, struggling manfully against a flood of sentimental rubbish.[5]

The inability of twentieth-century critics either to appreciate the complexity and scope of a novel like Stowe's, or to account for its enormous popular success, stems from their assumptions about the nature and function of literature. In modernist thinking, literature is by definition a form of discourse that has no designs on the world. It does not attempt to change things, but merely to represent them, and it does so in a specifically literary language whose claim to value lies in its uniqueness. Consequently, works whose stated purpose is to influence the course of history, and which therefore employ a language that is not only not unique but common and accessible to everyone, do not qualify as works of art. Literary texts, such as the sentimental novel, that make continual and obvious appeals to the reader's emotions and use technical devices that are distinguished by their utter conventionality, epitomize the opposite of everything that good literature is supposed to be. "For the literary critic," writes J. W. Ward, summing up the dilemma posed by *Uncle Tom's Cabin*, "the problem is how a book so seemingly artless, so lacking in apparent literary talent, was not only an immediate success but has endured."[6]

How deep the problem goes is illustrated dramatically by George F. Whicher's discussion of Stowe's novel in *The Literary History of the United States.* Reflecting the consensus view on what good novels are made of, Whicher writes: "Nothing attributable to Mrs. Stowe or her handiwork can account for the novel's enormous vogue; its author's resources as a purveyor of Sunday-school fiction were not remarkable. She had at most a ready command of broadly conceived melodrama, humor, and pathos, and of these popular elements she compounded her book."[7] At a loss to understand how a book so compounded was able to "convulse a mighty nation," Whicher concludes—incredibly—that Stowe's own explanation that "God wrote it" "solved the paradox." Rather than give up his bias against "melodrama," "pathos," and "Sunday-school fiction," Whicher takes refuge in a solution that, even according to his lights, is patently absurd.[8] And no wonder. The modernist literary aesthetic cannot account for the unprecedented and persistent popularity of a book like *Uncle Tom's Cabin*, for this novel operates according to principles quite other than those that have been responsible for determining the currently sanctified American literary classics.

It is not my purpose, however, to drag Hawthorne and Melville from their pedestals, nor to claim that the novels of Stowe, Fanny Fern, and Elizabeth Stuart Phelps are good in the same way that *Moby-Dick* and *The Scarlet Letter* are; rather, I will argue that the work of the sentimental writers is complex and significant in ways *other than* those that characterize the established masterpieces. I will ask the reader to set aside some familiar categories for evaluating fiction—stylistic intricacy, psychological subtlety, epistemological complexity—and to see the sentimental novel not as an artifice of eternity answerable to certain formal criteria and to certain psychological and philosophical concerns, but as a political enterprise, halfway between sermon and social theory, that both codifies and attempts to mold the values of its time.

The power of a sentimental novel to move its audience depends upon the audience's being in possession of the conceptual categories that constitute character and event. That storehouse of assumptions includes attitudes toward the family and toward social institutions; a definition of power and its relation to individual human feeling; notions of political and social equality; and above all, a set of religious beliefs that organizes and sustains the rest. Once in possession of the system of beliefs that undergirds the patterns of sentimental fiction, it is possible for modern readers to see how its tearful episodes and frequent violations of probability were invested with a structure of meanings that fixed these works, for nineteenth-century readers, not in the realm of fairy tale or escapist fantasy, but in the very bedrock of reality. I do not say that we can read sentimental fiction exactly as Stowe's audience did—that would be impossible—but that we can and should set aside the modernist prejudices which consign this fiction to oblivion, in order to see how and why it worked for its readers, in its time, with such unexampled effect.

Let us consider the episode in *Uncle Tom's Cabin* most often cited as the epitome of Victorian sentimentalism—the death of little Eva—because it is the kind of incident most offensive to the sensibilities of twentieth-century academic critics. It is on the belief that this incident is nothing more than a sob story that the whole case against sentimentalism rests. Little Eva's death, so the argument goes, like every other sentimental tale, is awash with emotion but does nothing to remedy the evils it deplores. Essentially, it leaves the slave system and the other characters unchanged. This trivializing view of the episode is grounded in assumptions about power and reality so common that we are not even aware they are in force. Thus generations of critics have commented with condescending irony on little Eva's death. But in the system of belief that undergirds Stowe's enterprise, dying is the supreme form of heroism. In *Uncle Tom's Cabin*, death is the equivalent not of defeat but of victory; it brings an access of power, not a loss of it; it is not only the crowning achievement of life, it *is* life, and Stowe's entire presentation of little Eva is designed to dramatize this fact.

Stories like the death of little Eva are compelling for the same reason that the story of Christ's death is compelling; they enact a philosophy, as much political as religious, in which the pure and powerless die to save the powerful and corrupt, and thereby show themselves more powerful than those they save. They enact, in short, a *theory* of power in which the ordinary or "common sense" view of what is efficacious and what is not (a view to which most modern critics are committed) is simply reversed, as the very possibility of social action is made dependent on the action taking place in individual hearts. Little Eva's death enacts the drama of which all the major episodes of the novel are transformations, the idea, central to Christian soteriology, that the highest human calling is to give one's life for another. It presents one version of the ethic of sacrifice on which the entire novel is based and contains in some form all of the motifs that, by their frequent recurrence, constitute the novel's ideological framework.

Little Eva's death, moreover, is also a transformation of a story circulating in the culture at large. It may be found, for example, in a dozen or more versions in the evangelical sermons of the Reverend Dwight Lyman Moody which he preached in Great Britain and Ireland in 1875. In one version it is called "The Child Angel" and it concerns a beautiful golden-haired girl of seven, her father's pride and joy, who dies and, by appearing to him in a dream in which she calls to him from heaven, brings him salvation.[9] The tale shows that by dying even a child can be the instrument of redemption for others, since in death she acquires a spiritual power over those who loved her beyond what she possessed in life.

The power of the dead or the dying to redeem the unregenerate is a major theme of nineteenth-century popular fiction and religious literature. Mothers and children are thought to be uniquely capable of this work. In a sketch entitled

"Children," published the year after *Uncle Tom* came out, Stowe writes: "Wouldst thou know, o parent, what is that faith which unlocks heaven? Go not to wrangling polemics, or creeds and forms of theology, but draw to thy bosom thy little one, and read in that clear trusting eye the lesson of eternal life."[10] If children because of their purity and innocence can lead adults to God while living, their spiritual power when they are dead is greater still. Death, Stowe argues in a pamphlet entitled *Ministration of Departed Spirits*, enables the Christian to begin his "real work." God takes people from us sometimes so that their "ministry can act upon us more powerfully from the unseen world."[11]

> The mother would fain electrify the heart of her child. She yearns and burns in vain to make her soul effective on its soul, and to inspire it with a spiritual and holy life; but all her own weaknesses, faults and mortal cares, cramp and confine her till death breaks all fetters; and then, first truly alive, risen, purified, and at rest, she may do calmly, sweetly, and certainly, what, amid the tempest and tossings of her life, she labored for painfully and fitfully.[12]

When the spiritual power of death is combined with the natural sanctity of childhood, the child becomes an angel endowed with salvific force.

Most often, it is the moment of death that saves, when the dying child, glimpsing for a moment the glory of heaven, testifies to the reality of the life to come. Uncle Tom knows that this will happen when little Eva dies, and explains it to Miss Ophelia as follows:

> "You know it says in Scripture, 'At midnight there was a great cry made. Behold the bridegroom cometh.' That's what I'm spectin now, every night, Miss Feely,—and I could n't sleep out o' hearin', no ways."
> "Why, Uncle Tom, what makes you think so?"
> "Miss Eva, she talks to me. The Lord, he sends his messenger in the soul. I must be thar, Miss Feely; for when that ar blessed child goes into the kingdom, they'll open the door so wide, we'll all get a look in at the glory, Miss Feely."[13]

Little Eva does not disappoint them. She exclaims at the moment when she passes "from death unto life": "O, love,—joy,—peace!" And her exclamation echoes those of scores of children who die in Victorian fiction and sermon literature with heaven in their eyes. Dickens' Paul Dombey, seeing the face of his dead mother, dies with the words: "The light about the head is shining on me as I go!" The fair, blue-eyed young girl in Lydia Sigourney's *Letters to Mothers*, "death's purple tinge upon her brow," when implored by her mother to utter one last word, whispers "Praise!"[14]

Of course, it could be argued by critics of sentimentalism that the prominence of stories about the deaths of children is precisely what is wrong with the literature of the period; rather than being cited as a source of strength, the presence of such stories in *Uncle Tom's Cabin* could be regarded as an unfortunate concession to the age's fondness for lachrymose scenes. But to dismiss such scenes as "all tears and flapdoodle" is to leave unexplained the popularity of the novels and sermons that are filled with them, unless we choose to believe that a generation of readers was unaccountably moved to tears by matters that are intrinsically silly and trivial. That popularity is better explained, I believe, by the relationship of these scenes to a pervasive cultural myth which invests the suffering and death of an innocent victim with just the kind of power that critics deny to Stowe's novel: the power to work in, and change, the world.

This is the kind of action that little Eva's death in fact performs. It proves its efficacy not through the sudden collapse of the slave system, but through the conversion of Topsy, a motherless, godless black child who has up until that point successfully resisted all attempts to make her "good." Topsy will not be "good" because, never having had a mother's love, she believes that no one can love her. When Eva suggests that Miss Ophelia would love her if only she were good, Topsy cries out: "No; she can't bar me, 'cause I'm a nigger!—she'd's soon have a toad touch her! There can't nobody love niggers, and niggers can't do nothin'! *I* don't care."

> "O, Topsy, poor child, *I* love you!" said Eva, with a sudden burst of feeling, and laying her little thin, white hand on Topsy's shoulder; "I love you, because you have n't had any father, or mother, or friends;—because you've been a poor, abused child! I love you, and I want you to be good. I am very unwell, Topsy, and I think I shan't live a great while; and it really grieves me, to have you be so naughty. I wish you would try to be good, for my sake;—it's only a little while I shall be with you."
>
> The round, keen eyes of the black child were overcast with tears;— large, bright drops rolled heavily down, one by one, and fell on the little white hand. Yes, in that moment, a ray of real belief, a ray of heavenly love, had penetrated the darkness of her heathen soul! She laid her head down between her knees, and wept and sobbed,—while the beautiful child, bending over her, looked like the picture of some bright angel stooping to reclaim a sinner. (XXV, 330–331)

The rhetoric and imagery of this passage—its little white hand, its ray from heaven, bending angel, and plentiful tears—suggest a literary version of the kind of polychrome religious picture that hangs on Sunday-school walls. Words like "kitsch," "camp," and "corny" come to mind. But what is being dramatized here bears no relation to these designations. By giving Topsy her love, Eva initiates a process of redemption whose power, transmitted from heart to heart, can change the entire world. And indeed the process has begun. From that time on, Topsy is "different from what she used to be" (XXVI, 335) (eventually she will go to Africa and become a missionary to her entire race), and Miss Ophelia, who over-hears the conversation, is different, too. When little Eva is dead and Topsy cries out "ther an't *nobody* left now," Miss Ophelia answers her in Eva's place:

> "Topsy, you poor child," she said, as she led her into her room, "don't give up! *I* can love you, though I am not like that dear little child. I hope I've learnt something of the love of Christ from her. I can love you; I do, and I'll try to help you to grow up a good Christian girl."
> Miss Ophelia's voice was more than her words, and more than that were the honest tears that fell down her face. From that hour, she acquired an influence over the mind of the destitute child that she never lost. (XXVII, 349)

The tears of Topsy and of Miss Ophelia, which we find easy to ridicule, are the sign of redemption in *Uncle Tom's Cabin*; not words, but the emotions of the heart bespeak a state of grace, and these are known by the sound of a voice, the touch of a hand, but chiefly, in moments of greatest importance, by tears. When Tom lies dying on the plantation on the Red River, the disciples to whom he has preached testify to their conversion by weeping.

> Tears had fallen on that honest, insensible face,—tears of late repentance in the poor, ignorant heathen, whom his dying love and patience had awakened to repentance. . . . (XLI, 485)

Even the bitter and unregenerate Cassy, moved by "the sacrifice that had been made for her," breaks down; "moved by the few last words which the affectionate soul had yet strength to breathe, . . . the dark, despairing woman had wept and prayed" (XLI, 485). When George Shelby, the son of Tom's old master, arrives too late to free him, "tears which did honor to his manly heart fell from the young man's eyes as he bent over his poor friend." And when Tom realizes who is there, "the whole face lighted up, the hard hands clasped, and tears ran down the cheeks" (XLI, 486). The vocabulary of clasping hands and falling tears is one which we associate with emotional exhibitionism, with the overacting that kills off true feeling through exaggeration. But the tears and gestures of Stowe's characters are not in excess of what they feel; if anything they fall short of expressing the ex-periences they point to—salvation, communion, reconciliation.

If the language of tears seems maudlin and little Eva's death ineffectual, it is because both the tears and the redemption that they signify belong to a conception of the world that is now generally regarded as naive and unrealistic. Topsy's salvation and Miss Ophelia's do not alter the anti-abolitionist majority in the Senate or prevent southern plantation owners and northern investment bankers from doing business to their mutual advantage. Because most modern readers regard such political and economic facts as final, it is difficult for them to take seriously a novel that insists on religious conversion as the necessary precondition for sweeping social change. But in Stowe's understanding of what such change requires, it is the *modern* view that is naive. The political and economic measures that constitute effective action for us, she regards as superficial, mere extensions of the worldly policies that produced the slave system in the first place. Therefore, when Stowe asks the question that is in every reader's mind at the end of the novel—namely, "what can any individual do?"—she recommends not specific alterations in the current political and economic arrangements, but rather a change of heart.

> There is one thing that every individual can do—they can see to it that *they feel right.* An atmosphere of sympathetic influence encircles every human being; and the man or woman who *feels* strongly, healthily and justly, on the great interests of humanity, is a constant benefactor to the human race. See, then, to your sympathies in this matter! Are they in harmony with the sympathies of Christ? or are they swayed and perverted by the sophistries of worldly policy? (XLV, 515)

Stowe is not opposed to concrete measures such as the passage of laws or the formation of political pressure groups, it is just that, by themselves, such actions would be useless. For if slavery *were* to be abolished by these means, the moral conditions that produced slavery in the first place would continue in force. The choice is not between action and inaction, programs and feelings; the choice is between actions that spring from the "sophistries of worldly policy" and those inspired by the "sympathies of Christ." Reality, in Stowe's view, cannot be changed by manipulating the physical environment; it can only be changed by conversion in the spirit because it is the spirit alone that is finally real.

The notion that historical change takes place only through religious conversion, which is a theory of power as old as Christianity itself, is dramatized and vindicated in *Uncle Tom's Cabin* by the novel's insistence that all human events are organized, clarified, and made meaningful by the existence of spiritual realities.[15] The novel is packed with references to the four last things—Heaven, Hell, Death, and Judgment—references which remind the reader constantly that historical events can only be seen for what they are in the light of eternal truths. When St. Clare stands over the grave of little Eva, unable to realize "that it was his Eva that they were hiding from his sight," Stowe interjects, "Nor was it!—not Eva, but only the frail seed of that bright, immortal form with which she shall yet come forth, in the day of the Lord Jesus!" (XVII, 350). And when Legree expresses satisfaction that Tom is dead, she turns to him and says: "Yes, Legree; but who shall shut up that voice in thy soul? that soul, past repentance, past prayer, past hope, in whom the fire that never shall be quenched is already burning!" (XL, 480). These reminders come thick and fast; they are present in Stowe's countless quotations from Scripture—introduced at every possible opportunity, in the narrative, in dialogue, in epigraphs, in quotations from other authors; they are present in the Protestant hymns that thread their way through scene after scene, in asides to the reader, apostrophes to the characters, in quotations from religious poetry, sermons, and prayers, and in long stretches of dialogue and narrative devoted to the discussion of religious matters. Stowe's narrative stipulates a world in which the facts of Christ's death and resurrection and coming day of judgment are never far from our minds because it is only within this frame of reference that she can legitimately have Tom claim, as he dies, "I've got the victory!" (XLI, 486).

The eschatological vision, by putting all individual events in relation to an order that is unchanging, collapses the distinctions among them so that they become interchangeable representations of a single timeless reality. Groups of characters blend into the same character, while the plot abounds with incidents that mirror one another. These features are the features, not of classical nineteenth-century fiction, but of typological narrative. It is this tradition rather than that of the English novel that *Uncle Tom's Cabin* reproduces and extends; for this novel does not simply quote the Bible, it rewrites the Bible as the story of a Negro slave. Formally and philosophically, it stands opposed to works like *Middlemarch* and *The Portrait of a Lady* in which everything depends on human action and decision unfolding in a temporal sequence that withholds revelation until the final moment. The truths that Stowe's narrative conveys can only be reembodied, never discovered, because they are already revealed from the beginning. Therefore, what seem from a modernist point of view to be gross stereotypes in characterization and a needless proliferation of incident, are essential properties of a narrative aimed at demonstrating that human history is a continual reenactment of the sacred drama of redemption. It is the novel's reenactment of this drama that made it irresistible in its day.

Uncle Tom's Cabin retells the culture's central religious myth—the story of the crucifixion—in terms of the nation's greatest political conflict—slavery—and of its most cherished social beliefs—the sanctity of motherhood and the family. It is because Stowe is able to combine so many of the culture's central concerns in a narrative that is immediately accessible to the general population that she is able to move so many people so deeply. The novel's typological organization allows her to present political and social situations both as themselves and as transformations of a religious paradigm which interprets them in a way that readers can both understand and respond to emotionally. For the novel functions both as a means of describing the social world and as a means of changing it. It not only offers an interpretive framework for understanding the culture, and, through the reinforcement of a particular code of values, recommends a strategy for dealing with cultural conflict, but it is itself an agent of that strategy, putting into practice the measures it prescribes. As the religious stereotypes of "Sunday-school fiction" define and organize the elements of social and political life, so the "melodrama" and "pathos" associated with the underlying myth of crucifixion put the reader's heart in the right place with respect to the problems the narrative defines. Hence, rather than making the enduring success of *Uncle Tom's Cabin* inexplicable, these popular elements which puzzled Whicher and have puzzled so many modern scholars—melodrama, pathos, Sunday-school fiction—are the *only* terms in which the book's success can be explained.

The nature of these popular elements also dictates the terms in which any full-scale analysis of *Uncle Tom's Cabin* must be carried out. As I have suggested, its distinguishing features, generically speaking, are not those of the realistic novel, but of typological narrative. Its characters, like the figures in an allegory, do not change or develop, but reveal themselves in response to the demands of a situation. They are not defined primarily by their mental and emotional characteristics— that is to say, psychologically—but soteriologically, according to whether they are saved or damned. The plot, likewise, does not unfold according to Aristotelian standards of probability, but in keeping with the logic of a preordained design, a design which every incident is intended, in one way or another, to enforce.[16] The setting does not so much describe the features of a particular time and place as point to positions on a spiritual map. In *Uncle Tom's Cabin* the presence of realistic detail tends to obscure its highly programmatic nature and to lull readers into thinking that they are in an everyday world of material cause and effect. But what pass for realistic details—the use of dialect, the minute descriptions of domestic activity—are in fact performing a rhetorical function dictated by the novel's ruling paradigm; once that paradigm is perceived, even the homeliest details show up not as the empirically observed facts of human existence but as the expressions of a highly schematic intent.[17]

This schematization has what one might call a totalizing effect on the particulars of the narrative, so that every character in the novel, every scene, and every incident, comes to be apprehended in terms of every *other* character, scene, and incident: all are caught up in a system of endless cross-references in which it is impossible to refer to one without referring to all the rest. To demonstrate what I mean by this kind of narrative organization—a demonstration which will have to stand in lieu of a full-scale reading of the novel—let me show how it works in relation to a single scene. Eva and Tom are seated in the garden of St. Clare's house on the shores of Lake Pontchartrain.

> It was Sunday evening, and Eva's Bible lay open on her knee. She read,—
> "And I saw a sea of glass, mingled with fire."
> "Tom," said Eva, suddenly stopping, and pointing to the lake, "there 't is."

"What, Miss Eva?"

"Don't you see,—there?" said the child, pointing to the glassy water, which, as it rose and fell, reflected the golden glow of the sky. "There's a 'sea of glass, mingled with fire.' "

"True enough, Miss Eva," said Tom; and Tom sang—

> "O, had I had the wings of the morning,
> I'd fly away to Canaan's shore;
> Bright angels should convey me home,
> To the new Jerusalem."

"Where do you suppose new Jerusalem is, Uncle Tom?" said Eva.

"O, up in the clouds, Miss Eva."

"Then I think I see it," said Eva. "Look in those clouds!—they look like great gates of pearl; and you can see beyond them—far, far off—it's all gold. Tom, sing about 'spirits bright.' "

Tom sung the words of a well-known Methodist hymn,

> "I see a band of spirits bright,
> That taste the glories there;
> They all are robed in spotless white,
> And conquering palms they bear."

"Uncle Tom, I've seen *them*," said Eva. . . .

"They come to me sometimes in my sleep, those spirits;" and Eva's eyes grew dreamy, and she hummed, in a low voice,

> "They are all robed in spotless white,
> And conquering palms they bear."

"Uncle Tom," said Eva, "I'm going up there."

"Where, Miss Eva?"

The child rose, and pointed her little hand to the sky; the glow of evening lit her golden hair and flushed cheek with a kind of unearthly radiance, and her eyes were bent earnestly on the skies.

"I'm going *there*," she said, "to the spirits bright, Tom; *I'm going, before long*." (XXII, 303–307)

The iterative nature of this scene presents in miniature the structure of the whole novel. Eva reads from her Bible about a "sea of glass, mingled with fire," then looks up to find one before her. She reads the words aloud a second time. They remind Tom of a hymn which describes the same vision in a slightly different form (Lake Pontchartrain and the sea of glass become "Canaan's shore" and the "new Jerusalem") and Eva sees what he has sung, this time in the clouds, and offers her own description. Eva asks Tom to sing again and his hymn presents yet another form of the same vision, which Eva again says she has seen: the spirits bright come to her in her sleep. Finally, Eva repeats the last two lines of the hymn and declares that she is going "there"—to the place which has now been referred to a dozen times in this passage. Stowe follows with another description of the golden skies and then with a description of Eva as a spirit bright, and closes the passage with Eva's double reiteration that she is going "there."

The entire scene itself is a re-presentation of others that come before and after. When Eva looks out over Lake Pontchartrain, she sees the "Canaan of liberty" (VII, 70) Eliza saw on the other side of the Ohio River, and the "eternal shore" (XLIII, 499) Eliza and George Harris will reach when they cross Lake Erie in the end. Bodies of water mediate between worlds: the Ohio runs between the slave states and the free; Lake Erie divides the United States from Canada, where runaway slaves cannot be returned to their masters; the Atlantic Ocean divides the North American continent from Africa, where Negroes will have a nation of their own; Lake Pontchartrain shows Eva the heavenly home to which she is going soon; the Mississippi River carries slaves from the relative ease of the middle states to the grinding toil of the southern plantations; the Red River carries Tom to the infernal regions ruled over by Simon Legree. The correspondences between the episodes I have mentioned are themselves based on correspondences between earth and heaven (or hell). Ohio, Canada, and Liberia are related to one another by virtue of their relationship to the one "bright Canaan" for which they stand; the Mississippi River and the Ohio are linked by the Jordan. (Ultimately, there are only three places to be in this story: heaven, hell, or Kentucky, which represents the earthly middle ground in Stowe's geography.)

Characters in the novel are linked to each other in exactly the same way that places are—with reference to a third term that is the source of their identity. The figure of Christ is the common term which unites all of the novel's good characters, who are good precisely in proportion as they are imitations of him. Eva and Tom head the list (she reenacts the last supper and he the crucifixion), but they are also linked to most of the slaves, women, and children in the novel by the characteristics they all share: piety, impressionability, spontaneous affection—and victimization.[18] In this scene, Eva is linked with the "spirits bright" (she later becomes a "bright, immortal form," XXVII, 350) both because she can see them and is soon to join them, and because she, too, always wears white and is elsewhere several times referred to as an "angel." When Eva dies, she will join her father's mother, who was also named Evangeline, and who herself always wore white, and who, like Eva, is said to be "a direct embodiment and personification of the New Testament" (XIX, 263). And this identification, in its turn, refers back to Uncle Tom who is "all the moral and Christian virtues bound in black morocco, complete" (XIV, 179). The circularity of this train of association is typical of the way the narrative doubles back on itself: later on, Cassy, impersonating the ghost of Legree's saintly mother, will wrap herself in a white sheet.[19]

The scene I have been describing is a node within a network of allusion in which every character and event in the novel has a place. The narrative's rhetorical strength derives in part from the impression it gives of taking every kind of detail in the world into account, from the preparation of breakfast to the orders of the angels, and investing those details with a purpose and a meaning which are both immediately apprehensible and finally significant. The novel reaches out into the reader's world and colonizes it for its own eschatology: that is, it not only incorporates the homely particulars of "Life among the Lowly" into its universal scheme, but it gives them a power and a centrality in that scheme, thereby turning the socio-political order upside down. The totalizing effect of the novel's iterative organization and its doctrine of spiritual redemption are inseparably bound to its political purpose: to bring in the day when the meek—which is to say, women—will inherit the earth.

The specifically political intent of the novel is apparent in its forms of address. Stowe addresses her readers not simply as individuals but as citizens of the United States: "to you, generous, noble-minded men and women, of the South," (XLV, 513) "farmers of Massachusetts, of New Hampshire, of Vermont," "brave and generous men of New York," "and you, mothers of America" (XLV, 514). She speaks to her audience directly in the way the Old Testament prophets spoke to Israel, exhorting, praising, blaming, warning of the wrath to come. "This is an age of the world when nations are trembling and convulsed. A mighty influence is abroad, surging and heaving the world, as with an earthquake. And is America safe? . . . O, Church of Christ, read the signs of the times!" (XLV, 519). Passages like these, descended from the revivalist rhetoric of "Sinners in the Hands of an Angry God," are intended, in the words of a noted scholar, "to direct an imperiled people toward the fulfillment of their destiny, to guide them individually toward salvation, and collectively toward the American city of God."[20]

These words are from Sacvan Bercovitch's *The American Jeremiad*, an influential work of modern scholarship which, although it completely ignores Stowe's novel, makes us aware that *Uncle Tom's Cabin* is a jeremiad in the fullest and truest sense. A jeremiad, in Bercovitch's definition, is "a mode of public exhortation . . . designed to join social criticism to spiritual renewal, public to private identity, the shifting 'signs of the times' to certain traditional metaphors, themes, and symbols."[21] Stowe's novel provides the most obvious and compelling instance of the jeremiad since the Great Awakening, and its exclusion from Bercovitch's book is a striking instance of how totally academic criticism has foreclosed on sentimental fiction; for, because *Uncle Tom's Cabin* is absent from the canon, it isn't "there" to be referred to even when it fulfills a man's theory to perfection. Hence its exclusion from critical discourse is perpetuated automatically, and absence begets itself in a self-confirming cycle of neglect. Nonetheless, Bercovitch's characterization of the jeremiad provides an excellent account of how *Uncle Tom's Cabin* actually worked: among its characters, settings, situations, symbols, and doctrines, the novel establishes a set of correspondences which unite the disparate realms of experience Bercovitch names—social and spiritual, public and private, theological and political—*and*, through the vigor of its representations, attempts to move the nation as a whole toward the vision it proclaims.

The tradition of the jeremiad throws light on *Uncle Tom's Cabin* because Stowe's novel was political in exactly the same way the jeremiad was: both were forms of discourse in which "theology was wedded to politics and politics to the progress of the kingdom of God."[22] The jeremiad strives to persuade its listeners to a providential view of human history which serves, among other things, to maintain the Puritan theocracy in power. Its fusion of theology and politics is not only doctrinal—in that it ties the salvation of the individual to the community's historical enterprise—it is practical as well, for it reflects the interests of Puritan ministers in their bid to retain spiritual and secular authority. The sentimental novel, too, is an act of persuasion aimed at defining social reality; the difference is that the jeremiad represents the interests of Puritan ministers, while the sentimental novel represents the interests of middle-class women. But the relationship between rhetoric and history in both cases is the same. In both cases it is not as if rhetoric and history stand opposed, with rhetoric made up of wish fulfillment and history made up of recalcitrant facts that resist rhetoric's onslaught. Rhetoric *makes* history by shaping reality to the dictates of its political design; it makes history by convincing the people of the world that its description of the world is the true one. The sentimental novelists make their bid for power by positing the kingdom of heaven on earth as a world over which women exercise ultimate control. If history did not take the course these writers recommended, it is not because they were not political, but because they were insufficiently persuasive.

Uncle Tom's Cabin, however, unlike its counterparts in the sentimental tradition, was spectacularly persuasive in conventional political terms: it helped convince a nation to go to war and to free its slaves. But in terms of its own conception of power, a conception it shares with other sentimental fiction, the novel was a political failure. Stowe conceived her book as an instrument for bringing about the day when the world would be ruled not by force, but by Christian love. The novel's deepest political aspirations are expressed only secondarily in its devastating attack on the slave system; the true goal of Stowe's rhetorical undertaking is nothing less than the institution of the kingdom of heaven on earth. Embedded in the world of *Uncle Tom's Cabin*, which is the fallen world of slavery, there appears an idyllic picture, both utopian and Arcadian, of the form human life would assume if Stowe's readers were to heed her moral lesson. In this vision, described in the chapter entitled "The Quaker Settlement," Christian love fulfills itself not in war, but in daily living, and the principle of sacrifice is revealed not in crucifixion, but in motherhood. The form that Stowe's utopian society takes bears no resemblance to the current social order. Man-made institutions—the church, the courts of law, the legislatures, the economic system—are nowhere in sight. The home is the center of all meaningful activity; women perform the most important tasks; work is carried on in a spirit of mutual cooperation; and the whole is guided by a Christian woman who, through the influence of her "loving words," "gentle moralities," and "motherly loving kindness," rules the world from her rocking chair.

> For why? for twenty years or more, nothing but loving words, and gentle moralities, and motherly loving kindness, had come from that chair;—head-aches and heart-aches innumerable had been cured there,—difficulties spiritual and temporal solved there,—all by one good, loving woman, God bless her! (XIII, 163)

The woman in question *is* God in human form. Seated in her kitchen at the head of her table, passing out coffee and cake for breakfast, Rachel Halliday, the millenarian counterpart of little Eva, enacts the redeemed form of the last supper. This is holy communion as it will be under the new dispensation: instead of the breaking of bones, the breaking of bread. The preparation of breakfast exemplifies the way people will work in the ideal society; there will be no competition, no exploitation, no commands. Motivated by self-sacrificing love, and joined to one another by its cohesive power, people will perform their duties willingly and with pleasure: moral suasion will take the place of force.

> All moved obediently to Rachel's gentle "Thee had better," or more gentle "Hadn't thee better?" in the work of getting breakfast. . . . Everything went on so sociably, so quietly, so harmoniously, in the great kitchen,—it seemed so pleasant to every one to do just what they were doing, there was such an atmosphere of mutual confidence and good fellowship everywhere. . . . (XIII, 169–170)

The new matriarchy which Isabella Beecher Hooker had dreamed of leading, pictured here in the Indiana kitchen ("for a breakfast in the luxurious valleys of Indiana is . . . like picking up the rose-leaves and trimming the bushes in Paradise," [XIII, 169]), constitutes the most politically subversive dimension of Stowe's novel, more disruptive and far-reaching in its potential consequences than even the starting of a war or the freeing of slaves. Nor is the ideal of matriarchy simply a daydream; Catherine Beecher, Stowe's elder sister, had offered a ground plan for the realization of such a vision in her *Treatise on Domestic Economy* (1841), which the two sisters republished in an enlarged version entitled *The American Woman's Home* in 1869.[23] Dedicated "To the Women of America, in whose hands rest the real destinies of the republic," this is an instructional book on homemaking in which a wealth of scientific information and practical advice are pointed toward a millenarian goal. Centering on the home, for these women, is not a way of indulging in narcissistic fantasy, as critics have argued,[24] or a turning away from the world into self-absorption and idle reverie; it is the prerequisite of world conquest—defined as the reformation of the human race through proper care and nurturing of its young. Like *Uncle Tom's Cabin*, *The American Woman's Home* situates the minutiae of domestic life in relation to their soteriological function: "What then, is the end designed by the family state which Jesus Christ came into this world to secure? It is to provide for the training of our race . . . by means of the self-sacrificing labors of the wise and good . . . with chief reference to a future immortal existence."[25] "The family state," the authors announce at the beginning, "is the aptest earthly illustration of the heavenly kingdom, and . . . woman is its chief minister."[26] In the body of the text, the authors provide women with everything they need to know for the proper establishment and maintenance of home and family, from the construction of furniture ("The [bed] frame is to be fourteen inches from the floor . . . and three inches in thickness. At the head, and at the foot, is to be screwed a notched two-inch board, three inches wide, as in Fig. 8," [30]), to architectural plans, to chapters of instruction on heating, ventilation, lighting, healthful diet, preparation of food, cleanliness, the making and mending of clothes, the care of the sick, the organization of routines, financial management, psychological health, the care of infants, the managing of young children, home amusement, the care of furniture, planting of gardens, the care of domestic animals, the disposal of waste, the cultivation of fruit, and providing for the "Homeless, the Helpless, and the Vicious" (433). After each of these activities has been treated in detail, they conclude by describing the ultimate aim of the domestic enterprise. The founding of a "truly 'Christian family' " will lead to the gathering of a "Christian neighborhood." This "cheering example," they continue,

> would soon spread, and ere long colonies from these prosperous and Christian communities would go forth to shine as "lights of the world" in all the now darkened nations. Thus the "Christian family" and "Christian neighborhood" would become the grand ministry, as they were designed to be, in training our whole race for heaven.[27]

The imperialistic drive behind the encyclopedism and determined practicality of this household manual flatly contradicts the traditional derogations of the American cult of domesticity as a "mirror-phenomenon," "self-immersed" and "self-congratulatory."[28] *The American Woman's Home* is a blueprint for colonizing the world in the name of the "family state" (19) under the leadership of Christian women. What is more, people like Stowe and Catherine Beecher were speaking not simply for a set of moral and religious values. In speaking for the home, they speak for an economy—a household economy—which had supported New England life since its inception. The home, rather than representing a retreat or a refuge from a crass industrial-commercial world, offers an economic *alternative* to that world, one which calls into question the whole structure of American society which was growing up in response to the increase in trade and manufacturing.[29] Stowe's image of a utopian community as presented in Rachel Halliday's

kitchen is not simply a Christian dream of communitarian cooperation and harmony; it is a reflection of the real communitarian practices of village life, practices
which depended upon cooperation, trust, and a spirit of mutual supportiveness
which characterize the Quaker community of Stowe's novel.

One could argue, then, that for all its revolutionary fervor, *Uncle Tom's Cabin*
is a conservative book, because it advocates a return to an older way of life—
household economy—in the name of the nation's most cherished social and religious beliefs. Even the emphasis on the woman's centrality might be seen as
harking back to the "age of homespun" when the essential goods were manufac-
tured in the home and their production was carried out and guided by women.
But Stowe's very conservatism—her reliance on established patterns of living and
traditional beliefs—is precisely what gives her novel its revolutionary potential.
By pushing those beliefs to an extreme and by insisting that they be applied
universally, not just to one segregated corner of civil life, but to the conduct of
all human affairs, Stowe means to effect a radical transformation of her society.
The brilliance of the strategy is that it puts the central affirmations of a culture
into the service of a vision that would destroy the present economic and social
institutions; by resting her case, absolutely, on the saving power of Christian love
and on the sanctity of motherhood and the family, Stowe relocates the center of
power in American life, placing it not in the government, nor in the courts of
law, nor in the factories, nor in the marketplace, but in the kitchen. And that
means that the new society will not be controlled by men, but by women. The
image of the home created by Stowe and Beecher in their treatise on domestic
science is in no sense a shelter from the stormy blast of economic and political
life, a haven from reality divorced from fact which allows the machinery of industrial capitalism to grind on; it is conceived as a dynamic center of activity,
physical and spiritual, economic and moral, whose influence spreads out in ever-
widening circles. To this activity—and this is the crucial innovation—men are
incidental. Although the Beecher sisters pay lip service on occasion to male supremacy, women's roles occupy virtually the whole of their attention and dominate
the scene. Male provender is deemphasized in favor of female processing. Men
provide the seed, but women bear and raise the children. Men provide the flour,
but women bake the bread and get the breakfast. The removal of the male from
the center to the periphery of the human sphere is the most radical component
of this millenarian scheme, which is rooted so solidly in the most traditional
values—religion, motherhood, home, and family. Exactly what position men will
occupy in the millennium is specified by a detail inserted casually into Stowe's
description of the Indiana kitchen. While the women and children are busy preparing breakfast, Simeon Halliday, the husband and father, stands "in his shirt-
sleeves before a little looking-glass in the corner, engaged in the anti-patriarchal
operation of shaving" (XIII, 169).

With this detail, so innocently placed, Stowe reconceives the role of men in human history: while Negroes, children, mothers, and grandmothers do the world's primary work, men groom themselves contentedly in a corner. The scene, as critics have noted is often the case in sentimental fiction, is "intimate," the backdrop is "domestic," the tone at times is even "chatty";[30] but the import, as critics have failed to recognize, is world-shaking. The enterprise of sentimental fiction, as Stowe's novel attests, is anything but domestic, in the sense of being limited to purely personal concerns. Its mission, on the contrary, is global and its interests identical with the interests of the race. If the fiction written in the nineteenth century by women whose works sold in the hundreds of thousands has seemed narrow and parochial to the critics of the twentieth century, that narrowness and parochialism belong not to these works nor to the women who wrote them; they are the beholders' share.[31]

NOTES

This chapter is a slightly revised version of the essay that originally appeared in *Glyph, 8.* I would like to thank Sacvan Bercovitch for his editorial suggestions.

1. Johanna Johnston, *Runaway to Heaven* (Garden City, N.Y.: Doubleday and Co., 1963).

2. Edward Halsey Foster, for example, prefaces his book-length study *Susan and Anna Warner* (Boston: Twayne Publishers, n.d.), p. 9, by saying: "If one searches nineteenth-century popular fiction for something that has literary value, one searches, by and large, in vain." At the other end of the spectrum stands a critic like Sally Mitchell, whose excellent studies of Victorian women's fiction contain statements that, intentionally or not, condescend to the subject matter. For example, in "Sentiment and Suffering: Women's Recreational Reading in the 1860's," *Victorian Studies*, 21, No. 1 (Autumn 1977), p. 34, she says: "Thus, we should see popular novels as emotional analyses, rather than intellectual analyses, of a particular society." The most typical move, however, is to apologize for the poor literary quality of the novels and then to assert that a text is valuable on historical grounds.

3. Ann Douglas is the foremost of the feminist critics who have accepted this characterization of the sentimental writers, and it is to her formulation of the antisentimentalist position, *The Feminization of American Culture* (New York: Alfred A. Knopf, 1977), that my arguments throughout are principally addressed. Although her attitude toward the vast quantity of literature written by women between 1820 and 1870 is the one that the male-dominated tradition has always expressed—contempt—Douglas' book is nevertheless extremely important because of its powerful and sustained consideration of this long-neglected body of work. Because Douglas successfully focused critical attention on the cultural centrality of sentimental fiction, forcing the realization that it can no longer be ignored, it is now possible for other critics to put

forward a new characterization of these novels and not be dismissed. For these reasons, it seems to me, her work is important.

4. These attitudes are forcefully articulated by Douglas, p. 9.

5. The phrase, "a damned mob of scribbling women," coined by Hawthorne in a letter he wrote to his publisher, in 1855, and clearly the product of Hawthorne's own feelings of frustration and envy, comes embedded in a much-quoted passage that has set the tone for criticism of sentimental fiction ever since. As quoted by Fred Lewis Pattee, *The Feminine Fifties* (New York: D. Appleton-Century Co., 1940), p. 110, Hawthorne wrote:

> America is now wholly given over to a d****d mob of scribbling women, and I should have no chance of success while the public taste is occupied with their trash—and should be ashamed of myself if I did succeed. What is the mystery of these innumerable editions of *The Lamplighter*, and other books neither better nor worse? Worse they could not be, and better they need not be, when they sell by the hundred thousand.

6. J. W. Ward, *Red, White, and Blue; Men, Books, and Ideas in American Culture* (New York: Oxford University Press, 1961), p. 75.

7. George F. Whicher, "Literature and Conflict," in *The Literary History of the United States*, ed. Robert E. Spiller et al., 3rd ed., rev. (London: Macmillan, 1963), p. 583.

8. Whicher, in *Literary History*, ed. Spiller, p. 586. Edmund Wilson, despite his somewhat sympathetic treatment of Stowe in *Patriotic Gore: Studies in the Literature of the American Civil War* (New York: Oxford University Press, 1966), pp. 5, 32, seems to concur in this opinion, reflecting a characteristic tendency of commentators on the most popular works of sentimental fiction to regard the success of these women as some sort of mysterious eruption, inexplicable by natural causes. Henry James gives this attitude its most articulate, though perhaps least defensible, expression in a remarkable passage from *A Small Boy and Others* (New York: Charles Scribner's Sons, 1913), pp. 159–160, where he describes Stowe's book as really not a book at all but as "a fish, a wonderful 'leaping' fish"—the point being to deny Stowe any role in the process that produced such a wonder:

> Appreciation and judgment, the whole impression, were thus an effect for which there had been no process—any process so related having in other cases *had* to be at some point or other critical; nothing in the guise of a written book, therefore, a book printed, published, sold, bought and "noticed," probably ever reached its mark, the mark of exciting interest, without having at least groped for that goal *as* a book or by the exposure of some literary side. Letters, here, languished unconscious, and Uncle Tom, instead of making even one of the cheap short cuts through the medium in which books breathe, even as fishes in water, went gaily roundabout it altogether,

as if a fish, a wonderful "leaping" fish, had simply flown through the air.

9. Reverend Dwight Lyman Moody, *Sermons and Addresses*, in *Narrative of Messrs. Moody and Sankey's Labors in Great Britain and Ireland with Eleven Addresses and Lectures in Full* (New York: Anson D. F. Randolph and Co., 1975).

10. Harriet Beecher Stowe, "Children," in *Uncle Sam's Emancipation; Earthly Care, a Heavenly discipline; and other sketches* (Philadelphia: W. P. Hazard, 1853), p. 83.

11. Harriet Beecher Stowe, *Ministration of Departed Spirits* (Boston: American Tract Society, n.d.), pp. 4, 3.

12. Stowe, *Ministration*, p. 3.

13. Harriet Beecher Stowe, *Uncle Tom's Cabin; or, Life among the Lowly*, ed. Kathryn Kish Sklar (New York: Library of America, 1982), p. 344. All future references to *Uncle Tom's Cabin* will be to this edition; chapter and page numbers are given in parentheses in the text.

14. Charles Dickens, *Dombey and Son* (Boston: Estes and Luriat, 1882), p. 278; Lydia H. Sigourney, *Letters to Mothers* (Hartford: Hudson and Skinner, 1838).

15. Religious conversion as the basis for a new social order was the mainspring of the Christian evangelical movement of the mid-nineteenth century. The emphasis on "feeling," which seems to modern readers to provide no basis whatever for the organization of society, was the key factor in the evangelical theory of reform. See Sandra Sizer's discussions of this phenomenon in *Gospel Hymns and Social Religion* (Philadelphia: Temple University Press, 1978), pp. 52, 59, 70–71, 72. "It is clear from the available literature that prayer, testimony, and exhortation were employed to create a *community* of intense *feeling*, in which individuals underwent similar experiences (centering on conversion) and would thenceforth unite with others in matters of moral decision and social behavior." "People in similar states of feeling, in short, would 'walk together,' would be agreed." "Conversion established individuals in a particular kind of relationship with God, by virtue of which they were automatically members of a social company, alike in interests and feelings." Good order would be preserved by "relying on the spiritual and moral discipline provided by conversion, and on the company of fellow Christians, operating without the coercive force of government."

16. Angus Fletcher, *Allegory, The Theory of a Symbolic Mode* (Ithaca, N.Y.: Cornell University Press, 1964), discusses the characteristic features of allegory in such a way as to make clear the family resemblance between sentimental fiction and the allegorical mode. See particularly his analyses of character, pp. 35, 60, symbolic action, pp. 150ff., 178, 180, 182, and imagery, p. 171.

17. Fletcher's comment on the presence of naturalistic detail in allegory, pp. 198–199, is pertinent here:

> The apparent surface realism of an allegorical agent will recede in importance, as soon as he is felt to take part in a magical plot, as soon as his causal relations to others in that plot are seen to be magically based. This is an important point because there has often been confusion as to the function of the naturalist detail of so much allegory. In terms I have been outlining, this detail now appears not to have a journalistic function; it is more than mere record of observed facts. It serves instead the purposes of magical containment, since the more the allegorist can circumscribe the attributes, metonymic and synecdochic, of his personae, the better he can shape their fictional destiny. Naturalist detail is "cosmic," universalizing, not accidental as it would be in straight journalism.

18. The associations that link slaves, women, and children are ubiquitous and operate on several levels. Besides being described in the same set of terms, these characters occupy parallel structural positions in the plot. They function chiefly as mediators between God and the unredeemed, so that, e.g., Mrs. Shelby intercedes for Mr. Shelby; Mrs. Bird for Senator Bird; Simon Legree's mother (unsuccessfully) for Simon Legree; little Eva and St. Clare's mother for St. Clare; Tom Loker's mother for Tom Loker; Eliza for George Harris (spiritually, she is the agent of his conversion), and for Harry Harris (physically, she saves him from being sold down the river); and Tom for all the slaves on the Legree plantation (spiritually, he converts them) and for all the slaves of the Shelby plantation (physically, he is the cause of their being set free).

19. For a parallel example, see Alice Crozier's analysis of the way the lock of hair that little Eva gives Tom becomes transformed into the lock of hair that Simon Legree's mother sent to Simon Legree. *The Novels of Harriet Beecher Stowe* (New York: Oxford University Press, 1969), pp. 29–31.

20. Sacvan Bercovitch, *The American Jeremiad* (Madison: University of Wisconsin Press, 1978), p. 9.

21. Bercovitch, p. xi.

22. Bercovitch, p. xiv.

23. For an excellent discussion of Beecher's *Treatise* and of the entire cult of domesticity, see Kathryn Kish Sklar, *Catherine Beecher, A Study in American Domesticity* (New York: W. W. Norton and Co., 1976). For other helpful discussions of the topic, see Barbara G. Berg, *The Remembered Gate: Origins of American Feminism, The Woman and the City, 1800–1860* (New York: Oxford University Press, 1978); Sizer; Ronald G. Walters, *The Antislavery Appeal, American Abolitionism after 1830* (Baltimore: The Johns Hopkins University Press, 1976); and Barbara Welter, "The Cult of True Womanhood, 1820–1860," *American Quarterly*, 18 (Summer 1966), pp. 151–174.

24. For Douglas' charges of narcissism against Stowe and her readers, see *The Feminization of American Culture*, pp. 2, 9, 297, and 300.

25. Catherine Beecher and Harriet Beecher Stowe, *The American Woman's Home: or, Principles of Domestic Science; Being a Guide to the Formation and Maintenance of Economical, Healthful, Beautiful, and Christian Homes* (New York: J. B. Ford and Co., 1869), p. 18.

26. Beecher and Stowe, *The American Woman's Home*, p. 19.

27. Beecher and Stowe, *The American Woman's Home*, pp. 458–59.

28. These are Douglas' epithets, p. 307.

29. For a detailed discussion of the changes referred to here, see Christopher Clark, "Household Economy, Market Exchange and the Rise of Capitalism in the Connecticut Valley, 1800–1860," *Journal of Social History*, 13, No. 2 (Winter 1979), pp. 169–189; and Nancy F. Cott, *The Bonds of Womanhood: "Woman's Sphere" in New England, 1780–1835* (New Haven: Yale University Press, 1977).

30. Douglas, p. 9.

31. In a helpful article in *Signs*, "The Sentimentalists: Promise and Betrayal in the Home," 4, No. 3 (Spring 1979), pp. 434–46, Mary Kelley characterizes the main positions in the debate over the significance of sentimental fiction as follows: (1) the Cowie-Welter thesis, which holds that women's fiction expresses an "ethics of conformity" and accepts the stereotype of the woman as pious, pure, submissive, and dedicated to the home, and (2) the Papashvily-Garrison thesis, which sees sentimental fiction as profoundly subversive of traditional ideas of male authority and female subservience. Kelley locates herself somewhere in between, holding that sentimental novels convey a "contradictory message": "they tried to project an Edenic image," but their own tales "subverted their intentions" by showing how often women were frustrated and defeated in the performance of their heroic roles. My own position is that the sentimental novelists are both conformist and subversive, but not, as Kelley believes, in a self-contradictory way. They used the central myth of their culture—the story of Christ's death for the sins of mankind—as the basis for a new myth which reflected their own interests. They regarded their vision of the Christian home as the fulfillment of the Gospel, "the end . . . which Jesus Christ came into this world to secure," in exactly the same way that the Puritans believed that their mission was to found the "American city of God," and that Christians believe the New Testament to be a fulfillment of the Old. Revolutionary ideologies, typically, announce themselves as the fulfillment of old promises or as a return to a golden age. What I am suggesting here, in short, is that the argument over whether the sentimental novelists were radical or conservative is a false issue. The real problem is how we, in the light of everything that has happened since they wrote, can understand and appreciate their work. See Alexander Cowie, "The Vogue of the Domestic Novel, 1850–1870," *South Atlantic Quarterly,* 41 (October 1942), p. 420; Welter; Helen Waite Papashvily, *All the Happy Endings: A Study of the Domestic Novel in America, the Women Who Wrote It, the Women Who Read It, in the Nineteenth Century* (New York: Harper and Bros., 1956); and Dee Garrison, "Immoral Fiction in the Late Victorian Library," *American Quarterly,* 28 (Spring 1976), pp. 71–80.

10

"MAKE MY DAY!": SPECTACLE AS AMNESIA IN IMPERIAL POLITICS

MICHAEL ROGIN

I

The thief hides the purloined letter, in Edgar Allen Poe's story, by placing it in plain sight. His theft is overlooked because no attempt is made to conceal it. The crimes of the postmodern American empire, I want to suggest, are concealed in the same way. Covert operations actually function as spectacle. So let us begin like Poe's Inspector Dupin, and attend to the evidence before our eyes.[1]

The last president of the United States was a Hollywood actor. His vice president, the man who succeeded him, was the director of the Central Intelligence Agency. To understand how the career paths of these two men, rather than discrediting either them or the political system in which they had risen to the top, uniquely prepared them for the presidency is to name the two political peculiarities of the postmodern American empire: on the one hand the domination of public politics by the spectacle and on the other the spread of covert operations and a secret foreign policy. "Going public," Samuel Kernell's phrase for the shift from institutionalized, pluralist bargaining among stable, elite coalitions to appeals to the mass public, coexists with going private, the spread of hidden, unaccountable decision making within the executive branch. How are we to think about the relationship between the two?[2]

It may seem that spectacle and secrecy support each other by a division of labor, one being public and the other private, one selling or disguising the foreign policy made by the other. The Iran/Contra exposure broke down that division, on this view, by revealing a secret foreign policy that not only violated public law against aiding the Contras but also contradicted public denunciations of the Ayatollah Khomeini and of bargaining with terrorists. The privatization of American foreign policy that characterized Iran/Contra signified, in this interpretation, the takeover of policy by private, unaccountable arms merchants and state terrorists by means of private, secret operations. Although the executive junta owed its

229

power to officials in high public positions, the argument continues, it was not a public body.

Such an interpretation, which divides public image from secret operations, ignores secrecy's role beyond covert operational borders, producing signals for elite and mass audiences. To begin with, the "neat idea[s]" that produced Iran/Contra (to recall Oliver North's apt phrase) were acted out as a film scenario in the heads of the junta, who, along with the right-wing ideologues let in on parts of the story, formed the audience for their own movie. ("Ollie was a patriot," remarked former Reagan press spokesman Larry Speakes. "But I sometimes felt he thought he was playing some kind of role, that he was watching a movie on the screen with himself the star in it.")[3] And just as Iran/Contra was acted out as a spectacle within the junta, other covert operations have been intended to function as spectacle for relevant audiences—enemies and allies abroad, mass public and opinion makers at home. Political spectacle in the postmodern empire, in other words, is itself a form of power and not simply window dressing that diverts attention from the secret substance of American foreign policy.

To introduce the entanglement between the two apparent opposites, spectacle and secrecy, let us consider their conjunction in the modus vivendi of the two presidential figures, the Ronald Reagan of spectacle and the George Bush of covert operations. "Plausible deniability," as the phrase used to exculpate Reagan inadvertently admitted, points to a president whose operations in front of the camera were meant to render plausible the denial that he also operated behind it. That has been true since Hollywood, when President Reagan of the Screen Actors Guild engaged in two covert actions: first, he informed on his coworkers to the FBI and helped organize the anti-Communist blacklist whose existence he denied; second, he negotiated the exemption for Music Corporation of America that allowed it alone among talent agencies to produce movies and television shows and simultaneously to represent actors. The former covert action launched Reagan's political career. The latter, putting him in front of the camera on the GE Television Theater, moved him from movies to TV; helped him perfect the intimate, living-room image that would be crucial to his political success; and gave him the capital and capital-producing friendships that would underwrite his political career.[4]

These examples, which reverse the usual image of Reagan as mere entertainer, make covert action into the source of his power. Reagan's domination of American politics has come, however, not from his compartmentalized mastery of either covert action or spectacle but from his confusion of the two. Just as it facilitated his rise from Hollywood acting to Washington power, that confusion also protected the president from the worst consequences of the Iran/Contra exposure. When Reagan took responsibility for Iran/Contra with the words "It happened on my watch," he placed himself on the permeable border between public display and covert operation. "My watch" identified him as commander-in-chief, standing on the bridge as he did in the role of submarine commander in his last Hollywood movie, *Hellcats of the Navy*. Just as the script of that movie freed the fictional commander from responsibility for the loss of his ship, so "It happened on my watch" allows the real president to evade responsibility by assuming it. The line first separates the visible commander-in-chief from the guilty parties in charge of operations down in what one former presidential chief-of-staff has called the "engine room." Second, the line identifies the president not simply as the object at whom we look but as one of the watchers as well. "My watch" makes the president just another ordinary American spectator, as much or as little responsible as the rest of us—there and not there at the same time—as in the head and upper body shot of Reagan at the 1984 Republican convention. At once on camera and part of the television audience, the president lounged in shirt sleeves and watched his wife (a tiny image much smaller than he) raise her arms and, saying "Win one for the Gipper," turn toward the giant image of presidential head and torso lounging and watching his wife—an infinite regression that drew the convention and television audience into the picture, identifying that audience as one of and as subject to the one of itself it was watching. Reagan's managers planned every detail of that scene, including the special podium built without a single edge or straight line—"Curves everywhere," as its creator described it, "brown, beige, nothing jarring. . . . The eye comes to rest there. Earth tones and rounded shapes are peaceful." "The podium was a giant womb," comments Garry Wills, "into which the country would retreat along with Reagan."[5]

The Reagan spectacle points, then, neither to the insignificance nor to the autonomy of the sign but rather to its role in producing power. By the same token, the former CIA director was no more a powerful invisible presence before he became chief of state than the former actor was a powerless visible one. That is not because, as Robert Dole charged, Bush is the perennial good-boy marionette who doesn't pull his own strings. Bush has had, after all, a substantial relationship to the CIA. He was, first, the former director who brought in Team B to politicize intelligence judgments, to exaggerate the extent of the Soviet military and political threat to the United States, and thereby to lay the groundwork for the massive military buildup and expanded covert operations that together define the Reagan Doctrine in foreign policy. And, second, his national security adviser, Donald Gregg, was (according to Congressional testimony) linked through CIA agent Felix Rodriguez to the illegal Contra supply operation, including the ill-fated Eugene Hassenfuss and probably to Contra drug running as well. Moreover, Bush has falsely denied his substantial involvement in trading arms for hostages. Bush's claims of ignorance and privileged communication, like Reagan's assumption of responsibility, evidence plausible deniability rather than the absence of either president or vice president from the scene of the crime.[6]

Bush, like Reagan, calls into question the distinction between mass spectacle and covert power. He does so in two ways. First, Bush's evasions exemplify the public use of the claim of secrecy, in the name of national security, that allows men like Bush, John Poindexter, and Oliver North to avoid political responsibility. And, second, Bush reminds us of the set of beliefs of the men (and women like Jeane Kirkpatrick) who carry out and defend covert operations. Whether or not Bush is a figurehead, he stands for fantasies about our enemies that—I have cited Reagan and the Reagan Doctrine, Bush and Team B to suggest—operate not in the first place in popular culture but at the most secret levels of decision making. These fantasies, reinforced by being shared among the covert operators, constitute the spectacle they produce for one another.

In a recent review, Ian Baruma agrees that Ronald Reagan's jokes, *Rambo*, and Jerry Falwell "tell us something about popular culture in America, but it would be simplistic to say that they directly account for United States foreign policy—even though the link might exist somewhere in the president's own mind."[7] In dismissing the organizing principle of the president's mind, however, Baruma is making a big mistake. For if the link exists not only in Reagan's mass mind—the public spectacle—but in the minds of those who think up and implement our foreign policy, then to separate fantasy from policy works simply to preserve a realm of public discourse for reasonable men like Baruma to speak to power.

The public Reagan/Bush relation to secret operations also introduces a third form of power, the power of amnesia. The secret, retroactive finding that President Reagan forgot he signed, like the incessant "I don't recall"s of John Poindexter and Edwin Meese, may seem merely to disconnect high public officials from secret, illegal activities. Amnesia of this sort slides into claims of privileged communication on the one hand—Bush cannot tell us what, as vice president, he advised the president about arms and hostages—and ignorance on the other—Bush denies he knew Noriega was trafficking in drugs although that was commonplace information in the CIA when he was in charge of it—"not a smoking gun," one former NSC staffer has remarked, "but rather a twenty-one-gun barrage of evidence." Amnesia here severs the link between what goes on behind the scenes and what in front of the camera, as when Reagan forgets the movie origins of the lines he delivers as his own, or is just as surprised as the rest of us to learn that he never spoke to Mikhail Gorbachev the words that Larry Speakes attributed to him.[8] If we disbelieve those claims of forgetting, we see them as protecting secret complicity. If we believe them, the reality principle disappears. Let us not dismiss the latter hypothesis too quickly, for I am going to suggest that memory loss is not confined to the president and his men, and that it sustains not only the covert actions hidden from public view but also the imperial spectacles that we have all seen. Covert actions derive from the imperatives of spectacle, not secrecy. They owe their invisibility not to secrecy but to political amnesia. What is displayed and forgotten in imperial spectacle is the historical content of American political demonology.

II

If spectacle and secrecy define the political peculiarities of the post-modern American empire, racial and political demonology define the peculiarities of the historic American empire. Countersubversion and racism, I will argue, provide the content for the covert, specular form. But this content is hidden by the form that seems to reveal it. Racism and countersubversion, like the actor and the CIA director, are concealed from contemporary eyes by being in plain sight. I am calling this forgetting of what one continues to see political amnesia, in order to yoke together the arguments of Russell Jacoby's *Social Amnesia* with those of Fredric Jameson's *The Political Unconscious.*[9] In this motivated forgetting, that which is insistently represented becomes, by being normalized to invisibility, absent and disappeared. Instead of distinguishing circuses for the mass mind from secret, elite maneuvers, as if the former merely covered over the forces that drive the latter, we need to see how the links between going public and going private are strengthened by amnesia. Consider two illustrations from a source I have been trying to legitimate, the movies that matter to Ronald Reagan. Instead of reporting only my own interpretations of these motion pictures, as if the films were self-enclosed texts, let me practice some informal reception analysis.

"Go ahead. Make my day!" President Reagan invited Congress, promising to veto a threatened tax increase. Reagan was quoting Clint Eastwood as Dirty Harry, of course. But it turned out to be hard to remember in which of the four Dirty Harry movies the lines appeared and in what context Eastwood delivered them. Like many others, I first thought the lines came from the original movie, *Dirty Harry* (1971), in the scene where Eastwood holds a gun on a killer and dares him to draw, neither the killer nor the audience knowing whether there is a bullet left in Eastwood's gun. But although that scene opens and closes the movie (the first time the killer fails to call Eastwood's bluff, the second time he is blown away), Eastwood says "Make my day!" neither time. He speaks that line in *Sudden Impact* (1983) to a hoodlum holding his gun to a female hostage's head. In the scene that closes the movie the hoodlum is a rapist; in the scene that opens the movie he is black. Eastwood is daring a black man to murder a woman, in other words, so that Dirty Harry can kill the black. No question this time about whether his gun is empty and Eastwood at risk. The lives he proves his toughness by endangering are female and black, not his own.

When the president says "Make my day!" he is aspiring to Eastwood's power, but the audience is in a more complicated position. Theories of the male gaze notwithstanding, viewers are passive spectators closer to the helpless, female hostage position than to Eastwood's. This is not only because of their passivity in theater or living room but because of their larger, political helplessness as well. "Make my day!" blames that impotence on the criminal threat to women. By reinscribing race and gender difference and identifying with the rescuer, Clint Eastwood, the film offers viewers imaginary access to power.

The audience's relationship to this particular scene, however, is more complicated yet. Eastwood made *Sudden Impact* during the Reagan presidency, as the racial and sexual antagonisms of the 1980s put women and blacks into the picture at their own expense. The president who quoted Eastwood's line had made women and blacks his targets, notably through the tax cuts that eviscerated their welfare-state benefits and that he was defending when he said "Make my day!" But my claim here is not only that women and blacks were present in the presidential unconscious but also that they were absent from the memories of those who had seen the picture. Whenever I spoke on Reagan and the movies after seeing *Sudden Impact,* to student and nonstudent audiences, in my own classes and in public lectures, I asked whether anyone remembered the context of the famous words. Everyone recognized the line, for it has become a cultural cliché. But those who thought they had seen the movie foundered on the scene. Some wrongly placed the words in the episode, between men alone, of the first movie. Others got the movie and general setting right, but forgot key characters. As my sample reached the thousands, only one person remembered either the black man or the woman. That exception was himself a black man; he forgot the woman. Amnesia allows Eastwood and Reagan to have their race and gender conflict and digest it too. The white hero is remembered; the context that produced him is buried so that it can continue to support *Standing Tall* (the title of yet another Reagan-quoted movie) in the world. In the American myth we remember, men alone risk their lives in equal combat. In the one we forget, white men show how tough they are by resubordinating and sacrificing their race and gender others. The white man dares Moamar Qadaffi to blow up a café (maybe he did and maybe he didn't) so that he can drop bombs on men, women, and children of color. "Go ahead. Make my day!"

My first example of political amnesia concerns race and gender; my second is about countersubversion. In his 1940 movie *Murder in the Air,* Ronald Reagan plays an undercover member of the Secret Service (forerunner of the wartime OSS and the postwar CIA). The secret agent, Brass Bancroft, penetrates a Nazi/Communist plot to steal the plans for a secret, defensive superweapon that bears an uncanny (and, I have argued, not accidental) resemblance to Star Wars. I introduced my book *"Ronald Reagan," the Movie* with that film. But I told the story of sabotage, subversives, House Un-American Activities Committee investigation, and secret weapon as if I were describing history and not a movie. In the fall of 1987, after *"Ronald Reagan," the Movie* appeared, I visited a college freshman English class that was studying political writing and had read the Reagan essay. One student asked whether I had wanted readers to believe I was telling a true story, and since that was indeed my intention I asked other members of the class whether it had worked. An Asian-American responded that he had been taken in at first but realized the tale was fiction and not fact when I brought in the House Un-American Activities Committee. Relying on intelligence and common sense to compensate for historical ignorance, this student assumed that HUAC could only be made up; how could he know that it was also American history? It was a history, moreover, that operated with particular force, if not against the parents or grandparents of this student then against other Asian-Americans who were, from the point of view of the makers of that history, indistinguishable from them.

These responses to *Sudden Impact* and *Murder in the Air* point to two amnesias whose forgettings are hardly identical. One is personal, the other social, since ignorance of American history is not the same as forgetting what one has actually seen. Millions of Americans familiar with "Make my day!" never have seen the movie, moreover. They may know the line from television trailers that do not show the actual scene, or from computer "toy" programs in which a digitalized voice speaks the words. As "Make my day!" enters the common culture its roots disappear, and HUAC and *Sudden Impact* come to resemble each other as instances not of individual forgetting but of historical memory loss. At the same time film, by functioning in Reaganite politics to confuse the historical with the imaginary, also preserves an objective memory of scenes that have now entered history. *Sudden Impact* allows us to hold to account the culture that voices the movie's most famous words.

That is not to damn all speakers of the line, however. "Make my day!" declares an aggression that leads back in American culture to racial and sexual inequality, even if many have used the phrase without knowing its filmic source or historical meaning. (The same would apply, for an earlier generation, to Theodore Roosevelt's injunction to speak softly and carry a big stick.) No one wants to be accused of knowing and forgetting the origin of "Make my day!" But instead of exculpating the innocently ignorant and sending those who have forgotten their guilty knowledge to hell, the concept of a political amnesia points to a cultural structure of motivated disavowal. That structure will vary in implicating individuals (from those who want others to forget; to whose who forgot; to those who, with varying degrees of willfulness, never allowed themselves to know) and events (readers of earlier drafts of this essay have been more willing to acknowledge race and amnesia in Bush's use of Willie Horton, with which I will conclude, than in Reagan's invocation of Clint Eastwood).

It is not necessary to agree about who and what fit within the structure of political amnesia to understand how it works. Since amnesia means motivated forgetting, it implies a cultural impulse both to have the experience and not to retain it in memory. Political amnesia signifies not simply memory loss but a dissociation between sensation and ego that operates to preserve both. Amnesia signals forbidden pleasure or memory joined to pain. It permits repetition of pleasures that, if consciously sustained in memory over time, would have to be called into question. From this perspective, the political spectacle opens a door the viewer wants to close so that it can be opened again. There is, first, the forbidden pleasure in the sensations themselves, a sensory overstimulation that in political spectacle is more typically violent than sexual (or sexual by being violent). Amnesia disconnects from their objects and severs from memory those intensified, detailed shots of destruction, wholesaled on populations and retailed on body parts. There is, second, the historical truth exposed by the mythic effort to cannibalize it—that the white male sacrificed women and people of color, for example, in the name of his own courage. Historical amnesia allows race and countersubversion to continue to configure American politics by disconnecting current practices from their historical roots. Political amnesia works, however, not simply through burying history but also through representing the return of the repressed. An easily forgettable series of surface entertainments—movies, television series, political shows—revolve before the eye. The scopic pleasure in the primal, illegitimate scenes produces infantile amnesia once the images themselves threaten to enter the lasting, symbolic realm.[10] The recovery of historical memory exposes these processes.

Spectacle is the cultural form for amnesiac representation, for specular displays are superficial and sensately intensified, short lived and repeatable. Spectacle and amnesia may seem at odds, to be sure: *amnesia*, a term from depth-historical analysis, points backward, to the nineteenth century's concern with the past. *Spectacle*, by contrast, names the spatial pleasures of contemporary visual entertainment. But this opposition, underlined in modernist and postmodernist analysis, is what enables spectacle to do its work.

Spectacles, in the Marxist modernist view, shift attention from workers as producers to spectators as consumers of mass culture. Spectacles colonize everyday life, in this view, and thereby turn domestic citizens into imperial subjects. Spectacle goes private by organizing mass consumption and leisure; it attaches ordinary, intimate existence to public displays of the private lives of political and other entertainers. Spectacles, in the postmodern view, define the historical rupture between industrial and postindustrial society—the one based on durable goods production, the other on information and service exchange. With the dissolution of individual subjects and differentiated, autonomous spheres, not only does the connection between an object and its use become arbitrary, in this view, but skilled attention to display also deflects notice from the object to its hyperreal, reproducible representation. The society of the spectacle provides illusory unification and meaning, Guy Debord argues, distracting attention from producers and from classes in conflict. Simulacric games have entirely replaced the real, in Jean Baudrillard's formulation, and offer not even a counterfeit representation of anything outside themselves.[11]

Spectacle is about forgetting, for the Marxist modernist, since it makes the tie to production invisible. The historicizing concept of amnesia suggests that the forgotten link in political spectacle is the visible tie to the past. Spectacle contrasts to narrative, for the postmodernist, as fragmented and interchangeable individuals, products, and body parts replace the subject-centered story. Political spectacles display centrifugal threats—threats to the subject and threats to the state—to contain as well as to enjoy them. Instead of dissolving the subject into structures or discourses, the concept of amnesia points to an identity that persists over time and that preserves a false center by burying the actual past.

American imperial spectacles display and forget four enabling myths that the culture can no longer unproblematically embrace. The first is the historical organization of American politics around racial domination. Once openly announced, American political racialism must now give unacknowledged satisfactions. The second is redemption through violence, intensified in the mass technologies of entertainment and war. The third is the belief in individual agency, the need to forget both the web of social ties that enmesh us all and the wish for an individual power so disjunctive with everyday existence. And the fourth is identification with the state, to which is transferred the freedom to act without being held to account that in part compensates for individual helplessness but in part reflects state weakness as well.

Covert spectacles, the Reagan Era's main contribution to American imperial representation, display state-supported American heroes in violent, racial combat. Covert spectacles—movies like *Rambo* (which begins, "A covert action is being geared up in the Far East") and political schemes like aid to the Nicaraguan "freedom fighters"[12]—preserve the fiction of a center. It is not just that America occupies that center, but that international politics comprises a coherent narrative where secret agents—the word *agent* has a double meaning—are at once connected to a directing power and also able to act heroically on their own. In a world of impersonal forces, massive suffering, and individual helplessness, the covert spectacle provides the illusion, through violence, of personal control. The visual character of the story, moreover, encourages immediate audience identification, elevating a visionary ideal above chaotic, ordinary, daily existence.[13]

Political spectacles incorporate fragmentary surface pleasures—the crotch shot in *Rambo*, for example, where the camera pulls back to reveal that it was showing not female private parts but the crease inside the hero's elbow, now safely tucked between biceps and forearm; or the explosions of violence in *First Blood, Part I* and *Part II*—into a larger whole. Resuscitating the center rather than disintegrating it, political spectacle provides the pleasure of meaning-giving order. In so doing, political spectacle heals the rift between present and past. Mass advertising has marketed reassurance about historical connectedness since its origins in the 1920s.[14] The covert operator, bringing the past into the present, offers that reassurance as well. Entering racially alien ground, he regresses to primitivism in order to destroy the subversive and appropriate his power.

Two American histories support the covert spectacle, the history of racial demonology and the emergence of a specular foreign policy. I want briefly to outline those histories, suggesting at greater length how World War II provides the missing link between them. World War II, by joining demonology to the covert spectacle, configured both the first Cold War and its revival under Reagan. Finally, since amnesia itself must be historicized, I will conclude with the connection established in the 1960s between racial demonology and imperial spectacle. For the display and forgetting of that link produced both the Reagan Doctrine in foreign policy and the Bush presidential campaign.

III

As with the career paths of the current president and his predecessor, so with our historical origins, the obvious is rendered invisible by being taken for granted. The United States is a settler society. America began in European imperialism against people of color. The American empire started at home; what was foreign was made domestic by expansion across the continent and by the subjugation, dispossession, and extermination of Indian tribes. Other settler societies—South Africa, now Israel—came to depend on the labor of indigenous populations. The American colonies, after experimenting with Indian workers, enslaved Africans instead. The United States was built on the land and with the labor of peoples of color.

Academic divisions between domestic and international politics separate the American empire from its domestic, imperial base. With the end of the continental frontier, the racial basis of American expansion carried forward into the Philippines, the Caribbean, Latin America, and eventually the Asian mainland, with full consciousness (since forgotten) of the continuity between the triumph of civilization over savagery at home and the white man's burden abroad. (Rudyard Kipling urged America to take up the white man's burden in the Philippines, connecting that war to European imperialism as well.) The distinction between European powers that held colonies and the United States, which generally did not, wrongly locates the imperial age in the late nineteenth century instead of three centuries earlier, at the dawn of the modern age. Imperial expansion to extend the area of freedom (in Andrew Jackson's words) was integral to American politics from the beginning. The linkage of expansion to freedom instead of to the acquisition of colonies prepared the United States to see itself as the legitimate defender of freedom in the postcolonial Third World.

To trace a line from Columbus to, say, Elliott Abrams hardly proves the racial motivations of America's Third World interventions—Iran in the 1950s, Zaire in the 1960s, Vietnam in the 1960s and 1970s, Nicaragua and El Salvador today, to name some prominent examples. Race enters in three ways, however. First, most subjects of American intervention are peoples of color, and the racial history of the United States makes it easier to dehumanize and do away with them. Second, American political culture came into being by defining itself in racialist terms. And third, categories that originated in racial opposition were also imposed on political opponents, creating an American political demonology.

To illustrate these three points, I borrow an example from Jonathan Kwitny's *Endless Enemies*.[15] Walter Cronkite opened the CBS evening news on 19 May 1978 with these words: "Good evening. The worst fears in the rebel invasion of Zaire's Shaba province reportedly have been realized. Rebels being routed from the mining town of Kolwezi are reported to have killed a number of Europeans." Easy to pass right over that remarkable "worst fears," which, as Kwitny says, makes it better to kill blacks than whites. Colored deaths, my first point, do not count the way white ones do. That is because the history of imperialism and slavery has encoded a nightmare of racial massacre so that it speaks even through Walter Cronkite. That nightmare of red and black murdering white inverts actual history, in which massacres (certainly in the big, world-historic picture and in most individual cases as well) were usually the other way around. There was, as Kwitny shows, neither a rebel invasion of Zaire nor a massacre of whites. Far more blacks were killed than whites in the fighting that did occur, and "the worst massacre of Europeans in modern African history" was a historically produced figment of the imagination of the *Washington Post*. It never happened.

Imaginary racial massacres make peoples of color not simply disposable but indispensable as well, for—and this is my second point—the fantasy of savage violence defines the imperial imagination. Racial inversions, in which victims metamorphose into killers, may seem at most to justify Euro-American interventions in the Third World, not to cause them. Surely the color of the minerals in Zaire, not the people, provoked the covert American intervention of the early 1960s that was responsible for killing Patrice Lumumba and making Joseph Mobutu the dictator of the postcolonial state. If Vietnamese oil won't do the work of Zairian copper, then geopolitical conflict will. Or the domino effect? Or anti-Communism? Or unconsummated male bonding? Why *were* we in Vietnam? As the procession of explanations moves farther and farther from solid, mineral ground, it moves closer to race. Not race as a natural category of difference (and even minerals acquire value from culture and not nature) but as a cultural field, inseparable from the economic and political forces it has helped to constitute.

Racial conflict, as Richard Slotkin, Richard Drinnon, and I among many others have argued, created a distinctive American political culture. It linked freedom to expansion in nature rather than to social solidarity, to violent conquest of the racial other rather than peaceful coexistence. The covert operator, "consummating an act of racial revenge or rescue," is the mythic hero of American expansion.[16] The rescue of the helpless female hostage from peoples of color established sexual as well as racial difference—against the threats of racial uprising, female independence, and the feminization of helpless white men, *Sudden Impact* transports the frontier myth into the city as well. "Make my day!"

The impact of the racial history of the United States transcends race—my third point—contaminating our political culture as a whole. The conflict in the New World between protestant bourgeois white men and peoples of color not only produced a racial demonology but underlies the broader countersubversive tradition in American politics. Racial and political demonology are often explicitly linked, as in the hostility to aliens in *Murder in the Air*, and as among the government officials and media spokespeople who fantasized a racial massacre in Zaire. Zaire illustrates the interconnection between race and countersubversion because Cuban troops in Angola were held responsible for a conflict with which they had nothing to do. Balunda who had fled to Angola after the defeat of their effort to create an independent state (which put them on the "Right" in the Cold War procrustean bed during the 1960s) were in 1978 trying to return home (which put them on the "Left").[17]

"The crisis of ethnocentricity in the beginning of the sixteenth century (and for a long time afterward)," to borrow Carlo Ginzburg's phrase, came about when Europeans discovered other places and peoples that did not revolve around them. But Europeans in the New World used this Copernican revolution in politics to make themselves the center again.[18] The claims of the Reagan Doctrine to roots in American history should thus not be lightly dismissed. The distinctiveness of Reagan's foreign policy lies elsewhere, not in its demonological vision per se but in the character of its Cold War revival. For the Cold War, by centering countersubversion in the national security state, marked a break with the past. That shift, in turn, had its origins in World War II, both structurally at the beginning of the Cold War and in the career patterns and mentality of those who revived the Cold War under Reagan. World War II, moreover, is the distinctive historical moment when the United States seems innocent of the charges of racial and political demonology. The birth of the national security state from out of "the good war" (as Studs Terkel has labeled it) produced the Cold War's specular foreign policy.[19]

IV

Beginning with the Cold War's origins in World War II, demonology has been used to dramatize and justify the covert spectacle. But if racial demonology organized American politics before the war, and if the war has organized our politics since, then the grip of the good war has importantly to do with how it seemed at once to justify demonology and to free American politics from the stigma of race.

World War II justified demonology because in that war we confronted a truly demonic foe. It is easy enough to show how the presence of Nazism distorted postwar politics; how the concept of totalitarianism promoted a binary division between the extremes of Right and Left on the one hand and the Free World on the other; how the resulting distinction between authoritarianism and totalitarianism, well before Jeane Kirkpatrick resuscitated it,[20] was an empty placeholder faithful neither to the actual domestic qualities of the regimes it contrasted nor to their ambitions abroad but rather to their relationship to the United States; and how anti-Communism justified both coups against democratic regimes— Guatemala, Iran, Chile—to protect them from totalitarianism and the embrace of merely authoritarian regimes that (with our help) use death squads and massive bombing against their own populations. A thought experiment might be able to reproduce all these effects in the absence of World War II. In real historical time, however, World War II offered an objective correlative for the countersubversion that preceded and succeeded it by providing a genuinely demonic enemy bent on world conquest.

In so doing, in addition, the good war shifted the stigma of racialism from the United States to its enemies, Germany and Japan. Jim Crow continued at home, of course, notably in the armed forces. American participation in the war had nothing to do with saving European Jewry, moreover, and was, as David Wyman has shown, actively hostile to efforts to do so.[21] That was hardly the dominant postwar perception, however, and since racial murder was the centerpiece of Nazism and at worst a sideshow for America, the good war seemed to bring to an end the racial underpinnings of American demonology. Racialism had spread from peoples of color to Southern and Eastern Europeans during the alien and Red scares of the industrializing United States; before 1930 American history was more dominated than was German by racism. But the New Deal and World War II could be seen as reversing the racialist direction of American politics and as beginning to bring American racism to an end.

That is its effect on Ian Baruma, whom I quoted earlier and to whom I now want to return. John Dower's recent book, *War Without Mercy: Race and Power in the Pacific War*, shows the brutalizing, murderous impact of racial hysteria on American and Japanese policy. Baruma disagrees; he believes that "Dower overstates . . . the moral equivalence of both sides"; that what racism emerged against the Japanese "was more the result of war . . . than the cause of it"; that the propaganda required by a mass war should not be confused with the causes of the war; and that the easy, postwar resumption of friendship with Japan shows the superficiality of negative racial stereotypes during the war. One has to distinguish, Baruma writes, the Nazi war against the Jews and the American conflict with Japan. "Jews were killed because they were Jews. Japanese got killed because they were part of a nation bent on military conquest." My quarrel is not with the distinction between Nazi genocide and American racism, but with using that distinction to obliterate the racial character of America's war with Japan and— Baruma's explicit project—the character of subsequent American foreign policy.[22]

To take first the war against Japan: surely Baruma would at least acknowledge the racist basis for the internment of Japanese-Americans during the war. However, he suggests instead that the differing attitudes toward Germans and Japanese were based on "logical reasons that Dower does not take into account. Japanese-Americans, being relatively recent immigrants, still lived in highly visible, culturally distinct communities," explains Baruma. " 'Good' Germans were acknowledged simply because there were more of them," that is, refugees from Nazi terror.[23]

Why does Baruma normalize Japanese internment? The good war has wiped out of his historical memory the exclusion of Japanese from America and the racially based residential segregation of those who were here. It has made him forget that the Italians, more recent immigrants than the Japanese, were not rounded up, deprived of their liberty and property without due process of law, and placed in concentration camps. Baruma suppresses not only the racially based exclusion of thousands of good Germans, Jews, from the United States but also the presence of many bad Germans, the thousands of organized and active supporters of Nazism in the German-American Bund who were not rounded up and jailed. He has forgotten that, underneath the fantasies about Japanese aliens, about the disloyalty not only of Japanese born in Japan but of those born in the United States as well, there simply were no bad Japanese. He fails to cite the racist justifications for Japanese internment by high United States and West Coast state officials who could cite no evidence at all of Japanese disloyalty or of any danger to American security. Baruma neglects one of Dower's most telling findings, that although cartoons and propaganda against Germany during the war depicted Hitler and Nazism rather than the Germans as the enemy, the demon in the Pacific war was the depersonalized "Jap." Thus a July 1942 *Washington Post* cartoon captioned "Mimic" shows Hitler destroying the towns of Lidice and Lezaky in the foreground, while in the background a gorilla labelled "Jap" tramples Cebu. Cartoon Japanese are apes and rodents; American leaders (sounding like cartoon figures but wielding real power) call for their extermination. "The Japs will be worried about all the time until they are wiped off the face of the map," warned Lt. Gen. John Dewitt, who headed the Western Defense Command and interned the Japanese-Americans. Marines wore "Rodent Exterminator" on their helmets, and a *Leatherneck* cartoon in March 1945 showed a Japanese "lice epidemic." "To the Marine Corps," reads the caption, "was assigned the gigantic task of extermination." That cartoon appeared the same month that the firebombing of Tokyo killed on a single night 80,000 to 100,000 Japanese—fewer than would soon die on a single night in Hiroshima, more than Nagasaki.[24]

Dresden and Hamburg were firebombed before Tokyo, to be sure; World War I's depersonalized, mass killing preceded them all. But instead of citing indiscriminate mass slaughter to minimize the significance of racism, one might better remember the racially imperialist prehistory of World War I, a war produced not only from imperialist rivalries in Lenin's sense but also from the brutalizations of colored peoples, Slavs, Jews, and others viewed as racially inferior.[25]

The Tokyo firebombing, defended as an effort to break the Japanese fighting will, was aimed at no material, military targets. It was psychological warfare, a spectacle to terrorize, demoralize, and destroy the civilian, Japanese mass public. And that firebombing produced another spectacular during the Cold War. In the Hollywood, anti-Communist parable *Them!*, the Japanese rodents reappeared as giant ants, mutations from a desert atomic explosion. In history the atom bomb destroyed those labeled rodents; in fantasy it created them in order to destroy them again. At the climax of *Them!*, the ants are traced to their breeding ground, with its strong "brood odor," in the storm drains under Los Angeles. They are obliterated in a holocaust of fire. What looks like futuristic science fiction is actually, in the service of anti-Communism, a record of the firebombing of the past. Gordon Douglas, who had also directed *I Was a Communist for the FBI*, was putting on screen the injunction in *Leatherneck* that, "before a complete cure may be effected, the origins of the Plague, the breeding grounds in the Tokyo area, must be completely annihilated." Failing to accept responsibility for the hundreds of thousands of Japanese deaths by firebombs and atomic destruction, Hollywood made nuclear explosions reproduce the rodents who, now become Communists, had to be wiped out all over again.[26]

The firebombing of Tokyo also produced movies of another sort. Unlike *Them!*, which was made for a mass audience, these were part of a covert operation, "one of the better-kept secrets of the war, ranking up with the atomic bomb project." "Everyone who has ever seen a picture based on World War II" will, according to their narrator, recognize the briefing in which he supplied the voice-over. To prepare real pilots to bomb Tokyo, Hollywood special effects men built a complete miniature of the city for simulated bombing runs. They "intercut their movies of the model with real scenes taken from flights over Tokyo," thereby creating a series of movies that taught pilots about the real thing. Each movie concluded when the narrator said, "Bombs away." The narrator who has been describing his role in World War II is Capt. Ronald Reagan. After I read this account in his autobiography and then wrote about it, I stressed how, to make himself a partic-ipant in the war while he was actually stationed in Hollywood, Reagan had broken down the distinction between filmed war and real war, simulated bombing runs and real bombs: "As a result, none of the explosives in his account, from the bombs he narrates to the atomic bomb, fall on real targets."[27] But I was still being taken in, for Reagan is not simply pretending to have participated in a war but is also distancing himself from the real bombs his movie instructions helped drop. The actual people at risk were the inhabitants of Tokyo; as Reagan tells the story, he becomes the secret agent close to danger. Turning his covert operation into spectacle, Reagan has made invisible the real, obliterated Japanese. The white man, in no danger himself, cinematically participates in killing men, women, and children of color. "Make my day!"

When the Japanese government mercilessly bombed the civilian population of China in 1938, the United States Senate denounced "this crime against humanity . . . reminiscent of the cruelties perpetrated by primitive and barbarous nations upon inoffensive peoples."[28] The rhetoric of this condemnation blamed modern total war on American Indians. It helped prepare the United States, in the name of fighting savages, to imitate them, or rather, *Them!*—not historical Indians, but the monsters recreated in the imperial mind.

V

World War II laid the structural foundations in politics for the modern American empire. First, the good war established the military industrial state as the basis for both domestic welfare and foreign policy. Second, it made surveillance and covert operations, at home and abroad, an integral part of the state. Third, it drew the political parties together behind an interventionist, bipartisan foreign policy directed by Democrats during the major wars (World War II, Korea, and Vietnam), and by the former Democrat, Ronald Reagan, in the 1980s. Fourth, the good war's popularity linked the mass public to the structures of power. Mass enthusiasm for the national security state could not be mobilized for subsequent hot wars and was actually threatened by them. Nevertheless, only for a few years during and after the American defeat in Vietnam were the fundamental assumptions about America's role in the world established during World War II ever challenged by significant sectors within American politics. Finally, World War II celebrated the undercover struggle of good against evil, and thereby prepared the way for the covert spectacle.

World War II slid easily into the Cold War, as Communism replaced Nazism and one Asian enemy, China, took the place of another, Japan (so that the Japanese demons of World War II movies could be recycled within the decade as Hollywood North Koreans and Chinese).[29] But the Cold War was fought mainly with symbols and surrogates. It organized politics around ideology and conspiracy (Communists in government at home, secret interventions abroad) just as ideology was supposed to be coming to an end. It may be, as Fred Block argues, that the state recognized its need to play a foreign, economic role as the alternative to domestic social reconstruction, and recast economic challenges as Cold War and military ones to mobilize popular support. In any case, Richard Barnet suggests, the permanent mobilization of the American population—to sustain high taxes, foreign aid, interventionist state policies, and ongoing international alliances— marks a fundamental break with the peacetime past. The worry in the now famous

National Security Council memorandum no. 68 as the Cold War began—that America would be crippled by internal weakness at the moment of its greatest strength—reflected the state's new economic and security role and the fear that the population would not support it. Genuinely covert actions were one response to fears of popular flaccidity; the politics of spectacle as political mobilization was the other.[30]

The spread both of covert operations and of foreign policy as spectacle responded to the tensions among economy, state, organs of public opinion, and instruments of nuclear war that emerged in the shift from World War II to the Cold War and that were accentuated at the end of the first Cold War period with the American defeat in Vietnam. Postwar worries about the weakness of the American state nonetheless presumed an American hegemony that more recent economic and political developments have called into question. A multinational-dominated internationalized economy that resists state control sets the stage for defensive, American nationalism. The sources for that nationalism lie in state structures that lack the power either to control the economy or to mobilize the populace and so turn to covert action and the spectacle; in the political economy of the military-industrial complex; in a nuclear-dominated military strategy, where weapons function as symbols of intentions in war games rather than as evidence of war-fighting capabilities; and in the permeation of public and private space by the fiction-making visual media.[31]

Public anti-Communist mobilization operated alongside genuinely covert operations in the early Cold War years, the one to engage masses, the other to serve the interests of elites. That separation broke down with John Kennedy, however, for whom the theory and practice of foreign interventions served less to preserve imperial interests than to demonstrate the firmness of American will. Vietnam functioned as the most important theater of destruction, from Kennedy's Green Beret adventurism through Nixon's expansion of the war to test our resolve to meet a future "real crisis."[32] But Vietnam failed as symbolic foreign policy, not just because the United States lost the war but also because American suffering and turmoil could not immediately be dissolved into spectacle.

The full-fledged absorption of American foreign policy by symbolic gesture, therefore, awaited the Reagan presidency. The men whose consciousness was formed by World War II revived the American empire after Vietnam—Paul Nitze and the other members of the Committee on the Present Danger, who prepared the ideological ground for the Reagan administration; William Casey, who moved from the wartime OSS to direct first Reagan's presidential campaign and then the CIA (and, as he shifted from electoral spectacle to secrecy, to subordinate intelligence collection to covert activities); and Reagan himself, who made training and morale movies during the war and who met the crisis in his personal and professional life after it by leading the fight against Hollywood Communism.[33] The Reagan Doctrine—inspired by the ideological adventurer Jack Wheeler, known as the "Indiana Jones of the right"[34]—recuperated in political theater what had been lost in imperial substance. A foreign policy run from the expanded, hidden, militarized National Security Council aimed, by reversing Vietnam ("Do we get to win this time?" Rambo wants to know), to reenact the good war as a movie.

The covert spectacle thus reflects the persistence of dreams about American dominance in the face of the erosion of the material and ideological sources for American preeminence in the world. The budgetary and political demands that the American government inflicts on its people in the name of military and national security contribute, to be sure, to trade and budget deficits and economic decay. But at the same time the decline in a solidly based American preeminence has generated efforts at symbolic recovery that center around military and national security. This combat with the Soviet Union takes two forms: a visible military buildup in weapons that cannot be used, and low-intensity (as they are called) military interventions in the Third World. Together these demonstrate American resolution without substantial risks at home. Foreign policy is conducted by theatrical events—Grenada invasion, Libyan bombing, Persian Gulf flagging, Honduran "show of force"—staged for public consumption. These interventions may well succeed, but their significance lies less in stopping the local spread of "Communism" than in convincing elite and mass publics that America has the power to have its way. Substituting symbols for substance, these staged events constitute the politics of postmodernism, so long as one remembers that symbols produced for consumption at home and abroad have all too much substance for the victims of those symbols, the participant-observers on the ground in the Third World.[35]

Individual covert operations may serve specific corporate or national-security-clique interests, and the operations themselves are often (like Iran/Contra) hidden from domestic subjects who might hold them to political account. But even where the particular operation is supposed to remain secret, the government wants it known it has the power, secretly, to intervene. The payoff for many covert operations is their intended demonstration effect. The covert spectacle is a form of therapeutic politics. By focusing attention on itself, it aims to control not simply political power but knowledge.

Most obviously, the specular relation to political life has implications for democratic governance. Spectators gain vicarious participation in a narrative that, in the name of national security, justifies their exclusion from information and decision making. Covert operations as spectacle pacify domestic as well as foreign audiences, for they transform the political relation between rulers and citizens from accountability to entertainment. Vicarious participation, moreover, is also granted to the rulers themselves, for those who sponsor and promote covert action almost never place themselves at risk. Vicarious participation in the spectacle of the covert heals in fantasy and preserves in fact the separation of those who plan from those who kill and are killed, the separation that Richard Barnet has called bureaucratic homicide.[36]

Secrecy is a technique not just for vicarious inclusion and political exclusion, however, but also for defining the real. Covert actions, obscured by disinformation, require the state to lie. When John Poindexter denied that the Libyan bombing aimed to kill Qadaffi, and defended the spread of disinformation about alleged Libyan terrorism as a strategy to keep the Libyan leader off balance, he also had a domestic purpose. He was orchestrating an entertainment that, in winning popular applause, would underline for the mass audience the need for secret planning, accountable to no one and to no standard of truth outside itself. Poindexter wanted a mass public that stopped asking what was true and what false because it knew which side it was on. The term for the psychology at which Poindexter aimed is *identification with the aggressor*. Destabilizing orienting cues from any source, the state was to become the single anchor in the midst of the shifting realities it displayed. And that would increase trust in government, for the less one experiences alternatives to power, the more one needs to see it as benign.

Aggression is thus not opposed to intimacy but rather a technique for producing it—much as, conversely, intimacy in the American president normalizes the violence he authorizes. The benign version of spectacle plays on our ontological insecurity by offering trust in the sources of information. That answers the question James Lardner recently asked in his review of *Broadcast News*: "Why are the networks' anchormen so much more vivid to us than the stories they present?"[37] Presidential intimacy, as in the "giant womb" Garry Wills described at the 1984 Republican convention, or Bush's call for a "kinder, gentler nation" four years later, offers us the security of trusting the head of state as much as we trusted Walter Cronkite.

The form promoted by political infantilization is reliance on central power; its content is reassurance that we can continue to live in the (fantasized) past. Aspirations to appropriate basic trust may well fall short, into mass cynicism and withdrawal. But they do succeed in investing the imaginary with as much truth effect as the real—or rather, I have been arguing, the other way around. Where political spectacles compel attention and are not turned off, they acquire the power of fiction. For why should the mass audience be able to tell the difference between TV series and movies and the political spectacles that also appear on the screen, so long as the reality principle never reaches, directly and forcefully, into their lives (as it did, for example, in the 1930s depression or the 1960s draft)? The spectacle aims either to keep the reality principle entirely at bay (Star Wars as invisible shield) or to seize control of the interpretations placed on its intrusions (Star Wars shifts the terms of political debate from aggressive American preparations to win a nuclear war to the pros and cons of nuclear defense).

The covert spectacle thus breaks down the distinction between politics and theater (or rather, movies)—from the one side in police, spy, adventure, and science-fiction thrillers (including old movies starring Ronald Reagan) where the audience is privy to the hidden world of counterinsurgency warfare, and from the other side in Reagan's invocation of lines from such movies and reenactments of their plots—in his praise to Oliver North on the day he fired him that the events that had made North a "national hero" would "make a great movie."[38]

This movie reenactment of history, whether directed from Hollywood or from Washington, puts few Americans at risk. Instead of actually refighting the Second World War, it enlists Third World peoples as surrogates. The covert spectacle is thereby grounded in the history of American expansion, not eastward against established European powers but westward and southward against vulnerable racial others. But the 1960s, by recovering imperial history in civil rights struggle and Vietnam, challenged the racial constitution of American national identity. The Reagan doctrine had to forget, therefore, the moment in which American history was remembered.

VI

"The crisis in ideological confidence of the 70s, visible on all levels of American culture and variously enacted in Hollywood's 'incoherent texts,' has not been resolved," writes Robin Wood in *Hollywood from Vietnam to Reagan*. "Instead it has been forgotten." Wood is referring to the shocks administered to the dominant (white male) politics and culture by black protest, Vietnam, and the emergence of a mass-based feminism. Two 1967 Sidney Poiter movies, as Ed Guerrero has argued, represented Hollywood's last effort to incorporate race into liberalism. These twin celebrations of the black, middle-class professional, *Guess Who's Coming to Dinner* and *In the Heat of the Night*, together won seven Academy Awards. But Hollywood containment exploded the next year—in the Tet offensive, on the streets of America's inner cities, at the Chicago Democratic National Convention, and with the assassinations of Robert Kennedy and Martin Luther King, Jr. Wood analyzed the Hollywood movies that registered cultural breakdown without being able to resolve it. Ella Taylor has offered a comparable interpretation of the (more domesticated) space opened up on 1970s television, undercutting the traditional family and finding refuge in imagined workplace communities. The Carter presidency would lend itself to similar treatment.[39]

The Reagan regime put America back together again by exploiting and disavowing the 1960s. On the one hand, Reagan capitalized on the sharpest electoral polarization in American history along race and gender lines. Beginning in 1968, a large majority of whites (overwhelming in every election but 1976) has opposed the presidential choice of a large majority of peoples of color. Beginning in 1980 men have voted more strongly Republican for president than have women. No president since James Monroe has received as enormous a share of the white male vote as Reagan received in 1984—75 percent by my rough calculation, if Jewish voters are excluded—and the gap between men and women was as large or larger in the presidential vote four years later. On the other hand, since the 1960s subversive, colored, and female voices have called into question the racial and political demonology that often silenced such voices in the past.

The response to this double pressure, which undercuts the Reagan regime's claims to universality as they are being made, is regression. 1980s Hollywood has been dominated, writes Wood, by "children's films conceived and marketed largely for adults," an analysis that applies to Washington as well. Even if not technically science fiction (like *Star Wars*, the movie, and Star Wars, the weapon), 1980s films restore traditional race and gender divisions by abandoning pretensions to verisimilitude. "The audiences who wish to be constructed as children also wish to regard themselves as extremely sophisticated and 'modern,'" Wood explains, and they do so by admiring the skills with which they have been infantilized. Production is not hidden as the real source of power; it rather appears on the surface as one more display. Taking pleasure from production numbers, in film terminology, from the special effects of spin doctors, in the language of political campaigns, audiences enjoy at once the effects produced on them and the way those effects are produced. "We both know and don't know that we are watching special effects, technological fakery," Wood writes, suggesting that being in on the infantilizing tricks allows one to regress and enjoy them.[40]

The self-aware quality of the mass spectacle, to which postmodernism points, should thus be read not as a sign of maturity but as an escape from troubling depths so that their residues can safely appear on the surface. As the mass public withdraws from political engagement to spectacles, lo and behold it watches self-ironizing—*Indiana Jones*—or self-pitying—*Rambo*—displays of racial demonology. Fredric Jameson once distinguished entrapping displays of nostalgia, which emphasize the beauty and accuracy of surface reproductions, from self-knowing forms of pastiche that create distance from the past.[41] He wrote before the politics and the movies of the Reagan years used self-knowingness to allow us to return to the past (or go *Back to the Future* in another movie invoked by the president) without having time travel remind us of what we now know we must not do. When an imperial white male wins a white woman in violent combat with evil, dark tribes, as in the Indiana Jones movies, everyone knows that these surface cartoons are not meant to be taken seriously. So we don't have to feel implicated in their displays, can think they are sendups of 1930s serials rather than precipitates of current covert operations, and forget what we have seen. "Go ahead. Make my day!"

VII

George Bush might have borrowed his film criticism during the 1988 campaign from Robin Wood. "We have turned around the permissive philosophy of the

70s," Bush boasted, so that a society that once enjoyed movies like *Easy Rider* now prefers "Dirty Harry" films. "Clint Eastwood's answer to violent crime is 'Go ahead, make my day,'" Bush continued. "My opponent's answer is slightly different. His motto is, 'Go ahead, have a nice weekend.'" Bush was invoking, of course, the Massachusetts weekend furlough program under which Willie Horton, the black convicted murderer, had been allowed to leave prison. Horton, as the Bush campaign was making sure every American knew, had terrorized a white couple and raped the woman. The black criminal and white rapist whom Eastwood had dared to make his day had merged in the figure of Horton; Bush was casting Dukakis as the impotent liberal who could not protect his wife. The buddies who went seeking America, according to the advertising campaign for *Easy Rider*, and "couldn't find it anywhere" had in Bush's movie reviews turned into Dukakis and Horton.[42]

Bush's campaign was not the first attempt to organize American politics around the specter of interracial rape. Repeated ads showing a revolving prison door, combined with the Horton victim's well-advertised campaign tour for Bush, reproduced *The Birth of a Nation*.[43] Attacking Dukakis as weak on defense as well as on violent crime, moreover, the Bush campaign linked imperial to domestic racial politics, for the Dukakis of Bush's television ads would make Americans vulnerable to aliens abroad and at home. Open racist appeals were now forbidden, however, and Bush (and his supporters in my presidency class) denied that Bush's version of "Make my day!" had anything to do with race. But the Republican candidate had succeeded in replacing Jesse Jackson with Willie Horton as the dominant black face in the campaign. For the first time, several of my students then remembered the racial and sexual context for "Make my day!"

That memory of the racial antagonism he promoted posed a problem for Bush, however, to which he offered a solution after his victory. The solution was amnesia. Along with two other movie phrases popularized by President Reagan— "Win one for the Gipper," from *Knute Rockne, All American*, and "the Evil Empire," from *Star Wars*—"Make my day!" will be included in the new edition of *Bartlett's Book of Famous Quotations*. If Bush has his way, however, the words will be severed from their meaning. "The American people," the new president reassured us after his election, "are wonderful when it comes to understanding when a campaign ends and the work of business begins." Bush wanted Americans to believe that his campaign spectacle would have nothing to do with his conduct of government. He was making his business that "great act of American amnesia," as political scientist James Barber called it on election night, by which our politics forgets the forces that drive it. The new president brushed off Barbara Walters's questions about the campaign on the eve of his inauguration. "That's history," said George Bush. "That doesn't mean anything any more."[44]

NOTES

An earlier version of this paper was presented in the series "The Peculiarities of the American Empire," sponsored by the History Department, Rutgers University, 29 April 1988. The title of the session for which this paper was written was "The Postmodern Empire." I am grateful for the responses of Richard Barnet, Fred Block, Victoria de Grazia, and Michael Schaffer, who share responsibility for the differences between the paper they heard and this one. I have also benefited from the comments of Ann Banfield, Kathleen Moran, H. Bradford Westerfield, and members of the *Representations* editorial board.

1. There are risks in adopting the Inspector Dupin position, as D. A. Miller has pointed out to me most forcefully. It will position me as the subject supposed to know, detecting crimes that others overlook. Given the direction of the argument, this will cast me as the double of my white, male target, not only antagonizing white men who do not see themselves defined by imperial American political culture but also speaking for women and people of color in the name of coming to their defense. Acknowledging this risk hardly disarms it. But being unable to envision criticism without a place to stand, the best response I can make to such suspicions is the argument of the essay itself.

2. Samuel Kernell, *Going Public: New Strategies of Presidential Leadership* (Washington D.C., 1986). The depiction of imperial political culture on which I am about to embark identifies operating mentalities, powerful forces, and individuals in whom they reside. I am concentrating on extreme tendencies that came to a head during the Reagan years and, as the current legal indictments facing some of these individuals attest, however powerful in our history and politics and however sanitized in respectable accounts thereof, they have not always gotten their way. Nonetheless, the Bush regime represents the normalization of the politics of the Reagan era, not their reversal. Anti-Communism undergirded the Reaganite shift from domestic welfare to military spending, the expansion of secret government, and the conduct of foreign policy as spectacle. The advertised end of the cold war has reversed none of these developments, and, insofar as the drug war and the defense of traditional family values inherit the role of anti-Communism, that will intensify what I link here to going public and going private in foreign policy, the racialist basis of American politics.

3. *San Francisco Chronicle*, 19 March 1987, 15.

4. The sources for this paragraph are Don Moldea, *Dark Victory* (New York, 1986); Garry Wills, *Innocents at Home* (New York, 1987); and Michael Rogin, *"Ronald Reagan," the Movie, and Other Episodes in Political Demonology* (Berkeley, 1987), 1–43.

5. On *Hellcats* and the 1984 Republican convention, see Rogin, *"Reagan," the Movie*, 40–42; Garry Wills, "More Than a Game," *New York Review of Books*, 28 April 1988, 3.

6. Robert Scheer, *With Enough Shovels: Reagan, Bush, and Nuclear War* (New York, 1982), 36–65; *Contra Watch* 4–5 (May–June 1987): 3; Christopher Hitchens, "Minority Report," *Nation,* 17 October 1988, 333–34.

7. Ian Baruma, "Us and Others," *New York Review of Books,* 14 August 1986, 24.

8. *San Francisco Examiner,* 24 April 1988, A-6; *New York Times,* 30 April 1988, 11; Rogin, *"Reagan," the Movie,* 7–8; *San Francisco Chronicle,* 13 April 1988, 9; 14 April 1988, 20.

9. Russell Jacoby, *Social Amnesia* (Boston, 1975); and Fredric Jameson, *The Political Unconscious* (Ithaca, N.Y., 1981).

10. Thanks to Kathleen Moran for this argument, which is expanded in the following section.

11. Cf. T.J. Clark, *The Painting of Modern Life: Paris in the Art of Manet and His Followers* (Princeton, N.J., 1984), 9, 68–69; Guy Debord, *Society of the Spectacle* (1967; Detroit, 1983); Jean Baudrillard, *Simulations* (New York, 1983), and "The Ecstasy of Communication," in *The Anti-Aesthetic: Essays in Postmodern Culture,* ed. Hal Foster (Port Townsend, Wash., 1983), 126–34; Dana Polan, *Power and Paranoia: History, Narrative, and the American Cinema, 1940–1950* (New York, 1986), 293–98; Fredric Jameson, "Postmodernism; or, the Cultural Logic of Late Capitalism," *New Left Review* 146 (July 1984), 58–69.

12. For linking *Rambo* to Iran/Contra, I am indebted to Ronald Reagan, and I have analyzed the connection between Iran/Contra and *First Blood, Part I* and *Part II,* in "Ronbo," *London Review of Books,* 13 October 1988, 7–9.

13. This formulation is indebted to Debord, *Society of the Spectacle,* and to Jacques Lacan, "The Mirror Stage as Formative of the Functions of the I as Revealed in Psychoanalytic Experience," *Ecrits,* trans. Alan Sheridan (New York, 1977), 1–7.

14. Roland Marchand, *Advertising the American Dream: Making Way for Modernity, 1920–1940* (Berkeley, 1985).

15. Jonathan Kwitny, *Endless Enemies* (New York, 1986), 11–14.

16. Richard Slotkin, *Regeneration Through Violence* (Middletown, Conn., 1973), and *The Fatal Environment* (New York, 1985); Richard Drinnon, *Facing West* (Minneapolis, 1980); Michael Rogin, *Fathers and Children: Andrew Jackson and the Subjugation of the American Indian* (New York, 1975), and *"Reagan," the Movie.* The quotation in the text is from Richard Slotkin, "The Continuity of Forms: Myth and Genre in Warner Brothers' *The Charge of the Light Brigade,*" in this issue, pp. 1–23.

17. Kwitny, *Endless Enemies,* 13–15.

18. Carlo Ginzburg, *The Cheese and the Worms* (London, 1980), 78, 92. On the history of American demonology, see Rogin, "Political Repression in the United States," in *"Reagan," the Movie,* 44–80 and passim.

19. Studs Terkel, *"The Good War"* (New York, 1984).

20. Jeane Kirkpatrick, "Dictatorships and Double Standards," *Commentary* 68 (November 1979): 34–45.

21. David Wyman, *The Abandonment of the Jews* (New York, 1984).

22. See John Dower, *War Without Mercy: Race and Power in the Pacific War* (New York, 1986); and Baruma, "Us and Others," 23–25.

23. Baruma, "Us and Others," 24.

24. Dower, *War Without Mercy,* 34, 38–39, 78–92. See also Richard Drinnon, *Keeper of Concentration Camps: Dillon S. Myer and American Racism* (Berkeley, 1986); and Peter Irons, *Justice at War* (New York, 1983).

25. See Dower, *War Without Mercy,* 325; Baruma, "Us and Others," 25; Hannah Arendt, *The Origins of Totalitarianism* (New York, 1951).

26. I analyzed *Them!* in "Kiss Me Deadly: Communism, Motherhood, and Cold War Movies," *"Reagan," the Movie,* 264–66, but did not make the connection to the Tokyo firebombing until reading *War Without Mercy;* see Dower, 174–75; and, on depictions of Asians in Hollywood from World War II to Vietnam, Tom Engelhardt, "Ambush at Kamikazi Pass," *Bulletin of Concerned Asian Scholars* 3 (Winter-Spring 1971): 64–84.

27. Rogin, *"Reagan," the Movie,* 24.

28. Dower, *War Without Mercy,* 38–39.

29. Engelhardt, "Ambush at Kamikazi Pass."

30. Fred Block, "Empire and Domestic Reform" (Paper delivered at the conference on "The Peculiarities of the American Empire," Rutgers University, 29 April 1988); Richard Barnet, comments at the same conference; James Fallows, *National Defense* (New York, 1981), 162–63.

31. Of the enormous literature on these subjects, I have found particularly helpful Jonathan Schell, *The Time of Illusion* (New York, 1975); and Fallows, *National Defense.*

32. Cf. Garry Wills, *The Kennedy Imprisonment* (Boston, 1982); Bruce Miroff, *Pragmatic Illusions: The Presidential Politics of John F. Kennedy* (New York, 1976), 35–166; Schell, *Time of Illusion,* 90–95.

33. See Scheer, *With Enough Shovels;* and Rogin, *"Reagan," the Movie,* 27–37.

34. Ben Bradlee, *Guts and Glory: The Rise and Fall of Oliver North* (New York, 1988), 153–55.

35. Richard J. Barnet, "Reflections (National Security)," *New Yorker,* 21 March 1988, 104–14; "Talk of the Town," *New Yorker,* 4 April 1988, 23.

36. Richard J. Barnet, *The Roots of War* (New York, 1972).

37. James Lardner, "Films," *Nation,* 28 January 1988, 94–98.

38. *New York Times,* 30 November 1986, 12-Y.

39. Robin Wood, *Hollywood from Vietnam to Reagan* (New York, 1986), 162;

Edward Villaluz Guerrero, *The Ideology and Politics of Black Representation in U.S. Narrative Cinema* (Ph.D. diss., University of California, Berkeley, 1989), 68–79; Ella Taylor, *Prime-Time Families* (Berkeley, 1989).

40. Wood, *Hollywood*, 163–66.

41. Fredric Jameson, "The Shining," *Social Text* 4 (Fall 1981): 114.

42. Maureen Dowd, "Bush Boasts of Turnaround from 'Easy Rider' Society," *New York Times*, 7 October 1988, A-11; Elizabeth Drew, "Letter from Washington," *New Yorker*, 31 October 1998, 94; Wood, *Hollywood*, 228.

43. Cf. Micheal Rogin, " 'The Sword Became a Flashing Vision': D. W. Griffith's *Birth of a Nation*," in *"Reagan," the Movie*, 190–235. Having written on the political significance of *Birth*, I was suffering from amnesia, and the connection between *Birth* and Willie Horton was pointed out to me by Martin Sanchez-Jankowski.

44. *New York Times,* 28 November 1988, B-4; *New Yorker*, 21 November 1988, 41; *International Herald Tribune*, 21 January 1989, 4.

SOME FRACTURES AND FUTURES OF THE NEW HISTORICISM

11

THE LOGIC OF THE TRANSVESTITE

MARJORIE GARBER

> *Bottom.* I will aggravate my voice so that I will roar
> you as gently as any sucking dove; I will roar you and
> 'twere any nightingale.
> (Midsummer Night's Dream 1.2.76–78)

> The phenomenology that emerges from analytic
> experience is certainly of a kind to demonstrate in
> desire the paradoxical, deviant, erratic, eccentric,
> even scandalous character by which it is
> distinguished from need.[1]

Materialist and historicist feminist critics have tended, recently, to read Middleton and Dekker's play *The Roaring Girl* thematically as a play about the economic injustices of the sex-gender system. These critics see female cross-dressing as a metaphor for the changing condition of women. As we will see, the play's anxiety about clothing and fashion, which is omnipresent, is indeed conjoined with a related anxiety about sexuality, but that anxiety is not so much based upon women's emancipatory strategies as upon the sexual inadequacies of men. In an effort to explore the relationship between transvestism and desire, then, let us look at *The Roaring Girl*, a less readily allegorized text than cross-dressing plays like *As You Like It* or *Twelfth Night*, with its urban setting, canter's slang, and biographical subtext, the "real-life" story of Mary Frith. For in this play the historical figure herself functions as an unmasterable excess, and thus opens the question of transvestism's relationship to the embodiment of desire.

Born in 1584, Mary Frith, better known as Moll Cutpurse, was a notorious London figure, who dressed in men's clothes throughout her long life (she died at 75, after a career that spanned professions from pickpocketing to prostitution and bawdry, and ultimately—long after the play—to tavernkeeping). Her predilection for male attire, and the angry resistance of Jacobean society to women in men's clothing, is strongly attested to in *The Consistory of London Correction Book*, where dressing as a man is one of the offenses with which the historical Moll was charged.[2]

Moll had appeared on the stage in a scandal of self-display, unseemly for women of any class but the aristocracy—in this case, the public stage of the Fortune Theater, where, according to court records, she "sat there upon the stage in the publique viewe of all the people there p[rese]nte in mans apparrell and playd upon her lute & sange a songe."[3] The Epilogue to the play seems to promise a return of this spectacle, dissolving the artifice of the false or fictive Moll in the anticipation of the "real" one: if the writers and actors have disappointed the expectations of the audience, "The Roaring Girl herself, some few days hence, / Shall on this stage give larger recompense." Yet this is as likely to be a sly glance backward at the first scandalous appearance as a genuine offer to display Moll's body again for public delectation. The lute playing incident may also be behind the episode of Moll's singing and playing upon a viol in 4.1. where jokes are made upon her taking down the gentleman's instrument and playing upon it, and reference is made to censorious dames who think the viol "an unmannerly instrument for a woman." In any case, the play is clearly grounded in social history as well as literary and formal precedent. Like David Hwang's *M. Butterfly*, which capitalized on the real story of a French diplomat's love affair with a Chinese "woman" who turned out to be a man,[4] *The Roaring Girl* was produced at a time when the cultural referent, the "real" Moll, was in the news; as Mary Beth Rose notes, it is probable that Middleton and Dekker were "attempting to benefit from the *au courant* notoriety of the actual Moll in the timing of their play."[5]

That the play itself is concerned with clothing, and with the commutability of class and gender as categories capable of anxious social disruption, is manifest not only from its titular heroine but also from Middleton's note to the "Comic Play-Readers" in the 1611 Quarto:

> The fashion of play-making I can properly compare to nothing so naturally as the alteration in apparel; for in the time of the great cropdoublet, your huge bombasted plays, quilted with mighty words to lean purpose, was only then in fashion; and as the doublet fell, neater inventions began to set up. Now, in the time of spruceness, our plays follow the niceness of our garments; single plots, quaint conceits, lecherous jests, dressed up in hanging sleeves; and those are fit for the times and the termers. Such a kind of light-colored summer stuff, mingled with divers colors, you shall find this published comedy; . . . Venus, being a woman, passes through the play in doublet and breeches; a brave disguise and a safe one, if the statute untie not her codpiece point.[6]

The "statute" referred to in this last phrase is of course the code of sumptuary laws that prohibited both cross-dressing and sartorial class-jumping from one station to another.[7] *Should* the statute untie her codpiece point, of course, the audience would see more than it had perhaps bargained for, since the wearer of the codpiece, the player dressed as Moll the roaring girl, would have been a boy actor. Venus in doublet and breeches might have suggested the goddess's cross-dressed appearance in the *Aeneid*, where her buskins, quiver, and tucked-up gown made her resemble a huntress, a Spartan or Thracian girl, one of the followers, not of Venus, but of Diana, an Amazon *in potentia*, and a mortal rather than a goddess—a class distinction of some moment. But not to her son. That Aeneas reads beneath the disguise, does not interpret the clothes except as a ruse, is itself some indication of Middleton's take on the pervasive, indeed obsessive, concern with clothing in this play. The sense of this passage is that bulky clothing styles and bulky, weighty plays are likewise out of fashion. "The alteration in apparel" is made deliberately analogous to other alterations in public taste; anxiety about clothing, as well as anxiety about *sexual* alteration (sexual identity and sexual performance) will predominate throughout the play.

Thus Mary Fitzallard, daughter of Sir Guy and beloved of the young hero, Sebastian Wengrave, makes her initial appearance (and the first appearance of any actor in the play) "disguised like a sempster," or seamstress, carrying a case of "falling bands," or flat collars, a style that had replaced the ruff. "Sempster" is immediately glossed as "needle-woman" by Sebastian's servant, (1.1.51), presumably with a glance at the phallic woman who is the boy actor playing Mary Fitzallard. As for "falling bands," a sartorial joke is made on them, too, since "bands" are also "bonds" and "banns"; face to face with Sebastian, Mary reproves him for his neglect of their "bond fast sealed"; "Is this bond canceled? Have you forgot me?" (1.1.57–60)—in effect, she accuses him of the "falling bands" that she has emblematically chosen as her wares. Later in the play Mary Fitzallard will appear in another disguise, that of a page, the traditional Renaissance stage role for the woman-dressed-as-a-man; in 4.1. Mary, Sebastian, and Moll Cutpurse are *all* dressed as men, and as Sebastian kisses Mary, Moll comments drily that it seems strange for one man to kiss another. The homoerotic subtext here, like the en-coding of sartorial/class consciousness, is not merely thematic or illustrative, but intrinsic to the inner dynamics of the play, to what might be called the play's "unconscious."

What else is in the play's unconscious? What does it know?

The Roaring Girl is a play about the circulation of parts, about women with penises and testicles and men who lack them. Thus, for example, when in Act 2 scene 2 Sir Alexander overhears a tailor designing a costume for Moll, he realizes that the design is not only for a pair of breeches, but, in effect, for a phallus, one that will stand round and full (if somewhat stiffly) between the legs (2.2.80–100). Moll is to be a "codpiece daughter." No wonder he is disconcerted; this is what has always been feared about women who wear the pants. "Normalized" or tamed by a dramatic genre which seems reassuringly realistic and socio-economic (the emergent middle class, the male and female shopkeepers of the City, the moneyed urban aristocracy with their conservative mores, the tavern underclass, and, in this context, the woman who rebels against social and economic constraints) this play, looked at hard, discloses a dangerous, carnivalized fantasia of dislocation, in which the fetishization of commodities is the cover for the fetishization of body parts. It is a play that theorizes the constructedness of gender in a disconcertingly literal way through the construction of bodies—and of clothes. The tailor makes the man (and the tail); but the tailor also wields the shears.

Consider the character of the suggestively named Laxton. Laxton is described by Rose as a "lecherous, misogynistic gallant" (380), and by Jean Howard as a "gentleman rake,"[8] but a joke as broad as the one about Moll's extra "yard" of cloth in the tailor scene ("yard" of course is also slang for penis) is made by Sir Alexander the first time he appears onstage:

> SIR ALEXANDER.   Furnish Master Laxton
> With what he wants, a stone—a stool, I would say,
> A stool.
> LAXTON.   I had rather stand sir.
> SIR ALEXANDER.   I know you had, good Master Laxton.
>
>   *(1.2.56–60)*

Laxton is in fact "lack-stone," the fellow without testicles, who would stand if he could, but may not be capable of doing so. Sir Alexander's parapraxis (Laxton "wants," that is both *lacks* and desires, a *stone*) suggests his estimate of his companion's virility. "Stone" as testicle recurs throughout the play—a stallion is a "stone-horse" (2.1.86) (something Moll tells Laxton derisively that she knows how to ride), and the dandies in the feather shop are informed by no less an authority than Mistress Tiltyard that certain feathers are "most worn and most in fashion / Among the beaver gallants, the stone riders, / The private stage's audience" (2.1.156–59). (Beaver hats were notoriously expensive—Stubbes in the *Anatomie of Abuses* cites prices of 20, 30, and 40 shillings[9]—and were worn at one time by both men and women; it seems possible that the modern slang meaning of "beaver" may also be anticipated here, especially since a "beaver" is a hat.[10])

It may be worth noting that the New Mermaid editor, Andor Gomme, looks resolutely away from this reading of Laxton's sexual etymology, preferring an entirely different onomastic code; Laxton's name, he says, "suggests that . . . all his lands are sold."[11] This is in the context wholly reasonable, since, as we will see, the marriage/property system in this play is located in, and exists as a sign for, the register of the symbolic (one of the play's merchant aristocrats is named "Lord Noland"). Laxton's name foregrounds him as a figure of "lack," and the recognition of this lack permits or requires his entry into the socio-economic world of patriarchy and commerce. But to deny or repress the specific sexual elements of "lack" in Laxton by regarding these passages as merely general proofs that "Middleton is a master of . . . sexual innuendo"[12] is like labeling the dirty jokes as "bawdy" or "obscene punning" and leaving them at that. In a similar way Gomme (whose own name means "eraser") comments on Moll's assertion, upon the appearance of Mary Fitzallard as Sebastian's true bride "thank me for't; I'd a forefinger in't" (5.2.169) that "despite Moll's skill with instruments we should probably resist a sexual innuendo here." His decision to register this resistance in a footnote is more interesting than the "innuendo" itself. In short, *The Roaring Girl's* omnipresent references to castration, emasculation, penises and testicles worn (like clothing; extra "yards," "codpieces," "trinkets") by women rather than men tell a story—a story somewhat different from the progressivist narrative of economic and cultural reconfiguration urged by both modern British editors and modern American feminists.

Nor is Laxton the only ambivalent (or ambivalently named) male figure in the play: the gallants are named Jack Dapper, Sir Beauteous Ganymede, and Sir Thomas Long—this last yet another familiar reference to the penis yet again (cf. *Lady Chatterley's* "John Thomas"; Sir Thomas—Sir Thomas *Long*—would seem to be a walking penis), while the interest of the men in fashion (Dapper, Beauteous) is related by the text to their questionable (bi)sexuality. Jack Dapper's father, who jokes in a complex pun (based on the name of a law court and debtors' prison, the "Counter") that he will make his son a "counter-tenor" (equating castration with loss of economic power [3.3.81]) laments further that "when his purse jingles, / Roaring boys follow at's tail, fencers and ningles" (3.3.67). Ningles, or ingles, are homosexual boy-favorites, whose attractiveness as love-objects offers a strong homoerotic subtext. In the beginning of Act 4 Moll sees Sebastian kissing Mary Fitzallard when Mary is dressed as a page boy (Gomme, apparently uncomfortable with the implications of this scene, describes it as a "dubiously suggestive piece of something near perversity"[13]). Moll herself notes wryly that it's strange to see one man kissing another (she of course is also dressed as a man in that scene, and both women's parts are played by men).

The anxiety of lack and the circulation of simulacra are, for Jacques Lacan, the very insignia of human sexuality. Because the human being is a *speaking* being, he or she must articulate desire and identity in language, must have recourse to the dimension of the Other in the constitution of a self. Thus, body parts take on the value of signifiers and can enter into circulation in multiple, figurative, displaced forms. The system of desire is organized around the phallus, which is neither a phantasy nor an organ but "a signifier . . . intended to designate as a whole the effects of the signified. . . . It can play its role only when veiled, that is to say, as itself a sign of the latency with which any signifiable is struck when it is raised . . . to the function of signifier."[14] In learning that the mother does not have the phallus (that is, in interpreting the difference between the sexes in terms of lack), the subject, according to Lacan, gains access to the desire of the Other ("designating by the Other the very locus evoked by the recourse to speech"). Lacan goes on:

> One may, simply by reference to the function of the phallus, indicate the structures that will govern the relations between the sexes.
> Let us say that these relations will turn around a "to be" and a "to have," which, by referring to a signifier, the phallus, have the opposed effect, on the one hand, of giving reality to the subject in this signifier, and, on the other, of derealizing the relations to be signified.
> This is brought about by the intervention of a "to seem" that replaces the "to have," in order to protect it on the one side, and to mask its lack in the other, and which has the effect of projecting in their entirety the ideal or typical manifestations of the behaviour of each sex, including the act of copulation itself, into comedy. (289)

In other words, there is a profound connection between theatricality and sexuality, between having, being, and "seeming." Once "seeming" enters the picture, it is capable of coming to substitute for all other terms, and everything is "derealized"; anything can be a simulacrum, a "comedy." Lacan makes the theatricality of sexuality even more explicit in what follows:

> Paradoxical as this formulation may seem, I am saying that it is in order to be the phallus, that is to say, the signifier of the desire of the Other, that a woman will reject an essential part of femininity, namely, all her attributes in the masquerade. . . . (290)

> The fact that femininity finds its refuge in this mask, by virtue of the fact of the *Verdrangung* [repression] inherent in the phallic mark of desire, has the curious consequence of making virile display in the human being itself seem feminine. (291)

"Having" and "being" the phallus are alike conditions of lack. It is that lack which constitutes desire, and which calls into play the "masquerade." In *The Roaring Girl* the lack is multiply overdetermined, in the masquerade of Moll Cutpurse in male attire (even her name), in Laxton's multiple lacks and *his* emblematic name, in the dandyism of Laxton and the other gallants, Dapper, Ganymede, and so on, whose displays of virility (in the feather shop, in the sempstresses', in swordplay with Moll) precisely "has the curious consequence of making virile display in the human being itself seem feminine."

As the play has been trying to tell us all along ("yard," "stones," "trinkets," "stiff," "stand," at tiresome length), Moll is the phallus. The mark of desire in the Symbolic. The signifier that is constituted by, and in, a split.

Over and over again *The Roaring Girl* draws attention to the fact that its two heroines have the same name: Mary. Moll says that she pitied Mary Fitzallard "for name's sake, that a Moll / Should be so crossed in love" and therefore arranged for her to dress (*cross*-dress) as a page: "My tailor fitted her; how like you his work?" (4.1.68–71). Sir Alexander, convinced by his son's stratagem that Sebastian wants to marry Moll Frith (rather than Mary Fitzallard), remonstrates that "Methinks her very name should fright thee from her":

SEBASTIAN. Why is the name of Moll so fatal, sir?
SIR ALEXANDER. Mary, one, sir, where suspect is entered;
For seek all London from one end to t'other,
More whores of that name than of any ten other.
(2.2.156–61)

Marylebone Park, called here (as if for emphasis) "Marybone," is the dubious district where, Laxton instructs his coachman, they are likely to find Moll Frith.[15] The name of the district, derived from "Mary le bon" (originally a reference to the Virgin) ironically incorporates both "good" and "bad" Maries (as well as the vexed question of virginity itself, and the contiguity of madonna and whore as object types of male desire[16]). In a play in which, as we have already seen, names take on a humorous or allegorical significance (Lack-stone, Dapper, Beauteous Ganymede), this doubling of Moll and Mary Fitzallard (both Mary.F.s) extends the range of the psychoanalytic reading suggested by Laxton's lack and the phallicized Moll. The figure of the transvestite, in dream-logic terms already a figure *for*—as well as *of*—overdetermination, here becomes split into the apparently marginal and separable, and the apparently central. But it does so, again, in an insidious and disturbing way, by substitution and replacement. Sebastian wants one girl, and so pretends to want the other; he substitutes Moll for Mary in order to get Mary. But what he gets may be a Mary who is no longer separable—if she ever was—from Moll.

Let us see how this works within the text. The play begins, and ends, with Mary Fitzallard's betrothal to Sebastian; in the opening scene it is covert and contested, opposed by Sir Alexander in his role as patriarch; in the last scene Mary and Sebastian are openly reunited, with Mary publicly welcomed as young Wengrave's "wife" and "bride." In between these two scenes comes Sebastian's subterfuge (he pretends to be in love with Moll in order to make his father see how much better off he would be with Mary), Moll's arrangement with her tailor for a new pair of breeches and her (offstage) employment of that same tailor to dress Mary in a page's costume, and the denouement in which Moll appears in her role as Sebastian's fiancée dressed as a man, is greeted with horror by Sir Alexander because of her clothes ("Is that your wedding gown?" [5.2.101] he asks, and his friend Goshawk, with a gesture toward the homoerotic subtext of the boy actor, replies: "No priest will marry her, sir, for a woman/Whiles that shape's on; and it was never known/Two men were married and conjoined in one./ Your son hath made some shift to love another" [106–109]) and is finally replaced in the wedding tableau by Mary Fitzallard. Sir Alexander, who could be said to represent the stereotypical male gaze throughout the play, now asks her pardon for his misreading:

Forgive me, worthy gentlewoman; 'twas my blindness:
When I rejected thee, I saw thee not.

(5.2.192–193)

But Sir Alexander's apology, though gracious, is misdirected. He *did* see Mary Fitzallard when he looked at the cross-dressed Moll Frith; the conflation of the two figures, as in dream logic, tells its own suggestive truth about who and what Sebastian is marrying. (We might here remember that other Sebastian, in Shakespeare's *Twelfth Night*, who was also "betrothed unto a maid and man"). Both Rose and Jean Howard read Mary Fitzallard as a much more conventional, female character than Moll; Howard remarks that though Moll sees marriage as a straightjacket for herself, she nonetheless promotes it for Mary, "and if comedy demands a marriage, it gets the marriage of Mary Fitzallard and Sebastian, but not the marriage of Moll" (Howard, 438–39). Rose recognizes a strategy of displacement, but locates it on the level of conscious choice and dramatic convention: Moll, she claims, takes on the social and psychological freedom of the traditional disguised heroine "without providing the corresponding reassurance implicit in that heroine's eventual erotic transformation. These functions are instead displaced onto Mary Fitzallard, who, disguised as a page, joyously sheds the disguise to take her place as Sebastian's wife in the final scene. Moll, on the other hand, having served as the instrument who brings about the happy ending, is nonetheless excluded from the renewed comic society" (Rose, 389).

In effect, these feminist historicist readings, despite themselves, reinstate the patriarchal aesthetics of closure, by separating (or keeping separated) the figures of Moll and Mary. But I would contend that in doing so they reinscribe the politics the play deconstructs. If Moll *is* Mary, if the similarity of their names indicates that one is a projection of the other, then Moll is not so much a role model as a recognition and a phantom, not a sign of the road not taken or a metaphor for the aspirations of early modern feminists but a sign of the double division of the concept of the "roaring girl" (female/male; Mary/Moll). Not either/or but both/and. The *in*divisibility of the subject-as-object, the female transvestite as that which puts in question the traditional gender divisions, is present not only in Moll, the liminal, lower-class outsider who outspokenly dismisses marriage as social enslavement, but also, and already, in the apparently more conventional Mary Fitzallard, whose desire for marriage compels her, through the play's logic, to cross-dress.

The scene in which Moll, Mary, and Sebastian all appear onstage in men's clothes is, in one sense, the exposure of the transvestite theatrical structure and its homoerotics (Moll: "How strange this shows, one man to kiss another?" Sebastian: "I'd kiss such men to choose, Moll, / Methinks a woman's lip tastes well in a doublet" [4.1.47–49]), but in another sense it is the navel of the dream, the *mise en abyme*, the place where "truth" is disclosed—or "disclothed." The play splits the figure of the "roaring girl" into acceptable and less acceptable, socially integrated and outlaw, upper class and lower, Mary-the-good and Mary-the-not-so-good. But, as in a dream, this split is a defensive acknowledgment of what is not so readily separated in waking life, or in history, or in any other configurations of the self-designated "real." However assured Sir Alexander may be to the contrary, Sebastian does marry Moll Frith, as surely as he does kiss a man.

Thus the conception of Moll-as-politically-correct-marginal is a construct that reinscribes what it purports to challenge. The point is not that Moll represents a brave but legible and separable element of the play's populace, one whose self-avowed chastity (in contrast with the historical Moll's prostitution) protects against promiscuity in the past and self-replication in the future, but rather that in getting Mary Sebastian gets Moll, too—and in getting Moll (as heroine, as role model, as proto-feminist) the reader or audience gets Mary, the monogamous heterosexual woman who cross-dresses—in a way frequently recorded in historical cases from the period[17]—in order to be with her man.

The editor of the New Mermaid edition of Dekker and Middleton's play commented as recently as 1974 that "the revival of interest in Jacobean comedy has largely passed *The Roaring Girl* by."[18] Despite approving comments by Swinburne and T. S. Eliot, wrote Andor Gomme at that time, "*The Roaring Girl* has dropped back into obscurity." Yet ten years afterward the play was already enjoying a new vogue.[19] In the manner of such things, it has now become the one cross-dressing play (other than Shakespeare's) most students of the period study. I can't help but think that that is at least in part because of the positive-role-model-challenge-to-the-sex-gender-system-disruption-of-the-old-verities view of the play. Moll Cutpurse is indeed, as is often noted, a cross-dresser who differs from Rosalind and others in that she is not in disguise; she is what sexologists today would call a (relatively) continuous or constant cross-dresser, rather than an episodic one,[20] though she does not cross-dress to pass (everyone onstage knows she is a woman—although everyone offstage, presumably, also knew she was played by a boy). She has been extensively cleaned up from the original, "historical" Moll, as is also noted; her virginity—in fact, a fairly common choice on the part of female-to-male cross-dressers in the early modern period[21]—and the fact that she gives back stolen money make her an attractive rogue heroine of the Robin Hood (or Paladin) type. She is not really anti-social or disturbingly transgressive to a modern reader, though she stands as a placeholder for the energies of transgression. By looking backward at Moll's place in "history," contemporary readers can look forward to their own struggles with sex-gender inequalities, and also (though this sounds trivial) to their own struggles with gender-inflected dress codes. The female professor in pants, the female undergraduate in blue jeans, finds in Moll (and even in Mary) an attractively innovative predecessor.

Furthermore, *The Roaring Girl* occupies a position in the Elizabethan-Jacobean canon quite analogous to the position occupied by Moll within the play. Like her it is marginal, a kind of outsider, hard to contextualize and integrate into the old rules (in this case, the conventional rules of comedy), doubled (the "shared authorship" question: which part is by Dekker and which by Middleton? do they represent distinct literary, cultural, and class interests, and if so can their contributions to the text be separated from one another?), but finally not disruptive to the canon itself. Again like Moll, it is the exception that proves the rule.

Even the play's fathers, patriarchal and phallocentric arbiters of the law, show the lack which is common to New Comedy, as Sir Alexander tries in vain to forbid his son's marriage to Mary, and thereby invites all the subterfuge that follows. Sebastian's "courtship" of Moll Cutpurse, the several maskings and unmaskings of the final scene (which is the bride? Moll or Mary? the one in pants or the one dressed like a woman?) all stem from this paternal repression, which is (needless to say) only an externalization of repressions that could as well be located within Sebastian—or within seventeenth-century London—or within the "sex-gender" system. The phallus is the mark of desire, and the sign of the entry into the Symbolic (the world of commerce, of land, of law, of marriage contract). Its lack, or the consciousness of its lack, is what motors the play. And if, as I have already suggested, the transvestite, specifically here the female transvestite, is the complexly overdetermined marker of that lack—is, in fact, a sign of overdetermination *itself*, as well as itself an overdetermined sign—then the play's appropriation of the locally celebrated story of Moll Frith makes *literary* sense, interpretive sense, not only sense as a historical reminder of shifting class and gender roles and *their* attendant anxieties. The anxiety here is not—or not only—about the rising power of women and the middle class, the breakdown of legible cultural distinctions as signified in dress codes governing class and gender decorum, but about something that underlies those specific cultural anxieties: an anxiety about the ownership of desire.

Critics of *The Roaring Girl* emphasize that Moll is not in disguise. Whether in pants or her frieze jerkin and black safeguard she is always read as a woman, unlike Rosalind/Ganymede, or Viola/Cesario, or any of the dozens of female pages who turn up in the cross-dressing plays of the period. What this means is that she does not, will not, cannot disappear into the fictively "real" identity of the "woman" she is supposed to be, her transvestite "other" going underground, or becoming incorporated into the dominant fiction of womanhood (femininity, object of desire). Mary Beth Rose notes that Moll "is human and will not disappear from social life" (Rose, 389). Unlike Ganymede, the transvestite who "vanishes," or who "escapes," Moll remains. She is not a figure but a subject.

Moll's existence on the "outside" or fold of the text of *The Roaring Girl* is thus a strong argument against the domestication or taming of transvestism as metaphor. "Enter Moll like a man," says the stage direction to Act 3 scene 1. The force of the theatrical moment comes from 1) the audience's awareness that this is *not* a man (i.e., is Moll), 2) the audience's awareness that this *is* a man (i.e., is a boy actor), 3) the audience's awareness that Laxton will likely be deceived, at first, by her disguise (he has just said, with sublime self-confidence, "I see none yet dressed like her; I must look for a shag ruff, a frieze jerkin, a short sword, and a safeguard"), 4) the audience's awareness that there *is* (or *was*) a cross-dressed historical personage of this same name who walked the London streets, and 5) the audience's awareness that this "Moll" is *not* that Moll, is a representation. That the play's Moll is cross-dressed, but not in disguise—that her recognizable, semi-legendary identity (in London, in literary and cultural history) as "Moll Cutpurse" is indivisible from her men's clothing—that Moll "unmasked" (SD 5.2.142) is Moll in transvestite garb suggests that the appropriation of "transvestite" and "masquerade" as enabling figures for women—for feminist critics as well as for female spectators[22]—is itself an act of phallogocentric mastery. The pleasurable tease of being a woman in masquerade, a "transvestite" in imagination, still refers back to the male as norm and hence is still itself a hegemonic move. The question is whether, in calling Moll the "phallus," we ourselves have escaped that move.

NOTES

1. Jacques Lacan, "The Significance of the Phallus," in *Ecrits: A Selection*, trans. Alan Sheridan (New York: W. W. Norton, 1977), p. 286.

2. P. A. Mulholland, "The Date of *The Roaring Girl*," *Review of English Studies* 28 (1977), 20–21, 30–31.

3. Mulholland, "The Date of *The Roaring Girl*," 22, 30–31.

4. See "The Occidental Tourist," in Marjorie Garber, *Vested Interests: Cross-Dressing and Cultural Anxiety* (Routledge, forthcoming) for an extensive discussion of Hwang's play.

5. Mary Beth Rose, "Women in Men's Clothing: Apparel and Social Stability in *The Roaring Girl*," *ELR* 14 (1984), 379.

6. Thomas Middleton, "To the Comic Play-Readers, Venery and Laughter." Cited from Russell A. Fraser and Norman Rabkin, *Drama of the English Renaissance, II: The Stuart Period* (New York: Macmillan, 1976). All references to *The Roaring Girl* are from this edition.

7. See, for example, Frances Elizabeth Baldwin, *Sumptuary Legislation and*

Personal Regulation in England (Baltimore: Johns Hopkins University Press, 1926), and Wilfred Hooper, "The Tudor Sumptuary Laws," *English Historical Review* 20 (1915), 433–39.

8. Jean E. Howard, "Crossdressing, The Theatre, and Gender Struggle in Early Modern England," *Shakespeare Quarterly* 39:4 (Winter, 1988), 437.

9. Andor Gomme, ed., *The Roaring Girl* (London: Ernest Benn, Ltd. 1976), p. 32.

10. See Sigmund Freud, *Interpretation of Dreams, Standard Edition* (London: Hogarth Press, 1901), 5:360–62.

11. Gomme, *Roaring Girl*, p. xxviii.

12. Gomme, *Roaring Girl*, p. xxx. Christopher Ricks, "The Moral and Poetic Structure of *The Changeling*," *Essays in Criticism* X (July 1960), 291.

13. Gomme, *Roaring Girl*, p. xxiv.

14. Lacan, "The Signification of the Phallus," p. 288.

15. Gomme's note reads: "Until 1611 Marlybone Manor was crown property: the gardens (ultimately incorporated into Regent's Park) were said in *A Fair Quarrel* (IV.iv.217ff.) to be suitable as a burial ground for whores and panders because it was near Tyburn. The point of Laxton's quip, however, is enriched by the linking of a pun on Marybone (= marrow bone [popularly thought of as an aphrodisiac] and park in the sense of 'the female body as a domain where the lover may freely roam' (*Shakespeare's Bawdy*, 163; cf. *Venus and Adonis* 231ff.)."

16. See Sigmund Freud, "A Special Type of Choice of Object made by Men," *SE* 11:165–175.

17. Rudolf M. Dekker and Lotte C. van der Pol, *The Tradition of Female Transvestism in Early Modern Europe* (London: Macmillan, 1988), pp. 27–30. Under the heading of "Romantic Motives" Dekker and van der Pol report the cases of numerous women who cross-dressed as sailors, marines, or soldiers in order not to be separated from their lovers or husbands. They summarize this section with a matter-of-fact statement that registers the extraordinary difficulty of interpreting cross-dressing, even in a given historical period, as "meaning" something rather than its opposite: "In short, for the women whom we know to have been married, transvestism appears to have been either a means to remain with their husbands, or escape from them" (30).

18. Gomme, *Roaring Girl*, p. xix. The "Acknowledgments" to Gomme's edition carry a date of November, 1974, which is why I give that date (rather than the publication date of 1976) as the time frame for his opinion here.

19. See not only Rose and Howard, but also Linda Woodbridge, *Women and the English Renaissance* (Urbana: University of Illinois Press, 1986), and an excellent essay by Jonathan Dollimore, "Subjectivity, Sexuality, and Transgression: The Jacobean Connection," in *Renaissance Drama* 17, *Renaissance*

Drama and Cultural Change, ed. Mary Beth Rose (Evanston: Northwestern University Press, 1986), pp. 53–81.

20. John Money, *Gay, Straight, and In-Between: The Sexology of Erotic Orientation.* (New York: Oxford University Press, 1988), p. 85.

21. Dekker and van der Pol, *Tradition of Female Transvestism*, pp. 35–39. They observe that, even though many of their cases are derived from judicial archives, and would therefore present the stories of cross-dressing criminals, a documentable criminal subculture did exist in Dutch cities in the seventeenth and eighteenth centuries, in which cross-dressing women did play a prominent role. Male disguises, pseudonyms, and nicknames were obviously good cover, but Dekker and van der Pol suggest that both cross-dressers and criminals are already disposed to violate social norms. "For women who had already crossed one fundamental social boundary, that between men and women, it must have been relatively simple to set aside other norms. On the other hand, women who had already attempted criminal paths felt less intensely the social pressure which impelled individuals to behave in a way consistent with their sexes, and they must have found it relatively easy to make the decision to begin cross-dressing." The data generated by Dekker and van der Pol's research is fascinating, and gives an invaluable sense of the frequency and variety of female-to-male transvestism in the period. Nonetheless, I remain somewhat skeptical about the elements of "must have been" and "must have found" that go into this analysis, and indeed about any easy "psychologizing" of tendencies among cross-dressers, in the early modern period as in the modern (or post-modern) one.

22. For transvestism as metaphor in film theory see Mary Ann Doane, "Film and the Masquerade: Theorizing the Female Spectator," *Screen* 22, nos. 3–4 (September–October 1982), 81. Laura Mulvey, "Afterthoughts . . . inspired by *Duel in the Sun*," *Framework* 6, nos. 15–17 (Summer, 1981), 13. Joan Riviere, "Womanliness as a Masquerade," in *Formations of Fantasy*, ed. Victor Burgin and Cora Kaplan (New York: Methuen, 1986) is a key founding text for these film theorists, and for their deployment of "transvestism" as a figure. I regard the relegation of "transvestism" and "transvestite" to the status of a metaphor or an analogy as an appropriation. It is striking that materialist feminists and film theorists both arrive—from such different directions—at this point, of utilizing transvestism as a metaphor, rather than confronting its transgressive power to destabilize and reconfigure.

12

ADAM BEDE AND HENRY ESMOND: HOMOSOCIAL DESIRE AND THE HISTORICITY OF THE FEMALE

EVE KOSOFSKY SEDGWICK

The discussions of novels from the paranoid Gothic tradition, in chapters 5 and 6 [of *Between Men*], were based on two important assumptions about historical periodization. The first, discussed explicitly in chapter 5 and based largely on scholarship about sexuality per se—signally male sexuality—and often specifically about attitudes toward male homosexuality, locates a crucial but temporally elusive historical fulcrum somewhere in or since the late seventeenth century. This fulcrum is the transfer of sexual regulation from religious institutions and ideologies to a complex of secular institutions and ideologies such as the state and the sciences of medicine and individual psychology. As we have seen, this transfer of assignment entailed an increasingly stressed and invasive homophobic division of the male homosocial spectrum. Our discussion so far has focused on the resultant changes in men's experience of living within the shifting terms of compulsory heterosexuality. It has been clear that women had a kind of ultimate importance in the schema of men's gender constitution—representing an absolute of exchange value, of representation itself, and also being the ultimate victims of the painful contradictions in the gender system that regulates men. This conception of women's role may be an unwarrantably flat and ahistorical one, however, even within the limits of a study of *male* homosocial desire.

The second assumption about periodization, which has more tacitly undergirt our readings so far in the novel, and became more active with *The Princess* in the last chapter, has to do with the changing constitution of the family under emerging industrial capitalism. In various ways, a hypothesis about the increasing importance and the changing ideological significance of the so-called nuclear family will be a referent for our reading of masculinity in nineteenth-century England. Because of the strong identification of women's roles with the family during this period, it is to this hypothesis that we can look in shifting our focus temporarily from the historicity of men's bonds themselves to the historicity of women's relations to men's bonds.

The feminist periodization that hypothesizes an important change in European femininity, and in the European family, under industrialism, goes back at least as far as Engel's *Origins of the Family, Private Property, and the State.* Some version of it is by now a staple in virtually all historically oriented feminist scholarship. It is closely tied to the importance that feminist social scientists (most influentially anthropologists) place on the different shapes and intensities, in different cultures, of the distinction between the "domestic" and the "public."[1] As Joan Kelly-Gadol describes cultures that are "at the end of the scale where the domestic and public orders are clearly distinguished from each other,"

> Women . . . steadily lose control over private property, products, and themselves as surplus increases, private property develops, and the communal household becomes a private economic unit, a family (extended or nuclear) represented by a man. The family itself, the sphere of women's activities, is in turn subordinated to a broader social or public order— governed by a state—which tends to be the domain of men. This is the general pattern presented by historical or civilized societies.[2]

Feminist historical scholarship, following Engels, has tended to see eighteenth-century England, leading toward industrial capitalism and toward a newly narrow focus on the nuclear family, as an especially symptomatic point in the consequential, growing split between "public" and "domestic" spheres.

Although historically oriented feminism (which I will here condense as "Marxist feminism," overriding for the purposes of this argument many very serious differences of approach among many scholars and thinkers) finds this change real and important, the forms of feminism that I have been grouping together under the rubric "radical" (see Introduction iii [of *Between Men*]) deemphasize its importance. In the recent give-and-take between Marxist and radical feminism, an important crux has been the issue of priority—chronological priority, explanatory priority, *or* functional/teleological priority—between industrial capitalism and the male-dependent family household. The following questions, coarsely formulated as they are, are among the immediate, practical feminist issues at stake in this discussion of priority: Is it men as a group, or capitalists as a class, that chiefly benefit from the modern sexual division of labor? How close is the fit between the functions of the gendered family and the needs of capitalism? Is the gendered family necessary for capitalism? Will changes in one necessarily effect changes in the other, and if so, how?

Alternative reconstructions of the *pre*capitalist family naturally accompany each move in this debate. In another coarse formulation, one could say that radical feminism tends to see within history a relatively unchanging family, in which not only the fact but the basic structures of patriarchal domination have remained stable by resisting or assimilating economic difference or change; while Marxist feminism, again caricaturally, tends to historicize the gendered family catastroph-ically, to see it as taking its present oppressive form or forms relatively late, chiefly under the pressure of capitalism, and in a fairly direct response to the needs of capital.

In the more sophisticated middle ground that is emerging between these po-sitions, it is appearing that European capitalism was, as it were, born into, or bred in, a pre-existent language of the family. (By "language" here I do *not* mean only ideology, but a complex structure for combining actual persons and functions along the axes of kinship and cohabitation.)[3] Like most languages, this one was multiple, contradictory, and redundant; also like most European languages, it was already intensively and complexly gendered. On the other hand, to the actual speakers of a language, if not the forms themselves then at least the salience, rationale, and meaningfulness of its inherited gender forms are always to some extent up for grabs. And just so did the coming of industrialism reopen negoti-ations on the salience, rationale, and meaning of pre-existent gender divisions in what was to become the class-marked family of industrial capitalism.

I am using a linguistic metaphor for this process, but, again, not because I mean to suggest that the ideological realm was the theater in which it mainly was enacted. The pattern by which wage work came to take place at a distance from the home, by which men were paid a "family" wage and women a "supplementary" wage for what might be the same work, by which women became a reserve labor force and at the same time had almost sole responsibility at home for the repro-duction of male and female labor power; the differentials of salary, occupation, and often even of food consumption; the institution of childbearing by a single person of a single sex—these facts are obviously not ideological constructions in any very hermetic sense of "ideology." At the same time, complicated processes of meaning and reinterpretation must clearly have been close to the very center of mutual class and gender foundation during this period. To that extent it is certainly appropriate for us, as students of the relations of meaning, to work at tracing out the stitchery of ideology in its "invisible reweaving" of future to past and of class to gender.

My project in this chapter is, of course, more modest and much more specific than to adjudicate the issues between a "radical-feminist" and a "Marxist-femi-nist" reading of the transition to the nineteenth century in England. It is more modest because of the many limitations involved in working on historical ques-tions through the reading of literature; it is much more specific because it is ultimately aimed at the question of male homosocial desire. I am going to be looking here at Thackeray's *Henry Esmond* and Eliot's *Adam Bede*, still against the background of [Alfred, Lord Tennyson's] *The Princess*: three nineteenth-cen-tury narrative fictions that consciously offer historical or mock-historical accounts of women's changing family roles in relation both to women's own sexuality and to male homosocial desire. *Bede* and *Esmond*, like *The Princess*, end with a ratification of the female role usually identified with the bourgeois Victorian "angel in the house." On the way to that ratification, however, each offers a very different genealogy in preindustrial, feudal relations for what by the end of each has turned into the normative, male-headed nuclear family. Each presents family structure and the meaning of femininity and of masculinity as needing to be redefined in newly "modern" terms. In *Bede* and *Esmond*, a magnetic and preemptive drama of heterosexual transgression occasions even as it obscures a transfer of power between classes. And in all three, the tableau of legitimation of "modern" class and gender arrangements is something that takes place on firmly male-homosocial terms: it is a transaction of honor between men over the dead, discredited, or disempowered body of a woman.

I am going in this chapter to be using the two novels, *Henry Esmond* and *Adam Bede*, to embody a dialectic between Marxist-feminist and radical-feminist views of the historicity of women's status in relation to male homosocial desire. In *Adam Bede*, as in any serious historical novel, a trajectory of myth organizes landscapes of sociology. In *Adam Bede*, both the exquisite sociology and the overarching myth have the same catastrophic structure that we have already seen in the Marxist-feminist account of the economic foundations of the gendered middle-class family. Of course, it is more than arguable whether Eliot would have accepted the *disastrous* connotations of the word "catastrophic" to describe this shift. Nevertheless, a (relatively speaking) big bang theory of class and gender foundation is so finely articulated here, that the feminist scholar/professor *moyen marxisante* can comfortably base half of her women's studies survey on this text alone.

The explanatory power of this novel for our current theoretical crux comes from the authority and fullness with which it places its characters in relation to apparently timeless gender roles; but then from the specificity with which it anchors those roles in the productive and conservative economy of particular families at particular nodes of the social fabric; and finally from the resolute directionality with which the mythic plot pushes those families into new relations that, for some of the familial roles, mean extinction, and for others radical and alienating reorganization.

In the survey of preindustrial society at the beginning of the novel, it is of course the Poysers' farm that most strikingly represents the integrated agricultural workplace described by Marxist feminists, in which the spheres of men's work and women's work overlap substantially.[4] Partly because commodities and services rather than cash are the main medium of exchange, the dairy and textile products over whose production Mrs. Poyser reigns are never clearly differentiated as being for domestic use as against market trade. Neither is Mr. Poyser's farming. Not only are the home and the workplace not physically distinct, that is, but the modes of production and consumption that characterize them are very similarly structured and, hence, similarly valued.

Demographically, as well, the Poyser family is very elastic. A muse of cliometry alighting on the hearth would have her evening's work cut out for her in cataloging and categorizing the group. There are three direct generations of the Poyser family; then there are Dinah and Hetty, two nieces, one living there as a guest, but the other as a servant; then there are the real servants and farm-laborers. But again, in this omni-industrious household everyone not only works hard, but works relatively similarly. Surely it matters, economically, whether one is or is not in line to inherit the tenancy of the farm or ownership of the splendid linens; but in a household economy where manual and managerial labor are only barely distinguished, and more importantly where commodities, services, room and board, companionship, and training in skills are exchangeable on a complex market that does not claim to translate them all into one common rationalized measure, the different capacities in which groups of people live or work in the same household do not easily fit into the gross alternatives, "family" and "servant," or again "men's sphere" and "women's sphere." The family in this sense stretches along the axes of both kinship and cohabitation, apparently not reducing either to the terms of the other.[5]

Of course, Mrs. Poyser's personal authority and incisiveness make the warmest of sense in the context of this economically integrated family. She is not sparing of her words, but pointedness rather than diffuseness is their trait: they are pointed because her pointing hand is a visibly consequential one; her say in the production of family goods and power requires no dilation or mystique. In this we could compare her with Lisbeth Bede, Adam's mother, whose speech, by contrast, shows so many of the traits associated by Robin Lakoff[6] with "female language": repetitiousness, querulousness, self-deprecation, insistence on irrelevant details, "anxious humours and irrational persistence," and, in addition, "a sort of wail, the most irritating of all sounds where real sorrows are to be borne, and real work to be done."[7] Her speech is always vexingly beside the point of the "real"—apologetic and defiant at the same time, "at once patient and complaining, self-renouncing and exacting, brooding the live-long day over what happened yesterday, and what is likely to happen tomorrow, and crying very readily both at the good and the evil" (I,4). "But," Eliot adds to this description, as if to contradict herself, "a certain awe mingled itself with her idolatrous love of Adam, and when he said, 'leave me alone,' she was always silenced."

When we first see Lisbeth, she is standing at the door of her house, where she lives with only her husband and sons. She is watching with practiced eyes "the gradually enlarging speck which for the last few minutes she has been quite sure is her darling son Adam" (I,4), on his way home from the shop where he works as a carpenter. Lisbeth, we are told, is a hard worker herself—she knits "unconsciously," she cleans compulsively, she carries pails of water on her head in from the spring. But it is hard not to associate the fearful hemorrhage of authority and consequentiality from her language, with the physical alienation from her household of the male workers and, by the same economic process, of the emerging monetary nexus. The work she performs in the household is descriptively circumscribed as "domestic" and conservative, *as opposed to* economically productive. Her voice, correspondingly, which presents itself as that of maternity, is really that of perceived dependence, of the talking dog: "We are apt to be kinder to the brutes that love us than to the women that love us," here remarks George Eliot (not then known to be a women). "Is it because the brutes are dumb?" (I,4) Mrs. Poyser, too, is an energetic lover of her children, but the fretful category of "the women that love us" could never be applied to her; her language is incapable of irrelevance, because she in *her* home is in a position to create relevance.

Fertile and continuous as the Poysers' arrangement originally looks, and fragile and ill-assorted as the Bedes' does, the basic historical trajectory of *Adam Bede* is to move the novel's normative vision of family from the Poysers' relatively integrated farm to the Bedes' highly specified nuclear household. *As part of this transition*, the normative female role must change from Mrs. Poyser's to one like Mrs. Bede's. By the Epilogue of the novel, no one is left in the Poyser household who seems likely to grow up into Mrs. Poyser; Arthur Donnithorne's only child is, of course, dead; but Dinah and Adam have their baby Adam and their baby Lisbeth, whose function is to refract their parents' and namesakes' values on into the future. Of course, the degree to which the novel is not a feminist one in its *valuations* is clear from the lengths to which it goes to make this change seem palatable; but the full measure of the lengths which, as it also clearly shows, there are to go for that purpose, demonstrates the thoroughness of its feminist *analysis*.

The main vehicle for this change in the normative female role is Dinah Morris. Dinah's career in the novel has been extraordinarily full, not only in its intensity, but in its aptitude for catching up the important strands of women's fate as a gender during this period. Although she is Mrs. Poyser's niece, and one of the inhabitants of the Hall Farm as the novel begins, she is also the only character in the novel who has a direct experience of the concentration of industry: she supports herself by working at a cotton mill in Snowfield. At the same time, she is visiting her aunt at the Hall Farm as part of a round of itinerant Methodist preaching. Dinah's mode of life, then, when the novel begins, seems to exemplify certain promises of individualism and autonomy held out to young working women around the time of the beginning of the industrial revolution. Her pay for the work at the mill is, as she puts it, "enough and to spare" (I,8) for her individual needs; orphaned early, she lives alone by choice; and no institutional constraints, and no very potent ideological ones, seem to offer to interfere with the mobility and resoluteness with which she can publicly dedicate her talents to the cause she has chosen.

Dinah's Methodism, predictably, is a two-edged sword in the service of her autonomy. At the beginning of the novel, though, the terms that Methodism offers the young female preacher seem to be fairly clear and fairly advantageous, even by the standards of a worldly individualism: by offering a heightened submission to a single, divine male authority, omniscient and omnipotent, she is to be able to function on at least equal terms with *all* the creatures, men as well as women, on the reduced plane of the human. The seriousness of her vocation justifies her independence from her aunt's family and her geographical mobility, and it also permits her to decline a very eligible offer of marriage without being subject to undue social pressure to accept. Her eloquence as a preacher is a source of attention, prestige, and great influence for her. The terms in which she describes her eloquence to others, however, always de-emphasize her own control over it:

> "[I]t seemed as if speech came to me without any will of my own, and words were given to me that came out as the tears come, because our hearts are full and we can't help it. . . . But, sir, we are led on, like the little children, by a way that we know not." (I,8)

Or Dinah's exercise of her art and influence may be recuperated through the image of maternal compulsion: she tells Mrs. Poyser,

> "I can no more help spending my life in trying to do what I can for the souls of others, than you could help running if you heard little Totty crying at the other end of the house." (I,7)

Plainly, the price to be paid for the extraordinary authority carried by Dinah's voice, which is public in a way that even Mrs. Poyser's is not, is just the insistence that that voice is the instrument of a higher patriarchal utterance not her own. The source of this authority is so very high, nevertheless, that it gives her for the moment a concrete and potent leverage over mere human men. At this *particular* juncture, that is to say, as so often in history, "patriarchy" is not a monolithic mechanism for subordinating "the female" to "the male"; it is a web of valences and significations that, while deeply tendentious, can historically through its articulations and divisions offer both material and ideological affordances to women as well as to men. "She for God only, he for God in her" seems for a long time to be the structure of Dinah's relationship with at any rate the Methodist men in the novel, and to a large extent with the other men as well. And the power that goes with that position is not a merely circumscribed and transcendent one, but a secular one as well.

But given that the story must end, as Milton's does, with the modern male-dominated nuclear family, what is to be done, ideologically, with a paradise in which Eve was created first and stronger, she for God only, he for God in her? Of course, in novels, that is what love is for. The change in Dinah as she "falls in love" with the impervious Adam begins with the emergence of a new, silent, doglike eros whose only expressive faculty is through the eyes, and whose main erogenous zone is the feather-duster:

> . . . how the duster behaved in Dinah's hand—how it went into every small corner, and on every ledge in and out of sight—how it went again and again round every bar of the chairs, and every leg, and under and over everything that lay on the table, till it came to Adam's papers and rulers, and the open desk near them. Dinah dusted up to the very edge of these, and then hesitated, looking at them with a longing but timid eye. (II,26)

Interestingly, it is only around this part of the novel that the Biblical/ Miltonic associations of Adams's given name, as opposed to the stolid Saxon associations of his surname, begin to become salient in relation to Dinah. This occurs as Dinah begins to ask herself with a new urgency and uncertainty who is, after all, really for God in whom.

> "Nay, Adam; it seems to me that my love for you is not weak; for my heart waits on your words and looks, almost as a little child waits on the help and tenderness of the strong on whom it depends. If the thought of you took slight hold of me, I should not fear that it would be an idol in the temple. But you will strengthen me." II,28)

The scene in which Dinah finally accepts Adam carries this tendency to its extreme, for she seems to hear his voice, not as that of the Biblical Adam, but as God's. He comes upon her climbing a hill:

> It happened that just as he walked forward, Dinah had paused and turned round. . . . Adam was glad; for, with the fine instinct of a lover, he felt that it would be best for her to hear his voice before she saw him. He came within three paces of her and then said, "Dinah!" She started without looking round, as if she connected the sound with no place. "Dinah!" Adam said again. He knew quite well what was in her mind. She was so accustomed to think of impressions as purely spiritual monitions, that she looked for no material visible accompaniment of the voice.
>
> But this second time she looked round. What a look of yearning love it was that the mild grey eyes turned on the strong dark-eyed man! She did not start again at the sight of him; she said nothing, but moved towards him so that his arm could clasp her round. (II,30)

Although earlier in the novel, splits of signification and institutional structure between the heavenly father and the earthly male had offered Dinah the space and leverage for some real power of her own, those enabling gaps are closing up here. In fact, the regime of meaning that had empowered her forms precisely the ground for her present surrender. Dinah finds here that her heavenly Master's voice *is*, simply, Her Master's Voice; now voiceless herself, she can only quiver, whimper, or gaze humidly in response to it.

Importantly, too, the circumscription of Dinah's power and sphere at the end of the novel is far from taking place only in the realm of individual psychology, even though that is where the novel has most scope for making it appear voluntary and exciting. Changes in the composition of the industrial workforce, apparently enforced as much by working men as by capitalists, severely curtailed women's access to well-paid or steady industrial work as the factory system developed during this period, although the novel masks this fact by the assumption that marriage would in any case mean, for Dinah, settling down for good in her husband's village and a cessation of wage work. The novel does make explicit, however, that even had Dinah never married, she would have had to give up the preaching that had been the source of her independence and power, since in 1803 the right to preach was taken away from Methodist women. Chillingly, it is only in Adam's voice, in the Epilogue, that we hear what he claims is Dinah's defense of this rule:

"Most o' the women do more harm nor good with their preaching—they've not got Dinah's gift nor her sperrit; and she's seen that, and she thought it right to set th'example o'submitting. . . . And I agree with her, and approve o' what she did." (II, 374)

Also chillingly, the Epilogue begins with Dinah in just the same canine posture in which we first saw Lisbeth Bede: poised on the threshold of a house, straining her eyes out to catch the first possible glimpse of a returning Adam. In fact, Seth points out the continuity:

"Trust thee for catching sight of him if he's anywhere to be seen. . . . Thee't like poor mother used to be. She was always on the look-out for Adam, and could see him sooner than other folks, for all her eyes got dim." (II, 372)

If one listens to Top-40 radio, one thinks here irresistibly of Sheena Easton's hit from several years ago, "My baby takes the morning train/ He works from nine to five and then/ He takes another home again/ To find me wa-a-a-aiting," with its insinuating whisper between the choruses—"Only when he's with me— I come to life!/ Everything he gives me—makes me feel all right!"[8] That nine-to-five regularization of productive work, as much as its alienation from the household, is an underpinning of the statutory tableau of sphere ideology, in which the woman who cannot venture out of "her" sphere stands poised waiting for the man who, owning it, enters it freely but at regularly foreseeable hours specified by the needs of his own masters.

In fact, an especially incisive although tendentiously handled locus of Eliot's sociology in *Adam Bede* is the growing rationalization, the placing on a basis of measurable and interchangeable units, of male work, as it is increasingly differentiated from the increasingly feminized sphere of the household. The hours are not yet "nine to five," but the very first scene of the novel shows a conflict between a pre-industrial task orientation and a factorylike time discipline: as the church clock strikes six, all the carpenters in the Burge workshop throw down their tools from their unfinished tasks—all but Adam, who chides, "I hate to see a man's arms drop down as if he was shot, before the clock's fairly struck, just as if he'd never a bit o' pride and delight in 's work" (I,1). Adam's ideological appeal here, as often in the novel, is to the values of an individualized, pre-industrial artisanry, in which the maker is unproblematically identified with the artifact, and extracts from it the full value of his labor in it. It is important, though, that Adam is speaking from the position of heir-apparent to Jonathan Burge who owns the workshop, and therefore as a prospective beneficiary of the alienated profits of this more collectivized labor. It makes economic sense *for him* to want to reimpose the now emptied-out values of "pride and delight" in work; but the sharp differentiation made by Wiry Ben, his colleague and soon-to-be-employee, between the time for "work" and the time for "play," corresponds more closely to the immediate, less mystified situation of the salaried workers. Outside the sphere of labor relations, the "stiff and masterful" (I,11) Adam is actually a hero of abstraction and rationalization: he "wrote a beautiful hand that you could read off, and could do the figures in his head—a degree of accomplishment totally unknown among the richest farmers of that countryside" (I,9). And what is perhaps clearest about Adam's personality is how fully it is shaped by the leverage on the world given him by rationalized work.

> "There's nothing but what's bearable as long as a man can work. . . . the natur o' things doesn't change, though it seems as if one's own life was nothing but change. The square o' four is sixteen, and you must lengthen your lever in proportion to your weight, is as true when a man's miserable as when he's happy; and the best o' working is, it gives you a grip hold o' things outside your own lot." (I,11)

In contrast to that, the work of the (diminished) household, now become "women's work," remains stubbornly task-oriented and unrationalized: care of children, the sick, or the elderly cannot stop when the clock strikes, nor does the square root of a potroast give one a grip hold o' things outside her own lot. The result of these historical dislocations of work, as Eliot shows, is that the space and time of women's work are ideologized as not only separate but anachronistic in relation to the realm of "real" work. In other words, the ideological soil for Dinah's relegation to the narrow sphere of "angel in the house" had been amply prepared by her early ministry, but that ministry could have borne very different fruit, as well; it is only on the material ground of catastrophic change in the economic structure and functions—and context—of the family, that her particular worldly relation to the transcendent becomes the engine of so narrow and specialized a fate.

Eliot's choice of the rural artisan class rather than representatives of urban industrialism as the vehicle for her genealogy of the English middle-class family was a shrewd one for her gentle defense of the status quo: as we mentioned in the last chapter, it permits her to suggest that the values of modern industrial society are genetically—and appropriately—individualistic, couched in the mode of private property. Furthermore, the terminological slippage "bourgeois family"–"middle-class family"–"working-class family," a slippage that is both a crucial tool of capitalist ideology *and* a yet-unmet challenge to Marxist analysis,[9] is hand-somely accommodated by Adam's quiet slippage upward from worker to owner, which is much less emphatically presented than the more clearly "historical" shift of his economic base away from personal aristocratic patronage.

So far we have been using *Adam Bede* to exemplify a proto Marxist-feminist view of the inextricability of gender arrangements from economic division. A corollary of that view is that the one-directional development of economic forms toward industrial capitalism in the eighteenth and nineteenth centuries had cor-respondingly deep and irreversible effects on the construction of femininity, and of gender relations, as we now experience them. In *Adam Bede*, the most revealing locus of this change will be the fate of Dinah Morris, as she moves from a position of relative power and independence in a loose relation to an agriculture-based extended family, to a much more circumscribed position as mother of an inten-sively gendered bourgeois nuclear family that is in a marginal relation to the site of economic production.

Henry Esmond, like *The Princess*, while it seems to dramatize a related shift at the level of the transfer of power from the aristocracy to the bourgeoisie, actually, as we shall see, grounds this apparent shift in a preexistent division of power and roles between men and women, the structure and content of which are already those of the bourgeois nuclear family. Because it shows a relatively constant form of gender division and subordination as *presiding* over historical change in other areas, *Henry Esmond* is perhaps most appropriately considered a proto radical-feminist novel. The main locus in the novel for the reproduction and conservation of gender roles and of male ascendancy is the question of female sexuality. Female sexuality itself, however, is meaningful in the novel chiefly within the context of the exchange of power and of symbolic goods between men; and the scene of female sexuality, whether it be that of the virgin or of the whore, seems regularly and fittingly to end, with the banishment of the woman, in an "affair of honor" between men.

Eliot chooses the rural artisan class for her mythic genealogy of the family; Thackeray has a very different idea. The characters in *Henry Esmond* come from a different class and play for much higher stakes—Earldoms and Marquisates. In some important respects, however, the basic trajectory is the same. In each novel, at any rate, the perceived norm moves from a demographically elastic, untidy family led by an incisive woman, to a small, well-defined family led by a man, and in which the woman's role is both economically undercut and intensively and circumscriptively moralized.

In *Henry Esmond*, a family that begins as rakish, reactionary, Catholic, Jacobite aristocracy, in the picturesque and (in this rendering) chivalric England of Queen Anne, turns within a few years to a piously Protestant, Whiggish, obsessionally domestic home circle of, essentially, solid mid-Victorian citizens.[10] Isabel, the dominant woman of the first, Jacobite family, had been one of those old women in whom Thackeray specialized: a childless selfish Catholic pagan matriarch, powerful, wealthy, semiliterate, with the ruins of beauty and coquetry, a checkered and fairly explicit sexual history, and absolutely no natural ingredients. Rachel, the normative mother of the final family, on the other hand, joys in nursing her loved ones back to health, uses no makeup, studies foreign literatures in her spare time (although "she was a critic, not by reason but by feeling"),[11] is sexually both repressive and possessive to an almost murderous or suicidal degree, has no money of her own . . . in short, the beloved, avenging Angel in the House.

The actual historical legitimation of this new family and new female role in *Henry Esmond* is more graphic and explicit than in *Adam Bede*, because the aristocratic siting of the tale makes familial legitimacy a more available image.[12] Henry Esmond, the new paterfamilias, legitimates the new form of family in two ways: first, he turns out, unexpectedly, to *be*, not a bastard as had been thought, but the legitimate heir to the family's title, the 5th Viscount Castlewood; but second, from that position of power he renounces the title and withdraws from the aristocratic world, symbolically casting his lot instead with the future, with the more modest and private values of the respectable bourgeoisie.

It is characteristic of Thackeray's bravado to underline the historicism of his myth of familial history by intertwining it with genuine world-historical events and persons—world-historical at least at the summer-stock or touring-company level. Most notably, the Jacobitism that is the badge of the old aristocratic values and gender roles is called into question in the very concrete form of the Pretender James Edward. The climactic night when the Pretender squanders, for a sexual adventure, his chance to succeed Queen Anne on the English throne marks the very moment that Henry Esmond becomes a Whig, and the very moment that his plans and desires fall conclusively on Rachel. Surely here, if anywhere, is a portrayal of the bourgeois family as the result of the catastrophic, one-way devolution of the forces of class conflict.

But so much that is most Thackeray in the novel goes in another direction. The problem here is not that he is not a feminist. Of course Thackeray was no more a feminist than David Ricardo was a communist; but Thackeray, like George

Eliot, was an inspired specialist in the analysis of gender roles as forms of power, and for that reason it behooves feminists to situate our theoretical formulations in some intelligible relation to their findings. The contradiction in *Henry Esmond* is something more oblique: that for all the novel's finely wrought thematization of historical change in gender relations, the feminism that its analysis truly prefigures is instead the radical and *a*historical critique of patriarchy. If anything, the structure of other kinds of political change is itself subordinated to what is seen as the stable and self-reproducing structure of the gendered family.

For instance, the *The Virginians*, the sequel to *Henry Esmond*, one character says, "Every woman is a Tory at heart. Pope says a rake, but I think t'other is the more charitable word."[13] The remark is symptomatic of Thackeray's insistent yoking-together of the sexual and the political, so that "rake" and "Tory" become exchangeable quantities. No less symptomatic, though, is his fondness for the "*every* woman is—" formulation to begin with; and its effect in turn is to dehistoricize, and hence *de*politicize, the term "Tory," so that political parties themselves come to represent not a struggle of interests but an assignment of static personality types. Besides, one might ask, if *Henry Esmond* showed the once-and-for-all weaning-away of the modern bourgeois family from forms of sexuality and gender relations shaped by a "reactionary" feudalism, then why, in this novel that is its sequel, are we hearing once again about the "naturally" reactionary sexuality of women? And the embarrassments posed by the later novel to the earlier one are only beginning with this question; for from start to finish, *The Virginians* is only an explicit reprise, in the terms of cynical farce, of the grave drama that had first been played, in the terms of catastrophe, in the novel set two generations before.[14]

In fact, what makes *Esmond* plausible as a great *historical* novel, as a novel in which something changes, is only the cleverness with which it is framed, with which it seems to show us that its events happen and could happen only once. But as *The Virginians* makes clear, a slip of the frame, by which *Esmond* might have ended a few years later, or even only a few weeks later, would have shown the dead alive again, lost reputations found or done without, the shattered pitcher back at the well for more. *Henry Esmond* shows us the pastoral cat let out of the bag; *The Virginians* offers us, so to speak, the Cats Repastured. Yet oddly, the great strength of *Esmond*, not as a historical novel perhaps but as a novel of gender constitution, is exactly here, in its presentation of gender roles as things that cannot help but reproduce themselves. If *Adam Bede* offers a sociology of sexual change, *Henry Esmond* is almost in spite of itself an analysis of the mechanisms of sexual continuity.

The great question of *Henry Esmond* seems, as we have said, to be whether the modern family will keep the raffish "reactionary" shape of the Jacobite feudal aristocracy, with its loose ends of both male and female power, filiation, and desire, or take on the tighter and chaster form that is seen as appropriate to bourgeois work and values. The most dramatic form in which this apparent question is enacted is the choice that Henry himself has to make between two women: Rachel, who, as we have seen, already embodies the new-style angel in the house; and her daughter Beatrix, who takes after her aunt Isabel and is growing up to be hell on wheels in the promiscuous old style. (By the time of *The Virginians*, it is patent that Beatrix, with age, has quite simply turned into Isabel.) Now, so far as *Esmond* merely dramatizes the terms of a single moment of choice, it does pose and enact this historical crux of the family. But as a novel that moves through time, even aside from its relation to *The Virginians*, it does something quite different: it shows, with extraordinary continuity and force, old-style Beatrix *as* the daughter of new-style Rachel. The kind of woman Beatrix turns into is both so brilliantly the result of her mother's style of nurturance, and at the same time so clearly the mirror of the ancien regime of femininity whose overthrow *by* her mother it is the novel's apparent purpose to record, that one is left with the image, not of determinate historical change, but of a self-reproducing and incessant narrative of schism within femininity itself, unraveling backwards into the past.

Thackeray's great, inexhaustible subject is the poetry of the unhappy family, but the accent must be on *the* unhappy family. They are not exactly all alike, but the lines of conflict and the personality conformations seem most often to reflect the Victorian bourgeois family, even when the setting of time, rank, place, or even demographic composition might suggest something very different. So that even the household of Rachel's first marriage, when she is Viscountess of Castlewood, with an extended entourage that includes, among others, the chaplain's entire family and the apparently illegitimate son of her husband's cousin, is pure Biedermeier: the inner enforcing mechanism of sphere ideology is firmly in place in her. Her unhappiness is in the first place about her husband's absences from home; her consolations come through cultivation of mind and soul, and these inevitably divide her ever more completely from her husband's sphere of physical action and physical pleasure; her most piercing emotions are attached to jealousy and to the suppression or concealment of sexual desire (I,7; I,11). It is made explicit that her jealousy is caused by the accurate perception of a simple scarcity of love or power available to women (I,11; I,13); and responding to this scarcity, Rachel in turn, although as an idealized mother she is supposed to be an *embodiment* of familial love, turns out to be a cripplingly narrow channel for it (Preface, p.7). Rachel not only monopolizes the love of the men around her, but reserves all *her* love for *them*—first for her husband and son, but soon for Henry Esmond, the saturnine little changeling in the domestic nest. Beatrix, in adulthood, says in one of her revelatory outbursts to Henry,

> "she cares more for Frank's little finger than she does for me—I know she does: and she loves you, sir, a great deal too much; and I hate you for it. I would have had her all to myself; but she wouldn't. In my childhood, it

was my father she loved—(oh, how could she? I remember him kind and handsome, but so stupid, and not being able to speak after drinking wine). And then it was Frank; and now, it is heaven and the clergyman. How I would have loved her! From a child I used to be in a rage that she loved anybody but me; but she loved you all better—all, I know she did." (III,3)

In a family whose first principle is a radical cleavage of concerns between father and mother, bridged only by the mother's jealousy, Beatrix is taught early to feel jealousy—which, "if spoken in the presence of Lord Castlewood, tickled and amused his humour; he would pretend to love Frank best, and dandle and kiss him, and roar with laughter at Beatrix's jealousy" (I,8). Unlike her mother, however, and under the tutelage of her seductive father, Beatrix learns not only to feel jealousy, but to manipulate it in others.

She had long learned the value of her bright eyes, and tried experiments in coquetry. . . . not a little to . . . the joy of her father, who laughed his great laugh, and encouraged her in her thousand antics. Lady Castlewood watched the child gravely and sadly. . . . From her mother's sad looks she fled to her father's chair and boozy laughter. She already set the one against the other: and the little rouge delighted in the mischief which she knew how to make so early. (I,11)

Beatrix's sexual manipulativeness will prove, however, not only a necessary strategy for survival in the gendered family, but at the same time the grounds for the denial to her of love and authority within the same family.

In short, the first brilliance of *Henry Esmond* is to show with apparently timeless authority, in a past tense that keeps turning to present tense, and through a third-person that keeps turning to the first person, the process by which the virgin and the whore beget each other. Thackeray's description is remarkable for not depending on any crudely hydraulic channeling of a reified substance called Sexual Desire, be it male or female: that is, men do not turn some women into whores because they have turned others into virgins but still require their natural quota of sexual discharge; nor do women split between a virginal superego that says no and a whorish id that is raring to go. Instead, in an analysis that strikingly dramatizes some recent feminist readings of Freud (see Introduction ii and iii, and chapter 1 [of *Between Men*]), Thackery depicts sexuality as a highly charged and volatile signifier for differentials of power that take their shape from the social/political concommitants of gender difference. Specifically, both woman-as-virgin and woman-as-whore take on sexual significance within the context of circulation, exchange, and the gift; and what women make of women, as moral or social creatures but most signally as sexual creatures, occurs primarily (though not exclusively) under the pressure of a signifying relation in which both the sender and the intended recipient of the message are male.

Beatrix's erotic situation is an exquisitely detailed double bind. We can begin (but *only* begin) by examining the female homosocial bond in which it seems most immediately to reside. The most sustained and consistent and (at least after the first reading) dramatically visible pressure of desire in *Henry Esmond* is that of Rachel, her mother, for Henry himself. But Rachel's desire occurs entirely within, and in the terms of, the enforcing familial dichotomies of prohibition/transgression, fidelity/infidelity, repression/revelation; if it is potentially subversive of those, it subverts them only from within, and therefore silently, apolitically, and in a mode that permits no solidarity with other women. Thus, although—extraordinarily—her mother's desire for Henry is fully visible to Beatrix, it offers no legitimation to any desires of her own. Instead, the moralistic discourse which the mother silently though agonistically circumvents in her own life is imposed all the more monolithically on the daughter. Beatrix's situation is like Satan's or the Frankenstein monster's: Satan wants only what God wants (and has), but because God writes the lexicon of good and evil, Satan in laying claim to his desires is reduced to two unsatisfactory alternatives: first, a belated, servile, secondhand acquiescence in "the good," which can not get him what he wants, or second, a posing of himself in opposition to God ("Evil be thou my good"[15]), in terms that because they are already taken from God's lexicon put him in an unstable semiotic situation that is bound to degenerate in terms ripe for moralization. In each case, Beatrix's and Satan's, the disabling, unadmitted split between the parental practice and the prescriptive parental definitions is the same, and the two adult children share a similar range of tones among the plangent, the hollow/defiant, and the abject (e.g., III,3; III,7). What is different is that Rachel, as a woman, is not the author of her lexicon nor even an important beneficiary of it. Instead, although this excruciating woman-to-woman relationship is the novel's great distinction, it functions as only half of a scissors mechanism, holding poor Beatrix and her would-be sexuality against the far sharper blade of male homosocial desire.

What is the situation of the men in the novel? In contrast to the mixed messages that Beatrix gets, and the room for (need for) manipulation between the male and female parental spheres, "The young heir of Castlewood," at any rate, "was spoiled by father and mother both. He took their caresses as men do, as if they were his right" (I,11). After his father's death, Frank takes over his father's role of describing Beatrix to herself "indulgently" in the most damagingly sexualized terms; he both promotes her, and reserves the right always to condemn her, as someone who manipulates her sexual allure to advantage. "Look who comes here!—ho, ho! . . . 'Tis Mistress Trix, with a new riband; I knew she would put one on as soon as she heard a captain was coming to supper" (II,7). Rachel, as we have seen, displays the same rapidity in crystallizing her damning judgment of the traits in which she has educated her daughter; but it is perhaps less damaging because less genial, obtuse, and impersonal, the vessel of jealousy in her throbbing so close to the translucent surface of ethical judgment (e.g., II,8; II,15; III,3).

In fact, Henry himself plays the same game with Beatrix: what he defines as *lovable* in her is exactly the same catalog of traits that he defines as morally damning, and to which he holds out a contrast in her mother (e.g., II,15); so that his erotic servitude to her, compulsive as it feels, exists only on the ground of a more or less willed suspension of judgment, a judgment with which he is always free to threaten her and which he finally allows to descend on her with extraordinary punitive force.

As I have suggested, the whipsaw noose of condemning women and desiring them for exactly the same traits is drawn tightest in certain triangular transactions for women between men. The prototype of this transaction in *Esmond* has occurred early in the novel: in Rachel's position in the middle of her first husband's passionate friendship for the dissolute Lord Mohun. Castlewood's infatuation is sudden and imperious, "my Lord Castlewood kissing the other lord before he mounted on horseback, and pronouncing him the best companion he had met for many a long day";

> and when my Lady said there was something free in the Lord Mohun's looks and manner of speech which caused her to mistrust him, her lord burst out with one of his laughs and oaths; said . . . that Mohun was the prettiest fellow in England; . . . and that he would let Mohun know what my Lady Prude said of him. (I,12)

Determining that "Mohun is the best fellow in England; and I'll invite him here, just to plague that . . . frigid insolence" (I,12), Castlewood asserts his mastery over his wife by thrusting her at his friend, who, once arrived,

> was no sooner in his nightcap and dressing-gown than he had another visitor whom his host insisted on sending to him: and this was no other than the Lady Castlewood herself with the toast and gruel, which her husband bade her make and carry with her own hands in to her guest. (I,13)

Needless to say, although there seems to be no serious threat to Rachel's physical fidelity as far as her own feelings are concerned, this triangular relationship becomes a dangerously freighted conduit of all kinds of apparently exchangeable symbolic goods: of money in the form of Castelwood's gambling debts to Mohun, of religion in the form of Rachel's desire to reform Mohun, of sexual one-upmanship in the form of Mohun's desire to cuckold Castlewood. The result is a duel in which Rachel becomes a widow, even though her husband has had no serious doubts about her fidelity.

> "Did I ever doubt that she was pure? It would have been the last day of her life when I did. Do you fancy I think that *she* would go astray? No, she hasn't passion enough for that. She neither sins nor forgives. I know her temper—and now I've lost her, by Heaven I love her ten thousand times more than ever I did—yes, when she was young and beautiful as an angel— . . . when she used to look with her child more beautiful, by George, than the Madonna in the Queen's Chapel. I am not good like her, I know it. . . . And I felt she didn't belong to me: and the children don't. And I besotted myself, and gambled, and drank, and took to all sorts of devilries out of despair and fury." (I,14)

With these words, Castlewood at the end of his life makes clear that it is exactly her purity, the commodity that made the whole point of his thrusting her at Mohun in the first place, that is at the same time the ground of her value for him and the ground of his continuing, and now conclusive, abandonment of her.

Just as Rachel's sexual *goodness* both takes on exchange value, and becomes a strangling double bind for her, in the context of an intense, transactive homosocial desire between men, so Beatrix's sexual *badness* is activated in the same ways by the same male homosocial structure. We have seen how her brother Frank both promotes and criticizes her carefully nurtured aptitude for judicious flirtations; but he does more than that. When Beatrix seems in a position to make an advantageous match with his friend, the young Lord Blandford, Frank acts as an aggressive go-between, giving Blandford a lock of her hair, extorting a signed avowal of love from him, and threatening Blandford with a duel if he does not acknowledge the Castlewood family to be worthy of his hand; though at the same time, Frank feels free to condemn "Trix" for her worldliness in affairs of the heart (II,8).

The political climax of the novel, the crisis of the Jacobite plot, is also the climax of this plot that founds Beatrix's sexuality in a detour of male homosocial desire. The Castlewood family's involvement with the dynastic claims of the Stuarts is long-standing, and has historically been expressed through the gift of women, for instance in the form of Isabel's sexual services to Charles II and his brother (I,2). The strands that tie Beatrix's menfolk to the young Pretender are complicated; but among them is Henry's determination that his suit for Beatrix will "stand or fall" (III,8) by the success of his scheme to smuggle James Edward into England and onto the throne; while the scheme itself depends on James Edward's sharing a birthday with Frank Castlewood, resembling him physically, having his portrait painted as Frank, and finally impersonating him. The prospective rewards for this exploit would include James's retroactive ability to make good the marquisate secretly granted by his father to the Castlewood family; as well as, Henry thinks, Beatrix's ultimate acceptance of himself.

Impelled by this intoxicating blend of upwardly mobile personal identification, romantic patriotism, family tradition, political ambition, and sexual desire, Henry and Frank smuggle the young prince into the Castlewood household. Henry watches the women's preparations for him with approval:

> The chamber was ornamented with flowers; the bed covered with the very finest of linen; the two ladies insisting on making it themselves, and kneeling down at the bedside and kissing the sheets out of respect for the web that was to hold the sacred person of a King. (III,9)

What is more, it is arranged that the ladies themselves will wait on the young visitor; and when he arrives, Beatrix is wearing the family diamonds given to her by Esmond, for "it had been agreed between them, that she should wear these brilliants on the day when the King should enter the house, and a queen she looked, radiant in charms, and magnificent and imperial in beauty" (III,9).

Of course, no sooner have the Castlewood men succeeded, through their exertions both practical and imaginative, in bringing this "King" and "Queen" together in the service of Castlewood family ambitions, than the terrified scapegoating of female sexuality begins.

> She appeared . . . radiant, and with eyes bright with a wonderful lustre. A pang, as of rage and jealousy, shot through Esmond's heart, . . . and he clenched his hand involuntarily, and looked across to Castlewood, whose eyes answered his alarm-signal, and were also on the alert. (III,9)

And that night,

> "I have done the deed," thought [Esmond], sleepless, and looking out into the night; "he is here, and I have brought him; he and Beatrix are sleeping under the same roof now. Whom did I mean to serve in bringing him? Was it the Prince? was it Henry Esmond? . . ." The eager gaze of the young Prince, watching every movement of Beatrix, haunted Esmond and pursued him. The Prince's figure appeared before him in his feverish dreams many times that night. (III,9)

Spurred by his jealousy, Henry finally leads Frank and Rachel in a horrifying, irreparable scene of not-quite-accusation of Beatrix, aimed at getting her out of London and "harm's way." Her denunciations of them are wrenching and undeniable: to Henry she says "you are the chief of the conspiracy against me"; "I give back these family diamonds, which belonged to one king's mistress, to the gentleman that suspected I would be another"; to Frank, "Keep your oaths, my lord, for your wife"; to her mother,

> "Farewell, mother; I think I never can forgive you; something hath broke

> between us that no tears nor years can repair. I always said I was alone:
> you never loved me, never—and were jealous of me from the time I sat
> on my father's knee." (III,10)

No wonder the victors in this scene are left "scared, and almost ashamed of our victory. It did seem hard and cruel that we should have conspired the banishment and humiliation of that fair creature. We looked at each other in silence."

In the upshot, Beatrix is proved to be indeed the whore she has been made into. With a note hidden in *Eikon Basilike*, she tempts the Prince out to the place of her imprisonment, on what by coincidence turns out to be the very night that he most needs to be in London; and the damnation pronounced on her character by each member of the remaining family is entirely beyond appeal. None of them ever sees her again. Interestingly, however, the generations-long male homosocial transaction, in which this destructive heterosexual relationship had been a brief detail, proves at this juncture more durable—even, within certain terms, *successful*. Henry, as head of the family, angry at the Pretender, formally renounces the Castlewood family's fealty to the Stuart succession, and there is a brief, formal gesture that represents a duel; after which Esmond

> falling back a step dropped his point with another very low bow, and de-
> clared himself perfectly satisfied.
> "Eh bien, Vicomte," says the young Prince, who was a boy, and a
> French boy, "il ne nous reste qu'une chose a faire": he placed his sword
> upon the table, and the fingers of his two hands upon his breast:—"We
> have one more thing to do," says he; "you do not divine it?" He stretched
> out his arms:—"*Embrassons nous!*" (III,13)

If this male embrace does not represent the triumph of the Castlewood ambitions in the anticipated, Jacobite, form, it does however ratify a more authoritative social foundation. It represents the ultimate moral legitimation, the passing on of the torch of history from the discredited old order to Henry Esmond and the small, male-headed, prescriptively gendered bourgeois nuclear family that he seems about to found. This tableau of bonding, in which an aristocratic male hands over his moral authority to a newly bourgeois male, over the sexually discredited body of a woman, offers an arresting image of what appears to be a distinct historical moment of class foundation. Its apparent historical distinctness is, however, in the context of this novel, apparently illusory; since, as we have seen, the transhistorical structure by which female sexuality itself is defined and reproduced, and used and discredited, is condensed in exactly the same triangular and male-homosocial terms, which the novel also shows as repetitious and incessant.

Explicit in our discussion of the not-quite historical genealogies of femininity in *Henry Esmond* and *The Princess* has been a focus on what we have treated as a transhistorical, or perhaps more problematically ahistorical, triangular structure of male exchange of women. Even when we look in our proto "Marxist-feminist" historical novel for "radical-feminist" sexual structure, however, we have not far to go. In *Adam Bede*, the signally sexual plot is the one around Hetty. Like the Jacobite plot of *Henry Esmond*, too, this one culminates in what I have been describing as a tableau of male homosocial bonding—"in which an aristocratic male [Arthur in this case] hands over his moral authority to a newly bourgeois male [Adam], over the sexually discredited body of a woman [Hetty]." This scene in *Adam Bede*, which is the last in the novel and in fact occurs offstage, has the same claims as the *Henry Esmond* scene to being historically constitutive: its ideological purpose is clearly to ratify the authority of the bourgeois male both in economic/political terms, and as head of the emerging nuclear family. In each novel, however, the supposedly foundational nature of this tableau is undermined because it occurs, for one reason or another, ex post facto. In *Henry Esmond* it is ex post facto because the entire, generations-long chain of events that has led up to it has apparently all along been shaped by almost exactly the same forms of almost exactly the same divisions that are supposedly just now being constituted. In *Adam Bede*, it is ex post facto because the novel in its other plot, the Dinah plot, has already done such a careful job of siting these changes—*as* changes—historically in economic and demographic terms.

Thus the specifically sexual power plot of each novel, though it may seem substantively to echo or mirror the more overtly political plot of historical gender and class relations, does so in a form that is temporally both displaced and condensed. In other words, as we have already discussed in section ii of the Introduction [in *Between Men*], sex as such not only resembles and conveys but represents power, including—but not only—the power relations of gender. This signifying relation of sex to the various forms of power is very intimate and often direct, but it is neither simple nor innocent.

Even the condensation alone of a sexual plot, in the context of a directly historical fiction, can be wildly tendentious. Let me exemplify this briefly in terms of the marriage plots, the plots of family foundation, that we have already treated in *Adam Bede*, *The Princess*, and *Henry Esmond*. In each of these fictions the condensed evolution of the family proceeds at such a clip, and the "accidents" of the story are arranged in such a way, that each hero "happens" to marry a woman who appears at a crucial moment to be more powerful than he is: Rachel because she is, to all intents and purposes, Henry Esmond's mother; Dinah because Adam is shattered over Hetty's fate, and because her own religious mandate has temporarily let her seem to represent an authority more forceful and patriarchal even than his own; Princess Ida because she is more single-minded, more passionate, more educated, more eloquent, more emotionally forceful, and of course, at the end, much healthier than the Prince. Like Princess Ida, Rachel in *Esmond* has fallen in love with, while nursing, a delirious, utterly dependent invalid who appeared to be dying. Dinah, in *Bede*, imagining her religious power to be inalienable, has fallen in love with a man who bitterly needs her consolations. In each case, it has been the woman who has appeared to be *more* closely tied to the sources of political, intellectual, material, and/or rhetorical authority. The watchword of Ida's feminism is "Better not be at all / Than not be noble"[16]—and when she first propounds this doctrine, its ethical meaning is firmly tied to its grounding in political power.

Of course, each of these forms of apparent power is destined to undergo a direct translation into a form of bourgeois female powerlessness. The physical vigor of the healthy survivor becomes the humility of the nurse. The vocal authority of the preacher becomes the marginality of the religious quietist. The political clout of the nobility becomes the paralysis of the ethically "noble" (i.e., silent) Victorian heroine. However, for the brief moment of the genealogical fiction, the transaction by which the woman binds herself over to the man, which is presented in each of these fictions as coinciding with the transaction by which the feudal order gives over to the bourgeois—for that brief moment, the transaction appears to be between a woman so powerful, and a man so powerless, that no subsequent use of the power that has been ceded to the man could ever endanger the woman's interests.

And indeed the language of transcendence that continued to disguise the relative powerlessness of bourgeois women kept the same ideological shape: the power of women was assigned the same metaphysical, superstitious, ungrounded status that was supposed also, in the nineteenth century, to inhere in the power of the hereditary aristocracy. In each case, the *displacement* of power relations onto a historical fiction of class relations, and their temporal *condensation* in an erotic narrative, was a way of rationalizing gender inequality, and other inequalities, in the face of an egalitarian public rhetoric.

One important result of this mutual mapping onto each other of class and gender was that bourgeois women became publicly allegorized, in mystifying and for the most part disempowering ways, as representing the traits of a class higher than their husbands'. Women's sexuality, in these marriage plots, has been the space of a chiasmic switching between gender and class power. As in our ideological archetype "A man's home is his castle" (Introduction iii [of *Between Men*]), an archaizing image of control—in these cases condensed as the women's disposal of their own bodies—has been used as a cover under which the material grounds of that control can be prospectively withdrawn.

The more signally, because transgressively, *sexual* plots of the two historical novels—the Beatrix and Hetty plots—display this figure even more insistently. As we have noted, each sexual plot can seem to represent a transhistorical, graphic absolute of Structure: the triangular traffic in women, that busy, transactive stasis that is the setpiece of every form of structuralism. At the same time, however, it

is important that these transactions in the two novels occur within a fictive, tendentious, but none the less historically meaningful and purposeful, European class
discourse about the vicissitudes of aristocratic *droit de seigneur*. The class discourse
of "seduction," here, is distinct from for instance the discourse of rape that has
insistently characterized American racism (see Introduction ii [of *Between Men*]).

The frame called sexuality in these historical myths offers a privileged space
for the emptying and filling of "external" forms with profoundly and specifically
manipulative meanings. The mechanism of this, in the transgressively sexual plots,
is easy to see. It is the crossing by which women like Hetty and Beatrix enter
into sexuality, not as an avenue to pleasure but as the only avenue to power; and
emerge from it, far more abject and denuded of power, retroactively identified as
embodiments of sexuality itself. This plot is familiar from *Paradise Lost*. For each
woman, the sexual narrative occurs with the overtaking of an active search for
power of which she is the *subject*, by an already-constituted symbolic power exchange between men of which her very misconstruction, her sense of purpose-
fulness, proves her to have been the designated *object*.

This crossing of subjects within "female" sexuality is congruent with Freud's
account of the retroactive constitution of individual sexuality itself.[17] Historically,
as well, however, the very inclusions and definitions of the sexual are variable and
themselves political. In a sense, none of the plots we have discussed is a sexual
one: the marriage plots are about marriage, an institution, hence clearly economic
and political, while the heroines of the "sexual" plots are both clearly described
as being sexually numb, but ambitious. Conversely, look at the relationships that
embody what we have been calling here "male homosocial desire"—between
Adam and Arthur, say, or between the Prince and Florian, or between the Prince
and the tight band of men who "speak" him, or between Castlewood and Mohun,
or between all the Castlewood men and their Stuart hero. Political as these relationships clearly are, fraught with the exchange of every kind of symbolic, economic, and cultural meaning and power, each relationship also could be—not
only theoretically, but under different historical configurations might have been—
classified as sexual, and for reasons themselves tendentious. In such a case, not
only the prestige but the "heterosexual" force, the power of these men and these
bonds to organize the lives of women, could have been compromised and qualitatively changed, even had the relationships themselves been exactly the same.

From a twentieth-century American perspective, however, these three mainstream early- and mid-Victorian texts, unlike the paranoid Gothic texts discussed
in chapters 5 and 6 [of *Between Men*], seem not to engage the homosex-
ual/homophobic division of the male homosocial spectrum in especially marked
ways. Each treats the compulsory routing of homosocial desire through heterosexual love more or less as a matter of course. Nevertheless, in each text that
routing is both stressful and heavily freighted with political meaning. Perhaps the
most generalizable and important for our ongoing narrative is this: that in the

presence of a woman who can be seen as pitiable or contemptible, men are able to exchange power and to confirm each other's value even in the context of the remaining inequalities in their power. The sexually pitiable or contemptible female figure is a solvent that not only facilitates the relative democratization that grows up with capitalism and cash exchange, but goes a long way—for the men whom she leaves bonded together—toward palliating its gaps and failures.

NOTES

1. On this see, for instance, Michelle Zimbalist Rosaldo, "Women, Culture, and Society: A Theoretical Overview," in *Women, Culture, and Society,* ed. Michelle Z. Rosaldo and Louise Lamphere (Stanford: Stanford University Press, 1974), pp. 17–42.

2. Joan Kelly-Gadol, "The Social Relation of the Sexes: Methodological Implications of Women's History," *Signs* 1.4 (1976), p. 819.

3. My formulations here are most directly indebted to the incisive survey of this ground in Michèl Barrett, *Women's Oppression Today: Problems in Marxist Feminist Analysis* (London: Verso, 1980), pp. 160–86.

4. For example, Nancy Chodorow summarizes this argument: "In precapitalist and early capitalist times, the household was the major productive unit of society. Husband and wife, with their own and/or other children, were a cooperative producing unit. A wife carried out her childcare responsibilities along with her productive work, and these responsibilities included training girls—daughters, servants, apprentices—for their work. Children were early integrated into the adult world of work. . . . Until very recently, women everywhere participated in most forms of production. Production for the home was in, or connected to, the home." ("Mothering, Male Dominance, and Capitalism," in *Capitalist Patriarchy and the Case for Socialist Feminism,* ed. Zillah Eisenstein (New York: Monthly Review Press, 1979). p. 88.)

5. On this two-axis understanding of the family, see Barrett, *Women's Oppression,* pp. 200–3.

6. Robin Lakoff, *Language and Women's Place,* (New York: Harper & Row, 1975), esp. pp. 53–57. My understanding of the bearings of "women's language" is additionally derived from William M. O'Barr and Bowman K. Atkins, " 'Women's Language' or 'Powerless Language'?" in *Women and Language in Literature and Society,* ed. Sally McConnell-Ginet, Ruth Borker, and Nelly Furmin (New York: Praeger, 1980), esp. p. 96.

7. George Eliot, *Adam Bede,* Illustrated Cabinet Edition, 2 vols. (Boston: Dana Estes, n.d.), vol. I, ch. 4, p. 52. Further citations will be incorporated in the text and designated by volume and chapter number. (Vol. I of this two-volume edition ends with ch. 34.)

8. Unichappell Music BMI, © 1980, 1981 EMI Records, Ltd.

9. For more on this see Jeffrey Weeks, "Capitalism and the Organisation of

Sex," pp. 11–20 in *Homosexuality: Power and Politics*, ed. Gay Left Collective (London: Allison & Busby, 1980), esp. pp. 14–15.

10. John Sutherland's brief but suggestive description of Henry Esmond himself as both "eighteenth-century man" and nineteenth-century man," in his Introduction to the Penguin Edition (Hammondsworth, Sussex, 1970), pp. 20–21, along with Harry Shaw's discussion cited below, offer a useful, male-centered counterpart to the feminist historical argument.

11. William Makepeace Thackeray, *The History of Henry Esmond, Esq. Written by Himself*, Biographical Edition (New York: Harper, 1903), Bk. I, ch. 9, p. 89. Further citations will be incorporated in the text and designated by book and chapter numbers.

12. A good discussion of the general problems of *Henry Esmond's* historicity, which however fails to question the historical status of femininity and the family in the novel, is in Harry E. Shaw, *The Forms of Historical Fiction: Sir Walter Scott and His Successors* (Ithaca: Cornell University Press, 1983), pp. 56–70.

13. William Makepeace Thackeray, *The Virginians*, Biographical Edition, New York: Harper, 1899), ch. 22.

14. For a related formulaton of the relationship between the two novels, see Jack P. Rawlins, *Thackeray's Novels: A Fiction That Is True* (Berkeley: University of California Press, 1974), p. 190.

15. Milton, *Paradise Lost*, iv, 1. 110.

16. Alfred, Lord Tennyson, *The Princess: A Medley*, ii, 79–80.; in *The Poems of Tennyson*, ed. Christopher Ricks (London: Longmans, 1969).

17. See Introduction ii–iii, and, for instance, Jean Laplanche and J.-B. Pontalis, "Deferred Action; Deferred," in *The Language of Psychoanalysis*, tr. Donald Nicholson-Smith (New York: Norton, 1973), pp. 111–14.

13

MISMĀR GOHA: THE ARAB CHALLENGE TO CULTURAL DEPENDENCY

BARBARA HARLOW

Goha is a popular figure of folk wit and people's humor throughout the Arab world. Known as Si Djeha in Morocco or Djuha in Palestine and Syria, Goha has long animated the jokes and fables told in Egypt, where he often triumphs over superior odds by his sheer cleverness and wiles. The story of "Goha's nail" (*mismār Goha*) has widespread currency. According to this story, Goha offered his house for sale, but attached one condition: that he retain ownership of just one of the nails in the house. This condition did not dissuade the prospective purchaser at the time, but he was surprised somewhat later when Goha appeared at the door of his house, asking to check on his nail. Whatever his misgivings, the owner allowed Goha to see to the safety of his nail. Goha, for his part reassured, departs, only to return a few weeks afterward in the midst of a severe storm, this time with his blanket, and requesting now to spend the night guarding his nail from any elemental threat. Soon Goha has moved back into the house, lodging there as the permanent custodian of his nail. The story of *mismār Goha* was used by the Egyptian journalist Fikri Abaza in an editorial in the 1950s to describe the Egyptian reaction to the British offer to evacuate Egypt, on the condition that they retain their base in the Suez Canal.[1] Eventually "Goha's nail" came to represent in the Arab popular political imagination any attempt by the dominant Western powers to maintain, however discreetly or blatantly, their active presence in the Arab Middle East.

Popular humor is often introduced as political critique in all parts of the Arab world, and *mismār Goha* resonates as such a critique, from Morocco to Saudi Arabia, in Palestine no less than in Egypt. Even given the different circumstances of independence and local postindependence development, the Western powers, in particular the United States, continue to exert powerful military, economic, political, and cultural control over the contemporary Arab world—like Goha, retaining many nails in the Arab house. If "Goha's nail" circulates widely across the Middle East as a proverb or joke, it is also reformulated on multiple levels and in a variety of disciplinary vocabularies by Arab intellectuals, writers, and political theorists. In seminars, journals, novels, and stories, the issue of economic dependency and its correlate of cultural dependency figures critically in determining the ideological parameters of debate, its narrative forms and thematic paradigms. This debate, however, which contests insistently the supremacist imposition of Western militarism, technology, and marketing practices, furthermore represents the complex heterogeneity of political and theoretical positions within the Arab world. While thus acknowledging for their part the significance of theories of dependency and world systems, Arab and other critics of Western imperial tactics also demand the recognition of the internal historical and ideological dynamics of the Arab political arena in its own terms. It is those dynamics and internal contradictions that sustain the historicity and active agency of the "dependent" countries.

The Arab critical debate has its roots, of course, in the Arab past, in Islam, as well as in the confrontation with Western imperialism and European colonialism in the nineteenth and early twentieth centuries. The appeal to this past, whether in order to revive it or to challenge it, remains critical today. The philosophy of Pan-Arabism or Arab nationalism, which in the 1950s and 1960s, under the charismatic leadership of Egypt's first president, Gamal Abdel Nasser, had sought to unify the postcolonial Arab world, has been in the last two decades seriously fractured as a result of the combination of outside pressures and internal conflicts and tendencies. Egyptian nationalism, for example, acquired some ascendancy immediately following Anwar Sadat's separate peace with Israel after his 1977 trip to Jerusalem. Two years later, in 1979, the success of Ayatollah Khomeini's revolution in Iran provided a significant catalyst for other Islamic movements of differing kinds throughout the region whose broad appeal suggests an imminent threat to many existing regimes. This tension between Arabism and Islam, between religion and nationalism, as a unifying force in the Arab world, was commented on in an editorial by the Moroccan philosopher Muhammad Abd al-Jabari, "Theses . . . and Counter-Theses," which appeared in *Al-Yaum al-Sābi'*, an Arabic weekly published in Paris. Al-Jabari concluded his essay with the suggestion that "Questions of this sort are for the most part either one of the manifestations of movement and change, whose governing logic is the logic of development, the logic of controversy, in which the confrontation and struggle between the sides is concluded and negation leads to the negation of negation . . . or they are spurious questions whose falseness goes back to the fact that their spokespersons do not speak one 'language,' do not understand terms in the same way. They speak from different locations governed by conflicting and dissimilar authorities, powers, knowledge and ideology." For al-Jabari, "what is required is not the valorization of a given position, but a re-examination of all the positions by an investigation into their epistemological interpretations and historical origins. So that the dialogue goes on."[2]

A variation on the conflict between Arabism and Islam as philosophies contending for the power to represent the past, present, and future choices of the Arab Middle East is the ongoing, indeed perennial, debate over "traditionalism" and "modernism." Partisans of traditionalism insist that only a return to the authentic values and mores of the past, of the ancestors (al-aslāf), will restore the integrity of Arab character and society. Modernism's proponents, on the other hand, maintain that the Arab world must adapt to and adopt the demands of the present, usually articulated by the Western powers, if they are to enter the history of the future. The definitions assumed by the debate are in turn informed by the specific character and conditions of the immediate historical setting. In Lebanon, for example, the heralded past might be Phoenician, as for the Lebanese Christians who prefer to identify themselves as European rather than as Arabs, or it might be Islamic, as for either the Shi'ite or Sunni Muslims of Lebanon. Whether Ali or Muhammad is recognized as the prophet of the past, however, is part of Lebanon's internecine conflict. Or again, Pharaonic, Coptic, or Islamic culture is introduced, depending on the circumstances and the claimants, as constitutive of the Egyptian national identity. These debates have ramifications beyond the national borders in determining the larger Arab world's tenuous, if tendentious, relationship to the dominant Western regimes.

Like the Arabism/Islam split, the divisive dichotomy between traditionalism and modernism has been subjected to critical challenges. In a recent article entitled "National Culture and Dependent Culture: Preliminary Observations,"[3] the Palestinian writer Faysal Daraj anathematized the use current among certain Arab thinkers and pedagogues of the conventional distinction between "traditionalism" (asāla) and "modernism" (hadātha) as delimiting the choices available to Arab cultural critics and theorists as well as their counterparts in other areas of the third world. According to Daraj, whose 1985 article appeared in the Egyptian journal Al-Muwājaha (Confrontation), the distinction itself is complicit with cultural dependency and its deployment only reinforces that dependency. The traditionalism/modernism alternative which found expression in the critiques of early Arab reformers such as al-Afghani and Muhammad Abduh in the first decades of this century when Western imperial influence was altering what the English orientalist E. W. Lane had already referred to in 1836 as the "manners and customs of the modern Egyptians,"[4] is, in its contemporary implementation, part of that dominant Western influence and its implied historical narrative. As Ronald Charles Benge, a Nigerian critic, points out in his study Cultural Crisis and Libraries in the Third World, "Related to the linear 'stages of development' view of events was a concept called 'modernization,' largely produced by the knowledge industry in the United States." The concept, "modernization," had its antecedents, Benge goes on, "in the social anthropology of the nineteenth century, when it was customary to distinguish between traditional and modern attitudes. The traditional outlook was designated pre-scientific or pre-logical and it was believed

that this type of thinking was non-linear in the sense that it is devoid of causal-
ity. . . . Emphasis was also put on attitudes to time."[5] As a concept, "modernization" allowed not only Western politicians, entrepreneurs, and statesmen, but
the intellectuals as well, to theorize and thereby justify their economic and political
program of ascendancy and advantage granted by what was considered "historical
necessity." Benge writes that it is the "developmentalists" who are "producing an
ideology for neo-colonialism."[6]

Economic dependency, or "combined and unequal development" as it has been
called, between first and third world countries, between core and periphery, me-
tropole and colony, has important concomitants in the cultural arena. No less
important than the armed liberation struggles of organized resistance movements
had been against colonial regimes in the two and a half decades between 1952
and 1977, critical challenges to national dependency in the postcolonial period
are now a significant part of contemporary Arab cultural production, as in the
third world more generally. The very effort to deny what Faysal Daraj, for example, insists on as the "relationship between culture on the one hand and society
and production on the other" is crucial to the dependent system which, Daraj
claims, "substitutes dependent consumption for production."[7] Pointing to the
changes that have taken place within the Arab social structure and its relationship
to Western economic and political culture, the Syrian writer Hana Mina, during
a round-table discussion on "the consumer society and the Arab world" which
was published in the leftist journal *Al-Nahj*, claimed that "whereas the national
bourgeoisie in the 50s protected and developed—to a certain extent—production,
the parasitic bourgeoisie of today is nothing more than a broker and agent for
foreign companies."[8]

Hana Mina described a socioeconomic transformation within the Arab world
that witnessed the replacement of a national (*wataniya*) bourgeoisie by a parasitic
(*tufailiya*) bourgeoisie and that has engaged the debate over traditional-
ism/modernism in the cultural arena. According to Faysal Daraj, that is, "the
relations of dependency not only combat any national endeavor, but also work to
establish objective conditions which will not permit the development of science
and culture."[9] Neither the recourse to "traditionalism" nor an appeal for "modernization," Daraj goes on, is adequate to reactivate the historical aspirations of
the dependent society. Whereas traditionalism (*asāla*), on the one hand, is "incapable of studying the classical heritage in that any scientific ability must begin
from a knowledge of the present,"[10] modernism (*hadātha*) is only the "importation
of a European-American system of social relations, the dissemination of imperialist culture, nothing more, nothing less."[11] The problem for the critic is that
neither alternative acknowledges the necessary specific and material historical development of the given country, both within the global system and in terms of
its own inherited past. The alternative must be located elsewhere, then, than in
the same dichotomous distinction, itself both inherited and imported, which had

been critiqued a decade earlier by the Moroccan historian Abdallah Laroui in his book, *The Crisis of the Arab Intellectual.* Playing on the Arabic words *i'tirāb* (Arabization) and *ightirāb* (alienation or Westernization) in the chapter on historicism and modernization, Laroui wrote: "Now there are two types of alienation: the one is visible and openly criticized, the other all the more insidious as it is denied on principle. Westernization indeed signifies an alienation, a way of becoming other, an avenue to self-division. . . . But there exists another form of alienation in modern Arab society, one that is prevalent but veiled: this is the exaggerated medievalization obtained through quasi-magical identification with the great period of classical Arab culture. The cultural policy of all the Arab states combats the alienation of Westernization by two means: the sanctification of Arabic in its archaic form and the vulgarization of classic texts (the resurrection of the cultural legacy)."[12]

Crucial to this cultural policy is the separation of cultural consumption from the sphere of dependent economic and political relations with the West as practiced by the bourgeois Arab regimes. As for "Westernization," these Arab regimes, notes Saad Allah Wannus, have been largely successful only in "modernizing the repressive apparatus of the state and the control of information."[13] For Faysal Daraj, "what is new in literature in the dependent societies classified as such within the framework of national policy and their efficacy in the sphere of national aspirations, must be a literature that speaks for revolution, not for modernism."[14]

The two and a half decades defined by the years 1952 and 1977 mark a crucial period in the history of contemporary Egypt and its relationship to the rest of the Arab world. In July 1952 the Free Officers took control of Egypt's government, toppling the monarchy and forcing King Farouq to flee the country. Under the leadership of its first president, Gamal Abdel Nasser, Egypt then entered a period in which the nation sought, in often conflicting, controversial, at times even erratic ways, to provide the basis for its own development and to play an exemplary role in the Middle East. Nasser's socialism and his Pan-Arab ideals, like his aborted practical engagement through the United Arab Republic from 1958 to 1961 with Syria or his military intervention in the civil war in Yemen in the early 1960s, were ultimately dashed in the June War of 1967, when Israel inflicted a stunning defeat on the Egyptian army and its national honor. The establishment of the historical narrative—the marking of crises, turning points, and culminations—is part of the interpretation of these devolutions. Egyptian historian Anouar Abdel Malek explains that Egypt's national revolution took place between two "black Fridays": 25 January 1952, which preceded the burning of Cairo, and 9 June 1967, when Abdel Nasser addressed the people of Egypt during the June War. Raymond Baker, on the other hand, a United States political scientist, sees Sadat's presidency as continuous with, albeit with different emphases, Nasser's rule in his book *Egypt's Uncertain Revolution Under Nasser and Sadat.* Egyptian popular humor had its own analysis. According to one joke which circulated soon after Nasser's death, Sadat answered Nasser's chauffeur as to what direction he wanted to travel with the instruction, "whichever way Nasser went." When the chauffeur informed him that Nasser always went left, Sadat's reply was, "Well, put on the left-turn signal and go right."[15]

Anwar Sadat, who succeeded Nasser after his death in 1970, sought, particularly following the 1973 October War with Israel, to realign Egypt's position within the parameters of Western, largely United States, interests in the region. The policy of *infitāh*, or economic "open door," which Sadat initiated in the 1970s, achieved its political fruition in November 1977, when Sadat visited Jerusalem and spoke before the Israeli Knesset, thus beginning the Camp David "peace process" involving Egypt, Israel, and the United States and isolating Egypt from its Arab neighbors. These events in Egypt, in conjunction with other national chronologies in the region, delineate the immediate historical context within which the Arab debate on Arabism/Islam, traditionalism/modernism devolved. They serve, too, to organize contemporary Arab "literary history," not in the reductive terms of dependency, nor within the abstract categories of aestheticism, but rather within the framework of the direct encounter between cultural production and economic domination.

In a poem, for example, written by Ahmad Fuad Negm and sung by Shaykh Imam, two popular Egyptian resistance poets who have been alternately banned, tolerated, and imprisoned by Egyptian authorities, the 1974 visit to Egypt by the United States president Richard Nixon is derisively commemorated. The song, which begins "You came, Papa Nixon / The son of Watergate," goes on to describe the pillage of the Egyptian people, who live on *fūl bi-l-zayt* (beans and oil), to provide the luxurious and decadent reception for the visiting dignitary. The reception, recite Negm and Shaykh Imam, became a "wandering circus," a "ceremony of exorcism," replete with prostitutes, pederasts, pimps, Shamhurash and spiders, "arranged in order, of course."[16]

The force of such events—Nixon's visit to Egypt, the 1956 Tripartite Aggression, the wars of 1967 and 1973, the Camp David Accords in 1979, or the Israeli invasion of Lebanon in 1982—demands the displacement of the almost mythic representation of historical time implied in the distinction between traditional and modern. The writers, critics, and poets of the Arab world who question the formulations of dependency are contributing to a rearrangement of the "order of importance" signaled by Nixon's Egypt visit and contested by Shaykh Imam and Ahmad Fuad Negm.

Yahya Taher Abdullah's short story, "The Story of the Upper Egyptian who, overcome by fatigue, went to sleep under the wall of the old mosque,"[17] first published in 1976 and part of the collection of stories, *Tales for the Prince, so that he can sleep*, contains an important critique of economic dependency and the ideology of "modernization" purveyed in Sadat's Egypt, especially following the

1973 October War. Making use of traditional storytelling forms, Yahya Taher Abdullah interrogates in his narrative of an Upper Egyptian *fellah* transported in his sleep, as if in a dream or by magic, to the capital city of Cairo, the effects of Egyptian society of Sadat's policy of *infitāh*. The conventional distinction between "country and city," like that between traditionalism and modernism, and which Sadat himself manipulated rhetorically in order to gain support for his own political programs and personal ambitions, is here exhibited as failing to account for the changes in the contemporary Egyptian social order.

According to a report issued in 1969 by the United Nations Population Division on the evolution of cities in the third world, "The process of urbanization may come to surpass itself and give rise to geographic and social forms of human settlement to which current vocabulary can no longer be validly applied."[18] The storyteller of "The Story of the Upper Egyptian" responds to the demands of describing and narrativizing this process of transformation, which the United Nations report suggests may require a new vocabulary, through recourse to apparently traditional and popular wisdom, combining allegory with chronological referencing:

> The Great Hand, O my Emir, had marked out for him the way: two iron lines over which trains ran, with their wooden poles along which were stretched telegraph wires. When the Upper Egyptian found the way marked out in front of him, he walked along it. He continued to walk, with Allah's lands passing by, until he reached the Mother of Cities, which he entered on the fifth day of *Dhu 'l-Hijja,* and the year was that of the wolf and the bears. In a sea of iron and fire he saw human beings hopping about and asking for alms, saw them on bicycles, saw them going on all fours, saw them in buses, in trams, in trolley-buses, saw them flying, saw them driving cars.[19]

The assimilation of historical necessity to mythic or religious destiny, however, only demonstrates the failure to provide an explanation adequate to the circumstances of the Upper Egyptian migrants to Cairo. The issues of rural-urban migration and their impact on the local and indigenous social structures have been much debated in the social science literature and in the reports of various funding and development agencies, which cite "urban bias" theses and the "rural-urban divide" hypothesis while often neglecting the cultural evidence available from within the society and its traditions. As John Berger points out in his study of migrant workers in Europe, *A Seventh Man,* "his migration is like an event in a dream dreamt by another. As a figure in a dream dreamt by an unknown sleeper, he appears to act autonomously, at times unexpectedly; but everything he does— unless he revolts—is determined by the needs of the dreamer's mind. Abandon the metaphor. The migrant's intentionality is permeated by historical necessities of which neither he nor anybody he meets is aware. That is why it is as if his life were being dreamt by another."[20] Yahya Taher Abdullah abandons the metaphor, and "The Story of the Upper Egyptian" in Cairo becomes the story of the migrant worker who must admit when he gets there: " 'I've got no money for buying anything to sell.' He said: 'I own nothing but my body.' They said: 'Then go to the building workers,' and they described to him how to get there."[21]

The dependency theory of Andre Gunder Frank and the world systems theory of Immanuel Wallerstein continue to be critical influences in maintaining among analysts and policymakers a global perspective on the distorted relationships of power on the international level. According to an early formulation by Samir Amin, these theories contended that "the economic system of the periphery cannot be understood in itself, for its relations with the center are crucial; similarly, the social structure of the periphery is a truncated structure that can only be understood when it is situated as an element in a *world* social structure."[22] The analytical position represented by this formulation is in the process of being modified by focusing attention on the internal contradictions and dynamics within the peripheral social formations, asking about the ways in which these dynamics—which Armand Mattelart has referred to as "resistance, adaptation, recuperation, offensives and mimicry,"[23] or "anti-systemic movements" in Wallerstein's terminology[24]—can influence the construction of the world system. Within this framework, the conventional, even traditional, tension between country and city plays a significant role, and its popular connotations are often deployed in order to manipulate acquiescence in given strategies of development within a particular historical context.

Anwar Sadat introduced his autobiography, *In Search of Identity,* by identifying himself with the Egyptian peasantry and thus, with the course of modern Egyptian history. "I, Anwar el-Sadat," he dictated, "a peasant born and brought up on the banks of the Nile—where man first witnessed the dawn of time—present this book to readers everywhere. This is the story of my life, which is at the same time the story of Egypt since 1918—for so destiny has decreed."[25] At the same time, however, that Sadat professed his intimate personal and historical identification with the *fellahin* of Egypt and legislated the infamous "law of shame" (*qānūn al-'aib*) in early 1980 purportedly to safeguard traditional "village values," he was negotiating terms of economic and military dependency with the West in the name of development and modernization in Egypt. It is this transfer of the traditional/modern rhetorical currency into the Arab political and cultural arena that Faysal Daraj attacks as itself complicit with dependency. When Lenin proposed "abolishing the village idiot" (although this may have been part of the Soviet industrialization debate), he nonetheless most probably referred not to the peasant himself, but, as Ronald Benge points out, to a "concept by means of which it is possible to idealize him."[26]

Egypt and its planners have been much criticized from within and without for the unequal development which has supervised the unchecked growth of the urban metropolis at the expense of the rural periphery. Some critics have even suggested that "instead of Cairo urbanizing the migrant peasantry, the latter are ruralizing the city," and invented a word, *taryīf* ("ruralization," from *rīf,* countryside) for the process.[27] And in a recent study of the Egyptian education system by Abd al-Azim Anis, from the opposition party of Hizb al-Tajammu', the discrepant allocation of material resources and teachers between city and countryside, as well as between male and female students, is analyzed. Anis begins his article, "Educational Reform or Further Decline," by pointing to the fact that the Egyptian government tends to examine issues and problems "from the point of view of the parasitic *infitāhists* and the foreign exploiters, the point of view of the IMF (International Monetary Fund) or USAID (United States Agency for International Development)." They thus find that the major disadvantage to the Egyptian education system is the large number of students who participate in it (as if the solution were, as usual, in the end, a mere matter of better birth control methods).[28] According to Anis's statistics for student enrollment in vocational schools, which highlight the issue of economic dependency as well as the "urban bias," 63 percent of Egyptian students were in commerce, 27 percent in industry, and 10 percent in agriculture.[29] The unbridled optimism of development displayed by such United States social scientists as Robert Reich, who writes for *Foreign Affairs,* is challenged by Anis's report. Reich says that

> [j]ust as the main source of comparative advantage changed over a century ago from static natural endowments to slowly accumulated capital stocks, so now the new importance of a skill intensive production makes comparative advantage a matter of developing and deploying human capital. This second change is more dramatic than the first. In a very real and immediate way, a nation chooses its comparative advantage. The flexibility of its institutions and the adaptability of its work force govern the scope of choice. Decisions on human capital development define a nation's competitive strategy.[30]

According to Anis, however, Egypt has "chosen" to develop its educational institutions "against the countryside (*rīf*) in favor of the town (*hadr),* against the Sa'id in favor of the Delta, against women in favor of men, and finally against the poor in favor of the rich."[31]

Within this "urban bias" debate set in the Egyptian context of development and underdevelopment, the early stories by Yahya Taher Abdullah of peasant life in Upper Egypt suggest a critical examination of the forms of exploitation and brutality inherent in village social structures and hierarchies. While not partisan to the idea once expressed by Marx of the "idiocy of rural life," Yahya Taher Abdullah nonetheless insists in his narration on the inequalities of gerontocracy and the internal repression and violence of village life. In "The Tattoo," written in 1974, Gaber, dispossessed by the tribe when his father dies and his mother remarries outside her first husband's tribe, is unable to marry Fatima because he cannot afford the camel to give as dowry money to Abdul Rassoul. At the end of the story, after visions of starvation and prison as the probable result of whatever efforts he might make to obtain the dowry, Gaber departs for the encampment of the gypsies, to "deliver up his forearm to the old gipsy woman sitting in front of her tent under the two date-palms, for her to adorn upon his flesh, with skilled hand and needle, a heart and inside it, a standing camel with a human face."[32]

In "The Lofty One," another story written a year earlier, the structures of authority in the village are made manifest when Grandad Hasan bellows orders to Jad al-Maula the Lame, who passes on the directives to the boy al-Bistawi known as the Bald One, who in turn goes off to Mohammedani the Leprous One. In the end, it is Mohammedani who climbs the date-palm, the Lofty One, to gather the dates demanded by Grandad Hasan for his guest. While the city may exploit the resources of the countryside, beatings and feudal authority as well as inherited traditions are shown here to hold the village structure together.

The economic and cultural dichotomy between country and city, the "rural-urban divide," which allows for the systematic exploitation of the peasantry to the benefit of the town dwellers is reformulated in the different historical and ritualized narratives which condition the two regions. It is summed up in a brief anecdote reported by Husayn Ahmad Amin in his study, *Guidebook to the Sad Muslim*: "In the Egyptian countryside (*rif*) you find the fellah with several packages of cigarettes in his pocket. A package of Egyptian cigarettes—which are good cigarettes—for his own use. And a package of costly American cigarettes which he will present to an 'effendi' visitor from Cairo. He offers you an American cigarette and then takes a cigarette from his own package for himself. All the while he believes that he is establishing the existence of a bond between himself and the visiting 'son of the city.' "[33] If the city has been assimilated into a dependent relationship within the "linear 'stages of development' view of events" described by Benge, the countryside maintains, against its exploited incorporation into that world system, its own rhythms and chronology. The interference between the two narratives disrupts the coherence of countryside represented in Yahya Taher Abdullah's stories. In the courtyard of "Rhythms in Slow Time" from 1969, the "white hen had spread its wings," while "a white aeroplane ran along the ground of the small airport," flying off to "some unknown land."[34] Meanwhile, inside the house,

The air that penetrated through the aperture in the wall grew cooler; the aperture was blocked up with the cover of a wall diary. The diary had writing on it and pictures of people in military uniforms, also congratulations to the Egyptian people on their glorious army from the owner of the sweet factories who had sponsored the calendar.[35]

The defeat of the Egyptian army in 1967 had not reached the village, but in the story of "Grandad Hasan" (1975), the season of Ramadan has arrived in both village and town and Grandad Hasan, who spends his days on the bench outside his home, is most solicitous to see that one and all in the village are observing the fast until sundown, when the evening prayer is announced and the fast can be broken. The Ramadan fast unites Muslims throughout the world, but the Upper Egyptian countryside maintains its own rhythms, consonant with a natural order that has its own relentlessness:

> The voices of the boys come through with a faint clamour. They are over there at Mohammed ibn Makiyya's ship, and over there is a mulberry tree which is still alive, while Ahmed Mabrouk who planted it died ten years ago. The boys' rowdiness means that the gun for breaking the fast has been heard on the radio of Hajj Mohammed, the eldest of Grandad Hasan's brothers, in accordance with Cairo time. The time has thus come round for breaking the fast for those living under the protection of Sayyida Zeinab and Sayyidna Hussein, and when One-eyed Yusuf gives the call to prayer from high up on the Abdullah Mosque the time will have come for the people of both New and Old Karnak to break the fast.[36]

Yahya Taher Abdullah is a native of Karnak, in the Sa'id, or Upper Egypt, who lived and wrote in Cairo until 1981, when he was killed in an automobile accident while returning from a visit to al-Bahriyya Oasis. Refusing to work for any of the government agencies or bureaucracies in Egypt, or to perform any of the tasks which generally provide clerks' salaries to many of Egypt's writers, Yahya Taher Abdullah lived a life of simplicity and considerable poverty. As his English translator, Denys Johnson Davies, points out in his introduction to *The Mountain of Green Tea*, Yahya Taher Abdullah makes very few concessions to his readers, be they foreign or Egyptian. His stories draw demandingly on the traditional patterns of Arabic literature and Egyptian folklore, but insist uncompromisingly as well on the current historical and political conjuncture of Egypt as the condition of their writing: the "urban bias" of Egypt's dependent condition, the distorted authoritarian hierarchies within the society, the relevant location of Upper Egypt in the Egyptian national and popular imagination. Whether set in the Sa'id or in Cairo, the tales probe the ambiguities of economic and cultural development and the forms of exploitation and repression these ambiguities produce.

Following the writer's death, *Al-Khatwa*, an independent periodical in Cairo, devoted a special issue to the life and work of Yahya Taher Abdullah to which many of the major critics and poets of Egypt contributed their testimonials. Salah 'Issa, an Egyptian historian, began his essay, "Funeral Roll on the Tambourines of the Sixties," by setting the news of Yahya Taher Abdullah's death within the context of the "news of the day," mentioning in particular a story about Mena- chem Begin and Israel, a report on consumerism, and news of the trial of three Palestinians which was taking place in Egypt. For Salah 'Issa, Yahya Taher Ab- dullah's life and death were intricately complicated within the circumstances of Egypt's present condition, and he cites frequently in the course of his article the storywriter's description of himself: "From the world of the market I come." Just as importantly he cites Yahya Taher Abdullah's description of his relationship to the Sa'idi world: "I understood them—my system—amongst the pillars of Karnak. They clash with each other in this small new village, isolated in the cages of their enemies, hungry for food, for love, for sex, and for certainty, repulsed from within and from without. I read them like paintings in the place of the gods of Amon. I saw them, wrinkles on a man's eye and his scowl in dreaming of the breast. . . . And then when (I read them—wrote them—materialized them) I didn't find them modern (mu'āsir), and since I was modern, I historicized them. I read the 'runūk' [symbol of the Mameluke sultans] on their bodies: Hyksos, Ptolemy, the Romans, the Turks, the Circassians, the French, the English, the Americans and the Zionists . . . from every creed and religion, with protective nails, I pounded here: on the head."[37]

Like Yahya Taher Abdullah, Aml Dunqul, the popular Egyptian colloquial poet, began his writing career in the 1960s, in Nasser's Egypt. Like Yahya Taher Abdullah, he lived to contest in his writing the changes wrought in Egyptian society by Sadat's policies of infitāh and Camp David. Aml Dunqul died in 1983. Like Yahya Taher Abdullah, Aml Dunqul was born and raised in Upper Egypt and his wife, 'Abla al-Ruwini, entitled her memoirs The Southerner (Al-Gunūbi). In a chapter headed "Republic of the Sa'id," she described Dunqul's committed loyalties to the south. "His clothes and his words and greatest pride were in his Sa'idi soul. It makes me remember the joke he always told whenever he saw a Sa'idi in Cairo: 'What we need is independence from the North, the creation of a Republic of the Sa'id.' It's not so funny. The Sa'id is the beginning and the end of existence."[38] The generation of Egyptian "writers of the 60s," to which Yahya Taher Abdullah and Aml Dunqul belonged, who had responded then to the call for revolution, condemned Sadat's policies of dependency on the West and total capitulation to United States stratagems in the Middle East, and questioned the new role being assigned by such policies to cultural production. Al-Ruwini recalls the contradictions and compromises imposed on writers like Aml Dunqul and Yahya Taher Abdullah: "In the shadow of the conditions of the seventies, man became anxious. If the poet called the people to revolution and change, they thought he wanted them to go back to poverty and socialism. If he called to the people to refuse a bogus peace, that meant a call to sacrifice for the sake of war and death. And if the poet called to the people to make their lives more beautiful and affluent, that meant emigration and not staying in the country."[39] The "new in literature," called for by Faysal Daraj, of revolution, not modernism, is situated within this historical and political context of struggle in Egypt and the "third world" against the domination of the West.

When the Upper Egyptian in "The Story of the Upper Egyptian" reaches Cairo with only his body to sell, he goes to the construction sites where he finds work in the company of his Sa'idi compatriots who are building the modern capital of Egypt. One night he is invited to a circumcision party where there is dancing, hashish, and entertainment. Part of this entertainment is the traditional song competition, where the audience pays for the privilege of greeting his favorite party. The Upper Egyptian asks for " 'Greetings to the Upper Egyptians, the men who put up buildings and construct the Mother of the Cities.' " But then a Cairene pays his quarter of a pound and announces, " 'O masters of crafts, it is the men from the Mother of the Cities who construct the Mother of the Cities.' " The rural-urban divide that threatens the festivities is deflected when another Upper Egyptian pays and greets both the Sa'idis and the Cairenes. The divide is then transformed into class solidarity when a Cairene concludes the ceremonial with his announcement: " 'We and the Upper Egyptians put up the buildings and construct the Mother of the Cities, but we don't live in the buildings, so greetings to those who live in the buildings.' "[40] Yahya Taher Abdullah's variation on the classical *mu'arada* challenges the cultural and economic situation of dependency enforced and underwritten by such categorical and prescriptive distinctions as those between traditionalism and modernism, rural and urban, and their sectarian variations in the rhetoric of Islam vs. Arabism. In Arabic, *mu'arada* means confrontation or opposition, but it is also the name of a literary genre, wherein one poet repeats the lines of a previous poet, altering them just enough to "go the poet one better." The contemporary *mu'arada* between Upper Egyptians and Cairenes becomes a contest between third and first worlds, a contribution to the challenge to cultural dependency.

Samir Amin, in *Unequal Development,* writes that "it is only the ideology of 'universal harmonies' that sees in these migrations [from the hinterland to the coast in Africa] anything but movements that impoverish the zones of origin of the migrants."[41] The shantytowns that grow up around the major urban metropolises in many third world countries, now euphemistically referred to by planners and developers as the "informal sector," absorb much of the migrant labor and peasant population which has emigrated from the countryside. Perhaps, like Yahya Taher Abdullah's Upper Egyptian in Cairo, they find temporary employment with the conglomerated contractors who have already made their personal fortunes as migrants in the oil-rich countries of the Arabian Gulf (a pipeline of Egyptian livelihood which is now slowly being cut off) and are now building with "Goha nails" their private fiefdoms as agents for United States development pro-

grams and multinational corporations, whose interests span the skyline from ho-
tels and high-rise office buildings to plazas and subway systems.

Surveying the Egyptian topography and demographic scene in the mid-1970s,
John Waterbury, then representative of the American Universities Field Staff,
wrote that "Egypt is locked inextricably in the grips of three crises: transportation,
housing and hostilities with Israel, or so one would conclude judging by the
amount of newspaper coverage given them. All that the first two share with
the last is their seeming insolubility."[42] A decade later, it would seem clear that
the three "crises" facing Egypt have more in common than their apparent "insolubility." Already to an Arab observer writing in 1968 the interconnections were
patent. According to Abdallah Laroui, in his essay on "Tradition and Tradition-
alization" reprinted in *The Crisis of the Arab Intellectual*, "To a far greater extent
than the various struggles for independence, the problem of Palestine, because of
its complexities and objective contradictions, is allowing the Arabs, while demanding much of them, to become truly conscious of history. Each one of us
must applaud this awakening and see to it that it does not come to naught; for
not only is the Arab's future at stake, but the interests of other peoples as well."[43]

Since 1968, many have been the nails of Goha pounded into the economic,
political, and cultural structures of the Arab Middle East and in the larger third
world. *Mismār Goha* is told as a joke, a popular witticism, to thwart the effects
of the British base in the Suez Canal, the United States Rapid Deployment Forces
in Oman or Morocco, the joint military maneuvers between the United States
and Egypt, the marines in Lebanon, the multinational corporations throughout
the region, the state of Israel on the land of Palestine. But *mismār Goha* is also a
conundrum, with its own exhortations. In a popular song by the Lebanese resistance singer Marcel Khalifeh, "They stopped me on the border," there is the
suggestion that the challenge to economic and cultural dependency lies in the
reconstructing of historical narratives:

> They stopped me on the border and demanded my identity card.
> I said to them, "By the prophet, uncle, my grandmother hid it."

Khalifeh's song narrates the dilemma of Palestinian identity as it is confronted
by a young Palestinian asked to produce his "papers" by Israeli border guards.
Half of him stands on the border, his other half is hidden by his grandmother in
a house. He does not know which house, but he does know that "surely they wish
to destroy it . . . efface it altogether." The promise of resistance is the conclusion
of the song: "On some winter night, we will join together. . . ." But, Abdallah
Laroui reminds us, "To make and unmake—to recombine the facts of history—
takes time."[44]

NOTES

1. Khalid Kishtainy, *Arab Political Humor* (London, 1985), 127.

2. Muhammad Abd al-Jabari, "Theses . . . and Counter-Theses," *Al-Yaum al-Sābi'*, 22 July 1985. In Arabic.

3. Faysal Daraj, "National Culture and Dependent Culture: Preliminary Observations," *Al-Muwājaha* 5 (1985). In Arabic.

4. E. W. Lane, *An Account of the Manners and Customs of the Modern Egyptians* (New York, 1973).

5. Ronald Charles Benge, *Cultural Crisis and Libraries in the Third World* (London, 1979), 16.

6. Ibid., 20.

7. Daraj, "National Culture," 21.

8. Hana Mina, " 'The Consumer Society' and the Arab Countries: Cultural, Intellectual and Social Reflections," *Al-Nahj* 9 (1985): 240. In Arabic.

9. Daraj, "National Culture," 21.

10. Ibid.

11. Ibid., 22.

12. Abdallah Laroui, *The Crisis of the Arab Intellectual: Traditionalism or Historicism?* trans. Diarmid Cammell (Berkeley, 1976), 156.

13. Mina, " 'Consumer Society,' " 244.

14. Daraj, "National Culture," 25.

15. Anouar Abdel Malek, *Egypt: Military Society,* trans. Charles Lam Markmann (New York, 1968), vii; Raymond Baker, *Egypt's Uncertain Revolution Under Nasser and Sadat* (Cambridge, Mass., 1978); cited in Hassan al-Shamy, *Folktales of Egypt* (Chicago, 1980), 228.

16. The songs by Shaykh Imam and Marcel Khalifeh came to me by the circuitous route of copying and recopying cassette tapes, a means for the dissemination of culture much practiced in the Arab Middle East. I am grateful to many people who both brought these to my attention and helped in transliterating and translating. Here as elsewhere the task of the critic was a collective one.

17. Yahya Taher Abdullah, "The Story of the Upper Egyptian . . . ," in *The Mountain of Green Tea,* trans. Denys Johnson-Davies (London, 1984). All of Yahya Taher Abdullah's stories discussed here are taken from this collection which selects from the seven volumes of stories published by the writer.

18. Cited in John Waterbury, *Egypt: Burdens of the Past, Options for the Future* (Bloomington, 1978), 125.

19. Abdullah, *Mountain of Green Tea,* 51.

20. John Berger and Jean Mohr, *A Seventh Man: Migrant Workers in Egypt* (New York, 1975), 43.

21. Abdullah, *Mountain of Green Tea,* 20.

22. Samir Amin, *Unequal Development: An Essay on the Social Formations of Peripheral Capitalism,* trans. Brian Pearce (New York, 1976), 294.

23. Armand Mattelart, *Transnationals and the Third World: The Struggle for Culture,* trans. David Buxton (South Hadley, MA., 1983), 17.

24. Immanuel Wallerstein, "Crisis as Transition," in *Dynamics of Global Crisis,* ed. Amin et al. (New York, 1982).

25. Anwar el-Sadat, *In Search of Identity: An Autobiography* (London, 1978), 9.

26. Benge, *Cultural Crisis,* 122.

27. Waterbury, *Egypt,* 125.

28. Abd al-Azim Anis, *Educational Reform or Further Decline* (Cairo, 1984), 1. In Arabic.

29. Ibid., 14.

30. Robert B. Reich, "Beyond Free Enterprise," *Foreign Affairs* 61 (Spring 1983): 782.

31. Anis, *Educational Reform,* 2.

32. Abdullah, *Mountain of Green Tea,* 24.

33. Husayn Ahmad Amin, *Guidebook to the Sad Muslim: On the Necessity of Conduct in the Twentieth Century* (Cairo, 1983). In Arabic. I am grateful to Jane Ferson for bringing this work to my attention.

34. Abdullah, *Mountain of Green Tea,* 31.

35. Ibid., 33.

36. Ibid., 45–46.

37. Salah 'Issa, "Funeral Roll on the Tambourines of the Sixties," *Al-Khatwa* 2 (n.d.): 21. In Arabic.

38. Abla al-Ruwini, *The Southerner* (Cairo, n.d.), 131. In Arabic.

39. Ibid., 118–19.

40. Abdullah, *Mountain of Green Tea,* 54–55.

41. Amin, *Unequal Development,* 331.

42. Waterbury, *Egypt,* 145.

43. Laroui, *Crisis of the Arab Intellectual,* 32.

44. Ibid.

14

HISTORY IS LIKE MOTHER

JANE GALLOP

Within the literary academy, the term "criticism" refers to what, by the 1960s, was certainly the most commonly practiced form of scholarship: textual interpretation. Outside of literary studies, "literary criticism" is more likely to mean some form of evaluation (the book review) and "criticism" unmodified has the primarily negative sense of fault-finding. When, within the academy, the term "criticism" takes on objective, neutral connotations, the word "critique" takes over the negative functions served by "criticism" outside academic discourse. Feminists writing about literature described our practice as "criticism" in order, I believe, to take advantage of the double sense of the word. It could imply, when necessary, that we were engaged in a negative evaluation, a "critique," of a cultural institution; it could also signify, when appropriate, that we were simply doing what students of literature did. This double sense worked well for a group located on the margins of an institution, expressing our position as at once critical of and obedient to the discipline.

The last anthology we will consider, published in 1987, is entitled *Feminist Issues in Literary Scholarship*. The word "scholarship" in this title replaces the ambiguous "criticism" of the earlier collections. Inside the volume, "scholarship" is most frequently used in an essay by Lillian Robinson, itself entitled "Feminist Criticism." Robinson's thoughts in that piece come out of her "experience as one of five collaborators on a . . . study of feminist scholarship in its first decade." Five feminists working in different academic disciplines produce a book called *Feminist Scholarship: Kindling in the Groves of Academe.*[1] However volatile "feminist scholarship" might be, it is clearly to be found *within* "the groves of academe." "Scholarship" is a general term to describe the practice of academics in diverse disciplines. The phrase "literary scholarship," used by Robinson in her essay and picked up in the anthology's title, locates criticism as one among other academic disciplines.

For the first time, an anthology of feminist literary criticism names itself as academic. These are "Feminist Issues," but they are "Feminist Issues *in* Literary Scholarship." This 1987 anthology is located in the aftermath of the institution-alization of feminist literary study.

In *Feminist Issues* Jane Marcus cites an earlier essay by the collection's editor: "Shari Benstock suggests . . . that academic feminist critics are not marginal in the least."[2] The Benstock essay cited refers to "those of *us* inside the circle (academics who practice feminist literary criticism)."[3] This 1983 essay, Benstock's first statement as editor of *Tulsa Studies in Women's Literature,* notes that Marcus's "work has informed this editorial in a way that will become more apparent, I think, with the publication of Volume 3 of *Tulsa Studies,* a special issue . . ., a volume to which Jane Marcus is contributing an essay" (p. 149 n. 7). This 1983 editorial is also the call for papers for "Volume 3," the 1984 special double issue called "Feminist Issues in Literary Scholarship" which is republished in 1987 as an anthology by the same name. Not just a contributor among others, Marcus "informs" that volume's very conception.

Marcus's contribution to *Feminist Issues* points to another connotation for the title's "scholarship" besides the academic identity we have been pursuing. Earlier in the history of literary studies, criticism and scholarship had been polemically opposed alternatives. By the time feminist "criticism" enters the scene, the terms can be used synonymously to refer to the literary academic's production.[4] Although scholarship and criticism are no longer at odds, by the 1980s a new opposition polarizes literary studies. Marcus opposes "scholarship" to "theory."

Marcus takes theorists to task for slighting scholars: "At present the scholars generously acknowledge the theorists, but theorists, like their brothers, follow the fashionable practice of minimalism in footnoting, often slighting years of scholarship, textual editing, and interpretation without which their own work could not begin" (p. 90). Feminist theorists, no better than their brothers, are modish, impolite, and ungrateful. As bad as all that might be, it is in fact worse. What in the text appears a breach of etiquette, in the footnotes gets politically colored as exploitation:

> This minimalism in annotation has the political effect of isolating the critic or theorist from scholars and from the history of scholarship. If present practice in footnoting is a legacy of nineteenth-century capitalist recognition of the ownership of ideas, the minimalism of theorists, as opposed to scholars, represents a new economy of critical exchange in which the work of scholars is fair game (like exploitation of third world countries) and the Big White Men only acknowledge each other. (p. 96 n. 23)

Theorists slight not only scholarship but also "interpretation," i.e., criticism, yet "the critic or theorist" can be isolated from scholars and scholarship. In the polarization of literary studies, the "critic" can go either way. Marcus wants her sister critics, socialist feminist critics she usually calls us, to align ourselves with the scholars. She is acutely aware of the historical antagonism between criticism and scholarship: "It is an ironic turn of events when one declares that a socialist feminist criticism should defend its old enemies, the very bibliographers, editors, textual scholars, biographers, and literary historians who wrote women writers out of history to begin with. But without the survival of these skills and the appropriation of them, women will again lose the history of their own culture. Theory is necessary and useful but is not superior to other literary practice or immune to historical forces" (p. 87). At this point in the history of literary studies, Marcus fears that the old antagonism may lead criticism to a fatal misalliance.

Marcus is not so much attacking theory (she notably concedes here that it is "necessary and useful") as she is arguing against a critical siding with theory against scholarship. The anthology's titular substitution of "scholarship" for "criticism," cementing an alliance between the two terms, is most certainly "informed by Marcus's work." This collection has been taken as an attack on theory,[5] but I see it more precisely, here in Marcus's specification, as a resistance to an alliance with theory that would isolate criticism from scholarship. And what is rather insistently at stake, according to Marcus's formulation, is "history."

"Theory is not immune to historical forces." If Marcus needs to assert something so obvious, it is because she fears that theory is, precisely, passing as trans-historical. "Why this defensive bristling at the historical nature of our enterprise?" she asks (p. 90).

Debunking theory's transcendent immunity, Marcus constructs an intriguing family romance:

> I would also like to see a more sisterly relationship develop between feminist theorists and feminist scholars. At present the scholars generously acknowledge the theorists, but theorists, like their brothers, follow the fashionable practice of minimalism in footnoting, often slighting years of scholarship, textual editing, and interpretation without which their own work could not begin. This is a denial of the place of one's own work in literary history, asserting as virgin births interpretations which have ancestry. As Virginia Woolf claimed of art, "masterpieces are not single and solitary births," so one may claim that criticism itself has a familial and cultural history. Perhaps theorists, like the characters in Oscar Wilde's plays, want to be orphaned. It increases the cachet of avant-gardism. (p. 90)

This passage begins by treating theorists and scholars as "sisters," albeit as estranged sisters. The next sentence, quoted earlier, adds brothers to the family. The theorists, not close enough to their sisters, are all too close to their brothers. At this point although the relations are familial, all parties are of the same generation; the significant difference is gender. With the third sentence, theorists are now denying not sisters but "ancestry." Other generations enter the portrait along with "history." "Criticism has a history," and that history is not only cultural but "familial." Returning to the ingrate modishness of "theorists," Marcus claims they want to be not only "virgin births" but "orphans." The scholars who began as unacknowledged sisters have become scorned, denied, or wished-dead parents. The denial of history is here synonymous with the refusal of filial obligation; cultural history parallels familial.

Marcus's essay cites one of the other essays in the anthology. The editor's own essay also cites only one of the other contributions, the same one as Marcus does, Judith Newton's "Making—and Remaking—History." Newton's article is a fine example of research into cultural and familial history. She too is troubled by an ahistorical tendency in feminist criticism. Newton urges us, whom she might with Marcus call "socialist feminist critics," to resist this trend: "We have implicitly committed ourselves to resist English Department formalism—the view that literature and literary critics are divorced from history—a view still perpetuated, despite their air of currency and French fashionableness, by the forms of criticism now dominant in Britain and the United States."[6]

As in Marcus's discussion, denial of history is accompanied by "fashionableness." Newton, however, expects something better from "fashion": "*despite* their fashionableness." Fashionableness after all is precisely the embrace of the historical moment, the rejection of the "unchanging." The problem here is not modishness but that the "currency" is simply an "air," a surface affectation below which remains the conservative belief in the unchanging. Whereas for Marcus, trendiness is negative in its rejection of the past, for Newton it might be, if it were not a sham, a commitment to change and the historical moment. Yet Newton too drapes her cultural history in the trappings of family romance. Where Marcus is offended by a lack of respect for older generations, Newton would set us against "divorce."

Catharine Stimpson's Introduction to this anthology mentions Newton's article first of the volume's essays, before she even gets to the presentation of the collection's contents: "We must . . . act, politically and culturally, in order to change history. Theory and practice must meet, engage each other, wed. Judith Newton's strong essay . . . details such an imperative" (p. 2). In a move explored at length in the preceding chapter, Stimpson would resolve the theory/practice dilemma through matrimonial metaphor. Although she likely means that Newton's essay "details [the] imperative" to change history, the intervening sentence also suggests that Newton's text carries a matrimonial imperative. Such an imperative might indeed view "divorce" in a negative light.

Newton is not the only writer in *Feminist Issues* explicitly to resist divorce from history. Elizabeth Fox-Genovese concludes: "The account of the black woman's self cannot be divorced from the history of that self or the history of the people among whom it took shape."[7] I am not questioning the necessity, which Newton and Fox-Genovese are here affirming, of thinking texts in relation to history. I am, however, interested in the way that, in a feminist context, a separation which is considered objectionable is repeatedly imaged as "divorce."

Fox-Genovese's essay is the first of three at the end of the 1987 volume which were not in the original *Tulsa Studies* special issue, the only one of the three not previously published elsewhere. It is in fact a slightly different version of a chapter in another anthology edited by Benstock a year later.[8] In the context of the 1987 collection whose title locates us within the literary academy and in the context of the present study, we might note that Fox-Genovese, alone of all the writers anthologized in the volumes we have been studying, is from another academic discipline: she is a historian.

Along with Gerda Lerner, Joan Kelly-Gadol, and Nancy Cott, Fox-Genovese is cited as a "theorist of feminist historiography," in Elaine Showalter's contribution to *Feminist Issues.*[9] Appearing immediately after the editor's own contribution, Showalter's essay is an attempt, as its subtitle puts it, at "Writing the History of Feminist Criticism." In this anthology, feminist criticism must attend not only generally to history but first and foremost to its own historicity. Marcus asserts, "criticism itself has a familial and cultural history" (p. 90); and Showalter can be seen precisely as mapping that double history for us.

Showalter begins by claiming for feminist criticism an anomalous family history: "There is no Mother of Feminist Criticism" (p. 31). The absence of a mother is not in itself, in this context, anomalous; the other modern criticisms to which she compares us have no mother either, but they all have, according to her, a father. "We do not derive our charter from a single authority or a body of sacred theoretical texts. There is no . . . fundamental work against which one can measure other feminisms."[10] Feminist criticism is, in the familial terms with which this book likes to express our cultural history, an orphan. Showalter clearly considers this a real advantage; we are freer because we have no model to obey.

Not every feminist critic prefers us unmothered. In 1981 Jane Marcus asserts: "As a literary critic, Virginia Woolf is the mother of us all."[11] Toril Moi, in her 1985 book, shares Marcus's sense of the homage due Woolf: "she has yet to be adequately welcomed and acclaimed by her feminist daughters in England and America. . . . A feminist criticism that would do both justice and homage to its great mother and sister: this, surely, should be our goal."[12]

In Benstock's volume, Marcus's discussion of the desire to be orphaned focuses specifically on two theorists who "reject explicitly Woolf's role as foremother of feminist criticism in *A Room of One's Own*. There she outlines 'thinking back through our mothers' as writing practice for feminist critics . . . and shows us how to do feminist criticism. . . . What they seem unable to accept is their own daughterhood as critics to Woolf's role as the mother of socialist feminist criticism" (p. 89). For Marcus, there is a mother as well as a "fundamental work against which one can measure other feminisms." That "foremother" prescribes, precisely, that we "think back through our mothers."

The 1978 anthology *Feminist Criticism* opens with Margaret Andersen's statement: "the literary critic who first used feminism as a criterion was, to my knowledge, Christine de Pisan."[13] Pisan, Andersen goes on to tell us, was born in 1364. We are then led on a quick tour of six centuries of feminist criticism which concludes: "It is evident from this brief survey that a tradition of feminist critique exists" (p. 4). A decade later, Stimpson—introducing *Feminist Issues in Literary Scholarship*—repeats Andersen's gesture, upping the *ante*. The 1987 anthology opens: "Feminist literary criticism in the West . . . begins with Sappho in the mid-seventh century B.C." (p. 1). After some verses from Sappho, Stimpson's second paragraph begins: "Despite the length of its lineage, feminist criticism did not become a force with a name until the mid-twentieth century A.D. One of its two major texts was *A Room of One's Own* . . . the second was *The Second Sex*. . . . Signifying the lack of a history that might have bonded women to each other was the brevity of *The Second Sex*'s one-sentence response to the prior text."

For the presentation of feminist criticism, Andersen and Stimpson go back and claim a long "lineage" precisely to repair the absence of a "history." The difference between the two terms is not so much that "lineage" is familial, since feminist critics repeatedly cast our history in familial terms, but rather a matter of record, of recognition and "naming." When Marcus's theorists deny their ancestry, they refuse to record their lineage in "history."

Stimpson's Beauvoir bears a certain resemblance to Marcus's theorists. Not only does she slight the work that went before her, but "notably, even notoriously, Beauvoir's language . . . balloon[s] towards 'brotherhood' while jettisoning 'sisterhood.' . . . *The Second Sex* erases women from history" (p. 2). Stimpson sees contemporary feminist critics "negotiating between" Beauvoir and Woolf, "although writers within colleges and universities are more apt to resemble Beauvoir." Herself well within the academy—at the time of publication, a dean; as I write, the president of the MLA—Stimpson clearly prefers Woolf, and not just for reasons of style. "Woolf's grasp of history, if narrower than de Beauvoir's, is often hardier" (p. 1).

Having taken us from Sappho to Beauvoir and Woolf, having shown us where Woolf goes beyond Beauvoir, Stimpson, in a move typical of anthology introductions, segues from the lineage to a discussion of the essays which follow: "Such ideas form the matrix for much of the thinking in *Feminist Issues in Literary Scholarship*. In 'Still Practice . . .' an act of homage to Virginia Woolf, Jane Marcus calls for critics to accept the '. . . authority of the female text.' Marcus must be read against Judith Kegan Gardiner's study of the ambivalence of one female creator, Doris Lessing, towards the mother, an authority in the female text and time" (p. 3, second ellipsis Stimpson's).

"Such ideas" is ambiguous: it might refer to Woolf's ideas in *A Room,* discussed in the paragraph which immediately precedes this statement; it might refer to all the ideas of the lineage discussed up to this point in the Introduction. In either case, the "matrix" is a sort of "thinking back through our mothers"; we might recall the etymological sense of "matrix." Stimpson then, immediately, mentions Marcus's essay. The phrase Stimpson quotes from Marcus directs us to this sentence: "these critics deny the authority of the female text, they deny the motherhood of the author of the text" (p. 89). "Marcus must be read against Gardiner's study": Stimpson wants us to attend to this contrast in attitudes toward female authority. If some critics prefer us mothered, some writers are ambivalent on that head.

Stimpson's appositive to the mother in Gardiner's study—"an authority in the female text and time"—is quite puzzling. The phrase "authority in the female text" recalls the previous sentence's "authority of the female text," bringing the two close together so we might better read them "against" each other. The "time," however, both evocative and ambiguous in the extreme, does not refer to anything else in the paragraph. Does "and time" mean "in the female text and the female time" or does it mean "and an authority in time"?

The first reading does not strike me as particularly likely, but it does connect to the phrase "women's time," which Showalter features prominently in her essay:

> We need to begin by seeing feminist criticism from within . . . women's time instead of as a subset of standard critical time. The history of feminist criticism is more than a history of ideas or institutions; it takes in events on many levels of women's daily lives. But to limit ourselves to women's time would be equally misleading, since feminist criticism is also constituted by the histories of the academy, the discipline, and modern criticism itself. . . . [F]eminist criticism . . . has both a Mother and a Father time. (Showalter, p. 33)

"Women's time" would seem to refer to the "many levels of women's daily lives" as opposed to "a history of ideas or institutions." At the end of this passage it is personified as Mother Time. "Mother" here might be said to be, in a certain uncertain interpretation of Stimpson, "an authority in the female time."

Showalter is playing with the classic personification of time as Father Time, reminding us that history has been "his story," not hers. A similar gesture is made in the 1978 anthology which begins with Christine de Pisan where the dedication reads: "To MOTHERTIME whose pendulum is beginning to swing." Yet Showalter also makes women's time a mother in order rhetorically to strengthen her assertion that we need two models: one male and one female. "Women's time" could remain separate from what she calls not "men's time" but "standard critical time"; these two phrases belong to radically different associations. But when she wants to persuade us not to "limit ourselves" but to embrace both models, her metaphor appeals to our ideological "common sense": you can't have (or you wouldn't want?) a mother without a father. Mother Time ought not be divorced from Father Time?

Let us return to the second possible interpretation of Stimpson's phrase: "the mother, an authority in time." This reading, which seems the more likely to me, is unclear in its reference. Half a page later, Stimpson again uses the word "time," equally ungarnished, when she lists differences among women not yet sufficiently addressed by feminist critics: "religion matters; colonization matters . . . time matters" (p. 3). In this case, "time" would seem to mean something like "historical moment," and she would thus be calling for an attention to historical change and specificity like Newton does. In any case, I assume that "time," in the maternal authority context, must be connected to "history." Such a vague yet powerful connection echoes an entire register of Gardiner's article which functions as a sort of matrix for the present chapter. Although Gardiner often, and variously, links mother and "history," only once does she use the word "time" in connection to the mother, and then in the most offhand of manners.

"Time" shows up in Gardiner's discussion of Lessing's potboiler *Particularly Cats*: "Talking of cats, it seems, Lessing allows herself to slip into careless conventions that she otherwise examines more scrupulously. This carelessness helps the critic, because it means that here Lessing leaves unprocessed chunks of ideology lying exposed in her prose. . . . Time and time again, Lessing judges her cats by how well they mother their kittens."[14]

What Lessing is careful not to say directly about human females, she feels free to say about cats. One of the "chunks of ideology" exposed is Lessing's subscription to the belief that, to be good, a woman must be a good mother. Gardiner throws in the phrase "time and time again" to emphasize repetition. The phrase itself is, to be sure, utterly marginal to the discussion of motherhood and ideology Gardiner is pursuing, but the very notion of repetition, the idea that "time again" will be just like "time," is in fact central to the difficult nexus she is here trying to think through.

These "unprocessed" chunks of ideology are lying around, it is implied, because Lessing has not yet worked them through. The ideology is residual, belonging to an earlier idea of women than otherwise characterizes Lessing's thinking. Lessing repeats these ideas, unprocessed, unwittingly. She repeats them precisely because she does not process them. In order not to repeat we must process: "History is like mother: if we don't understand her, we are doomed to repeat her" (p. 121).

Gardiner's consideration of Lessing's cats is also a reconsideration of "mothering theory." We could take as the fundamental text of mothering theory Chodorow's 1978 *The Reproduction of Mothering* which, as the title implies, is about repetition. The ideologically supported mode of parenting produces daughters with fluid boundaries between themselves and their mothers. This prepares those daughters to grow up to be good mothers, capable of the sort of empathy which the institution of motherhood demands. Thus, time and time again, motherhood reproduces itself.

Gardiner finds mothering theory useful but also critiques it: "I think the chief defect of mother-daughter theory is that it separates empathy from history, according to conventional stereotypes: women become their mothers; whereas men go off to conquer the world. . . . According to this theory, empathy belongs to women, history to men" (p. 117). Mothering theory supports a gendered dichotomy: one can either become mother or join history. Four pages later, in her closing paragraph, Gardiner provocatively asserts "history is like mother," insisting upon a connection between the separate spheres.

If, in her discussion of Gardiner's essay, Stimpson uses the word "time" with such vague reference it is perhaps because there is an aspect of Gardiner she wants to represent even if she doesn't precisely know how. "Gender, Value, and Lessing's Cats" is centrally about both mother and history. Gardiner closes her essay with a plea to connect the two. The final paragraph begins with the stunning "History is like mother," then briefly summarizes the relation between history and empathy in the works by Lessing she has considered. Then, without even a paragraph break, she goes on: "And this returns us to the importance of the paradigms through which we understand our world. If we do not incorporate gender into our model of history, we may relapse into . . . sexism. . . . But if, on the other hand, we feminists do not incorporate history into our model of gender, we are doomed to simple repetition" (p. 122). Not only must we, living our lives, try to connect the separate domains of empathy and history, but our theorizing must likewise attempt to combine mothering theory with the study of history.

Gardiner's essay ends here, with this call to double our paradigms, and is immediately followed by Judith Newton's essay. Newton's first two pages decry feminist criticism's tendency toward unchanging, essentialist constructions, and then she begins a new paragraph on a positive note: "there have been important counters to this." The "important counters" to ahistorical formalism are represented as dual by Newton's next two sentences:

> Theories of gender construction advanced by feminist theorists like Nancy Chodorow, Dorothy Dinnerstein, and Jane Flax have re-emphasized the idea that gender identity and ideologies of gender . . . are socially constructed. . . . Feminist history by historians like Mary Ryan and Judith Walkowitz, meanwhile, has countered the ahistorical quality of much feminist psychoanalytic theory by illuminating the ways in which constructions of gender . . . have changed with changing historical situations. (pp. 125–26)

After these two separate if not quite equal sentences, Newton's paragraph concludes: "Together these developments in feminist theory and feminist history . . .

provide a more adequate and helpful model . . . than our current implicit focus on the unchanging, the universal, and the monolithic." All three of the "feminist theorists" listed in the first sentence in fact specifically do "mothering theory." Like Gardiner, Newton proposes a combination of mothering theory and history as the basis for feminist criticism.

That Judith Gardiner and Judith Newton should take up this same position is particularly interesting when read against the roles they play in the roughly con-temporaneous Greene and Kahn anthology. *Making a Difference* came out in 1985; *Feminist Issues in Literary Scholarship* was published in 1987, but both Gar-diner's and Newton's essays were included in the 1984 *Tulsa Studies* special issue. In the Greene and Kahn volume, where each essay represents a different trend within feminist criticism, Gardiner's contribution represents psychoanalytic fem-inism, in particular mothering theory and its impact on literary criticism. Not a contributor to the 1985 anthology, Newton nonetheless plays a major role in the article immediately following Gardiner's, Cora Kaplan's consideration of socialist feminist criticism. Discussing the split between the social and the psychic in feminist criticism, Kaplan contrasts Newton's reading of *Villette* with Mary Ja-cobus's: Jacobus's is psychoanalytic, Newton's historical.

In 1985 Kaplan is longing for a feminist criticism that could combine psycho-analysis with history. Gardiner, who could speak for psychoanalysis with not a worry about history, and Newton, who is seen as disregarding the psychic for the sociohistorical, meet to express the same wish as Kaplan, in another book, but at the same moment in the history of feminist criticism. When we join Newton not to Jacobus but to Gardiner, we bring history together not only with the psyche but with mother.

Gardiner closes her essay in *Making a Difference* by bringing us back to her title, "Mind mother," commenting, "as daughters and sons, we automatically re-sent such a demand."[15] Contrasting Marcus and Gardiner in *Feminist Issues,* Stimpson repeats the word "authority": "Marcus calls for critics to accept the 'authority of the female text.' Marcus must be read against Judith Kegan Gardi-ner's study of the ambivalence of one female creator, Doris Lessing, towards the mother, an authority in the female text and time" (p. 3). Accepting authority, especially maternalized authority, can mean obeying, minding mother. The moth-er's "authority in time" might mean that since she is older, has more experience, she must be accepted as knowing better, and followed. That obedience can be conservative, dooming the daughter to repeat the mother. History might function as the same sort of authority. The phrase "history tells us" has been used to rule out possibilities, keeping us within the confines of what has already been.

Both mother and history, for Gardiner, function as models. There are two ways to embrace a model: imitate it or study it. In "thinking back through our mothers," as Marcus recommends in Woolf's words, do we think in identification with our mothers? Or do we think them through, analyze them, so we, in Gardiner's words, "can understand [our] mothers and change to become better mothers than [our] own mothers were" (p. 122)? A decade earlier Gardiner wrote: " 'We think back through our mothers.' . . . We have yet to think forward through them."[16]

Feminist Issues in Literary Scholarship resounds with the call to history. Sometimes history is opposed to theory, in this volume; sometimes there is the demand or the wish that the two be conjoined. In either case, the call and its intrication with the question of theory typifies this moment of academic feminist criticism, a moment we might locate around 1985.

In the pages of this anthology, Stimpson, Showalter, Nina Baym, Marcus, Gardiner, Newton, Robinson, and Fox-Genovese all call feminist literary criticism to an accounting with history. Beside this clarion call can also be found traces of a quiet rebellion against history. Whereas Newton and Fox-Genovese insist that literature ought not to be divorced from it, a few critics in the collection seem to find some sort of liberation in an escape from history.

Between Marcus's and Gardiner's essays lies Josephine Donovan's cultural feminist program, "Toward a Women's Poetics." In this attempt to characterize a women's writing practice, appearing first in the 1984 *Tulsa Studies* special issue, Donovan refers to another article she published that same year on Sarah Orne Jewett: "Using [the] notion that the traditional woman's sense of time is repetitive or cyclic rather than linear (the time of the quest), I suggest that Jewett's plots be understood as reflective of the traditional woman's consciousness. Ultimately, I argue, Jewett's greatest works concern an escape from the androcentric time of history into transcending gynocentric space."[17]

The gendered contrast between repetitive and quest time is the same one we find in Gardiner between reproducing mother and "going off to conquer the world." But whereas Gardiner urges us to escape repetition and become part of history, Donovan seems to value the escape from history. The notion of women's time here resembles the one used by Showalter. Showalter recommends constructing a history according to women's time, but Donovan sees this time leading us ultimately, and in the best cases, beyond history, perhaps even beyond time itself. The framing of the escape—"from the androcentric time of history into gynocentric space"—does not logically imply but nonetheless rhetorically suggests that time itself, in contradistinction to space, is androcentric.

Although cultural feminism might wish to escape time, and thus history as change through time, as well as history as dramatic world-conquering event, it does not seek to escape the past. On the contrary. Donovan's women's poetics is based in "traditional women's experience and practice in the past" (p. 100). Cultural feminist theory tends to imply that what women have been and done is what women ought to do or be. Respect for our history in the sense of what has been here threatens our participation in history in the sense of movement in time.

Jewett's escape from time into space is echoed elsewhere in the volume. Showalter divides feminist literary criticism into two types, gynocritics and gynesis: "Gynocritics is, roughly speaking, historical in orientation. . . . Gynesis rejects . . . the temporal dimension of women's experience . . . and seeks instead to understand the space granted to the feminine in the symbolic contract" (p. 37). "Gynocritics," her own coining, is used to name what Showalter herself and others like her do. She borrows Alice Jardine's word "gynesis" to represent feminist critics working under the sign of French poststructuralist theory.[18] Showalter's "gynesis" closely resembles what Marcus calls theory. Marcus's two examples of theorists who deny their own history—Gayatri Spivak and Peggy Kamuf—are avowed poststructuralists both. Although Showalter makes an attempt to be fair to this other side, and is certainly less dismissive of poststructuralist feminism than she was in 1979 or 1981,[19] her preference remains unmistakable.

Donovan's challenge to history could perhaps be overlooked as merely a token inclusion of the cultural feminist perspective which, if a major force in 1980s feminist thought, is wrong-headed and ahistorical ("comedic essentialism," Newton calls it, p. 125). Gynesis's rejection of the temporal dimension is likewise included as part of an attempt to give some time (if not quite equal) to the other side. Neither of these seriously challenge the hegemony of historicism in *Feminist Issues in Literary Scholarship*. But there are two other escapes from history in the volume, which cannot be dismissed quite so easily: one from the periphery and the other echoing it from the very center. I will turn to the margins first.

Laurie Finke's 1986 response to the 1984 "Feminist Issues in Literary Scholarship" locates in that *Tulsa Studies* special issue a "center" and "margins": "The 'center' of the issue is taken up with nine articles, all by prominent white female critics. . . . In the margins of the text are the book reviews to which are relegated women of color (there is one review on works by black feminist critics), lesbians (there is one review of a book on Radclyffe Hall), men (three of the reviewers are men and four books by men are reviewed), and women writers before 1800 (three reviews)" (Finke, p. 254). When the issue comes out as a book in 1987, none of the reviews are included, but one of the reviewers now has an article in the collection. The only one to survive marginal status is Hortense Spillers, author of the "one review on works by black feminist critics."[20]

Finke's tableau is slightly more complicated than its binary distinction might suggest. When Finke turns to the margins, it at first appears that subject matter is what counts. For the first two marginal categories she mentions only subject, however when she reaches the third category, she counts both author and subject. In the final category, she need not specify. Finke, in fact, is the author of a book review, on writers before 1800, in this issue of *Tulsa Studies*.

Finke does not mention the subject matter of the "central" articles; here she focuses instead on the author's identity. Aside from the issue of author versus subject, only two of her marginal categories reply directly to her portrait of the center. She does not comment on the sexual orientation of the central critics and she could hardly complain that they all write after 1800. Finke characterizes the center as "articles by prominent white females." Benstock publishes Finke's critique in *Tulsa Studies* in 1986. Looking at the 1987 version, following Finke, I would say that Benstock seems interested in remedying the "white" but not the "female."[21]

The nine articles of the *Tulsa Studies* special issue are, in the 1987 anthology, followed by three additional articles, which thus literally occupy the place of the 1984 book reviews. All three of these new articles deal with black women and/or race. But the middle one is also written by a "woman of color," by the only nonwhite female writing in the 1984 *Tulsa Studies,* Hortense Spillers.

Spiller's essay, originally published in *Feminist Studies* in 1983, is a study of three novels: Zora Neale Hurston's *Their Eyes Were Watching God* (1937), Margaret Walker's *Jubilee* (1966), and Toni Morrison's *Sula* (1973). Before turning to the novels, Spillers warns her readers: "The scheme of these observations . . . is not strictly chronological."[22] In fact, Spiller's "scheme" is in rebellion against chronological order. One of her central points is that Janie, the heroine of the 1937 novel, is located midway between Walker's Vyry Ware and Morrison's Sula. And in terms that have to do with development and progress: *Jubilee's* female protagonist is traditional; Sula is something new; Hurston's heroine falls right in-between. Spiller's explicitly anti-chronological method runs directly counter to Judith Newton's exhortations to understand a work in its time.[23]

Ending the paragraph which begins with her warning that she will not be "strictly chronological," Spillers makes it clear that this is not a casual gesture but implies a certain politics: "Ironically, it is exactly the right *not* to accede to the simplifications and mystifications of a strictly historiographical time line that now promises the greatest freedom of discourse to black people, to black women, as critics, teachers, writers, and thinkers" (p. 183). Her repetition of the adverb "strictly" contrasts effectively with "freedom" to suggest history might also be a discipline in the sense of that which keeps us in line.[24]

Spillers is not the only critic in the volume to suggest violating chronological order. The first essay in the collection, "Beyond the Reaches of Feminist Criticism," proposes we read Hurston's contemporary, Gerturde Stein, out of order: "If we take Stein out of her modernist setting . . . Stein seems to be one of our contemporaries" (pp. 25–26). This critic is working to free Stein from other feminist critics: "Her work had been recovered by . . . feminist critics who, however refreshing their sensitivity to Stein as a woman within a patriarchal framework, have continued to discuss her work within the confines of the modernist project. That is, her work has been viewed as the product of her historical situation; she has remained 'contemporary' with her contemporaries" (p. 25). The word "confines" here could suggest, like Spiller's "strictly," that respect for historical context can operate as a form of constraint.

I have used Finke's mapping to show how Spillers exemplifies the margins of

Benstock's anthology. We might be prepared to see this black challenge to historicism join cultural feminism and poststructuralism as token inclusions, of restricted effect upon the volume's hegemonic center. But the reader of Stein who joins Spillers in her lack of respect for chronology is none other than Shari Benstock, the volume's editor, herself.

In counting nine articles as the center, Finke does not include Benstock's which, presented as "From the Editor's Perspective" in the 1984 *Tulsa Studies*, looks like some sort of introduction. Although Finke never mentions Benstock's essay, we might still use her mapping to locate it. If the book reviews, after the articles proper, are a marginal edge of the special issue, so too is this text, preceding the real articles, which is about Gertrude Stein and treats her writing as specifically lesbian. We might thus keep Finke's notion that lesbians are relegated to the margin. But we would be forced to contemplate the possibility of an editor marginalizing herself.

In 1987, when the issue is republished as a book, Benstock's text is essentially unchanged. But the tag "From the Editor's Perspective" has been removed and the piece is now preceded by Stimpson's Introduction. Like Spillers, Benstock moves from margin to full-fledged article. Yet it strains our notions of tokenism to see the editor's inclusion as merely token. In order to understand this editor and her "marginal" place in her own anthology we may have to rethink marginality and editorial authority. In 1983, Benstock's first text under the tag "From the Editor's Perspective" ends with her call for the special issue that would become "Feminist Issues in Literary Scholarship." In the last sentence of that first editorial, she writes: "Most especially, I hope that *Tulsa Studies* will resist the reestablishment of the old centrality under a new guise."[25]

In the present study, "around 1981" locates a moment when feminist criticism attains some sort of centrality. And, in the present study, that moment is centrally connected to the figure of Elaine Showalter. Showalter is, in every sense of the word, framed by the present book which describes a structure radiating from that moment. In that moment, the first section of this book, are two anthologies: Showalter's *New Feminist Criticism* and Abel's *Writing and Sexual Difference*. Showalter's strategy as an editor is unabashedly to claim centrality for herself. Her anthology contains not only her introduction but two other pieces by her, each heading a section, each interpreting and directing the path of feminist criticism. One of those Showalter texts, the one dating from 1981 ("Feminist Criticism in the Wilderness"), also appears in Abel's anthology, immediately following Abel's introduction. At the back of Benstock's 1987 collection, in the notes on contributors, we read that Elaine Showalter "is editor of *Writing and Sexual Difference* and an anthology, *The New Feminist Criticism*" (p. 234).

Showalter's essay in *Feminist Issues in Literary Scholarship*, like her essay in *Writing and Sexual Difference*, appears directly after the editor's text and is, like "Feminist Criticism in the Wilderness," an overview of feminist literary criticism.

Benstock repeats Abel's placement of Showalter; the lapsus in the contributors' notes might then imagine the most dramatic marginalizing of an editor from her own anthology.

Of all the anthologies we have considered, *Feminist Issues in Literary Scholarship* is the only one to have an introduction by someone other than the editor. Benstock has given up the privilege (or the responsibility) of taking stock of and speaking for the collection as a whole. Her own contribution is entitled "Beyond the Reaches of Feminist Criticism: A Letter from Paris," thus doubly suggesting something from outside American feminist criticism. And if "gynesis" names something marginalized in this volume, it is worth noting that Benstock opens with an epigraph from Jardine's "Gynesis."[26]

Referring to the male theoretical masters (French, poststructuralist) behind "gynesis," Benstock has occasion to discuss marginality: "If some of these men align themselves and their theoretical practice with *les marginaux* in western culture, we suspect it is only to secure for themselves a firmer grip on the center of theoretical discourse" (p. 9). She thus suggests one possible motive for self-marginalization: in order better to occupy the center. Yet Benstock does not simply align herself with the margins.

Benstock explicitly asks: "Do we claim the center for ourselves (taking up the modernist project) or do we redefine the limits of authority by which the center constitutes itself (taking up the post-modernist project)? Or do we, like Gertrude Stein, try to do both?" (p. 12). Refusing to claim the center for herself, Benstock would be a thoroughly postmodern editor. Yet it is pretty clear that, to the extent that Benstock marks one of the alternatives as superior, the right answer is "try to do both, like Gertrude Stein."

Virginia Woolf is Marcus's model for feminist criticism; Benstock's model is Gertrude Stein. Benstock's essay cites Catharine Stimpson as someone "currently at work on a book-length study of Stein." If Benstock asks Stimpson to replace her in the Introduction, it undoubtedly has something to do with the Stein connection. In the Introduction Stimpson names Stein as a model for the feminist criticism she would like to see and links that model to a certain Woolf: "Calling its own premises and proto-canons into question, such a revisionary feminist criticism would *honor* both the more ironic, lucid Virginia Woolf and the radically innovative Gertrude Stein. It would *follow Stein's injunction:* . . . 'Act so that there is no use in a center' " (p. 5, emphasis added). Despite the anticentric content of her "injunction," Stein, like Marcus's Woolf, appears here as an authority we ought to follow.

How does one *follow,* especially how does one *honor* "radical innovation"? Where Stimpson asks us to "follow" Stein, giving her priority, Benstock's rebellion against history might make it possible to think of Stein as following us. When she imagines Stein as a postmodernist, as one of our contemporaries, she recreates Stein in our image; we become the model for Stein.

Benstock would seem to belong to the perhaps marginal camp in this collection who rebel against authority in time. Marcus, on the other hand, is squarely among those who call us to account for being disrespectful of history and our elders. Yet we cannot in any way simply polarize Benstock and Marcus. Not only does the editor credit Marcus with "informing the conception" of the anthology, but there is also a solidarity between Marcus's model feminist critic and Benstock's post-modern Stein.

Marcus proposes an approach she calls "still practice": "*A Room of One's Own* is 'still practice.' . . . This concept of 'still practice' . . . is a model for feminist criticism. It demands the suppression of the critic's ego in a genuine attempt at explicating the signs of the subject, her body, her text. It is a frustrating and selfless activity" (p. 80). It is precisely this selflessness which rejoins Benstock's Stein: "Oddly enough, this new reading of Stein writes an ironic afterword to that early Stein criticism that accused her of having an ego as big as the Ritz. In order to make the kind of . . . discoveries I am claiming she did make, Gertrude Stein had to renounce ego" (p. 26).

Whereas Marcus's feminist critic renounces ego in order to listen to "oppressed women," Stein "submitted her will to language" (pp. 80, 16–17). I do not want to deny the crucial differences between these two renunciations: the one moral, the other postmodernist. Yet I find the connections striking and I credit them particularly because of the way Benstock and Marcus cite each other in such comradely fashion. Whether or not Marcus's "selfless activity" can describe Stein, it might more properly characterize Benstock, the heterosexual critic speaking in defense of a lesbian's power. According to Marcus, the feminist critic ought to speak on behalf of her more marginalized sisters, "women of color and lesbians" (p. 79).

Marcus's title—"Still Practice, A/Wrested Alphabet"—comes from Shakes-peare's *Titus Andronicus.* Raped, without tongue or arms, Lavinia makes bodily gestures to Titus, her father, who asserts: "I, of these, will wrest an alphabet, / And by still practice learn to know thy meaning."[27] Marcus comments: "The story is not a pretty one, but it does give us a vivid image for the feminist critic and her relation to oppressed women" (p. 80). I am struck by Marcus's placing "the feminist critic" outside the category of "oppressed women." "Oppressed women" are those not only raped but silenced: because the feminist critic still has her tongue and arms she is not oppressed. It is our responsibility to speak for, care for, and defend "oppressed women," like Titus, the father.

Perhaps Titus can be the father of feminist criticism because his "still practice" in attending to his daughter is so motherly. Unlike fathers or children, mothers have traditionally been valued for their selfless activity in caring for others. It is this resemblance to the ideological construction of the good woman as good mother even more than Titus's gender that disturbs me in Marcus's construction of the good feminist as selfless caretaker of those who cannot speak for themselves.

Stimpson's Introduction asks us to read Marcus against Judith Gardiner. The latter seems particularly aware of the ideological functioning of motherliness. Her study of Lessing's work begins with the 1960 story "Our Friend Judith." Her reading of that story concludes with a paragraph that contains one or two of the enigmatic but suggestive phrases that I consider Gardiner's critical signature:

> The story does not devalue Judith for being unmarried; rather, it shows her an admirable new woman. However, its attitudes to motherhood are ambivalent. . . . [T]he incident of the cat who killed her kitten exposes Judith's thwarted maternity as the essence of her character. Only in attending the birthing cat . . . does she evoke our sympathy. . . . We, the motherly, understand people as do the narrator and her friend Betty. Judith does not. . . . [S]ince she cannot understand others, she is doomed to remain a fictional character, not a motherly creator. (p. 119)

Suddenly, in the middle of the interpretation, a first person plural pronoun appears, representing a community of readers. Its first occurrence is ordinary enough: "evoke *our* sympathy." But with its next appearance this collective subject particularizes itself in a rather startling way: "we, the motherly." Not just those who may have read the story but those who are, as opposed to those who aren't, "motherly."

I find the phrase—"we, the motherly"—powerful and puzzling. It probably is to be taken ironically since Gardiner criticizes a certain ideological complicity here. It clearly includes Gardiner and is perhaps part of some sort of self-criticism. I recall that, in the biographical sketches of the 1978 anthology *Feminist Criticism*, the entry for Judith Kegan Gardiner concludes: "Her mother and two daughters are among her heroines, she states" (p. 354).

Gardiner concludes her reading of Judith on the diacritical distinction "a fictional character, not a motherly creator." Here the irony is even less certain. The categories are theoretically fascinating if not referentially clear. My association is to Gardiner's pithy and evocative formulation "The hero is her author's daughter," the refined distillation of her attempt to apply psychoanalytic to literary theory.[28] Since "creator" seems the more attractive category, "motherly" would be a positive trait. Or else, and I cannot disallow this possibility, the irony has extremely wide repercussions.

"A fictional character, not a motherly creator" joins "the hero is her author's daughter" and "history is like mother" as phrases by Gardiner which unleash in me a flood of thought. Gardiner tends to set these jewels in her prose with little explanation. For me they sparkle with the promise of a wealth of understanding, like minimalist poems, tight and compact, set in but discontinuous from a discursive context. Of all these, "we, the motherly" is probably the most minimalist of all. I can barely begin to imagine what Gardiner wishes to suggest by it. But, if puzzling, it is nonetheless pertinent, for it is not the only "motherly we" in the volume.

Criticizing the place allotted to the mother in psychoanalytic feminist theory, Nina Baym writes: "Of course we all know, in our rational moments, that the mother's influence lasts far beyond the age of five. But even if we were to grant its waning at that age, we surely know that the mother's role in the child's earliest life is not so simple as this pre-Oedipal model makes it out to be. (At least we who have been mothers know.)"[29] The passage begins by evoking a community of reasonable people, or at least of people who have rational moments. The first "we" is broadly inclusive, rhetorically calling her readers to join her in finding this psychoanalytic model ridiculous. The "we" insists, occurring four times in the space of three sentences. The insistence builds ("we all know," "we surely know"), implicitly mocking not only the pre-Oedipal model, but anyone who might abstain from the "we." And then the parenthesis renders the "we" exclusive.

Baym's "motherly we" reads mothering theory: "recent feminist literary work on mothers and daughters . . . provides testimony, often unwitting and in contradiction to its stated intentions, of the deep-seated hostility of daughters to mothers. (Mothers do not speak of daughters in this discourse.) Adrienne Rich's *Of Women Born* . . . is strikingly cold when not silent on the writer's own mother. Nor does Rich's poetry speak to her mother" (p. 57). The parenthesis in this passage perhaps refers to the one a page earlier, quoted above. In contradistinction to Baym's text, mothering theory is not spoken by a motherly subject. "We who have been mothers" read this disclosure and remark the hostility to mothers: "What purpose does the theory . . . serve? It minimizes the mother" (p. 56). The motherly reading ultimately unveils the pre-Oedipal mother as itself Oedipal, constructed according to the daughter's classic Oedipal wish: "The matricidal impulse could not be plainer" (p. 58).

The citation of Rich is surprising. Rich, after all, writes *Of Woman Born* explicitly as a mother, albeit as a mother of sons. Baym, however, reads not Rich the mother but Rich the daughter. The latter is not appreciative enough. The comments about Rich bespeak another aspect of motherly discourse; the flip side of self-suppression is bitterness and resentment. Here is a tone likely to produce guilt in "today's feminist daughter-critic" (p. 58).

Baym is worried about the future: "There is no future for a commonality of women if we cannot traverse the generations" (p. 58). Marcus specifically closes her essay on a model of generational traversal: "One after the other [feminist critics] have climbed in the pantry window of literary criticism taking note of the muddy footprints of their predecessors. It is in this way that literary criticism moves from one generation to the next, affirming its mothers' works and moving them along" (p. 94).

Although Baym's explicit complaint, and Marcus's too, would seem to be with theory, that protest is accompanied by a psychologically more effective complaint:

feminist critics are not good daughters to their mothers. Whereas Baym largely restricts herself to negative examples, Marcus cites appropriate daughterly behavior. If Woolf is the mother of feminist criticism, Marcus nominates Sylvia Townsend Warner as number one daughter: "[Townsend Warner's] 'Women as Writers' is not a seductive sapphistry like *A Room of One's Own,* but in its own dry, wryly ironic way it continues the work of its predecessor as feminist criticism. It modestly apprentices itself (we might say 'daughters itself') to its mother text and brings up to date the history of women writers" (p. 92).

The feminist critic must renounce ego not only in the service of (more) oppressed women but also in apprenticeship to the predecessor. Daughterliness is next to motherliness. If the good daughter modestly apprentices herself to the good mother, then she will be a good feminist. We, the daughterly, resemble the motherly, but as pale imitations, dry rather than seductive, lacking the mother's power, except through identification.

Feminist Issues in Literary Scholarship gives another example of good daughterly writing. According to Spillers, *"Jubilee* is, in effect, the tale translated of the author's female ancestors. This is a story of the foremothers, a celebration of their stunning faith and intractable powers of endurance. . . . The source material for the novel is based on the life story of the author's great-grandmother, told to her by her grandmother in the best tradition of oral his/herstory" (pp. 191, 205). Walker's heroine, Vyry Ware, is heroically maternal: "Vyry and Randall Ware . . . have two children . . . and Ware makes plans for their liberation. His idea is that he or Vyry will return for the children later, but Vyry refuses to desert them. Her negotiation of a painful passage across the countryside . . . groans with material burden. . . . Vyry travels with the two children——Jim toddling and the younger child Minna in her arms" (p. 190). Not only a literal good mother, Vyry is figuratively and symbolically motherly: "Vyry Ware belongs to, embodies, a corporate ideal. The black woman in her characterization exists for the race, in its behalf, and in maternal relationship to its profoundest needs and wishes" (p. 182).

Neither the daughterly Walker nor the motherly Ware are Spiller's heroes. Sensitive and appreciative with all three of the novels she considers, Spillers makes her preference clear, from the first paragraph: "*Sula* . . . is, to my mind, the single most important irruption of black women's writing in our era. . . . the novel inscribes a dimension of being, moving at last in contradistinction to the tide of virtue and pathos that tends to overwhelm black female characterization in a monolith of terms and possibilities. I regard Sula the character as a literal and figurative *breakthrough* toward the assertion of what we may call, in relation to her literary 'relatives,' new female being" (p. 181).

Spillers celebrates Sula as a "breakthrough" precisely in contradistinction to the "ideal" exemplified by Walker's Vyry Ware. "If Vyry is woman-for-the-other, then Sula is woman-for-self" (p. 182). This contrast is articulated specifically in relation to motherliness: "Vyry Ware . . . embodies a corporate ideal. The black woman in her characterization exists for the race . . . and in maternal relationship to its profoundest needs. . . . Sula, on the other hand, lives for Sula and has no wish to 'mother' anyone, let alone the black race in some symbolic concession to a collective need" (p. 182).

Sula is a bad woman. Her "badness" (p. 183) involves her "nubile *singleness* and refusal of the acts and rites of maternity" (p. 200). A white academic critic articulates her own badness in similar terms: "I enjoyed thinking of myself as a bad woman; never until recently, did I admit that it was never 'bad' to refuse to be 'good' in the self-mutilating way young women were raised to be in the 1950s. I never wanted to be a caretaker; I never saw myself as a wife or a mother, and I never was one."[30]

Like the article on Sula, this statement by Nina Auerbach was not in the 1984 version of "Feminist Issues in Literary Scholarship." The acknowledgments to the 1987 volume state that, of the original *Tulsa Studies* articles, Auerbach's and Baym's are "in slightly altered forms." Although the alterations to Baym's piece are indeed "slight," not noticeable in a casual reading, Auerbach's 1987 piece is a substantially different text. In fact only about a quarter of her 1984 text is even included in the much longer 1987 text.

Between 1984 and 1987, Auerbach, like Spillers and Benstock, moves from the periphery toward the center of the volume. If the center of the *Tulsa Studies* special issue was made up of nine articles, Auerbach's was the last of these, right before the book reviews. Just as we might see Spillers as central to the margins, Auerbach, in 1984, was at the edge of the center. Spiller's was the only book review to have endnotes; Auerbach's was the only of the central texts with no notes. Auerbach's 1984 text was not actually a full-fledged article: it was a mere four pages long, shorter, in fact, then Spiller's six and one-half page Review Essay. In 1987, Auerbach's text is not only more than doubled in length, with fourteen endnotes; it is followed by three additional articles so it is no longer on the edge.

According to Finke's typology, relegated to the margins of the 1984 issue are not only women of color, lesbians, and writers before 1800, but also men. Both versions of Auerbach's contribution make the point that, unlike the mainstream of feminist criticism, unlike gynocriticism, she writes about men's books.

Auerbach's 1987 text associates gynocriticism with Sandra Gilbert and Elaine Showalter. Auerbach contrasts not only her work but her life with these two other feminists of her generation. Showalter, for example, was an "obedient good woman" and "a caretaking faculty wife" (p. 151). Auerbach is referring to the 1983 English Institute talk published in *Feminist Issues in Literary Scholarship,* where Showalter opens her life history: "In 1968 I was a faculty wife with a small child" (p. 34). Auerbach's adjective "caretaking" specifically refers to Showalter's motherhood. Gynocritics here lines up with "we who have been mothers."

Between 1984 and 1987 Auerbach gives her contribution a new title: "Engorging the Patriarchy." One of the few passages remaining essentially unchanged from her 1984 essay glosses this title: "Probably, I share the primitive superstition that by writing about the patriarchy, as by eating it, I engorge its power."[31] This sentence would suggest that reading men could be an act of dominance rather than submission. As a sister hearty appetite, I am, first of all, taken with the oral character of her act. Where the caretaking woman feeds others, this woman eats. The good woman nurtures men; the bad woman feeds off them.

This hearty oral scenario is shadowed by another I find more troubling. When, in 1987, Auerbach elevates the verb "engorge" to her title, presenting it thus first of all out of context, it becomes even more likely that a phallic double entendre might occur to us. One of the meanings of "engorge" is "to congest or fill to excess, as with blood." But even if we bracket the phallic possibility, the oral scene itself can become ambiguous. "Engorge" as a transitive verb can mean "to devour greedily," but it can also mean "to feed (as an animal) to repletion."[32] Auerbach does not comment on these shadow meanings. How can we know for sure if her "engorging" consumes the patriarchy or feeds it full?

Whatever the status of this ambiguity in and for Auerbach specifically, it resonates more generally in the position of the bad woman in patriarchy. Does the bad girl break out of the strictures demanding women's obedience or does she just titillate the patriarchs? Engorging their power?

The valence of the bad girl left ambiguous, the good girl turns out to be no less trouble. Although this anthology seems at any moment ready to range us in good girls against bad (we, the motherly, against the bad daughters; scholars against theorists), the oppositions neither hold nor actually break down. There is angry, moral discourse and ironic, superior discourse, both of which have the effect of dividing the world into opposing camps. But, taking the volume as a whole, it is hard to tell not only who is good and who bad, but what set of values might consistently apply.

As I have constructed the volume, Baym and Auerbach would represent opposite poles on the scale of good womanhood as motherliness. Yet to leave the two Ninas in opposition would be to ignore a major commonality: both term themselves "pluralists" and are angered by an orthodox position which would define what a feminist critic should or should not do.[33] In 1984, Auerbach defines feminist pluralism as "insisting on the differences that allowed us to say no in the first place to what we were told women were" (p. 153). This pluralism could be seen as a bad girl's stance.

As I have constructed the volume, Baym is in league with Marcus in shaming us into appropriate daughterly behavior. Others have grouped Baym and Marcus together in an anti-theory camp; yet this togetherness can only be achieved by ignoring what Baym explicitly says about Marcus.[34] Baym begins her final paragraph: "I am, evidently, a pluralist. Essays in feminist journals are permeated with musts and shoulds" (p. 59). At this point, we are directed to her final note: "See Jane Marcus in her attack on pluralism, 'Storming the Toolshed' . . . : 'she must

... she must ... she must.' If that *she* is *me*, somebody (once again) is telling me what I *'must'* do to be a true woman. . . . I've been here before" (p. 61, Baym's ellipses in internal quotation). Baym rebels against Marcus's prescription of appropriate behavior.

When Auerbach presents herself as a pluralist in 1984, she explicitly derives the term from Annette Kolodny's 1980 article "Dancing through the Minefield." Baym never explicitly mentions Kolodny's article but, in introducing the concept of pluralism, writes: "Pluralists 'dance'; theorists 'storm' " (p. 45). The first verb would seem to allude to Kolodny's article; the second to Marcus's "Storming the Toolshed" which appears in Baym's final note. Marcus's "Storming" in fact discusses Kolodny's "Dancing" and her pluralism: "In 'Dancing through the Minefield,' Kolodny's liberal relaxation of the tensions among us and the tensions between feminists and the academy reflects a similar relaxation on the part of historians and political activists. What this does is to isolate Marxist feminists and lesbians on the barricades while 'good girl' feminists fold their tents and slip quietly into the establishment."[35] Whereas with Baym and Auerbach pluralists were the bad girls rebelling against authority, when we turn to Marcus pluralists are the "good girls."

Perhaps there are two kinds of good girls: good daughters of the mother and good daughters of the father. The " 'good girl' feminists" who "slip quietly into the establishment" are, presumably, good in the sense of respectful of paternal authority. On the other hand, Marcus and Baym would have us respect *maternal* authority. Marcus makes that quite explicit. Yet when she complains that theorists "assert as virgin births interpretations which have ancestry" or that theorists "want to be orphaned" (p. 90), the issue begins to seem not maternal as opposed to paternal authority but recognition of parental authority.

The good/bad split, in feminist discourse, is shot through with irony. First of all, it is, by and large, bad to be a "good girl." Probably no feminist wants to be a "good girl," although no one really wants to be bad. Probably most every feminist fears that she is good and/or that she is bad. Out of that double bind we get feminists accusing other feminists of being "good girls" which implies that they are bad feminists, i.e., bad girls.

Center and margins interact with the good/bad dichotomy. If we take the center/margin structure straight, the center defines itself as good and relegates its others, presumed bad, to the margins. But in feminist (or postmodernist) discourse the center tends to be suspect, i.e., bad, and the margins have the moral authority, that is, it is good to be marginal. Thus marginalized by her badness, the bad girl is good.

The center/margins dichotomy also interacts with pluralism. Marcus quotes Gayatri Spivak: "Pluralism is the method employed by the *central* authorities to neutralize opposition by seeming to accept it. The gesture of pluralism on the part of the *marginal* can only mean capitulation to the center."[36] Pluralism's valence depends upon whether one is located in the center or the margins. Like the poststructuralist identification with *les marginaux,* pluralism enhances the center's power. On the other hand, it diminishes the margin's resistant force. If pluralism has become a focus for debate in the academic feminist critical community, if it seems to carry with it the highly moralized if nonetheless ambiguous opposition of good and bad girls, it is probably because feminist literary criticism is no longer simply marginal while still not comfortably central.

The final essay in the 1987 anthology is a telling case in point. Three essays were added to the 1987 collection, replacing the book reviews: the first two consider African-American women's writing; the last article is on the Euro-American modernist poet H. D. Given much attention by more than a decade of feminist criticism, H. D. has practically entered the bisexual modernist canon. The supplementary articles in the 1987 volume seem like an attempt to include the margins. What, we might ask, is H. D. doing in those margins?

The most immediate answer to this question is that Susan Stanford Friedman is examining H. D.'s relation to African-Americans. Friedman, who has written two books on H. D. and edited a volume of her letters, gives an exhaustive account of the places in the poet's life and writings where black people appear. In many ways, this gesture of returning to a canonical white writer after considering black women's texts seems right. First of all, it ensures that black women are not completely on the periphery of the volume. But beyond that superficial gesture, if we white women are going to turn to racial questions, it is essential that we counteract "the implication that only women of color possess a racial identity that has to be understood by the critic" (Robinson, p. 147). As Robinson goes on to say, "[i]n fact, in a society divided not only by racial differences but by racism, all writers have a significant racial identity." It would seem that the anthology absorbs Robinson's lesson and goes on from the consideration of those women who have had expressly to bear the burden of race to see what light such considerations might shed on a member of the default race.[37]

But as much as turning the question of race on ourselves and our white sisters seems an appropriate response to the awareness that black feminists have forced upon us, I find myself embarrassed by Friedman's essay. Friedman supplies us with detailed evidence from life and work, calling the two sections of her essay "The Biographical Record" and "The Literary Record." But this evidence is "for the record" not so much in the sense of an objective study but in the sense of a legal brief, not scholarship but advocacy. Friedman explicitly sets out to defend H. D. from charges of "political escapism." She theoretically locates the case within the feminist questioning of a gendered understanding of political activism which excludes a lot of women's more personal style of political practice. Although the theoretical point is certainly well-taken, this defense appears at the end of the 1987 anthology not because of the general issue of political engagement but because of the almost exclusive concentration on the single political issue of

334 / JANE GALLOP

white/black race relations. Friedman musters all her documentation to prove that, in her relations to black people and in her views on race, H. D. was good, perhaps not perfect by our 1980s standards, but definitely better than the others in her milieu.

A few examples will demonstrate the tone of unabashed advocacy: (1) "Although Bryher's wealth and the interracial erotics in H. D.'s circle constituted the conditions of white paternalism, the Harlem Renaissance did not function for H. D. as a fashionable excursion into the dangerously exotic and erotic world of Otherness." (2) "A narrative that focuses on a young white girl who loves the family's black servant dangerously evokes the conventional stereotyped script. . . . What is interesting about the issue of race in *HER* is the degree to which H. D. avoids the familiar pattern." (3) "This focus on politics as it permeates the inner life is partially responsible for the degree to which H. D. avoided exploitative objectification of blacks that characterized the fascination of so many wealthy white liberals involved in the Harlem Renaissance."[38]

In a remarkably bland sentence, Stimpson's Introduction links Friedman's essay to another in the collection: "Susan Stanford Friedman and Paula A. Treichler show specifically how being a woman can mark poems and stories" (p. 3). Nothing else is said in the Introduction about either of these essays. The sentence closes a paragraph; the next paragraph discusses the danger in universalizing the category of woman and not attending to things like sexual orientation and race.

Treichler's essay is a reading of Charlotte Perkins Gilman's "The Yellow Wall-paper," a text canonized by feminist criticism. In 1989, Susan S. Lanser discusses Treichler's article along with other feminist readings of the story published between 1973 and 1986 (the very period covered by the present study) as a way of tracing the mainstream of feminist literary criticism through its discussion of this privileged text. Pointing out that none of these diverse and inspired interpretations ever wondered why the wallpaper was yellow, Lanser connects the color to racial questions and carefully documents Gilman's racism. Lanser does not demonize Gilman or her later day feminist critics but rather calls upon us to recognize her and our contradictory places as subjects *in* ideology and history. Lanser's reading of Gilman responds to the same historical forces as Friedman's reading of H. D. but seems willing to look upon our foremothers' shame in order not to repeat, unwittingly, their errors.[39]

Friedman had published an earlier attempt to show that H. D. was "good," although in quite a different sense. A 1975 article argues for her inclusion in the (male) modernist canon, emphasizing her commonalities with those already included:

> H. D. is part of the same literary tradition that produced the mature work of the "established" artists—T. S. Eliot, Ezra Pound . . ., D. H. Lawrence. She in fact knew these artists well. . . . Like these artists, H. D. began

> writing in the aestheticism . . . characteristic of the imagists; and like them, she turned to epic form and to myth. . . . I . . . insist . . . that H. D. was a serious prolific poet exploring the same questions as her famous counterparts and thus inviting comparison with them.[40]

In the essay included in the Benstock anthology, first published in 1986, Friedman worries about these same connections: "No one has yet associated H. D.'s politics with the view of many of the male modernists she knew well—Ezra Pound's anti-Semitic fascism, T. S. Eliot's reverant [sic] Toryism . . . , D. H. Lawrence's flirtations with racism and fascism. . . . It is possible, however, that people will come to regard H. D.'s politics as a gentler version of the generally reactionary direction of these men" (p. 209). Friedman's essay is a concerted attempt to forestall this very possibility.

Although I am contrasting Friedman's two defenses of H. D., I do not believe they contradict each other. It is not Friedman's understanding of H. D. that has changed; it is the critical context in which a white academic feminist critic writes about a white woman poet. In the mid-seventies, the critic wanted to prove her poet was "good" by male modernist aesthetic standards; by the mid-eighties she wants to prove her poet "good" by color-conscious feminist political standards. Or, to put the same story another way: in the mid-seventies white women modernists were marginal and critics struggled to make them central; by the mid-eighties white women modernists are practically central and critics want to align them with the margins.

Friedman's 1986 essay concludes: "Working through issues of race played a significant role in the development of [H. D.'s] political syncretism, a modernism of the margins rather than the reactionary center. H. D.'s particular modernism developed out of her identification with all the others who have been 'dispersed and scattered' by the forces of history: blacks, Jews, Indians, homosexuals and lesbians, women, even artists" (p. 227). "The reactionary center" is the modernism of Eliot, Pound, and Lawrence. What is H. D. doing in the margins, I asked? Hers is a "modernism of the margins," replies Friedman; she identifies with "all the others" that Benstock, in her Letter from Paris, calls "les marginaux."

The first article in *Feminist Issues in Literary Scholarship* defines the modernist project as "claiming the center" and, defying chronological order, saves Stein as a postmodernist. The last article in the anthology finds, in addition to "a modernism of the center," a "modernism of the margins" and locates H. D. there. In the first article, the volume's editor defines the modernist project as centrist explicitly in relation to the question of where we, today's feminist critics, should position ourselves: "Do we claim the center for ourselves (taking up the modernist project)"? (p. 12). At the end of the volume, as Friedman pleads for H. D.'s marginal identity, she does so, I would wager, for the sake of our position as prominent white female critics.

"With all this jostling in the margins," asks Marcus, "who is in the center?" She then supplies a sort of answer: "Shari Benstock . . . suggests that academic feminist critics are not marginal in the least, compared to black outsiders or writers excluded from the academy" (p. 87). Marcus is referring to Benstock's 1983 editorial, the seed text for *Feminist Issues in Literary Scholarship,* the text where Benstock gives Marcus credit for informing her conception of the collection. Somewhere around the birth of this 1984/1987 anthology, somewhere between Shari Benstock and Jane Marcus, is a recognition that academic feminist critics are no longer marginal. We might read the anthology as a very complex response to this ambiguous fact.

Citing but not quoting Benstock, Marcus lists two sorts of writers more marginal than academic feminists: "black outsiders or writers excluded from the academy." The first group is, at least in a token way, included between 1984 and 1987. And looking beyond this specific anthology, I would say that a major gesture of academic feminist literary criticism in the mid-1980s has been the inclusion of "black outsiders." White feminist critics by the dozens have turned to writing about black women writers. Finally, we started listening to what black feminists had been saying for at least a decade (if not a century), although too often listening just long enough to rush out and quickly try to do the right thing. It is possible that, not long after I write these words in 1990, we might envision an inclusion of black women writers in the literary academy paralleling the inclusion of white women writers in the 1980s. But Marcus's second category, "writers excluded from the academy," could pose a more troubling problem for us academic feminists, if we understand it not as those contingently excluded (the writers we fight to get into the canon) but as the structural, institutional exclusion of the nonacademic, of those who might challenge our values, those who are excluded by the processes which constitute our inclusion.

It is specifically in relation to our centrality and its complicity with this exclusion that Marcus suggests we identify with Titus Andronicus: "It is a frustrating and selfless activity that must include, as in the case of Titus, a recognition of one's own complicity in the silencing of the subject" (p. 80). If I am embarrassed by Friedman's attempt to prove that H. D. is (and by implication we prominent white female critics are) good and marginal, I find myself equally uncomfortable with Marcus's moral imperative that, in recognition of our guilty centrality, we suppress our selves in the service of our silenced, marginalized sisters.

According to Friedman, H. D. learns her own marginalization and finds her feminism by identifying with racially oppressed others. Auerbach's 1987 text tells a similar story: "Putting aside my private, lifelong and often enjoyable rebellion, I accepted my oppression as a woman after living with a racist and class oppression that included men as well. I recognized myself as a victim when I saw others victimized. In the best female, caretaking tradition, I learned to fight for myself by fighting for others" (pp. 154–55). This is definitely *the* "female tradition": in the nineteenth century, white women got the idea of fighting for their "emancipation" by working for the abolition of slavery; in the 1960s, white women got the idea of fighting for our "rights" from working in the black "civil rights" movement.

A page earlier, Auerbach states: "I never wanted to be a caretaker; I never saw myself as a wife or a mother, and I never was one." Never wanting to be a caretaker, she finds herself "in the best female, caretaking tradition." We are more familiar with the feminist story of "good women" learning to claim something for themselves. Auerbach is telling a different story: about how a "bad woman" gave up her private rebellion, in order to fight as a woman for women. But in going from rebellious to caretaking, Auerbach is not simply crossing the line from bad girl to good. Auerbach redefines the "female, caretaking tradition" so it is not synonymous with self-suppression, so it includes fighting "for myself."

"It was never 'bad,'" Auerbach realizes, "to refuse to be 'good' in the self-mutilating way" (p. 152). The opposition between good girls and bad has historically set women against each other. Although the standards that determine good girls have varied over the last century or so, and in relation to specific subcultures, the moralized, adversarial opposition has remained powerful in its ability to paralyze individual women and to obstruct alliances between women of differing groups.

Within our ideology of normative femininity, middle-class and white, as it has played itself out since the 1830s, the black female has not only been excluded from pink femininity, she has been suspended as the "bad woman" from the burning cross of sex and race. Dialectically attempting to free her sisters from that violent marginalization, the African-American woman writer has, since she started writing, constructed the black heroine as good woman. Yet if the bad woman is marginalized, the good woman approaches the center only at the expense of her self. For Spillers, Sula takes the risk of being bad so that the black woman not be confined to the self-sacrifice of good womanhood.

Not only race, but class difference, sexual orientation, ethnicity, among other less theorized differences, all have been interpreted through the bad girl/good girl dichotomy. The split serves patriarchy not only by marginalizing disloyal women, not only by setting women nearer the center of power against those less domesticated, but by ensuring that the women closest to power renounce their selves in order to keep that proximity. One of the constants behind the good girl/bad girl dichotomy is that it is bad to have power. The moralized split, if left unanalyzed, unfortunately reappears within feminism, interpreting differences between women, for example, marginalizing some women as not feminist (enough): bad or "good girl." And I fear, as some few women approach a sort of peripheral centrality, specifically for our present concern, as some feminist critics find a secure place within the literary academy, we will be forced to choose between selfish individualism and selflessness for the sake of our more oppressed sisters.

I have, throughout my career as an academic feminist, enjoyed the role of bad girl. Yet if to affirm one's identity as bad girl can be a first step in breaking out of obedient femininity, it seems necessary to get beyond that posture in order to challenge the good/bad divide that makes the assertion of female self too often private and destructive, too often at the expense of other women.

History is like mother. As I read the 1984 special issue "Feminist Issues in Literary Scholarship," "history" seemed very much "like mother." Both words, differently but in insistent if not fully articulated connection, seemed to carry moral imperatives, produced guilt/resistance/resentment in me, the bad daughter-critic, not daughterly or motherly enough, insufficiently historical. When I read the 1987 volume, I noted in Spillers a rebellion against both history and the motherly. I wanted to use Spillers/Sula to break the power of the volume's center, to rebel against maternal authority. I wanted this newly included black critic to speak my rebellion, rendering it not bad but good, giving it another sort of authority. Marcus, on the other hand, correctly urges us: "The white woman critic must be careful not to impose her own alphabet on the art of women of color" (p. 80).

History is like mother. Gardiner and Newton, polarized in *Making a Difference*, surprisingly coincide in the wish for a feminist criticism both psychologically and historically informed. If indeed I could bring those two terms together, then I could also bring together two different versions of my own project. One version dates from around 1984 and is centered in psychological categories, interpreting feminist critical relations in familial and psychoanalytic terms, in particular the mother-daughter relation. The other version dates from around 1987 and sees feminist critical positions in terms of institutional history.

History is also not like mother. Despite my attraction to Gardiner's oracular pronouncement, I am beginning to realize that feminists need to stop reading everything through the family romance. If we are going to understand our relation to the academic institution within which we think and teach and speak, we need to recognize its specific dynamics which are obscured in the recourse to familial metaphor.

We must again risk being "bad" and recognize that we are operating outside the family, outside the realm of romance, outside woman's traditional place, that we are "pros," workers and authorities, in the literary academy and that what we can most effectively say and do as feminists is mediated through the institution, its ideologies, values, structures, and its location in the world.

NOTES

1. Ellen Carol DuBois, Gail Paradise Kelly, Elizabeth Lapovsky Kennedy, Carolyn W. Korsmeyer, and Lillian S. Robinson, *Feminist Scholarship: Kindling in the Groves of Academe* (Urbana: University of Illinois Press, 1986). The

quotation is from Lillian S. Robinson, "Feminist Criticism: How Do We Know When We've Won?" in Shari Benstock, ed., *Feminist Issues in Literary Scholarship* (Bloomington: Indiana University Press, 1987), p. 143.

2. Jane Marcus, "Still Practice, A/Wrested Alphabet: Toward a Feminist Aesthetic" in *Feminist Issues in Literary Scholarship,* p. 87.

3. Shari Benstock, "The Feminist Critique: Mastering Our Monstrosity," *Tulsa Studies in Women's Literature,* 2 (Fall 1983), p. 141, emphasis added.

4. For an extremely readable account of the history of literary studies, highlighting the dialectic between "criticism" and "scholarship," see Gerald Graff, *Professing Literature.*

5. See for example, Laurie Finke, "The Rhetoric of Marginality: Why I Do Feminist Theory," *Tulsa Studies* 5 (1986), pp. 251–72; and Elizabeth A. Meese, "(Ex)Tensions: Feminist Criticism and Deconstruction," ch. 1 of *Ex-Tensions: Re-Figuring Feminist Criticism* (Champaign: University of Illinois Press, 1990).

6. "Making—and Remaking—History: Another Look at 'Patriarchy' " in *Feminist Issues in Literary Scholarship,* p. 124.

7. Elizabeth Fox-Genovese, "To Write My Self: The Autobiographies of Afro-American Women" in *Feminist Issues in Literary Scholarship,* pp. 176–77.

8. Elizabeth Fox-Genovese, "My Statue, My Self: Autobiographical Writings of Afro-American Women" in *The Private Self: Theory and Practice of Women's Autobiographical Writings,* Shari Benstock, ed. (Chapel Hill: University of North Carolina Press, 1988), pp. 63–89.

9. Elaine Showalter, "Women's Time, Women's Space: Writing the History of Feminist Criticism" in *Feminist Issues in Literary Scholarship,* p. 31.

10. Showalter, pp. 30–31. K. K. Ruthven shares this sense of our history: "Unlike psychoanalysis and marxism, of course, feminism does not have the equivalent of a founding 'father'—nor could it have, seeing that that in itself is a patriarchal notion of how knowledge is created and authorized"—*Feminist Literary Studies,* p. 25.

11. Jane Marcus, Introduction, *New Feminist Essays on Virginia Woolf,* ed. Jane Marcus (Lincoln: University of Nebraska Press, 1981), p. xiii.

12. *Sexual/Textual Politics,* p. 18.

13. Margret Andersen, "Feminism as a Criterion of the Literary Critic" in Brown and Olson, eds., *Feminist Criticism,* p. 1.

14. Judith Kegan Gardiner, "Gender, Values, and Lessing's Cats" in *Feminist Issues in Literary Scholarship,* pp. 119–20.

15. Judith Kegan Gardiner, "Mind mother: psychoanalysis and feminism" in Greene and Kahn, eds., *Making a Difference,* p. 139.

16. Judith Kegan Gardiner, "The Heroine as Her Author's Daughter" in Brown and Olson, eds., *Feminist Criticism,* p. 252.

17. Josephine Donovan, "Toward a Women's Poetics" in *Feminist Issues in Literary Scholarship*, p. 105. Donovan is referring to her own "Sarah Orne Jewett's Critical Theory: Notes Toward a Feminine Literary Mode" in *Critical Essays on Sarah Orne Jewett*, ed. Gwen L. Nagel (Boston: G. K. Hall, 1984). She takes the notion of women's time as repetitive or cyclic from Kathryn Allen Rabuzzi, *The Sacred and the Feminine: Toward a Theology of Housework* (New York: Seabury, 1982).

18. For a sense of how Jardine herself uses this coining, see Alice A. Jardine, *Gynesis: Configurations of Women and Modernity* (Ithaca: Cornell University Press, 1985).

19. See Showalter, "Toward a Feminist Poetics" and Showalter, "Feminist Criticism in the Wilderness," both collected in Showalter, ed., *The New Feminist Criticism*.

20. Hortense Spillers, "Review Essay: 'Turning the Century': Notes on Women and Difference," *Tulsa Studies in Women's Literature,* Vol. 3, Nos. 1–2 (1984), pp. 178–85.

21. Finke does not explicitly counter the "prominent" with her marginal categories and the 1987 book version adds four more "prominent" feminist critics, with three additional articles and the Stimpson introduction.

22. Hortense J. Spillers, "A Hateful Passion, A Lost Love" in *Feminist Issues in Literary Scholarship*, p. 182.

23. Following gender ideology in British culture from 1798 to 1880, Newton shows us major shifts around 1830 and 1860 in order to argue for the necessity of understanding literature in its specific historical context.

24. No one can, at this moment in academic theoretical time, play on these two senses of the word "discipline" without referring to the work and the effect of Michel Foucault.

25. Benstock, "The Feminist Critique," p. 148.

26. Alice Jardine, "Gynesis," *Diacritics,* 12 (1982).

27. William Shakespeare, *Titus Andronicus,* III, ii, 44–45.

28. Judith Kegan Gardiner, "On Female Identity and Writing by Women" in Abel, ed., *Writing and Sexual Difference,* pp. 179, 187, 191. For an early version of this, see Gardiner, "The Heroine as Her Author's Daughter" in Brown and Olson, eds., *Feminist Criticism,* pp. 244–53.

29. Nina Baym, "The Madwoman and Her Languages: Why I Don't Do Feminist Literary Theory" in *Feminist Issues in Literary Scholarship,* p. 56.

30. Nina Auerbach, "Engorging the Patriarchy" in *Feminist Issues in Literary Scholarship,* pp. 152–53.

31. Auerbach, "Engorging the Patriarchy," p. 158. Auerbach, "Why Communities of Women Aren't Enough," *Tulsa Studies in Women's Literature,* Vol. 3, Nos. 1–2 (1984), p. 156. The only difference between the two versions of this sentence is the addition of a comma after "probably."

32. Dictionary meanings gleaned from *The American Heritage Dictionary of the English Language,* p. 434 and *Webster's Third New International Dictionary,* p. 753.

33. Baym, pp. 45, 59; Auerbach, "Why Communities of Women Aren't Enough," p. 153. Auerbach's tone in 1987 is no longer angry but even-handed. She moves from calling herself a pluralist while raging at orthodoxy to speaking with pluralist tolerance.

34. See, for example, Finke, op.cit. pp. 225, 258. Finke does cite Baym's opposition to Marcus.

35. Jane Marcus, "Storming the Toolshed" in Nannerl O. Keohane et al, eds., *Feminist Theory: A Critique of Ideology* (Chicago: University of Chicago Press, 1982), p. 218.

36. Gayatri Spivak, "A Response to Annette Kolodny," unpublished paper, 1980, quoted in Marcus, "Storming the Toolshed," p. 218. We might recall that in "Still Practice," Marcus finds Spivak bad for not recognizing Woolf's authority as the mother of socialist feminist criticism but also finds her a model ("no more perfect example of 'still practice' ") feminist critic for her essay on and translation of "Draupadi" (p. 89).

37. I am indebted to my colleague Carol Quillen of the History Department, Rice University for this phrase.

38. Susan Stanford Friedman, "Modernism of the 'Scattered Remnant': Race and Politics in H. D.'s Development" in *Feminist Issues in Literary Scholarship,* pp. 218, 227. Bryher is the close friend with whom H. D. lived and traveled for many years. *HER* is a novel H. D. wrote in 1927.

39. Susan S. Lanser, "Feminist Criticism, 'The Yellow Wallpaper,' and the Politics of Color in America," *Feminist Studies,* Vol. 15, No. 3 (1989), pp. 415–42.

40. Susan Friedman, "Who Buried H. D.? A Poet, Her Critics, and Her Place in 'The Literary Tradition' " in Brown and Olson, eds., *Feminist Criticism,* pp. 93–94.

15

POSTCOLONIALITY AND THE ARTIFICE OF HISTORY: WHO SPEAKS FOR "INDIAN" PASTS?

DIPESH CHAKRABARTY

Push thought to extremes.
—Louis Althusser

I

It has recently been said in praise of the postcolonial project of *Subaltern Studies* that it demonstrates, "perhaps for the first time since colonization," that "Indians are showing sustained signs of reappropriating the capacity to represent themselves [within the discipline of history]."[1] As a historian who is a member of the *Subaltern Studies* collective, I find the congratulation contained in this remark gratifying but premature. The purpose of this article is to problematize the idea of "Indians" "representing themselves in history." Let us put aside for a moment the messy problems of identity inherent in a transnational enterprise such as *Subaltern Studies,* where passports and commitments blur the distinctions of ethnicity in a manner that some would regard as characteristically postmodern. I have a more perverse proposition to argue. It is that insofar as the academic discourse of history—that is, "history" as a discourse produced at the institutional site of the university—is concerned, "Europe" remains the sovereign, theoretical subject of all histories, including the ones we call "Indian," "Chinese," "Kenyan," and so on. There is a peculiar way in which all these other histories tend to become variations on a master narrative that could be called "the history of Europe." In this sense, "Indian" history itself is in a position of subalternity; one can only articulate subaltern subject positions in the name of this history.

While the rest of this article will elaborate on this proposition, let me enter a few qualifications. "Europe" and "India" are treated here as hyperreal terms in that they refer to certain figures of imagination whose geographical referents remain somewhat indeterminate.[2] As figures of the imaginary they are, of course, subject to contestation, but for the moment I shall treat them as though they were given, reified categories, opposites paired in a structure of domination and subordination. I realize that in treating them thus I leave myself open to the charge of nativism, nationalism, or worse, the sin of sins, nostalgia. Liberal-minded scholars would immediately protest that any idea of a homogeneous, uncontested "Europe" dissolves under analysis. True, but just as the phenomenon of orientalism does not disappear simply because some of us have now attained a critical awareness of it, similarly a certain version of "Europe," reified and cele-brated in the phenomenal world of everyday relationships of power as the scene of the birth of the modern, continues to dominate the discourse of history. Anal-ysis does not make it go away.

That Europe works as a silent referent in historical knowledge itself becomes obvious in a highly ordinary way. There are at least two everyday symptoms of the subalternity of non-Western, third-world histories. Third-world historians feel a need to refer to works in European history; historians of Europe do not feel any need to reciprocate. Whether it is an Edward Thompson, a Le Roy Ladurie, a George Duby, a Carlo Ginzburg, a Lawrence Stone, a Robert Darnton, or a Natalie Davis—to take but a few names at random from our contemporary world—the "greats" and the models of the historian's enterprise are always at least culturally "European." "They" produce their work in relative ignorance of non-Western histories, and this does not seem to affect the quality of their work. This is a gesture, however, that "we" cannot return. We cannot even afford an equality or symmetry of ignorance at this level without taking the risk of appearing "old-fashioned" or "outdated."

The problem, I may add in parenthesis, is not particular to historians. An unselfconscious but nevertheless blatant example of this "inequality of ignorance" in literary studies, for example, is the following sentence on Salman Rushdie from a recent text on postmodernism: "Though Saleem Sinai [of *Midnight's Children*] narrates in English . . . his intertexts for both writing history and writing fiction are doubled: they are, on the one hand, from Indian legends, films, and literature and, on the other, from the West—*The Tin Drum, Tristram Shandy, One Hundred Years of Solitude*, and so on."[3] It is interesting to note how this sentence teases out only those references that are from "the West." The author is under no obligation here to be able to name with any authority and specificity the "Indian" allusions that make Rushdie's intertexuality "doubled." This ignorance, shared and un-stated, is part of the assumed compact that makes it "easy" to include Rushdie in English department offerings on postcolonialism.

This problem of asymmetric ignorance is not simply a matter of "cultural cringe" (to let my Australian self speak) on our part or of cultural arrogance on the part of the European historian. These problems exist but can be relatively easily addressed. Nor do I mean to take anything away from the achievements of the historians I mentioned. Our footnotes bear rich testimony to the insights we have derived from their knowledge and creativity. The dominance of "Europe" as the subject of all histories is a part of a much more profound theoretical condition under which historical knowledge is produced in the third world. This condition ordinarily expresses itself in a paradoxical manner. It is this paradox that I shall describe as the second everyday symptom of our subalternity, and it refers to the very nature of social science pronouncements themselves.

For generations now, philosophers and thinkers shaping the nature of social science have produced theories embracing the entirety of humanity. As we well know, these statements have been produced in relative, and sometimes absolute, ignorance of the majority of humankind—i.e., those living in non-Western cultures. This in itself is not paradoxical, for the more self-conscious of European philosophers have always sought theoretically to justify this stance. The everyday paradox of third-world social science is that *we* find these theories, in spite of their inherent ignorance of "us," eminently useful in understanding our societies. What allowed the modern European sages to develop such clairvoyance with regard to societies of which they were empirically ignorant? Why cannot we, once again, return the gaze?

There is an answer to this question in the writings of philosophers who have read into European history an entelechy of universal reason, if we regard such philosophy as the self-consciousness of social science. Only "Europe," the argument would appear to be, is *theoretically* (i.e., at the level of the fundamental categories that shape historical thinking) knowable; all other histories are matters of empirical research that fleshes out a theoretical skeleton which is substantially "Europe." There is one version of this argument in Edmund Husserl's Vienna lecture of 1935, where he proposed that the fundamental difference between "oriental philosophies" (more specifically, Indian and Chinese) and "Greek-European science" (or as he added, "universally speaking: philosophy") was the capacity of the latter to produce "absolute theoretical insights," that is "*theoria*" (universal science), while the former retained a "practical-universal," and hence "mythical-religious," character. This "practical-universal" philosophy was directed to the world in a "naive" and "straightforward" manner, while the world presented itself as a "thematic" to *theoria,* making possible a praxis "whose aim is to elevate mankind through universal scientific reason."[4]

A rather similar epistemological proposition underlies Marx's use of categories like "bourgeois" and "prebourgeois" or "capital" and "precapital." The prefix *pre* here signifies a relationship that is both chronological and theoretical. The coming of the bourgeois or capitalist society, Marx argues in the *Grundrisse* and elsewhere, gives rise for the first time to a history that can be apprehended through a philosophical and universal category, "capital." History becomes, for the first time, *theoretically* knowable. All past histories are now to be known (theoretically, that is) from the vantage point of this category, that is in terms of their differences from it. Things reveal their categorical essence only when they reach their fullest development, or as Marx put it in that famous aphorism of the *Grundrisse:* "Human anatomy contains the key to the anatomy of the ape."[5] The category "capital," as I have discussed elsewhere, contains within itself the legal subject of Enlightenment thought.[6] Not surprisingly, Marx said in that very Hegelian first chapter of *Capital,* vol. 1, that the secret of "capital," the category, "cannot be deciphered until the notion of human equality has acquired the fixity of a popular prejudice."[7] To continue with Marx's words:

> Even the most abstract categories, despite their validity—precisely because of their abstractness—for all epochs, are nevertheless . . . themselves . . . a product of historical relations. Bourgeois society is the most developed and the most complex historic organization of production. The categories which express its relations, the comprehension of its structure, thereby also allow insights into the structure and the relations of production of all the vanished social formations out of whose ruins and elements it built itself up, whose partly still unconquered remnants are carried along within it, whose mere nuances have developed explicit significance within it, etc. . . . The intimations of higher development among the subordinate animal species . . . can be understood only after the higher development is already known. The bourgeois economy thus supplies the key to the ancient.[8]

For "capital" or "bourgeois," I submit, read "Europe."

II

Neither Marx nor Husserl spoke—not at least in the words quoted above—in a historicist spirit. In parenthesis, we should also recall here that Marx's vision of emancipation entailed a journey beyond the rule of capital, in fact beyond the notion of juridicial equality that liberalism holds so sacred. The maxim "From each according to his ability to each according to his need" runs quite contrary to the principle of "Equal pay for equal work," and this is why Marx remains— the Berlin Wall notwithstanding (or not standing!)—a relevant and fundamental critic of both capitalism and liberalism and thus central to any postcolonial, postmodern project of writing history. Yet Marx's methodological/epistemological statements have not always successfully resisted historicist readings. There has always remained enough ambiguity in these statements to make possible the emergence of "Marxist" historical narratives. These narratives turn around the theme of "historical transition." Most modern third-world histories are written within problematics posed by this transition narrative, of which the overriding (if often implicit) themes are those of development, modernization, capitalism.

This tendency can be located in our own work in the *Subaltern Studies* project. My book on working-class history struggles with the problem.[9] Sumit Sarkar's (another colleague in the *Subaltern Studies* project) *Modern India,* justifiably regarded as one of the best textbooks on Indian history written primarily for Indian universities, opens with the following sentences:

> The sixty years or so that lie between the foundation of the Indian National Congress in 1885 and the achievement of independence in August 1947 witnessed perhaps the greatest transition in our country's long history. A transition, however, which in many ways remains grievously incomplete, and it is with this central ambiguity that it seems most convenient to begin our survey.[10]

What kind of a transition was it that remained "grievously incomplete"? Sarkar hints at the possibility of there having been several by naming three:

> So many of the aspirations aroused in the course of the national struggle remained unfulfilled—the Gandhian dream of the peasant coming into his own in *Ram-rajya* [the rule of the legendary and the ideal god-king Ram], as much as the left ideals of social revolution. And as the history of independent India and Pakistan (and Bangladesh) was repeatedly to reveal, even the problems of a complete bourgeois transformation and successful capitalist development were not fully solved by the transfer of power of 1947.(4)

Neither the peasant's dream of a mythical and just kingdom, nor the Left's ideal of a social[ist] revolution, nor a "complete bourgeois transformation"—it is within these three absences, these "grievously incomplete" scenarios that Sarkar locates the story of modern India.

It is also with a similar reference to "absences"—the "failure" of a history to keep an appointment with its destiny (once again an instance of the "lazy native," shall we say?)—that we announced our project of *Subaltern Studies*:

> It is the study of this *historic failure of the nation to come to its own,* a failure due to the *inadequacy* [emphasis added] of the bourgeoisie as well as of the working class to lead it into a decisive victory over colonialism and a bourgeois-democratic revolution of the classic nineteenth-century type . . . or [of the] "new democracy" [type]—*it is the study of this failure which constitutes the central problematic of the historiography of colonial India.*[11]

The tendency to read Indian history in terms of a lack, an absence, or an incompleteness that translates into "inadequacy" is obvious in these excerpts. As a trope, however, it is an ancient one, going back to the hoary beginnings of colonial rule in India. The British conquered and represented the diversity of "Indian" pasts through a homogenizing narrative of transition from a "medieval" period to "modernity." The terms have changed with time. The "medieval" was once called "despotic" and the "modern," "the rule of law." "Feudal/capitalist" has been a later variant.

When it was first formulated in colonial histories of India, this transition narrative was an unashamed celebration of the imperialist's capacity for violence and conquest. To give only one example among the many available, Alexander Dow's *History of Hindostan*, first published in three volumes between 1770 and 1772, was dedicated to the king with a candor characteristic of the eighteenth century when one did not need a Michel Foucault to uncover the connection between violence and knowledge: "The success of Your Majesty's arms," said Dow, "has laid open the East to the researches of the curious."[12] Underscoring this connection between violence and modernity, Dow added:

> The British nation have become the conquerors of Bengal and they ought to extend some part of their fundamental jurisprudence to secure their conquest. . . . The sword is our tenure. It is an absolute conquest, and it is so considered by the world. (I:cxxxviii)

This "fundamental jurisprudence" was the "rule of law" that contrasted, in Dow's narrative, with a past rule that was "arbitrary" and "despotic." In a further gloss Dow explained that "despotism" did not refer to a "government of mere caprice and whim," for he knew enough history to know that that was not true of India. Despotism was the opposite of English constitutional government; it was a system where "the legislative, the judicial and the executive power [were] vested in the prince." This was the past of unfreedom. With the establishment of British power, the Indian was to be made a legal subject, ruled by a government open to the pressures of private property ("the foundation of public prosperity," said Dow) and public opinion, and supervised by a judiciary where "the distributers of justice ought to be independent of everything but law [as] otherwise the officer [the judge] becomes a tool of oppression in the hands of despotism" (I:xcv, cl, cxl-cxli).

In the nineteenth and twentieth centuries, generations of elite Indian nationalists found their subject positions, as nationalists, within this transition narrative that, at various times and depending on one's ideology, hung the tapestry of "Indian history" between the two poles of the homologous sets of oppositions, despotic/constitutional, medieval/modern, feudal/capitalist. Within this narrative shared between imperialist and nationalist imaginations, the "Indian" was always a figure of lack. There was always, in other words, room in this story for characters who embodied, on behalf of the native, the theme of "inadequacy" or "failure." Dow's recommendation of a "rule of law" for Bengal/India came with the paradoxical assurance (to the British) that there was no danger of such a rule "infusing" in the natives "a spirit of freedom":

> To make the natives of the fertile soil of Bengal free, is beyond the power of political arrangement. . . . Their religion, their institutions, their manners, the very disposition of their minds, form them for passive obedience. To give them property would only bind them with stronger ties to our interests, and make them our subjects; or if the British nation prefers the name—more our slaves. (I:cxl-cxli)

We do not need to be reminded that this would remain the cornerstone of imperial ideology for many years to come—subjecthood but not citizenship, as the native was never adequate to the latter—and would eventually become a strand of liberal theory itself.[13] This was of course where nationalists differed. For Rammohun Roy as for Bankimchandra Chattopadhyay, two of India's most prominent nationalist intellectuals of the nineteenth century, British rule was a necessary period of tutelage that Indians had to undergo in order to prepare precisely for what the British denied but extolled as the end of all history: citizenship and the nation state. Years later, in 1951, an "unknown" Indian who successfully sold his "obscurity" dedicated the story of his life thus:

> To the memory of the
> British Empire in India
> Which conferred subjecthood on us
> But withheld citizenship;
> To which yet
> Everyone of us threw out the challenge
> "Civis Britanicus Sum"
> Because
> All that was good and living
> Within us
> Was made, shaped, and quickened
> By the same British Rule.[14]

In nationalist versions of this narrative, as Partha Chatterjee has shown, it was the peasants and the workers, the subaltern classes, who were given to bear the cross of "inadequacy," for, according to this version, it was they who needed to be educated out of their ignorance, parochialism, or, depending on your preference, false consciousness.[15] Even today the Anglo-Indian word *communalism* refers to those who allegedly fail to measure up to the "secular" ideals of citizenship.

That British rule put in place the practices, institutions, and discourse of bourgeois individualism in the Indian soil is undeniable. Early expressions—that is, before the beginnings of nationalism— of this desire to be a "legal subject" make it clear that to Indians in the 1830s and 1840s to be a "modern individual" was to become a "European." *The Literary Gleaner,* a magazine in colonial Calcutta, ran the following poem in 1842, written in English by a Bengali schoolboy eighteen years of age. The poem apparently was inspired by the sight of ships leaving the coast of Bengal "for the glorious shores of England":

> Oft like a sad bird I sigh
> To leave this land, though mine own land it be;
> Its green robed meads,—gay flowers and cloudless sky
> Though passing fair, have but few charms for me.
> For I have dreamed of climes more bright and free
> Where virtue dwells and heaven-born liberty
> Makes even the lowest happy;—where the eye
> Doth sicken not to see man bend the knee
> To sordid interest:—climes where science thrives,
> And genius doth receive her guerdon meet;
> Where man in his all his truest glory lives,
> And nature's face is exquisitely sweet:
> For those fair climes I have the impatient sigh,
> There let me live and there let me die.[16]

In its echoes of Milton and seventeenth-century English Radicalism, this is obviously a piece of colonial pastiche.[17] Michael Madhusudan Dutt, the young Bengali author of this poem, eventually realized the impossibility of being "European" and returned to Bengali literature to become one of our finest poets. Later Indian nationalists, however, abandoned such abject desire to be "Europeans" themselves. Nationalist thought was premised precisely on the assumed universality of the project of becoming individuals, on the assumption that "individual rights" and abstract "equality" were universals that could find home anywhere in the world, that one could be both an "Indian" and a "citizen" at the same time. We shall soon explore some of the contradictions of this project.

Many of the public and private rituals of modern individualism became visible in India in the nineteenth century. One sees this, for instance, in the sudden flourishing in this period of the four basic genres that help express the modern self: the novel, the biography, the autobiography, and history.[18] Along with these came modern industry, technology, medicine, a quasibourgeois (though colonial) legal system supported by a state that nationalism was to take over and make its own. The transition narrative that I have been discussing underwrote, and was in turn underpinned by, these institutions. To think this narrative was to think these institutions at the apex of which sat the modern state,[19] and to think the modern or the nation state was to think a history whose theoretical subject was Europe. Gandhi realized this as early as 1909. Referring to the Indian nationalists' demands for more railways, modern medicine, and bourgeois law, he cannily remarked in his book *Hind Swaraj* that this was to "make India English" or, as he put it, to have "English rule without the Englishman."[20] This "Europe," as Michael Madhusudan Dutt's youthful and naive poetry shows, was of course nothing but a piece of fiction told to the colonized by the colonizer in the very process of fabricating colonial domination.[21] Gandhi's critique of this "Europe" is compromised on many points by his nationalism, and I do not intend to fetishize his text. But I find his gesture useful in developing the problematic of nonmetropolitan histories.

III

I shall now return to the themes of "failure," "lack," and "inadequacy" that so ubiquitously characterize the speaking subject of "Indian" history. As in the practice of the insurgent peasants of colonial India, the first step in a critical effort must arise from a gesture of inversion.[22] Let us begin from where the transition narrative ends and read "plenitude" and "creativity" where this narrative has made us read "lack" and "inadequacy."

According to the fable of their constitution, Indians today are all "citizens." The constitution embraces a classically liberal definition of citizenship. If the modern state and the modern individual, the citizen, are but the two inseparable sides of the same phenomenon, as William Connolly argues in *Political Theory and Modernity*, it would appear that the end of history is in sight for us in India.[23] This modern individual, however, whose political/public life is lived in citizenship, is also supposed to have an interiorized "private" self that pours out incessantly in diaries, letters, autobiographies, novels, and, of course, in what we say to our analysts. The bourgeois individual is not born until one discovers the pleasures of privacy. But this is a very special kind of "private"—it is, in fact, a deferred "public," for this bourgeois private, as Jürgen Habermas has reminded us, is "always already oriented to an audience [*Publikum*]."[24]

Indian public life may mimic on paper the bourgeois legal fiction of citizenship—the fiction is usually performed as a farce in India—but what about the bourgeois private and its history? Anyone who has tried to write "French" social history with Indian material would know how impossibly difficult the task is.[25] It is not that the form of the bourgeois private did not come with European rule. There have been, since the middle of the nineteenth century, Indian novels, diaries, letters, and autobiographies, but they seldom yield pictures of an endlessly interiorized subject. Our autobiographies are remarkably "public" (with constructions of public life that are not necessarily modern) when written by men, and they tell the story of the extended family when written by women.[26] In any case, autobiographies in the confessional mode are notable for their absence. The single paragraph (out of 963 pages) that Nirad Chaudhuri spends on describing the experience of his wedding night in the second volume of his celebrated and prize-winning autobiography is as good an example as any other and is worth quoting at some length. I should explain that this was an arranged marriage (Bengal, 1932), and Chaudhuri was anxious lest his wife should not appreciate his newly acquired but unaffordably expensive hobby of buying records of Western classical music. Our reading of Chaudhuri is handicapped in part by our lack of knowledge of the intertextuality of his prose—there may have been at work, for instance, an imbibed puritanical revulsion against revealing "too much." Yet the passage remains a telling exercise in the construction of memory, for it is about what Chaudhuri "remembers" and "forgets" of his "first night's experience." He screens off intimacy with expressions like "I do not remember" or "I do not know how" (not to mention the very Freudian "making a clean breast of"), and this self-constructed veil is no doubt a part of the self that speaks:

> I was terribly uneasy at the prospect of meeting as wife a girl who was a complete stranger to me, and when she was brought in . . . and left standing before me I had nothing to say. I saw only a very shy smile on her face, and timidly she came and sat by my side on the edge of the bed. I do not know how after that both of us drifted to the pillows, to lie down side by side. [Chaudhuri adds in a footnote: "Of course, fully dressed. We Hindus . . . consider both extremes—fully clad and fully nude—to be modest, and everything in-between as grossly immodest. No decent man wants his wife to be an *allumeuse*."] Then the first two words were exchanged. She took up one of my arms, felt it and said: "You are so thin. I shall take good care of you." I did not thank her, and I do not remember that beyond noting the words I even felt touched. The horrible suspense about European music had reawakened in my mind, and I decided to make a clean breast of it at once and look the sacrifice, if it was called for, straight in the face and begin romance on such terms as were offered to me. I asked her timidly after a while: "Have you listened to any European music?" She shook her head to say "No." Nonetheless, I took another chance and this time asked: "Have you heard the name of a man called Beethoven?" She nodded and signified "Yes." I was reassured, but not wholly satisfied. So I asked yet again: "Can you spell the name?" She said slowly: "B, E, E, T, H, O, V, E, N." I felt very encouraged . . . and [we] dozed off.[27.]

The desire to be "modern" screams out of every sentence in the two volumes of Chaudhuri's autobiography. His legendary name now stands for the cultural history of Indo-British encounter. Yet in the 1,500-odd pages that he has written in English about his life, this is the only passage where the narrative of Chaudhuri's participation in public life and literary circles is interrupted to make room for something approaching the intimate. How do we read this text, this self-making of an Indian male who was second to no one in his ardor for the public life of the citizen, yet who seldom, if ever, reproduced in writing the other side of the modern citizen, the interiorized private self unceasingly reaching out for an audience? Public without private? Yet another instance of the "incompleteness" of bourgeois transformation in India?

These questions are themselves prompted by the transition narrative that in turn situates the modern individual at the very end of history. I do not wish to confer on Chaudhuri's autobiography a representativeness it may not have. Women's writings, as I have already said, are different, and scholars have just begun to explore the world of autobiographies in Indian history. But if one result of European imperialism in India was to introduce the modern state and the idea of the nation with their attendant discourse of "citizenship," which, by the very idea of "the citizen's rights" (i.e., "the rule of law"), splits the figure of the modern individual into "public" and "private" parts of the self (as the young Marx once pointed out in his *On the Jewish Question*), these themes have existed—in contestation, alliance, and miscegenation—with other narratives of the self and community that do not look to the state/citizen bind as the ultimate construction of sociality.[28] This as such will not be disputed, but my point goes further. It is that these other constructions of self and community, while documentable in themselves, will never enjoy the privilege of providing the metanarratives or teleologies (assuming that there cannot be a narrative without at least an implicit teleology) of our histories. This is so partly because these narratives often themselves bespeak an antihistorical consciousness; that is, they entail subject positions and configurations of memory that challenge and undermine the subject that speaks in the name of history. "History" is precisely the site where the struggle goes on to appropriate, on behalf of the modern (my hyperreal Europe), these other collocations of memory.

To illustrate these propositions, I will now discuss a fragment of this contested history in which the modern private and the modern individual were embodied in colonial India.[29]

IV

What I present here are the outlines, so to speak, of a chapter in the history of bourgeois domesticity in colonial Bengal. The material—in the main texts produced in Bengali between 1850 and 1920 for teaching women that very Victorian subject, "domestic science"—relates to the Bengali Hindu middle class, the *bhadralok* or "respectable people." British rule instituted into Indian life the trichotomous ideational division on which modern political structures rest, e.g., the state, civil society, and the (bourgeois) family. It was therefore not surprising that ideas relating to bourgeois domesticity, privacy, and individuality should come to India via British rule. What I want to highlight here, however, through the example of the *bhadralok,* are certain cultural operations by which the "Indians" challenged and modified these received ideas in such a way as to put in question two fundamental tenets underlying the idea of "modernity"—the nuclear family based on companionate marriage and the secular, historical construction of time.

As Meredith Borthwick, Ghulam Murshid, and other scholars have shown, the eighteenth-century European idea of "civilization" culminated, in early nineteenth-century India, in a full-blown imperialist critique of Indian/Hindu domestic life, which was now held to be inferior to what became mid-Victorian ideals of bourgeois domesticity.[30] The "condition of women" question in nineteenth-century India was part of that critique, as were the ideas of the modern individual, "freedom," "equality," and "rights." In passages remarkable for their combination of egalitarianism and orientalism, James Mill's *The History of British India* (1817) joined together the thematic of the family/nation and a teleology of "freedom":

> The condition of women is one of the most remarkable circumstances in the manners of nations. . . . The history of uncultivated nations uniformly represents the women as in a state of abject slavery, from which they slowly emerge as civilisation advances. . . . As society refines upon its enjoyments . . . the condition of the weaker sex is gradually improved, till they associate on equal terms with the men, and occupy the place of voluntary and useful coadjutors. A state of dependence more strict and humiliating than that which is ordained for the weaker sex among the Hindus cannot be easily conceived.[31]

As is well known, the Indian middle classes generally felt answerable to this charge. From the early nineteenth-century onward a movement developed in Bengal (and other regions) to reform "women's conditions" and to give them formal education. Much of this discourse on women's education was emancipationist in that it spoke the language of "freedom," "equality," and "awakening," and was strongly influenced by Ruskinian ideals and idealization of bourgeois domesticity.[32] If one looks on this history as part of the history of the modern individual in India, an interesting feature emerges. It is that in this literature on women's education certain terms, after all, were much more vigorously debated than others. There was, for example, a degree of consensus over the desirability of domestic "discipline" and "hygiene" as practices reflective of a state of modernity, but the word *freedom,* yet another important term in the rhetoric of the modern, hardly ever acted as the register of such a social consensus. It was a passionately disputed word, and we would be wrong to assume that the passions reflected a simple and straightforward battle of the sexes. The word was assimilated to the nationalist need to construct cultural boundaries that supposedly separated the "European" from the "Indian." The dispute over this word was thus central to the discursive strategies through which a subject position was created enabling the "Indian" to speak. It is this subject position that I want to discuss here in some detail.

What the Bengali literature on women's education played out was a battle between a nationalist construction of a cultural norm of the patriarchal, patrilocal, patrilineal, extended family and the ideal of the patriarchal, bourgeois nuclear family that was implicit in the European/imperialist/universalist discourse on the "freedoms" of individualism, citizenship, and civil society.[33] The themes of "discipline" and "order" were critical in shaping nationalist imaginings of aesthetics and power. "Discipline" was seen as the key to the power of the colonial (i.e., modern) state, but it required certain procedures for redefining the self. The British were powerful, it was argued, because they were disciplined, orderly, and punctual in every detail of their lives, and this was made possible by the education of "their" women who brought the virtues of discipline into the home. The "Indian" home, a colonial construct, now fared badly in nationalist writings on modern domesticity. To quote a Bengali text on women's education from 1877:

The house of any civilised European is like the abode of gods. Every household object is clean, set in its proper place and decorated; nothing seems unclean or smells foul. . . . It is as if [the goddess of] order [*srinkhala,* "order, discipline"; *srinkhal,* "chains"] had become manifest to please the [human] eye. In the middle of the room would be a covered table with a bouquet of flowers on it, while around it would be [a few] chairs nicely arranged [with] everything sparkling clean. But enter a house in our country and you would feel as if you had been transported there by your destiny to make you atone for all the sins of your life. [A mass of] cowdung torturing the senses . . . dust in the air, a growing heap of ashes, flies buzzing around . . . a little boy urinating into the ground and putting the mess back into his mouth. . . . The whole place is dominated by a stench that seems to be running free. . . . There is no order anywhere, the household objects are so unclean that they only evoke disgust.[34]

This self-division of the colonial subject, the double movement of recognition by which it both knows its "present" as the site of disorder and yet moves away from this space in desiring a discipline that can only exist in an imagined but "historical" future, is a rehearsal, in the context of the discussion of the bourgeois domestic in colonial India, of the transition narrative we have encountered before. A historical construction of temporality (medieval/modern, separated by historical time), in other words, is precisely the axis along which the colonial subject splits itself. Or to put it differently, this split *is* what is history; writing history is performing this split over and over again.

The desire for order and discipline in the domestic sphere thus may be seen as having been a correlate of the nationalist, modernizing desire for a similar discipline in the public sphere, that is for a rule of law enforced by the state. It is beyond the scope of this paper to pursue this point further, but the connection between personal discipline and discipline in public life was to reveal itself in what the nationalists wrote about domestic hygiene and public health. The connection is recognizably modernist, and it is what the Indian modern shared with the European modern.[35] What I want to attend to, however, are the differences between the two. And this is where I turn to the other important aspect of the European modern, the rhetoric of "freedom" and "equality."

The argument about "freedom"—in the texts under discussion—was waged around the question of the Victorian ideals of the companionate marriage, that is, over the question as to whether or not the wife should also be a friend to the husband. Nothing threatened the ideal of the Bengali/Indian extended family (or the exalted position of the mother-in-law within that structure) more than this idea, wrapped up in notions of bourgeois privacy, that the wife was also to be a friend or, to put it differently, that the woman was now to be a modern individual. I must mention here that the modern individual, who asserts his/her individuality over the claims of the joint or extended family, almost always appears in nineteenth- and early twentieth-century Bengali literature as an embattled figure, often the subject of ridicule and scorn in the same Bengali fiction and essays that otherwise extolled the virtues of discipline and scientific rationality in personal and public lives. This irony had many expressions. The most well-known Bengali fictional character who represents this moral censure of modern individuality is Nimchand Datta in Dinabandhu Mitra's play *Sadhabar ekadashi* (1866). Nimchand, who is English-educated, quotes Shakespeare, Milton, or Locke at the slightest opportunity and uses this education arrogantly to ignore his duties toward his extended family, finds his nemeses in alcohol and debauchery. This metonymic relationship between the love of "modern"/English education (which stood for the romantic individual in nineteenth-century Bengal) and the slippery path of alcohol is suggested in the play by a conversation between Nimchand and a Bengali official of the colonial bureaucracy, a Deputy Magistrate. Nimchand's supercilious braggadocio about his command of the English language quickly and inevitably runs to the subject of drinks (synonymous, in middle-class Bengali culture of the period, with absolute decadence):

> I read English, write English, speechify in English, think English, dream in English—mind you, it's no child's play—now tell me, my good fellow, what would you like to drink?—Claret for ladies, sherry for men and brandy for heroes.[36]

A similar connection between the modern, "free" individual and selfishness was made in the literature on women's education. The construction was undisguisedly nationalist (and patriarchal). *Freedom* was used to mark a difference between what was "Indian" and what was "European/English." The ultra-free woman acted like a *memsahib* (European woman), selfish and shameless. As Kundamala Devi, a woman writing for a women's magazine *Bamabodhini patrika*, said in 1870: "Oh dear ones! If you have acquired real knowledge, then give no place in your heart to *memsahib*-like behaviour. This is not becoming in a Bengali housewife."[37] The idea of "true modesty" was mobilized to build up this picture of the "really" Bengali woman.[38] Writing in 1920, Indira Devi dedicated her *Narir ukti* [A Woman Speaks]—interestingly enough, a defense of modern Bengali womanhood against criticisms by (predominantly) male writers—to generations of ideal Bengali women whom she thus described: "Unaffected by nature, of pleasant speech, untiring in their service [to others], oblivious of their own pleasures, [while] moved easily by the suffering of others, and capable of being content with very little."[39]

This model of the "modern" Bengali/Indian woman—educated enough to appreciate the modern regulations of the body and the state but yet "modest" enough to be unselfassertive and unselfish—was tied to the debates on "freedom." "Freedom" in the West, several authors argued, meant *jathechhachar*, to do as one pleased, the right to self-indulgence. In India, it was said, *freedom* meant freedom from the ego, the capacity to serve and obey voluntarily. Notice how the terms *freedom* and *slavery* have changed positions in the following quote:

> To be able to subordinate oneself to others and to *dharma* [duty/moral order/proper action] . . . to free the soul from the slavery of the senses, are the first tasks of human freedom. . . . That is why in Indian families boys and girls are subordinate to the parents, wife to the husband and to the parents-in-law, the disciple to the guru, the student to the teacher . . . the king to *dharma* . . . the people to the king, [and one's] dignity and prestige to [that of] the community [samaj].[40]

There was an ironical twist to this theorizing that needs to be noted. Quite clearly, this theory of "freedom-in-obedience" did not apply to the domestic servants who were sometimes mentioned in this literature as examples of the "truly" unfree, the nationalist point being that (European) observers commenting on the unfree status of Indian women often missed (so some nationalists argued) this crucial distinction between the housewife and the domestic. Obviously, the servants were not yet included in the India of the nationalist imagination.

Thus went the Bengali discourse on modern domesticity in a colonial period when the rise of a civil society and a quasimodern state had already inserted the modern questions of "public" and "private" into middle-class Bengali lives. The received bougeois ideas about domesticity and connections between the domestic and the national were modified here in two significant ways. One strategy, as I have sought to demonstrate, was to contrapose the cultural norm of the patriarchal extended family to the bourgeois patriarchal ideals of the companionate marriage, to oppose the new patriarchy with a redefined version of the old one(s). Thus was fought the idea of the modern private. The other strategy, equally significant, was to mobilize, on behalf of the extended family, forms and figurations of collective memory that challenged, albeit ambiguously, the seemingly absolute separation of "sacred" and "secular" time on which the very modern ("European") idea of history was/is based.[41] The figure of the "truly educated," "truly modest," and "truly Indian" woman is invested, in this discussion of women's education, with a sacred authority by subordinating the question of domestic life to religious ideas of female auspiciousness that joined the heavenly with the mundane in a conceptualization of time that could be only antihistorical. The truly modern housewife, it is said, would be so auspicious as to mark the eternal return of the cosmic principle embodied in the goddess Lakshmi, the goddess of domestic well-being by whose grace the extended family (and clan, and hence, by extending the sentiment, the nation, *Bharatlakshmi*) lived and prospered. Thus we read in a contemporary pamphlet: "Women are the Lakshmis of the community. If they undertake to improve themselves in the sphere of *dharma* and knowledge . . . there will be an automatic improvement in [the quality of] social life."[42] Lakshmi, regarded as the Hindu god Vishnu's wife by about A.D. 400, has for long been held up in popular Hinduism, and in the everyday pantheism of Hindu families, as the model of the Hindu wife, united in complete harmony with her husband (and his family) through willful submission, loyalty, devotion, and chastity.[43] When women did not follow her ideals, it was said, the (extended) family and the family line were destroyed by the spirit of Alakshmi (not-Lakshmi), the dark and malevolent reverse of the Lakshmi principle. While women's education and the idea of discipline as such were seldom opposed in this discourse regarding the modern individual in colonial Bengal, the line was drawn at the point where modernity and the demand for bourgeois privacy threatened the power and the pleasures of the extended family.

There is no question that the speaking subject here is nationalist and patriarchal, employing the clichéd orientalist categories, "the East" and "the West."[44] However, of importance to us are the two denials on which this particular moment of subjectivity rests: the denial, or at least contestation, of the bourgeois private and, equally important, the denial of historical time by making the family a site where the sacred and the secular blended in a perpetual reenactment of a principle that was heavenly and divine.

The cultural space the antihistorical invoked was by no means harmonious or nonconflictual, though nationalist thought of necessity tried to portray it to be so. The antihistorical norms of the patriarchal extended family, for example, could only have had a contested existence, contested both by women's struggles and by those of the subaltern classes. But these struggles did not necessarily follow any lines that would allow us to construct emancipatory narratives by putting the "patriarchals" clearly on one side and the "liberals" on the other. The history of modern "Indian" individuality is caught up in too many contradictions to lend itself to such a treatment.

I do not have the space here to develop the point, so I will make do with one example. It comes from the autobiography of Ramabai Ranade, the wife of the famous nineteenth-century social reformer from the Bombay Presidency, M. G. Ranade. Ramabai Ranade's struggle for self-respect was in part against the "old" patriarchal order of the extended family and for the "new" patriarchy of companionate marriage, which her reform-minded husband saw as the most civilized form of the conjugal bond. In pursuit of this ideal, Ramabai began to share her husband's commitment to public life and would often take part (in the 1880s) in public gatherings and deliberations of male and female social reformers. As she herself says: "It was at these meetings that I learnt what a meeting was and how one should conduct oneself at one."[45] Interestingly, however, one of the chief sources of opposition to Ramabai's efforts were (apart from men) the other women in the family. There is of course no doubt that they, her mother-in-law and her husband's sisters, spoke for the old patriarchal extended family. But it is quite instructive to listen to their voices (as they come across through Ramabai's text), for they also spoke for their own sense of self-respect and their own forms of struggle against men:

> You should not really go to these meetings [they said to Ramabai]. . . . Even if the men want you to do these things, you should ignore them. You need not say no: but after all, you need not do it. They will then give up, out of sheer boredom. . . . You are outdoing even the European women.

Or this:

> It is she [Ramabai] herself who loves this frivolousness of going to meetings. Dada [Mr. Ranade] is not at all so keen about it. But should she not have some sense of proportion of how much the women should actually do? If men tell you to do a hundred things, women should take up ten at the most. After all men do not understand these practical things! . . . The good woman [in the past] never turned frivolous like this. . . . That is why this large family . . . could live together in a respectable way. . . . But now it is all so different! If Dada suggests one thing, this woman is prepared to do three. How can we live with any sense of self-respect then and how can we endure all this? (84–85)

These voices, combining the contradictory themes of nationalism, of patriarchal clan-based ideology, of women's struggles against men, and opposed at the same time to friendship between husbands and wives, remind us of the deep ambivalences that marked the trajectory of the modern private and bourgeois individuality in colonial India. Yet historians manage, by maneuvers reminiscent of the old "dialectical" card trick called "negation of negation," to deny a subject position to this voice of ambivalence. The evidence of what I called "the denial of the bourgeois private and of the historical subject" is acknowledged but subordinated in their accounts to the supposedly higher purpose of making Indian history look like yet another episode in the universal and (in their view, the ultimately victorious) march of citizenship, of the nation state, of themes of human emancipation spelled out in the course of the European Enlightenment and after. It is the figure of the citizen that speaks through these histories. And so long as that happens, my hyperreal Europe will continually return to dominate the stories we tell. "The modern" will then continue to be understood, as Meaghan Morris has so aptly put it in discussing her own Australian context, "as *a known history*, something which has *already happened elsewhere*, and which is to be reproduced, mechanically or otherwise, with a local content." This can only leave us with a task of reproducing what Morris calls "the project of positive unoriginality."[46]

V

Yet the "originality"—I concede that this is a bad term—of the idioms through which struggles have been conducted in the Indian subcontinent has often been in the sphere of the nonmodern. One does not have to subscribe to the ideology of clannish patriarchy, for instance, to acknowledge that the metaphor of the sanctified and patriarchal extended family was one of the most important elements in the cultural politics of Indian nationalism. In the struggle against British rule, it was frequently the use of this idiom—in songs, poetry, and other forms of nationalist mobilization—that allowed "Indians" to fabricate a sense of community and to retrieve for themselves a subject position from which to address the British. I will illustrate this with an example from the life of Gandhi, "the father of the nation," to highlight the political importance of this cultural move on the part of the "Indian."

My example refers to the year 1946. There had been ghastly riots between the Hindus and the Muslims in Calcutta over the impending partition of the country into India and Pakistan. Gandhi was in the city, fasting in protest over the behavior of his own people. And here is how an Indian intellectual recalls the experience:

> Men would come back from their offices in the evening and find food prepared by the family [meaning the womenfolk] ready for them; but soon it would be revealed that the women of the home had not eaten the whole day. They [apparently] had not felt hungry. Pressed further, the wife or the mother would admit that they could not understand how they could

go on [eating] when Gandhiji was dying for their own crimes. Restaurants and amusement centres did little business; some of them were voluntarily closed by the proprietors. . . . The nerve of feeling had been restored; the pain began to be felt. . . . Gandhiji knew when to start the redemptive process.[47]

We do not have to take this description literally, but the nature of the community imagined in these lines is clear. It blends, in Gayatri Spivak's words, "the feeling of community that belongs to national links and political organizations" with "that other feeling of community whose structural model is the [clan or the extended] family."[48] Colonial Indian history is replete with instances where Indians arrogated subjecthood to themselves precisely by mobilizing, within the context of "modern" institutions and sometimes on behalf of the modernizing project of nationalism, devices of collective memory that were both antihistorical and antimodern.[49] This is not to deny the capacity of "Indians" to act as subjects endowed with what we in the universities would recognize as "a sense of history" (what Peter Burke calls "the renaissance of the past") but to insist at the same time that there were also contrary trends, that in the multifarious struggles that took place in colonial India, antihistorical constructions of the past often provided very powerful forms of collective memory.[50]

There is then this double bind through which the subject of "Indian" history articulates itself. On the one hand, it is both the subject and the object of modernity, because it stands for an assumed unity called the "Indian people" that is always split into two—a modernizing elite and a yet-to-be-modernized peasantry. As such a split subject, however, it speaks from within a metanarrative that celebrates the nation state; and of this metanarrative the theoretical subject can only be a hyperreal "Europe," a "Europe" constructed by the tales that both imperialism and nationalism have told the colonized. The mode of self-representation that the "Indian" can adopt here is what Homi Bhabha has justly called "mimetic."[51] Indian history, even in the most dedicated socialist or nationalist hands, remains a mimicry of a certain "modern" subject of "European" history and is bound to represent a sad figure of lack and failure. The transition narrative will always remain "grievously incomplete."

On the other hand, maneuvers are made within the space of the mimetic—and therefore within the project called "Indian" history—to represent the "difference" and the "originality" of the "Indian," and it is in this cause that the antihistorical devices of memory and the antihistorical "histories" of the subaltern classes are appropriated. Thus peasant/worker constructions of "mythical" kingdoms and "mythical" pasts/futures find a place in texts designated "Indian" history precisely through a procedure that subordinates these narratives to the rules of evidence and to the secular, linear calendar that the writing of "history" must follow. The antihistorical, antimodern subject, therefore, cannot speak itself as "theory" within the knowledge procedures of the university even when these knowledge procedures acknowledge and "document" its existence. Much like Spivak's "subaltern" (or the anthropologist's peasant who can only have a quoted existence in a larger statement that belongs to the anthropologist alone), this subject can only be spoken for and spoken of by the transition narrative that will always ultimately privilege the modern (i.e., "Europe").[52]

So long as one operates within the discourse of "history" produced at the institutional site of the university, it is not possible simply to walk out of the deep collusion between "history" and the modernizing narrative(s) of citizenship, bourgeois public and private, and the nation state. "History" as a knowledge system is firmly embedded in institutional practices that invoke the nation state at every step—witness the organization and politics of teaching, recruitment, promotions, and publication in history departments, politics that survive the occasional brave and heroic attempts by individual historians to liberate "history" from the metanarrative of the nation state. One only has to ask, for instance: Why is history a compulsory part of education of the modern person in all countries today including those that did quite comfortably without it until as late as the eighteenth century? Why should children all over the world today have to come to terms with a subject called "history" when we know that this compulsion is neither natural nor ancient?[53] It does not take much imagination to see that the reason for this lies in what European imperialism and third-world nationalisms have achieved together: the universalization of the nation state as the most desirable form of political community. Nation states have the capacity to enforce their truth games, and universities, their critical distance notwithstanding, are part of the battery of institutions complicit in this process. "Economics" and "history" are the knowledge forms that correspond to the two major institutions that the rise (and later universalization) of the bourgeois order has given to the world—the capitalist mode of production and the nation state ("history" speaking to the figure of the citizen).[54] A critical historian has no choice but to negotiate this knowledge. She or he therefore needs to understand the state on its own terms, i.e., in terms of its self-justificatory narratives of citizenship and modernity. Since these themes will always take us back to the universalist propositions of "modern," (European) political philosophy—even the "practical" science of economics that now seems "natural" to our constructions of world systems is (theoretically) rooted in the ideas of ethics in eighteenth-century Europe[55]—a third-world historian is condemned to knowing "Europe" as the original home of the "modern," whereas the "European" historian does not share a comparable predicament with regard to the pasts of the majority of humankind. Thus follows the everyday subalternity of non-Western histories with which I began this paper.

Yet the understanding that "we" all do "European" history with our different and often non-European archives opens up the possibility of a politics and project of alliance between the dominant metropolitan histories and the subaltern peripheral pasts. Let us call this the project of provincializing "Europe," the "Europe" that modern imperialism and (third-world) nationalism have, by their collaborative venture and violence, made universal. Philosophically, this project must ground itself in a radical critique and transcendence of liberalism (i.e., of the bureaucratic constructions of citizenship, modern state, and bourgeois privacy that classical political philosophy has produced), a ground that late Marx shares with certain moments in both poststructuralist thought and feminist philosophy. In particular, I am emboldened by Carole Pateman's courageous declaration—in her remarkable book *The Sexual Contract*—that the very conception of the modern individual belongs to patriarchal categories of thought.[56]

VI

The project of provincializing "Europe" refers to a history that does not yet exist; I can therefore only speak of it in a programmatic manner. To forestall misunderstanding, however, I must spell out what it is *not* while outlining what it could be.

To begin with, it does not call for a simplistic, out-of-hand rejection of modernity, liberal values, universals, science, reason, grand narratives, totalizing explanations, and so on. Frederic Jameson has recently reminded us that the easy equation often made between "a philosophical conception of totality" and "a political practice of totalitarianism" is "baleful."[57] What intervenes between the two is history—contradictory, plural, and heterogeneous struggles whose outcomes are never predictable, even retrospectively, in accordance with schemas that seek to naturalize and domesticate this heterogeneity. These struggles include coercion (both on behalf of and against modernity)—physical, institutional, and symbolic violence, often dispensed with dreamy-eyed idealism—and it is this violence that plays a decisive role in the establishment of meaning, in the creation of truth regimes, in deciding, as it were, whose and which "universal" wins. As intellectuals operating in academia, we are not neutral to these struggles and cannot pretend to situate ourselves outside of the knowledge procedures of our institutions.

The project of provincializing "Europe" therefore cannot be a project of "cultural relativism." It cannot originate from the stance that the reason/science/universals which help define Europe as the modern are simply "culture-specific" and therefore only belong to the European cultures. For the point is not that Enlightenment rationalism is always unreasonable in itself but rather a matter of documenting how—through what historical process—its "reason," which was not always self-evident to everyone, has been made to look "obvious" far beyond the ground where it originated. If a language, as has been said, is but a dialect backed up by an army, the same could be said of the narratives of "modernity" that, almost universally today, point to a certain "Europe" as the primary habitus of the modern.

This Europe, like "the West," is demonstrably an imaginary entity, but the demonstration as such does not lessen its appeal or power. The project of provincializing "Europe" has to include certain other additional moves: 1) the recognition that Europe's acquisition of the adjective *modern* for itself is a piece of global history of which an integral part is the story of European imperialism; and 2) the understanding that this equating of a certain version of Europe with "modernity" is not the work of Europeans alone; third-world nationalisms, as modernizing ideologies *par excellence,* have been equal partners in the process. I do not mean to overlook the anti-imperial moments in the careers of these nationalisms; I only underscore the point that the project of provincializing "Europe" cannot be a nationalist, nativist, or atavistic project. In unraveling the necessary entanglement of history—a disciplined and institutionally regulated form of collective memory—with the grand narratives of "rights," "citizenship," the nation state, "public" and "private" spheres, one cannot but problematize "India" at the same time as one dismantles "Europe."

The idea is to write into the history of modernity the ambivalences, contradictions, the use of force, and the tragedies and the ironies that attend it. That the rhetoric and the claims of (bourgeois) equality, of citizen's rights, of self-determination through a sovereign nation state have in many circumstances empowered marginal social groups in their struggles is undeniable—this recognition is indispensable to the project of *Subaltern Studies.* What effectively is played down, however, in histories that either implicitly or explicitly celebrate the advent of the modern state and the idea of citizenship is the repression and violence that are as instrumental in the victory of the modern as is the persuasive power of its rhetorical strategies. Nowhere is this irony—the undemocratic foundations of "democracy"—more visible than in the history of modern medicine, public health, and personal hygiene, the discourses of which have been central in locating the body of the modern at the intersection of the public and the private (as defined by, and subject to negotiations with, the state). The triumph of this discourse, however, has always been dependent on the mobilization, on its behalf, of effective means of physical coercion. I say "always" because this coercion is both originary/foundational (i.e., historic) as well as pandemic and quotidian. Of foundational violence, David Arnold gives a good example in a recent essay on the history of the prison in India. The coercion of the colonial prison, Arnold shows, was integral to some of the earliest and pioneering research on the medical, dietary, and demographic statistics of India, for the prison was where Indian bodies were accessible to modernizing investigators.[58] Of the coercion that continues in the names of the nation and modernity, a recent example comes from the Indian campaign to eradicate smallpox in the 1970s. Two American doctors (one of them presumably of "Indian" origin) who participated in the process thus describe their operations in a village of the Ho tribe in the Indian state of Bihar:

> In the middle of gentle Indian night, an intruder burst through the bamboo door of the simple adobe hut. He was a government vaccinator, under orders to break resistance against smallpox vaccination. Lakshmi Singh awoke screaming and scrambled to hide herself. Her husband leaped out of bed, grabbed an axe, and chased the intruder into the courtyard. Outside a squad of doctors and policemen quickly overpowered Mohan Singh. The instant he was pinned to the ground, a second vaccinator jabbed smallpox vaccine into his arm. Mohan Singh, a wiry 40-year-old leader of the Ho tribe, squirmed away from the needle, causing the vaccination site to bleed. The government team held him until they had injected enough vaccine. . . . While the two policemen rebuffed him, the rest of the team overpowered the entire family and vaccinated each in turn. Lakshmi Singh bit deep into one doctor's hand, but to no avail.[59]

There is no escaping the idealism that accompanies this violence. The subtitle of the article in question unselfconsciously reproduces both the military and the do-gooding instincts of the enterprise. It reads: "How an army of samaritans drove smallpox from the earth."

Histories that aim to displace a hyperreal Europe from the center toward which all historical imagination currently gravitates will have to seek out relentlessly this connection between violence and idealism that lies at the heart of the process by which the narratives of citizenship and modernity come to find a natural home in "history." I register a fundamental disagreement here with a position taken by Richard Rorty in an exchange with Jürgen Habermas. Rorty criticizes Habermas for the latter's conviction "that the story of modern philosophy is an important part of the story of the democratic societies' attempts at self-reassurance."[60] Rorty's statement follows the practice of many Europeanists who speak of the histories of these "democratic societies" as if these were self-contained histories complete in themselves, as if the self-fashioning of the West were something that occurred only within its self-assigned geographical boundaries. At the very least Rorty ignores the role that the "colonial theater" (both external and internal)—where the theme of "freedom" as defined by modern political philosophy was constantly invoked in aid of the ideas of "civilization," "progress," and latterly "development"—played in the process of engendering this "reassurance." The task, as I see it, will be to wrestle ideas that legitimize the modern state and its attendant institutions, in order to return to political philosophy—in the same way as suspect coins returned to their owners in an Indian bazaar—its categories whose global currency can no longer be taken for granted.[61]

And, finally—since "Europe" cannot after all be provincialized within the institutional site of the university whose knowledge protocols will always take us back to the terrain where all contours follow that of my hyperreal Europe—the project of provincializing Europe must realize within itself its own impossibility. It therefore looks to a history that embodies this politics of despair. It will have been clear by now that this is not a call for cultural relativism or for atavistic, nativist histories. Nor is this a program for a simple rejection of modernity, which would be, in many situations, politically suicidal. I ask for a history that deliberately makes visible, within the very structure of its narrative forms, its own repressive strategies and practices, the part it plays in collusion with the narratives of citizenships in assimilating to the projects of the modern state all other possibilities of human solidarity. The politics of despair will require of such history that it lays bare to its readers the reasons why such a predicament is necessarily inescapable. This is a history that will attempt the impossible: to look toward its own death by tracing that which resists and escapes the best human effort at translation across cultural and other semiotic systems, so that the world may once again be imagined as radically heterogeneous. This, as I have said, is impossible within the knowledge protocols of academic history, for the globality of academia is not independent of the globality that the European modern has created. To attempt to provincialize this "Europe" is to see the modern as inevitably contested, to write over the given and privileged narratives of citizenship other narratives of human connections that draw sustenance from dreamed-up pasts and futures where collectives are defined neither by the rituals of citizenship nor by the nightmare of "tradition" that "modernity" creates. There are of course no (infra)structural sites where such dreams could lodge themselves. Yet they will recur so long as the themes of citizenship and the nation state dominate our narratives of historical transition, for these dreams are what the modern represses in order to be.

NOTES

Many different audiences in the United States and Australia have responded to versions of this paper and helped me with their criticisms. My benefactors are too numerous to mention individually but the following have been particularly helpful: the editorial board of *Representations* for criticisms conveyed through Thomas Laqueur; Benedict Anderson, Arjun Appadurai, David Arnold, Marjorie Beale, Partha Chatterjee, Natalie Davis, Nicholas Dirks, Simon During, John Foster, Ranajit Guha, Jeanette Hoorn, Martin Jay, Jenny Lee, David Lloyd, Fiona Nicoll, Gyanendra Pandey, Craig Reynolds, Joan Scott, and Gayatri Spivak. And very special thanks to Christopher Healy for sharing both the intellectual and the physical labor that went into this paper.

1. Ranajit Guha and Gayatri Chakravorty Spivak, eds., *Selected Subaltern Studies* (New York, 1988); Ronald Inden, "Orientalist Constructions of India," *Modern Asian Studies* 20, no. (3 1986): 445.

2. I am indebted to Jean Baudrillard for the term *hyperreal* (see his *Simulations* [New York, 1983]), but my use differs from his.

3. Linda Hutcheon, *The Politics of Postmodernism* (London, 1989), 65.

4. Edmund Husserl, *The Crisis of European Sciences and Transcendental Philosophy,* trans. David Carr (Evanston, Ill., 1970), 281–85. See also Wilhelm Halbfass, *India and Europe: An Essay in Understanding* (New York, 1988), 167–68.

5. See the discussion in Karl Marx, *Grundrisse: Foundations of the Critique of Political Economy,* 3 vols. (Moscow, 1971), 3:593–613.

6. See Dipesh Chakrabarty, *Rethinking Working-Class History: Bengal, 1890–1940* (Princeton, N.J., 1989), chap. 7.

7. Marx, *Capital,* 1:60.

8. Marx, *Grundrisse,* 105.

9. See Chakrabarty, *Rethinking Working-Class History,* chap. 7, in particular.

10. Sumit Sarkar, *Modern India, 1885–1947* (Delhi, 1985), 1.

11. Guha and Spivak, *Selected Subaltern Studies,* 43. The words quoted here are Guha's. But I think they represent a sense of historiographical responsibility that is shared by all the members of the Subaltern Studies collective.

12. Alexander Dow, *History of Hindostan,* 3 vols. (London, 1812–16), dedication, vol. 1.

13. See L. T. Hobhouse, *Liberalism* (New York, 1964), 26–27.

14. Nirad C. Chaudhuri, *The Autobiography of an Unknown Indian* (New York, 1989), dedication page.

15. Partha Chatterjee, *Nationalist Thought and the Colonial World: A Derivative Discourse?* (London, 1986).

16. *Mudhusudan rachanabali* [Bengali] (Calcutta, 1965), 449. See also Jogindranath Basu, *Michael Madhusudan Datter jibancharit* [Bengali] (Calcutta, 1978), 86.

17. My understanding of this poem has been enriched by discussions with Marjorie Levinson and David Bennett.

18. I am not making the claim that all of these genres necessarily emerge with bourgeois individualism. See Natalie Zemon Davis, "Fame and Secrecy: Leon Modena's *Life* as an Early Modern Autobiography," *History and Theory* 27 (1988): 103–18; and Davis, "Boundaries and Sense of Self in Sixteenth-Century France," in Thomas C. Heller et al., eds., *Reconstructing Individualism: Autonomy, Individuality, and the Self in Western Thought* (Stanford, Calif., 1986), 53–63. See also Philippe Lejeune, *On Autobiography,* trans. Katherine Leary (Minneapolis, 1989), 163–84.

19. See the chapter on Nehru in Chatterjee, *Nationalist Thought.*

20. M. K. Gandhi, *Hind swaraj* (1909), in *Collected Works of Mahatma Gandhi,* vol. 10 (Ahmedabad, 1963), 15.

21. See the discussion in Gauri Visvanathan, *Masks of Conquest: Literary Studies and British Rule in India* (London, 1989), 128–41, passim.

22. Ranajit Guha, *Elementary Aspects of Peasant Insurgency in Colonial India* (New Delhi, 1983), chap. 2.

23. William E. Connolly, *Political Theory and Modernity* (Oxford, 1989). See also David Bennett, "Postmodernism and Vision: Ways of Seeing (at) the End of History" (forthcoming).

24. Jürgen Habermas, *The Structural Transformation of the Public Sphere: An Inquiry into a Category of Bourgeois Society* (Cambridge, Mass., 1989), 49.

25. See Sumit Sarkar, "Social History: Predicament and Possibilities," in Iqbal Khan, ed., *Fresh Perspective on India and Pakistan: Essays on Economics, Politics, and Culture* (Oxford, 1985), 256–74.

26. For reasons of space, I shall leave this claim here unsubstantiated, though I hope to have an opportunity to discuss it in detail elsewhere. I should qualify the statement by mentioning that in the main it refers to autobiographies published between 1850 and 1910. Once women join the public sphere in the twentieth century, their self-fashioning takes on different dimensions.

27. Nirad C. Chaudhuri, *The Hand, Great Anarch!: India, 1921–1952* (London, 1987), 350–51.

28. See Karl Marx, *On the Jewish Question,* in *Early Writings* (Harmondsworth, Eng., 1975), 215–22.

29. For a more detailed treatment of what follows, see my paper "Colonial Rule and the Domestic Order," to be published in David Arnold and David Hardiman, eds., *Subaltern Studies,* vol. 8.

30. Meredith Borthwick, *The Changing Role of Women in Bengal, 1849–1905* (Princeton, N.J., 1984); Ghulam Murshid, *Reluctant Debutante: Response of Bengali Women to Modernisation, 1849–1905* (Rajshahi, 1983). On the history of the word *civilization,* see Lucien Febvre, "*Civilisation:* Evolution of a Word and a Group of Ideas," in Peter Burke, ed., *A New Kind of History: From the Writings of Febvre,* trans. K. Folca (London, 1973), 219–57. I owe this reference to Peter Sahlins.

31. James Mill, *The History of British India,* vol. 1, ed. H. H. Wilson (London, 1840), 309–10.

32. Borthwick, *Changing Role.*

33. The classic text where this assumption has been worked up into philosophy is of course *Hegel's Philosophy of Right,* trans. T. M. Knox (Oxford, 1967), 110–22. See also Joanna Hodge, "Women and the Hegelian State," in Ellen Kennedy and Susan Mendus, eds., *Women in Western Philosophy* (Brighton, Eng., 1987), 127–58; Simon During, "Rousseau's Heirs: Primitivism, Romance, and Other Relations Between the Modern and the Nonmodern" (forthcoming); Joan B. Landes, *Women and the Public Sphere in the Age of the*

French Revolution (Ithaca, N.Y., 1988); Mary Ryan, *Women in Public: Between Banners and Ballots, 1825–1880* (Baltimore, 1990).

34. Anon., *Streesiksha,* vol. 1 (Calcutta, 1877), 28–29.

35. I develop this argument further in Dipesh Chakrabarty, "Open Space/Public Place: Garbage, Modernity, and India," *South Asia* (forthcoming).

36. *Dinabandhu racanabali,* ed. Kshetra Gupta (Calcutta, 1981), 138.

37. Borthwick, *Changing Role,* 105.

38. I discuss this in more detail in Chakrabarty, "Colonial Rule."

39. Indira Devi, *Narir ukti* (Calcutta, 1920), dedication page.

40. Deenanath Bandyopadhyaya, *Nanabishayak prabandha* (Calcutta, 1887), 30–31. For a genealogy of the terms *slavery* and *freedom* as used in the colonial discourse of British India, see Gyan Prakash, *Bonded Histories: Genealogies of Labor Servitude in Colonial India* (Cambridge, 1990).

41. Peter Burke, *The Renaissance Sense of the Past* (London, 1970).

42. Bikshuk [Chandrasekhar Sen], *Ki holo!* (Calcutta, 1876), 77.

43. David Kinsley, *Hindu Goddesses: Visions of the Divine Feminine in the Hindu Religious Tradition* (Berkeley, 1988), 19–31; Manomohan Basu, *Hindu acar byabahar* (Calcutta, 1873), 60; H. D. Bhattacharya, "Minor Religious Sects," in R. C. Majumdar, ed., *The History and Culture of the Indian People: The Age of Imperial Unity,* vol. 2 (Bombay, 1951), 469–71; Upendranath Dhal, *Goddess Lakshmi: Origin and Development* (Delhi, 1978). The expression *everyday pantheism* was suggested to me by Gayatri Chakravorty Spivak (personal communication).

44. See the chapter on Bankim in Chatterjee, *Nationalist Thought.*

45. *Ranade: His Wife's Reminiscences,* trans. Kusumavati Deshpande (Delhi, 1963), 77.

46. Meaghan Morris, "Metamorphoses at Sydney Tower," *New Formations* 11 (Summer 1990): 10.

47. Amiya Chakravarty, quoted in Bhikhu Parekh, *Gandhi's Political Discourse* (London, 1989), 163.

48. Gayatri Chakravorty Spivak, "Can the Subaltern Speak?," in Cary Nelson and Lawrence Grossberg, eds., *Marxism and the Interpretation of Culture* (Urbana, Ill., 1988), 277.

49. See *Subaltern Studies,* vols. 1–7 (Delhi, 1982–91); and Ashis Nandy, *The Intimate Enemy: Loss and Recovery of Self Under Colonialism* (Delhi, 1983).

50. *Subaltern Studies,* vols. 1–7, and Guha, *Elementary Aspects.*

51. Homi Bhabha, "Of Mimicry and Man: The Ambivalence of Colonial Discourse," in Annette Michelson et al., eds., *October: The First Decade, 1976–1986* (Cambridge, Mass., 1987), 317–26; also Bhabha, ed., *Nation and Narration* (London, 1990).

52. Spivak, "Can the Subaltern Speak?" Also see Spivak's interview published in *Socialist Review* 20, no. 3 (July–September 1990): 81–98.

53. On the close connection between imperialist ideologies and the teaching of history in colonial India, see Ranajit Guha, *An Indian Historiography of India: A Nineteenth-Century Agenda and Its Implications* (Calcutta, 1988).

54. Without in any way implicating them in the entirety of this argument, I may mention that there are parallels here between my statement and what Gyan Prakash and Nicholas Dirks have argued elsewhere. See Gyan Prakash, "Writing Post-Orientalist Histories of the Third World: Perspectives from Indian Historiography," *Comparative Studies in Society and History* 32, no. 2 (April 1990): 383–408; Nicholas B. Dirks, "History as a Sign of the Modern," *Public Culture* 2, no. 2 (Spring 1990): 25–33.

55. See Amartya Kumar Sen, *Of Ethics and Economics* (Oxford, 1987) . Tessa Morris-Suzuki's *A History of Japanese Economic Thought* (London, 1989) makes interesting reading in this regard. I am grateful to Gavan McCormack for bringing this book to my attention.

56. Carole Pateman, *The Sexual Contract* (Stanford, Calif., 1988), 184.

57. Fredric Jameson, "Cognitive Mapping," in Nelson and Grossberg, *Marxism and the Interpretation of Culture,* 354.

58. David Arnold, "The Colonial Prison: Power, Knowledge, and Penology in Nineteenth-Century India," in Arnold and Hardiman, *Subaltern Studies,* vol. 8. I have discussed some of these issues in a Bengali article: Dipesh Chakrabarty, "Sarir, samaj, o rashtra: Oupanibeshik bharate mahamari o jana-sangskriti," *Anustup,* 1988.

59. Lawrence Brilliant with Girija Brilliant, "Death for a Killer Disease," *Quest,* May/June 1978, 3. I owe this reference to Paul Greenough.

60. Richard Rorty, "Habermas and Lyotard on Postmodernity," in Richard J. Bernstein, ed., *Habermas and Modernity* (Cambridge, Mass., 1986), 169.

61. For an interesting and revisionist reading of Hegel in this regard, see the exchange between Charles Taylor and Partha Chatterjee in *Public Culture* 3, no. 1 (1990). My book *Rethinking Working-Class History* attempts a small beginning in this direction.

BIBLIOGRAPHY

Arac, Jonathan. "F. O. Matthiessen: Authorizing an American Renaissance"; Sel. Papers from the Eng. Inst., 1982–83. In *The American Renaissance Reconsidered,* edited by Walter Benn Michaels, Donald E. Pease (introduction). Baltimore: Johns Hopkins University Press, 1985.

Bann, Stephen. "The Sense of the Past: Image, Text, and Object in the Formation of Historical Consciousness in Nineteenth-Century Britain." In *The New Historicism,* editor and introduction, H. Aram Veeser, Stanley Fish, commentary. New York: Routledge, 1989.

Berger, Harry, Jr., and Louis Montrose (introduction). *Revisionary Play: Studies in the Spenserian Dynamics.* Berkeley: University of California Press, 1988.

Bercovitch, Sacvan. "Investigations of an Americanist." *Journal of American History* 78 (December 1991): 972–87.

Boyarin, Daniel. " 'Language Inscribed by History on the Bodies of Living Beings': Midrash and Martyrdom." *Representations* 25 (Winter 1989): 139–51.

Cesarini, Remo. "Nuove strategie rappresentative: La scuola di Berkeley." *Belfagor* (Florence, Italy) 39 (30 November 1984): 665–85.

Chakrabarty, Dipesh. "The Death of History? Historical Consciousness and the Culture of Late Capitalism." *Public Culture* 4 (Spring 1992): 47–65.

Chartier, Roger, and Christian Jouhaud. "Pratiques historiennes des textes." *Etudes de Lettres.* 2–3 (Apr.–Sept. 1988): 53–79.

Cohen, Walter. "Political Criticism of Shakespeare." In *Shakespeare Reproduced: The Text in History and Ideology,* edited by Jean E. Howard and Marion F. O'Connor. New York and London: Methuen, 1987.

Davis, Natalie Zemon. *The Return of Martin Guerre.* Cambridge: Harvard University Press, 1983. Originally in French, with a *"recit romanesque"* written by the screenwriter Jean-Claude Carriere and the director Daniel Vigne (*Le Retour de Martin Guerre).* Paris: Robert Laffont, 1982.

———. *Fiction in the Archives: Pardon Tales and Their Tellers in Sixteenth-Century France.* Stanford: Stanford University Press, 1987.

Dimock, Wai-chee. "Scarcity, Subjectivity, and Emerson." *boundary 2* 17 (Spring 1990): 83–99.

370

——. "Feminism, New Historicism, and the Reader." *American Literature: A Journal of Literary History, Criticism and Bibliography* 63 (December 1991): 601–22.

——. "The Economy of Pain: Capitalism, Humanitarianism, and the Realistic Novel." In *New Essays on the Rise of Silas Lapham*, edited by Donald E. Pease. Cambridge: Cambridge University Press, 1991.

During, Simon. "New Historicism." *Text and Performance Quarterly* 11 (July 1991): 171–89.

Evans, Malcolm. *Signifying Nothing*. Brighton: Harvester, 1986.

Fineman, Joel. "The Turn of the Shrew," in *Shakespeare and the Question of Theory* edited by Patricia Parker and Geoffrey Hartman. New York and London: Methuen, 1985: 138–59.

——. "Shakespeare's Will: The Temporality of Rape." In *Representations* 20 (Fall 1987): 25–76.

——. "The History of the Anecdote: Fiction and Fiction." In *The New Historicism*, editor and introduction, H. Aram Veeser, Stanley Fish, commentary. New York: Routledge, 1989.

Fish, Stanley. "Commentary: The Young and the Restless." In *The New Historicism*, editor and introduction, H. Aram Veeser. New York: Routledge, 1989.

Fox-Genovese, Elizabeth. "Literary Criticism and the Politics of the New Historicism." In *The New Historicism*, editor and introduction, H. Aram Veeser, Stanley Fish, commentary. New York: Routledge, 1989.

Fukuyama, Francis. *The End of History and the Last Man*. New York: Free Press, 1992.

Gallagher, Catherine. *The Industrial Reformation of English Fiction: Social Discourse and Narrative Form, 1832–1867*. Chicago: University of Chicago Press, 1985.

——. "Embracing the Absolute: The Politics of the Female Subject in Seventeenth-Century England." *Genders* 1 (March 1988): 24–29.

——. "Marxism and the New Historicism." In *The New Historicism*, editor and introduction, H. Aram Veeser, Stanley Fish, commentary. New York: Routledge, 1989.

Gallop, Jane. *Reading Lacan*. Ithaca, N.Y.: Cornell University Press, 1985.

Garber, Marjorie. " 'What's Past Is Prologue': Temporality and Prophecy in Shakespeare's History Plays." In *Renaissance Genres: Essays on Theory, History, and Interpretation*, edited by Barbara Kiefer Lewalski. Cambridge: Harvard University Press, 1986.

——. "Descanting on Deformity: Richard III and the Shape of History." In *The Historical Renaissance*. Edited by Heather DuGrow and Richard Strier. Chicago: University of Chicago Press, 1989.

Gearhart, Suzanne. "History as Criticism: The Dialogue of History and Literature." *Diacritics* 17 (1987): 56–65.

Goldberg, Jonathan. "The Politics of Renaissance Literature: A Review-Essay." *ELH* 49 (1982): 514–42.

——. *James I and the Politics of Literature: Jonson, Shakespeare, Donne, and Their Contemporaries*. Baltimore: Johns Hopkins University Press, 1983.

Goux, Jean-Joseph. *Symbolic Economies: After Marx and Freud*. Tr. Jennifer C. Gage. Ithaca: Cornell University Press, 1990.

Graff, Gerald. "Co-optation." In *The New Historicism*, editor and introduction, H. Aram Veeser, Stanley Fish, commentary. New York: Routledge, 1989.

Greenblatt, Stephen. *Renaissance Self-Fashioning: From More to Shakespeare.* Chicago: University of Chicago Press, 1980.

———. "Invisible Bullets: Renaissance Authority and Its Subversion, Henry IV and Henry V." In *Political Shakespeare: New Essays in Cultural Materialism,* edited by Jonathan Dollimore, Alan Sinfield, and Raymond Williams. Manchester: Manchester University Press, 1985.

———. "Fiction and Friction." In *Reconstructing Individualism: Autonomy, Individuality, and the Self in Western Thought.* Edited by Thomas C. Heller, Morton Sosna, and David E. Wellbery, with Arnold I. Davidson, Ann Swidler, and Ian Watt, editors. Stanford: Stanford University Press, revised and expanded, in Stephen Greenblatt, *Shakespearean Negotiations.* Berkeley: University of California Press, 1986.

———. "Psychoanalysis and Renaissance Culture." In *Literary Theory/Renaissance Texts,* edited by Patricia Parker and David Quint. Baltimore: Johns Hopkins University Press, 1986.

———. "Marginal Notes." *Village Voice Literary Supplement* 68 (October 1988).

———. "Towards a Poetics of Culture." In *The New Historicism,* editor and introduction, H. Aram Veeser, Stanley Fish, commentary. New York: Routledge, 1989.

———. *Marvelous Possessions: The Wonder of the New World.* Chicago: University of Chicago Press, 1991.

———. "Introduction.: *The Forms of Power and the Power of Forms in the Renaissance. Genre* 7 (1982): 3–6.

Guillory, John. "Dalila's House: *Samson Agonistes* and the Sexual Division of Labor." *Rewriting the Renaissance: The Discourse of Sexual Differences in Early Modern Europe.* Edited by Margaret W. Ferguson, Maureen Quilligan, Nancy J. Vickers. Chicago: University of Chicago Press, 1986.

———. "Memory and Historical Record: The Literature and Literary Criticism of Beirut, 1982." In *Left Politics and the Literary Profession,* edited by Lennard J. Davis and Bella M. Mirabella. New York: Columbia University Press, 1990.

Harpham, Geoffrey Galt. "Foucault and the New Historicism." *American Literary History* 3 (Summer 1991): 360–75.

Hawkes, Terence. *That Shakespeherian Rag: Essays on a Critical Process.* London: Methuen, 1986.

Horwitz, Howard. " 'I Can't Remember': Skepticism, Synthetic Histories, Critical Action," *SAQ* 87 (Fall 1988): 787–820.

Howard, Jean E. "The New Historicism in Renaissance Studies." *ELR* 16 (1986): 13–43.

———. "Feminism and the Question of History: Resituating the Debate." *Women's Studies: An Interdisciplinary Journal* 19 (1991): 149–57.

Hulme, Peter. "Hurricanes in the Caribbees: The Constitution of the Discourse of English Colonialism." In *1642: Literature and Power in the Seventeenth Century,* edited by Francis Barker, Jay Bernstein, John Coombes, Peter Hulme, Jennifer Stone, and Jon Stratton. Colchester: University of Essex, 1981.

Hunt, Lynn, ed. *The New Cultural History.* Berkeley: University of California Press, 1989.

Javitch, Daniel. "The Impure Motives of Elizabethan Poetry." *Genre* 7 (1982): 225–38.

Jay, Gregory S. "American Literature and The New Historicism: The Example of Frederick Douglass." *boundary 2* 17 (Spring 1990): 211–42.

Jehlen, Myra. "The Story of History Told by the New Historicism." In *Reconstructing*

American Literary and Historical Studies, edited by Gunter H. Lentz, Hartmut Keil, Sabine Brock-Sallah. Frankfurt: Campus Verlag, 1990.

Klancher, Jon. "English Romanticism and Cultural Production." In *The New Historicism,* editor and introduction, H. Aram Veeser, Stanley Fish, commentary. New York: Routledge, 1989.

———. "Romantic Criticism and the Meanings of the French Revolution." *Studies in Romanticism* 28 (Fall 1989): 463–91.

LaCapra, Dominick. "On the Line: Between History and Criticism." *Profession 89* (1989): 4–9.

Leinwand, Theodore B. "Negotiation and New Historicism." *PMLA: Publications of the Modern Language Association of America* 105 (May 1990): 477–90.

Lentricchia, Frank. "Foucault's Legacy: A New Historicism?" In *The New Historicism,* editor and introduction, H. Aram Veeser, Stanley Fish, commentary. New York: Routledge, 1989.

Levin, Richard. "Unthinkable Thoughts in the New Historicizing of English Renaissance Drama." *New Literary History* 21 (Spring 1990): 433–47.

Levinson, Marjorie. *Wordsworth's Great Period Poems.* Cambridge: Cambridge University Press, 1986.

———. "Keats and His Readers: A Question of Taste." In *Subject to History,* edited by David Simpson. Ithaca and London: Cornell University Press, 1991.

———. "The New Historicism: Back to the Future." In *Rethinking Historicism: Critical Readings in Romantic History,* edited by Marjorie Levinson, Marilyn Butler, Jerome McGann, Paul Hamilton. Oxford: Basil Blackwell, 1989.

Litvak, Joseph. "Back to the Future: A Review Article on the New Historicism, Deconstruction, and Nineteenth-Century Fiction." *Texas Studies in Language and Literature* 30 (Spring 1988): 120–49.

Liu, Alan. "The Power of Formalism: The New Historicism." *ELH* 56 (Winter 1989): 721–71.

———. "Local Transcendence: Cultural Criticism, Postmodernism, and the Romanticism of Detail." *Representations* 32 (Fall 1990): 75–113.

Lytle, Guy Fitch and Stephen Orgel, editors. *Patronage in the Renaissance.* Princeton: Princeton University Press, 1981.

Mailloux, Steven. "Misreading as a Historical Act: Cultural Rhetoric, Bible Politics, and Fuller's 1945 Review of Douglass's Narrative." In *Readers in History: Nineteenth-Century American Literature and the Contexts of Response,* edited by James L. Machor. Baltimore and London: Johns Hopkins University Press, 1993.

———. "The Rhetorical Use and Abuse of Fiction: Eating Books in Late Nineteenth-Century America." *boundary 2* 17 (Spring 1991): 133–57.

Marcus, Jane. "The Asylums of Antaeus: Women, War, and Madness—Is there a Feminist Fetishism?" In *The New Historicism,* editor and introduction, H. Aram Veeser, Stanley Fish, commentary. New York: Routledge, 1989.

Marcus, Leah S. *Puzzling Shakespeare: Local Reading and Its Discontents.* Berkeley: University of California Press, 1988.

McGann, Jerome. *The Beauty of Inflections: Literary Investigations in Historical Method and Theory.* Oxford: Clarendon Press, 1985.

Michaels, Walter Benn, and Donald E. Pease. *The American Renaissance Reconsidered:*

Selected Papers from the English Institute, 1982–83. New Series, 9. Baltimore: Johns Hopkins University Press, 1985.

———. *The Gold Standard and the Logic of Naturalism: American Literature at the Turn of the Century.* Berkeley: University of California Press, 1987.

———. "The Souls of White Folk." In *Literature and the Body: Essays on Populations and Persons,* edited by Elaine Scarry. Baltimore: Johns Hopkins University Press, 1988.

Montrose, Louis Adrian. "The Purpose of Playing: Reflections on a Shakespearean Anthropology." *Helios* 32 (Spring 1980): 28–54.

———. " 'The place of a brother' in *As You Like It:* Social Process and Comic Form." *Shakespeare Quarterly* 32 (1981): 28–54.

———. Renaissance Literary Studies and the Subject of History." *English Literary Renaissance* 16 (Winter 1986): 5–12.

———. "Professing the Renaissance: The Poetics and Politics of Culture." In *The New Historicism,* H. Aram Veeser, editor and introduction, Stanley Fish, commentary. New York: Routledge, 1989.

———. "The Work of Gender in the Discourse of Discovery." *Representations* 33 (Winter 1991): 1–41.

Mullaney, Steven. "Strange Things, Gross Terms, Curious Customs: The Rehearsal of Cultures in the Late Renaissance." In Steven Mullaney, *The Place of the Stage: License, Play and Power in Renaissance England.* Chicago: University of Chicago Press, 1983.

Newton, Judith Lowder. "History as Usual? Feminism and the 'New Historicism.' " In *The New Historicism,* editor and introduction, H. Aram Veeser, Stanley Fish, commentary. New York: Routledge, 1989.

———. "Historicisms New & Old: 'Charles Dickens' Meets Marxism, Feminism, and West Coast Foucault." *Feminist Studies* 16 (Fall 1990): 449–90.

Orgel, Stephen. "Prospero's Wife." *Representations* 8 (1984): 1–13.

———. "Jonson and the Amazons." In *Soliciting Interpretation: Literary Theory and Seventeenth-Century English Poetry,* edited by Elizabeth D. Harvey and Katherine Eisamon-Maus. Chicago: University of Chicago Press, 1990.

Orr, Linda. "The Revenge of Literature: A History of History." *New Literary History* 18 (Autumn 1986): 1–22.

Pateman, Carole. *The Sexual Contract.* Stanford: Stanford University Press, 1988.

Patterson, Annabel. *Censorship and Interpretation: The Conditions of Writing and Reading in Early Modern England.* Madison: University of Wisconsin Press, 1984.

Patterson, Lee. *Literary Practice and Social Change in Britain, 1380–1530.* Berkeley: University of California Press, 1990.

Pearce, Roy Harvey. *Historicism Once More: Problems and Occasions for the American Scholar.* Princeton: Princeton University Press, 1969.

Pease, Donald. *Visionary Compacts: American Renaissance Writings in Cultural Context.* Madison: University of Wisconsin Press, 1987.

———. "Toward a Sociology of Literary Knowledge: Greenblatt, Colonialism, and the New Historicism." In *Consequences of Theory,* edited by Jonathan Arac, Barbara Johnson. Baltimore: Johns Hopkins University Press, 1991.

Pecora, Vincent. "The Limits of Local Knowledge." In *The New Historicism,* editor and

introduction, H. Aram Veeser, Stanley Fish, commentary. Nev
1989.

Pigman, G. W., III. "Self, Subversion, and the New Historicism." *Hu*
Quarterly: A Journal for the History and Interpretation of English and
ilization 52 (Autumn 1989): 501–8.

Robbins, Bruce. *The Servant's Hand.* New York: Columbia University Press,

Rogin, Michael. "Recolonizing America." *American Literary History* 2 (Spr
144–49.

Rosenberg, Brian. "Historicizing the *New Historicism:* Understanding the Past in C
and Fiction." *Modern Language Quarterly* 50 (December 1989): 375–92.

Ross, Marlon B. "Contingent Predilections: The Newest Historicisms and the Qu
of Method." *The Centennial-Review* 34 (Fall 1990): 485–538.

Said, Edward. *Orientalism.* New York: Random House, 1979.

———. "The Imperial Spectacle ('Aida')." *Grand Street* 6 (Winter 1987): 82–104.

Sedgwick, Eve Kosofsky. *Epistemology of the Closet.* Berkeley: University of California Press
1990.

Scott, Joan W. *Gender and the Politics of History.* New York: Columbia University Press,
1988.

Simpson, David. "Literary Criticism and the Return to History." *Critical Inquiry* 14 (1987–
88): 721–47.

———. "Figuring Class, Sex, and Gender: What is the Subject of Wordsworth's 'Gipsies'?"
South Atlantic Quarterly 88 (Summer 1989): 541–68.

———, ed. *Subject to History: Ideology, Class, Gender.* Ithaca: Cornell University Press, 1991.

Spivak, Gayatri Chakravorty. "The New Historicism: Political Commitment and the Postmodern Critic." In *The New Historicism,* editor and introduction, H. Aram Veeser,
Stanley Fish, commentary. New York: Routledge, 1989.

Tennenhouse, Leonard. *Power on Display: The Politics of Shakespeare's Genres.* New York
and London: Methuen, 1986.

Terdiman, Richard. "Is there Class in this Class?" In *The New Historicism,* editor and
introduction, H. Aram Veeser, Stanley Fish, commentary. New York: Routledge,
1989.

Thomas, Brook. *The New Historicism and Other Old-Fashioned Topics.* Princeton: Princeton
University Press, 1992.

Tompkins, Jane. *Sensational Designs: The Cultural Work of American Fiction, 1790–1860.*
Oxford: Oxford University Press, 1985.

———. "Me and My Shadow." *New Literary History* 19 (Autumn 1987): 161–67.

———. "At the Buffalo Bill Museum." *South Atlantic Quarterly.* 89 (Summer 1990):
525–45.

Waller, Marguerite. "Academic Tootsie: The Denial of Difference and the Difference It
Makes." *Diacritics: A Review of Contemporary Criticism* 17 (Spring 1987): 2–20.

White, Hayden. "New Historicism: A Comment." In *The New Historicism,* editor and
introduction, H. Aram Veeser, Stanley Fish, commentary. New York: Routledge,
1989.

Wilentz, Sean and David Cannadine, editors. *Rites of Power: Symbolism, Ritual, and Politics
Since the Middle Ages.* Philadelphia: University of Pennsylvania Press, 1985.

...krabarty is Ashworth Reader in Social Theory and Director, Ashworth
...er for Social Theory, the University of Melbourne.

...ineman was Professor of English, the University of California, Berkeley.

...atherine Gallagher is Professor of English, the University of California, Berkeley.

Jane Gallop is Distinguished Professor of English and Comparative Literature, the University of Wisconsin, Milwaukee.

Marjorie Garber is Professor of English and Director of the Center for Literary and Cultural Studies, Harvard University.

Stephen Greenblatt is Class of 1932 Professor of English, the University of California, Berkeley.

Barbara Harlow is Associate Professor of English, the University of Texas, Austin.

Walter Benn Michaels is Professor of English and the Humanities, the Johns Hopkins University.

Louis Adrian Montrose is Professor of English Literature and Chairman of the Department of Literature, the University of California, San Diego.

Stephen Orgel is Jackson Eli Reynolds Professor of Humanities, Stanford University.

Donald E. Pease is Ted and Helen Geisel Third Century Professor in the Humanities and Professor of English, Dartmouth College.

Michael Rogin is Professor of Political Science, the University of California, Berkeley.

Eve Kosofsky Sedgwick is Newman Ivey White Professor of English, Duke University.

Brook Thomas is Professor of English, the University of California, Irvine.

Jane Tompkins is Professor of English, Duke University.